MAN vs MACHINE

Challenging Human Supremacy at Chess

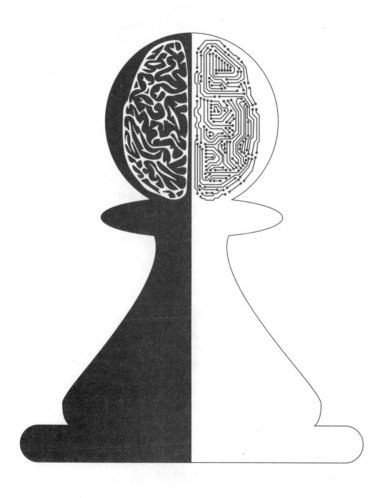

Foreword by Vladimir Kramnik

Karsten Müller & Jonathan Schaeffer

Man Versus Machine Challenging Human Supremacy at Chess
by Karsten Müller and Jonathan Schaeffer

© Copyright 2018
Karsten Müller and Jonathan Schaeffer

ISBN: 978-1-941270-96-7

Published by:
Russell Enterprises, Inc.
PO Box 3131
Milford, CT 06460 USA

http://www.russell-enterprises.com
info@russell-enterprises.com

Layout and cover design by Fierce Ponies, Brooklyn, NY

Printed in the United States of America

Acknowledgements

Karsten Müller:

I want to thank Joel Benjamin for answering many questions by e-mail and Raj Tischbierek for helping with a source from his excellent German magazine *Schach*. Thank you to Frederic Friedel from ChessBase for putting me in contact with the computer chess world by inviting me to operate a machine in the famous Kasparov 32:0 simultaneous exhibition in 1985 – those were the days! – and helping with my annotations of several man versus machine matches for the ChessBase website, which form the basis of the annotations. Andre Schulz, Dr. Ingo Althöfer, and Heiko Machelett also helped here. Publisher Hanon W. Russell did not only a great job as editor as usual but also to find a coauthor. I am very happy that Jonathan Schaeffer accepted. He made history when his Checkers program CHINOOK won against the human world champion in 1994 and his work *One Jump Ahead* about that journey is really excellent. I hope that you also enjoy the story of this battle in chess.

Special thanks to Pascal Simon of ChessBase and Lev Alburt.

Jonathan Schaeffer:

I thought my involvement with chess ended 25 years ago when I retired from competing in computer chess tournaments. However, Hanon Russell's idea for a book that told the story of computers challenging humankind for supremacy at chess was too good an opportunity to pass up. As a chessplayer myself, the chance to spend time playing over interesting games of chess, reading Karsten's wonderful annotations, diving into the historical literature, and reliving my experiences from the early days of this field was a lot of fun for me. This book was truly a labor of love – love for the game, love for the people in chess and computer chess that I have been privileged to know and work with, and love for the intellectual gratification (both from playing chess and researching computer chess). Thank you Hanon!

An important reason I decided to work on this book was the opportunity to collaborate with Grandmaster Karsten Müller. I have been a fan of his for many years, the result of reading his articles on ChessBase.com. I could not have asked for a better partner. Whatever I needed from his side, he was able to quickly provide it. Read his game annotations carefully – look for his insights and nuggets of gold. It has been a pleasure working with you Karsten.

Many people helped in the preparation of this book, and I especially want to single out the contributions of Elwyn Berlekamp, Murray Campbell, Frederic Friedel, David Levy, and Monroe Newborn.

This book is dedicated to Jennifer, my lovely wife and the source of my inspiration.

Some quotes have been edited for consistency. This includes changing descriptive chess notation to algebraic notation, as well as standardizing spelling and punctuation.

All chess games given in this book were played using tournament controls (typically 40 moves in 2 hours), except where indicated otherwise.

The authors thank 14th World Chess Champion Vladimir Kramnik for agreeing to write the foreword for this book. We had an engaging hour-long conversation with him – a highlight for both Karsten and Jonathan!

Thank you to Monroe (Monty) Newborn for permission to use his photographs. All ChessBase photographs come courtesy of Frederic Friedel. The photos by Mde Vincente and Gerhard Hund are used under the Creative Commons License. Additional permission from IBM, Carnegie Mellon University, and Semen Karpenko are appreciated.

Foreword

Technology has forever changed the world of chess. Today's player has access to… strong sparring partners whenever you want to play (and they never get tired); encyclopaedic opening books (that really aren't books); comprehensive games collections (that include virtually every game played by every player of note); and perfection in some endgames (that defy human understanding). As a young chess player growing up in Russia and honing my skills, I had access to none of these tools. I had to find willing opponents, annotate printed opening books, transcribe important games, and attempt to discover the mysteries of the endgames. I'm not complaining, just describing the not-so-distant past. Computers have changed so much in chess, as indeed they have transformed so much of the world today.

I was late to adopt computers into my training regime. At the beginning of my career I used computers only for their game databases. In 1995, while helping Garry Kasparov with his world championship match with Anand, I saw how important the use of computer applications were for his training. After working with Garry, I started to use computers quite regularly. However, it was mostly used for blunder checking. We were analyzing on the board and sometimes you could easily just simply blunder something, miss some cheap trick, and just make mistakes. At that time, the playing strength of the programs was quite weak, but still strong enough to embarrass us. Even Kasparov sometimes blundered in his analysis, and the computer was ruthless and impassionate about pointing out the mistakes. This was a humbling experience for a grandmaster! Simply having the ability to check for blunders was in itself a useful tool.

Then came Kasparov's famous matches against DEEP BLUE. Frankly, I was not taking computers too seriously at that time. Even though I understood that it was not that simple to beat the computer, I was sure that Garry was going to win both matches. Of course I analyzed the games. I found it unsurprising that he won the 1996 match by a score of 4-2 – the games were normal and logical. The 1997 match was dominated by a lot of PR that distracted Garry (but not DEEP BLUE) and this may have played a role in the final result. But I'm absolutely convinced that Garry was still a much stronger player than DEEP BLUE. The final result was bad luck on Garry's part, that he lost his nerves at some point. Even so, he was the better player.

My own fights with the machines also started around that time. I don't really know when I lost my first game against a machine. I was not a big fan of playing training games with computers, but I probably lost one such game. My first tournament with a computer participant was probably a rapid chess event in Mainz around 1999. My first classical chess game against a computer was in 2000 in Dortmund. This was a grandmaster round-robin tournament and the computer's participation was controversial. Some players were against including the machine; I didn't mind so much. I won the game in my first classical man-machine encounter.

Then I prepared for my first match against DEEP FRITZ, which was planned for 2001. The first step in my preparation was to analyze all the 1997 Kasparov-DEEP BLUE games, with FRITZ running on my laptop. Just a laptop – no special chess chips analyzing 100s of millions of positions per second. To my extreme surprise, FRITZ was simply playing better than DEEP BLUE. I was shocked. I couldn't understand how Garry managed to lose this match. When moves involved deep calculation, FRITZ made the same moves as DEEP BLUE nine times out of ten. When a move choice was based on a positional decision, FRITZ usually made a slightly better move than DEEP BLUE. I was puzzled -- I was expecting DEEP BLUE to be much stronger. I was even a bit frightened that I was going to play against FRITZ but with it using more computing power. After doing this analysis, I was really surprised that Gary managed to lose the match to DEEP BLUE.

The first match with DEEP FRITZ actually took place in 2002. It started very well for me with two draws and two wins. I was extremely happy. But then in game five I blundered a piece in basically one move. In game six I was leading by one point and so I sacrificed material. So in the end the match was drawn and the question of whether man or machine was the better player remained open. In my second match with DEEP FRITZ in 2006 things did not go as well and I ended up losing.

It was already difficult, but still not totally impossible, for a human to beat a top computer program. But within maybe two or three years it became completely impossible. I think by around 2010 there was no chance anymore for the human side. In the history of computer chess, there were three chapters. First the humans were better for a long time. Then the interesting chapter, where man and machine were close in strength, lasted maybe 10 to 15 years. And now, the final chapter, computers are stronger for good.

Computers have changed the game of chess, the world of chess, and even my profession. There are many pluses to what computers have brought to chess. Of most value is that they improved our understanding and appreciation of the game. The minuses are obviously that there is much less opportunity for the human side – less room to be creative. We must not forget that chess is, after all, a game between two humans. Computers may now be stronger than the human World Champion, but this achievement does not change the real value of the game: the pleasure that we humans get from playing one another at this beautiful intellectual game. And that will never change.

When I chose chess as my profession, I never imagined that one of the legacies of my career would be as a contributor to the field of artificial intelligence research. Both Garry and I put our titles and reputations on the line in the interests of Science. We both had early victories and eventually suffered painful defeats. I have no regrets. I enjoyed the challenge of playing against technology.

Grandmaster Karsten Müller and Professor Jonathan Schaeffer have managed to describe the fascinating history of the unequal fight of man against machine in an entertaining and instructive way. It evoked pleasant and not so pleasant memories of my own fights against the monsters. I hope that their work gives you as much pleasure as it has given me.

Vladimir Kramnik

14th World Chess Champion

Table of Contents

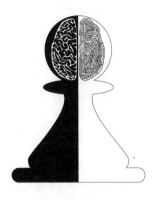

Pre-Game

The courtier stared at the chessboard, searching for a way out of his dilemma. Internally his mind was in turmoil, and externally it was starting to show. Faint hints of moisture could be seen on his forehead, above his knitted brow. He moved restlessly in his chair causing his frilly clothes to make rustling sounds. None of this, of course, bothered his adversary. Indeed, none of this was even noticed by him.

Across the chessboard was a man dressed in Middle Eastern clothes and wearing a turban. The opponent stared down at the board. He was emotionless in his expression, apparently unflappable, completely oblivious to the royalty and senior government officials watching his every move.

The courtier reached out and played a move. In less than a minute, the opponent replied, rather stiffly moving a piece.

"Oh no! I am losing!" thought the courtier in horror. "How is this possible? How can a mere machine, a combination of pulleys and wheels, best me, the creation of God? What wizardry makes this possible?" And then there was a surge of panic. There was no way out of his predicament. "I will be forced to resign in front of the Empress. How can I possibly recover from this public humiliation?"

The year was 1770 and people believed that technology had conquered the human game of chess.

Today's generation of chess players was raised on computers. To many of them, it is hard to imagine what life was like before cell phones, the Internet, Facebook, and Google. Technology now affects virtually every aspect of our daily life. Our love for the game of chess is not immune to the computer revolution. What serious player does not use a computer as a sparring partner or an analysis aid? Even if you are not a grandmaster, just to be able to play online whenever you want, against an opponent from literally anywhere in the world, allows you to indulge in your passion more so than ever before. Technology is helping us collectively to hone our skills through more practice and insightful analysis. Computers have helped discover secrets of the game and increased our appreciation of its beauty.

Although we take for granted that computers play strong chess, that was not always the case. In fact, grandmaster-level computer play did not happen until the late 1980s, and commercially available grandmaster programs arrived around the year 2000. In the fast-paced technology world of today, this seems like an eternity ago!

Today computers play at a level that is often called "super human"; they are stronger than the best human players (sorry, Magnus). The story of how computer chess programs grew from a whimsical idea into a 3300 ELO mega-grandmaster is intimately tied with the story of incredible technological advances that have happened over a 250-year period. The historical record, amazingly, started in the year 1770 when a brilliant engineer built a machine (named the TURK) that fooled people into thinking it played chess. Of course it was an illusion, but the seed of an idea was planted.

This book tells the story of the epic battle of man versus machine for supremacy at chess. From an entertainment-oriented beginning (1770), the foundational ideas

(1830-1952), the first programs capable of playing a complete game of chess (1960s), and the stunning victory of DEEP BLUE over World Champion Garry Kasparov (1997), the story of the scientific quest to build something many said was impossible is an important part of the history of computing, even the history of mankind.

This book tells the story of a cerebral battle between two remarkable groups of people.

The first are the scientists, who are passionate about developing new technology and pushing it to its limit. For the fledgling field of artificial intelligence research, building a chess-playing machine capable of competing with the strongest human players was one of the original "grand challenge" problems to tackle. Chess, it was felt, was a microcosm of more complex applications; if you could not satisfactorily address chess – a mere game – then what hope was there for harder problems? Fifty years of research, new ideas, improved computing hardware, and competitions against humans were needed to finally achieve this goal. It is an outstanding achievement and is justifiably regarded as a technological milestone.

The second group is the chess players, who are passionate about playing an intellectually stimulating game and improving their abilities. They are keen to demonstrate superiority over any opponent, whether man or machine. To excel at chess requires a rich set of highly refined skills, including imagination, calculation, reasoning, and learning. These skills set human chess players apart from mere calculating machines and, thus, human superiority at chess was unquestioned. Reality was something different and today it is acknowledged that the best chess players in the world are silicon based. Yet, the human achievement is impressive. Despite the onslaught of technology – computers analyzing millions of positions per second – humans remained on top for many years. The challenge coming from computers forced humans to up their game. Today's top players have achieved an unprecedented level of skill.

The motivations of these two sides are not all that different. The scientists did what they did in pursuit of knowledge (discover new ideas), ego (be first; be world champion), and, in some cases, financial gains. The chess players participated because of their competitive spirit (winning matters), ego (winning; be the best), and, in some cases, financial gains.

Man playing machine at chess was a scientific experiment, one that would have not been possible without human contestants. It would have been easy for the strongest chess players to say "no," and deprive the scientists of crucial performance data. Instead they bravely agreed to play. The stakes to them were enormous; a loss could hurt their reputation and pride in front of a global audience. In contrast, the scientists had little at stake; a lost game meant going back to the drawing board, searching for new ideas, or fixing a programming error.

These man-machine encounters have happened before and will happen again. It was only in March 2016 that the world watched in fascination as Lee Sedol, many-time World Champion at the Oriental game of Go, did battle with the computer ALPHAGO. In 2011 it was man versus machine at the question-answer game of *Jeopardy!*.

The man-machine battle for supremacy in chess is a landmark in the history of technology. There are numerous books that document the technical side of this epic story. The scientists, by definition, have a requirement to publish their work. Hence there are literally hundreds of articles documenting the ideas, advances, experiments, and competitive results achieved by chess-playing computers. The human side is not often told. Few chess players are inclined to write about their man-machine encounters, other than annotating the games played.

This book strives to bring the two sides together. It tells the stories of many of the key scientists and chess players that participated in a 50-year research project to advance man's understanding of computing technology.

To enrich the story, we include three types of sidebars throughout the book: technology (explanations of the ideas that advanced the technology for building chess programs), context (quotes from chess players and scientists giving their opinions and predictions), and computer game milestones (showing how the technological advances were affecting other games). This allows the reader to understand the broader context of the computer chess story.

Join us as we recount the epic battle of man versus machine for supremacy at the game of chess.

Opening

1
0000 (1770-1956)

Cast your mind back in time. Can you imagine what the world was like in the year 1900? Automobiles, airplanes, washing machines, and microwave ovens either did not exist or were novelties. What kind of quality of life was that? No televisions, computers, Internet, and cell phones. What could we possibly do for entertainment? The 20th century saw an unprecedented level of innovation, likely only to be superseded by what happens in the 21st century.

With the advent of technology, it was inevitable that the competitive spirit of humankind would come to the fore. After all, if these machines were capable of performing tasks that we could do, then the obvious question to ask was "Who can do it better?" The idea of besting an individual's physical capabilities using a machine goes back a long time. In the 1800s, there is the well-known story of John Henry who matched his skills at pounding steel spikes into rocks with that of a steam-powered drill. Henry won that initial contest, but his days as champ were numbered. Later on, there were examples of human runners racing against horseless carriages. Over short distances, man could win – but only for a little while.

The man-versus-machine battles at strength and endurance activities are in the distant past. But man still battles machine when it comes to other physical skills, such as dexterity. For example, humans can still play football (soccer) and table tennis better than machines.

What about in the intellectual domain? We regard the capabilities of our brains as what differentiates us from other life on our planet. Our ability to reason sets us apart. Yet with the advent of computers, we have to ask the thought-provoking and humbling question as to whether we are so special.

One of the profoundest contributions of the 20th century was the realization that human's intellectual abilities could be realized using a computer. Imagine being in the year 1900 and told that a little black box (with the whimsical name of "computer") could correct spelling mistakes in your writing, do your accounting, and help you with navigation. Hearsay! Yet all of this is commonplace today. These problems are solved using data as input to a well-defined formula, and a machine capable of executing that formula using the data.

What about playing a game of chess? Surely that is different. There is no well-defined formula for playing strong chess. Further, there are other intangible elements at play, including imagining, reasoning, learning, searching, applying knowledge, and using psychology. That makes the problem much harder, right?

The research field of artificial intelligence has been working to develop computer programs that exhibit behavior that one would normally call "intelligent." It does not mean that the programs are smart, just that their behavior appears to be smart. All computer programs use a well-defined specification – the software that they are given – and chess programs are no exception. However, unlike spell checking, accounting, and navigation, the mathematical formulas used for playing chess are not well defined.

Building a chess-playing machine that is stronger than any human chess player was one of the initial "grand challenge" problems for artificial intelligence researchers. For over 60 years, many researchers, commercial developers, and hobbyists around the world have worked on furthering progress on solving this fascinating problem. Progress was slow largely because achieving this goal depended on the invention of numerous other technologies. The DEEP BLUE victory over Garry Kasparov in 1997 would not have happened without amazing technological progress on many fronts over the past century. Some examples include:

- Computers. In 1900, the state of the art was an electro-mechanical machine that could count data on a punched card. A physical realization of a computer as we know it today did not emerge until the late 1940s.

- Engineering of the components needed to build microscopic devices. In the year 1900, who could imagine the precision required to build a computer chip at the nanometer level (one billionth of a meter)?

- Programming languages and tools for developing software. Imagine the wonder of sitting in a classroom in the year 1900 and being told that you could write a textual description of the solution to a problem (the "program") – and a machine would do exactly what you asked it to do!

- Algorithms that can be used for a chess program. What is an easy and/or efficient and/or practical way to use a computer to sort? Or sift through billions of possibilities? Optimize or maximize a computational result? Numerous algorithms (precise step-by-step methods) had to be invented.

- Devices for storing data. Data storage in the year 1900 consisted of paper in filing cabinets. One could manually manage hundreds or perhaps thousands of documents, but beyond that was a challenge. In 1956, the cost of a one-megabyte (one million bytes) disk was roughly $10,000 (US); by 1990 the cost of a one-gigabyte (billion bytes) disk was roughly $5,000; in 2016, a one-terabyte (thousand billion bytes) costs around $25!

- Electronic communication, the ability to send data anywhere in the world in an instant. This was superior to sending physical mail by car, train, and/or ship. Transmitting information that used to take several days (or weeks) now takes a fraction of a second.

- Chess knowledge. A century of studying the game has resulted in a deeper understanding of the theory and practice of strong play. The chess community learned much from studying Lasker, Nimzowitsch, Réti, and so on. Endgame technique has evolved considerably, starting with Rubinstein and Capablanca. Opening analysis has increased the breadth of playable openings and the depth of the analysis; some early names that come to mind include Grünfeld, Pirc, Alekhine, and Najdorf.

All of the above happened in the past century, most of it in the last half of the century.

Building a hardware/software entity capable of playing chess at a level higher than the very best human players is a remarkable feat. It is a testament to the incredible technology that has been built, and the passionate researchers and software developers who turned ideas into reality. It is also a testament to the brave grandmasters that were willing to do battle with the machine, allowing scientists to measure progress towards their goal. In turn, however, the capabilities of the computer were used by the chess players, allowing them to improve their game and advance towards unprecedented levels of human skill at a rich and complex game. This book tells the story of man versus machine for supremacy at chess, an "intellectual game *par excellence*" (Newell, Simon, and Shaw 1958).

Incredibly, the idea of a chess-playing machine goes back almost 250 years. Baron Wolfgang von Kempelen (1734-1804) was a respected scientist who held favor in the court of the Empress of Austria. In 1770, he made a bold promise to the Empress that he could build an automaton that was more impressive than anything she had ever seen. True to his word, six months later, he delivered a machine that appeared to play chess.

Von Kempelen was a genius. The contraption he conceived of and built was impressive! It consisted of an ornate wood desk with many compartments, some containing a mechanical contraption of numerous interacting wheels of various sizes. The top of the desk had a built-in chessboard, and the pieces could be found in one of the desk's compartments. Seated behind the desk was an automaton that looked like a man dressed in middle-eastern robes. When von Kempelen's creation was running, the wheels would turn giving rise to the impression that something was being calculated. Eventually the machine stopped, and the human-like figure reached out and played a move. Periodically, von Kempelen would approach the machine and wind some dials, planting the idea that the machine used springs for its energy. The machine had no official name, but because of the way the automaton was dressed – in a turban – it was often referred to as the Turk.

The machine was a stunning demonstration of human ingenuity, and everyone who witnessed it play was duly impressed (von Windisch 1783).

> The most daring idea that a mechanism could ever conceive would be without doubt that of a machine which would imitate by more than mere form and movement the masterpiece of all creation. Not only has Mr. von Kempelen conceived such a project, he has executed it, and his chess-player is without any contradiction the most amazing automaton which has ever existed.

The Turk toured Europe to great success and eventually travelled to the United States. During its illustrious career, the machine did battle with many well-known personalities, including Benjamin Franklin. It even went to the most famous mecca for chess in the 1800s, the *Café de la Régence*, to challenge with strongest players in Paris, eventually getting a chance to play the great Philidor. After the game, Philidor apparently claimed that it was "his most fatiguing game of chess ever!" Sadly, no record of the encounter has survived.

The Turk chess "machine."
(Von Windisch 1783)

Perhaps the Turk's most famous opponent was Napoleon Bonaparte (Wairy 1895):

> The automaton was seated in front of a table on which a chessboard was arranged
> for a game. His Majesty took a chair, and sitting down opposite the automaton, said,
> laughing: "Come on, comrade; here's to us two." The automaton saluted and made
> a sign with the hand to the Emperor, as if to bid him begin. The game opened, the
> Emperor made two or three moves, and intentionally a false one. The automaton
> bowed, took up the piece and put it back in its place. His Majesty cheated a second
> time; the automaton saluted again, but confiscated the piece. "That is right," said His
> Majesty, and cheated the third time. Then the automaton shook its head, and passing
> its hand over the chessboard, it upset the whole game.

This account of the game's start is likely apocryphal. It is hard to imagine a
man of Napoleon's stature (and ego) being toyed with by the machine. It seems
more plausible that Napoleon was the one sweeping the pieces off the board. He
played three times, losing badly; this was not the kind of treatment he was used to
receiving! For the record, here is one of their man versus "machine" encounters.

Napoleon Bonaparte – Turk

Irregular Open Game C23

Schönbrunn Palace, Vienna, 1809

**1.e4 e5 2.♕f3 ♘c6 3.♗c4 ♘f6 4.♘e2 ♗c5 5.a3 d6 6.0-0 ♗g4 7.♕d3
♘h5 8.h3 ♗e2 9.♕e2 ♘f4 10.♕e1 ♘d4 11.♗b3 ♘h3 12.♔h2 ♕h4
13.g3 ♘f3 14.♔g2 ♘e1 15.♖e1 ♕g4 16.d3 ♗f2 17.♖h1 ♕g3 18.♔f1
♗d4 19.♔e2 ♕g2 20.♔d1 ♕h1 21.♔d2 ♕g2 22.♔e1 ♘g1 23.♘c3 ♗c3
24.b×c3 ♕e2# 0-1**

Today, it is easy to see that the machine was an illusion. Von Kempelen cleverly designed his contraption to create the impression that the Turk calculated and then played chess moves. Of course, hidden inside the machine was a strong chess player (the chess master Allgaier, in Napoleon's case). The cleverness of the design was how a human could be inside and avoid detection even when, as part of von Kempelen's showmanship, many of the compartment doors were opened to reveal empty space or mechanical parts. Von Kempelen never revealed his secret, and much effort was devoted in the popular and scientific literature trying to figure out how the Turk worked. Some correctly figured out the mystery; most did not.

The Turk had an amazing career. It died in 1854, the victim of a fire. However, the idea of a chess automaton continued, in the likes of Ajeeb (Hastings 1895 winner Harry Nelson Pillsbury did time in the machine) and Mephisto (World Championship challenger Isidor Gunsberg was the computer for a while – a chess master has to do what needs to be done to pay the bills).

The Turk was the first example of using computers to cheat at chess. Here we had man impersonating a computer, a theme that continued to 1929 (when Ajeeb, oddly enough, also died due to a fire). Later on, of course, as computers became stronger at chess, we have a role reversal: humans misrepresented their playing abilities by using computers to decide on their moves.

While the Turk was a marvelous technological illusion, it actually inspired a technological revolution. While it was giving exhibitions in London in 1819, a young scientist named Charles Babbage came to see it and was intrigued. He returned the following year and played against the machine, losing of course. While Babbage understood that the Turk could not possibly be calculating moves on its own, it led him to imagine what it would take to have a machine do that for real. Thus was the inspiration for the dawn of the computer revolution.

Charles Babbage is rightly considered the father of computing. In the early to mid 1800s he envisioned building a mechanical device to perform calculations. Although the Turk had wheels and cogs rotating in such a way as to create the illusion of computation, Babbage's Difference Engine was the real thing – it used the same technology to actually calculate results. It could compute simple mathematical formulas and was used to accurately and quickly fill in numerical tables.

Babbage's experience with the Turk inspired him, and the idea of building a machine to play chess was at the back of his mind for much of his career. Later on he designed the Analytical Engine that, he believed, satisfied many of the computational abilities needed to play chess. It included things that we take for granted today: memory, input and output (punched cards), a computing engine, and an instruction set. Although Babbage's research concentrated on the architecture of machines that could compute, his muse, Ada, Countess of Lovelace, thought about algorithms – how to design a set of instructions that a computer could use to carry out a task. While Babbage is the father of computing, Ada Lovelace is the mother of computer programming.

Charles Babbage with a modern recreation of his Difference Engine.
(ChessBase)

In his autobiography, Babbage gives his reasoning about why he selected chess as a test-bed for his research and, impressively, the first algorithm for a computer to play a game (Babbage 1864). His thoughts on this matter were probably influenced by his work with Ada Lovelace.

After much consideration I selected for my test the contrivance of a machine that should be able to play a game of purely intellectual skill successfully; such as [tic-tac-toe], drafts [draughts/checkers], chess, &c.

I endeavoured to ascertain the opinions of persons in every class of life and of all ages whether they thought it required human reason to play games of skill. The almost constant answer was in the affirmative. Some supported this view of the case by observing, that if it were otherwise then an automaton could play such games. A few of those who had acquaintance with mathematical science allowed the possibility of machinery being capable of such work; but they most stoutly denied the possibility of contriving such machinery on account of the myriads of combinations which even the simplest games included.

On the first part of my inquiry I soon arrived at a demonstration that every game of skill is susceptible of being played by an automaton.

Further consideration showed that if *any position* of the men upon the board were assumed (whether that position were possible or impossible), then if the automaton could make the first move rightly, he must be able to win the game, always supposing that under the given position of the men that conclusion were possible.

Whatever move the automaton made, another move would be made by his adversary. Now this altered state of the board is *one* amongst the *many positions* of the men in which, by the previous paragraph, the automaton was supposed capable of acting.

Hence the question is reduced to that of making the best move under any possible combinations of positions of the men.

Now the several questions the automaton has to consider are of this nature:

1. Is the position of the men, as placed before him on the board, a possible position? That is, one which is consistent with the rules of the game?

2. If so, has Automaton himself already lost the game?

3. If not, then has Automaton won the game?

4. If not, can he win it at the next move? If so, make that move.

5. If not, could his adversary, if he had the move, win the game?

6. If so, Automaton must prevent him if possible.

7. If his adversary cannot win the game at his next move, Automaton must examine whether he can make such a move that, if he were allowed to have two moves in succession, he could at the second move have *two* different ways of winning the game;

and each of these cases failing, Automaton must look forward to three or more successive moves.

Now I have already stated that in the Analytical Engine I had devised mechanical means equivalent to memory, also that I had provided other means equivalent to foresight, and that the Engine itself could act on this foresight.

In consequence of this the whole question of making an automaton play any game depended upon the possibility of the machine being able to represent all the myriads of combinations relating to it. Allowing one hundred moves on each side for the longest game at chess, I found that the combinations involved in the Analytical Engine enormously surpassed any required, even by the game of chess.

As soon as I had arrived at this conclusion I commenced an examination of a game called [tic-tac-toe] usually played by little children. It is the simplest game with which I am acquainted.

Although the algorithm omits important details, at its core is the principle of look-ahead searching.

Babbage was never able to realize his dream of building the Analytic Engine, as he was continually plagued by a lack of funding. Although his design was purely mechanical (rotating wheels with cogs), the breadth of his vision and the depth of his ideas would have profound impact on the computing revolution a century later. Today's modern computer has a high-level architecture not that dissimilar from Babbage's 19th century design. Just as importantly, he envisioned a computing engine that did more than calculate numerical formulas. Without fully understanding the implications, Babbage's ideas were the forerunner of artificial intelligence research.

Fast-forward fifty years. The first real chess-playing machine was built by Leonardo Torres y Quevedo (1852-1936). Inspired by Babbage's work, in the early 1900s he had the idea of constructing a mechanical chess machine (*a la* Babbage) that was run using electronic circuits (a forerunner of modern computing). A machine-driven arm would be used to move a piece. This was impressive technology for its time.

Torres y Quevedo decided to demonstrate his invention using the endgame of king and rook versus king, with the human always playing the weaker side. He designed an electronic circuit that adopted the simple algorithm of boxing in the king and then delivering checkmate. If a win were possible, the program would always play a winning sequence. Its algorithm guaranteed the final result, although not necessarily using the minimal number of moves. As opposed to the TURK with its human fraudsters, Torres y Quevedo's creation was a real automaton, computing its moves without any human input.

The machine was named EL AJEDRECISTA, Spanish for chess player. Although it was built in 1912, it did not gain widespread attention until it was exhibited in Paris in 1914. As happened with the TURK, the machine captured the public's imagination and generated scientific discussion. World War I quickly ended the conversation. In 1920, Leonardo's son, Gonzalo, built a second, improved EL AJEDRECISTA. Of note was that each chess piece had a metal ball at its base, and movement of a magnet underneath the board was used to make a move by rolling a piece to its destination square.

Torres y Quevedo's invention was the first real chess-playing machine. In fact, many regard it as the first computer game in history. Both EL AJEDRECISTAS can be seen today at the *Colegio de Ingenieros de Caminos, Canales y Puertos* in Madrid.

Norbert Wiener (1948)
Renowned MIT mathematician

A chess machine could be built that "might very well be as good a player as the vast majority of the human race."

Leonardo Torres y Quevedo's first chess-playing machine.
(Mde Vincente)

Fred Reinfeld (1948)
Chess author

Fred Reinfeld, introducing the game between Savielly Tartakower and Lajos Steiner (Warsaw, 1935), wrote that: "When Professor Wiener of the Massachusetts Institute of Technology invented a calculating machine which requires only one ten-thousandth of a second for the most complicated computations, he was quoted as saying, 'I defy you to describe a capacity of the human brain which I cannot duplicate with electronic devices.'

"Up to the time these lines were written, the Professor had apparently not yet perfected an electronic device capable of making such chess moves as Tartakower's 20th... The day may yet come, however, when we shall see such books as Robot's 1000 Best Games, or when chess tournaments will have to be postponed because of a steel shortage."

The world saw amazing technological advances in the first half of the 20th century because of and in spite of the global political upheavals. The most profound advance was the invention of the computer. Researchers had known for a long time (even before Babbage) that it was possible to build mechanical devices to automate a series of mathematical calculations. However, the 1930s and in particular the 1940s saw a number of important ideas come together, giving birth to the modern computer. Key to this revolution was the notion of programmability – that the machine would input a series of instructions to execute. Change the instructions, and the machine would exhibit different behaviour. Contrast that with EL AJEDRECISTA, where it could do one and only one task. The notion of a computer was that it would be general purpose and do anything it was instructed to do.

Teams in the United States, Europe, and Great Britain worked independently to build the first computer. Depending on your definition of a computer, one can argue that each was first to the finish line! More importantly, people began to think about what you could make these machines do. The early applications developed for computers were, not surprisingly, military in nature. However, a number of dreamers had grander aspirations for this technology. For example, Konrad Zuse (1910-1995) in Germany, whose Z3 machine in 1941 has a strong claim to being the first programmable computer, developed a programming language and imagined how one might use it to program chess. Alan Turing, who worked on building a special-purpose machine that could crack Germany's secret wartime message encryption technology, had discussions with his scientific colleagues – all chess players – imagining how one might build artificially intelligence machines, including playing chess. But the first to get his ideas out to a wider audience was an American scientist, Claude Shannon.

Claude Shannon (1916-2001) was a researcher at Bell Telephone Laboratories in the 1940s. He is considered the father of information theory, having made profound contributions in a number of important areas of direct applicability to computing. He understood what computers could do and this led him to consider chess as an interesting application. In 1949 he gave a talk on the issues of getting a machine to play chess; this was later elaborated into his pioneering paper "Programming a Computer for Playing Chess." In the paper, he justified the research community's interest in chess with the following discussion (Shannon 1950):

> The chess machine is an ideal one to start with, since: (1) the problem is sharply defined both in allowed operations (the moves) and in the ultimate goal (checkmate); (2) it is neither so simple as to be trivial nor too difficult for satisfactory solution; (3) chess is generally considered to require "thinking" for skillful play; a solution of this problem will force us either to admit the possibility of a mechanized thinking or to further restrict our concept of "thinking"; (4) the discrete structure of chess fits well into the digital nature of modern computers.

If you add one more point – (5) that there are human opponents of varying skill levels that allow one to be able to assess the strength of the chess machine – then you have the introductory paragraph to most of the technical computer chess papers written in the next fifty years!

Shannon's paper touched on all the important aspects of a modern chess program. The contribution in the paper that is most often quoted is the two search strategies that he introduced:

Type A: consider all scenarios a fixed number of moves ahead. Shannon was concerned that a program built on this idea "would be both slow and a weak player." The mathematics supported his claim. If in a typical position a player had 40 moves to choose from, then looking ahead one full move (each side plays a move) would lead to 40x40 = 1,600 possibilities. This is certainly a manageable number. But what if you consider two full moves ahead? 40x40x40x40 = 2,560,000 scenarios. More work, but still doable. Three full moves ahead? 4,096,000,000. This is becoming a problem! This approach would soon be referred to as "brute-force search," usually with a derogatory connotation.

Type B: be smart about the move sequences considered. Shannon wanted to ensure that "the machine does not waste its time in totally pointless variations," thus only examine those lines of play that are "important." Of course, the whole idea hinges on defining what "important" means. How do you decide which move is relevant and which is irrelevant? Were that easy to decide, then chess would not be as intellectually challenging as it is. This approach is often called "selective search" – being selective (smart) about which moves are chosen to invest search effort in.

By so clearly differentiating the two search strategies, Shannon unwittingly set off a debate about the right approach for playing chess. Whereas Type B was a better reflection of how humans played chess, it had the serious disadvantage of trying to define "importance." On the other hand, a Type A approach was simple to program; it just got lost in the mathematical explosion of possibilities. As we shall see the question of the appropriate choice of search strategy dominated the discussion of computer chess for the next three decades.

Shannon concludes his paper with remarks that, with hindsight, are obvious yet profound:

> It is not being suggested that we should design the strategy in our own image. Rather it should be matched to the capacities and weakness of the computer. The computer is strong in speed and accuracy and weak in analytical abilities and recognition. Hence, it should make more use of brutal calculation than humans, but with possible variations increasing by a factor of [a thousand] every move, a little selection goes a long way forward improving blind trial and error.

Consider the human brain and the computer as being two information-processing architectures for intelligence. Each has strengths and weaknesses. Humans are very good at visual analysis, reasoning by analogy, learning, and so on. Computers are very good at doing repetitive tasks, precise calculations, memorizing vast amounts of information, and so on. It is easy to think that the best way to build a strong chess program is to copy the human approach – after all, it works! But the simplicity of the argument does not match the reality of an implementation. What is interesting is that many things that humans are good at are hard for computers to do, and *vice versa*. When trying to solve a problem, such as chess, it is best to exploit the strengths of the information-processing architecture and avoid the weaknesses. Thus if one wants to write a chess program, take advantage of the computer's ability to do repetitive tasks (look at millions of positions), do precise calculations (position evaluation), and memorization (openings and endgames). In effect, that is what Shannon is saying. Just because humans play chess does not mean it is a model we should copy for computers. Just because birds fly by flapping their wings does not mean we should build airplanes in a similar way.

Computing science is a fast-paced field. Many papers are obsolete within a few years of being published. Shannon's paper is one of these exceptional intellectual feats that stand the test of time. Reading the paper today, almost seven decades after it appeared in print, one cannot help but be impressed at how farsighted he was.

Shannon never wrote a chess program himself. He was a tinkerer and liked to build things. He did build a chess machine that allowed up to six pieces on the board. It is unclear how well (or even if) the machine worked, as it never gave a public demonstration. He was eclectic and inquisitive; he also built a machine to juggle balls.

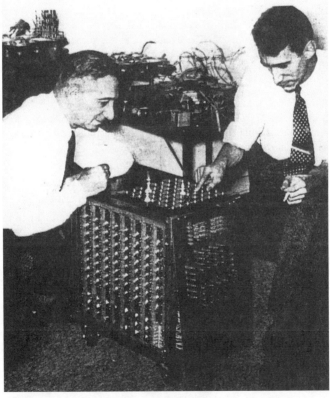

Claude Shannon (right) demonstrating his chess machine to chess master Edward Lasker.
(Monroe Newborn)

Look-ahead Search

When searching ahead, minimax is the fundamental principle used for determining the value of a chess move sequence. Pretend that the two players in a game are given the mathematical names Max (short for Maximum) and Min (abbreviation of Minimum). Max wants to achieve the best that is possible – winning a pawn (+1 in material) is better than losing a knight (-3 in material). Min also wants to achieve the best, but what is good for Min is bad for Max. Thus Min prefers a score of -3 (Max loses a knight; Min wins a knight) to 1 (Max wins a pawn; Min loses a pawn). In minimax search, given a choice of moves, Max always chooses the move to maximize the reward; Min chooses the move that minimizes Max's reward (or, conversely, maximizes Min's reward).

Consider a position, A, with White to move (the Max player). Assume, for simplicity, that both players only have two legal moves in each position. The example uses a simple material evaluation function, where a pawn is worth 1 point and a piece is worth 3.

In the diagram below, the White player has a choice of two moves, one leading to position B1 and the other to B2. Consider B1. Black has a choice of two moves, leading to C1 and C2. Now it is White to play. White could play to D1. Our evaluation of the position says material is equal, so the score is 0. Alternatively, White could try playing to D2. The evaluation is +1, meaning a pawn has been won. Now, given a choice of even material or winning a pawn, which would you choose? The value of position C1 is 1, the maximum of the values from D1 and D2. Similarly, the value of C2 is 3, the maximum of D3 (3) and D4 (1).

What is the value of position B1? It is Black to move, and Black wants White to do as poorly as possible. Given the choice of playing to C1 (1, White is up a pawn) or C2 (3, White is up a knight), Black will choose C1, the minimum of C1 and C2. A similar analysis can be done for position B2.

In our example below, the minimax value for position A is 1 – against Black's best defense White is guaranteed a score of 1 (a pawn ahead), the maximum of B1 and B2.

The above diagram is usually called a search "tree." If you turn the diagram upside down and use your imagination, then it looks like a tree. The starting position (A in this case) is called the root of the tree. The positions at the bottom of the tree, where the evaluation is done, are called leaves of the tree. And, of course, the lines that connect one position to the next represent moves and are called branches.

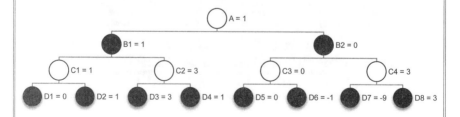

The above diagram is called a depth-3 search tree. All sequences of 3 moves (White moves; Black replies, White responds to Black's reply) were considered. However, the word "move" is ambiguous in chess, so computer programmers usually refer to a move by a player as a "ply." Thus the opening sequence 1.e4 e5 2.♘f3 ♘c6 is a game of two moves, but four ply.

After the war, Alan Turing ended up at Manchester University and worked in the fledgling fields of computer hardware and software. But chess-playing machines were never far from his thoughts. As far back as 1948 he wrote that, "One can produce 'paper machines' for playing chess. Playing against such a machine gives a definite feeling that one is pitting one's wits against something alive." This reflected the discussions he had with his wartime colleagues at Bletchley Park (where the German code-breaking work was done), including chess masters Conel Hugh O'Donel (CHOD) Alexander, Harry Golombek, and Stuart Milner-Barry.

Turing's presence at Manchester spurred interest in computer chess. In 1951, Dietrich Prinz wrote a program for solving mate-in-two problems. His program adopted a brute-force approach (Shannon Type A) – every move sequence of three ply (White's move, Black's reply, and White's move) was considered. The program looked for any White move for which every possible Black move White had a checkmating move. In other words, White (Max) could achieve checkmate because Black (Min) could not find anything better than being checkmated. This was the first use of computers to validate the correctness of human chess compositions.

1952: Checkers

Christopher Strachey (Manchester Computing Machine Laboratory) writes the first working checkers program. It plays complete games against human opponents.

Evaluation Function

In minimax search, the positions at the bottom of the tree (leaf nodes) need to be assigned a value. Some values are obvious: checkmate is a very high score, being checkmated is very low (negative), and a draw is probably assessed as a 0. But what about all the other positions? An evaluation function takes a chess position and describes how good or bad the position is by relating it to a single number, usually an integer. Some programs use the convention that a positive number means White has the advantage; negative is in Black's favor. Other programs use positive scores to indicate that the side to move has the advantage. The bigger the number (positive or negative) for one of the players, the larger the advantage or disadvantage. A score of zero usually means that the chances are even (or, in the extreme case, that the position is a draw).

In Shannon's paper, he described a reasonable starting point for a computer being able to assess the desirability of a position:

> The evaluation function...should take into account the "long term" advantages and disadvantages of a position, i.e. effects which may be expected to persist over a number of moves longer than individual variations are calculated. Thus

the evaluation is mainly concerned with positional or strategic considerations rather than combinatorial or tactical ones. Of course there is no sharp line of division; many features of a position are on the borderline. It appears, however, that the following might properly be included in [an evaluation function]:

(1) Material advantage (difference in total material).

(2) Pawn formation:

  (a) Backward, isolated and doubled pawns.

  (b) Relative control of centre (pawns at e4, d4, c4).

  (c) Weakness of pawns near king (e.g. advanced g pawn).

  (d) Pawns on opposite colour squares from bishop.

  (e) Passed pawns.

(3) Positions of pieces:

  (a) Advanced knights (at e5, d5, c5, f5, e6, d6, c6, f6), especially if protected by pawn and free from pawn attack.

  (b) Rook on open file, or semi-open file.

  (c) Rook on seventh rank.

  (d) Doubled rooks

(4) Commitments, attacks and options:

  (a) Pieces which are required for guarding functions and, therefore, committed and with limited mobility.

  (b) Attacks on pieces which give one player an option of exchanging.

  (c) Attacks on squares adjacent to king.

  (d) Pins. We mean here immobilizing pins where the pinned piece is of value not greater than the pinning piece; for example, a knight pinned by a bishop.

(5) Mobility.

These factors will apply in the middle game: during the opening and endgame different principles must be used. The relative values to be given each of the above quantities is open to considerable debate, and should be determined by some experimental procedure. There are also numerous other factors which may well be worth inclusion. The more violent tactical weapons, such as discovered checks, forks and pins by a piece of lower value are omitted since they are best accounted for by the examination of specific variations.

There really is not all that much difference between today's programs and what Shannon conjectured, with the important exception of additional terms in the evaluation function. This is a further testament to Shannon's amazing foresight.

Prinz's program was conceptually simple to write because it only needed to give one of two values to a position: it was either a checkmate or not – nothing else mattered. But Turing was interested in having a program to play complete games of chess against humans. He wrote the specifications for a chess evaluation function based on Shannon's ideas. He even tried programming it, but it was a large task for that time and never did get completed. However, in 1952 he decided to test his ideas out – if he could not write the program, then he would simulate it. Only someone anxious to see a chess program in action (and a little bit quirky) would have come up with the idea of having the human emulate the decision-making process of a computer. Basically, he would consider all moves in a position, manually calculate the evaluation function for each of the resulting positions using his algorithm, and then choose the move that led to the highest score. Of course this was a tedious and error-prone process, but Turing was just crazy enough (in a good way) to try it.

Turing tried his thought experiment at least twice. The first was against the wife of one of his students. Unfortunately the game score for this historic encounter has not survived. Turing annotates the second game in a paper published in 1953 but without naming the human opponent (Turing 1953). However, writer Alex Bell later tracked it done to a student named Alick Glennie. The following game represents the first game of "computer" versus human at chess. Whereas the TURK used a human to pretend to be a computer, Turing was a human actually emulating a computer. It was a step forward in technology, albeit one that was not so readily repeated!

Alan Turing with the edited text of his famous 1953 paper on Computer Games.

Alan Turing computer simulation – Glennie, Alick
Irregular Open Game C42
Manchester, England, 1952

1.e4 e5 2.♘c3 ♘f6 3.d4 ♗b4 4.♘f3 d6 5.♗d2 ♘c6 6.d5 ♘d4 7.h4 ♗g4 8.a4 ♘×f3+ 9.g×f3 ♗h5 10.♗b5+ c6 11.d×c6 0-0 12.c×b7 ♖b8 13.♗a6 ♕a5 14.♕e2 ♘d7 15.♖g1 ♘c5 16.♖g5 ♗g6 17.♗b5 ♘×b7 18.0-0-0 ♘c5 19.♗c6 ♖fc8 20.♗d5 ♗×c3 21.♗×c3 ♕×a4 22.♔d2 ♘e6 23.♖g4

♘d4 24.♕d3 ♘b5 25.♗b3 ♕a6 26.♗c4 ♗h5 27.♖g3 ♕a4 28.♗×b5
♕×b5 29.♕×d6 ♖d8 0-1

Turing (1953) summarized the game as follows:

> If I were to sum up the weakness of the above system in a few words I would describe it as a caricature of my own play. It was in fact based on an introspective analysis of my thought processes when playing, with considerable simplifications. It makes oversights which are very similar to those which I make myself, and which may in both cases be ascribed to the considerable moves being inappropriately chosen. This fact might be regarded as supporting the glib view which is often expressed, to the effect that 'one cannot programme a machine to play a better game than one plays oneself.'

Alex Bell interviewed Glennie many years after the game was played. Glennie seemed to have no appreciation that he had inadvertently become an important part of artificial intelligence history (Bell 1978).

> As I remember, he persuaded me over lunch to take part in his chess experiment. I just happened to be there and was willing to take part on the spur of the moment. It was played in the afternoon, in his office, a rather bare placed with a small untidy table with paper. We had a chessboard with pieces and Turing had his select rules written on about six sheets of paper somewhat mixed up with other paper.

> Laboratory gossip had told me that mechanical chess was one of Turing's interests so there were very few preliminaries before we started to play. He did explain briefly what he wanted. You can see the recorded game. It seemed to go rather slowly and I think I got slightly bored as I was not a keen player and had not played much before or since – I knew a few standard openings but none of the finer points of strategy. I was indeed a weak player: chess was for me a pleasant relaxation for odd moments with other weak players.

> During the game Turing was working to his rules and was clearly having difficulty playing to them because they often picked moves which he knew were not the best. He also made a few mistakes in following his rules which had to be backtracked. This would occur when he was pondering the validity of White's last move while I was considering my move. There may have been other mistakes in following the rules that escaped notice – possibly they could be detected from the record of the game. He had a tendency to think he knew the move the rules would produce and then have second thoughts. He would then try to find the piece of paper containing that section of the rules, and to do so would start juggling with all his papers. We were playing on a small table which did not help.

> The game took 2 or 3 hours. Turing's reaction to the progress of the play was mixed; exasperation at having to keep to his rules; difficulty in actually doing so; and interest in the experiment and the disasters into which White was falling. Of course, he could see them coming. I remember it as a rather jolly afternoon and I believe Turing must have enjoyed it too – in his way.

Unfortunately Turing died tragically at age 41. In his two decades of his work, he was extremely productive: decoding German war-time messages, defining the boundaries for what was and was not computable (today called the Turing machine), and creating the Turing Test for deciding whether a computer program was exhibiting intelligent behavior. And, of course, playing the first game of "computer" chess.

In 1956, a group of scientists at Los Alamos National Research Laboratory, home of the atomic bomb, were looking for a creative outlet (James Kister, Paul Stein, Stanislaw Ulam, William Walden, and Mark Wells). They had access to state-of-the-art computing technology and wanted to try programing something other than physics calculations. They hit upon the idea of writing a chess program. Unfortunately the computer they used, MANIAC I (Mathematical Analyzer, Numerical Integrator, and Computer), was slow and had a small memory. This limited what they could accomplish with chess. To compensate, they decided to program a simpler version of the game – a 6x6 board without the bishops, no castling, and pawns move only one square at a time (Kister *et al.* 1957). The program, initially called MANIAC, was later referred to as the Los Alamos Chess Program.

The Los Alamos program reportedly only played three games. The first game had the program play itself. The second was against Martin Kruskal, a strong player who later on became a famous mathematician and physicist. Kruskal gave the program queen odds and eventually won. In the final game, the program defeated a lady who learned to play the game a few days before. This is the first known instance of a non-simulated computer program defeating a human opponent at a chess variant.

Los Alamos Chess Program – Unnamed Opponent
Los Alamos, USA, 1956
Played on a 6x6 board. Remove all the bishops.

1.d3 b4 2.♞f3 d4 3.b3 e4 4.♞e1 a4 5.b×a4 ♞×a4 6.♚d2 ♞c3 7.♞×c3 b×c3+ 8.♚d1 f4 9.a3 ♖b6 10.a4 ♖a6 11.a5 ♚d5 12.♛a3 ♛b5 13.♛a2+ ♚e5 14.♖b1 ♖×a5 15.♖×b5 ♖×a2 16.♖b1 ♖a5 17.f3 ♖a4 18.f×e4 c4 19.♞f3+ ♚d6 20.e5+ ♚d5 21.e×f6 ♞c5 22.♛×d4+ ♚c6 23.♞e5 1–0

In 1956, it had been almost 200 years since von Kempelen was inspired to build the first chess automaton. In that time, amazing progress had been made at turning his illusion into reality. The preliminaries were over. All the key technologies were in place:

- Calculating hardware. The first general-purpose computing machine had been built, and year after year they would be improved. Further since the early 1950s, machines were commercially available, albeit at a price that few could afford. Each year the machines would get faster and the prices would drop.

- Data. Computers had internal storage and external storage. Like all computing hardware of that era, the size of the data devices and their speed of access would improve and the cost would drop.

- Software tools. 1956 was the dawn of the software age. The first mainstream compiled programming language – FORTRAN – was about to be released.

- Algorithms. Many of the key ideas needed to for a computer program had been envisioned. Computers were now available to scientists. It remained for an adventurous person to write the first functioning chess program.

- Interest. Numerous groups were interested in artificial intelligence (AI). The Dartmouth AI conference was held in 1956, heralding the start of an aggressive AI research program. Building a program to play a strong game of chess was one of the original challenge problems arising from the Dartmouth discussions.

All the technical ingredients needed to build a chess-playing program were available. Shannon supplied the recipe. Now someone had to create an entrée.

2
1600 (1957-1969)

Writing a chess program in the late 1950s was a challenging task. First, programming languages were in their infancy. FORTRAN was a huge step up from machine language, but the early program translators had a limited feature set, were buggy, and generated code that was slow to execute. Second, the machines had limited memory. A machine with 100,000 bytes of memory was exceptional, but much of this precious resource was given to the operating system and program code. Third, debugging tools were non-existent. When something went wrong, or you suspected something was not right, there was little to help the programmer find the problem. Finally, computers were costly and access was limited. Much of the early efforts in chess programming were hampered by the challenge of getting access to expensive computing hardware. Under these difficult conditions, progress in developing strong chess programs was understandably slow.

Not surprisingly, much of the early work in computer chess was to be done by people who were either an employee of a computer hardware company or worked for a university. Both had limited access to precious computer time (especially in the middle of the night).

IBM was a company who had access to the key ingredient for building a chess program: state-of-the-art computers. All they needed were programmers – a skills' set that was hard to find in those days. So, IBM did what was necessary to find these people (Wall 2014):

> IBM put an ad in the December 1956 issue of *Scientific American* and the *New York Herald Tribune* newspaper seeking anyone interested in computer programming. The ad featured a black knight chess piece, and said that "those who enjoy playing chess or solving puzzles will like this work." One of the applicants that responded to the ad was US chess champion Arthur Bisguier (1929-2017). Bisguier was then hired as an IBM programmer. ... Another applicant was Alex Bernstein, a U.S. Intercollegiate champion. ... Another applicant was Don Schultz, who became president of the United States Chess Federation. He was with IBM from 1957 to 1987.

Alex Bernstein joined IBM and ended up leading a team (Michael de Van Roberts, Timothy Arbuckle, and Martin Belsky) that developed the first program capable of playing a complete game of chess. Soon-to-be grandmaster Arthur Bisguier became the chess advisor for the project.

The program combined Shannon's Type A approach (search four ply ahead) with Type B (be selective and only consider seven "plausible" moves per position). These limits reflected the technology available at the time (Bernstein and de Van Roberts 1958):

> These limits – four half-moves ahead with seven choices at each step – are dictated by the time factor. It takes the machine close to eight minutes to decide on each move

in most cases. If it had to weigh eight plausible moves instead of seven at each level, it would take about 15 minutes for a move. If it carried the examination to one more level ahead, a single move would take some six and a half hours.

It is hard to imagine such search constraints today, where the calculation that Bernstein describes would take a fraction of a second using a modern computer.

In 1958 a movie was made of Bernstein playing a game against his program. The narrator describes this encounter, one of the first chess games ever played by a computer against a human (Education Testing Service 1958):

> To find out how good a game of chess a machine might play, Mr. Bernstein and his collaborators prepared a chess-playing program for the IBM 704, a digital computer that has performed one billion calculations in a single day in computing the orbit of an artificial satellite. The chess-playing program is given to the 704 on a reel of magnetic tape.

> On the chessboard itself the moves are made by Mr. Bernstein for both players. As he makes a move, he communicates it to the machine. The machine prints out the position of all the pieces: its own and its opponents, to correspond with the chessboard on every move. In calculating its moves, the machine considers the board square by square. Is the square occupied? By whose man? Is it under attack? Can it be defended? Can it be occupied? All this has taken a long time by computer standards: one-tenth of a second. Now the computer proceeds to select its move. It has about 30 possible moves.

> After asking eight preliminary questions about each of them, it selects seven of the 30 for further analysis. It tests each of the seven through four moves ahead, considering its opponent's possible replies and its own possible counter responses in each case. It examines 2,800 positions in eight minutes. Now the machine prints out its move. It elects to take the opponent's knight with its own bishop. Mr. Bernstein takes the machine's bishop with his queen. The move is recorded. But the machine rejects the move as illegal. The difficulty is an incorrect coding, which is corrected.

> The game continues with the machine playing methodically and tirelessly. It's never absent-minded and never makes an obvious blunder. In individual moves, it often plays like a master. In a complete game, it can defeat an inexperienced player, but can be outwitted by a good one. This game has gone up to the 21st move. Mr. Bernstein attacks strongly, threatening the machine's knight with his castle. He records the move. The machine's response is a useless pawn move. Its unprotected knight is lost to Mr. Bernstein's castle. The machine recognizes its position as hopeless and resigns.

> After losing a game, the machine will still make the same moves again and lose in the same way. Some day, though not soon, Mr. Bernstein feels, a program may be designed that will enable the computer to profit by its own mistakes and improve its chess game on the basis of its experience against human opponents.

Note some of the amazing statements in the text. The computer did one billion calculations in a single day. In contrast, modern computers will do several billion in a second. The chess program analyzed 2,800 positions in eight minutes. That works out to almost six positions per second. These numbers help explain the weak play of the chess programs of that era. How strong would KOMODO, STOCKFISH, or

HOUDINI be if they could only analyze six positions per second?

The following game illustrates the limitations of the program's search algorithm. The opponent is described as "skillful" (Bernstein and de Van Roberts 1958).

BERNSTEIN CHESS PROGRAM – Unnamed Opponent
Irregular Open Game C96
Undated

1.e4 e5 2.♗c4 b6 3.d3 ♘f6 4.♗g5 ♗b7 5.♗×f6 ♕×f6 6.♘f3 c6 7.0-0 d5 8.e×d5 c×d5 9.♗b5+ ♘c6

This clearly shows the disadvantage of the program's search constraints. 10.♘×e5 wins a pawn as ♕×e5 11.♖e1 loses. The material win is missed either because one of the key moves is not in the seven possibilities considered per position, or after Black's 11th move, say 11... 0-0-0, Black is up a piece – the four-ply limit has been reached!

10.c4 d×c4 11.♗×c6+ ♕×c6 12.d×c4 e4 13.♘g5 ♕g6 14.♘h3 e3 15.f3 ♗c5 16.♖e1 0-0 17.♘c3 e2+

Such a horrendous ending is the result of the search limitations discussed above.

0-1 (in 22 moves)

Alex Bernstein and Michael de Van Roberts (1958)
Chess program developers

Even with much faster computers than any now in existence it will be impractical to consider more than six half moves ahead, investigating eight possible moves at each stage.

Concurrent with Bernstein *et al.*'s work, the team of Allen Newell (1927-1992), John Cliff Shaw (1922-1991),[1] and Herbert Simon (1916-2001) began using chess as a model application for their research in creating human-like approaches to computer problem solving. Newell and Simon worked at Carnegie Tech (later Carnegie Mellon University) and Shaw worked at the RAND Corporation (a non-profit research organization).

Newell and Simon shared a strong belief that artificial intelligence success could be achieved by having computers loosely mimic the problem solving strategies used by humans. Thus a brute-force Shannon Type A search approach was not of interest to them. Simon (1978) expressed his philosophy as such:

Information processing theories envisage problem solving as involving very selective search through problem spaces that are often immense. Selectivity, based on rules of thumb or "heuristics," tends to guide the search into promising regions so that solutions will generally be found after search of only a tiny part of the total space.

The result of their research was the NSS program, named using the initials of their last names. It used goals to guide the search. Human experience was translated into heuristics to help inform the program's understanding. Heuristics were used to help select subsets of moves to consider, decide on how deep to analyze a line of play, and to assess a position. Simon provided the chess expertise, while Newell and Shaw integrated this knowledge into the program.

From Newell and Simon's writing, we know that they understood that some of the positions considered by a minimax search were provably irrelevant: the outcome of evaluating those positions could have no effect on the final result of the search. Hence, they should be ignored; they were a waste of computational resources. This idea later became known as the alpha-beta (α-β) algorithm. The historical record is not clear as to whether Newell and Simon understood this algorithm in its full generality to eliminate all possible irrelevant positions.

NSS pioneered the use of a high-level programming language for chess; all efforts to date had used machine/assembly language. If programming chess was not enough of a challenge, Newell, Shaw, and Simon had to design and implement their own programming language! Their language, IPL (Information Processing Language), was running in 1957 and the following year it was used to create the NSS chess program.

The following game has Herbert Simon testing NSS.

NSS – Simon, Herbert
Irregular Closed Game D00
Undated

1.d4 ♘f6 2.♘c3 d5 3.♕d3 b6 4.e4 ♗b7 5.e×d5 ♘×d5 6.♘f3 e6 7.♗e2 ♗e7 8.♗e3 0-0 9.0-0 ♘d7 10.♖fe1 c5 11.♖ad1 ♕c7 12.♘×d5 ♗×d5 13.a4 ♖ac8 14.♕c3 ♗f6 15.♗b5 ♗×f3 16.g×f3 ♖fd8 17.♗×d7 ♕×d7 18.b3 c×d4 19.♕d2 ♕c6 20.♗f4 ♕×c2 21.♕×c2 ♖×c2 22.♖c1 ♖dc8 23.♖cd1 ♖c8c3 24.b4 ♖×f3 25.♗g3 d3 26.♖c1 ♗g5 27.♖×c2 d×c2 28.♗e5 c1♕ 29.♖×c1 ♗×c1 0-1

In 1958, NSS achieved a milestone by defeating a human player at chess. History was made – never mind that the opponent was taught the rules of chess shortly before the game was played. However, as quickly as NSS came on the scene and achieved an important milestone, it just as quickly disappeared. Progress in realizing Newell and Simon's artificial intelligence objectives were slow and the researchers moved on to other applications.

There is no Nobel Prize in Computer Science. To address that concern, in 1966 the Association of Computing Machinery (ACM) created the Turing Award, in recognition of the pioneering work of Alan Turing. The 1975 winners were Newell and Simon, in part for their artificial intelligence research that was applied to chess. Herbert Simon had an amazing career, as he also won the Nobel Prize for Economics (1978) and the Outstanding Lifetime Contributions to Psychology prize (1993).

Herbert Simon (seated) and Allen Newell.
(Carnegie Mellon University)

Herbert Simon (1957)
Scientist and Nobel Laureate

Within 10 years a digital computer will be the world's chess champion unless the rules bar it from competition.

Next on the scene was MIT undergraduate student Alan Kotok (1941-2006). He took an undergraduate programming course from MIT junior professor John McCarthy (1927-2011) in 1959. Fellow classmate Elwyn Berlekamp recounts that course (Berlekamp 2016):

> It may have been one of the first courses in programming that was taught anywhere that I was aware of, in the United States at least. It was the spring of 1959 and it was a freshman elective for which a bunch of us signed up. And McCarthy… got people doing various projects and four of us got together and decided to write a program to play chess.

Question: Who were the four?

> Me., Kotok, [Charles] Niessen, and [Michael] Lieberman.

> We divided this project up… I remember I got very excited about and did a piece that related to searching for very quick mates… [The program] certainly made legal moves which itself was something of an achievement… It might be ranked a beginner All the programmers could easily beat it.

> So, we turned it in and McCarthy gave all four of us "A"s for the project. We all went

our separate ways except for Kotok who really became attached to this and did several upgrades to the program. Although it started as a project in which all of us were more-or-less equal contributors, it ended with a program that was largely Kotok's, I'd say 90%.

Kotok and new collaborators Paul Abrahams, Robert Wagner, and B.F. Wells continued to refine the program for a few years. It was largely written in FORTRAN, which would become the programming language of choice for chess programs for most of the next two decades. The resulting effort is often referred to as the Kotok chess program in part because of Kotok's major role in developing it, but also because he documented it for his B.Sc. thesis.

McCarthy was in the Newell and Simon camp when it came to artificial intelligence, so it is not surprising that the Kotok program used a Shannon Type B search strategy. The selectivity was achieved much like Bernstein's effort, by limiting the number of moves considered in a position. Of historical importance was the elimination of positions from the search that had no impact on the final result. John McCarthy introduced this idea to the project, but it is unclear whether this was an independent idea of his or inspired by Newell and Simon. However there is no question about the name of the idea – "alpha-beta" came from McCarthy. In his 1962 B.Sc. thesis, Kotok tries to describe the algorithms (Kotok 1962):

> The program was tested late in the spring of 1961. The [IBM] 709 took about 5 to 20 minutes per move, depending on the complexity of the situation. Although the machine did not do too badly, we noted that it was looking at many irrelevant positions. We therefore attempted to find a method of pruning the move tree, without discarding good as well as bad moves.
>
> Prof. McCarthy proposed a heuristic for this purpose, called "alpha-beta." It operates as follows: Alpha is a number representing the value of the best position which white can reach, using a pessimistic evaluation. Beta represents the best position white can reach, using an optimistic evaluation, due to the fact that black can hold him to this position. Under normal circumstances, alpha starts at -infinity, and beta at +infinity. At each level, optimistic and pessimistic evaluations are made, and compared to alpha and beta in the following way. If a white move is optimistically less than alpha, it is discarded, since a better alternative exists elsewhere. Likewise, if a white move pessimistically is better than beta, it too is discarded, since black had a better alternative previously; furthermore we revert two levels since no other white moves are worth considering at that position. The reverse strategy is applied for black.

Can you understand this? From this description it is hard to figure out what is really happening. Further the alpha-beta idea is described as a heuristic whereas it is in fact stronger than a heuristic – it is a provably correct way of reducing the search effort. Thus, although Newell/Simon and McCarthy had the right idea, it is unlikely either group understood the full potential of what would soon become known as the alpha-beta (α-β) algorithm.

The program only played a few partial games – ugly chess by both sides – before Kotok graduated. He concluded "From our analysis of the results, we have found that in its present state, the program is comparable to an amateur with about 100 games experience" (Kotok 1962). A doubtful claim, to say the least.

1962: Checkers

Arthur Samuel's checkers program (IBM) plays a six-game exhibition match against Robert Nealey, a future Connecticut State Champion. Nealey wins the match by a score of two wins to one with three draws. This is the first time a computer defeats an opponent of creditable strength in an official competition.

Alpha-Beta Algorithm

The alpha-beta search algorithm is an enhancement to Minimax search. By keeping track of two numbers, the best score that each player can achieve, large parts of the search tree can be proven to be irrelevant to the final result.

Alpha-beta search can be thought of in terms of an obvious principle: once you know you can do no better, then stop. Let us return to our two chess friends, Max and Min. As before, consider that each position has 40 moves to consider and that a position is evaluated solely by material. Max considers the first move and it wins a pawn. On to the second move, which wins nothing. So far so good. Now the third move leads to checkmate. Wonderful! What do we do now? There is no point in doing more analysis here; we know the result. The remaining 37 moves can be ignored.

This idea can be generalized. Consider a position with Min to move. Assume that Min analyzes the first move and finds that he loses a pawn. Clearly Min wants to do better; a line of play that loses a knight is irrelevant. Min tries a move. Max analyzes his first move and it wins a knight. Now, you might think that Max should keep searching, hoping to win more than a knight. In fact, there is no point to doing any more work. From Min's point of view, this line of play is irrelevant. By playing this move, Min loses at least a knight and possibly more. Min will always prefer to take the move that loses the pawn to the move that loses the knight (or more).

The idea is illustrated in the following search tree. At position B1 Min (Black) knows that the first move leads to the loss of a pawn (C1). Can he do better with the second move? At position C2, Max (White) wins a knight by playing to D3. Now we know that further improving this score is irrelevant to Min (Black) at B1 – Min will always choose to lose a pawn over a knight. Hence, position D4 can be ignored. Using the tree analogy, such branches (moves) in the search are said to be "pruned."

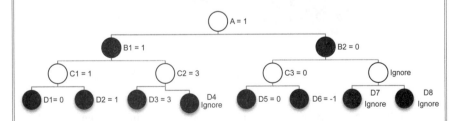

In this example, three of the eight leaf nodes do not need to be considered (D4, D7, and D8), a saving of 37.5%. Can you do better than that? Pretend that every position has 40 possible moves and that a search program wants to look ahead

10 ply. The number of leaf nodes in this search tree is the staggering 10^{10} = 10,485,760,000,000,000. If one is fortunate enough to eliminate the maximum possible leaf nodes, then the search tree shrivels down to the reasonable size of 10^5 = 102,400,000. In practice, one cannot obtain the maximum possible savings. However, modern programs usually search within a small factor of the minimum search tree size.

The alpha-beta algorithm is amazing. Searching 10 ply with Minimax in a reasonable amount of computer time is not possible. If your chess program could analyze 100 million positions in a second, then this Minimax search would take over 1,000 days to produce a result. Add in the alpha-beta enhancement and, voilà, the seemingly impossible becomes easy! The search takes one second.

Who invented the alpha-beta algorithm? There are four competing claims, but there is not enough information available to identify a "winner." Newell, Shaw, and Simon certainly discussed the notion of eliminating provably irrelevant positions from the search tree. Alan Kotok mentions the algorithm in his 1962 thesis and credits it to John McCarthy. A 1961 short paper by D.J. Edwards and T.P. Hart demonstrates "The α-β Heuristic." Also, Arthur Samuel (1901-1990) had a variant of the idea in his 1962 checkers program. In 1963, Russian researcher Alexander Brudno (1918-2009) published a paper describing and analyzing the algorithm, which he says he discovered a few years earlier. However, in the early 1960s the Cold War was in full force, and Brudno's work was not known in the West until many years later. A formalization and thorough analysis of the algorithm did not appear until 1975.

Alan Kotok (seated) programming the PDP 6 computer. Computing pioneer Gordon Bell looks on. (ComputerHistory.org)

Alan Kotok graduated and went on to an illustrious computing science career. In 1962 John McCarthy moved to Stanford University where he became the leader of their fledgling artificial intelligence research program. The Kotok program came with him, and McCarthy tinkered with improving it. This new version is often called the Kotok-McCarthy program in the literature.

In 1965, McCarthy visited Moscow and found out about a chess program being developed at the Institute for Theoretical and Experimental Physics (ITEP). The team consisted of Georgy Adelson-Velsky (1922-2014), Vladimir Arlazarov, Anatoly Uskov, and Alexander Zhivotovsky, with chess expertise from former World Champion Mikhail Botvinnik (1911-1995) and master Alexander Bitman. ITEP Director Alexander Kronrod and John McCarthy agreed to a four-game correspondence match between their programs. Given the tensions between the two countries, the match became more than just a scientific experiment; it became a competition between the USSR and the USA.

The match began in November 1966 and lasted nine months. Every few days a move would be telegraphed to the opposing side; access to computing resources being the limiting factor. The Soviet program won by a score of two wins and two draws. At the time it was not appreciated that the result was to portend the future of computer chess. First, the Soviet program (which had no formal name) used a Type A search whereas the Kotok-McCarthy program used a Type B. Science had its first data point suggesting which approach was better. Second, the Soviet program played two games with a search limitation of three ply; both were draws. Two games were played with a five-ply limit; both were wins. Thus there was the first evidence of a strong correlation between computational resources and chess performance.

As an historical footnote, it is sad to report that Dr. Kronrod was demoted at ITEP due to complaints that too much valuable computing time was being squandered on chess. In contrast, John McCarthy won the Turing Award in 1971, in part for his work on computer chess.

Georgy Adelson-Velsky (left) and John McCarthy playing chess.
Perhaps this game was the human version of the USSR versus USA match.
(Semen Karpenko)

It is not surprising that with Kotok's and McCarthy's work on computer chess at MIT getting some scientific exposure that a new leader would emerge. Undergraduate student Richard Greenblatt (1962) recounts his start in chess and computer chess:

> I got involved in computer chess after I visited the Stanford Artificial Intelligence Laboratory during a trip to the Fall Joint Computer Conference in November 1966, which was held in San Francisco. I had played chess in grade school, and used to play against university students at the Student Union of the University of Missouri in Columbia, Missouri, where I grew up; but I had never played in a tournament and did not play significantly after I came to MIT as a freshman in the fall of 1962.
>
> At that time there was an ongoing match between the Kotok program (that had moved to Stanford with Prof. John McCarthy) and a Russian program. Examining some computer printouts, it was immediately evident to me that the standard of play and analysis were very low, and I returned to [MIT in] Boston and resolved to do better. After one month, I had the computer playing chess, and the following [January]

we decided to enter a human tournament, feeling then, as I still do, that human competition is the best way to measure progress in computer chess, particularly from the AI point of view.

Unlike previous efforts, Greenblatt was able to quickly build a complete program (weeks, instead of many months or years). He had the advantage of Kotok's work as a model, as it was completely published in his thesis.

The program was given the rather esoteric name MACHACK VI, the amalgamation of three components of the work. First, Greenblatt did his work under the umbrella of the MIT research program called Project MAC (Multiple Access Computing to some; Machine-Aided Cognition to the artificial intelligence researchers). Second, what he was doing with his software development was "Hack"ing, a term that had its origins in the early 1960s MIT computer culture. Greenblatt was one of the new generation of sophisticated computer experts. The word had none of the negative connotations that it sometimes has today. Finally, he wrote his program to run on the Digital Equipment Corporation (DEC) computer PDP 6 (VI). Hence the formal name MACHACK VI, although usually referred to simply as MACHACK.

The combination of a more powerful computer, tuned program code, and the alpha-beta algorithm allowed MACHACK to search deeper and to consider more moves in a position than previous attempts. The standard program search was 5-ply deep. Like Kotok's program, at each ply it only considered plausible moves: 15 moves at the first ply, 15 at the second, 9 at the third, 9 at the fourth, and 7 at the fifth (Greenblatt *et al.* 1967). The extra breadth reduced the probability of making a catastrophic blunder because of missing a plausible move. Leaf nodes values included the result of a quick check for any obvious tactics (such as following all capture sequences), often called a quiescence search.

The MACHACK program pioneered two important computer chess ideas. The first was the use of an opening book. Why compute the opening moves every game when there were plenty of books available giving the main lines of play for each of the openings? Larry Kaufman (then a master, and later a grandmaster) and Alan Baisley created the opening book. Greenblatt recalls the opening book effort: "By later standards it wasn't so big, but at the time it was pretty good sized. I don't know I think it was probably 8,000 or 10,000 moves in there" (Greenblatt 2005).

The second idea was the use of a transposition table. During a search, the same position can arise multiple times. The first time a position is analyzed, remember the result. If you encounter the same position again later on in the search, you may be able to use the result of the previous computation. It is an obvious observation, but no one had yet done it. Transposition tables, named as such because the same position could arise as a result of move transpositions, had the potential to eliminate duplicate parts of the search.

An important consideration in a chess program is when to stop the analysis of a line of play and evaluate the resulting position. The ideal position to assess is one that is quiet, or *quiescent*. Shannon already figured this out in his amazing paper:

> A very important point about the simple type of evaluation function given above (and general principles of chess) is that they can only be applied in relatively quiescent positions. For example, in an exchange of queens White plays, say, ♕×♕ (×=captures) and Black will reply while White is, for a moment, a queen ahead, since Black will immediately recover it. More generally it is meaningless to calculate an evaluation function of the general type given above during the course of a combination or a series of exchanges.

There are several obvious rules the one might use for deciding if a position is not quiescent: the side to move is in check, the side to move can give check, the side to move can immediately recapture a piece, a valuable piece is *en prise*, and multiple pieces are attacked (e.g., a fork). In effect, the program is trying to resolve what looks like a forced sequence of moves. Part of the art/science of building a chess program is deciding on the rules for determining if a position is quiescent.

Modern chess programs will search until some criterion is met (e.g., a prescribed search depth is reached). Before doing the evaluation, a quiescence search will be done. This search is restricted to only the moves that help resolve quiescence. The goal is to extend the analysis until a quiet position is reached – only quiet positions should be evaluated.

Greenblatt was ambitious and he was able to get MacHack entered into the monthly Boylston Chess Club Tournament in Boston. On January 21, 1967, in the first round, MacHack VI, using the pseudonym of "Robert Q" was paired against Carl Wagner. Wagner, with a 2190 rating, had no problem winning this historic game.

Wagner, Carl (2190) – Robert Q (unrated)
Irregular Opening A00
Boylston Chess Club Tournament (1), 1967

1.g3 e5 2.♘f3 e4 3.♘d4 ♗c5 4.♘b3 ♗b6 5.♗g2 ♘f6 6.c4 d6 7.♘c3 ♗e6 8.d3 e×d3 9.♗×b7 ♘bd7 10.e×d3 ♖b8 11.♗g2 0-0 12.0-0 ♗g4 13.♕c2 ♖e8 14.d4 c5 15.♗e3 c×d4 16.♘×d4 ♘e5 17.h3 ♗d7 18.b3 ♗c5 19.♖ad1 ♕c8 20.♔h2 ♘g6 21.♗g5 ♖e5 22.♗×f6 g×f6 23.♘e4 f5 24.♘f6+ ♔g7 25.♘×d7 ♕×d7 26.♘c6 ♖be8 27.♘×e5 ♖×e5 28.♕c3 f6 29.♖d3 ♖e2 30.♖d2 ♖×d2 31.♕×d2 ♘e5 32.♖d1 ♕c7 33.♗d5 ♔g6 34.b4 ♗b6 35.♕c2 ♘c6 36.♗e6 ♘d4 37.♖×d4 ♗×d4 38.♕×f5+ ♔g7 39.♕g4+ ♔h6 40.♕×d4 ♕e7 41.♕h4+ ♔g6 42.♗f5+ ♔f7 43.♕×h7+ ♔f8 44.♕h8+ ♔f7 45.♕a8 ♕c7 46.♕d5+ ♔g7 47.♔g2 ♕e7 48.h4 ♔h6 49.g4 ♔g7 50.h5 ♕e2 51.h6+ ♔f8 52.h7 ♕×f2+ 53.♔×f2 ♔e7 54.h8♕ a6 55.♕e6# 1-0

But there was a positive note at the end of the event (Krakauer 2010):

Although we entered our first five-game tournament with high hopes, the program lost its first four games. In the fifth, though, it arrived at the endgame in decent shape, and the programmers decided to offer the opponent a draw. The opponent, an elderly man who perhaps imagined that the computer would be very strong in the endgame, accepted. In fact, the program was rather bad in its endgame play at the time, and the opponent might well have prevailed had he persisted. Richard Greenblatt noted, in a recent e-mail message, "The opponent was an older guy who was a local chess legend and rated about 1400. He was also a bit of a promoter, so although the game appeared legit, we were a bit leery about 'counting' it too much."

The program finished with a score of one draw and four losses, achieving a United States Chess Federation (USCF) rating of 1239. This was sufficient to win the Class D championship of the tournament, and Robert Q (aka MacHack VI) received a trophy. The era of man-machine competition was officially under way!

Greenblatt's appetite was whetted and a few months later MacHack VI competed in the Massachusetts State Championship. It was amazing what a few program enhancements and bug fixes could do.

MacHack VI (unrated) – Unnamed Opponent (1510)
Irregular Sicilian B21
Massachusetts State Championship (2), 1967

1.e4 c5 2.d4 c×d4 3.♕×d4 ♘c6 4.♕d3 ♘f6 5.♘c3 g6 6.♘f3 d6 7.♗f4 e5 8.♗g3 a6 9.0-0-0 b5 10.a4 ♗h6 11.♔b1 b4

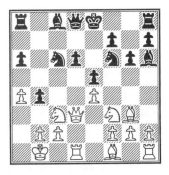

12.♕×d6 ♗d7 13.♗h4 ♗g7 14.♘d5 ♘×e4 15.♘c7+ ♕×c7 16.♕×c7 ♘c5 17.♕d6 ♗f8 18.♕d5 ♖c8 19.♘×e5 ♗e6 20.♕×c6+ ♖×c6 21.♖d8 #

History was made!

Lawrence Krakauer was a witness to the exciting days of MacHack's tournament adventures. Here he recalls a game that illustrates the emotional side of watching your programming creation compete (Krakauer 2010):

> In the particular game I'm describing, the computer was doing quite well, and it looked as if it would win. On the other hand, it could be weak in the endgame, so we knew that it might not pull it off. A master-level player working with the team was observing the game with us. I think it may have been Larry Kaufman, a student at

MIT who was a national master, but I'm not sure of that. Suddenly, he said something like, "Wow, look at this!," and he pointed out a mating combination for the program – the game was won! Except, of course, there was the question of whether or not the program would "see" the same possibility he had spotted. After all, of all the people following the game, only he had seen it.

We ran over to the line printer, and looked at the plausible move list, which had already been printed. The initial move of the mating combination was on the list, of course, since *all* moves are on the list. But it was ranked dead last - the Plausible Move Generator module of the program considered it to be absolutely the least-likely move for the computer to choose. This was not surprising, since it was a queen sacrifice. We knew that if the computer looked ahead a few ply… it would have been likely to see the mating combination. But of course, you can't see it if you don't look, and why waste time looking at a move that will result in the immediate capture of your queen?

Oh, well. How could we expect the program to find a tricky mating combination that only one observer had noticed, and he was a master-level player?

We waited for the program's move, but the program seemed to be taking longer than usual to do its analysis. Finally, the line printer chattered, and we knew that at the same time, the move was being typed out at the tournament site. It was the queen sacrifice, and the program's board evaluation, the large positive number that we considered to be "plus infinity," indicated that the program had seen the forced mate, and thus "knew" that the game was definitely won. That, in fact, accounted for the extra time the program had taken to announce its move. Upon seeing what looked like a mating combination, the program had evaluated all possible responses of the opponent at each level of the look-ahead, to be certain that the checkmate could not possibly be avoided.

We were all delighted, of course, but Greenblatt's delight was tempered by puzzlement. We could understand how the program had seen the mate once it had looked in depth at the queen sacrifice, but why had it evaluated that move at all, the lowest of the low in terms of its likelihood of success? If I'm recalling correctly, Greenblatt actually pulled out the thick source code listing, and started looking through the program to figure out what might have happened.

And then it hit him. There's an old chess adage, "When in doubt, check." The queen sacrifice was a checking move, and the program had been written to evaluate *ALL* checking moves, no matter how dubious they seemed. Nobody had particularly noticed that the queen move was a check. I mean, we saw it, obviously, but it's hardly important that the queen checks the opponent when the queen is going to be immediately captured. But it was that incidental attribute of the move that had caused it to be evaluated by the look-ahead module, which had exposed the mate.

The phone rang. It was one of our representatives at the tournament, all upset. The computer had been winning, he wailed, and now it's throwing away the game by giving up its queen! I was glad to know that I wasn't the only one who hadn't seen the mating combination.

Watch and learn, we told him, watch and learn.

MacHack's tournament career was short. Greenblatt (1992) summarized it by saying that, "MacHack went on to play in about half a dozen human chess tournaments. Its best results were drawing an 1880 player and beating a 1720 player. Its best performance rating in a tournament was 1820 and I believe its official USCF rating was 1523." In recognition of the program's trailblazing success, it was made an honorary member of the USCF.

Transposition Tables

Consider a search where the line of play 1.d4 d5 2.♘f3 is followed by a five-ply analysis. Later on in the same search, the program considers the sequence 1.♘f3 d5 2.d4. The second line of play is said to transpose into the first. If the five-ply result of the first piece of analysis has been saved somewhere, then when the second move sequence occurs, the transposition can be detected and the five-ply value that has already been calculated can be used.

The idea of a transposition table is intuitively obvious. Whenever you search a position, save the position and the search result. When you come across a new position, check to see if it has been previously searched and, if so, you may be able to reuse the result. Note that just because a transposition has been detected does not automatically mean one can throw away the repeated position. It might be that the first time the position is searched to, say, a depth of five, but when the transposed position arises, a search to depth seven is required. In this case the previous result cannot be used.

It turns out that the analysis done by chess programs is full of transpositions. The simple trick of not repeating a calculation can result in a large reduction in the search effort. Depending on properties of the position being analyzed and the depth of search, it is possible to see scenarios where the program runs hundreds of times faster. In complex middlegame positions, the savings are much smaller but still substantial.

Transposition tables are sometimes called hash tables, a name that describes the implementation rather than the idea. Hashing is a computer science algorithm that takes a chess position and "hashes" it into a number. This number is used to specify the table row in which the position is to be stored. The search typically proceeds as follows:

- Take the current position and turn it into a number N.
- Look in table entry N to see if the position is present.
- If present use the result to possibly end further search of this line of play.
- If not present, search this position and at the end of the search store the position and the result into table entry N.

Clearly the larger the transposition/hash table, the more information that can be saved, and the greater the likelihood that transpositions can be detected. Most chess programs will fill all of available memory with the table.

We conclude MacHack's tournament record with a game showing that Greenblatt's fear of the endgame was well founded. In the following game, MacHack squanders a winning position. Note that the program is referred to as MacHack VII, a reflection of the newer and faster computer (PDP 10) that the program was using.

Haley, Philip – MacHack VII
Reti Opening A08
Labor Day Open (3), Toronto, 31.08.1969

1.♘f3 ♞f6 **2.**g3 d5 **3.**♗g2 c5 **4.**d3 ♞c6 **5.**♗f4 ♝f5 **6.**0-0 ♛b6 **7.**♞c3 ♛×b2 **8.**♕d2 d4 **9.**♞e4 ♞×e4 **10.**d×e4 ♝×e4 **11.**♖fb1 ♛c3 **12.**♕×c3 d×c3 **13.**♖×b7 ♞b4 **14.**♖b8+ ♖×b8 **15.**♗×b8 ♞×c2 **16.**♖c1 ♞d4 **17.**♞×d4 ♗×g2 **18.**♞b5 ♗h3 **19.**♗×a7 ♗d7 **20.**♞c7+ ♚d8 **21.**♞d5 c4 **22.**♞×c3 e5 **23.**♞e4 ♗b5 **24.**♖b1 ♗c6 **25.**♞c3 ♗d7 **26.**a4 ♗f5 **27.**e4 ♗c8 **28.**a5 ♗a6 **29.**♖b6 ♚c8 **30.**♞d5 f6 **31.**♖c6+ ♚d7 **32.**♖×a6 ♚c8 **33.**♖b6 ♚d7 **34.**♖b8 ♚c6 **35.**♗e3 c3 **36.**♞×c3 **1-0** (in 47 moves)

Despite MacHack's successes, objectively the program's play was no better than Class C.

MacHack's most famous game was not played in a tournament. In 1965, MIT professor Hubert Dreyfus published an article titled "Alchemy and Artificial Intelligence." As the title suggests, it was a scathing critique of the progress made and the potential for success of artificial intelligence research. Dreyfus singled out the work of Newell, Shaw, and Simon. He is particularly barbed in his comments about their progress, predictions, and reporting of results (Dreyfus 1965):

> The chess-playing story is more involved and might serve as a study of the production of intellectual smog in this area. …

> In fact, in its few recorded games, the NSS program played poor but legal chess, and in its last official bout (October 1960) was beaten in 35 moves by a ten-year old novice. Fact, however, had ceased to be relevant. Newell, Shaw, and Simon's claims concerning their still bugged program had launched the chess machine into the realm of scientific mythology. …

> While their program was losing its five or six poor games – and the myth they had engendered was holding its own against masters in the middle game – Newell, Shaw, and Simon kept silent. When they speak again, three years later, they do not report their difficulties and disappointments … [and] gives the impression that the [within 10 years] chess prediction is almost realized. With such progress, the chess championship may be <u>claimed</u> at any moment. Indeed a Russian cyberneticist, upon hearing of Simon's 10-year estimate, called it "conservative." And Fred Gruenberger at RAND has suggested that a world champion is not enough – that we should aim for "a program which plays better than any man could." This output of confusion makes one think of the French mythical beast which is supposed to secrete the fog necessary for its own respiration.

And this is only the introduction of the paper! Dreyfus had made the astute observation that the field of artificial intelligence, not just computer chess, suffered from unrealistic expectations and unfulfilled predictions. Not surprisingly, this was a message that many did not want to hear, and the article attracted few friends but many fierce opponents. Dreyfus later expanded on his ideas in the widely read book *What Computers Can't Do*.

Dreyfus was a bit unlucky in that within a year of writing his paper, Greenblatt produced a reasonably strong chess program. And, since Dreyfus enjoyed playing chess, there was but one way to settle the score: on the chessboard. Richard Greenblatt recounts MacHack's most famous game (Greenblatt 2005):

> Well, there was a guy at MIT in those days named Hubert Dreyfus, who was a prominent critic of artificial intelligence, and made some statements of the form, you know, computers will never be any good for chess, and so forth. And, of course, he was, again, very romanticized. He was not a strong chess player. However, he thought he was, or I guess he knew he wasn't world class, but he thought he was a lot better than he was. So anyway, I had this chess program and basically Jerry Sussman, who's a professor at MIT now, … brought over Dreyfus and said, well, how would you like to have a friendly game or something. Dreyfus said, oh, sure. And sure enough, Dreyfus sat down and got beat. So this immediately got quite a bit of publicity.

Dreyfus, Hubert – MᴀᴄHᴀᴄᴋ VI
Italian Game C50
Dreyfus match, MIT, 1967

1.e4 e5 2.♘f3 ♘c6 3.♗c4 ♘f6 4.♘c3 ♗c5 5.d3 0-0 6.♘g5 ♘a5 7.♗d5 c6 8.♗b3 ♘×b3 9.c×b3 h6 10.♘h3 d5 11.e×d5 ♗g4 12.f3 ♗×h3 13.g×h3 ♘×d5 14.♘×d5 ♕×d5 15.♗d2 ♕×d3 16.b4 ♗e7 17.♖g1 e4 18.f×e4 ♗h4+ 19.♖g3 ♗×g3+ 20.h×g3 ♕×g3+ 0-1 (in 37 moves)

Although the game was not well played (especially by Dreyfus), all that really mattered was the result. Herbert Simon (1967) was particularly sarcastic in his response to the game:

> What are the facts? A man who exhibited great zest in writing that a "ten-year old novice" had beaten a particular chess program was himself beaten, and beaten roundly, by MᴀᴄHᴀᴄᴋ. Neither fact by itself proves much about the present or future of chess programs, but the two facts may interest and arouse emotions in persons already passionately committed to conclusions (pro or con) on these mutters. To protest amused comment on the MᴀᴄHᴀᴄᴋ victory shows either a desire to apply the rules of rhetoric asymmetrically, or such deep emotional involvement as to cause blindness to the asymmetry. You should recognize that some of those who are bitten by your sharp-toothed prose are likely, in their human weakness, to bite back; for though you have considerable skill in polemic, you have no patent on it.
>
> The discussion of the philosophy and status of artificial intelligence would benefit from de-escalation. Since you have contributed some of the most vivid prose on the subject, may I be so bold as to suggest that you could well begin the cooling – a recovery of your sense of humor being a good first step. You see, the real humor in the Dreyfus-MᴀᴄHᴀᴄᴋ game, as any chess player who plays it over will tell you, is not that you were beaten, the humor is that the Greenblatt program exhibited in this game many of the same human failings that you did (failing to see obvious impending

mates, for example), and still clobbered you by the skin of its teeth. It was a real cliffhanger, in which one fringe unconsciousness was outdone by another. MACHACK behaved not like an "omniscient computer" (to quote you out of context), but like a frail and sometimes desperate humanoid even, shall we say, as you and I.

Academic debates are usually not so spirited! In the end, it would be fair to say that both sides agreed to disagree. Dreyfus was a pariah to much of the AI community for many years. However, with hindsight, the AI community begrudgingly will admit that much of what Dreyfus wrote was correct.

In 1992, Richard Greenblatt reflected back on his pioneering work in computer chess (Greenblatt 1992):

> We say a system is wedged if there exists a binding, a clashing deep within its bowels, that prevents progress that you would otherwise expect. ...

> Looking back, I believe the field of computer chess was wedged when I got involved in it 26 years ago. It was not merely the state of ignorance, although that was great, but a certain "romantic" ideal, among philosophers and mathematicians, that was inhibiting progress. Most of these individuals were not strong chess-players, but some were. Former World Champion Botvinnik wrote a book claiming to be about computer chess, which devolved into a discussion of his famous combination against Capablanca. Thus, we may say, the philosophers, the mathematicians and the chess grandmasters of that time were all more or less equally wedged.

Much like Alan Kotok. Richard Greenblatt was given the opportunity to turn his work on computer chess into his B.Sc. thesis. Unlike Kotok, Greenblatt never got around to it and did not get academic credit for his groundbreaking work. Of course, what he lacked in a degree, he more than made up for in international recognition for his work.

MACHACK was developed for the PDP series of computer, a line of products that became immensely popular. The program was made freely available to PDP users. To that point in time, all chess programs developed had a user community of one – the team that developed the program. MACHACK could now be played by thousands of people.

Greenblatt's work was a major milestone in the history of computer chess. He pioneered the participation of computers in human tournaments. He invented new ideas that would improve a chess program's performance. He advanced the state of the art in arguably the biggest leap forward in computer chess history.

Mikhail Botvinnik (1968)
Former World Chess Champion

I forecast an unprecedented period of popularity for the game. When an electronic machine has started playing chess and played it successfully this will be such a momentous event that every schoolboy will want to know about it. In world history, it will perhaps fall not far short in importance of the discovery of fire.

The young will have to study not only computer technique and programming but also chess itself. And then when a hundred times more young people study chess, when many of them devote their lives to it, then we shall have a real chance of getting a new generation of [Mikhail] Tals and [Boris] Spasskys.

While Greenblatt's program generated considerable media and research community interest, little was heard from the Soviet Union. The ITEP program remained hidden behind the Iron Curtain; progress, if any, was a secret. Nevertheless, others took up the challenge. Another Russian chess program appeared in the late 1960s. Not much is known about it, but in 1968 it played a game against the readers of *The Ural Weekly* (*Uralsky Rabochny*) newspaper. Each week the program played a move, and the readers would vote on a response (majority rules). Although the program's play is weak, it is noteworthy that elite grandmaster Lev Polugaevsky annotated the game for the magazine *Chess in the USSR* (*Shakhmanty v USSR)*. A selection of his annotations is included below (Polugaevsky 1968).

Readers of *The Ural Worker* newspaper – RUSSIAN PROGRAM
Nimzowitsch Defense B00
Ural region, USSR, 1968

1.e4 ♘c6

A move suggested by Nimzowitsch. It is not very popular and has almost disappeared from tournaments, but the computer has its own 'theoretical taste,' which does not coincide with the conclusions of contemporary chess theory.

2.d4 d5 3.♘c3 d×e4 4.d5 ♘e5 5.♗f4 ♘g6 6.♗g3 f5?

It seems that a computer also has human weaknesses – it can be just as greedy as a human being.

7.♗b5+ ♗d7 8.♘h3!

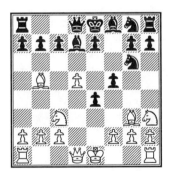

8...c6!

A natural move, but since it was made by a computer it deserves an exclamation mark. This move bears witness to the great possibilities of the electronic chess player. Evidently the computer is able to assess the position correctly. Black's Achilles' heel is the square e6 and the computer correctly decides not to allow the exchange of his white-squared bishop, which is the only piece defending that square.

9.♗c4 ♛b6 10.♕d2 ♛c5

The computer is alert. It avoids the trap prepared by the humans: 10...0-0-0 11.♘a4 and the queen has nowhere to go. The computer also refuses the 'Greek gift' – the pawn on b2: 10...♛xb2 11.♖b1 ♛a3 12.♖xb7 with an overwhelming advantage for White. Who could say after this move that the computer thinks in a primitive way?

11.d×c6 ♗×c6 12.♗e6! ♘h6

What would a chess player have played in this position? He would have chosen the lesser evil: 12.... ♖d8 13.♗f7+ ♚xf7 14.♕xd8 h6, but the computer cannot part with the exchange. We should note however that the computer's combinative ability is not too bad: it saw the piquant variation: 12.... h6 13.0-0-0 ♘f6 14.♗c7 and then 15.♕d8+.

13.0-0-0 ♘e5 14.♘g5 ♘h6g4 15.f3 g6

It has to give up the knight. The fight is over, but the computer (like some chess players) does not like resigning in time.

16.f×g4 ♗g7 17.♗×e5 ♛×e5

This leads to an attractive finish. ... Could the computer have seen the final combination? Perhaps, but even a computer is entitled to count on his opponent's mistakes...

18.♕d8+ ♖×d8 19.♗f7+ 1-0

Such experiments of pitting a chess player against a voting audience had been done before. However, this was a first for computer chess.

Horizon Effect

What happens when a program is told to look ahead a fixed number of moves? Trouble. The horizon effect is the colorful name given by Hans Berliner to the phenomenon of a computer playing an obviously bad move because of its limited search horizon of vision. Consider the following position and assume that Black is only searching three ply ahead.

Black is in check but has a massive material advantage. The correct sequence is

1...♚g8 2.♗×h8 ♚×h8 – but Black loses a queen for a bishop! This is a terrible result, hence the program searches for something better (within the three-ply horizon).

1…c3 The program sees that c3 2.♗×c3+ ♚g8 gives up only a pawn. This is a much better result than the line above. The material advantage is preserved.

2.♗×c3+ d4 Again, a three-ply search only loses a pawn.

3.♗×d4+ e5 And another pawn is lost. Black is still "winning."

4.♗×e5+ ♚g8 5.♗×h8 and White wins.

Having a fixed depth at which to stop searching clearly is wrong. Hence, considerable effort was devoted to identifying when to extend the search. For example, a common heuristic used is to never stop searching in a position where a piece is *en prise*. That would have solved the problem shown above but, of course, more such rules are needed.

In 1957, Herbert Simon predicted that chess programs would be world-championship caliber by 1967. That milestone came and went without much note, except perhaps by Hubert Dreyfus. But a new prediction soon came forward.

David Levy was a young master chess player with an interest in computing science and artificial intelligence. The confidence of youth met up with the over-optimism of research (Levy 2005):

In August 1968 John [McCarthy] and I started a bet that became a milestone in computer chess history. We were at a cocktail party in Edinburgh during one of the machine intelligence workshops organized by Donald Michie who was founder and head of the first AI university department in Britain. During the party, John invited me to play a game of chess which I won. And when the game was over, John said to me, "Well, David, you might be able to beat me, but within 10 years there'll be a program that can beat you." And I was somewhat incredulous at this suggestion.

I'd recently won the Scottish championship and it seemed to me that programs had a very, very long way to go before they got to master level. I knew of course of John's position in the world of AI for which I had the greatest respect, but I felt that he simply underestimated how difficult it is to play master level chess and I was also a bit brash and I've always had a tendency to make somewhat large bets. So I offered to make a bet with John that he was wrong and he asked me how much I wanted to bet and I suggested £500 which at that time was a little more than a thousand dollars. Now to put that into perspective, in those days I was in my first job after graduating university and the bet represented more than six months' salary for me.

So John wasn't quite sure whether to take the bet so he called over to our host, Donald Michie, for advice. And Donald was sitting on the floor a few feet away from us and he asked Donald what he thought. And Donald immediately said to John, "Could I take half the action?" And that of course gave John a lot of confidence and so we started the bet, we shook hands, and that's how it started with each of them betting me £250 that I would lose a match to a computer program within 10 years. Later the bet grew bigger. The following year, [MIT researcher] Seymour Papert and [scientist and computer chess program developer] Edward Kozdrowicki joined the list of opponents and the final amount at stake when we ended the bet was £1,250. But I had never felt that I was going to be in any trouble.

HAL 9000 (1968)
Computer

I'm sorry Frank, I think you missed it. Queen to bishop three, bishop takes queen, knight takes bishop, mate.

At the end of the 1960s, academic interest in building chess-playing computer programs was high. In part this was a consequence of the media and academic attention that Greenblatt's work attracted. The result was several North American computer chess efforts being launched. This work needed a catalyst to increase the efforts invested in the project, attract sponsors, bring in research grants, and advance artificial intelligence research. All this came together in 1970.

Middlegame

3
2000 (1970-1978)

The publicity generated by MacHack helped increase the level of interest in creating chess-playing programs. Tony Marsland, a graduate student at the University of Washington, enjoyed playing chess and this interest motivated him write a chess program. After graduating, he went to Bell Telephone Labs in New Jersey where he continued tinkering with his program in his spare time. He came up with an idea for helping to popularize computer chess research at the upcoming Association for Computing Machinery (ACM) conference (Marsland 2007):

> ... I wrote to Monty Newborn, who was working at Columbia University in Manhattan and was an organizer for the upcoming ACM Fall Joint Computer Conference, suggesting that we provide some kind of a Computer Chess Exhibit. I had in mind a demonstration of computer vs. human play. Instead, Monty came up with a better idea of a computer chess tournament and we met with Keith Gorlen and David Slate (Northwestern University) in a Howard Johnson's cafe on the Garden State Parkway and hammered out a proposal that Monty took to the ACM for their blessing...

And so was born the 1970 ACM Computer Chess Tournament. This event was meant to generate publicity for computer chess, help foster and support research in this area, facilitate the exchange of ideas, and benchmark the progress of developing strong chess-playing programs. In the end, the event was a tremendous success and became an annual event through to 1994. It was soon renamed as the North American Computer Chess Championship. The 1970 event was the start of a 25-year experiment that documented the gradual improvement in the playing abilities of chess computers.

The first tournament attracted six entrants. Of interest in the lineup was Hans Berliner, then a Ph.D. student at Carnegie Mellon University. He was a strong over-the-board chess master, and was the World Correspondence Chess Championship from 1965-1968. In 1956 he won the Eastern States Open, ahead of a promising junior player named Bobby Fischer. Berliner was the first strong chess player to write a chess program – in this case J. Biit (Just Because It Is There) was the first program he had ever written!

MacHack was noticeably absent from the lineup. Greenblatt explains why his program did not participate (Van den Herik and Greenblatt, 1992):

> Basically I was not particularly excited by the idea of computer-vs-computer chess. That plus the fact that I was busy at that time I think are the two reasons. I felt then and I still feel now to a great extent that it is better for the field if anybody can go to the local tournament and play any time when ready. The whole thing, where there is an event once a year, and you come in and play 4 or 5 games, is not a particularly

positive situation. But on the other hand I also understand that from the point of view of sponsorship and people's interest and so forth, maybe that helps promote the game and promote computer chess.

Max Euwe (1970)
Former World Chess Champion

The question is not merely whether a computer can be taught to play chess, but whether a computer can replace human perception to any great extent. If it is possible to arrive at an answer using chess as an example, a great contribution will have been made to the understanding of how the mind functions.

The first game to finish achieved one of the tournament's goals immediately – publicity. Programming errors resulted in the MARSLAND CP quickly succumbing to J. BIIT (Marsland 2007):

> The first ACM …Computer Chess Championship took place in New York. Meanwhile I was busy driving across the continent (probably I was in North Dakota when the first round started). However, I had arranged with my local sponsors [to have someone operate the program for me]. I am sure he would have had a happier time had [the MARSLAND CP] performed better, but at least we recognized the value to the advertising world of a *New York Times* headline like "Computer Loses in King-sized Blunder"! Any mention of computer chess in the [*New York Times*] was better than none, I guess.

The participants quickly realized another goal: the exchange of ideas. David Levy, who started in 1971 to be the guest commentator at the ACM events, observed this first hand (Levy, 2005):

> And one of the things that was very noticeable to me very quickly was the friendly atmosphere at the tournaments, in which the programmers would chat to each other while the games were in progress and between rounds. And they would get ideas from each other. So that after each tournament, the programmers would go away not only with more knowledge about their own programs, but with knowledge about how other people were doing things. And this, in my view, was the main factor in increasing the strength of programs steadily year on year. It was just an acquisition of important knowledge by most of the people in the field. So I think the importance of these tournaments cannot be underestimated in the whole history of the progress of computer chess.

The tournament was won by CHESS 3.0, developed by a team of students at Northwestern University. The program's win was decisive, not only by winning all three of its games but, more importantly, the quality of its play was noticeably above that of the other entries. This program, often called CHESS x.y to avoid having to remember their numbering scheme, was to dominate the annual computer chess tournament for a decade.

Program	Authors	Score
Chess 3.0	Larry Atkin, Keith Gorlen, David Slate	3-0
Daly CP	Chris Daly, Ken King	2-1
COKO III	Dennis Cooper, Ed Kozdrowicki	1½-1½
J. Biit	Hans Berliner	1½-1½
SCHACH	Franklin Ceruti, Rolf Smith	1-2
Marsland CP	Tony Marsland	0-3

Chess 3.0 wins the 1st ACM Chess Championship, 1970.
Left to right: Monroe Newborn, Larry Matsa (ACM President), David Slate, Larry Atkin (Chess 3.0), and Ben Mittman
(Northwestern University). (Monroe Newborn)

In 1968 undergraduate students Larry Atkin and Keith Gorlen wrote a chess program. Physics graduate student and 2050 USCF rated player David Slate heard of this effort and wrote his own program. In 1969, the two teams joined forces with the resulting effort named Chess 2.0. In 1970 Gorlen left Northwestern University and the Chess team (although he stayed in touch and occasionally made contributions).

Robert Fischer (1972)
Former World Chess Champion

Up till now they've only had computer scientists developing such programs, and they won't get anywhere until they actually involve some good chess players.

David Bronstein (1973)
Grandmaster

Whatever you might say and whatever I might say, a machine which can play chess with people is one of the most marvelous wonders of our 20th century!

There was nothing unusual about the early versions of the program. Yet it showed complete dominance in winning the first three ACM tournaments. Larry Atkin and David Slate (1977) described CHESS 3.6 as:

> ...the last in a series of evolutionary changes to our original chess program, written in 1968-1969, and it faithfully carried most of the original design deficiencies. CHESS 3.6 was, like the dinosaur, a species about to become extinct. Basically, a Shannon Type B program, it had a depth-first [alpha-beta algorithm], more-or-less fixed depth tree search. A primitive position evaluation function scored the endpoints and also doubled as a plausible move generator earlier in the tree by selecting the "best *n*" moves for further exploration. Rudimentary as they were, CHESS 3.6's evaluation and tree search were just adequate to make "reasonable-looking" moves most of the time and not hang pieces to one- or two-move threats. Apparently this was enough to play low class C chess and, for a while, to beat other programs.

Samuel Reshevsky (1973)
Grandmaster

Until you can engage a grandmaster of high repute, the computer will never get anywhere.

In 1973, faced with the prospect of trying to make incremental improvements to the program's code that had become increasingly messy over the years, Slate and Atkin opted for a complete rewrite and a new tree-searching strategy. This change to the search algorithm, although cosmetically simple and suggested by Claude Shannon almost 25 years previously, had profound ramifications for the future. Their reasoning went as such (Slate and Atkin, 1977):

> ... CHESS 3.6 had a plausible move generator based on its evaluation function. ... At first we were going to implement a similar scheme in CHESS 4.0. However, with only a month or two remaining before the [1973 ACM] tournament, we changed our minds. Although our plausible-move generator sounded plausible enough, and differed not very much from methods employed in several other chess programs, we had built up profound dissatisfaction with it over the years. A suggestion by Peter Frey triggered some thoughts on this matter, and as a result we dumped selective searching in favor of full-width searching, ostensibly a more primitive algorithm.[2] In CHESS 4.5, all legal moves are searched to the same depth. Beyond that depth, only a limited "quiescence" search of captures and some checks is conducted. ...

The principal motivation for switching to full-width searching was a desire for simplicity. Simplicity was important to ease the testing and debugging that had to be crammed into a short period of time. The easiest way to avoid all the complexities of generating plausible moves is to do away with the plausible-move generator. The trouble with plausible-move generators is that they have to be very clever to avoid discarding, at ply 1, good moves whose merit even a meager 5-ply search would discover. This is true for both tactical and strategic moves. Thus a move that appears "quiet" (to a naïve plausible-move generator) at ply 1 may pose a threat at ply 3 and win outright at ply 5. With CHESS 3.6, and other Shannon Type B programs, whether the right move is played often depends on whether, by sheer accident, that move is inadvertently included in the "best n," n being about 8 or so moves, at the base of the tree. ...

The notion of considering all moves had, of course, been discussed by researchers going back to Shannon (his Type A approach). Usually this idea was met with derision since it was clearly not how humans approached game-tree searching. Further, the combinatorial explosion of possible scenarios seemed to make the idea impractical. Slate and Atkin were willing to try it. They did not have to wait long to get feedback on the idea (Slate and Atkin, 1977):

> The implementation of full-width searching had immediate beneficial results. At last we had a program whose behavior we could explain simply. When it searched to 5 ply it found everything within that range, including both tactical combinations and positional maneuvers, some of which were obscure and ingenious.

> Besides simplicity, a full-width search rewards its creators with "peace of mind." The following daydream (or nightmare) illustrates the psychological hazards associated with the standard "best n" tree-search approach.

> Imagine yourself at a computer chess tournament. In a complicated position your program has the opportunity to shine by finding the right continuation or to embarrass you by making a blunder. You are reduced to a mere agent of the machine – communicating moves between it and its opponent and reporting the time on request. While anxiously waiting for the machine's decision, you speculate about what move it will make. It is difficult to infer the program's thinking processes. By combining an estimate of the machine's ability with an analysis of the structural features of the position you decide that:

> 1. The program will very likely make the right move.

> 2. The program will very likely make the wrong move.

> 3. The machine's move will depend on seemingly irrelevant factors that are difficult to estimate.

> In Cases 1 and 2 the suspense is relieved – one has peace of mind. Case 3, however, is hard on the nerves. Often one likes to be surprised by one's program, but not in positions where there is something straightforward to be done. A full-width search sharply reduces the number of incidents of Case 3 by eliminating the "seemingly irrelevant factor" of whether a tactically crucial move at a low ply level happens to lie just within the best-n group or outside of it.

From the debugging point of view, things were enormously simplified. If one did an n-ply search and did not find the winning combination, all you had to do was play out the move sequence to see if it should be found in n ply or less. If so, then this probably indicated a programming problem. As computer chess programmers discovered over and over, sometimes there was bug in their code, but equally likely was their inability to do chess analysis (and count ply)!

Another innovation in the CHESS series of programs was iterative search. For its decision-making process, the program would search to a fixed depth. This depth limit was set at the start of the search and, for many programs, was the same depth for all searches. However, some searches are easy (there is one obvious best move) and others are more difficult (many promising moves to choose from). The former might result in a 5-ply search that takes a few seconds, while the latter might be many minutes (using 1970s computer hardware). How do you choose a search depth that reflects the amount of effort required?

The idea of iterative search is to keep increasing the search depth until sufficient time has been used. The Northwestern program would do a 1-ply search. Once completed and assuming they still had more time in which to make a move, they would repeat the search but this time to a depth of 2 ply. Again, if the search completes and there is more time available, try doing 3 ply, and so on. Thus the final search depth does not have to be set in advance; the program keeps going until a time limit is reached.

Another important idea used by the Northwestern team was "bit boards." The idea is to use one computer bit for each square on the board – 64 bits of information, or 8 bytes. Bit 0 might represent the square a1; bit 1, a2; bit 3, a3; and so on with bit 63 representing h8. By manipulating the bit board with logic operations – Boolean and, or, not, exclusive-or, and shift – new information about the current position could be efficiently computed. For example, consider generating all the legal moves for the white pawns. If one takes a bit board representing all the white pawn locations (e.g., a2, bit 1, and c2, bit 17), shift the bits to the left one position (effectively adding one to each), and then logically "and"ing it with a bit board of all the empty locations (turning bits off for locations that are occupied), then one has a new bit board showing all the legal one-square-forward moves by white pawns.

Bit boards can be used to quickly compute many properties on the chessboard. Some of the more popular uses of bit boards include move generation (what are the set of legal moves), king safety (determining the squares near the king that are under attack), and evaluating pawn structure (finding doubled, isolated, or backward pawns).

Iterative Deepening

The idea of iterative deepening (ID or iterative search) is to repeat a search over and over again, each time increasing the search depth. This is a counter-intuitive idea since the only thing that matters is the result of the final completed search; the earlier searches represent repeated/wasted effort. So what is the appeal of iterative deepening?

There are four important observations one can make about the importance of iterative deepening:

(1) The early search depths are irrelevant. Assume that adding one to the search depth increases the search time by a factor of 5 – e.g., searching to depth 5 takes 10 seconds, but to depth 6 takes 50. The vast majority of the time is spent in the last iteration. In this example, the time taken by the searches to depths 1, 2, 3, 4, and 5 is dwarfed by the cost of the 6-ply search.

(2) Time control. Given a fixed amount of time, ID allows the program to find the maximum search depth achievable. Most programs use ID to decide when to

---

stop searching. For example, in the scenario above, should the program search to depth 7 if it has to make a move in at most a total of two minutes? If depth 6 takes 50 seconds and it might take a factor of 5 to reach depth 7, then there is no point in starting the search – it is unlikely to complete in the time required.

(3) Move ordering. The alpha-beta algorithm is most efficient (builds the smallest search trees) when it considers the best move first. In older programs, a plausible move generator would be used to order the moves; more often than naught the best move was not in the #1 position. But ID solves this. The results from the 1-ply search are used to order the moves for the 2-ply search, and so on. In most cases, the best move from an n-ply search is the best move for the $n+1$-ply search. Thus, even though ID does additional (smaller) searches, the information gleaned from this work usually makes the overall search effort less than had ID not been used!

(4) Results from an earlier search can be used in a later search. Whenever a position is searched, the best move found can be saved in the transposition table. When that position is reached again, possibly on a subsequent iteration (larger search depth), the best move can be retrieved and searched first – it was best previously, so it has a good chance of still being best.

Iterative deepening helps the program manage time and also improve search efficiency. Further it is simple to implement. It is a winner all around!

The name iterative deepening appears to have been first suggested by Jim Gillogly, the author of the TECH chess program, a many-time competitor in the ACM tournaments.

Slate and Atkin (1977) succinctly capture the frustration they felt in developing their series of chess programs in the 1970s: "The lack of programming tools has plagued the whole field of computer chess. With the proper tool one might accomplish in a day a job that had been put off for years." The truth is that 40 years later, their comment is still valid!

The above program enhancements (added at various times throughout the 1970s) and the later move to a fast computer (a Control Data Cyber machine, one of the fastest commercial computers of that era) allowed the CHESS X.Y programs to stay consistently ahead of the rest of the competition at the ACM tournaments::

1970: CHESS 3.0, first (3 wins, 0 draws, 0 losses)

1971: CHESS 3.5, first (3 wins, 0 draws, 0 losses)

1972: CHESS 3.6, first (3 wins, 0 draws, 0 losses)

1973: CHESS 4.0, first (3 wins, 1 draw, 0 losses)

1974: CHESS 4.2, second (3 wins, 0 draws, 1 loss – to RIBBIT)

1975: CHESS 4.4, first (4 wins, 0 draws, 0 losses)

1976: CHESS 4.5, first (4 wins, 0 draws, 0 losses)

1977: CHESS 4.6, first, tied with DUCHESS (3 wins, 1 draw, 0 losses)

1978: CHESS 4.7, second (3 wins, 0 draws, 1 loss – to BELLE)

1979: CHESS 4.9, first (3 wins, 1 draw, 0 losses)

It is remarkable how consistently well their program played over the first 10 North American Computer Chess Championships (1970-1979). Given the small number of games in each event, the closeness of the competition in terms of playing strength, and the presence of programming bugs, their dominance is a testament to Slate's and Atkin's innovative ideas, careful programming, and attention to details.

Killer Heuristic

Pretend in some position White plays the move ♕f5 and it is refuted by Black's fork ♘d6. ♘d6 is said to be the "killer" move for ♕f5. Now assume sometime later in the search, in a different position, White plays ♕f5. The program has not seen this position before and does not know what move is best for Black. The idea behind the killer heuristic is the following reasoning – ♘d6 refuted ♕f5 before, so maybe it will do it again. Hence, the program tries ♘d6 first, if it is legal in the position.

The killer heuristic is just that, a heuristic. It knows that ♘d6 worked before and hopes that it will work again. The heuristic does not take into account any of the surrounding context. For example, in the first instance, ♘d6 may have been a checking move, resulting in a win of the queen. In the second instance, ♘d6 may be a bad move because the square is attacked by a pawn.

Regardless, given a position with no information as to what move to try, some knowledge is better than no knowledge. Slate and Atkin (1977) characterize the idea as "basically an inexpensive attempt, based on superstition, to find a quick refutation move." They did not invent the idea, but they helped popularize it.

The program was also successful in human tournaments. In 1974 CHESS 4.0 played in an event held at Northwestern University. In a field of 50 players, it scored 4½ out of 6 with a performance rating of 1736. By the end of 1975 it had a USCF rating of 1572. In other words, it was not yet clear whether the Northwestern program has stronger than MACHACK.

In 1976, all doubt was removed. CHESS 4.5 played in the Class B (1600-1800 ratings) section of the Paul Masson tournament in California. Peter Frey (1978) recounts that the program:

> ...played against 5 human opponents with USCF ratings between 1693 and 1784. The program had a perfect 5-0 score. Nobody was more surprised at this outcome than the authors, David Slate and Larry Atkin. They have consistently maintained that the program is about C class in strength. One of the human opponents at the Paul Masson tournament remarked that the program was the "strongest 1572 player that he had ever seen."

David Slate (left) and Larry Atkin at the 1975 North American Computer Chess Championship
(Monroe Newborn)

CHESS 4.5 – Chu, Herbert (1784)
Owen's Defense B00
Paul Masson ACC California (5), 25.07.1976

1.e4 e6 2.d4 b6 3.♘f3 ♗b7 4.♘c3 ♗b4 5.♗d3 ♘f6 6.♗g5 h6 7.♗×f6 ♛×f6 8.0-0 g5?! 9.♛d2?

White just completes the development and misses the very strong 9.♘b5! ♛d8 (9...♘a6 10.c3 ♗e7 11.♛d2 ♛g7 12.♘c4) 10.c3 ♗e7 11.a4 g4 12.♘d2 ♖g8 13.f4 a6 14.♘a3 Shchekachev-Bacrot, Calatrava 2006, in both cases with a strong initiative.

9...♘c6 10.a3?! ♗e7 11.♘b5?! Now this comes too late.

11...♗d8?! After the natural 11...0-0-0, Black is much better as ...g4 is coming.

12.e5?! This does not feel right, but Black is probably still slightly better anyway.

12...♛g7 13.♛e3 a6 14.♘c3 g4 15.♘e1 ♗g5 16.f4

So far Black's strategy has worked well, but now comes the crucial phase.

16...♗e7?! 16...g×f3 17.♕×f3 0-0-0 is even better as 18.♕×f7? runs into 18...♕×f7 19.♖×f7 ♘×d4 −+ .

17.f5?

White is not ready for this advance yet. After 17.♘e4 d5 18.e×d6 c×d6 19.c3, he is slightly better as Black's king has problems finding a safe harbor.

17...e×f5? Both miss the very strong 17...♕g5!, after which Black is clearly better.

18.♗×f5

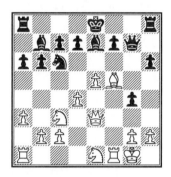

18...♘×d4?

This runs into a powerful shot. The normal 18...0-0-0= was called for.

19.♗×d7+! ♔×d7 20.♕×d4+ ♔c8 21.♘d3 ♔b8?

After this slow move, the computer gives Black no chance and controls the game. 21...♖d8 22.♕f4 ♖d7 was the last chance to fight.

22.♕d7 ♕g5?

This just gives up a pawn. 22...g3 23.h3 and 22...♕f8 were more tenacious.

23.♖×f7 ♕e3+?! 23...g3 offers more resistance.

24.♔h1 ♗d8 25.♕×g4 25.♖e1!?+− .

25...♔a7 26.e6 ♗g5?! 27.♖e1 ♖hg8 28.♖×e3 ♗×e3 29.♖g7 ♖af8 30.h4 1-0

With a 1950 performance rating, CHESS 4.5 now had a USCF rating of 1822. Why the sudden improvement? As much as the program creators would love to say it was the result of brilliant ideas, thorough testing, and careful programming, the answer in this case was simpler. No doubt all of the above contributed, but the real reason was the move to a Control Data Corporation (CDC) 170 computer. This was one of the fastest commercial computers in the world, and allowed the program to do an unprecedented amount of searching for each move decision. The days of 5-ply searches under tournament conditions were coming to an end. The faster computer and better search algorithms allowed 6-ply in the middlegame and deeper in endgames. Deeper searching clearly enabled stronger play. But what was the value of an extra ply of search? It would be a few years before that question was answered.

The following year CHESS 4.5 played in the Minnesota Open Championship. Its impressive score of five wins and one loss included the first tournament victory over a player with a 2000+ rating.

CHESS 4.5 – Fenner, Charles (2016)
Sicilian Defense B42
84th Minnesota Open (2), 19.02.1977

1.e4 c5 2.♘f3 e6 3.d4 c×d4 4.♘×d4 a6 5.c4 ♘f6 6.♗d3 ♕c7 7.0-0 ♗c5 8.♘b3 ♗a7 9.♘c3 ♘c6 10.♗g5 ♘e5 11.♗×f6 g×f6 12.♕e2 d6 13.♔h1 ♗d7 14.f4 ♘×d3 15.♕×d3 0-0-0 16.♖ad1 ♗c6?!

The beginning of a wrong plan. 16...h5 is more in the spirit of the position as 17.♕×d6 ♕×d6 18.♖×d6 h4 19.h3 ♗c6 20.♖×d8+ ♖×d8 gives Black compensation for the pawn.

17.f5 ♗b8?! 18.g3?!

Slightly weakening. 18.♕h3 is more precise.

18...h5 19.f×e6 h4?

19...f×e6 20.♘d4 ♗d7 limits the damage.

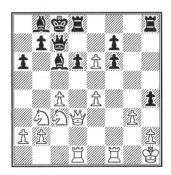

20.♖×f6?

Very greedy. 20.♘d5 wins, e.g., 20...♗×d5 21.c×d5 ♗a7 22.♖c1 ♗c5 23.♘d4+−.

20...h×g3?!

This is too ambitious. After 20...f×e6 21.♘d4 (21.♖×e6 is met by 21...d5) 21...♕g7, Black is not worse.

21.♕×g3 Objectively 21.♖×f7! is better, but very messy, e.g., 21...♕b6 22.♖d2 ♖dg8 23.♕d4 and White is for choice.

21...♖dg8?

Based on a miscalculation. After 21...f×e6 22.♖×e6 ♕f7, Black has more than enough compensation for the two pawns.

22.e×f7! The computer shows tactical alertness.

22...♕×f7 22...♖×g3?! 23.f8♕+ ♖×f8? runs into 24.♖×f8+ ♔d7 25.♖f7++−.

23.♖×f7 ♖×g3 24.♘d5 Fenner offers a draw, which is declined.

24...♗e8?

Desperation. 24...♖gh3 is necessary.

25.♘b6+ ♔d8 26.♖×b7 ♗c6 27.♖×b8+ ♔c7 28.♖c8+ ♖×c8 29.h×g3 ♗×e4+ 30.♔g1 ♖h8 31.♘d5+ ♔c6 32.♘a5+ 1-0 A very good game by the machine for those times.

The only loss was to a player rated 2175. With a 2271 performance rating, the chess and computer-chess worlds were stunned to realize that master-rated chess programs were not that far off.

The highlight of 1978 was the Twin Cities Open in Minneapolis. CHESS 4.5 blitzed the field, winning all five games. The program's USCF rating climbed past the magical barrier of 2000. With a 2014 rating, CHESS 4.5 held the official title of Expert.

And then there was speed (blitz) chess. In March 1977, CHESS 4.5 scored 2 points out of 4 in an exhibition blitz match against David Levy, a 2300+ performance rating. This was followed up in September with an exhibition game in London against Grandmaster Michael Stean (2485). User interfaces were not as user friendly then as they are today, so Levy acted as the conduit for transferring the computer's moves from the screen to the chessboard. Stean was given five minutes for the game; the program had five seconds per move (because of the user interface issue) and would forfeit if the game did not end by move 60.

CHESS 4.6 – Stean, Michael (2485)
Owen's Defense B00
Blitz game London, 18.09.1977

1.e4 b6 2.d4 ♗b7 3.♘c3 c5?!

Experimental. 3...e6 is the main move.

4.d×c5

A good choice under the circumstances. 4.d5 scores better in human games.

4...b×c5 5.♗e3 d6 6.♗b5+ ♘d7 7.♘f3 e6 8.0-0 a6 9.♗×d7+?

A mistake that reduces White's potential. After 9.♗a4, White's lead in development is very dangerous.

9...♕×d7 10.♕d3 ♘e7 11.♖ad1

Stean: "The damned computer has one of my pawns." But he does find a defense.

11...♖d8 12.♕c4?

This and the next moves show that the computer has no concrete idea of how to play the position. 12.♘d2 ♘c6 13.♗f4 ♗e7 14.♕g3 0-0 15.♘b3 applies much more pressure.

12...♘g6 13.♖fe1? 13.♗×c5? is met by 13...♕c6–+ .

13...♗e7 14.♕b3? White should try to halve the bishop pair with 14.♗g5.

14...♕c6 15.♔h1?

An odd move. White should not waste time and continue the initiative with 15.♘d2 but Black is better also in this case.

15...0-0 16.♗g5 ♗a8 16...♗xg5 17.♘xg5 h6 18.♘f3 ♖b8 is more precise.

17.♗×e7 ♘×e7 18.a4 ♖b8 19.♕a2 ♖b4 20.b3 White's queen looks very odd now.

20...f5 21.♘g5 f×e4 22.♘c×e4

22...♖×f2?

Flashy, greedy and wrong. After 22...d5 23.♘g3 ♖f6 24.c3 ♖g4 Black has a strong attack coming up.

23.♖×d6?

Also too greedy. Stopping the attack first with 23.♔g1 is called for.

23...♕×d6?

It is better to sacrifice the exchange or a pawn with 23...♕c7 24.♖dd1 (24.♘xf2 ♕xd6 25.c4 ♘f5 26.♖e6 ♕f8) 24...♖xe4 25.♘xe4 ♖f4 with compensation in both cases as a result of White's offside queen.

24.♘×d6 ♖×g2?

This is "easily" parried by the machine. 24...h6 25.♘ge4 ♗xe4 26.♘xe4 ♖xe4 27.♕b1 ♖g4 28.♖g1 ♖e4 29.♕d1 ♘f5 is much more active and gives practical drawing chances.

25.♘ge4 ♖g4 25...♖xe4 26.♘xe4 ♖g4 27.♕a3 ♗xe4+ 28.♖xe4 ♖xe4 29.♕xc5 +−

26.c4 ♘f5 27.h3 Stean: "This computer is a genius."

27...♘g3+?! 27...♘xd6 28.hxg4 ♘xe4 offers more resistance.

28.♔h2 Stean: "Help."

28...♖×e4 29.♕f2 h6 29...♖e1? 30.♕f7+ ♔h8 31.♕f8#

30.♘×e4 ♘×e4 31.♕f3

The computer knows no fear and sees no ghosts.

31...♖b8 32.♖×e4 ♖f8 33.♕g4 ♗×e4 34.♕×e6+ ♔h8 35.♕×e4 ♖f6 36.♕e5 ♖b6 37.♕×c5 ♖×b3 38.♕c8+ ♔h7 39.♕×a6 1-0

This was the first time that a grandmaster had lost to a computer chess program. It was a watershed year for CHESS 4.6, defeating GM Robert Hübner and IMs Hans Berliner, Lawrence Day, and Zvonko Vranešić at speed chess.

Another milestone was reached when CHESS 4.6 won against United States Champion Walter Browne in a game played in a 44-board simultaneous exhibition. With another grandmaster scalp to the computer's credit, it was now just a matter of time before grandmasters would lose at tournament time controls.

Then there was the idea of creating a man-machine chess-playing team. David Levy recounts of an interesting game played at the 1979 ACM tournament:

> The game against Slate playing in combination with [CHESS 4.9], that was the first example of what is now called advanced chess. And it was interesting because it was an innovation at the time to have a chess master playing against a program together with a human chess player. The idea was that both the program and Slate were weaker than me, but the idea was to see whether together they could make a formidable pair. I don't remember the game itself, but I remember that it was quite easy for me to win. But what's interesting is that about 20 years after that, Kasparov came out with the idea of, as it's now called, advanced chess, with a strong grandmaster plus a chess program, against another strong grandmaster with a chess program.

Meanwhile, on the other side of the planet, the Russians had not abandoned their interest in computer chess. Mikhail Botvinnik continued to report that he was working on a program, but little of substance on what he was doing reached the West. However, the ITEP program made famous by the 1966-1967 USSR-USA match was still of interest to Russian scientists. In 1971 Arlazarov and Uskov worked on a successor program, and were joined by an experienced programmer, Mikhail Donskoy (1948-2009). Now working at the Institute of Control Sciences in Moscow, the team felt confident enough in their program that in 1972 they braved exposing it to the public. A two game correspondence match was played between the program and the readers of *Komsomolskaya Pravda*, the youth newspaper for the All-Union Leninist Young Communist League. Moves were played once a week, with the move receiving the most votes from the readers being the one selected. A journalist at the newspaper suggested a name for the program – KAISSA after Caissa, the goddess of chess. Donskoy (undated) recounts:

> The match took almost a year – from January to November – and ended in victory for [the] people with a score of 1.5 to 0.5. Those who remember the hot summer of 1972 envied the authors of KAISSA who spent a couple of days a week in an air-conditioned machine room – the coolest place in Moscow.

KAISSA – Readers of *Komsomolskaya Pravda*
Sicilian Defense Rossolimo Variation B50
Correspondence match (1), 1972

1.e4 c5 2.♘c3 ♘c6 3.♘f3 d6 4.♗b5 ♗d7 5.0-0 g6 6.d4 c×d4 7.♘×c6 d×c3 8.♗×b7 ♖b8 9.♗d5 ♗g7 9...c×b2? runs into 10.♗×b2 ♖×b2 11.♕d4 and both rooks are attacked.

10.b3 ♘f6 11.♗e3 ♕c7 12.♕d4 a5 13.♗c4 0-0 14.♖ae1 ♗c6 15.e5 ♗×f3 16.e×d6 e×d6 17.g×f3 ♘h5 18.♕d3 ♗e5 19.♗d4 ♔g7 19...♗×d4!? 20.♕×d4 ♖fd8 21.a4 d5 22.♗b5 ♘g7 is slightly more precise.

20.♖e3 f6 21.♖fe1 ♘f4 22.♕×c3 ♖bc8 23.a4? White does not have time for this. After 23.♕d2, Black has compensation for the pawn but not more.

23...♕d7 24.♗×e5? This only opens the f-file for Black's attack. 24.♔h1 limits the damage.

24...f×e5 25.♔h1 ♕h3 26.♖g1

26...♘d5? A tactical miscalculation. After 26...♖f5, Black's attack crashes through sooner or later, e.g., 27.♖g3 ♕h6 28.♕a1 ♖h5 29.♕g1 d5 30.♗d3 ♘×d3 31.♖×d3 ♖×c2−+ .

27.♕×a5 ♖c5 28.♕a7+ ♖c7 29.♕a5 ♖c5 30.♕a7+ ♖f7?! 31.♕×c5 d×c5 32.♗×d5 ♖f4 33.♖×e5 ♖×f3?! 34.♗×f3 Modern engines want to continue here with 34.♖e7+!? ♔f8 35.♖×h7 ♕×h7 36.♗×f3 when only White can play for a win. **34...♕×f3+ 35.♖g2 ½-½**

Readers of *Komsomolskaya Pravda* – KAISSA

Nimzo-Larsen Opening A01
Correspondence match (2), 1972

The second game showed the value of finding a good opening setup. The computer plays too slow and does not manage to solve the problems of the light-squared bishop and gets crushed.

1.b3 e5 2.♗b2 ♘c6 3.c4 f6 4.♘c3 ♗b4 5.♘d5 ♘ge7 6.a3 ♗d6 7.g3 0-0 8.♗g2 ♘g6 9.e3 f5 10.♘e2 ♖e8 11.♕c2 e4 12.d3 e×d3 13.♕×d3 ♖f8 14.f4 ♗e7 15.h4 h6 16.h5 ♘h8 17.e4 d6 18.0-0-0 ♖f7 19.♘×e7+ ♕×e7 20.♘c3 ♗e6 21.♘d5 ♕d7 22.♘e3 f×e4 23.♗×e4 ♘e7 24.♗×b7 ♖b8 25.♗e4 ♘f5 26.♘d5 a5 27.g4 ♘e7 28.♘×e7+ ♖×e7 29.g5 h×g5 30.f5 ♘f7 31.f×e6 ♕×e6 32.♗d5 ♕e3+ 33.♕×e3 ♖×e3 34.♖df1 1-0

Not much else was known about KAISSA until it made its competitive debut in 1974. From discussions with the programmers, some important innovations were in Kaissa:

- Sophisticated time management, including thinking on the opponent's time;
- Extensive use of bit boards, probably predating the CHESS X.Y work;
- Use of the null-move search; and
- Searching using "human-like" reasoning.

Null-move searching was an important idea, whose real strength was not to be realized for another 15 years. The basic idea is for one side to make an illegal move in chess – to pass. Forfeiting the move allows the opponent the opportunity to realize whatever threat they may have in the position. Thus a null-move search is seen as providing a worst-case scenario. The reasoning goes like this: "If I do not move and my opponent then wins a knight, then with my move I better find a way to parry the threat to win my knight." In other words, a null-move search can give the program valuable information about the opponent's threats. Of course, the above reasoning breaks down in a *zugzwang* position.

The human-like reasoning, called the Method of Analogies, was especially intriguing to the research community. The idea was to use analogies to eliminate parts of the search. Consider a position where a sequence of moves allows White to win a knight. Suppose later on in the search a similar position is reached – it is identical except for a pawn having moved one square forward. The question is whether White can play the same sequence of moves to win a knight. The Method of Analogies analyzes all the preconditions needed for a combination to work. If an irrelevant move does not change any of the preconditions, then the original combination should still work.

Clearly there was innovative computer chess research going on in the Soviet Union. Other than the two correspondence games above, the West had no inkling as to how strong the KAISSA program might be. How do you get an unknown program in Russia to compete with the top programs in the rest of the world? David Levy (2005) recounts what happened:

I remember very well in 1973 when we had the ACM tournament in Atlanta, and after the tournament was over, you [Monty Newborn] and Ben Mittman and I were in the bar at the Hyatt Regency, and Ben said, "Gee, guys, this is such great fun. What can we do next?" And I thought for a moment, and I said, "Why don't we have a world championship?" And so we started talking about it, and then I explained to the two of you that how FIDE organizes its world championship every three years, which it did at that time. And we all agreed that would be a lot of fun. And so we started thinking about where we could hold it, and who would sponsor it. I can't remember whether it was you or Ben mentioned that the following year there was going to be an IFIP [International Federation for Information Processing] Congress in Sweden, in Stockholm. And so somehow contact was made with IFIP, and they liked the idea. So they put up the money for sponsoring the championships in Stockholm, and we all went off to Stockholm. That was very interesting, because we not only had most of the top programs from the ACM tournament, we also had some European programs who were able to get there more easily. One of those was KAISSA, the Russian program, about which we knew nothing before it entered for Stockholm.

The first World Computer Chess Championship (1974) had 13 entries, representing the United States (3 programs), Great Britain (3), Canada (2), Soviet Union (1), Austria (1), Norway (1), Switzerland (1), and Hungary (1). KAISSA won the tournament, winning all four games. The pre-tournament favorite, CHESS 4.0, was handed a defeat in round 2 by CHAOS (Ira Ruben, Fred Swartz, Joe Winograd, Victor Berman, William Toikka). CHESS 4.0, CHAOS and RIBBIT tied for second place with 3 points. After the event, a friendly game was played between CHESS 4.0 and KAISSA; the Northwestern program was unable to convert a winning position and drew the game.

Mikhail Donskoy (KAISSA) at the 1974 World Computer Chess Championship
(Monroe Newborn)

CHESS 4.0 with its Type A search approach lost a beautiful game to CHAOS, a Type B searcher. In the following position, CHAOS played ♘xe6, a move that is obvious to masters but fraught with danger for a computer program that cannot search deep enough to see the full consequences. Using positional factors to compensate for the lost material, CHAOS found the right move. At the time, ♘xe6 was called the most beautiful move by a computer chess program.

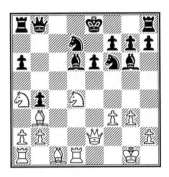

The KAISSA team returned triumphant to Moscow. With them they carried the prize for first place (Donskoy undated):

> I was awarded the "Caissa" gold (in the sense of pure gold) medal of the world champion among chess programs, [and] then deposited [it] in the [Institute of Control Sciences]. In the years of perestroika, its trace was lost in the museums of various chess clubs, where she was transferred without the consent of the authors' team members.

The next year, the Russian computer-chess community achieved another milestone – helping a grandmaster win an adjourned position (Levy 1988):

> Certain standard endgames have been programmed in such a way as to allow perfect or near-perfect play by computers. This work started in the Soviet Union, with a routine to play the endgame of king, queen and g-pawn (or b-pawn) against king and queen. International Grandmaster David Bronstein, who was once a challenger for the World Championship, actually reached this endgame in the Soviet Union in 1975. During the adjournment he telephoned the programmers who looked up their database and told Bronstein how to play. When the game was resumed, Bronstein followed the program's recommendation and eventually won (the opponent deviated from the expected line of play). After the game it was discovered that the program actually had an error in the key variation, overlooking a stalemate possibility, but I understand that this mistake was immediately corrected.

In 1977, KAISSA returned to competition at the Second World Computer Chess Championship in Toronto against a field of 16 competitors. This time there was role reversal between KAISSA and CHESS 4.6. CHESS 4.6 won the event with four wins and KAISSA tied for second place with DUCHESS (Eric Jensen, Tom Truscott, Bruce Wright) after an early loss to DUCHESS. As in 1974, after the event was over there was a friendly game between CHESS 4.6 and KAISSA. This time the American program won. With its world championship title, track record in North American computer chess events, and strong play in human events, CHESS X.Y was clearly the strongest program of its day.

One position at the world championship caused quite a stir. The following position is from the game DUCHESS versus KAISSA. DUCHESS had just played 34.♕a8+ and to the surprise and amusement of the spectators, KAISSA relied with the incomprehensible 34...♖e8. Clearly this was an enormous blunder, the result of a programming error. Even the chess experts in the audience had a good laugh, including former World Champion Mikhail Botvinnik. It was only after the game that it became known that ♖e8 was forced – the obvious ♔g7 is refuted by 35.♕f8+ leading to mate. This illustrates the strength of the computer's "brute-force approach" to search; by considering all moves, nothing is missed within the search depth. In this case, the human heuristic approach failed to consider the non-obvious move ♕f8.[3]

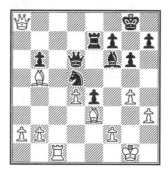

KAISSA participated in the 1980 World Computer Chess Championship but finished in the middle of the pack. By then the team members had moved on to other projects.

Monroe Newborn (1977)
Computer chess developer and event organizer

Masters used to come to computer chess tournaments to laugh. Now they come to watch. Soon they will come to learn.

Personality

Often a chess player – man or machine – is characterized by their playing style. For example, Mikhail Tal excited audiences with his aggressive attacking approach to the game, while Tigran Petrosian was admired for his subtle positional play. Computer chess programs also have styles, as Shannon noted in his famous paper:

It is interesting that the "style" of play of the machine can be changed very easily by altering some of the coefficients and numerical factors involved in the evaluation function and the other programs. By placing high values on positional weaknesses, etc., a positional-type player results. By more intensive examination of forced variations it becomes a combination player. Furthermore, the strength of the play can be easily adjusted by changing the depth of calculation and by omitting or adding terms to the evaluation function.

Thus by changing as little as a single number in a program, one could transform a Tal into a Petrosian, or a *patzer* into a grandmaster. In other words, computer programs have the advantage of being able to take on multiple personalities – and without needing psychiatric help.

During these exciting days of computer chess interest, little was heard from Richard Greenblatt. MacHack was available on the PDP computers, and was still arguably the most widely played chess program in the world. However, Greenblatt had moved on to other projects, most notably designing and building a special-purpose computer to run programs efficiently that were written in the Lisp programming language (a John McCarthy creation). Eventually this work would lead to Greenblatt creating a company to commercialize this work.

MacHack continued to attract attention. In 1977, it was not the strongest program but, in many circles, was better known than Chess x.y. This reputation led to an unexpected encounter. In 1977, former World Champion Bobby Fischer (1943-2008) showed up at MIT wanting to play MacHack. Since defeating Boris Spassky for the world title in 1972, Fischer had played no public games. In 1975 he refused to defend his title against Anatoly Karpov. And then, surprise, he wanted to play games against a computer.

Not much is known about the circumstances under which the games were played. Greenblatt was not present. No pictures were taken. The program's logs of the game have not been published. Fischer submitted the game scores to a fledgling publication, the *Computer Chess Newsletter*, without comments.

MacHack – Fischer, Robert
Sicilian Defense B92
Exhibition match (1), MIT, 1977

1.e4 c5 2.♘f3 d6 3.d4 c×d4 4.♘×d4 ♘f6 5.♘c3 a6 6.♗e2 e5 7.♘b3 ♗e7 8.♗e3 0-0 9.♕d3 ♗e6 10.0-0 ♘bd7 11.♘d5 ♖c8

12.♘×e7+?

A big mistake probably caused by overestimating the pair of bishops. But now Black's dynamics get out of control. 12.c4 is the main move to keep stability, which also scores quite good for White.

12...♕×e7 13.f3?!

13.♘d2 d5 14.e×d5 ♘×d5 15.c4 ♘×e3 16.♕×e3 is not as weakening.

13...d5 14.♘d2 ♕b4 14...d4!?

15.♘b3? Black initiative gets very dangerous now.

15.♕b3, to trade queens, eases the defensive task, e.g., 15...♕×b3 16.c×b3 d4 17.♗g5 ♖c2 18.♖ab1 h6 19.♗d3 ♖c6 20.♗×f6 g×f6 21.f4 and White is only slightly worse.

15...d×e4 16.♕d1?! ♘d5

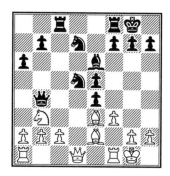

17.♗a7?

A typical computer mistake in those days. The bishop will either not see the light of day again or White will have to invest more material to free it. 17.c3 ♕e7 18.♕d2 limits the damage.

17...b6 18.c3 ♕e7 19.f×e4 ♘e3 20.♕d3 ♘×f1 21.♕×a6 21.♖×f1 ♖c7 22.♕×a6 ♖a8−+

21...♘e3 22.♗×b6 ♕g5 23.g3 ♖a8 24.♗a7 h5 25.♕b7 h4 26.♔f2 h×g3+ 27.h×g3 f5 28.e×f5 ♖×f5+ 29.♔e1 ♖af8 30.♔d2 ♘c4+ 31.♔c2 ♕g6 32.♕e4 ♘d6 33.♕c6 ♖f2+ 34.♔d1 ♗g4 35.♗×f2 ♕d3+ 36.♔c1 ♗×e2 37.♘d2 ♖×f2 38.♕×d7 ♖f1+ 39.♘×f1 ♕d1# 0-1

One can only imagine what went through Fischer's mind as he saw the numerous weak moves played by the program. Two more games were played that day, each an easy win for the former World Champion.

In 1978, MACHACK played a correspondence game (one move per week) against the readers of a German computer magazine, *Computerwoche* (Computer Week). The game was even until MACHACK self-destructed, the result of not searching deep enough.

CW-Leser − MACHACK
Petroff Defense C42
Schach dem Computer, Computerwoche, 1978

1.e4 e5 2.♘f3 ♘f6 3.♘×e5 d6 4.♘f3 ♘×e4 5.d4 d5 6.♗d3 ♗e7 7.h3 0-0

**8.0-0 ♘c6 9.♘c3 ♘xc3 10.bxc3 ♗e6 11.♗f4 ♖e8 12.♖e1 ♕d7 13.♖b1
♖ab8 14.♘g5 ♗f5 15.♕h5 ♗xg5 16.♕xg5 ♖xe1+ 17.♖xe1 ♗e6 18.♕g3
♖c8 19.♗h6 g6 20.♕h4 f5 21.♕f6 ♘xd4 22.cxd4 c6 1-0**

Greenblatt realized early on that a faster computer meant deeper searches, and
deeper searches meant stronger play. He knew what he could achieve on a
commercially available computer, but he wondered what might be possible on
a computer that was specially designed for computer chess. In the late 1970s
MIT professor Edward Fredkin and Greenblatt worked on developing computer
hardware that was specifically designed to facilitate the needs of a chess-playing
program. Their system, CHEOPS (CHEss-Orientated Processing System), was in
some sense a throwback to the EL AJEDRECISTA approach. The hardware included an
8x8 board, allowing for fast parallel generation of legal moves. Unfortunately the
machine could only be as fast as its slowest component – the position evaluation
function – that was done largely in software. This went against Amdahl's Law, a
well-known computing limit to performance. Assume that a chess search takes 100
seconds, and that 60% of the time is spent doing position evaluation. If you reduce
the 40% component to zero – say by building a special-purpose computer – you
still are limited by the 60% that is not any faster. Your 100 seconds becomes 60,
1.67 times faster, but no better. And so it was with CHEOPS. Although a working
prototype of the machine was completed, it did not play many games before the
project was abandoned.

Meanwhile, 1978 was fast approaching, the deadline for David Levy's bet. It was
pretty clear that he would win – none of the programs were playing close to 2000
ELO in 1977. Levy dutifully began to play two-game matches against the leading
computer program "threats." First up was CHESS 4.5 in April 1977. Levy easily
won the first game thereby clinching at least a draw in the match; the second game
was not played. Next up was KAISSA in December 1977. An easy win in game one
negated the need for the second game.

Levy, David (2320) – KAISSA
English Opening A20
Montreal, 17.12.1977

**1.d3 ♘c6 2.c4 e5 3.g3 ♗c5 4.♗g2 ♘f6 5.♘c3 0-0 6.e3 ♕e7 7.♘ge2
♗b6 8.0-0 d6 9.a3 ♗g4 10.b4 ♕e6 11.♘d5 ♗xe2 12.♕xe2 ♘g4
13.♗d2 ♖ab1 14.a4 a6 15.a5 ♗a7 16.b5 axb5 17.cxb5 e4 18.bxc6
♕xd5 19.♕xg4 ♕xd3 20.♖fd1 f5 21.♕g5 bxc6 22.♗f1 ♕b3 23.♖dc1
h6 24.♕g6 ♕b7 25.a6 ♕c8 26.♖c3 ♖f6 27.♕h5 ♕d7 28.♖ac1 ♗c5
29.♖c1xc5 dxc5 30.♖xf6 gxf6 31.♕g6+ ♕g7 32.♕xf5** (adjudicated 1-0)

Then it was MACHACK's turn in August 1978, this time using CHEOPS. Same
result: a Levy win in game one and a won match.

MacHack/CHEOPS – Levy, David (2320)
Sicilian Dragon B71
Cambridge, Massachusetts, 23.08.1978

1.e4 c5 2.♘f3 d6 3.d4 c×d4 4.♘×d4 ♘f6 5.♘c3 g6 6.f4 ♗g7 7.e5 ♘h5 8.♗b5+ ♗d7 9.e6 f×e6 10.♘×e6 ♗×c3+ 11.b×c3 ♕c8 The end of MacHack's book. **12.♕d4 ♘f6 13.♕c4 ♘c6 14.♘d4 ♘×d4 15.c×d4 ♕×c4 16.♗×c4 ♗f5 17.♗b5+ ♔f7 18.♗c4+ d5 19.♗d3 ♖fc1 20.0-0 ♖c7 21.♖b1 ♖ac8 22.♗e3 ♘e4 23.♖f3 ♘d6 24.♖b2 b6 25.a4 ♗×d3 26.c×d3 ♖c3 27.♖h3 h5 28.♗d2 ♖c2 29.♖×c2 ♖×c2 30.♗e1 ♘f5** (0-1 in 43 moves)

Immediately after playing MacHack, Levy went to Toronto for one final match. The opponent was Chess 4.7, a stronger opponent than Chess 4.5 that he played the year before. The faster computer that it used was already paying dividends in human tournaments, and it was realistic to expect the program to be playing at a 2000 USCF level. Still, Levy was rated 2320 ELO, a large gap. The apparent difference in strength had to be tempered by Levy's lack of play in the past few years. Like most strong chess players, he had quickly discovered the life of a chess professional was financially challenging, and he had moved on to other pursuits (including a prolific career writing chess books).

On August 26, 1978, the 6-game match between David Levy and Chess 4.7 began. At stake was pride and the value of the infamous bet. Levy recounts the playing conditions (Levy 2005):

> The match was played in a soundproof glass booth at the Canadian National Exhibition, which is a big exhibition held every year in Toronto. And I had to wear a tuxedo, which is not normal for me. In the 19th century, grandmasters used to wear tuxedos when they played important tournaments, and the early part of the 20th century, so it was sort of nice. And I was playing against the Slate and Atkin program, Chess 4.7, running on a CDC Cyber computer, a very powerful computer located in Minneapolis. When I turned up to play the first game, and sat down, I was expecting David Slate or Larry Atkin to be sitting opposite me making the moves. Instead of which, they wheeled in this really attractive young lady. They clearly decided that they were going to distract me. And she sat there smiling at me the whole time. It was really quite difficult. I had to sort of do what I do in human tournaments, and put my hands like this [shielding his eyes] and look down at the board when I was thinking. And then between moves when I was relaxing, I was sitting there, and she just sat there smiling at me. It wasn't the easiest circumstance under which to play.

Clearly the Chess 4.7 team had adopted an interesting psychological strategy. But Levy also had prepared a strategy, one that he felt could exploit the known limitations of his opponent:

> But I worked out my strategy beforehand, and I developed this sort of anti-computer strategy. And in those days the strategy was very successful, because programs could see a certain distance ahead, but they couldn't see very far ahead. So what you had to be careful of is, you had to be careful of very short-term tactical tricks. You had to just check that there wasn't some sequence of three or five, or maybe even seven moves, that the program could win material, or do something really unpleasant to you.

And once you got past that, if you could accomplish that safely, then you just have to develop a long-term strategy for the game. And so I developed a very sort of super long-term strategy. I made moves that appeared to have no point at the time, but they were moves which I knew if the game developed as I expected it would, would have a point much later on. But so far into the future that the program couldn't understand it. And the result of that was that the program basically had no idea what was going on. It was just playing the current position with no regard for long-term strategy. Every now and again, it would make a move that created a slight weakness in its position, or move the piece from one part of the board away to where it wasn't defending some area that I wanted to go into much later.

This idea of devising an anti-computer strategy was quite popular for several decades. Even today, with super-human chess-playing programs, work continues on devising ways to exploit perceived weaknesses in the machine's play. All is fair in love and war.

If Levy expected an easy match, he quickly had a rude awakening:

Well, the first game was almost a disaster. Because I did it [making moves that appeared to have no point at the time] too much, and I was in serious trouble, and I very nearly lost the first game. But I managed to draw.

Levy, David (2320) – Chess 4.7
Reti Opening A07
Toronto match (1), 26.08.1978

1.g3 d5 2.♗g2 e5 3.d3 ♘f6 4.♘f3 ♘c6 5.0-0 ♗d7?!

Very strange for the human eye.

6.b3?!

6.d4 e4 7.♘e5 ♗d6 8.♘×d7 ♕×d7 9.c4 d×c4 10.♘c3 ♕f5 11.♕a4 is more in the spirit of the position.

6...♗c5 7.♗b2 ♕e7 8.a3?!

This allows Black to take the initiative.

8...e4! 9.♘e1 0-0 10.d4 ♗d6

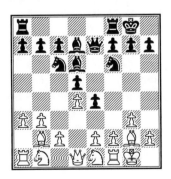

11.e3?

This slow move weakens the light squares. 11.c4 is called for.

11...♘g4 12.h3?

Inviting the following strong strike. But good advice is hard to give.

12...♘×e3!

A correct sacrifice.

13.f×e3 ♕g5 14.g4?

14.♘f3 ♕×e3+ 15.♔h2 e×f3 16.♖×f3 ♕h6 17.♘c3 limits the damage, but Black is of course on top after 17...♗g4.

14...♕×e3+

14...f5!?.

15.♖f2

15...♗g3?!

This should also win in the long run. But the direct attack, 15...f5, pays much higher dividends, e.g., 16.♗c1 ♕g3 17.g5 f4 18.♘d2 ♗×h3 19.♘f1 ♕×g5 20.♘h2 ♕g3−+.

16.♕e2 ♕×f2+ 17.♕×f2 ♗×f2+ 18.♔×f2 f5!

Opening inroads against White's king.

19.g×f5

19.g5 f4 20.♘c3 ♖f5 is also very grim.

19...♘e7 20.c4 ♖×f5+ 21.♔g1 c6 22.♘c3 ♖h5 23.♔h2 ♖f8 24.♘d1 ♘g6 25.♖c1 ♗×h3 26.♗×h3 ♖f1 27.♘g2

27.♘e3 ♖f2+ 28.♔g1 ♖×b2−+.

27...♖f3 28.c×d5 ♖h×h3+ 29.♔g1 c×d5 30.♖c8+ ♘f8

30...♖f8!?, to try to exchange White's active rook, is also very strong.

31.♗c3 ♖d3

31...♔f7!? 32.♖c7+ ♔f6 33.♖×b7 ♘e6 was easier.

32.♘de3 ♖h×e3 33.♘×e3 ♖×e3 34.♗b4 ♖f3 35.♖d8 h6 36.♖×d5

36...♖×b3?!

This greedy capture has no priority. The knight should be activated by 36...♘e6 37.♖d7 ♖×b3 38.d5 ♘d4 39.d6 e3, which wins relatively easily. In the following endgame phase, CHESS 4.7 underestimates the importance of activity in general. Modern programs would doubtlessly win it but in the game Levy even gets a chance to win it.

37.♖d8 ♖f3 38.♖a8 g5?! 39.d5?!

39...h5?!

This makes the technical task much more difficult by giving up winning potential which should be preserved by 39...a6!? 40.♖e8 b6 41.♖×e4 a5 42.♗d6 ♘g6−+.

40.d6

40.♖×a7 b6 41.♖e7 ♘g6 42.♖×e4 ♔f7 should also win in the long run.

40...♔g7 41.♖×a7 ♖f7 42.♖a5 ♔f6 43.♗c3+ ♔g6 44.♖e5 ♖f3 45.♗b4

45...♖f4?

Black's rook should help its own pawns with 45...♖e3, with excellent winning chances.

46.♖e7 ♖f7 47.♖×e4

47...♖d7

47...♘d7 is more logical from a human point of view, as the knight is a better blockader than the rook. But White's activity most probably saves him here as well.

48.♖e7 h4 49.♔g2 g4 50.♔h2 b6 51.♔g2 ♖d8 52.a4 ♘d7 53.a5 ♘f6 54.a×b6 ♘d5 55.b7

55...♘×e7?

This greedy capture is probably a result of the horizon effect as the *zwischenschach*
55...h3+ draws, e.g., 56.♔g3 ♘×e7 57.d×e7 ♖h8 58.♗c3 ♖g8 59.♗a5 ♖h8
60.♗d8 h2 61.b8♕ h1♕ 62.♕d6+=.

56.d×e7 ♖h8

57.♗d6?

Levy rushes to win the rook but misses winning the game with 57.♗c3 ♖g8 (57...
h3+ 58.♔h1 +−) 58.♗a5 h3+ 59.♔h1 ♖b8 60.♗c7 ♖e8 61.♗d8+− .

**57...♔f6 58.b8♕ ♖×b8 59.♗×b8 ♔×e7 60.♗f4 ♔f6 61.♗d2 ♔g6
62.♗e1 ♔g5 63.♗f2 ♔h5 64.♗e1 ½-½**

Despite the close call, Levy stuck to his strategy and it paid off – he won games
two and three:

> But pretty soon in the match, my strategy worked, and I was winning game after game
> very comfortably. I remember in particular one of the games where I played an English
> opening, but I played it as though I was playing a Sicilian defense but with white. ... I
> knew exactly what the long-term strategy was. The long-term strategy in the Sicilian
> is that you play to reach an endgame; an endgame with a particular kind of formation,
> which if you can get there in the Sicilian defense, you stand pretty well. So with the
> extra move, you would stand even better. That was my long-term goal, and I pushed the
> program off the board.

Levy, David (2320) – Chess 4.7

English Opening A00
Toronto match (3), 28.08.1978

1.c4 ♘f6 2.a3 ♘c6 3.♘c3 d5 4.cxd5 ♘xd5 5.d3 ♘xc3 6.bxc3 e5 7.g3 ♗e7 8.♗g2 ♕d6?! 9.♘f3 ♗e6 10.0-0 0-0 11.♕a4 ♕c5?! 12.♗d2 b5?!

Bad from a positional point of view. It just weakens too many squares.

13.♕c2 f6 14.♖fb1 ♖ad8?!

15.♕b2?!

Levy misses or intentionally avoids the tactical possibility 15.♗e3 ♘d4 16.♕d1 ♘xf3+ 17.♗xf3 ♕xc3 18.♖xb5 c6 19.♖bb1 ±.

15...♖b8 16.♗e3 ♕d6 17.♘d2 ♗d5 18.♗xd5+ ♕xd5 19.♕b3!?

Levy knows that the endgame is a weakness of the program and heads for it.

19...♕xb3 20.♘xb3 f5 21.♗c5 ♗d6 22.♖b2

22...♔h8?

The wrong direction, as an endgame is not a middlegame. 22...♔f7 is called for.

23.♖ab1 a6 24.♗xd6 cxd6 25.♘d2

84

In the early days of computer chess, the endgame was a big problem for the machines because of the importance of long-term planning and thinking in patterns. Chess 4.7 plays the following ending badly.

25...f4?

This just weakens the e4-square and wastes precious time. From a human point of view, it is clear that 25...♚g8 should be played.

26.♚g2 f×g3?! 27.h×g3 ♖bd8?! 28.a4! ♘a7?!

28...b×a4! 29.♖b6 ♘e7 30.♘e4±

29.♘e4?

Opening the queenside directly with 29.c4 makes better use of White's better mobilization, e.g., 29...b×a4 (29...b×c4 30.♘×c4 ♘c8 31.♖b8 ♖fe8 32.♖a8 d5 33.♘e3+−) 30.♖b6 h6 31.♖×a6 ♖f7 32.♖bb6+−.

29...b×a4?!

29...d5 30.♘c5 ♖f6 31.♖a1 ♚g8 32.a×b5 ♘×b5 33.c4 d×c4 34.d×c4 ♘c7 is better but White remains for choice of course.

30.♖b6 d5 31.♘c5 ♘b5 32.♘×a4 ♖a8?

Passive. 32...♖c8 33.♖×a6 ♘×c3 34.♘×c3 ♖×c3 35.♖e6 e4 36.d×e4 d×e4 37.♖×e4 ♖c7 offers much better practical chances.

33.c4 d×c4 34.d×c4

34...♘d4?

CHESS 4.7 underestimates the danger posed by White's passed c-pawn. 34...♘c7 is necessary.

35.e3 ♘f3?! 36.c5 ♘g5 37.c6 ♘e4?!

37...♘e6 38.♖c1 ♖f7 39.♖b7 ♔g8 40.♘b6+–

38.c7 ♖×f2+ 39.♔g1 ♖ff8 40.♖b8 h5 41.♖×a8 ♖×a8 42.♖b8+ 1-0

With 2½ points, he needed only a draw in the remaining three games to win his bet. Things had gone so well for him in the previous two games that he became complacent and, well, that is when bad things usually happen.

> … I was feeling pretty confident. And then I decided to take a chance. I'd been very successful with my strategy. I felt very confident that I could use that strategy probably to win every game in the rest of the match if I needed to. So I decided to take the chance and see what would happen if I played very sharp tactical chess. I played a really unsound opening, and the position got very sharp, and the program just killed me.

CHESS 4.7 – Levy, David (2320)
Latvian Gambit C40
Toronto match (4), 29.08.1978

1.e4 e5 2.♘f3 f5 3.e×f5 e4 4.♘e5 ♘f6 5.♘g4

A rare sideline but maybe not bad. 5.♗e2 is the main line.

5...d5 6.♘×f6+ ♕×f6 7.♕h5+ ♕f7 8.♕×f7+ ♔×f7 9.♘c3 c6 10.d3 e×d3 11.♗×d3 ♘d7 12.♗f4 ♘c5 13.g4 ♘×d3+ 14.c×d3 ♗c5

15.0-0?

This castles into an attack. 15.h3 h5 16.♔e2 is a better location for the king in this endgame.

15...h5 16.♘a4?

Misplacing the knight. 16.♗e3 ♗d6 17.h3 is the lesser evil.

16...♗d4 17.♗e3 ♗e5 18.d4 ♗d6 19.h3 b6?

Too slow. After the direct 19...g6, Black is clearly better because of his bishops and his attack.

20.♖fe1?

It is better to try to escape from the danger zone with 20.♔g2, but king safety was a difficult issue for the computers in those days.

20...♗d7 21.♘c3?!

21.♔g2 is still preferable.

21...h×g4 22.h×g4 ♖h4 23.f3 ♖ah8 24.♔f1?! ♗g3?

24...♖h3 hits the Achilles' heel f3 directly and is much stronger. Black has a winning attack.

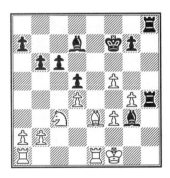

25.♖e2?

CHESS 4.7 underestimates Black's coming initiative. It had to exchange attacking potential with 25.♗f2 ♗×f2 26.♚×f2 ♖h2+ 27.♚g3 ♖×b2 28.♖e2 and White is not worse.

25...♗c8 26.♚g2 ♗d6?

The wrong order of moves. After 26...♖h3 27.♗g1, the bishop can retreat with 27...♗f4 which gives Black a strong initiative.

27.♗g1 ♖h3

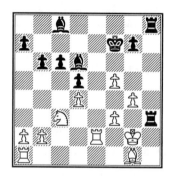

28.♖ae1?

Probably a more or less automatic choice for CHESS 4.7 as rooks belong on open files and the a1-rook was undeveloped. But the exchange sacrifice 28.♖e5!! is much stronger. But such sacrifices posed large problems for the programs for a very long time. But nowadays the programmers seem to have found ways to deal with this problem as the modern programs find it very quickly.

28...♖g3+ 29.♚f2 ♖hh3 30.♖e3

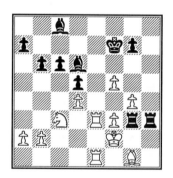

30...♗a6?

Levy miscalculates. After the direct 30...♗f4! 31.♖e7+ ♚f6, White faces a very unpleasant defensive task.

31.♘e2 ♗×e2 32.♖1×e2 c5!

Now it is too late for 32...♗f4? in view of 33.♖e7+ ♚g8 34.♖e8+ ♚h7 35.♖2e7 ♗g5 36.♖×a7 ♗f6 37.♖aa8 g6 38.f×g6+ ♚×g6 39.♖e6 ♖×f3+ 40.♚e2 ♖fg3 41.♖f8±.

33.f4! ⌐×e3

33...♗×f4? runs into 34.⌐×g3 ⌐×g3 35.♗h2 ⌐×g4 36.♔f3+−.

34.⌐×e3

34...⌐h4!

A very difficult decision as 34...⌐×e3 35.♔×e3 b5! also gives practical drawing chances. Against a computer, it is probably preferable as long-term planning plays a large role in the resulting bishop ending. With the rooks, the computer has more short-term goals.

35.♔g3 ⌐h1 36.♗f2 ⌐d1 37.⌐a3 c×d4 38.⌐×a7+

38...♔f8?

38...♔e8 was the last real chance to fight as ⌐d7 must be stopped.

39.⌐d7 ⌐d3+ 40.♔g2 ♗c5

40...♗f4 41.⌐×d5 ♗e3 42.♗×e3 ⌐×e3 43.♔f2 ⌐e4 (43...⌐h3 44.⌐b5+−) 44.♔f3 ⌐e3+ 45.♔f4 ⌐e2 46.⌐b5 d3 47.⌐×b6 d2 48.⌐d6+−.

41.⌐×d5 ⌐d2 42.b4 ♗×b4 43.⌐d8+?!

The direct 43.⌐×d4 is better technique and transposes to the game.

43...♔f7 44.⌐d7+

44...♔f8?

44...♗e7 45.♔f3 ♔e8 46.♖×d4 ♖×a2 47.♖d5 should be winning for White but it offers much more resistance than the game continuation.

45.♖×d4 ♖b2 46.♔f3 ♗c5?! 47.♖d8+ ♔e7

47...♔f7 48.♗×c5 b×c5 49.g5 ♖×a2 50.g6+ ♔e7 51.♖g8 ♔f6 52.♖f8++−.

48.♗h4+ ♔f7 49.g5 g6 50.♖d7+ ♔f8 51.f×g6 ♖×a2 52.f5 ♖a3+ 53.♔g4 ♖a4+ 54.♔h5 ♖d4 55.♖c7 ♗e7 1-0

This was the first time that an International Master had lost to a computer program under tournament conditions. Now the match was much more interesting to the chess world and to the media.

> So after that game I was still leading 2½ to 1½. So we played four of the games, and there were two more games to come. So then I said, "Okay, David, this is time to take it seriously." So I sort of buckled down, and in the fifth game I pushed it off the board again with my long-term strategy and the match was over, because I'd scored 3½ points.

The match was over; Levy had an unassailable lead. He later reflected on his opponent's ability:

> … How strong was the program? It was a lot weaker than me. I would say it was at least 200 points weaker than me. It was good enough that if I'd made a stupid mistake it would've beaten me. Or playing a very risky strategy, as I did in game four, it could beat me. But as long as I was careful, it had no chance.

Levy's historic 1968 bet had comes to an end: man triumphed over machine (Levy and Newborn 1980):

> Thus ended an era in the annals of computer chess. I had proved that my 1968 assessment had been correct, but on the other hand my opponent in this match was very, very much stronger than I had believed possible when I started the bet.

Then there was the matter of collecting his money:

> When sending me his cheque for £250 Professor John McCarthy expressed a sentiment [with] which I concurred – he said that had I lost to a brute-force program he would not have felt that the science of Artificial Intelligence was responsible for my defeat. McCarthy, Michie and Papert all paid promptly and with good sportsmanship, just as I would have done had I lost the bet. Only Edward Kozdrowicki did not.

Having won the match, albeit with a closer score than he anticipated in 1968, Levy remained confident. Perhaps another bet?

4
2200 (1979-1983)

People's careers often intersect in interesting ways. Elwyn Berklekamp worked on a course project with Alan Kotok in 1959. They eventually become life-long friends. Berlekamp received his Ph.D. in 1964 from MIT with Claude Shannon on his examining committee. He then took up a faculty position in the Mathematics Department at the University of California Berkeley. He would occasionally see John McCarthy, who was across the Bay at Stanford University. Berlekamp relates an unusual teaching experience and the aftermath (Berlekamp 2016):

> The first semester I was given this course in operating systems, because the department was understaffed. I did not know much about operating systems... learned enough to stay ahead of the class. So I taught this class – it was pretty big. It happened to have one student who already seemed to know the subject at least as well as me. His name was Ken Thompson. Fascinating. I assigned this programming assignment. It takes six weeks or so. He turned it in a week later. He just stayed up and did it. It was the best of all the people in the class...

> So I tried to recruit him. "What are you going to do? Where are you going to graduate school?" He didn't think he could get into graduate school. This was January of 1965. "Why not?" Well, his grade point average wasn't up to snuff...

> Clearly an A+ student... I look at his undergraduate transcript and he had no "B"s... His methodology was courses he was interested in he aced and courses he was not interested in his strategy was to do the minimal amount of work to pass. This was an unusual case...

> I was an Assistant Professor and I had just come here from MIT and I think, oh come on, this is kind of ridiculous... I did manage to get him into graduate school the next year. He stayed here as a graduate student and I was his advisor. Of course in graduate school he only took courses he liked and got all "A"s. And he wrote a thesis which already had early elements of the C [programming] language. I was very proud of him and helped him get a job at Bell Labs. It wasn't clear what he wanted to do. He didn't want to stay in graduate school after the Master's degree. He went to Bell Labs and that turned out spectacular!

From an early age, Thompson had an interest in games, something he shared with Berlekamp during his Berkeley days. At Bell Laboratories, perhaps inspired by the ACM computer chess tournaments, he started tinkering on a chess program, later named TINKER BELLE. Not surprisingly it was written in the C programming language and ran under the UNIX operating system. In 1983 Thompson and partner Dennis Ritchie would receive the Turing Award for their work on UNIX and C.

TINKER BELLE competed in the 1973 and 1974 ACM computer chess tournaments with good results. Thompson realized that computing speed played a large role in the program's performance and that the PDP computers he was using did not have the horsepower he desired. He envisioned a chess machine that would interface with his PDP computer – his version of CHEOPS-like hardware. Ideally all the computationally "expensive" components of the program would be in hardware – move generation, transposition tables, and evaluation function. However his first design, hardware for generating legal moves, did not deliver on the performance he wanted (Thompson 2005):

> So the hardware generates these moves fairly fast and then you pull them out meticulously and laboriously into the software. And then you sort them and by the time you do that the hardware is swamped by the sort and the [evaluations]. So it did speed things up, but not by what you'd normally think of as a hardware solution. It sped it up by two or three, something like that, instead of 100 which you'd expect out of hardware.

The program, now named BELLE, competed only once, finishing in the top half at the 1977 World Computer Chess Championship.

So, what to you do when your ambitious plans fall short of expectations? Go back to the drawing board. Thompson, never one to turn down a challenge, worked on a new machine design that would eliminate the performance bottlenecks:

> Joe Condon [(1942-2012)] and I teamed up and we built a small chess machine... [It] is maybe a cubic foot. It had...three cards [circuit boards], which is about a square foot each. One card was a move generator. It would generate the moves and sort them, and play them... It had another card that would evaluate the board and then it had a third one which was made out of memory chips... That was the transposition table, a big cache so that when you found the position you've seen before you can just cough up the answer instead of re-evaluating it, and cut off the search.

The BELLE brain trust in 1977: Joe Condon (left) and Ken Thompson.
(ComputerHistory.org)

The results were immediate and impactful: BELLE won the 1978 ACM event and tied for second in 1979 (behind CHESS 4.9 and tied with DUCHESS). But this was not good enough for Thompson; the machine could be made faster – much faster. Back to the drawing board. Thompson and Condon were determined to push the capabilities of their design as far as possible. The result was a new, faster BELLE (Thompson 2005):

> Joe and I then went off and designed another machine after that…. The next one was about the size of a small refrigerator, … a hip high refrigerator. It was built on the exact same principals but was much more parallel. It had three sections; one section was four boards which was [for] move generation. One section was evaluation, which was four more boards. There was one more board that was [program code in hardware that] ran the whole thing…. It had commercial memory at this point at 1 megabyte… of transposition memory…. It was probably 100 times faster than the [previous machine]. It ran about a 160,000 positions per second. A typical software [program] ran about 6,000 positions per second; that's on a fast machine.

David Levy (1979)[4]
International master

Ten years ago I would not have believed possible the progress that has since been made. Now nothing would really surprise me.

How many people would have the determination to write a software chess program and then follow through with several generations of building a chess-playing machine? Building, testing and debugging a complex software program is hard. Doing the same for a complex hardware machine is much harder. Yet Thompson and Condon persevered – multiple times. All this for the honor of reaching the pinnacle of the computer chess world.

How do you test the new machine? BELLE rarely played in human tournaments. Instead Thompson (2005) took a different approach, preferring to bring the machine to his local chess club:

> There was a hostility about computers and chess and humans and chess [playing] in the same tournament and whether they cheated or not and it was all a big philosophical [issue]. Some people were just adamant and mostly they were just apprehensive and afraid. So I made very, very slow inroads into the chess club and built my relationships. …Things like sponsored … tournaments and always refused prizes, always turned the prizes down if I ever won prizes. Played friendly games and played simultaneous exhibitions with the computer and then pass out … the analysis that the computer would print during its game with the people. … [The computer] was a part of the structure … of the club and … it was just there and [club members] always played it, … everybody played it. … If you have a chess machine like this or a program and you're trying to find out how well you're doing the best way to do that is to take it and play it and get it rated. The rating is a nice number [of] how well you're doing and if you haven't got a nice friendly place to do that, first off if you're

getting rating points from fear factor, which I don't think is fair, and secondly you're generating more heat than necessary in doing it. So anyway I had this local chess club, Westfield Chess Club, that I cultivated as a resource to play and I went nearly every week for ten years. ...

[BELLE] actually became Westfield Chess Club champ. It was clearly playing in the master level...

1979: Backgammon

BKG9.8, authored by Hans Berliner (Carnegie Mellon University), defeats World Champion Luigi Villa by a score of seven points to one in an exhibition match (the program won four of the five games; the other three points coming from the doubling cube). Because of the dice, backgammon is a game requiring both skill and luck. The consensus from the match was that BKG9.8 was lucky (Berliner agreed).

Thompson's determination immediately bore fruit. BELLE had impressive results in 1980, winning the ACM event and the World Computer Chess Championship. In the latter event, BELLE tied for first with CHAOS, but won the playoff game. Thompson (2005) describes the complications of using computers located half way around the world:

> It was too important to actually take the machine [to the World Championship], although it was portable enough to do that. Most of the computers were big main frames, were also called up by phone. After four rounds there was a tie; and so they ran out of money for phones after that and so what they did is they had both the winners – co-winners were in the United States, one was BELLE and one was CHAOS – and had them call each other up in the United States and then once every five or six moves they'd called us and read the moves off to us and we'd pretend like it was real time... BELLE won that, won the play-off. These are Swiss tournaments, very short Swiss tournaments, so actually who wins is remarkably close to the notion of who I thought was the strongest, even though they're pretty random events because of the very short tournaments and one loss and you're out.

This was the end of CHESS X.Y's decade-long dynasty at the top of the computer chess world. Larry Atkin and David Slate had done an incredible job staying ahead of the game, so to speak. Atkin moved on to other successful computing pursuits. Slate continued with a successor program, NUCHESS (Northwestern University Chess). It was one of the best programs of the 1980s but could not reach the impossibly high success standards of its predecessor.

1980: Othello/Reversi

The Othello (also called Reversi) program MOOR, authored by Mike Reeve and David Levy, win one of six games in an exhibition match against world champion Hiroshi Inoue. This is the first time that a World Champion is defeated in a public event by a computer.

The BELLE work made important contributions to computer chess progress. First, of course, was a hardware design for a high-performance chess machine. Thompson and Condon understood how to create a machine that reduced/eliminated many of the bottlenecks that could limit the speed. The design had many computations happening in parallel, something most commercial computers could not do. The performance results, measured in number of positions considered per second, were an enormous leap in computational power.

BELLE versus CHAOS at the 1980 World Computer Chess Championship. Seated (left to right) Ken Thompson, Vic Berman, and Fred Swartz.
(Monroe Newborn)

The second major contribution from this work was an innocuous two-page paper that Thompson published in 1982. In it he played versions of BELLE against each other, varying only the depth of search. His conclusion was that doubling the speed of a chess program was worth roughly 100 rating points. It sounds simple and obvious – more chess positions considered per move meant that the program was "seeing" more, leading to a higher probability of improved move selection. The implication of this result was profound. Perhaps the best way to improve your chess program was not to add more knowledge or tinker with the search algorithm. Maybe the best way was to make your code run faster. Better yet, the path of least effort was to find a faster computer.

TINKER BELLE was a software-only solution and it was capable of searching 200 positions per second (p/s). That led to a 1200 USCF rating. BELLE was a hardware solution galloping at 160,000 p/s, an 800-fold improvement. If going from 200 p/s to 400 p/s gives 100 rating points, and 400 to 800 another 100 points, and so on, then reaching 160,000 p/s requires 10 doublings. Thus one would expect to see an improvement of around $10 \times 100 = 1{,}000$ rating points. If Thompson's experiments are correct, he would expect BELLE to achieve a rating of $1200 + 1000 = 2200$.

The third notable innovation in BELLE was its opening book. Rather than hire someone to laboriously build a database of opening moves for the program,

Thompson took a more automated approach. Humans could read, study, and memorize opening books, like the *Encyclopedia of Chess Openings* (ECO). Why not computers? Thompson wrote a program that scanned each page in ECO and added the contents to BELLE's database of opening moves. He then had BELLE analyze the lines of play, looking to identify move sequences that the program seemed comfortable playing. Along the way, of course, numerous errors were found in ECO (to be avoided by BELLE, but perhaps used as bait to lure in unsuspecting opponents).

As should be already obvious, Ken Thompson was a determined man. Nothing was an obstacle for him!

Computer Chess Strength

Ken Thompson (1982) wrote a influential paper that demonstrated the impact of computing speed on chess program performance:

> The chess program BELLE was modified to search exactly 3 plies (half moves) and then enter its normal quiescence evaluation. This program (P3) was then entered into a match with program P4 (4 plies). The two programs played 20 games with each other. Each program took each side of the ten opening positions.

> The program P4 then faced P5 in 20 more games and so on through P7 vs P8. The results of the 5×20 games are tabulated [below]. …

> The program P5 was arbitrarily assigned a rating… of 1500. Then ratings were distributed to P4 and P6 based on the results with P5. The process was then iterated through all programs. The results show that a ply is equivalent to about 250 rating points. Since a ply costs about a factor of 6 in computing power, a factor of two in computing power is worth about 100 rating points.

	Rating	P3	P4	P5	P6	P7	P8
P3	1091		4				
P4	1332	16		5½			
P5	1500		14½		4½		
P6	1714			15½		2½	
P7	2052				17½		3½
P8	2320					16½	

The result – faster computers lead to better performance – had been known for quite some time. Intuitively it made sense; looking at more positions helped inform the decision-making process. Thompson's results quantified the (significant) impact of computer speed.

Now computer chess programs had a simple recipe for success: 1) make the program code and algorithms execute as efficiently as possible, and 2) find a faster computer. A chess-playing program could now become stronger without any effort whatsoever;

just wait for technology to improve the speed of computers. Of course, some people could not wait. If they could not have access to the world's fastest computer, then maybe they could build a fast machine to play chess.

In 1981, MIT Professor Edward Fredkin, who worked with Richard Greenblatt on CHEOPS, created a prize for the first program to achieve the following major milestones in computer chess:

1. $5,000 for achieving the USCF Master title;

2. $10,000 for becoming an International Master; and

3. $100,000 for defeating the World Champion.

BELLE was having results that suggested it could be playing at the USCF Master level, but as the following two games show, it still had a long way to go to be a serious threat to a strong player. Analysis of computer chess play – BELLE and other leading programs – clearly showed obvious weaknesses that humans were quick to exploit. So-called anti-computer strategies became popular; several books for chess players were written on the subject.

BELLE – Storey, Carl (2206)
Pirc Defense B06
Prize Match, Vancouver, 26.08.1981

Fredkin initiated periodic competitions to gauge the progress being made towards achieving the stages of the Fredkin Prize. In the inaugural Fredkin event, BELLE had a rough time. Peter Frey (1978) gives a succinct description of what happened in this game:

> Carl Storey, a Canadian with a USCF rating of 2206, defended the honor of human masters everywhere against the upstart computers by winning both games against BELLE and a $2,500 prize. He may have read a book or two on computer chess before the match. His playing style could be called "textbook" anti-computer technique: Play careful, quiet, positional chess, and wait for an opportunity to lure the machine into an endgame it doesn't understand. Probe the machine's defenses until it makes a strategic error and then infiltrate and mop up.

1.e4 g6 2.d4 ♝g7 3.♞f3 d6 4.♞c3 ♞f6 5.♝e2 0-0 6.0-0 c6 7.a4 ♛c7 8.h3 e5 9.♖e1 ♞bd7 10.♝f1 ♖e8 11.d5 a6 11...cxd5 is the main move.

12.♝g5 h6 13.♝e3 cxd5 14.♞xd5? 14.exd5 is objectively better, but for the computer this more closed position would also be more difficult to handle.

14...♞xd5 15.♛xd5 ♞f6 16.♛c4 ♛xc4 17.♝xc4 ♞xe4 18.♝xh6 ♝xh6 19.♖xe4 ♝f5 20.♖h4 ♝g7 21.♝d5 ♖e7 22.c3?! The rook should be brought back into the game with 22.♖c4=.

22...e4 23.♞d4 ♝xd4 24.cxd4 ♔g7 25.♖f4 ♖ae8 26.b4 ♝c8 27.♖a3?! f5 28.♖g3?

This misplaces the rook. 28.h4 ♖c7 29.g4 is more to the point and limits the damage.

28...e3?

This rushed advance frees White's forces. After 28...♖c7, Black is strategically winning.

29.f×e3 ♖×e3 30.♔h2 ♖×g3 31.♔×g3 ♖e1 32.♗b3? The rook should be activated with 32.♖f3 ♖d1 33.♖c3=.

32...b6 33.♖f3

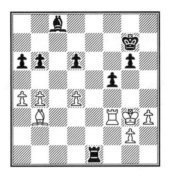

33...♖e4?

The rook should remain flexible and so 33...♗b7 is called for.

34.♖d3 ♗b7 35.♗d1 ♖e1 36.♔f2 ♖e7

Peter Frey (1978) writes:

> Who is winning here? Certainly an amateur chess player would not know. What should White do? Not an easy question at all. BELLE's problem is that there are no obvious short-range goals and therefore even a relatively deep look ahead does not find anything useful to do. To play this position properly, the program has to possess special knowledge about this type of endgame position. Computer chess programs currently do not have such knowledge.

37.♗f3?

The computer rushes. Occupying the open c-file with 37.♖c3 has priority and only after 37...♔f6 can White play 38.♗f3= safely.

37...♗×f3 38.♔×f3 ♖c7 This rook endgame should still be tenable, but it is very unpleasant to defend as White has no easy way to activate the forces.

39.♖b3 ♖c4 40.a5 b5 41.♔e3 g5 42.♔d3?

Purely passive play is usually not the way to hold rook endings. The more active 42.g4 ♔f6 43.g×f5 ♔×f5 44.♔d3 ♖c1 45.♔d2 ♖c7 46.♖f3+ ♔e4 47.♖g3 should be defendable.

42...♔f6

43.♖c3?

Very weak defense as the pawn endgame is easily winning. But White is so passive that the rook endgame should be lost as well, e.g., 43.g3 ♔e6 44.h4 g×h4 45.g×h4 ♔d5 46.♔e2 ♖×d4 47.♖h3 ♖×b4 48.h5 ♖b2+ 49.♔d1 ♖g2 50.h6 ♖g8−+ ; 43.g4 f4 44.♔e4 ♔e6 45.h4 d5+ 46.♔f3 g×h4 47.♖d3 ♔f6 48.♔×f4 ♖×b4 49.g5+ ♔g6 50.♔e5 ♔×g5 51.♔×d5 ♖c4−+ ; 43.♔e2 ♖×d4 44.♖c3 ♖×b4 45.♖c6 ♔e5 46.♖×a6 ♖a4 47.♖a8 ♔d4−+ .

43...♖×c3+ 44.♔×c3 f4 45.♔d3 ♔f5 46.d5 ♔e5 47.♔e2 ♔×d5 and **0−1** in view of 48.♔f3 ♔c4 49.♔g4 d5 50.♔×g5 d4−+ .

Hans Berliner commented on the endgame play (Frey 1978): "This game provides an apt demonstration for the computer chess community that going 11 plies deep in an endgame is not enough for Master play unless the [leaf positions] are evaluated with a lot of knowledge."

Adopting an anti-computer strategy is also evident in the following game against the colorful Dutch Grandmaster Jan Donner.

Donner, Jan Hein – Belle
Slav Defense D52
Exhibition game, Delft, 1982

1.d4 d5 2.c4 c6 3.♘f3 ♘f6 4.♘c3 e6 5.♗g5 ♘bd7 6.e3 ♕a5 7.♘d2 ♗b4 8.♕c2 0-0 9.♗e2 d×c4 10.♗×f6 ♘×f6 11.♘×c4 ♕c7 12.0-0 ♖d8 13.a3 ♗e7 14.b4 b6 15.♖fc1

Donner deviates from 15.♖fd1 as in Mikenas-Alekhine, Prague 1931. The opening went very well for Donner as he has control and more space and Black has problems with the light-square bishop, which Belle never managed to solve in the game.

15...♗b7 16.♗f3 a6 17.♖ab1 ♘d7 18.a4 ♖ab8 19.g3?

19.a5 b5 20.♘d2 is called for.

19...♔h8? BELLE misses the tactical shot 19...♗×b4!! after which Black is by no means worse, e.g., 20.♖×b4 c5 21.♗×b7 c×b4 22.♗×a6 b×c3 23.♕×c3 ♘f6.

20.♗g2 f5?! In the long run this just weakens the light squares on the kingside. Black should do nothing, but this is not easy at all.

21.♘e2 ♖e8 22.♘f4 ♗g5 23.♘d3 ♗f6 24.f4

24...♖ec8?!

Positions with static weaknesses should not be defended purely passively. 24...g5 25.♘de5 g×f4 26.e×f4 ♘×e5 27.d×e5 ♗e7 28.♕c3 ♔g8 injects more dynamics, but White is clearly better here as well of course.

25.a5! b5 26.♘d2

A good choice against the computer. 26.♘ce5!? ♗×e5 27.f×e5 ♕d8 28.♕a2 ♕e7 29.e4 applies even more direct pressure.

26...♗a8?! An odd square for the bishop, but good advice is hard to give already.

27.♘b3 ♕a7 28.♕e2 ♖c7 29.♘bc5 ♘f8?

The passive knight should be exchanged with 29...♘×c5 30.♖×c5 ♖e8 to reduce White's dynamic potential.

30.♖c2 ♖e8 31.♖bc1 ♔g8 32.♗f3 ♖d8 33.g4 ♖dc8 34.♖c3 f×g4 35.♗×g4 ♖e7 36.♕a2 ♖ce8 37.f5 ♖d8 38.♘f4 ♗×d4 Desperation.

39.e×d4 ♖×d4 40.f6! Donner opens the floodgates. It gets messy and tactical now, but White's pieces are so active that it just must work without the need to calculate too many concrete lines.

40...♖×f4 40...g×f6 41.♖g3 ♔h8 42.♕f2 +−

41.f×e7 ♖×g4+ 42.♖g3 ♖×g3+ 43.h×g3 ♕×e7 44.♕d2 h6 45.♖d1 ♕e8 46.♕d6 e5 47.♕c7 ♕h5 48.♖f1 ♕e8 49.♕d6 e4 50.♖f4 e3 51.♖e4 ♕c8 52.♖×e3 h5 53.♖e7 ♕f5 54.♕f4 ♕g6 55.♖a7 ♕e8 56.♕d4 ♕g6 1-0 in view of 57.♕d3 ♕e8 58.♕c3 ♕g6 59.♖×a8 ♕b1+ 60.♔g2 ♕a2+ 61.♔f1 ♕b1+ 62.♕e1 ♕f5+ 63.♕f2 ♕b1+ 64.♔g2 +− .

BELLE won the ACM tournament in 1981, finished in a four-way tie for first place in 1982 (winning on tiebreak), and was the favorite going into the 1983 World Championship. The Association for Computing Machinery hosted the event in the time slot usually reserved for their annual North American competition. Thus 1983 had a World Championship but no North American Championship.

The event started auspiciously for Ken Thompson. First, he and UNIX partner Denis Ritchie were presented with the Turing Award at the ACM conference. Second, BELLE was recognized as being a USCF Master – its October 1983 rating was 2203. This was first chess-playing program/machine to ever earn such a title and Thompson and Condon achieved the first Fredkin Prize.

However, things did not go so well for BELLE in the World Championship. In the third round, the machine lost to David Slate's NUCHESS. Going into the last round, BELLE was half a point behind the leader. With the title on the line, BELLE lost to CRAY BLITZ (Robert Hyatt, Albert Gower, and Harry Nelson).

Remember Thompson's winning recipe for a strong chess program? The BLITZ team followed it to perfection. BLITZ had participated in the ACM events in the late 1970s. In 1980 it moved to a Cray super-computer. The program began its steady climb to the top as it moved to an even faster Cray computer and the team rewrote the program to exploit the large-scale parallelism possible on this machine. CRAY BLITZ lost to BELLE in the 1980 and 1981 ACM events, drew in 1982, and finally beat its nemesis in 1983 – claiming the World Computer Chess Championship as a bonus.

There is one more major contribution from Ken Thompson: endgame databases. Using computers to help grandmasters understand endgame positions goes back to at least 1975 when Grandmaster David Bronstein asked the KAISSA team for help with an adjourned game. But Thompson had bigger aspirations than understanding just a single position: he wanted the computer to analyze *all* possible positions in an endgame. Although building his endgame databases did not add much to the strength of BELLE, it is an important chapter in the battle between man and machine, and a profound contribution to humankind's understanding of the nuances of chess.

Dignitaries at the 1983 World Computer Chess Championship.
Left to right: Samuel Reshevsky, Reuben Fine, and Mikhail Botvinnik.
(Monroe Newborn)

It all started with a chance conversation between Ken Thompson and David Levy at an ACM tournament during the TINKER BELLE days (Thompson 2005):

> After the games we were in the bar talking and [David Levy] was saying that computers can't play endgames, even simple endgames and they never will and he says "I'm an expert in the [rook and pawn against rook] endgame and a computer will never play a [strong] rook and pawn against a rook endgame." So I went to my room in the hotel… that evening and I was calculating the numbers and came to the conclusion that this was doable, that you could solve that game, absolutely solve it by a different mechanism but not…by…normal computer chess [algorithms] but by a different mechanism. You could just have the answer and look it up…. I came back the next day and told him about it and he says "No, takes too many ply," and I said, "It's a ply independent different method."… He just pooh poohed me and I got sort of angry…. So I went home and I worked probably for ten years on endgames from that…encounter one evening after the bar.

Thompson implemented an idea called retrograde analysis (first proposed by Thomas Ströhlein in 1970). Given an endgame, the goal is to classify each position as either a win, loss, or draw. This is done in an iterative fashion by first identifying all the positions that are a win in one move. Next, look at all the remaining positions searching for those that can forcibly lead to a win in one – thus, a win in two moves. Then look for wins in three, and so on. At the end of the computation any position which is not shown to be a win or a loss must be a draw.

Thompson demonstrated his work with the deceptively hard endgame of king and queen versus king and rook (KQKR). This endgame is usually a simple win for the strong side, or so the conventional wisdom would say. Not so, as Thompson's database easily showed (Thompson 2005):

[There was the] U.S. championship going on in Chicago at the Park Hotel and a friend of mine was there playing. I called him and he arranged [for] a bunch of the real strong masters from the…U.S. Open to play the computer queen against rook. … It held them all to a draw. They couldn't win with a queen and then [my friend] said, "Well let's find a real strong grandmaster." The U.S. champion at the time was Walter Browne and a friend knew Walter and says, "You know you can't get him to play this. He'll think it's stupid. But if you bet him money… because he's a better, then you've got it."

So we bet [Browne] fifty bucks he couldn't win queen against rook. So we set up a date and he had friends over and he was going to…just blow it away…in 30 minutes… But half way through he kicked the people out… He was silent. He started going over on time but we didn't call him… Then at some point we knew exactly how far we were to mate…and we knew he wasn't going to win because [of the 50-move rule]. …

He lost and so he wanted a rematch – 50 more bucks. And I thought, "I'll give you your 50 bucks back. I've made my point." "No, no. 50 bucks." … There are two "best" positions, or "worst" positions – whatever you call these [most number of moves required to win] positions – and we gave him one and kept the other one a secret. From the one we gave him we gave him perfect play to [win] and he went home and studied for a week on [the] perfect play. He's a studier and he studied I think the whole week. The next week…we set up again and it was much more serious and we played the second "best" position. … He said he wanted some more conditions: 50 moves he wins. 50 to 55 it's a draw and more than 55, some number like that,… lose. He actually he did it – he did it over the board, did it in exactly 50 moves right on the nose. One more move and it would've been a draw by the rules. There's one point right around 18 moves to the win where it's like a wall where people just hit it and bounce. They just don't know how to cope with this defense. … The computer makes two or three random move selections and one of them [allows] repeating move where he could move [closer to a win] by doing a set of checks. It wasn't optimal but it was human and that's how he got through that wall. Anyway it was fun.

The KQKR endgame was just the beginning. Thompson's work on 4- and 5-piece endgames inspired many to continue his work to larger, more complex endgames. That work continues to this day.

Retrograde Analysis

Chess is a game of move sequences that start at the beginning of the game and go to the end of the game (mate or draw). Retrograde analysis constructs move sequences that start at the end of the game and go backward towards the initial position. The intent is to compute which positions can be shown to be wins, losses, and draws.

The construction of endgame databases is conceptually simple. Start with known results (e.g. checkmate) and work backward. Consider the trivial endgame of White king and queen versus Black king (KQK). All positions where the lone king is checkmated are an immediate loss in 0 moves (scenario "a" below). Now consider how this could have happened. Scenario "b" shows one such example – White can move to a known checkmate, hence it is a win in one move. Scenario "c" shows the predecessor to "b" – Black is to move and lose in one move. Scenario "d" goes back another move to show one possible position where White to move can reach a win in one move ("c"), hence it is a win in two.

Note that retrograde literally means "backward." For chess pieces there is no sense of a backward move, since they can move forward or backward. For pawns it is a different story. Retrograde analysis implies being able to undo moves. If a White pawn moves to e5 delivering mate, then the endgame calculation requires that the move be undone (pawn moves backward to e4) to find the position that led to the mate.

a) BTM: loss in 0   b) WTM: win in 1   c) BTM: loss in 1   d) WTM: win in 2

Originally these computations were stored on the computer as a database. However the idea of a database is much more general than is needed here. Basically, given a position (mapped to a number), one needs only to find the corresponding entry and retrieve the associated value. In computing science terms, the structure that provides this simple functionality is called a table. Hence, the endgame results are stored in what is commonly called an endgame tablebase.

There are different values that can be stored in a tablebase:

1. Number of moves (distance) to conversion (DTC). This computes the minimum number of moves to win (maximum to lose) required to progress from one tablebase to the next. For example, in the KQKR endgame, the number stored would be the lesser of the number of moves to mate (if it occurs in the KQKR tablebase) or the number of moves to win the rook, converting to the KQK tablebase.

2. Number of moves (distance) to mate (DTM). The DTC metric will always lead to a win in a won position, but it may take many moves to achieve. For example, DTC for KQKR might say the rook is won in 10 moves, and then the DTC tablebase for KQK finds a mate in 6 more moves. This wins, but may miss a shorter mate (say, in 12 moves). DTM computes the minimum number of moves to checkmate. Unfortunately DTM requires considerably more resources to compute than DTC.

Today most of the seven-man chess endgames have been solved using retrograde analysis. Progress on the eight-man endgames is proceeding slowly because of computational and storage limitations. Adding one man to the computation causes the complexity of the computation to grow dramatically. Consider having seven pieces/pawns on the board and adding an eight man. The extra man can go on anyone of the 57 empty squares. Hence the computation time and storage required increases by over 50-fold!

Computing endgame tablebases has produced some fascinating results. Some of them are:

- KRKB endgames are harder to win than thought, with many not winnable within the 50-move rule (assuming the strongest defense).
- The hardest KPPPKPP endgame has a DTC of 296 moves.
- KQPKRBN has a position with a DTC of 549.

The impact of Ken Thompson on computer chess cannot be overstated. The ideas behind BELLE would underpin the design of the next generation of chess machines. His systematic analysis of the openings revealed the value of computers as a tool for opening preparation. Endgame tablebases would challenge our understanding of the endgame and question the appropriateness of the 50-move rule. And if that was not enough, his UNIX operating system and its C programming language became the mainstay for computer chess software development.

BELLE and CHESS 4.9 led the way by moving towards faster computing platforms for the their chess programs. Their metric of success was the number of positions considered per second. But there was another computer chess performance metric that quietly emerged in the 1970s: price. There were literally millions of chess players around the world who might be interested in owning an electronic sparring partner. In other words, there was a potential market waiting for the right product to come along.

The mid-1970s saw the beginning of the so-called microcomputer revolution for computer chess. Hardware technology had improved enough that it was possible to produce relatively affordable computers for the consumer market. Such machines were often called microcomputers, a nod to the microprocessors that were at the heart of the system. The first commercial chess program hit the market in 1976 – Peter Jennings' MICROCHESS – and within a few years there were numerous competitors for sale, widely differing in their strength of play, quality of user interface, and abilities to help students improve their game.

The early years of microcomputer chess were dominated by the husband-and-wife team of Dan and Kathleen (Kathe) Spracklen. They each had been previously married, but a mutual friend arranged a meeting and, as they say, the rest is history. Dan tells the story (Spracklen 2005): "The first time I saw Kathleen, she was hunched over a chess program, or a chessboard, in the cafeteria, studying a chess position. And I go, wow, that's interesting. The young lady likes chess." The Spracklens were to spend most of the next quarter century pursing their passion of programming chess.

Oddly enough, Kathleen's interest in computer chess predates her interest in chess (Spracklen 2005):

> I was in high school, and I discovered a Time/Life book that had a big discussion of Claude Shannon's work, and which was very interesting to me. But I wasn't a chess player at the time, so it was only a passing interest. The thing that really struck me about Claude Shannon was when I looked at the picture of him, it was like, what's my

dad's picture doing in this book? My father is an identical twin, and Claude Shannon looked more like my dad than his identical twin brother – but I don't know of any blood relationship. I've never met Claude Shannon. My maiden name is Shannon, and my father is Vern Shannon. So there may be some biological link.

Perhaps interest in computer chess is genetic?

Given their mutual fascination with computers and with chess, it was inevitable that the Spracklens would start tinkering with writing a chess program. In those days, microcomputers were slow (thousands of operations per second) and memory was small (thousands of bytes). Programmers were severely limited in what they could do and the performance they could expect. Still the Spracklens wrote a program that ran using a miniscule amount of memory (4K or 4,000 bytes) and was capable of "a one or two-ply search."

Kathleen heard of a computer chess tournament to take place in March 1978 in San Jose (Spracklen 2005):

Kathleen Spracklen: So I suggested…to Dan…that he ought to take his computer up and try it out. There's…a tournament going on, just for microcomputers. And so, we were kind of young and adventurous, so we packed the computer in the car, on a very, very wet and rainy day, and drove up [to] the [San Francisco] Bay area, for the tournament.

Danny Spracklen: We entered the computer tournament, and there was a lot of other people there. And we had no hopes of winning at the time.

Interviewer: But you thought it would just be fun, to try it.

Danny Spracklen: Yes, right. Just for the fun of it. And lo and behold, we ended up winning the tournament. We won all of our games. Although I'm not real proud of the games, we did win them though.

Kathe and Dan Spracklen competing in the 9th ACM tournament (1978).
(Monroe Newborn)

The Spracklens took their program, SARGON, to the 1978 ACM tournament in Washington D.C. There they had the unexpected result of finishing near the top of the crosstable, losing only to the veteran program CHAOS. However, they were in for an unexpected surprise (Spracklen 2005):

> Kathleen Spracklen: I think the most exciting part for us was the last round of the tournament, when we played Tony Marsland's program AWIT. It was a 6 million dollar Amdahl computer. And we won the game. And we were just amazed. I remember, at the time, we won it. And there was a huge audience there. There was like a hundred people sitting out there, watching it, and they just all started cheering and clapping. And then we woke up the following morning to a big article in the *Washington Post* that says, "Microcomputer Beats 6 Million Dollar Machine," or something like that.

So, how did the *Washington Post* happen to get this story?

> Kathleen Spracklen: Dan's trip to Washington, D.C. wasn't the only eventful one. I traveled from Florida, up to Washington, D.C., and my seatmate was [Watergate reporter] Bob Woodward's wife. And his little daughter was a toddler. As it turns out, I had the window seat and she was fascinated with looking out the window. So, I had Bob Woodward's 2-year-old daughter on my lap, most of the trip. And so I was chatting with his wife and we were talking and she was asking me what brought me to Washington, and I told her about the chess tournament. And so, lo and behold, on the very exciting moment where we beat the Amdahl computer, Bob Woodward happened to be in the audience. And he's the one who wrote the story.

One has to feel sorry for Tony Marsland. Two of the biggest media stories on computer chess had his program on the losing side (ACM 1970 and ACM 1978).

The surprising success of SARGON led the Spracklens to sell their program commercially. Eventually they received an offer they could not refuse, and were hired by Fidelity Electronics to produce chess programs. The best known of their products was CHESS CHALLENGER.

The International Computer Chess Association (ICCA) was founded in 1977 to bring the computer chess community together for tournaments, conferences, and to exchange ideas. One of their first actions was to create a World Microcomputer Chess Championship. The event was limited to programs that were running on computers using microprocessors. The Spracklen's program (under the FIDELITY name) won the world title in 1980, 1981, and 1983 (there was no event in 1982). Even better, in 1982 worldwide sales of chess software was estimated to be $100 million – not a bad business to be in at that time.

The program could be a formidable opponent, as World Champion Anatoly Karpov discovered how hard it was to win a simultaneous exhibition game.

Karpov, Anatoly (2720) – FIDELITY
French Defense C10
Simultaneous exhibition, Turin, 22.05.1982

1.e4 e6 2.d4 d5 3.♘d2 d×e4 4.♘×e4 ♗b4+?! This just loses a valuable tempo.

5.c3 ♗e7 6.♘f3 ♘f6 7.♘×f6+ ♗×f6 8.♗d3 0-0 9.♕e2 ♗e7 10.♗f4 ♗d6 11.♗g3 ♘c6 12.0-0-0 ♗d7 13.♘e5 ♖c8?! An odd move.

14.f4 ♗×e5 15.f×e5 ♕g5+ 16.♔b1 ♘a5?! 17.b4?! 17.♖hf1 +− is easier.

17...♘c6 18.♕e4 ♕h5 19.♗f4?! 19.♗h4 is more precise.

19...♖b8?

Slow and odd. 19...♘e7 is more or less forced.

20.h4 ♘e7 21.g4 ♕g6 22.♕e2 ♘d5

23.♗d2?

This runs into a nasty cross pin. 23.♕d2 is just clearly better for White as 23...
♕×g4 can even be met by 24.♗h6 +− .

23...♗b5 24.♖h3 f6?

This slow approach gives Karpov the initiative. 24...♗×d3+ 25.♖×d3 f5 26.e×f6
♖×f6 more or less equalizes.

25.h5 ♗×d3+ 26.♖×d3 ♕e8 27.e×f6 ♖×f6 28.♖e1 ♔h8?!

Very slow and slightly odd. 28...a5! is more confusing to face and also better.

29.g5 ♘f4?

The tactics backfire. 29...♖f5 is more tenacious.

30.♗×f4 30.♕g4! ♘×d3 31.g×f6 g×f6 32.♖×e6 wins directly.

30...♖×f4 31.h6?! 31.♖e3 +− **31...♕b5?!** 31...♕g6 keeps more pieces near
the king. **32.h×g7+?!** The direct 32.d5 +− is even stronger as the h6-pawn helps
White's attack.

32...♔×g7 33.d5 ♖e8 34.♕e5+ ♔g8 35.♖de3?!

35.♖dd1 is more precise.

35...♖c4? This loses more or less directly as Black's king has no defenders. After 35...♖f5! 36.♕xc7 (36.♕xf5 exf5 37.♖xe8+ ♔f7 38.♖1e7+ ♔g6 39.♖g8+ ♔h5 40.♖xh7+ ♔g4 41.♖xc7 ♕d3+ is just drawn.) 36...♕xd5 37.g6 hxg6 38.♖h3, White is better, but matters are not completely clear.

36.g6 hxg6 37.♖h1 1-0

In tactical fights the machines were already dangerous opponents as seen in the following game.

FIDELITY PRESTIGE – Jansen (first name unknown)
Sicilian Defense B84
8th Porz Open (1), 14.08.1982

1.e4 c5 2.♘f3 d6 3.d4 cxd4 4.♘xd4 ♘f6 5.♘c3 a6 6.f4 e6 7.♗e2 ♕c7 8.0-0 ♗e7 9.♗e3 ♘bd7 10.♕e1 b5 11.a4?

The following exchange of the b-pawn for the e-pawn favors Black. 11.a3 and 11.♗f3 are the main moves.

11...b4 12.♘a2 ♘xe4 13.♘xb4 ♗b7 14.♘d3 ♘df6 15.♕h4?! ♘d5 16.♕h3 h5 17.♔h1 e5?

Black rushes matters. After 17...g6, he is in control.

18.fxe5? 18.♘f5 ♗f6 19.♗f3 was much better as the f4-pawn is valuable, at times providing the option of f4-f5.

18...dxe5 19.♘f5 ♗f6 20.♖ac1?! g6 21.c4 ♘b6? 21...♘xe3 22.♘xe3 ♗g5 is better for Black.

22.♘g3? 22.♘b4 and 22.c5 should both win according to the modern engines.

22...♗e7?

Black does not have time for this retreat. 22...♘g5 23.♕h4 ♕c6 24.♖f2 ♘h7 25.♘xe5 ♗xe5 26.♗f3 ♕c7 27.♗xb6 ♕xb6 28.c5 ♕c7 29.♗xb7 ♕xb7 is more or less forced and Black can still fight.

23.♗xb6 23.c5!? +– .

23...♕xb6 24.♘xe4 ♗xe4 25.♘xe5 f5?! Black's king will never be safe now, but good advice was hard to give.

26.c5? 26.♗f3 ♗×f3 27.♕×f3 0-0 28.♖fe1 wins.

26...♕e6 27.♕g3 g5?

This is asking for trouble. 27...h4 28.♕×g6+ ♕×g6 29.♘×g6 h3 is forced, with practical drawing chances.

28.♗c4 h4 29.♕c3 ♕h6 30.♗f7+ ♔f8 31.♕d4? 31.♗g6 wins directly.
31...h3?

31...♖d8 limits the damage, e.g., 32.♘g6+ ♕×g6 33.♕×d8+ ♗×d8 34.♗×g6 h3 35.♔g1 h×g2 36.♖×f5+ ♔g7 37.♖f8 ♔×f8 38.♗×e4 ♗c7 with drawing chances.

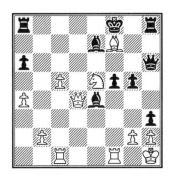

32.♕×e4?

This beautiful combination only leads to a draw. 32.♘d7+ ♔×f7 33.♕×e4 wins.

32...f×e4 33.♗d5+ ♗f6 34.♖×f6+ ♕×f6 35.♘d7+ ♔e7? 35...♔g7 36.♘×f6 ♖ad8 37.♘×e4 ♖×d5 38.g×h3 should lead to a draw.

36.♘×f6 h×g2+? 36...♖ad8 was the last chance to fight, albeit probably for a lost cause.

37.♔×g2 ♖ad8 38.♘g8+ ♖h×g8 39.♗×g8 ♖×g8 40.b4 ♖b8 41.♖c4 1-0

Here is a game against former World Champion Botvinnik. Although Botvinnik retired from competitive chess in 1970, he was still a formidable foe!

Botvinnik, Mikhail — SARGON
English Opening A21
Hamburg, exhibition game, 1983

**1.c4 e5 2.♘c3 d6 3.g3 ♗e6 4.♗g2 ♘c6 5.d3 ♘f6 6.f4 ♗e7 7.♘f3 0-0
8.0-0 ♕d7 9.e4 ♗g4 10.h3 ♗×h3 11.f5 ♗×g2 12.♔×g2 ♘b4 13.a3 ♘a6
14.b4 c5 15.b5 ♘c7 16.♖h1 a6 17.b6 ♘ce8 18.♘g5 ♕c6 19.♖b1 ♗d8
20.♘d5 h6 21.♘f3 ♘×d5 22.e×d5 ♕d7 23.g4 a5 24.♘d2 ♖a6 25.♘e4
♖×b6 26.♖×b6 ♗×b6 27.f6 ♘×f6 28.♘×f6 g×f6 29.♗×h6 ♖e8 30.♕f3
♗d8 31.♕h3 ♕a4 32.♗d2 ♔f8 33.♖f1 ♔g8 34.♕h6 ♕d7 35. ♔g3 f5
36.♖h1 f4+ 37.♔f3 1-0**

By the end of 1983, there was a vibrant, active, and growing computer chess community. Chess programs were getting stronger, a combination of faster hardware, better algorithms, additional chess knowledge, and lots of testing. From 1970 to 1983, the best chess programs had gained over 1,000 rating points allowing the milestone of an electronic chess master to be realized. During these heady days of computer processor development, where machines seemed to double in speed every 18 months, the next decade looked to be pivotal in the quest for a computer World Champion.

5
2500 (1984-1989)

What would the next period of computer chess history be without yet another David Levy bet?

In 1979 Levy jumped at the opportunity to taunt the AI community – this time it was for $1,000 in five years with Dan McCracken, a well-known computer scientist and author. The bet came due in 1984 and since CRAY BLITZ was the reigning world champion, their team was given the chance to play a four-game match against Levy.

Since moving to the Cray computer, CRAY BLITZ had been steadily improving. Robert Hyatt did most of the chess programming and Albert Gower provided much of the chess knowledge. But what pushed them to the top was a late addition to the team, Harry Nelson, who supplied expertise in programming the Cray computer. Moving the original BLITZ code to the machine was like trying to fit a square peg in a round hole. The Cray was architected to do a large number of computations at the same time – if the program could be re-structured to take advantage of this capability. Nelson's job was to "round the corners," so to speak, allowing what was originally a sequential program to be rewritten to achieve a high degree of parallelism. Harry Nelson (2005) describes how he became involved in the project:

> *Nelson*: [Robert Hyatt] had some connection with Cray. And Cray, which had the fastest machine in the world at that time, agreed to support the program of Hyatt's. [He] would be able to use their machines in the annual chess tournament. So Hyatt converted his program. Well, it was written in FORTRAN so it was no problem. He just moved it over to the Cray. … I was working at [Lawrence Livermore Laboratory] on Cray machines, and doing a lot of consulting between us and Cray, itself. So after Hyatt put [BLITZ] on [the Cray], then I heard about it, because I was connected with the Cray projects. And so I was able to get a copy of the program and use it and run it for my own purposes, just to see how good it was, and so forth.

> *Interviewer*: So Hyatt was happy to give the code out? He wasn't afraid of people.

> *Nelson*: No. He wasn't. That's no problem. He gave the code out. And so I did some tests with it. I was very surprised that some of the things it did very well, and some of the things it did very poorly, just for my own interest. So I contacted Hyatt myself and said, you know, I can help. I don't know a lot about chess. I'm not very good. But I know a lot about the Cray. And I'm sure I can improve the running speed of your program. Is that important? Yes, that's important. And so I was able to contribute a lot of hand-coded loops and things like that. And that result was that the program ran ten times as fast. And this was important, because you get to look ahead a whole other ply in the chess tournament. And then the BLITZ, which was then now called CRAY BLITZ, became very competitive, at the highest level of computer chess when they had found the ultimate machine, and the ultimate speed out of that.

Interviewer: And would you say – this might be in speculation – but do you think it was the strength of the algorithms of the software, or the strength of the speed of the computer that enabled it to become that world class?

Nelson: Okay. First of all, it had good algorithms. But it didn't become top echelon until it had the speed to go with it. So both were important.

A disadvantage of using a multi-million dollar supercomputer was that the machine was in high demand. This limited the opportunities for CRAY BLITZ to play in tournaments. However in 1981 the program achieved an impressive result by winning the Mississippi State Championship. It won all five games and achieved a performance rating of 2258. One of the victories was against a master, the first time a computer had defeated a human master in tournament play. The game was typical of many man-machine "upsets" of the time. The human built up what looked like a strong attack, sacrificed material, missed his way in the complications, and eventually lost. Computers had no fear when it came to exposing their king to abuse.

Sentef, Joe (2262) – CRAY BLITZ
English Opening A16
Mississippi State Championship (4), 1981

1.c4 ♘f6 2.♘c3 c6 3.♘f3 d5 4.c×d5 c×d5 5.d4 ♘c6 6.g3 ♘e4 Seldom encountered, but playable. 6...♗f5 is the main move. **7.♗g2 ♘×c3 8.b×c3 e6 9.0-0 ♗d6 10.♕c2 0-0 11.♘g5** 11.c4 is more natural. **11...f5 12.f4?! ♘a5 13.♕d3**

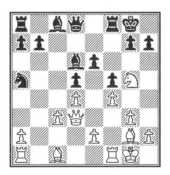

13...♕d7?

An odd move. The natural 13...♗d7 is called for.

14.♗d2? White misses the shot 14.♘×e6 ♕×e6 15.♕b5 ♗d7 16.♕×a5, with an extra pawn. **14...♘c4?!** 14...♕e8 15.♘f3 ♗d7 is slightly better for Black. **15.♗c1?** 15.e4!! f×e4 16.♘×e4 is more energetic. **15...♕a4?** The first step in the wrong direction. 15...♕c7 is called for.

16.g4! h6 17.g×f5 h×g5 17...♖×f5 was the alternative.

18.f×g5

18...♗a3? Now Black's king does not have enough defenders. Correctly evaluating long-term attacks against its king was one of the major computer weaknesses. 18...♛e8 19.g6 e×f5 20.♗×d5+ ♗e6 21.♗×c4 ♛×g6+ was forced, to limit the damage.

19.g6 ♗×c1 20.♖a×c1 ♘d6 21.♛h3 ♖×f5 22.♛h7+ ♔f8 23.♛h8+ ♔e7 24.♛×g7+ ♔d8 25.♖×f5 25.♛h8+!? ♔c7 26.g7 wins easier.

25...♘×f5 26.♛f6+ ♘e7 27.g7 ♛e8 28.♗f3 ♔d7 29.♖f1 ♘g8 30.♛g5 ♛e7 31.♛g6 ♔d6 32.e4 d×e4 33.♗×e4 33.♛g3+!? ♔d7 34.♗×e4 +−

33...♛h4

34.♛g3+? The endgame is not clear, while with queens White wins, e.g., 34.♖f8 ♛e1+ 35.♔g2 ♛e2+ 36.♔h3 ♘e7 (36...♛e3+ 37.♔h4 ♛e1+ 38.♛g3++−) 37.♗f3 ♛f1+ 38.♗g2 ♘×g6 39.♗×f1 e5+ 40.♔g3 +−.

34...♛×g3+ 35.h×g3 ♗d7 36.♖f8 ♖c8

37.♘h7? Too greedy. As the knight cannot really run away, 37.♘xb7! ♖e8 38.c4 was necessary, with practical chances.

37...♖xc3 38.♖xg8 ♖xg3+ 39.♔f2 ♖g5 40.♗e4 b6 41.♔e3 e5 42.♖a8?!
42.♗f5!? ♖xf5 43.♖d8 exd4+ 44.♔xd4 ♖d5+ 45.♔c3 ♖c5+ 46.♔b2 ♖b5+ 47.♔a1 ♖g5 48.g8♕ ♖xg8 49.♖xg8 is drawn but gives White practical chances.

42...♖g3+ 43.♔f2? 43.♗f3 exd4+ 44.♔xd4 should hold easily as White is very active.

43...♖xg7 44.dxe5+ ♔xe5 45.♗f3 ♗e6 46.a4? 46.♖e8 is necessary.

46...♖f7

47.♔e3? This runs into a direct blow and computers never miss such tactical shots. 47.♖e8 was the last chance to fight, albeit for a lost cause.

47...♖xf3+ 48.♔xf3 ♗d5+ 49.♔e3 ♗xa8 50.a5

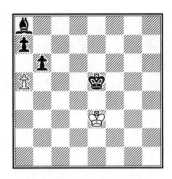

One last trick to test the computer's endgame abilities.

50...♗e4 Of course not 50...b×a5?? 51.♔d2 and it is drawn, as it does not matter how many wrong rook's pawns the attacker has if the defending king reaches the queening corner.

51.♔d2 ♔d4 52.♔c1 b5 53.♔b2 ♔c4 54.a6 b4 55.♔a2 ♔c3 0-1

In 1984 David Levy played CRAY BLITZ to satisfy the conditions for the bet. Levy (2005) describes the match:

> I beat CRAY BLITZ very easily. I think I won four-nil, but one of those [was] a forfeit because they had a hardware problem. But I never had any problem. I trained for that match very seriously. I had my friend Danny Kopec, who's also an international master. He worked with me for a bit, and we sort of developed the "do-nothing" strategy, as I called it. We developed that a bit further. Although I'd retired from competitive chess against humans in 1978, Danny sort of brought me back to speed a bit. We played a lot of fast games together to hone up my tactical ability, which had sort of got a bit rusty. I was in pretty good shape for that match and the program never stood a chance.

The playing conditions made CRAY BLITZ's task quite difficult. The match was played in London but the computer was located in Minnesota. This required communication by telephone, costing the program up to a minute per move. In addition there were computer hardware problems, leading to two losses. Still, Robert Hyatt (1984) was pragmatic in his overall assessment, "I don't think we could have won the match, even without the technical problems we had."

The CRAY BLITZ team. From left to right: Robert Hyatt, Albert Gower and Harry Nelson.

Another successful wager for Levy. Why quit while you are ahead? This time he was not so quick to commit himself. Levy (2005) recounts what happened next:

> Then I thought, "Well, there're all these programs out there, and they've all been striving for years to beat David Levy, and it's sort of unfair to take the target away. On the other hand, I didn't want to make any more bets... Ken Thompson was doing well with BELLE, and I could see that things were showing signs of some serious progress. Although I didn't think I would lose for a while, I thought I would really like to leave myself as a target. ... So I got in touch with *Omni Magazine*, and I said, "Look, this bet of mine has got a lot of publicity. I would like to set up a challenge now. I'd like to offer $1,000 to the first programmer or programming team that wins a match against me. And I'd like you to add another $4,000, so we have a $5,000 prize." And they agreed. So this prize became a sort of milestone that would last as long as I lived.

It was just as well that he did not make another 10-year bet. No one had any inkling of the dramatic advances that were about to happen in computer chess.

Hans Berliner (1929-2017) was thirteen years old when he discovered chess.[5] He embraced the game and quickly moved up in the rankings (Berliner 2005):

> In...'49 or '50 I became a master. And then I played on the U.S. [chess] Olympic team in 1952, and then in that period of time, through '55, '56, '57, I was one of the top ten players in the country. And I played regularly in the U.S. Invitational Championship, and I even [played] the year Bobby Fisher won it for the first time. I finished fifth, and I drew with Bobby.

In the 1960s he embraced correspondence chess, participating in the 5th World Championship. The tournament began in 1965 and ended three years later. Berliner won the title with the dominating score of an undefeated 14 points out of 16, three points ahead of the field. He abruptly retired from the game with the title of International Grandmaster of Correspondence Chess and International Master of over-the-board chess. In 1969, at the age of 40, he decided to go to graduate school to pursue his interests in artificial intelligence and computer chess. He went to Carnegie Mellon University, specifically to work with Alan Newell.

Berliner's first program was J. BIIT, a participant in the first ACM tournament in 1970, "which, in retrospect, was pretty woesome [*sic*]." Those first few years of computer chess games were painful to watch for someone of Berliner's chess abilities. At one event he recalls that "…all the good New York players came and laughed, 'cause they understood just how badly the programs were playing."

Berliner finished his Ph.D. in 1974, the first doctoral degree ever awarded for computer-chess related research. He took a job at Carnegie Mellon University in Alan Newell's group and was allowed to continue pursuing games-related research. Berliner's early interest was in backgammon. His program, BKG 9.8, played an exhibition match against the world champion, Luigi Villa. The decisive result in favor of the program, misrepresents the true strength of his program (Berliner 2005):

> By some very fortuitous set of circumstances, some entrepreneur…managed to arrange a match between the winner of the world backgammon championships in 1979 and my program. And sure enough, it played and it won! Now it wasn't nearly as good a player as he was, but the dice have something to do with the outcome, and it was lucky. But it played well.

This was the first time that a computer had defeated a world champion in any game.

The backgammon success may have led Ph.D. student Carl Ebeling to approach Berliner with the idea of building a set of computer chips to play chess. The timing was right – the technology to design and fabricate chips was just being made available to universities free of charge. Thus there was this new opportunity to turn software into special-purpose hardware. Ebeling realized this and jumped at the chance. Berliner agreed to supervise Ebeling's project, which eventually turned into his Ph.D. thesis. Berliner (2005) recounts the start of the effort:

> So anyway there was this idea for these chips… Carl Ebeling thought he would do this as a project…. You submitted a [chip] design and then maybe a month later you'd get back a chip or two to test and then you'd find the mistakes and fix them and go back, so it was a long process…. So here all of a sudden we had this set of chips that could do move generation and very fast; a microsecond[6] for a move generation. You could have 64 of them together and in a microsecond you'd know all the legal moves…. So we ultimately had a machine that had a six-microsecond cycle. In that period of time it could look at all the moves, pick one to do something with, and do some bookkeeping, and so forth and six microseconds later it would be finished processing that position. So that meant that we could do 160,000 positions per second.

The chess machine, soon to be named HITECH, was based on an 8×8 grid of Ebeling's chips. Each chip represented a square on the chessboard and was connected with its neighbors in such a way as to facilitate move generation (horizontal, vertical, and knight move). A piece on a square would radiate out in each of its legal direction as far as it could go. Each reachable square would be a legal move. The hardware design allowed all the legal moves to be extracted from the chip in sorted order, starting with capture moves. Further each chip knew its location on the board, and would exchange information with its neighbors to calculate positional scores. Thus all 64 chips worked in parallel to do the time-consuming move generation and position evaluation.

Hans Berliner demonstrating his backgammon program.
(Carnegie Mellon University)

Debugging complex software can be challenging and time consuming. That difficulty pales in comparison to that of debugging computer hardware. Thompson experienced this in building BELLE. However, his machine was built solely from commercially available computer chips. Ebeling's task was even more challenging. Not only was he building a chess machine, he was also creating the chips that it would use. Imagine designing a computer chip and having to wait a month (or more) to see if the chip worked... and then repeating that process until you get it right. Needless to say it requires lots of skill... and lots of patience. Berliner (2005) recognized the tremendous effort required to create the HITECH hardware:

> Carl Ebeling, a wonderful person, and he worked very, very hard to build this machine. I mean, he did five times as much effort as the average person does on a [Ph.D.] dissertation.

While the hardware was well in hand, the chess machine also needed software, including a search algorithm and evaluation function. Ph.D. students Murray Campbell (chess ideas, opening book) and Gordon Goetsch (systems software, search algorithms) played a large supporting role, and numerous other talented students made contributions.

So as not to limit the machine's speed, it was essential that the evaluation function also be in hardware. HITECH had the standard evaluation functionality, such as material balance, pawn structure, and king safety. However, from his experience studying computer chess games, Berliner understood that computers poorly understood certain chess patterns. Most common was a move that looked good in the short term, but had a long-term consequence.

Imagine a Black bishop taking off a White pawn on h2, only to be trapped by a White pawn moving to g3 protected by a pawn on f2 (as in game two of the 1972 Fischer – Spassky match). An evaluation function scoring the position after g3 will likely conclude that Black has won a pawn. This may be a huge assessment error. Unless there is an immediate way to free the bishop (search will be needed), the bishop could be lost or remain trapped for the rest of the game.

Berliner wanted to avoid such situations and conceived of the idea of adding well-known chess patterns to HITECH's hardware. Eventually the machine's knowledge base grew to include 40 patterns. Each position considered by HITECH would be matched against these patterns and, when a match occurred, an action would be taken. For example, the evaluation function assessment might be penalized to reflect danger, as in the trapped bishop example.

Success happened quickly for HITECH, as Berliner (2005) recounts:

> [There was this] period at the beginning of 1985 when you put together a chess machine, there's all these parts, and you see the part is working the way you want and then sooner or later the moment of truth comes where you put them all together and see what it does. And from the very beginning, I could see that it had the…potential to play better than any device that existed, and we had this wonderful group of people… So we had all these people and there was a set of tournaments that were easily accessible, and we played, like, one tournament every three weeks. And in those three weeks I used to work easily 100-hour weeks, and so did many of my cohorts. And we would have Monday morning meetings in which we discussed how things were going, what was wrong, if there had been a tournament over the weekend,… what had they discovered, and maybe we played some games against somebody or something. And there was always an agenda of things that needed to be done, progress report and things moved at an incredible rate…. I don't think people would believe the rate at which we progressed…. I think at the very beginning we were right around 2000, maybe a few points below, maybe a few points above. But in a period of a month and a half, we were playing master level chess. So that's a 200 point increase, which showed you [that] we were putting an awful lot of work in and a lot of good ideas too. There were a lot of bright people contributing good ideas…. And from that point on it slowed down a lot, but it kept on going.

HITECH was entered in numerous human chess tournaments, allowing the development team to identify and fix software and hardware errors. The early results were impressive, with the machine firmly establishing a rating over 2100. Berliner's analysis of the games led to the idea of pattern recognizers. They debuted in the hardware in late 1985 and the results were impressive. Within a year Hitech had climbed 200 rating points and was clearly a serious opponent for strong players.

HITECH made its debut in computer chess competitions at the 1985 North American Computer Chess Championship, winning all of its games including scoring a point against CRAY BLITZ (BELLE did not compete). But CRAY BLITZ had its revenge six months later. In May 1986 at the fourth World Computer Chess Championships, an undefeated HITECH lost in the last round to CRAY BLITZ in a controversial game. The result was a four-way tie for first place. CRAY BLITZ edged out HITECH, BEBE (Tony and Linda Scherzer), and SUN PHOENIX (Jonathan Schaeffer) on tiebreak to claim the World title for the second time. This event soured Berliner's enthusiasm for computer-only events, and Berliner concentrated his efforts on events with human opposition.

A year later, the second generation of pattern recognizers was debugged and HITECH easily scaled the 2400 barrier, achieving a USCF Senior Master title (2400+). A highlight was the 1987 Pennsylvania State Championship. HITECH scored 4½ out of 5 to win first place on tiebreak, an impressive 2559 USCF performance! The result was not a fluke; the program also won in 1988 and 1989.

The following game from 1986 shows that despite the program's accomplishments, strong grandmasters could still defeat the program (even with several important mistakes).

HITECH – Sax, Gyula (2545)
Sicilian Defense B89
Philadelphia, 1986

1.e4 c5 2.♘f3 e6 3.d4 c×d4 4.♘×d4 ♘f6 5.♘c3 d6 6.♗c4 ♗e7 7.♗e3 0-0 8.♕e2 a6 9.a3?! 9.0-0-0 is the main move.

9...♕c7 10.0-0-0 ♘c6 11.f4 b5 12.♘×c6 ♕×c6 13.♗d3 ♖b8

14.e5?

HITECH misjudges the resulting position. Black's attack is much quicker because of the hook on a3. 14.g4 is a better way to start White's attack.

14...d×e5 15.f×e5 ♘d5 16.♘×d5 e×d5 17.♗a7?! ♖b7 18.♗d4 b4 **19.♗×a6?** This just opens roads for Black's attack. 19.a4 b3 20.♔b1 was the last chance to fight.

19...♖b8 20.♗×c8 ♖f×c8?!

Objectively the amazing 20...b×a3!! is even better, e.g. 21.♕a6 a2 22.♔d2 ♗g5+ 23.♔d3 ♖b6 24.♗×b6 ♖×c8 –+ .

21.a×b4?

HITECH continues to open attacking roads for Black. 21.b3 b×a3 22.罝d3 was the last chance to fight. In some lines the a3-pawn can even be used to shield White's king.

21...罝×b4 22.曑b1 罝a8 23.e6

HITECH goes all in, but the position is also lost after 23.c3 罝b7 24.e6 f5−+ .

23...豛a4 24.e×f7+ 曑f8 25.奰×g7+ 25.b3 豛a2+ 26.曑c1 罝×d4−+

25...曑×g7 26.f8豛+ 奰×f8 27.豛e5+ 曑g8 28.豛×d5+ 曑h8 0-1

Consistent success against grandmasters proved to be elusive. In 1986, the machine defeated Women's Grandmaster Jana Miles in both games of a two-game match. The program drew against GM Michael Rhode at the 1986 Philadelphia World Open. In 1998, the program achieved a milestone by defeating a grandmaster in a match, a 3½-½ rout. Unfortunately, the opponent was well past his prime. Grandmaster Arnold Denker (2300) had been a force in American chess in the 1940s (winning the US Championship twice), but by 1988 he was more a living legend than a strong player.

HITECH – Denker, Arnold (2300)
Sicilian Defense B22
New York exhibition match, 1988

1.e4 c5 2.c3 d5 3.e×d5 豛×d5 4.d4 奰f6 5.奰f3 c×d4 6.c×d4 g6 7.奰c3 豛d8 8.奰c4 奰g7 9.豛a4+ 奰bd7?

Denker falls into the trap. 9...奰d7 10.豛b3 0-0 11.奰e5 奰e8 from Braga-Ricardi, Villa Gesell 1997 is forced.

10.奰×f7+! 曑×f7 11.奰g5+ 曑e8 12.奰e6 Even 12.0-0 wins.

12...豛b6 13.豛c4! The point of White's combination.

13...奰f8 13...罝g8 14.奰b5+−

14.奰×g7+ As the knight cannot be won White has the pawn and the compensation now.

14...曑d8 15.0-0 奰d7 15...罝g8 16.奰h6+−

16.罝e1 豛d6 17.奰g5 罝c8 18.豛f7 罝c6 19.奰b5 豛b4 20.d5 豛×b5 21.d×c6

♕×g5 22.c×d7 ♘6×d7 23.♖ac1 1-0

Searching 175,000 chess positions per second and aided by Berliner's deep knowledge of chess and his fastidious attention to detail, HITECH's position at the top of the computer chess world seemed assured. The barrier for would-be aspirants was high: to compete either you had to build your own chess machine, or you needed access to multi-million dollar supercomputers. Yet surprisingly HITECH was quickly eclipsed. Even more surprising was how this happened.

Feng-hsiung Hsu, or CB (short for Crazy Bird) to his friends, was born in Taiwan but came to the United States for his graduate studies (Hsu, 2005):

> I think I started playing chess when I was in primary school. I thought of it as just another game, and liked it the way kids always like to play games. But then when I was in college one day I bumped into a book in the library that was a classic for computer chess, called [*Chess Skill in Man and Machine*]. A chapter in it describes the structure of the program called CHESS 4.5, which was a very influential design and was pretty much the basic blueprint for all modern computer chess programs. But the main reason why I came to the States was to study how to design chips, and doing computer chess was actually the last thing on my mind.

He enrolled as a Ph.D. student at Carnegie Mellon University in 1984. All the media attention that HITECH generated piqued his interest; after all, the chess project was a good match for his interests. The results were surprising (Aung, 2010):

> In 1985, while doing secondary research for another professor, Feng-Hsiung Hsu discovered a method that could reduce the work done by [HITECH]'s move generator by simplifying the program's silicon chip design from a maximum of sixty-four distinct chips used by contemporary machines down to just one. While looking over the design of sixty-four chips, he discovered that the extensive amount of wiring could easily be reduced, decreasing the delay of the design and saving time and precious space on the chip. After further studying the design sketches, Hsu discovered that another large portion of the chip was redundant and could therefore be excised completely. Because he was only removing useless components, Hsu's new, reduced design did not lose the speed expected with his reduction in size. In fact, Hsu's proposal actually suggested a theoretical gain of speed by a factor of twenty due to the reduced complexity of his new chip. The single chip design that Hsu developed would evolve over time to form the backbone of DEEP BLUE's hardware.

His blueprint evolved into one that was an improved version of Ken Thompson's design for BELLE. Astonishingly, it took him only six months to go from concept to reality. The new chess machine, dubbed CHIPTEST, could search 50,000 positions per second. It debuted at the 1986 ACM tournament, scoring two wins and two losses.

Hsu, now partnered with fellow graduate student Tomas Anantharaman and supported by Murray Campbell (whose primary role was with the HITECH team), reworked the hardware and software bottlenecks, leading to a 10-fold increase in speed – 500,000 chess positions per second! The new version, called CHIPTEST-M, won the 1987 ACM event 4-0. As was evident from the games played, the program had a lot to learn about playing strong positional chess, but whatever weaknesses it had were compensated for by its deeper search.

One might think that with two world-class chess-playing machines being birthed at the same University – literally down the hall from each other – that this would create opportunities for cooperation and synergy. Such was not the case. Both Berliner and Hsu had strong personalities, and the consequence was that they developed into bitter rivals.

Murray Campbell (2005) was in the unusual, and at times uncomfortable, situation of being a member of both teams:

Interviewer: Can you evaluate the two machines that grew out of the department? The interactions maybe between the two teams, or the two architectures?

Campbell: HITECH came first and had some good initial results. ... It was, I guess, the first senior master level program, rating above 2400 on the U.S. Chess Federation scale.

Almost a competitive program was developed by this other group of students. There was no actual faculty member involved in that network, it was just students, and it was more or less scrounging up parts from around the computer science department to put together, borrowing a work station and putting it all together. There were some shared technologies between them, and some of the searching enhancements that we had come up with in DEEP THOUGHT or CHIPTEST made their way into HITECH. Certainly since I was on both teams -- I guess I was the only person that was on both teams -- there was some transfer that way through me into evaluation and into other ideas. But they were relatively independent projects at that point.

Interviewer: I don't want to open any old wounds, but there was some tension – a little bit maybe – between the teams.

Campbell: Sure. I think there was some tension between the two groups, and I was sort of caught in the middle of that. That was perhaps uncomfortable at times, but I think that I did help share technologies between the groups to some extent. It eventually became clear that the DEEP THOUGHT path was leading to better results than the HITECH system, which was limited in some ways. It was harder to parallelize and grow.

1986: Scrabble

Brian Shepherd's program MAVEN scores eight wins and two losses to tie for first place in the Matchups Tournament. The program's opposition included past and future national champions.

In 1987 Hsu started work on an improved chess chip, the basis for a new chess machine that would later be named DEEP THOUGHT. Murray Campbell (2005) notes the motivation for the redesign:

The CHIPTEST system – the first system based on Hsu's chip – used a very simplistic evaluation function which allowed it to evaluate positions. So it was a very strong searching system but [had] a limited capability to evaluate. DEEP THOUGHT addressed some of those concerns and created a more comprehensive evaluation function.

Feng-hsiung Hsu (2005) was not as subtle:

> [Brute-force searching] was my initial starting point, after reading a paper by Ken Thompson that experimentally verified how you can increase program playing strength by improving computation speed. So we decided to push speed, which we knew how to do and was interesting by itself from a computer science point of view.

The new machine was almost 50% faster – 720,000 positions per second. Computer opponents could not compete with that horsepower, and DEEP THOUGHT cruised to a win in the 1988 ACM tournament (defeating HITECH) and the 1989 World Computer Chess Championships (with wins against both CRAY BLITZ and HITECH).

1989 ACM tournament. In the foreground are Murray Campbell (left) and Feng-hsiung Hsu.
Hans Berliner is between them in the background.
(Monroe Newborn)

Null Move Searching

Not all lines of play in chess analysis require the same level of attention. Clearly lines that appear to be bad should be searched considerably less than lines that look good. How do you determine whether a line of play is of interest or not?

In chess, the side to move must move – there is no legal option to pass. Having the move is usually a major asset (except in rare *zugzwang* positions). What if the position being considered is so bad that even if you give the player two moves in a row (the opponent generously passes their turn), they still have a bad position? Then a reasonable conclusion is that further effort devoted to analyzing this position should be curtailed. That is the idea behind null move searching.

This idea can be easily implemented into a chess program. Consider a position where it is White to move, and previous analysis has shown that White can achieve a big advantage (say 70 points, where 100 is equal to a pawn). Is analyzing the current position to, say, 7-ply a good use of time? The null-move idea is to let White pass on making a move (illegal, but anything goes inside the program!), and then Black moves again – two Black moves in a row. Now we do our search and see how good the resulting score is. If the search score is not competitive (perhaps 10, 60 points less than the best line to date), then we conclude that this line of play is weak and further search effort is not needed. In other words, if Black cannot make anything happen even with the opportunity to play two moves in a row, then surely this must be a weak line of play for Black.

There are several important points to note. First, the savings come from reducing the search depth of null-move sequences. In the above example, if the search after the null move was also 7-ply, then we really have not saved any search effort. To make the idea practical, the searches after null moves use a reduced search depth, say 5-ply in this example. This represents a large reduction in search effort. Second, dropping a move from consideration because of a poor null-move search score is a heuristic. At best it indicates with a high probability that the line being considered is poor, but examples can be constructed where the null-move search allows one to infer a wrong conclusion. Third, if a null-move search returns a competitive value (e.g., 55 in the above example), then the move should be searched with the correct search depth to get a better picture of just how good the move is. Obviously if this happens often, then the advantage of null-move searching is negated (e.g., the 5-ply search has to be redone as a 7-ply search). Finally, the more aggressively the null-move search depth is reduced (e.g., use 3-ply above instead of 5-ply), the greater the savings, but the greater the risk of missing something important. Modern chess programs are very aggressive in their use of reduced null-move search depths.

The idea of using null moves goes back to at least the 1960s and a variant was used in Kaissa. Andy Palay used them to advantage in his 1983 Ph.D. thesis (Hans Berliner was the supervisor). Palay was at Carnegie-Mellon University during the early Hitech days and was an important contributor to the project. The ChipTest team turned the null-move search idea into a practical algorithm, which has been extended many times since.

Garry Kasparov (1988)
Former World Chess Champion

When asked if a computer could defeat the best player in the world by the year 2000, World Chess Champion Garry Kasparov replied, "No way and if any grandmaster has difficulties playing computers, I would be happy to provide my advice."

Deep Thought began competing regularly against humans in 1988. In the 1988 U.S. Open Championship, it made its mark with victories against strong players. In the following game, Igor Ivanov, one of the highest rated players in the United States at the time, gets crushed by his electronic opponent.

Deep Thought – Ivanov, Igor (2505)
Scandinavian Defense, Marshall Variation B01
U.S. Open, 1988

1.e4 d5 2.e×d5 ♘f6 3.d4 ♘×d5 4.c4 ♘f6 5.♘f3 ♗g4 6.♗e2 e6 7.♗e3 ♗b4+ 8.♘bd2 0-0 9.a3 ♗e7 10.h3 ♗h5 11.0-0 c6 12.g4 ♗g6 13.♘h4 ♘bd7 14.♘×g6 h×g6 15.f4 c5 16.g5 ♘e8 17.♘e4 ♘d6 18.♘×d6 ♗×d6 19.b4 c×b4 20.c5 ♗c7 21.a×b4 a6 22.♕c2 ♕e7 23.♕e4 b6 24.♕b7 ♖fc8 25.♗×a6 e5 26.f×e5 b×c5 27.♗c4 ♖ab8 28.♖×f7 ♖×b7 29.♖f4+ 1-0

The program scored 8½ points in 12 games, good enough to tie for 18th place. This was a harbinger of things to come.

The Deep Thought team was buoyed by their success, but realistic in their expectations. They succinctly summarized the dichotomy of machine versus man as follows (Hsu *et al.*, 1990):

> It may seem strange that our machine can incorporate relatively little knowledge of chess and yet outplay excellent human players. Yet one must remember that the computer does not mimic human thought – it reaches the same ends by different means. Deep Thought sees far but notices little, remembers everything but learns nothing, neither erring egregiously nor rising above its normal strength. Even so, it sometimes produces insights that are overlooked by even top grandmasters.

Deep Thought enjoyed multiple successes against human opponents in 1988, reaching the point where defeating International Masters was a routine event. At the Hall of Fame tournament, the machine won its first human event scoring 4½ out of five, conceding only a draw to Igor Ivanov. Ivanov's attempts to extract revenge for his U.S. Open loss almost backfired; in the end he was fortunate to escape with a draw.

In November, Deep Thought was permitted to play in the Software Toolworks Championship in California. The star-studded field featured former World Champion Mikhail Tal, former World Championship contenders Bent Larsen and Samuel Reshevsky, and strong grandmasters including Walter Browne and Tony Miles.

In round 3, Deep Thought was paired against the legendary Bent Larsen, affectionately known as the "Great Dane." Larsen had been one of the world's elite players throughout the 1960s and 1970s. In 1988 he was still a strong player (then ranked #96 in the world). The game was a clash of styles: the uncompromising man against the unorthodox machine.

Larsen, Bent (2580) – Deep Thought
English Opening A20
Software Toolworks, Long Beach, 11.1988

1.c4 e5 2.g3 ♘f6 3.♗g2 c6 4.♘f3 e4 5.♘d4 d5 6.c×d5 ♕×d5 7.♘c2 ♕h5 8.h4 ♗f5 9.♘e3 ♗c5 10.♕b3 b6

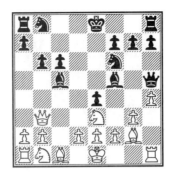

11.♕a4?!

Larsen wants to provoke the machine further, but this goes a bit far. 11.♘xf5 ♕xf5 12.0-0 ♘bd7 13.d3 is more natural.

11...0-0 12.♘c3 b5 13.♕c2 ♗×e3 14.d×e3 ♖e8 15.a4?

This is definitely too provocative. The normal 15.b3 ♘bd7 16.♗b2 is called for.

15...b4 16.♘b1 ♘bd7 17.♘d2

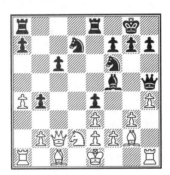

17...♖e6?

This slow approach gives White time to consolidate. 17...♘e5! was much better as also given by DEEP THOUGHT, JR. later according to Hsu, e.g., 18.b3 ♘f3+ 19.e×f3 e×f3 20.♗×f3 ♕×f3 21.♘×f3 ♗×c2−+ .

18.b3 ♖d8 19.♗b2 ♗g6 20.♘c4 ♘d5 21.0-0-0?!

White's king is not really safe on the queenside. 21.♖d1 was better.

21...♘7f6 22.♗h3?!

The coming bishop exchange makes Black's task easier as it frees his game. After the direct 22.♗d4 the position is more or less equal.

22...♗f5 23.♗×f5 ♕×f5 24.f3 h5 25.♗d4 ♖d7 26.♔b2?!

This blocks the bishop's retreat squares. The prophylactic 26.♖hf1 was more precise.

26...♖c7

26...♘c3!? also was interesting.

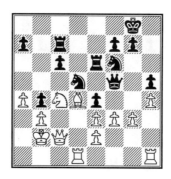

27.g4?

This activity backfires. White should wait by taking his last move back with 27.♔c1 when it is not clear if his walls can be stormed. But Bent Larsen was not the kind of player to take his moves back like this. He executes his ideas.

27...h×g4 28.♖hg1? 28.♔c1 was forced, but is hardly the point of the pawn sacrifice of course.

28...c5 29.f×g4 ♘×g4 30.♗×g7 ♖g6 31.♕d2 ♖d7 32.♖×g4 ♖×g4 33.♘e5 ♘×e3 34.♕×d7 ♘×d1+ 35.♕×d1 ♖g3 36.♕d6 ♔×g7 37.♘d7 ♖e3 38.♕h2 ♔h7 39.♘f8+ ♔h8 40.h5 ♕d5 41.♘g6+ f×g6 42.h×g6+ ♔g7 43.♕h7+ ♔f6 0-1

This was the first win by a computer against a strong human grandmaster under tournament conditions.

Several weeks later, David Levy interviewed Larsen and asked him what he thought of the computer's performance during the game. Larsen (1988) said that he "was not impressed at all. I thought it was rather ridiculous. For instance there is a point where it protects the pawn on c6. It has a weak pawn on c6 and it plays a clumsy rook move, 17...♖e6 I think it is, to protect the pawn. But it is a pawn I cannot take, so I don't understand why it protects it." Levy also asked him when was the first time he thought it was possible that he might lose to a computer, and Larsen responded that he still didn't "think that is possible! What happened to me [at the Software Toolworks Championship] was that I got very angry when I had to play the machine. And then I get even more angry when I was told that I could have signed a note saying that I did not want to be paired against it. I did not know that."

The next round provided a reality check, courtesy of many-time United States champion Grandmaster Walter Browne.

Deep Thought – Browne, Walter (2530)
Sicilian Defense B22
Software Toolworks, Long Beach, 11.1988

1.e4 c5 2.c3 ♘f6 3.e5 ♘d5 4.d4 c×d4 5.♘f3 ♘c6 6.♗c4 ♘b6 7.♗b3 d5 8.e×d6 ♕×d6 9.0-0 e6 10.c×d4 ♗e7 11.♘c3 0-0 12.♖e1 ♘d5 13.g3?

This just weakens the light squares. 13.♘xd5 scores best and 13.a3 is also logical.

13...♕d8 14.a3 ♘×c3 15.b×c3 b6 16.♕d3 ♗b7 17.♗c2 g6 18.♗f4?! ♖c8 19.♗h6 ♖e8

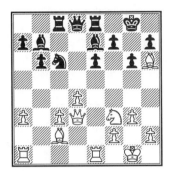

White must be very careful here in view of the weakened light squares in his camp.

20.♗d2? 20.♘d2 ♘a5 21.♗d1 limits the damage.

20...♘a5! 21.♗a4?! ♕d5! The pressure along the long diagonal will decide the game now. The computer has underestimated that it can never be neutralised.

22.♗×e8 22.♖e3 does not help because of 22...♘c4 23.♗b3 b5 24.♕e2 g5 25.h3 h5−+.

22...♖×e8 23.♔g2 ♘c4 24.♗c1 g5 25.h3 h5 26.g4 e5 27.♕d1

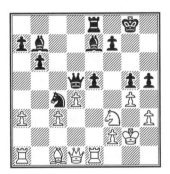

27...f5! 28.g×h5 g4 29.h×g4 f×g4 30.♔g1 ♕×f3 Finally the time has come to cash in.

31.♕×f3 ♗×f3 32.♗h6 ♔h7 33.♗d2 ♖f8 34.♖×e5 ♘×e5 35.♖e1 ♘c6 36.♖e6 0-1

A strong performance by Walter Browne! Hsu was philosophical: "Sometimes you give them lessons, and sometimes they give you lessons."

DEEP THOUGHT drew with IM Vincent McCambridge (2599 USCF) and won the remainder of its games. With 6½ points out of 8, it tied for first place with Grandmaster Tony Miles. The chess world was agog. DEEP THOUGHT's sudden ascendancy from a mere graduate student project a scant year before to challenging the elite of the chess world was unexpected and, to many, upsetting. Popular author

Jerry Hanken (1989) reported the event in *Chess Life* magazine:

> Although Miles won the $10,000 first place money, he was not clear first... Tying for first place with Miles was the computer program known as DEEP THOUGHT... No this is not Hans Berliner's HITECH. It is a completely different program...that peers almost two-ply deeper than HITECH... This inhuman beast begins to fulfill the dire predictions of those who expect Kasparov and Karpov to be taking notes at the 1995 World Computer Championship... In round three...the impossible happened! Bent Larsen, the Great Dane, was axed and fell like a mighty tree in the forest! For the first time ever, a computer program defeated a world championship candidate in a tournament...

DEEP THOUGHT had a 2745 USCF performance, boosting its USCF rating to the unprecedented level of 2551. The program was now one of the top 30 players in the United States.

Based on the outstanding results in 1988, DEEP THOUGHT was formally awarded the $10,000 Fredkin Prize for achieving the equivalent of International Master status. The program had achieved a USCF rating of over 2500 from its previous 25 games against human opposition.

The Software Toolworks success led to an unexpected result. While the chess world was stunned at the results of this new prodigy and the media embraced a looming showdown between man and machine, a technology giant watched from the sidelines. As Murray Campbell (2005) relates:

> I also think that that result got IBM's attention as well. There was an IBM employee, Peter Brown, who had taken time off to get his Ph.D. at [Carnegie Mellon University], and was there at the same time as the DEEP THOUGHT team. So he had gone back to his management back at IBM, and pointed out what was going on, and initiated IBM's interest in hiring the DEEP THOUGHT team to build the next generation chess machine.

Hans Berliner (1988)
Chess program developer and former World Correspondence Chess Champion

Computer experts vastly underestimate the time required to beat the World Champion. Chess experts, on the other hand, vastly overestimate the time involved.

Singular Extensions

Not all chess lines of play require the same attention. Clearly lines of play that are bad should be searched considerably less than lines that are good.

CHIPTEST team members Anantharaman, Campbell, and Hsu invented the idea of singular extensions: use the search to identify moves that are significantly better than the alternatives and then explore them deeper. Like null-move searches, the search is manipulated to discover something interesting about the position being analyzed. In the singular extensions case, having searched the first move in a position, the remaining moves are analyzed to see if all of them return scores that show they are significantly worse. If so, then the first move is "forced" and the program can decide to search this line of play an extra ply (or more) deeper. If the move is not a forced move, then the normal search occurs.

The following position illustrates the power of singular extensions (Anantharaman *et al.*, 1990):

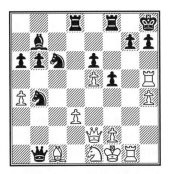

White to move has a sacrifice that leads to a forced mate in 18 moves (35 ply). The winning line is easy to find for a human, but the many delaying moves that Black can play make finding the mate a challenge for a computer. CHIPTEST was capable of finding the mate with a 19-ply search (checking moves get a 1-ply search extension). However, such a search would likely require thousands of hours to complete. Adding singular extensions to CHIPTEST resulted in an 8-ply search that found the mate in 65 seconds. Many of the moves by both sides are forced, resulting in the search going very deep exploring the main line of play.

In other words, singular extensions made computer chess programs an even more fearsome tactical foe.

Whereas 1988 was an amazing year for computer chess progress, 1989 proved to have its set of challenges. There was more to playing strong chess than just deep search, as was painfully demonstrated multiple times.

The Harvard Cup was set up by Harvard University to have periodic competitions between a team of humans and a team of computers. The idea was to benchmark computer progress over the years in a meaningful way. In the interest of expediency, the games were played at the rapid pace of 25 minutes per player, a speed that perhaps favored the computers.

For the first Harvard Cup in 1989, a team of four American grandmasters played a team of four computers. Despite the impressive results of DEEP THOUGHT and HITECH, the computer team was completely out-classed. In the following game, Boris Gulko has an easy time dispatching of DEEP THOUGHT.

Gulko, Boris (2605) – DEEP THOUGHT
King's Indian Attack A07
Harvard Cup, 1989

1.♘f3 d5 2.g3 ♘f6 3.♗g2 c6 4.d3 ♘bd7 5.0-0 e5 6.♘c3 d4 7.♘b1 ♗d6 8.e4 ♘c5 9.♘bd2 b5 10.♘×d4 e×d4 11.e5 ♗b7 12.e×d6 ♕×d6

13.♖e1+ ♘e6 14.a4 a6 15.♘e4 ♘xe4 16.♗xe4 0-0 17.♕h5 g6 18.♕h4 ♕b4 19.♗h6 ♖fb8 20.♗xg6 fxg6 21.♕f6 ♖f8 22.♗xf8 ♖xf8 23.♕xe6+ ♔g7 24.♕e7+ ♕xe7 25.♖xe7 ♖f7 26.♖ae1 bxa4 27.♖1e4 c5 28.♖4e5 c4 29.dxc4 1-0

Boris Gulko and Michael Rhode won all of their games against DEEP THOUGHT, HITECH, CHIPTEST, and MEPHISTO PORTOROSE (Richard Lang). DEEP THOUGHT scored a point against Maxim Dlugy, HITECH won against Lev Albert, and MEPHISTO drew against Alburt. CHIPTEST was shut out. Final score: Humans: 13½, Computers: 2½.

Chess knowledge: 1. Deep search: 0.

Garry Kasparov (1989)[7]
Former World Chess Champion

In 1989 Garry Kasparov offered some comments on chess computers in an interview with Thierry Paunin on pages 4-5 of issue 55 of *Jeux & Stratégie* (our translation from the French):

Question: ... Two top grandmasters have gone down to chess computers: Portisch against LEONARDO and Larsen against DEEP THOUGHT. It is well known that you have strong views on this subject. Will a computer be world champion, one day...?

Kasparov: Ridiculous! A machine will always remain a machine, that is to say a tool to help the player work and prepare. Never shall I be beaten by a machine! Never will a program be invented which surpasses human intelligence. And when I say intelligence, I also mean intuition and imagination. Can you see a machine writing a novel or poetry? Better still, can you imagine a machine conducting this interview instead of you? With me replying to its questions?

Since 1981 International Master Mike Valvo (1942-2004) had been the referee and commentator at most of the major computer chess tournaments, including the World Championships and ACM events. He observed DEEP THOUGHT play and heard technical presentations by the DEEP THOUGHT team. He felt there were weaknesses in the program's play and that given enough thinking time he could beat the program. He challenged the DEEP THOUGHT team to a two game correspondence match. Each side would have up to three days to think about each move. Valvo made his analysis public during the match, so that thousands of chess fans could follow his thoughts and emotions about the games.

Valvo, Michael (2385) – DEEP THOUGHT
Alekhine's Defense B03
Internet match (1), 1989

1.e4 ♘f6 2.e5 ♘d5 3.d4 d6 4.c4 ♘b6 5.f4 dxe5 6.fxe5 ♘c6 7.♗e3 ♗f5 8.♘c3 e6 9.♘f3 ♗g4 10.♗e2 ♗xf3 11.gxf3 ♕h4+ 12.♗f2 ♕f4 13.c5!
An improvement over 13.♕c1?! ♕xc1+ 14.♖xc1 0-0-0= Valvo-Alburt, Philadelphia 1988.

13...♘d7 14.♕c1 A good move to reduce Black's dynamic potential by exchanging queens.

14...♕f5 15.♕b1 ♕×b1+ 16.♖×b1 0-0-0 17.f4 ♗e7 18.♖d1 g5! Opening lines is correct as otherwise White's bishops will rule sooner or later.

19.f×g5 ♗×g5 20.♗f3

20...f5? The position becomes too static now and White can attack on the queenside in the long run for free. Black should open more lines with 20...♗e7 21.♔e2 f6 to find active roles for the knights as soon as possible.

21.0-0 Valvo gives 21.♔e2!? in *ChessBase MEGABASE* and this seems to be more precise as the king can later support White's center.

21...♘b4 22.♖fe1!? ♖hg8 23.♔h1

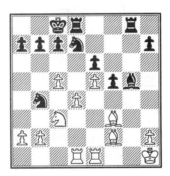

23...c6?! Now Black is very passive. 23...♖g6 24.a3 ♘c6 offers more options for counterplay, but White is much better also in this case.

24.a3 ♘a6 25.b4 ♘c7 26.a4 a6 26...♘a6!? was interesting as it gives Black more active options.

27.♖e2 ♗e7? This move looks odd as it is so passive. But good advice is already hard to give.

28.♖b2 ♘d5 29.♘×d5 c×d5 30.b5

30...a×b5?! Opening lines just helps White's attack. 30...a5 31.♗e1 b6 32.c×b6 ♔b7 33.♗h5 ♖g7 34.♗×a5 ♖a8 35.♗d2 ♖×a4 36.♗h6 ♖g8 37.♗f7 ♖g4 38.♗×e6 ♘×b6 is more tenacious.

31.a×b5 ♖g7 32.♖a1 ♘b8 33.♖ba2 ♖dg8 34.♖a8 ♗g5 35.b6 ♗d8 36.♗h5 ♖f8 37.♗e2 ♖fg8 38.♗e3 h5 39.♖b1 ♗e7 40.♗b5 ♗d8 40...♖g2 41.c6 b×c6 42.♗×c6 ♖c2 43.♗a4 ♖a2 44.♖a7 +– .

41.♗a4 f4 An odd move, but Black is lost in any case. 41...♖g4 42.c6 42.♗d1!? +– b×c6 43.♗×c6 f4 44.♗f2 ♖g2 45.b7+ 45.♗e8!? +– ♔c7 46.♖c1 ♖×f2 47.♗×d5+ ♔d7 48.♖×b8 e×d5 49.♖bc8 ♖gg2 50.♖×d8+ ♔e6 51.♖d6+ ♔f5 52.♖f6+ ♔e4 53.♖g6! +– (Valvo).

42.♗×f4 ♖f7 42...♖g4 43.♗e3 h4 44.♖f1 h3 45.♖f7 +– .

43.♗h6! h4 44.♗b5 ♗e7 44...h3 45.♖f1 +– .

45.c6 b×c6 46.♗×c6 ♖f3 47.♖ba1 ♗a3 48.♗d2 1-0 in view of 48...♖b3 (48...h3 49.♗b4 +–) 49.♗a5 h3 50.♗a4 ♖b2 51.♖c1+ +– .

Deep Thought – Valvo, Michael (2385)
Falkbeer Countergambit C31
Internet match (2), 1989

1.e4 e5 2.f4 d5 3.e×d5 c6 4.♘c3 e×f4 5.♘f3 ♗d6 6.d4 ♘e7 7.d×c6 ♘b×c6 8.d5 ♘b4 9.♗c4 0-0 10.a3 b5!! A strong sacrifice especially against the greedy computer.

11.♗b3 11.♗×b5? ♘b×d5 12.♘×d5 ♘×d5 13.♗c6 was Hoyos Milan-Garcia, New York 1987 and now 13...♘f6 –+ is even stronger than the game continuation, 13... ♗a6.

11...♘a6 12.♘×b5? This greedy capture is asking for trouble. 12.0-0 is called for.

12...♕a5+ 13.♘c3 ♘c5

14.♗a2? The computer underestimates Black's attack. 14.0-0 is more or less forced, when after 14...♘xb3 15.cxb3 ♗b7 (Valvo) Black is only slightly better.

14...♗a6! 15.b4 ♕c7 15...♕b6!? might be even stronger.

16.bxc5 ♖fe8! 17.♘e2 ♕xc5 18.c4

18...♘xd5!! 19.♕d4 19.♕xd5 is met by 19...♖xe2+ 20.♔d1 ♕xd5+ 21.cxd5 ♖xg2 (Valvo) and Black is better.

19...♕xd4 20.♘fxd4 ♗c5! 21.♔d2 21.♔d1 ♘b6 also gives Black more than enough compensation.

21...♘e3 22.♔c3?! 22.♖b1 ♘xc4+ 23.♗xc4 ♗xc4 24.♗b2 ♖ad8 25.♖he1 limits the damage.

22...♖ac8! Valvo invites all attackers to the party.

23.♗b2 ♘xg2 DEEP THOUGHT gave 23...♗b6!? which is also strong.

24.♖af1 ♖cd8 25.♖hg1 ♖e3+ 26.♔d2 f3 27.♖xf3 ♖xf3 28.♖xg2 ♖h3! However, not the greedy 28...♗xa3? because of 29.♔c2! (Valvo) and White regains coordination.

29.♔c1 g6 30.a4 ♗b7 31.♖f2 ♗a8!? The bishop clears the b-file for the rook.

32.♗b1 ♖b8 33.♗a2 ♖d3 34.♖f4 ♖d2 35.♔xd2 ♖xb2+ 36.♘c2 ♖xa2 37.♘c3 ♖b2 38.♗f6 ♔g7 39.♖f1 f5 40.♘d5 ♗xd5 41.cxd5 ♖b3 42.h4 ♔f6 43.♖c1 ♖h3 43...f4!? 44.♖e6+ ♔f5-+ is even better.

44.♖e6+ ♔f7 45.a5 ♖xh4 46.♖c6 ♗b4+ 47.♘xb4 ♖xb4 48.♖c7+ ♔f6

0-1 in view of 49.♔c3 (49.♖xh7 ♖d4+ 50.♔e3 ♖xd5 51.♖xa7 ♔g5 52.a6 f4+ 53.♔e4 ♖a5−+) 49...♖b5 50.♔d4 ♖xa5 51.♖c6+ ♔g5 52.♖c1 f4 53.d6 (53.♔e5 ♖a3−+) 53...♔f6 54.♖e1 ♖a2 55.♔c3 ♖a6 56.♖d1 ♖c6+ 57.♔b4 ♖c8−+

Two impressive games by Mike Valvo, and valuable lessons for the DEEP THOUGHT team.

Chess knowledge: 2. Deep search: 0.

Meanwhile, the efforts in developing strong commercial chess programs continued. In 1981, Richard Lang wrote his first chess program and then surprised everyone by winning the European Microcomputer Chess Championship a few months later (CYRUS). In 1984 he won his first World Championship, the start of a decade-long dominance of the microcomputer tournaments under various names including PSION, MEPHISTO, and CHESS GENIUS.

What was his secret? Usually a man of few words at computer chess events, Lang (1987) uncharacteristically reveals much in an interview:

> It searches 4-5 plies brute force plus up to 6-7 plies selective search. The program contains a lot of chess knowledge, which is used both in the tree and to create piece-value-tables. The chess knowledge was obtained from chess masters, who analyzed games played by the program. The program has an asymmetric evaluation function, which emphasis safety (has rules like 'do not start a wild attack, but worry a lot if the opponent does so'). The program searches about 4,000 nodes per second on a 28 MHz [Motorola] 68020 [computer], but this includes a thorough analysis at every node, including a swap-off evaluation (static analysis of captures instead of a capture search).

The above numbers are circa 1987. As his program moved to faster processors, he could search deeper. But his commitment to the refinement and addition of chess knowledge continued.

Richard Lang at the 1989 North American Computer Chess Championships.
(Monroe Newborn)

At the 1988 ACM tournament, Lang's MEPHISTO program surprised everyone by drawing its game against CRAY BLITZ. At the 1989 event, despite being out-searched by roughly a factor of 200, Mephisto knocked off Deep Thought.

Chess knowledge: 3. Deep search: 0.

The year 1989 was capped off by the unprecedented event of a two-game exhibition match between the human World Champion and Deep Thought. The resulting media frenzy was decidedly pro-human, and a confident Garry Kasparov did not let them down.

Deep Thought – Kasparov, Garry (2775)
Sicilian Defense B22
AGS Computer Challenge New York (1), 21.10.1989

1.e4 c5 2.c3 e6 3.d4 d5 4.e×d5 e×d5 5.♘f3 ♗d6 6.♗e3 c4 7.b3 c×b3 8.a×b3 ♘e7 9.♘a3 ♘bc6 10.♘b5 ♗b8 11.♗d3 ♗f5 12.c4 0-0 13.♖a4

Slightly odd. 13.0-0 is more natural.

13...♕d7 14.♘c3 ♗c7 15.♗×f5 ♕×f5 16.♘h4 ♕d7 17.0-0 ♖ad8 18.♖e1?! 18.♘f3= was more precise.

18...♖fe8 19.c5 ♗a5 20.♕d3 a6 21.h3 ♗×c3 21...f6!?.

22.♕×c3 ♘f5 23.♘×f5 ♕×f5 24.♖a2 ♖e6 25.♖ae2 ♖de8 26.♕d2 f6 27.♕c3 h5 28.b4 ♖8e7 29.♔h1?! 29.♕b2 ♘a7 30.♗c1 was called for to reduce the pressure.

29...g5 30.♔g1 g4 31.h4 ♖e4 32.♕b2 ♘a7 33.♕d2 ♖4e6 34.♕c1 ♘b5 35.♕d2 ♘a3 36.♕d1 ♔f7

37.♕b3? White should try to exchange attacking potential with 37.♗c1!, since with the rooks on board, Black's attack will crash through sooner or later.

37...♘c4 38.♔h2?! ♖e4 39.g3?! This weakens squares and gives Black a hook. But White is lost in any case.

39...♕f3 40.b5 a5?

Kasparov has the right plan, but implements it wrongly. 40...a×b5, 41.♕×b5 f5 wins, e.g. 42.c6 b×c6 43.♕×c6 ♖4e6 44.♕c8 f4 45.♗×f4 ♖×e2 46.♕f5+ ♔g8 47.♕g5+ ♖g7 48.♕d8+ ♔h7 –+. Kasparov (2017) writes that "I could have kept my crushing advantage with 40...f5."

41.c6 f5 The battering ram marches forward.

42.c×b7 ⌷×b7

43.⌷g1?

The coming combination is too deep for DEEP THOUGHT. 43.♛b1 was the last chance to fight. Kasparov (2017) calls this "a clever move I don't see mentioned in any of the many books and articles that covered the match."

43...f4! Kasparov opens the floodgates and the overloading will tell sooner or later.

44.g×f4 g3 45.♛d1 ⌷be7 46.b6 g×f2+ 47.⌷×f2 ♛×d1 48.⌷×d1 ⌷×e3 49.⌷g2 ♞×b6 50.⌷g5 a4 51.⌷×h5 a3 52.⌷d2 ⌷e2 0–1

Kasparov, Garry (2775) – DEEP THOUGHT
Queen's Gambit Accepted D20
AGS Computer Challenge New York (2), 22.10.1989

In the second game Kasparov's superior opening knowledge tells. The DEEP THOUGHT team was not yet ready to match him in opening preparation.

1.d4 d5 2.c4 d×c4 3.e4 ♞c6 4.♞f3 ♝g4 5.d5 ♞e5 6.♞c3 c6? 6...♞f6 is the main move.

7.♝f4 ♞g6 8.♝e3 c×d5 9.e×d5 ♞e5?! 10.♛d4 ♞×f3+ 11.g×f3 ♝×f3 12.♝×c4

12.♛×c4!? is also very strong.

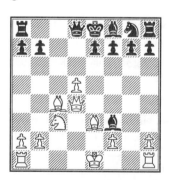

12...♛d6? This loses more or less by force, but White's compensation after 12...a6 13.♖g1 ♞f6 14.♖g3 ♝h5 15.♝f4 is also more than sufficient.

13.♞b5 ♛f6 13...♛d7 14.♞xa7+– **14.♛c5 ♛b6 15.♛a3 e6**

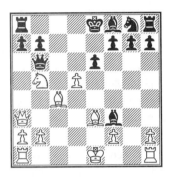

16.♞c7+ 16.♛c3!? ♝c5 17.dxe6+– is even better.

16...♛xc7 17.♝b5+ ♛c6 18.♝xc6+ bxc6 19.♝c5 ♝xc5 20.♛xf3 ♝b4+ 21.♔e2 cxd5 22.♛g4 ♝e7 23.♖hc1 23.♛xg7!? ♝f6 24.♛g4+– **23...♔f8 24.♖c7 ♝d6 25.♖b7 ♞f6 26.♛a4 a5?** 26...g6 was the last chance to fight.

27.♖c1 h6 28.♖c6 ♞e8 29.b4 ♝xh2 30.bxa5 ♔g8 31.♛b4 ♝d6 32.♖xd6 ♞xd6 33.♖b8+ ♖xb8 34.♛xb8+ ♔h7 35.♛xd6 ♖c8 36.a4 ♖c4 37.♛d7 1-0

Deep Thought was clearly not in the same class as Garry Kasparov.

Chess knowledge: 4. Deep search: 0.

The implications were clear. There were weaknesses that had to be addressed if computer programs wanted to continue climbing up the rating ladder.

A triumphant Garry Kasparov after defeating Deep Thought in a 2-game match.
(Monroe Newborn)

All good things eventually come to an end, and so it was with David Levy. After over 20 years of taunting the computer chess community, International Master Levy was finally humbled. On December 12, 1989 Levy sat down to play DEEP THOUGHT, then playing at a 2500 ELO level. Levy had not played competitive chess for many years and his official FIDE rating of 2320 did not reflect the years of inactivity. Although many people had faith that man would prevail over machine, virtually all the experts in computer chess knew what was about to happen.

The match took place in London, but DEEP THOUGHT was physically located at Carnegie Mellon University in Pittsburgh. DEEP THOUGHT team member Peter Jansen was responsible for sitting opposite David Levy during the match and relaying the moves to and from the computer. Jansen (1989) describes the setting for the match:

> Together with David Levy and Robert Wade (who was the arbiter for the match, as I learned right before the first game....) I was sitting up in a fifth-floor room of the old Victorian house the British Computer Society used for their offices. Everybody else was downstairs in two adjacent rooms on the second floor, watching the moves as they appeared on two demonstration boards which were linked via a [personal computer] to the intelligent sensor board we were playing on. The display also included approximate clock times. Commentary was provided by David Norwood... and Jonathan Speelman.

> Relaying the moves to [DEEP THOUGHT (DT)] was quite a bit more cumbersome, and the total delays ranged from about 15 to more than 40 seconds per move. Fortunately...we did not have to switch to voice communications.... Setting things up and agreeing about the exact course of action to take in case of problems turned out to be quite a headache, and among other things I missed the opening ceremony because of it...

> As to the match, it is clear that David Levy is no longer the player he was ten years ago. He consistently used too much time in the beginning of the first three games, and made rather embarrassing tactical mistakes. That he had to go all out after the first two games didn't help. Levy still believes he could have beaten DT ten years ago (i.e. before he quit tournament play), and perhaps he is right. In any case, 'doing nothing' seems to have become considerably more difficult...

> As a side note, several people were betting on the outcome of the match, as well as on the outcome of each individual game (with professional bookmakers and everything!). Odds before the match were strongly in favor of the 'Man.' Another indication of the way this match was hyped up are newspaper headlines such as "Dangerous moves in a brutal game," "Man fights machine in chess war," "Computer's win marks new stage in chess," and the like.

Levy, David (2320) – Deep Thought
Dutch Defense A80
London match (1), 12.12.1989

1.d4 f5 2.♗g5 h6 3.♗h4 g5 4.e3 ♘f6

Of course the machine parries the mate.

5.♗g3 d6 6.c3 ♗g7 7.♘d2 0-0 8.f3?! ♘c6 9.♗c4+ d5 10.♗d3 ♘h5 11.♗f2 e5

12.♕b3?!

It is better to enter the complications with 12.f4.

12...f4?!

It is more precise to insert 12...e×d4 13.c×d4 before playing 13...f4.

13.e4 e×d4

14.c×d4?

This gives Black a dangerous initiative. 14.♘e2 keeps the position dynamically balanced.

14...♗×d4 15.e×d5 ♘a5 16.♕c2 ♗×f2+ 17.♔×f2 ♕×d5 18.♘e2 ♗f5 19.♘e4 ♕c6

20.♘2c3?

Allowing Black to destroy White's coordination. After 20.b4, White has some compensation for the pawn because of his centralization.

20...♕b6+ 21.♔f1 ♖ad8 22.♖d1 ♖fe8 23.♗e2

23...♖×d1+?

23...♘c6, to meet 24.♘d5 with 24...♘b4, creates much more pressure.

24.♕×d1 ♗×e4 25.♘×e4?!

25.f×e4 ♘g7 26.h4 g4 27.♗×g4 ♘c6 28.♕d2 ♘e5 29.♗d1 was the lesser evil.

25...♘f6

26.♕a4?!

It was better to insert 26.h4 g4 before 27.♕a4, but Black retains the initiative with 27...♖×e4 28.f×e4 ♘c6.

26...♖e5 27.♕d1?

Losing by force. 27.♘×f6+ ♕×f6 28.h4 had to be played to activate the h1-rook.

27...♘d5 28.♕a4?!

28...♕×b2

"I would simply play 28...♘c6 here. The rook on h1 isn't exactly in the thick of battle. But a true computer has to be blindly materialistic" (Schüssler 1989). But taking the pawn is objectively best here.

29.♕d7 ♕c1+ 30.♔f2 ♕×h1 31.♕d8+ ♔g7 32.♕d7+ ♘e7 33.♕×c7 ♘ac6 34.♘d6 ♖×e2+ 35.♔×e2 ♕×g2+ 36.♔e1 ♕h1+ 0-1

Game two was a tough battle where Levy had his chances but eventually succumbed. The psychological battle was over and a discouraged Levy easily lost the last two games. The final result – 4 wins to 0 for the computer – led to a collective sigh of relief by the computer chess community. Although disappointed (but not surprised) at the final result, Levy was a graceful loser. The DEEP THOUGHT team collected the $5,000 Levy/*Omni Magazine* prize.

David Levy's bets moved the esoteric topic of computers playing chess into the public eye, causing an acceleration of research in the field. His 1968 bravado and repeated success was a reality check to the community, essentially an antidote to the unrealistic optimism of the 1950s and 1960s. He continues to be a force in computer chess. He is the long-serving president of the International Computer Chess (now Games) Association, organizer of many man-machine chess events, computer chess program co-author, and prolific writer.

The 22 years of being taunted by a retired International Master had finally come to an end. It was time to set sights on the ultimate goal, to challenge the very best of the best. The DEEP THOUGHT team had ambitious plans (Hsu *et al.*, 1990):

When the two opinions collide over the board, the ingenuity of one supremely talented individual will be pitted against the work of generations of mathematicians, computer scientists and engineers. We believe the result will not reveal whether machines can think but rather whether collective human effort can outshine the best achievements of the ablest human beings.

Spectators at the 1989 World Computer Chess Championship. The success of DEEP THOUGHT owed much to the pioneering efforts of (left to right) Ken Thompson, Claude Shannon, and David Slate.
(Monroe Newborn)

6
2650 (1990-1996)

One way to maximize your chances of winning a game is to prepare for your opponent. By replaying their games, you might discover useful information that can be leveraged to your advantage. For example, what kind of positions does he/she seem to like? Dislike? How strong is their tactical vision? Positional play? Endgame skills? What are their opening preferences? The elite chess players study all their potential opponents and often adopt opponent-specific strategies. For example, it might not be a good move to challenge Mikhail Tal to a tactical melee, nor would you want to question Tigran Petrosian's positional understanding. Simplistically, you should consider playing a quiet positional game against Tal (he might get impatient), and mix it up against Petrosian (tactical complications instead of positional subtleties).

It should not come as a surprise then that with computers playing at the level of a strong international master and even grandmaster strength, humans began to intensively study their games looking for weaknesses. The computer's strengths were obvious. Some of the more important ones included:

- Tactics *par excellence*. The programs are calculating monsters, analyzing forced sequences of play many moves into the future, often much deeper than many strong players can foresee given the constraints of a ticking clock. Woe unto him or her who pits their tactical analysis against the computer's deep search.

- No obvious blunders. A program that searches, say, eight-ply deep (ignoring search extensions) will not make a blunder that can be found within four moves aside.

- Unbiased. Computers are not subject to human biases as to what strong chess should look like. Computers can (and do!) play unorthodox moves that perhaps initially appear weak but turn out to be strong. By considering all possible moves, the computer does not eliminate unorthodox moves from consideration.

- The machine never gets tired. Humans get tired as the game progresses. Not much we can do about that!

Now, what about weaknesses in the computer's play? Clearly every program is different, but analysis of computer play suggest that the shortcomings fall into several categories:

- Closed positions. Here the strategic element is to maneuver the pieces behind the pawn wall waiting for the right moment to break the position open. This requires long-range understanding of where the pieces need to be to achieve maximum impact.

- Positional sacrifices of material. Most chess programs of this era would rarely allow positional considerations to outweigh the value of a pawn. Thus you might see a program accept a pawn, even though it destroyed its pawn structure or weakened its king's position. More extreme cases were also sources of computer difficulties, for example in positions where a knight was more valuable than a rook.

- Many types of endgames proved challenging to a computer. For example, deciding whether to transition into a rook-and-pawn endgame might require a deep understanding of the position. For a human, much of this is pattern based (known formations that are good or bad), but for a computer it often comes down to what can be seen within the search horizon.

- Trapped pieces and permanent features. Computers have difficulty understanding that some position features will not change. For example, consider a Black fianchetto position with the bishop on h8. If White has pawns on f6, g5, and h4, there may be no way out for the trapped piece. Although nominally Black has a bishop on the board, the value of the piece must be discounted.

- Quiet positions. Some humans adopt a do-nothing strategy, patiently waiting to see what the computer might do. Oftentimes the computer will make aggressive and/or weakening moves that lead to a long-term disadvantage. Many small mistakes can eventually add up. David Levy used such a strategy in his CRAY BLITZ match – "do nothing but do it very well" (Kopec, 1990).

- Getting the computer out of its opening book. By deviating from well-studied lines of play, one can force the computer to use its own analysis instead of just repeating published or pre-computed move sequences. The computer may not "understand" the resulting position, increasing the chances of a positional mistake being made.

With the success of HITECH and then DEEP THOUGHT, chess grandmasters took computer chess programs seriously and studied their games looking for weaknesses. This is the sincerest form of flattery and a tremendous accolade for the developers of strong chess-playing programs.

From 1986-1997, the Dutch organized an annual tournament in The Hague to assess computer program strength. These Aegon Man-Machine competitions (named after the sponsoring company) were organized as a Swiss tournament. There were an equal number of human and computer participants, with all games being a man-machine pairing. The human side was initially all local players, including some who prided themselves on their ability to beat computers using anti-computer strategies. For the early years of the event, a few International Masters led the human side; that was more than sufficient to produce decisive victories over their electronic opponents. For example, in 1988 there were 16 humans and 16 computers participating. The result was a 53 – 43 victory for the humans.

The 1989 event saw the first grandmaster participant, Hans Ree. Both HITECH and CHIPTEST participated that year, with each scoring less than 50%. Despite their presence, the computer side was crushed.

The next year saw a stronger human side, including Grandmasters Jerome Piket (four wins and two draws) and David Bronstein (four wins and two losses). The 67-year-old legendary Bronstein (1924-2006), Botvinnik's World Championship match opponent in 1951, had no reservations about putting his reputation on the line against a computer.

Bronstein, David (2445) – HITECH

Queen's Gambit Accepted D20
5th Aegon Man-Machine competition, 05.10.1990

1.d4 d5 2.c4 d×c4 3.e4 e5 4.♘f3 e×d4 5.♗×c4 ♘c6 6.0-0 ♗e6 7.♗×e6 f×e6 8.♕b3 ♕d7 9.♕×b7 ♖b8 10.♕a6 ♘f6 11.♘bd2 ♗b4 12.♕d3 ♗×d2 13.♘×d2 That White plays this move suggests his opening strategy (get the computer out of its book?) has been a failure. Black ruthlessly presses home the point. **0-0 14.a3 ♘e5 15.♕g3 ♘h5 16.♕h4** 16.♕×e5 fails to ♖b5 trapping the queen. Six of White's last nine moves have been by the queen. **16...♘f4 17.b4 ♘e2+ 18.♔h1 ♘d3 19.♘b3 ♕a4 20.♘c5 ♘×f2+ 21.♕×f2 ♖×f2 22.♖e1 ♕c2 23.♗g5 ♘g3+ 24.h×g3 ♖×g2 0-1**

The event was a resounding success for HITECH, with four wins (including against Bronstein) and two draws (including Piket). Hans Berliner was understandably jubilant (Carpenter 1990):

> HITECH, Carnegie Mellon University's chess-playing computer, scored what its handlers called "the greatest victory of its career" last month when it beat one of the world's highest-ranked chess players…

> "Everyone was utterly amazed," said Berliner. "It just burned up the track." …

> What made HITECH's victory over Bronstein particularly sweet was that it eclipsed previous wins by its more famous rival DEEP THOUGHT, another chess-playing computer also developed at CMU, Berliner said.

> DEEP THOUGHT, which uses speed rather than artificial intelligence to make its moves, beat International Master David Levy in [1989] and Grandmaster Bent Larsen in 1988, but Bronstein outranks them, Berliner said. …

> Can a computer have its good days and bad days?

> "Sure it can," Berliner said. "It had a couple of pretty good days in the Netherlands."

> "Or maybe David Bronstein had a bad day," he added. "At least he said he did."

Three years later, Bronstein took his revenge. He learned much about what to do – and what not to do – against computers. At an age when most grandmasters cannot compete at grandmaster strength, Bronstein played dominating chess to win the 1992 and 1993 Aegon events with a combined score of 11½ out of 12! The following game epitomizes his strategy for playing computers.

HITECH – Bronstein, David (2405)
French Defense: Winawer, Poisoned Pawn Variation General C18
8th Aegon Man-Machine competition, 1993

Bronstein (1996) writes about his strategy against computers:

> Now computers are so clever they can make brilliant moves that pose problems
> even to grandmasters! They have no expectations, no joy, no disappointment. They
> never tire. They have no idea who they are playing against and are not even afraid of
> someone like myself who once fought for the crown.

> Conventional wisdom holds that the best way to beat machines is to construct dull,
> closed positions, and I cannot disagree. However, I aim to complicate positions as
> much as possible. Intuition and experience tell me that even if machines see far ahead,
> they don't always find the best way to conduct the game.

> Now I will tell you the secret of my play against silicon foes. I use sheer psychology!
> I make them "feel good" by giving up a slight material advantage, like a pawn. In my
> opinion this lulls their evaluation function into a false sense of security and entices
> them into making overoptimistic moves that in reality are unwarranted. While they are
> happy to have a material edge, I try to attack their king. In many cases, but not always,
> I succeed.

**1.e4 e6 2.d4 d5 3.♘c3 ♗b4 4.e5 c5 5.a3 ♗×c3+ 6.b×c3 ♘e7 7.♕g4 ♘f5
8.♗d3 h5 9.♕h3 c4 10.♗×f5 e×f5 11.♘e2 f4 12.♕f3 g5 13.♗×f4 ♗g4
14.♗×g5 ♕×g5 15.♕×d5 ♘c6 16.♘g3 ♗e6 17.♕f3 0-0-0 18.0-0 ♕g4
19.♕f6 h4 20.f3 ♕g6 21.♕×g6 f×g6 22.♘e4 ♔c7 23.♖ab1 b6 24.♖fe1
♘e7 25.♖b4 ♖hf8 26.♘g5 ♗d5 27.♘h7 ♖f5 28.♘f6 h3 29.♘×d5+
♘×d5 30.♖×c4 ♔d7** HITECH does not understand that the ♖c4 is trapped and
cannot be extricated. Optically the material is balanced but, of course, Bronstein
knows better. **31.f4 ♖×f4 32.e6+ ♔d6 33.g×h3 a5 34.e7 ♘×e7 35.♔g2
♖df8 36.♖b1 ♘d5 37.♖e1 ♖f2+ 38.♔g1 ♖2f3 39.h4 ♘e3 40.♖×e3 ♖×e3
0-1**

Bronstein played in eight Aegon events (1990-1997), winning two of them and
always scoring at least four points out of six. He was a spectator's delight; he
could be counted on being entertaining over the board, in his analysis, and in his
commentary.

Aegon became a regular and popular event on the tournament circuit. Over
the years, the human side grew in strength as strong grandmasters enjoyed the
challenge of playing the machines. Participants included Larry Christiansen,
Vlastimil Hort, John Nunn, Susan Polgar, Yasser Seirawan, Gennadi Sosonko, and
Rafael Vaganian, several of whom were at one time rated in the world's top-10.

But the computer side grew stronger too, and at a faster rate than the human side.
Regular microcomputer competitors included CHESS CHALLENGER (Kathy and Dan
Spracklen), FRITZ (Franz Morsch and Mathias Feist), HIARCS (Mark Uniacke),
MCHESS (Marty Hirsch), MEPHISTO (Richard Lang), NIMZO (Chrilly Donninger),
REBEL (Ed Schröder), SOCRATES (Don Dailey and Larry Kaufman), and THE KING
(Johan de Koning) – a veritable who's who of the commercial computer chess

world. Without the HITECH and DEEP THOUGHT advantage of special-purpose hardware, these program developers instead relied on their ingenuity and attention to detail. Search algorithms were refined, especially search extensions (when to search deeper) and search reductions (when to curtail the search). But the heart of what they did was to work with chess knowledge. A little bit of knowledge applied in the right situation could make a huge difference. Thus various teams meticulously analyzed all the endgames – how to play a bishop-and-pawn endgame was different than a rook-and-pawn game. They added patterns to the program that better understood common middlegame position features. They had their computers use all the available resources to analyze the openings, looking for new moves and tailoring their opening repertoire to match the computer's playing style. All of this took time, patience, and effort.

David Bronstein and John Nunn won the 1993 Aegon event with 5½ out of 6. Despite their success, for the first time the computer side finished ahead of the humans, by a narrow score of 98½-93½. The 1994 event featured a stronger human side (more grandmasters) but the competition ended in a draw with 114 points aside. The computers won the 1995 and 1996 events handily, and narrowly won in 1997.

An anti-computer strategy often included simplifying into an endgame and then waiting for the computer to err. Grandmaster and soon-to-be World Women's Champion Zsuzsa (Susan) Polgar finds out the hard way that generalizations do not always work.

MCHESS PRO – Polgar, Zsuzsa (2545)
Sicilian Dragon B77
10th Aegon Man-Machine competition, 03.05.1995

1.e4 c5 2.♘f3 ♘c6 3.d4 c×d4 4.♘×d4 g6 5.♘c3 ♗g7 6.♗e3 ♘f6 7.♗c4 0-0 8.♗b3 a5 9.f3 d5 10.♗×d5 ♘×d5 11.♘×d5 f5 12.♘×c6 b×c6 13.♘b6 ♖b8 14.♕×d8 ♖×d8 15.♖d1 ♖×d1+ 16.♔×d1 f×e4 17.♘×c8 ♖×c8 18.b3 e×f3 19.g×f3 a4 20.♖e1 ♖a8 21.♖e2 ♔f7 22.♗c5 e6 23.♖d2 ♔e8 24.♔e2 ♗e5 25.♔e3 g5 26.♔e4 ♗f4 27.♖g2 ♔f7 28.h4 h6 29.♗b4 ♖b8 30.♗c3 ♖a8 31.♗d4 ♖a5 32.h×g5 h×g5 33.♗c3 ♖a8 34.♗e5 a×b3 35.c×b3 ♗×e5 36.♔×e5 ♔e7 37.a4 ♖b8 38.♖×g5 ♖×b3 39.♖g7+ ♔d8 40.f4 ♖b4 41.a5 ♖a4 42.♔×e6 ♖e4+ 43.♔d6 ♖d4+ 44.♔×c6 ♖×f4 45.a6 ♖c4+ 46.♔b5 ♖c7 47.♖g8+ ♔d7 48.a7 1-0

Grandmaster John van der Wiel's anti-computer strategy pays off. Here he plays a closed game and bides his time until he can break through.

HIARCS – Van der Wiel, John (2570)
French Defense Winawer Variation C16
Aegon, 03.05.1995

1.e4 e6 2.d4 d5 3.♘c3 ♗b4 4.e5 b6 5.♕g4 ♗f8 6.♗g5 ♕d7 7.h4 h6 8.♗f4 ♗a6 9.♗×a6 ♘×a6 10.♘f3 ♘e7 11.0-0 ♘f5 12.a3 ♘b8 13.h5

♘c6 14.♖fd1 ♖g8 15.♔h2 0-0-0 16.b4 ♗e7 17.♕h3 g5 18.h×g6 f×g6
19.g4 ♘g7 20.♗×h6 ♖h8 21.b5 ♘a5 22.♖h1 ♖h7 23.♔g2 ♖dh8 24.g5
♘f5 25.a4 ♘c4 26.♘e2 ♗×g5 27.♘×g5 ♖×h6 28.♕c3 ♕e7 29.♘f3 ♕h7
30.♖×h6 ♕×h6 31.♘eg1 ♕f4 32.♔f1 g5 33.a5 b×a5 34.♖×a5 ♘×a5
35.♕×a5 ♔b8 0-1

The Aegon tournaments were not a valid scientific experiment. There was too much
variability in the man and machine lineups each year to be able to interpret and
compare the results. However it was an invaluable contribution to the computer
chess community, being one of the few events where a chess program could do
battle with a grandmaster. Most importantly it was a fun competition and one that
the participants – both human players and computer chess developers – looked
forward to each year.

Mikhail Botvinnik (1994)
Computer chess program designer and former World Chess Champion

Question: What will be the influence of the computer on chess literature?

Answer: For the moment, none. Now the computer is a source of information, but
nothing more. But in the future the situation will change. I hope that in a few months
our chess program will be ready that was developed by my mathematicians in the
Botvinnik laboratory. This is the only program in the world that doesn't use brute
force. Instead of using brute force our program "thinks" in a similar manner as a
chess master thinks. DEEP THOUGHT analyses one hundred and fifty million positions
in three minutes. They are working on a program that will look at two billion
positions in three minutes. However, my program looks only at twenty or thirty
positions, just as a chess master would do. This allows the computer to show the
player with whom it is playing everything it's been analyzing, because it only looks
at a limited number of possibilities. Thus the opponent of the computer can learn
to play chess while playing the computer. I hope that this program will be further
improved in the future and that the computer will be able to make analyses. When
that happens no one will publish analyses anymore without consulting the computer.
This will drastically change the chess literature.

Not to be outdone, the Americans initiated their own version of an annual man-
machine competition. The Harvard Cup was held annually from 1989 to 1995, with
the exception of 1990. Unlike Aegon, this event restricted the human side to only
grandmasters, an attempt to get meaningful insight into the relative strength of the
computers. Further, to ensure that this was a spectator event, each side was given
25 minutes in which to play the game.

The first event in 1989 featured an exceptional lineup for both sides. The
grandmasters – Lev Alburt, Maxim Dlugy, Boris Gulko, and Michael Rohde – were
all in the upper echelon of US chess. The programs – CHIPTEST, DEEP THOUGHT,
HITECH, and MEPHISTO – were unquestionably the elite of the computer chess world.
A close match was expected in this battle of titans. To most people's surprise, it
ended in a crushing victory for humankind: 13½-2½. The excitement caused by

the spectacular tournament results of Deep Thought and Hitech now had a much-needed reality check.

Two years later the programs were stronger – and the humans better prepared. For the 1991 event, the top programs stayed away, perhaps a consequence of the previous debacle. Instead a team of microcomputers did battle with the grandmasters (substitute Patrick Wolff for Lev Alburt). Again, it was a resounding win for the human side: 12-4. In the following game, Michael Rohde outplays the Spracklen's program in the opening. Lack of development proves costly. This is a nice game by Rohde, marred only by the inaccuracies at the end likely a result of time trouble.

Rohde, Michael (2550) – Fidelity Mach 4
Reti Accepted A09
Harvard Cup, 05.03.1991

1.♘f3 d5 2.c4 d×c4 3.♘a3 c5 4.♘×c4 ♘c6 5.g3 ♘f6 6.♗g2 ♗e6 7.b3 ♗×c4 8.b×c4 e5 9.0-0 e4 10.♘g5 ♕d4 11.♖b1 h6 12.♕b3 ♖b8 13.♗b2 ♕×d2 14.♘×e4 ♘×e4 15.♗×e4 ♕d6 16.♖fd1 ♔c7 17.♕a4 ♖d8 18.♗e5 ♖×d1+ 19.♖×d1 ♕×e5 20.♗×c6+ ♔e7 21.♖d3 ♕a1+ 22.♔g2 ♔f6 23.♖f3+ ♔g5 24.h4+ ♔h5 25.♗e8 ♕b1 26.♗×f7+ g6 27.♕d7 ♕e4 28.♗d5 ♖h7 29.♗×e4 ♖×d7 30.♖f6 ♖d4 31.♗×g6+ ♔g4 32.f3 # 1-0

The 1992 event saw a breakthrough. The microcomputer program Socrates, the work of Don Dailey (1956-2013) and IM Larry Kaufman, impressively won three of its five games (Patrick Wolff, Maxim Dlugy, John Fedorowicz). Despite this success, the computer side lost again, this time by an 18-7 score. Michael Rhode won all five of his games.

In the following game, Fedorowicz gets into trouble in the opening and then succumbs to Socrates' precise handling of the tactics. It is not often that a grandmaster gets manhandled so easily. But then, maybe he should not have allowed the game to go in a direction that played to the computer's strength.

Fedorowicz, John (2530) – Socrates
English, Four Knights, Kingside Fianchetto A29
Harvard Cup, 1992

1.c4 ♘c6 2.♘f3 e5 3.♘c3 ♘f6 4.g3 ♗b4 5.♘d5 ♗c5 6.♗g2 0-0 7.0-0 d6 8.d3 ♘×d5 9.c×d5 ♘d4 10.♘d2 ♗g4 11.♖e1 ♕d7 12.♘c4 f5 13.♗d2 f4 14.b4 f×g3 15.h×g3 ♘e2+ 16.♖×e2 ♗×f2+ 17.♖×f2 ♗×d1 18.♖×d1 ♕g4 19.♘e3 ♕×g3 20.♘f5 ♕×d3 21.♗f1 ♕a3 22.♗g2 ♕×a2 23.♗e1 ♕b3 24.♖a1 ♖ae8 25.♖f3 ♕b2 26.♗c3 ♕c2 27.♗h3 g6 0-1

The 1993 competition was a six-round event with Socrates again leading the electronic side with three points (two wins, two losses, and two draws). Defeating 2500+ rating grandmasters with rapid time controls was no longer an exceptional event. Joel Benjamin scored 6-0 *en route* to a 27-9 win for the humans.

The next year saw an expanded event, with six humans playing eight computers.

Joel Benjamin again claimed top spot, conceding only three draws in eight games. WCHESS (David Kittinger) stunned the grandmasters by winning four games and drawing two. Despite this impressive result, the computer team lost, albeit by a closer 29½-18½ score. The event featured a playoff match between the top human and computer scorers, with Benjamin winning it.

Shabalov, Alexander (2590) – WCHESS
Center Game, Berger Variation C22
Harvard Cup, 1994

1.e4 e5 2.d4 An attempt to get WCHESS out of its opening book, a typical anti-computer strategy. **2...e×d4 3.♕×d4 ♘c6 4.♕e3 ♘f6 5.♘c3 ♗e7 6.♗c4 0-0 7.♗d2 d6 8.0-0-0 ♘e5 9.♗b3 ♗e6 10.f4 ♘c4 11.♗×c4 ♗×c4 12.♘f3 ♖e8 13.h3 b5 14.b3 b4 15.b×c4 b×c3 16.♗×c3 ♗f8** Role reversal! WCHESS gives up a pawn, with obvious positional compensation. Which player is the man and which is the machine? **17.e5 ♖b8 18.c5 ♕c8 19.♕d3 d×e5 20.f×e5 ♘h5 21.♘g5 g6 22.♕f3 ♖e7 23.g4 ♘g7 24.♖hf1 ♕a6 25.♘×f7 ♘e6 26.♕f6 ♕a3+ 27.♔d2 ♖d7+ 28.♘d6 ♘×c5 29.♕f3 ♕×a2 30.♔e1 c×d6 31.♖f2 d×e5 32.♖×d7 ♘×d7 33.♕c6 ♘c5 34.♗×e5 ♖b1+ 35.♔d2 ♗h6+ 36.♔e2 ♕×c2+ 37.♔f3 ♕d1+ 38.♔g3 ♕g1+ 39.♖g2 ♖b3+ 40.♔h4 g5+ 0-1**

WCHESS – Benjamin, Joel (2585)
Ruy Lopez, Berlin Defense, Open Variation C67
Harvard Cup playoff, 1994

1.e4 e5 2.♘f3 ♘c6 3.♗b5 ♘f6 4.0-0 ♘×e4 5.d4 ♘d6 6.♗×c6 d×c6 7.d×e5 ♘f5 8.♕×d8+ ♔×d8 Benjamin plays the solid Berlin defense, expecting the program to misplay this endgame. No such luck. **9.♖d1+ ♔e8 10.♘c3 ♗e6 11.b3 ♗b4 12.♗b2 ♗×c3 13.♗×c3 a5 14.♖d2 h5 15.♖ad1 ♔e7 16.h3 c5 17.♘g5 a4 18.♘×e6 ♔×e6 19.♖d5 b6 20.♖5d2 ♘e7 21.♖d7 ♖hc8 22.f4 h4 23.♔f2 a×b3 24.a×b3 ♖a2 25.♖1d2 ♘f5 26.♖7d3 ♖ca8 27.♔e2 ♖2a6 28.♔f3 b5 29.♗b2 ♖c6 30.c4 ♖b8 31.♗a3 b×c4 32.b×c4 ♖b1 33.♖d8 ♖b3+ 34.♖2d3 ♖×d3+ 35.♖×d3 g6 36.♖d8 ♖b6 37.♗×c5 ♖b3+ 38.♔e2 ♘g3+ 39.♔d1 ♘e4 40.♗a7 ♖g3 41.♖e8+ ♔d7 42.♖f8 ♔e7 43.♖c8 ♔d7 44.♖h8 ♖×g2 45.♖h7 ♔e6 46.♗b8 ♖g3 47.♗×c7 ♖×h3 48.♔e2 ♖c3 49.♖×h4 ♖×c4 50.♗b8 ♘g3+ 51.♔f3 ♘f5 52.♖h8 ♖c3+ 53.♔f2 ♖c2+ 54.♔f3 ♖c3+ 55.♔f2 ♖c2+ 56.♔f3 ½-½** Sometimes doing nothing well leads to, well, nothing!

The 1995 Harvard Cup turned out to be the last in the series. Benjamin and Rhode led the human side to another convincing victory, this time by the score of 23½-12½. The top computer was VIRTUAL CHESS (Marc-François Baudot and Jean-Christophe Weill) with 3½ out of 6 points.

Having scored 14 wins, five draws, and no losses against computers in his previous Harvard Cup appearances, Benjamin was the surprise of the event by losing to CHESSMASTER 4000 (Johan de Koning) in the first round. He roared back with four wins and a draw to again finish at the top of the crosstable. However, there was still blood to be spilled. The playoff match was played a few months later and Benjamin lost the first game, but came back to defeat VIRTUAL CHESS 2½-1½.

Benjamin, Joel (2570) – VIRTUAL CHESS
English, Mikenas-Carls, Flohr Variation A18
Harvard Cup playoff, 05.01.1996

1.c4 ♞f6 2.♞c3 e6 3.e4 d5 4.e5 d4 5.e×f6 d×c3 6.b×c3 ♛×f6 7.♞f3 ♝b4 8.♖b1 ♝d6 9.d4 h6 10.♝d3 c5 11.0-0 0-0 12.♛e2 ♞c6 13.♝e3 c×d4 14.c×d4 e5 15.d5 ♞b4 16.♝e4 b6 17.♖b2 ♝f5 18.♞d2 ♛g6 19.f3 ♖fd8 20.♝×f5 ♛×f5 21.♞e4 ♞a6 22.g4 ♛g6 23.h4 h5 24.♝g5 h×g4 25.f×g4 f6 26.h5 ♛f7 27.♞×f6+ g×f6 28.♖×f6 ♝c5+ 29.♚h1 ♛g7 30.♖g6 ♛×g6 31.h×g6 ♖d6 32.♛×e5 1-0

Despite his uneven result at the 1995 Harvard Cup. Joel Benjamin had quietly built a reputation as a player who understood how to beat chess computers. Little did he know that this reputation would have a profound influence on his career.

The Harvard Cup produced results that were easier to interpret than those of the Aegon events. The human team was consistently composed of strong grandmasters. The computer team was mostly composed of the top microcomputer programs. The series of Harvard Cups showed an unmistakable trend of improved computer performance over the years. Further, given that the computer side mostly featured single-processor commercial products, the unanswered question was "How would the top programs have fared?" In 1989, we had the answer. DEEP THOUGHT, HITECH, and CHIPTEST were crushed. Circa 1995, when the last Harvard Cup was held, there was no good answer to the question.

Meanwhile, what had the DEEP THOUGHT team been doing all this time?

Peter Brown, the IBM employee who was studying at Carnegie Mellon during the time of the DEEP THOUGHT successes, knew a great opportunity when he saw it. He convinced IBM management that bringing the chess project to IBM had huge potential for the company: attracting an outstanding team of talented people, doing interesting research, and a massive media opportunity. IBM made the DEEP THOUGHT team an offer they could not resist: access to immense IBM resources with the goal of bringing the chess project to a successful conclusion. Given the impressive results achieved by the DEEP THOUGHT team with a paucity of resources at Carnegie Mellon, this was too good an opportunity to pass up. Hsu and Campbell joined IBM in the summer of 1989; Anantharman followed at the end of the year after defending his Ph.D. thesis.

IBM deserves a lot of credit for seeing the commercial potential from building a world-championship-caliber chess-playing machine. It was a gamble with a huge upside and a small potential downside. As Murray Campbell (2005) relates:

> *Interviewer*: When I look at the history, from a corporate perspective, if I were IBM, it seems like one of those kind of "steeples of excellence," if you like. It's kind of a point project, and it was very well defined. But it's unusual, and you think of IBM as a fairly staid, conservative company. I've always been intrigued as to whether they saw

the public relations potential, or whether they had a genuine research interest, which I suspect is the case; they don't tend to waste their money. But I'm very interested in the business understanding, the business case, of sponsoring the DEEP BLUE Project, because it went on for quite a few years and took quite a few resources.

Campbell: It did. It went on for seven years, which is unusual for a project that isn't leading to direct revenue and income. I think there were at least two factors that came into play here. One is that at the time the Watson Research Center was, and still is, one of the top research facilities in the world – industrial research facilities. They were always looking to hire good people, and they saw that in the team of us, independent of whatever project we worked on. I believe that they thought we were people that could contribute to IBM research, and so it made sense independent of that. But…somebody had the foresight to say this project is sort of win-win. We can bring some good people to IBM, we can do some research on parallel algorithms, high performance computing, and there is this potential payoff down at the end, if we're successful, where we'll get a lot of recognition. Part of IBM Research's mission is to generate this awareness of IBM – the term they use is luster – the prestige of accomplishing scientific goals and awareness in the scientific community. Somebody had the foresight to see that there was a chance for this happening.

With financial and technical support from IBM, computer chess research would be able to progress in ways that were not possible previously. For the first time, there were realistic expectations that the end of human supremacy at chess was not far off. Campbell (2005) puts this into perspective:

Interviewer: Did you feel when you went to IBM that just based on, say, the number of rating points that chess programs seemed to be improving by every year or every two years, that you could almost draw [a line on a graph showing chess rating versus year] assuming there were no singularities or strange, bizarre meteors or whatever you want to call them, that you could almost tell, to the year plus or minus a couple of years, when you'd reach certain levels?

Campbell: Well, that's an interesting story. I guess people would draw that line and they'd say "But there's a tailing off effect" and it's going to tail off around, I want to say, 2200, master level. Then when you passed master level they say "Oh, it'll keep going up for a while but then there'll be a tailing off effect around 2400," and then "2500." Then eventually as it surpassed each of those levels, people redrew this graph and always said that "There'll be a tailing off effect." I guess now we're seeing that they just keep going up. If you keep taking advantage of faster hardware and improving – it doesn't even have to be revolutionary improvements in the programming but evolutionary – things keep improving. There may in fact be a tailing off. I think there is. If you plot the year versus rating, it's slowing down. If you take out outliers, in a sense like DEEP BLUE, which sort of pushed ahead several years in terms of speed over the curve that present day PCs are on, I think it is continuing to go up. I don't see any reason to believe it won't continue to go up for a while yet.

There was an initial flurry of computer chess competitive activity in the latter half of 1989, with both the two-game exhibition match against World Champion Garry Kasparov and then the match that closed the book on the David Levy saga. But

DEEP THOUGHT was a media darling at that point, and new opportunities for games kept arising. Unfortunately, all this activity meant the team was concentrating on Band-Aid approaches to improving their current chess player, and not enough time to do the serious work required to build their next generation machine. Feng-hsiung Hsu (2002a) describes the change in reality as he moved from academia to industry:

What I did not realize was that we could no longer take only a long-term view. Back at Carnegie Mellon, DEEP THOUGHT was not an official project and the faculty did not have high expectations abut how well we would do. Before we joined IBM, we had our own self-imposed milestones to meet, but we did not have to maintain a constant presence in the computer chess world. In theory, we could go back to the drawing board for years on end without showing up at any computer chess event. We did not have this luxury at IBM. Our arrival there was a high-profile one. Within two months, we were on the front page of the *New York Times* and *Wall Street Journal* as a result of the exhibition match with Garry Kasparov. Such a high profile came with a price. Providing short-term performance became an important concern for us even if it might be in conflict with long-term progress of the project.

So, when the opportunity to play someone of former World Champion Anatoly Karpov's caliber came along, the decision was a *fait accompli*. On February 2, 1990, DEEP THOUGHT played an exhibition game against Karpov. Few expected any result other than a decisive victory for the champion. Things were not quite as expected, as Hsu (1990) recounts:

Both GM Ron Henley and IM Mike Valvo called it a moral victory for computers, but, of course, the machine knows nothing about morals.

First, some personal impressions about the match and Karpov. … Karpov is a little bit more plump than I expected. During the press conference, he seemed to be somewhat nervous – his hands were twitching behind his back. Compared to Kasparov, Karpov appeared to be less comfortable with the press. His command of English is not as good as Kasparov's. Across the board, Karpov has a poker face, while Kasparov constantly shifts his expressions. Mike Valvo seemed to be able to tell Karpov's mood changes even from off the stage though.

Before the match, we were expecting to toss a coin to decide the color. GM Ron Henley… had a different idea. Suggesting that Karpov had not slept for 24 hours during the trip, he would like Karpov to have White. The decision was made without our consent, but given that we were fully expecting to lose with either color, we had no serious objection.

Karpov's play may have been hampered by the jet lag, but it was also evident that he was not as well prepared for the match as Kasparov. This might be in part due to [DEEP THOUGHT]'s selection of opening line. Over its entire career, it played Caro-Kann 3 times and none of the games have been widely circulated. Karpov might have been expecting Alekhine defense (surprisingly, the only Alekhine defense game that [DEEP THOUGHT] lost was the postal game against Valvo...). Valvo did tell Karpov the day before to expect Caro-Kann.

A slower but safer hardware configuration was used for the Karpov match. The 6-processor version that played Kasparov had been found to contain serious software bugs; some of them were fixed, but more bugs showed up right before the Karpov match, and the old 2-processor version was resurrected. The machine was operating from IBM T.J. Watson Lab.

Before the match, I predicted that the game would end in a clearly winning, at least to the titled players, endgame for Karpov and with me resigning for the machine somewhere between move 40 and 60. I was off by 5 moves and wrong about the nature of the endgame.

Karpov, Anatoly (2730) – Deep Thought
Caro-Kann Defense B12
Harvard, 1990

1.e4 c6 2.d4 d5 3.♘d2 g6 4.c3 ♗g7 5.e5 f6 6.f4 ♘h6 7.♘gf3 0-0 8.♗e2 f×e5 9.f×e5 c5 10.♘b3 c×d4 11.c×d4 ♘c6 12.0-0 ♕b6 13.♔h1 a5 14.a4 ♗f5 15.♗g5 15.♖a3!? **15...♗e4 16.♘c5**

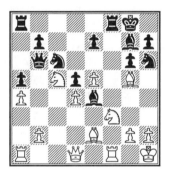

16...♕×b2?

This greedy capture is problematic, as the queen cannot so easily come back. After 16...♘f5, Black is not worse.

17.♘×e4 d×e4 18.♖b1 ♕a3 19.♗c1 ♕c3 20.♗d2 ♕a3 21.♗c1 ♕c3

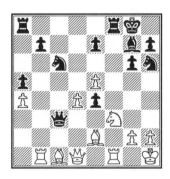

22.♖b3?

Karpov heads for an endgame that is objectively drawn. He could exploit Black's wayward queen with 22.♗b2 ♕e3 23.♕e1 ♕b3 24.♗a1 ♕e6 25.♗d1 with a clear advantage.

22...♛a1 23.♗c4+ ♚h8 24.♗×h6 ♛×d1 25.♗×g7+ ♚×g7 26.♖×d1 e×f3 27.g×f3

27...♖a7 Hsu (2002a): "On the 27th move, DEEP THOUGHT played a move that a first sight looked quite ugly and the audience laughed. After the game, Anatoly commented that the ugly move was the only good move." But the active 27...♖ad8 28.♖×b7 ♖×f3 should draw as well.

28.♗d5 ♖d8 29.♖b5 ♖a6 30.♗c4 ♖a7 31.♗d5 ♖a6 32.♖c5 ♖d7 33.♚g2 ♖b6 34.♗×c6 The resulting rook endgame is drawn, but there is nothing better and Karpov hopes to use his excellent endgame technique.

34...b×c6 35.♚f2 ♖d5 36.♖×d5 c×d5 37.♖c1 ♖b4 38.♚e3 ♖×a4 39.♖c5 e6 40.♖c7+ ♚g8 41.♖e7 ♖a3+ 42.♚f4 ♖d3 43.♖×e6 ♖×d4+ 44.♚g5 ♚f7 45.♖a6 a4 46.f4 h6+ 47.♚g4 ♖c4 48.h4 ♖d4 49.♖f6+ ♚g7 50.♖a6 ♚f7 51.h5 A typical lever.

51...g×h5+?!

This is asking for trouble. 51...g5 52.♖×h6 ♖×f4+ 53.♚×g5 ♖f1 draws relatively easily. "The machine thought it was down for the first time in the endgame. g5!? may or may not draw at this point. Right after the game, Karpov thought he would still be winning. Afterwards, on the cab back to hotel, he changed the assessment to slightly better for white. After the game move, Black is theoretically lost. According to [Mike] Valvo, 'now he (Karpov) is happy.' Karpov at this time was down to his last few minutes, but it was easy for him from now on." (Hsu 1990)

52.♔f5 Karpov's king comes to join the attack. **52...♔g7 53.♖a7+** 53.♖g6+!? was a dangerous try, but should also not win against best defense.

53...♔f8 54.e6 ♖e4 55.♖d7 ♖c4? 55...a3 56.♖a7 h4 57.♖×a3 ♔e7 58.♖a7+ ♔d6 59.♖d7+ ♔c5 60.♖h7 h3 61.♖×h6 ♖e3= **56.♖×d5 h4 57.♖d3?** 57.♖d8+ ♔e7 58.♖d7+ ♔f8 59.♔e5 +− **57...♔e7?**

This invites White's attack. 57...h3 58.♖×h3 ♔e7 59.♖×h6 ♖c5+ 60.♔e4 ♖c4+ 61.♔e5 ♖c5+ 62.♔d4 ♖a5 destroys the attacking coordination and draws.

58.♖d7+ ♔f8

59.♖h7? Short of time Karpov misses 59.♔e5 h3 60.f5 h2 61.f6 ♖e4+ 62.♔f5 +− . **59...h5?**

The computer returns the favor as this just loses one valuable tempo in the race. 59...h3 60.♖×h6 a3 61.♖×h3 ♖a4 draws.

60.♔e5 h3 60...♔g8 61.♖a7 h3 62.♖a8+ ♔g7 63.e7 +− **61.f5 ♔g8 62.♖×h5 a3 63.♖×h3 a2** 63...♖a4 64.f6 +− **64.♖a3 ♖c5+ 65.♔f6 1-0**

Deep Thought was competitive, but made too many mistakes. But the short-term exhibitions enabled the long-term vision. As Hsu (2002a) quickly discovered, there was also a big upside to moving from academia to industry:

> As a graduate student, I was used to operating with the minimum amount of outlay. We had a nil budget for ChipTest, and a $5,000 budget for Deep Thought. You had better be frugal when you have a budget as tight as we did. To me, it was already a big surprise that IBM agreed to hire a full team immediately…

IBM added personnel to the team, including senior management, hardware design (to help Hsu with his chess chip work), software developer (Joe Hoane, replacing Thomas Anantharaman who left for Wall Street in 1990), and chess expertise (including a short stint with GM Maxim Dlugy).

Deep Blue team. From left to right: Joe Hoane, Feng-Hsiung Hsu, Murray Campbell. (IBM)

IBM felt it was important to also keep in touch with the artificial intelligence research community. The DEEP THOUGHT team agreed to an exhibition game at the biennial International Joint Conference on Artificial Intelligence (IJCAI), one of the premier AI research events. Against a respectable Australian master, DEEP THOUGHT struggled, further evidence that serious work was needed to address the well-known weaknesses in its play.

Johansen, Darryl (2465) – DEEP THOUGHT
English Opening A22
International Joint Conference on Artificial Intelligence, Sydney, 1991

1.e3 e5 2.c4 ♘f6 3.♘c3 ♗b4 4.♘ge2 0-0 5.a3 ♗e7 6.d4 d6 7.d5!

White's pieces are not particularly well placed to support this advance but Johansen is aware that DEEP THOUGHT (and all chess computers of that time) handled closed positions badly, being unable to form a long-term plan.

7...c6 8.♘g3 ♗g4? 9.f3 ♗d7 10.♗e2 c×d5 11.c×d5 ♗e8?! 12.0-0 ♘bd7 13.♔h1 ♖c8 14.e4 a6 15.♗e3 ♔h8 16.♖c1 h6 17.♘f5 ♘c5

DEEP THOUGHT has completely run out of ideas and almost all its moves between moves 15 and 22 could be criticized. The basic problem is that Black's only active plan in this type of position is the ...f5 pawn advance, a concept which cannot be taught to a calculating machine such as DEEP THOUGHT. However, DEEP THOUGHT's waiting moves merely ensure that Johansen's queenside attack can be built up until it is utterly decisive.

18.b4 ♘cd7 19.a4 ♘g8 20.a5 ♘gf6 21.♕d2 ♖g8 22.♘a4 ♗f8? 23.♘b6
♘×b6 24.♗×b6 ♕d7 25.♖×c8 ♕×c8 26.♖c1 a8 27.♗c7 ♘h5 28.♘×d6
♗×d6 29.♗×d6 f6 30.♕e3 ♗a4 31.g3! ♖c8 32.♗c7 ♗e8 33.♕b6 ♗f7
34.b5 a×b5 35.♗×b5 ♗e8 36.d6 ♗×b5 37.♕×b5 1–0 Further material loss
through 38.d7 is inevitable.

Jaap Van den Herik and Richard Greenblatt (1992)
Computer chess program developers

Van den Herik: And how far do you think [computers] will reach [in performance]?

Greenblatt: I do not think there is any reason why it should stop at any particular level.

Van den Herik: So in the long run they will defeat the World Champion?

Greenblatt: Sure.

1992: Checkers

CHINOOK loses the first Man-Machine World Championship to Marion Tinsley by a
score of two wins and four losses in a 40-game match. The match was even closer
than portrayed by the score; CHINOOK defaulted one game due to technical problems,
and then lost the last game in an all-out attempt to win.

The chess machine continued to use the DEEP THOUGHT moniker despite the move to
IBM. With the team developing a newer, faster computer chip and improved chess
software, it was time to consider an appropriate name for the successor machine.
An internal IBM naming contest led to the selection of the name DEEP BLUE – an
obvious choice given IBM's nickname of "Big Blue," a reflection of the color
of their logo and, some would say, the synonymous blue suits worn by company
salesmen.

In 1993, the IBM chess machine was invited to play exhibition events in
Copenhagen. What was the program to be called? DEEP BLUE was the name of the
new machine, but the hardware was not ready. The games were played using the
DEEP THOUGHT II hardware (14 chess chips) running parts of the new DEEP BLUE
software – a DEEP BLUE prototype if you will. DEEP BLUE? DEEP THOUGHT II? In the
end, the decision was made to call this hybrid machine DEEP BLUE NORDIC.

Copenhagen featured two events: four-game matches against Bent Larsen and the
Danish national chess team. Here was a chance for Larsen to get revenge for his
1988 loss to the program. Robert Byrne (1993) summarized the event in the *New
York Times*.

> DEEP BLUE, IBM's successor to its world leader in chess computers, DEEP THOUGHT II,
> won one match and lost another in Copenhagen, Feb. 24 to 28. DEEP BLUE defeated
> the Danish national team by a 3-1 score, but lost to the top Dane, Grandmaster Bent
> Larsen, by 1½-2½ in a second, individual contest.

DEEP BLUE's programmers had hoped for a better result, but explained that they had made several errors that handicapped their machine. Dr. Murray Campbell said: "We were afraid that since we had upped it to 14 processors from the original DEEP THOUGHT's 2, it might use too much time. So we limited its search depth in complex positions." It went wrong in the first game against Larsen and in practice games with the other Danes.

His fellow programmer, Dr. Feng-hsiung Hsu, added, "It was also failing to open diagonals for the bishops." Once the proper adjustments to the program were made, DEEP BLUE easily drew its following games with Larsen and finished with two victories and a draw against the other Danes.

Dr. Campbell said, "Overall, it has the potential to play very well, but it needs more endgame knowledge."

In Game 1 against Larsen, it gave its weakest performance in years.

Larsen, Bent (2540) – DEEP BLUE NORDIC
Open Games Four Knights Variation C49
Exhibition match (1), Copenhagen, 24.02.1993

Hsu (1993):

Larsen adopted a very simple strategy that worked surprisingly well in the first match game. He traded off all the machine's knights, allowing the machine to have the bishop pair but without an open position to realize the potential of the bishop pair. This really should not have worked if the machine had been told explicitly to trade off some pawns to increase the scope of the bishop pair. This diagnosis, however, came a little bit late, as [in Game 2], Black's opening preparation was also too superficial.

1.e4 e5 2.♘f3 ♘c6 3.♘c3 ♘f6 4.♗b5 ♗b4 5.0-0 0-0 6.♗×c6 d×c6 7.d3 ♕e7 8.♘e2 ♗g4 9.♘g3 ♘h5 10.h3 ♘×g3 11.f×g3 ♗c5+ 12.♔h2 ♗c8 13.g4 ♗e6 14.♕e2 f6 15.♗e3 ♗×e3 16.♕×e3 h6 17.a4 ♕b4 18.b3 b6 19.♖f2 c5 20.♔g3 ♕a5 21.h4 ♕c3 22.♖af1 ♖ad8 23.g5 ♗×b3 24.c×b3 ♖×d3 25.♕e2 h×g5 26.h×g5 f×g5 27.♖d1 ♖e3 28.♕b2 ♕×b3 29.♕×b3+ ♖×b3 30.♖d5 ♖a3 31.♖×e5 g4 32.♔×g4 c4 33.♖d2 ♖×a4 34.♖d7 ♖c8 35.♘g5 ♖a2 36.♖×c7 ♖a8 37.g3 ♖f2 38.♖ee7 ♔h8 39.♖×g7 ♖h2 40.e5 ♖d8 41.♖h7+ ♖×h7 42.♘×h7 ♖g8+ 43.♘g5 1-0

Larsen had his moments of concern but was able to draw the three remaining games, scoring a nice 2½-1½ match victory. His post-match comment was (Larsen 2014) "You should not play computers in tournaments, but in laboratories and in circuses. I suppose this was a mixture of both." The venue was irrelevant – it was a most satisfying chess result for him!

Bent Larsen (1993)
Grandmaster

It's nonsense if they [the DEEP BLUE team] believe that they will be able to build a machine that can beat Garry Kasparov in 1994. Maybe in twenty more years.

Larsen's fourth game counted as part of the Danish national team result against Deep Blue Nordic. The computer beat two of the three Danish players. In a particularly nice game, the machine's positional maneuvering slowly outplayed Grandmaster Lars Bo Hansen. This is a game that would make any chess player proud!

Hansen, Lars Bo (2545) – Deep Blue Nordic
Queen's Gambit Declined D37
Danish National Team Match (3), Copenhagen, 27.02.1993

1.♘f3 ♘f6 2.c4 e6 3.♘c3 d5 4.d4 ♗e7 5.♗f4 0-0 6.e3 c5 7.d×c5 ♗×c5 8.♕c2 ♘c6 9.a3 ♕a5 10.♘d2 ♗e7 11.♗g3 ♗d7 12.♗e2 ♕b6 13.0-0 d4 14.♘a4 ♕d8 15.b4 ♖c8 16.♘b2 e5 17.♘b3 d×e3 18.f×e3 ♕e8 19.♖ad1 ♘g4 20.♕c3 ♗g5 21.♗×g4 ♗×g4 22.♖de1 f6 23.c5 ♘d8 24.♘d2 ♕c6 25.♕c2 b6 26.♘e4 ♘f7 27.♘c4 b×c5 28.♘×c5 ♗h5 29.e4 ♘d6 30.♘×d6 ♕×d6 31.♗f2 ♕d2 32.♕b3+ ♗f7 33.♕h3 ♖fd8 34.♗e3 ♗×e3+ 35.♖×e3 ♗c4 36.♖fe1 ♖b8 37.♕g3 a5 38.♖c3 ♕d4+ 39.♕e3 a×b4 40.♕×d4 ♖×d4 41.a×b4 ♖×b4 42.♔f2 ♖b5 43.♘a4 ♖a5 44.♘b6 ♗a6 45.♘d5 ♗b7 46.♘e7+ ♔f8 47.♘f5 ♖a2+ 48.♔f3 ♖dd2 49.♖c7 ♖f2+ 50.♔g4 ♖×g2+ 51.♘g3 ♖af2 52.h4 g6 0-1

Parallel Search

One computer processor can only analyze so many chess positions per second. But what if you had access to 100 computers? Could you get your program analyzing 100 times as many positions? If so, Ken Thompson's (1982) results suggest that this would be worth hundreds of rating points.

Some tasks are inherently sequential. For example, it takes nine months to give birth to a baby. Having nine mothers helping out will not reduce the time to delivery. In contrast, some tasks are inherently parallel. Painting a fence can be done much faster if you can persuade ten friends to help out: divide the fence into independent sections, one for each person.

Most real-world problems fall in-between these extremes. The task of searching for the best chess move can be broken up into pieces that are done on multiple computers running in parallel. However no one has yet found a way to effectively use hundreds of processors.

There are many algorithms for dividing up the work to be done, but they all suffer from inherent problems. First, some of the analysis ends up being irrelevant. For example, if you search two moves in parallel and the first one ends up producing a cutoff, then the effort expended on the second move was unnecessary. Second, much work might be repeated. For example, one processor might have searched a position and stored the result in its transposition table. A different processor might encounter the same position and, not knowing that the work had been done elsewhere, unwittingly repeat the computation. Third, some computers may have a lack of work. The larger the number of computers being used, the harder it is to generate enough work to keep all of them busy. Finally, the computers have to communicate with each other, whether it be sending/receiving tasks or to report results. All communication effort is time spent not doing chess analysis.

The performance measure for a parallel program is called the Speedup (S): the number of times faster a program can produce its results when using parallelism. Another measure is the Efficiency (E): the Speedup achieved relative to the number of processors used. A sequential program has an S of 1 (i.e., no improvement) and E of 1 (all resources are efficiently used). A highly parallel program might have S close to the number of processors used and E close to 1.0. A program with poor parallelism will have a small S and an E closer to 0 than to 1.

There are many research papers that show a chess program using 8 computers can produce results roughly 3 to 5 times faster. Pretend that the program runs 4 times faster. That means S is 4 and E is 0.5 (you are effectively getting only half of what is possible). As you add more processors, you see diminishing returns. For example, with 100 computers, having the search proceed 25 times faster would be considered an excellent result (S=25 and E=0.25)!

Murray Campbell did his Masters thesis on parallel game-tree search at the University of Alberta with Tony Marsland in 1980. Feng-hsiung Hsu proposed ideas for large-scale parallel search in his Ph.D. thesis. Keeping hundreds of DEEP BLUE chess chips busy in parallel was a research challenge for the team.

Feng-hsiung Hsu and his chess-playing computer chip.
(IBM)

The DEEP BLUE team spent most of their time in their laboratory: Hsu building the next generation of chess chips (to be tens, if not hundreds of times faster), Campbell working on the chess knowledge (endgames being of particular concern), and Hoane on the parallelism (efficiently using hundreds of chess chips would prove a challenge). Occasionally they would privately test their new system, as happened in August 1993 when they invited Judit Polgar to play a two-game exhibition match. The time control was game in 30 minutes.

Deep Blue Prototype – Polgar, Judit (2630)
Sicilian Defense Taimanov Variation B47
Exhibition match (1), T.J. Watson Research Center, 30.08.1993

**1.e4 c5 2.♘f3 e6 3.d4 c×d4 4.♘×d4 ♘c6 5.♘c3 ♛c7 6.♗e2 a6 7.0-0
♗b4 8.♘×c6 b×c6 9.♛d4 ♗d6 10.♛×g7 ♗×h2+ 11.♔h1 ♗e5 12.♗f4
♗×g7 13.♗×c7 d5 14.♖ad1 ♘e7 15.♘a4 ♖a7 16.♗d6 ♖a8 17.c3 ♘g6
18.♗c7 ♖a7 19.♗b8 ♖b7 20.♗g3 0-0 21.e×d5 c×d5 22.♖fe1 f5 23.♗d6
♖d8 24.♗a3 ♖c7 25.♗b4 ♖c6 26.♗a5 ♖f8 27.♗b6 ♖f7 28.♔g1 ♗f8
29.b3 ♗b7 30.♗h5 ♖e7 31.♔f1 ♔f7 32.c4 ♖c8 33.♗a5 d×c4 34.♘b6
♖b8 35.♘d7 ♖c8 36.♗b4 c×b3 37.♘×f8 ♖×f8 38.a×b3 ♖b8 39.♗×e7
♔×e7 40.♖d4 a5 41.♖a4 ♗c6 42.♖×a5 ♖×b3 43.♖a7+ ♔f6 44.♖×h7
♘f4 45.g3 ♗b5+ 46.♔g1 ♘h3+ 47.♔g2 ♘g5 48.♖h6+ ♔e7 49.♖e5
♗c6+ 50.♔f1 ♖b1+ 51.♖e1 ♖b2 52.♗e2 ♘e4 53.♖d1 ♗d5 54.♖c1
♘d2+ 55.♔e1 ♘e4 56.♖a1 ♘c3 57.♗d3 ♘a2 58.♔f1 ♘b4 59.♗×f5
♘c6 60.♖d1 ♗c4+ 61.♗d3 ♗b3 62.♖b1 ♖×b1+ 63.♗×b1 ♗d5 64.♖h7+
♔f6 65.♖h4 ♘e5 66.♔e2 ♗f3+ 67.♔e3 ♗c6 68.f4 ♘f7 69.g4 e5 70.g5+
♔g7 71.♖h7+ ♔g8 72.g6 e×f4+ 73.♔×f4 1-0**

The second game was drawn. Deep Blue had won an exhibition match against one
of the world's elite players!

Matches like this suggest that Deep Blue was making progress. Indeed it was, but
that progress was largely invisible to the public. As the team soon discovered, being
the best also meant having to prove you were best.

In May 1994, Fritz defeated Garry Kasparov in a 5-minute game, attracting
international media attention. To the chess world, the game was easy to discount
– after all it was speed chess where the quality of play was not so strong. But a
few months later, there was more bad news for mankind. Kasparov lost again, this
time to Richard Lang's Chess Genius program in a 25 minute per side game. It was
harder to make excuses this time.

Kasparov, Garry (2815) – Chess Genius
Queen's Gambit Declined Slav D11
London, 31.08.1994

**1.c4 c6 2.d4 d5 3.♘f3 ♘f6 4.♛c2 d×c4 5.♛×c4 ♗f5 6.♘c3 ♘bd7 7.g3
e6 8.♗g2 ♗e7 9.0-0 0-0 10.e3 ♘e4 11.♛e2 ♛b6 12.♖d1 ♖ad8 13.♘e1
♘df6 14.♘×e4 ♘×e4 15.f3 ♘d6 16.a4 ♛b3 17.e4 ♗g6 18.♖d3 ♛b4
19.b3 ♘c8 20.♘c2 ♛b6 21.♗f4 c5 22.♗e3 c×d4 23.♘×d4 ♗c5 24.♖ad1
e5 25.♘c2 ♖×d3 26.♛×d3 ♔e7 27.b4 ♗×e3+ 28.♛×e3 ♖d8 29.♖×d8+
♛×d8 30.♗f1 b6 31.♛c3 f6 32.♗c4+ ♗f7 33.♘e3 ♛d4 34.♗×f7+ ♔×f7
35.♛b3+ ♔f8 36.♔g2 ♛d2+ 37.♔h3 ♛e2 38.♘g2 h5 39.♛e3 ♛c4
40.♛d2 ♛e6+ 41.g4 h×g4+ 42.f×g4 ♛c4 43.♛e1 ♛b3+ 44.♘e3 ♛d3
45.♔g3 ♛×e4 46.♛d2 ♛f4+ 47.♔g2 ♛d4 48.♛×d4 e×d4 49.♘c4 ♘c6
50.b5 ♘e5 51.♘d6 d3 52.♔f2 ♘×g4+ 53.♔e1 ♘×h2 54.♔d2 ♘f3+
55.♔×d3 ♔e7 56.♘f5+ ♔f7 57.♔e4 ♘d2+ 58.♔d5 g5 59.♘d6+ ♔g6**

60.♔d4 ♞b3+ 0-1

Clearly the microcomputer programs had made enormous strides forward. Without the incredible hardware assist that DEEP BLUE enjoyed, they had to rely on skillful programming, clever algorithms (most of which were not published), and extensive chess knowledge. And it was working!

1994: Checkers

After six games, all drawn, Marion Tinsley resigns the Second Man-Machine World Championship to CHINOOK citing health concerns. Subsequent matches against Grandmaster Don Lafferty in 1994 and 1995 confirm CHINOOK's right to the title. Tinsley died in 1995. CHINOOK is retired in 1997, having dominated all human opposition.

1994: Go

Computer Go World Champion GO INTELLECT is given a massive handicap but still loses all three games against youth players.

The success of the microcomputers continued in 1995. DEEP BLUE entered the World Computer Chess Championship in Hong Kong (they skipped the 1992 event). Against FRITZ, they were out-booked, left on their own in a dangerous position, could not find the right moves, and lost. FRITZ was crowned World Computer Champion. It was a stunning setback for the IBM effort and the source of much soul searching by the DEEP BLUE team.

Which chess program was the strongest player? The answer was not obvious.

Franz Morsch and many of his computer chess products that led up the creation of FRITZ.

In May1995 IBM came to terms with Garry Kasparov for another match, planned for February 1996. There would be $500,000 at stake, with $400,00 going to the winner. Despite DEEP BLUE's wins against lower-ranked grandmasters, Kasparov must have been supremely confident of a decisive victory. The program's positional play was uneven and the positive results often came from a strong tactical game. Based on the public games to date, Kasparov must have viewed the match as easy money.

The match was to be billed as the world human chess champion against the world computer chess champion. But things did not go as expected. First, in June DEEP BLUE lost the world computer chess championship in an upset to FRITZ. Further, in September there were anxious moments for Kasparov as he defended his world title against Viswanathan Anand. He fell behind late in the match, raising the specter that neither competitor in the February event would be a world champion. The lost game to Anand awakened a sleeping giant and Kasparov blitzed out four wins to crush his opponent. Thus at least one of the man-machine competitors would be a champion.

Things did not go well for DEEP BLUE. They had an ambitious schedule for preparing a new version of their chess machine for the match. A combination of hardware problems and software issues plagued them, resulting in losing a two-game match to Spanish Grandmaster Miguel Illescas and drawing with Chinese women's Grandmaster Xie Jun.

The DEEP BLUE team recognized the need for chess expertise on the team. Murray Campbell had been a strong player in his student days, but was much more valuable to the team as a computer scientist than as a chess player. Now was the time to bring in grandmaster expertise.

Joel Benjamin was invited to play a pair of private games against DEEP BLUE. As he later recounted, "I didn't know the games would serve as auditions for a potential employer" (Benjamin 2007).

DEEP BLUE – Benjamin, Joel (2570)
Irregular Opening A45
Training match (1), T.J. Watson Research Center, 1995

1.d4 d6 2.e3 ♘f6 3.♘c3 g6 4.f4 ♕a5 5.♗d3 e5 6.d×e5 d×e5 7.f5 b5 8.♗g5

"This is dubious because White's dark squares will be too weak should White exchange on f6. After the game, I suggested that DEEP BLUE might be penalizing doubled pawns too much, or underrating the bishop pair, or not appreciating dark square weaknesses enough" (Benjamin 2007). Benjamin's insights give direction to the DEEP BLUE team on how to improve the program's play. Few chess players have the ability to talk to chess program creators in meaningful ways.

8...♘bd7 9.a3 ♘c5 10.b4 ♘×d3+ 11.c×d3 ♕b6 12.♗×f6 g×f6 13.♘f3 ♗b7 14.♕d2 c5 15.♖b1 c×b4 16.a×b4 ♖c8 17.♘d1 ♖d8 18.♘f2 h5 19.♕e2 a5 20.b×a5 ♕×a5+ 21.♕d2 ♕b6 22.♕b2 ♗a6 23.0-0 ♗c5 24.♕c2 b4 25.♘e1 ♖b8 26.♖b3 ♔e7 27.♔h1 ♖hc8 28.♕a2 ♖a8 29.♕e2

♗b5 30.♘d1 h4 31.♘c2 ♗a4 32.♖b1 ♗×c2 33.♘c3

"Now comes a move that computers had difficulty appreciating." An example of the computer not understanding that in this position the value of the pieces has changed.

33...♗×b1 34.♘d5+ ♚e8 35.♘×b6 ♗×b6 36.♖×b1 ♗d4 37.g3 h3 38.♕d1 ♖a2 39.♕h5 ♖cc2 40.♕×h3 b3 41.♕h7 ♚e7 42.♕h8 b2 43.♕b8 ♖a1 44.♕b4+ ♖c5 0-1

Joel Benjamin – Deep Blue
Training match (2), T.J. Watson Research Center, 1995

"I needed only a draw in the second game to clinch the match and the $500 bonus. With the White pieces, I had the power to steer for boredom. That was part of my anti-computer strategy anyway."

50...♗g1

"?? Deep Blue finds the only way to preserve material equality, but loses the game. It calculated 50...♗f4 51.♚f3 g5 52.♚g2 would put it in zugzwang, but didn't realize 52...♚b7 53.♗×a5 ♚a6 would produce an impenetrable fortress. The draw is not hard for humans to see; Murray [Campbell] pointed it out after the game. People can look ahead in their mind's eye and move the pieces all around the board. Computers do not understand permanent conditions; they only understand as far as their searchlight shines. No one has been able to address this problem satisfactorily – feed this position into your PC and see for yourself."

51.♗×e5 ♗×c5 52.♗c3 ♗b6 53.♚d3 ♚b7 54.♗d4 ♗d8 55.♚c4 ♚c8 56.♚c5 ♚c7 57.♗e5+ ♚d7 58.♗f4 ♗e7+ 59.♚b6 ♗b4 60.♚a6 c5 61.♚b5 ♗a3 62.♗g3 ♗b4 63.♗b8 ♗a3 64.♗a7 c4 65.♚×c4 ♚c6 66.♗d4 ♗e7 67.♗c3 ♗d8 68.e5 ♗b6 69.e6 ♗d8 70.♗d2 ♗c7 71.e7 ♚d7 72.♚b5 ♗d6 73.♚×a5 ♗×e7 74.♚b6 ♚c8 75.♚c6 ♗f6 76.♗e3 ♗c3 77.♗b6 ♗e1 78.a5 ♚b8 79.a6 ♚a8 80.♚d6 1-0

The Deep Blue team was impressed with Benjamin's abilities over the board, his communication skills (especially to non-chess players), his work ethic, and his personality, one that worked well with the members of the chess team. He became a member of the Deep Blue team in December 1995.

Key to success against Kasparov was the next generation of Hsu's chip. The new design would put more chess knowledge into silicon and streamline operations to improve speed. The formula was simple: add more knowledge, make faster chips, and use more of them. The chess knowledge would allow the program to better assess common positional features while the speed enabled the machine to search deeper, following Ken Thompson's recipe for success. Unfortunately, time was short and it was not possible to fully debug all aspects of the new chip in time for the match. In particular, some of the new knowledge capabilities were too risky to use, not having been adequately tested and integrated into the program.

IBM had made a huge investment in sponsoring the match, expecting to reap enormous publicity benefits. But they were almost scooped. Kasparov had sponsorship from Intel and as part of his agreement he had to play a two-game match against FRITZ in December 1995. This was the real match between the human and computer world champions, something that was not lost on the media. A win by FRITZ would take away much of the luster of the February match. In the lead-up to the event, IBM and the DEEP BLUE team must have endured some anxious moments before the result came in. Kasparov won the first game as a result of operator error (a move was incorrectly played and the mistake not detected until several moves later) and the second game was a draw.

The Kasparov – DEEP BLUE match began on February 10 in Philadelphia. Whereas the 1989 match between Kasparov and DEEP THOUGHT was viewed as entertainment (no one expected the computer to do well), the 1996 event was historic. The machine was of grandmaster strength and had to be respected. It was capable of winning a game against anyone.

Kasparov was clearly the favorite, as evidenced by having an estimated 200-250 ELO rating advantage. Almost all experts were unanimous in their prediction of a decisive victory for mankind. Not even the most optimistic computer chess developers expected less than a Kasparov win. But, some cautioned that anything could happen in a short match.

On stage was the human champion. On the other side of the chessboard was his adversary, a proxy for the challenger. Feng-hsiung Hsu, a weak chess player by his own admission, had the privilege of being seated across the table from arguably the greatest chess player in history (to that point in time). His job was to relay moves to/from the chessboard via a computer interface to a refrigerator-like black box located in a room offstage. Inside the box were 256 chess chips with an aggregate capacity of 150 million positions in a typical 3-minute move. In contrast, a human can do roughly 500 positions in the same time. It did not seem to be a fair fight. But, as we all know, chess is more than merely search…

1996 Kasparov – DEEP BLUE Match Predictions

International Master David Levy: 6-0 for Kasparov

Grandmaster Lev Albert: 6-0 for Kasparov

DEEP BLUE project manager C.J.Tan: 4-2 for DEEP BLUE

World Champion Garry Kasparov: 4-2 for Kasparov

Deep Blue – Kasparov, Garry (2795)

Sicilian Defense B22
Philadelphia match (1), 10.02.1996

1.e4 c5 2.c3 d5 3.e×d5 ♛×d5 4.d4 ♞f6 5.♞f3 ♝g4 6.♝e2 e6 7.h3 ♝h5 8.0-0

8.♝e3 c×d4 9.c×d4 ♝b4+ 10.♞c3 0-0 11.0-0 ♛a5 12.♛b3 ♞c6 13.a3 ♝×c3 14.b×c3 ♞d5 was equal in the rapid game Kramnik-Kasparov, Paris 1994.

8...♞c6 9.♝e3 c×d4 10.c×d4 ♝b4

10...♝e7 is the main line.

11.a3!?

11.♞c3 ♛a5 12.♛b3 transposes to the Kramnik game.

11...♝a5 12.♞c3 ♛d6 13.♞b5

13...♛e7

According to Hsu, Deep Blue was planning to answer 13...♛d8 with the retreat 14.♞c3 as it assessed the position to be in Black's favor. But Kasparov was most probably more afraid of something like the typical advance 14.d5 with a dangerous initiative.

14.♞e5 ♝×e2 15.♛×e2 0-0 16.♖ac1 ♖ac8 17.♝g5!

The pin is very annoying for Black.

17...♝b6?!

17...♖fd8 18.♞g4 ♝b6 is a more precise order of moves.

18.♗×f6!

DEEP BLUE seizes the moment when Kasparov must take with the pawn. After
18.♖fd1 ♖fd8 19.♘g4 ♗×d4 20.♖×c6 ♗×f2+ 21.♔×f2 b×c6 22.♗×f6 g×f6 23.♘d4,
a messy position arises.

18...g×f6

18...♕×f6? runs into 19.♘d7 ♕g5 20.♘×f8 ♘×d4? 21.♕g4 and White wins.

19.♘c4 ♖fd8

Of course not 19...♗×d4?? 20.♘×d4 ♘×d4 21.♕g4+. The computer does not give
away a pawn for free.

20.♘×b6 a×b6

21.♖fd1

The surprising 21.♕g4+!? is also interesting, e.g., 21...♔h8 22.♖fd1 ♖g8 23.♕e4 f5
24.♕e3 ♕f6 25.d5 f4 26.♕c3, with the initiative.

21...f5 22.♕e3 ♕f6

23.d5!?

The isolated pawn breaks free in typical fashion. "Kasparov was taken completely by surprise. This is the kind of positional sacrifice computers are not supposed to play. Later we found that by sheer brute force DEEP BLUE had calculated that it could win back the pawn by force." (Friedel 2016) The alternative 23.♕g3+!? should be met by 23...♔f8 (as 23...♔h8? runs into 24.♘d6 f4 25.♕g5 ♕×g5 26.♘×f7+).

23...♖×d5!

Kasparov rightly exchanges attacking potential. After 23...e×d5? 24.♕×b6 ♕×b2 25.♕×b7 ♖b8 26.♕×c6 ♖×b5 27.♖c3 f4 28.♖d4, Black's king is very vulnerable.

24.♖×d5 e×d5 25.b3

25.b4 looks more logical to the human eye.

25...♔h8!

As White's king does not have many defenders this plan to attack is logical. The alternative, 25...♖d8 26.♕×b6 ♖d7, to keep the queenside intact, is also interesting, but White retains a slight initiative with 27.♕e3. So Kasparov's choice at this point was probably best.

26.♕×b6 ♖g8 27.♕c5

A computer would of course never fall for 27.♕×b7?? ♕g5−+.

27...d4?

This is the wrong pawn advance as it does not support Black's attack. After 27...f4, the position is more or less balanced, as 28.♕×d5? f3 29.g4 runs into the double attack 29...♕h6.

28.♞d6 f4

29.♞×b7!

The computer has no fears. It just calculated that the knight will return in time.

29...♞e5 30.♕d5 f3 31.g3 ♞d3?

31...♕f4? is met by 32.♜c8!! (32.♔h2?? runs into 32...♜×g3) 32...♕g5 33.♜c5 (but not 33.h4?? ♜×c8 34.h×g5 ♜c1+ 35.♔h2 ♞g4+ 36.♔h3 ♞×f2+ 37.♔h2 ♜h1 #).
31...d3 was the last chance, but it is unlikely that Black can survive after 32.♕d4.

32.♜c7!

32.♜c6? runs into 32...♜g5 33.♕d8+ (33.♜×f6 ♜×d5 34.♞d6 ♞c5) 33...♕×d8 34.♞×d8 ♔g7, and in both cases Black is still fighting.

32...♜e8?!

32...♞f4?! is met by 33.♕×f3. More tenacious are 32...♕e5 33.♕×e5+ ♞×e5 34.♜e7 f6 35.♞d6 and 32...♜g5 33.♕×f7 ♕×f7 34.♜×f7 ♜d5 35.♔f1, but White will win in the long run in both cases.

33.♞d6!

Bringing the knight into the attack is the only way to win. The alternatives allow Black to hold: 33.♕×f7? ♜e1+ 34.♔h2 ♕×f7 35.♜×f7 ♞e5 36.♜f8+ ♔g7 37.♜d8

♖e2 38.♖×d4 ♖×f2+ 39.♔g1 ♖g2+ 40.♔f1 ♖b2 41.♘c5 ♖b1+ 42.♔f2 ♖b2+, and White's king cannot escape from the checks; or 33.♖×f7? ♖e1+ 34.♔h2 ♘×f2 35.♕×f3 ♘g4+ 36.♕×g4 ♕×f7 37.♕×d4+ ♔g8.

33...♖e1+ 34.♔h2 ♘×f2

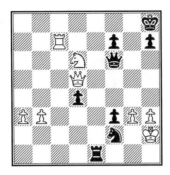

Black's attack looks dangerous, but the computer has of course calculated correctly.

35.♘×f7+ ♔g7

35...♕×f7 is refuted by the zwischenschach 36.♕d8+! ♔g7 37.♖×f7+ ♔×f7 38.♕d5+ ♔e7 39.♕×f3 ♘e4 40.♕d3 and the queen will win.

36.♘g5+ ♔h6 37.♖×h7+ 1-0

Kasparov resigned because of 37...♔g6 38.♕g8+ ♔f5 39.♘×f3 ♖h1+ 40.♔g2 ♔e4 41.♖f7 when his attack is stopped, while White's will be successful.

One of this book's authors (Schaeffer) had difficulty following the game from his home in Canada. IBM underestimated the interest that the first game would generate, and their web page with the game updates was slow to respond and kept crashing. Eager to see the moves in real time, he searched the web for another source for the game's moves. The page that he found had the colors mistakenly reversed; Kasparov was reported as playing White. At the end of the game, he shrugged his shoulders and thought that man had convincingly beaten machine. At dinner that night, friends asked him for his thoughts on DEEP BLUE's historic win, but he assured them that they were wrong – Kasparov had won a nice game. It was only the next morning that he discovered the reality of what had happened!

Media response to this historic game was muted. After the initial flurry of interest at the start of the game, few reporters stuck around to watch a game that most did not understand. Kasparov's resignation – the first time a computer had defeated a human world champion in chess under tournament conditions – did not get the front-page headlines that it deserved. The reporters did not make the same mistake twice. They came out in greater numbers for game two.

It is hard to imagine what went through Kasparov's mind as the reality of game one sunk in. What he expected to be a cakewalk was anything but that. It is a testament to his determination and focus that he was able to put the event of the day before behind him and pour all his energy into game two.

Kasparov, Garry (2795) – DEEP BLUE

Catalan Opening E04
Philadelphia match (2), 11.02.1996

1.♘f3 d5 2.d4 e6 3.g3 c5 4.♗g2 ♘c6 5.0-0 ♘f6 6.c4

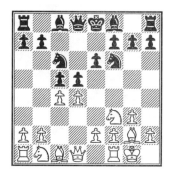

"Here the computer operator, Feng-hsiung Hsu, executed the move 6...c×d4 on the board. Garry's face lit up, he looked like a kid whose parents had given him a big box of candy. After some minutes, however, Hsu suddenly discovered that the computer had displayed 6...d×c4 on the screen. The rules allowed him to call the arbiter and correct the move, with a time adjustment for White. Kasparov was obviously quite upset to have the box of candy snatched away from him." (Friedel 2016)

6...d×c4 7.♘e5 ♗d7 8.♘a3 c×d4 9.♘a×c4 ♗c5 10.♕b3 0-0 11.♕×b7 ♘×e5 12.♘×e5 ♖b8 13.♕f3 ♗d6

This had all been played before; now comes a strong novelty by Kasparov. It should be noted that DEEP BLUE found the moves itself as it played this game from move 2 on without its traditional opening book, which was not uploaded correctly. It was using an "extended book" instead, which Murray Campbell had created based on grandmaster games. The basic concept was that a move that had been played by a strong grandmaster with good results would get a bias in its favor. But the computer still calculated itself and could also play new moves that gave better chances according to DEEP BLUE's own evaluation.

14.♘c6!? ♗×c6 15.♕×c6 e5 16.♖b1

16.b3?! weakens the dark squares too much.

16...♖b6?!

16...h6 prevents the coming inconveniences.

17.♕a4 ♕b8 18.♗g5

18...♗e7!

Trading structure for material with 18...♖×b2? 19.♖×b2 ♕×b2 20.♗×f6 g×f6 runs into 21.♕d7 ♕b6 22.♕g4+ ♔h8 23.♗e4 with a very powerful attack.

19.b4!

A very strong move which expands White's control of the queenside and which is difficult to answer, as Black must decide on which wing there should be concessions.

19...♗×b4

"This time DEEP BLUE cannot resist. Maybe this is because White's attack is not quite as direct and the computer cannot 'smell' the danger any more. Feng-Hsiung Hsu said this was a 'positional mistake caused in part by an evaluation weighting error that was not caught'." (Friedel 2016) But Black's position is quite difficult in any case, so this capture is objectively not a mistake.

20.♗×f6 g×f6 21.♕d7 ♕c8

DEEP BLUE gives the pawn back to divert White's queen from the kingside attack.

22.♛×a7

22...♖b8?

Black should force the exchange of queens with 22...♖a6 23.♛b7 ♛×b7 24.♗×b7 ♖b6 with better drawing chances than in the game. Hsu (2002a) explained: "Going into the 1996 match we definitely believed that Garry was the stronger player, and to increase our tactical chances, we gave DEEP BLUE a large penalty for trading the queens. The queen trade avoidance bias backfired in this game."

23.♛a4 ♗c3

Hsu (2002a) explained that DEEP BLUE massively overrated the importance of this bishop outpost: "Unfortunately the software code that assigned the values wrongly assigned unchallengeable bishops the same values as unchallengeable outposted knights." In reality, here it is the other way round: White's bishop has no unchallengeable outpost, but dominates the important light squares while Black's only hits air.

24.♖×b8 ♛×b8 25.♗e4 ♛c7

26.♕a6?

This is quite slow. 26.♖b1 ♖b8 27.♖×b8+ ♕×b8 28.♕d7 targets Black's weaknesses quicker and the a-pawn is still on the board.

26...♔g7

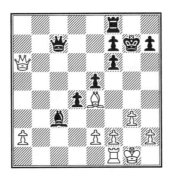

27.♕d3 ♖b8

28.♗×h7?!

28.♕f3!? is a serious alternative as it is now much more difficult for Black to force exchanges.

28...♖h2

White wants to keep as much attacking and winning potential on the board. But unfortunately he cannot avoid the exchange of rooks and the loss of the a-pawn:

29.♗e4

29.a4?! ♖d2 30.♕e4 ♕c4; 29.♖b1 ♖xa2 30.♔g2 ♖b2 and in both cases Black maintains good drawing chances.

29...♖xa2 30.h4 ♕c8 31.♕f3 ♖a1 32.♖xa1 ♗xa1 33.♕h5 ♕h8 34.♕g4+ ♔f8

"White has a dangerous passed pawn on the h-file, Black a weak pawn on f7 and an exposed king. Still the game could probably be held by a strong player, as Kasparov later admitted. However, this requires full understanding of the nature of the position and a strategy required to defend it. The computer lacks this and Kasparov is able to masterfully lure it to its destruction." (Friedel 2016)

35.♕c8+ ♔g7 36.♕g4+ ♔f8 37.♗d5 ♔e7 38.♗c6 ♔f8 39.♗d5 ♔e7 40.♕f3 ♗c3 41.♗c4 ♕c8?

It was better to have the king stay near the kingside with 41...♔f8, as in the game Black's king will become the target of attack from both sides.

42.♕d5 ♕e6

43.♕b5!

Kasparov must keep his queen to retain winning chances. His aim is to win the f7-pawn to weaken the shield of Black's king.

43...♕d7 44.♕c5+ ♕d6 45.♕a7+ ♕d7 46.♕a8 ♕c7 47.♕a3+ ♕d6 48.♕a2

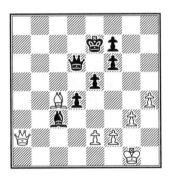

48...f5?

This advance in the end just weakens the f-pawn. After 48...e4!?, Black keeps practical drawing chances, e.g., 49.♕a7+ ♔d7 50.♕c5+ ♔d6 51.♕h5 d3 52.♕×f7+ ♔d8 53.e×d3 e×d3 54.♕g8+ ♔c7 55.♕h7+ ♔d7. But DEEP BLUE probably could not find the line as the c3-outpost is destroyed.

49.♗×f7 e4 50.♗h5! ♕f6

After 50...d3 51.e×d3 e×d3 52.♕f7+ ♔d8 53.♕×f5 d2, White stops the pawn with 54.♗d1 and wins.

51.♕a3+ ♔d7 52.♕a7+ ♔d8 53.♕b8+ ♔d7 54.♗e8+ ♔e7 55.♗b5 ♗d2

Finally the bishop leaves its unchallengeable outpost, but it is too late.

56.♕c7+ ♔f8 57.♗c4 ♗c3 58.♔g2 ♗e1 59.♔f1 ♗c3 60.f4!

Kasparov wants to fix the f5-weakness.

60...e×f3 61.e×f3 ♗d2

61...f4 is met by 62.g4.

62.f4 ♔e8 63.♕c8+ ♔e7 64.♕c5+ ♔d8 65.♗d3 ♗e3 66.♕×f5 ♔c6

67.♕f8+ ♔c7 68.♕e7+ ♔c8 69.♗f5+ ♔b8 70.♕d8+ ♔b7

71.♕d7+!

After the exchange of queens, Kasparov has an easy technical win.

71...♕×d7 72.♗×d7 ♔c7

Or 72...d3 73.♗f5 d2 74.♗c2 ♔c6 75.♔e2 and White wins.

73.♗b5 ♔d6 1-0

Kasparov summed it up as follows: "I tested the computer subtly, giving it chances to act like a machine and trade short-term advantages for long-term weaknesses… Against a very strong human, the result might have been a draw. But I simply understood the essence of the endgame in a way the computer didn't." (Keene 2002)

He was also complimentary: "I congratulate the researchers at IBM for a fantastic achievement. They have succeeded in converting quantity into quality…In certain kind of positions, it sees so deeply that it plays like god." While there is something to this, in general overestimating your opponent is very dangerous.

Deep Blue – Kasparov, Garry (2795)
Sicilian Defense B22
Philadelphia match (3), 13.02.1996

1.e4 c5 2.c3 d5 3.e×d5 ♕×d5 4.d4 ♘f6 5.♘f3 ♗g4 6.♗e2 e6 7.0-0 ♘c6 8.♗e3 c×d4 9.c×d4 ♗b4 10.a3 ♗a5 11.♘c3 ♕d6

12.♘e5

Joel Benjamin is responsible for the opening preparation and has prepared a new challenge for Kasparov, but Garry deals with it easily:

12...♗×e2

12...♘×e5? 13.d×e5 ♛×d1 14.♗×d1 ♗×d1 15.e×f6 ♗b3 16.f×g7 ♖g8 17.♗d4 f5 18.♖fe1 plays into White's hand.

13.♛×e2 ♗×c3 14.b×c3 ♘×e5 15.♗f4 ♘f3+ 16.♔×f3 ♛d5 17.♛d3 ♖c8

Preventing c4 to fix White's weaknesses.

18.♖fc1

"In this line Joel Benjamin had intended 18.♗e5?, but after 18...♘d7 19.♗×g7? ♖g8 20.♛×h7 ♘f6 21.♛h6 ♘h5, Black is winning a piece! Benjamin: 'Thank heavens we didn't put 18.♗e5 into the book.'" (Friedel 2016)

18...♛c4 19.♛×c4 ♖×c4

Now DEEP BLUE finds an amazing concept to avoid playing passively with its structural weaknesses:

20.♖cb1! b6 21.♗b8!!

"The computer played the only moves that don't lose," Garry told us later (Friedel 2016). "I'd like to know how many humans would find this plan." Hsu (2002a) explains the moves as follows: "Some of the 'inhuman' moves were not the result of deep searches at all, but of DEEP BLUE evaluating Garry's rook getting close to being trapped."

21...♖a4 22.♖b4 ♖a5 23.♖c4!

"Any human would play 23.c4, almost instinctively, without thinking." (Kasparov quoted in Friedel 2016)

23...0-0?!

Black has no winning chances with his king so far away. After 23...♔e7 24.♗e5 ♖d8, Black is more harmoniously placed than in the game and can press for a long time.

24.♗d6 ♖a8 25.♖c6

White is so active that Black cannot profit from the better pawn structure.

25...b5 26.♔f1 ♖a4 27.♖b1 a6 28.♔e2 h5 29.♔d3 ♖d8 30.♗e7 ♖d7 31.♗×f6 g×f6 32.♖b3 ♔g7 33.♔e3 e5 34.g3 e×d4+ 35.c×d4

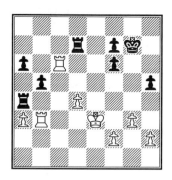

35...♖e7+

35...囯d×d4?! is met by 36.囯×a6.

36.♔f3 囯d7 37.囯d3 囯a×d4 38.囯×d4 囯×d4 39.囯×a6

and in view of 39...b4 40.♔e3 囯c4 41.a4 b3 42.囯b6 囯×a4 43.囯×b3 ♔g6, a draw was agreed. ½–½

Kasparov, Garry (2795) – Deep Blue
Slav Defense D46
Philadelphia match (4), 14.02.1996

1.♘f3 d5 2.d4 c6 3.c4 e6 4.♘bd2 ♘f6 5.e3 ♘bd7 6.♗d3 ♗d6 7.e4

Kasparov accepts the challenge and opens the position. As he has the initiative this fits his style well.

7...d×e4 8.♘×e4 ♘×e4 9.♗×e4 0-0 10.0-0 h6 11.♗c2 e5 12.囯e1 e×d4 13.♕×d4 ♗c5 14.♕c3 a5 15.a3 ♘f6

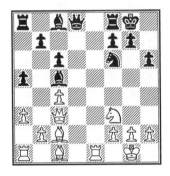

16.♗e3?!

Kasparov plays it safe and keeps a slight initiative. But the hammer-blow 16.♗×h6!! would have given him a very powerful attack. "Against a human, Kasparov confided, he would have seriously considered this sacrifice, but not against a machine running at… millions [of positions] per second. 'The slightest miscalculation and you are dead!'" (Friedel 2016) 16...g×h6 17.囯ad1 ♗d7 (17...♕b6? is refuted by 18.♕×f6 ♗×f2+ 19.♔h1 ♗×e1 20.♘g5 and wins (Friedel 2016); 17...♘d7 18.囯e4 h5 19.囯f4) 18.囯e2 囯e8 19.囯×e8+ ♘×e8 20.♘e5 and in all cases White is clearly better. After the match Kasparov analyzed this sacrifice together with Deep Blue and came to the conclusion that it is sound, but "…after seeing some of the attacking and defensive moves Deep Blue came up with, Garry was glad that he did not make the sacrifice" (Hsu 2002).

16...♗×e3 17.囯×e3 ♗g4 18.♘e5 囯e8 19.囯ae1 ♗e6 20.f4 ♕c8 21.h3 b5

22.f5?!

A risky and courageous decision by Kasparov. Objectively, 22.b3! is better, to fight for the important d5-squares. White keeps the initiative after, e.g., 22...a4 (22... b×c4 23.b×c4 a4 24.♗d1 c5 25.♗f3 ♖a6 26.g4 with an attack.) 23.b×a4 b×c4 24.♘×c4 ♕a6 (24...♘d5? runs into 25.♕d3 ♘×e3 26.♕h7+ ♔f8 27.♖×e3 and White wins.) 25.♘d6 ♖ed8 26.♖×e6 f×e6 27.♖×e6 ♘d5 28.♕g3 ♕b6+ 29.♔h2 ♕d4 30.♗b3, but it is not clear, if White can convert his advantage.

22...♗×c4!

"Before it could make this move the computer crashed. For about 20 minutes the team worked at the terminal in the playing hall, while a distraught Kasparov, torn out of his calculations, complained bitterly about the disturbance. To compound his displeasure, DEEP BLUE, in the end, plays a very good move. This looked a bit suspicious, but later we discovered that FRITZ finds the same move in about 30 minutes. DEEP BLUE, being about 500 times faster, must find it in about four seconds." (Friedel 2016) After 22...♗×f5?! White can and probably should choose the safe 23.♗×f5 (as the risky 23.♘×f7?!, which was planned by Kasparov, is met by 23...♖×e3 24.♘×h6+ g×h6 25.♖×e3 ♘h5 26.♗b3 a4 27.♗a2 ♗e6 28.♗b1 ♘g7) 23...♕×f5 24.♘×c6 ♕c5 25.c×b5 ♕b6 26.♕d4 ♕×b5 27.♘e7+ with a slight initiative.

23.♘×c4 b×c4 24.♖×e8+ ♘×e8

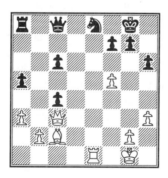

White's position looks better than it actually is. Black will be able to establish its knight on d5 and get counterplay via the b-file and against White's king on the dark squares.

25.♖e4

25.♕×c4 was better according to Kasparov, but after 25...♘f6, White has no real advantage.

25...♘f6 26.♖×c4 ♘d5 27.♕e5 ♕d7 28.♖g4 f6 29.♕d4 ♔h7 30.♖e4 ♖d8 31.♔h1 ♕c7 32.♕f2 ♕b8 33.♗a4 c5 34.♗c6

Kasparov had planned 34.♕e1? ♕×b2 35.♗e8 from afar, but now realized that 35...♘f4! gives Black the upper hand.

34...c4 35.♖×c4

35.♖d4 ♕b6 36.♗×d5 ♖×d5 37.♖d2 is playable as well.

35...♘b4!? 36.♗f3

36.a×b4? runs into the obvious 36...♖d1+ 37.♔g1 ♖×g1+ 38.♔×g1 a×b4.

36...♘d3

37.♕h4?

An error in time trouble, as the queen will be missed in the defense. 37.♕e2! ♘×b2 38.♖c1 ♘d3 39.♖d1 ♕b3 40.♕e3 ♘f2+ 41.♕×f2 ♖×d1+ 42.♗×d1 ♕×d1+ 43.♔h2 equalizes.

37...♕×b2 38.♕g3!

38...♛×a3?

This slows down Black's attack. DEEP BLUE should keep the initiative with 38...
♞e5 39.♖c7 ♛b1+ (the rook endgame after 39...♛a1+? 40.♚h2 ♞×f3+ 41.♛×f3
♛e5+ 42.♛g3 ♛×g3+ 43.♚×g3 ♖d3+ 44.♚g4 is only drawn.) 40.♚h2 ♞×f3+
41.♛×f3 ♖d1 and in this major piece endgame, Kasparov's task would have been
extremely unpleasant. Another disadvantage of DEEP BLUE's capture on a3 is that
only pawns on the kingside remain. Hsu (2002a) explains this as follows: "One key
endgame feature for this game was, that if all the pawns are on the same half of the
chessboard, the game is more likely to be drawn. The chess chip could recognize
this important endgame feature, but the software did not make use of this ability."

39.♖c7 ♛f8 40.♖a7 ♞e5 41.♖×a5 ♛f7

Kasparov's draw offer was turned down, so he decides to simplify matters by
giving the exchange.

**42.♖×e5!? f×e5 43.♛×e5 ♖e8 44.♛f4 ♛f6 45.♗h5 ♖f8 46.♗g6+ ♚h8
47.♛c7 ♛d4 48.♚h2 ♖a8 49.♗h5 ♛f6 50.♗g6 ♖g8 ½-½**

Kasparov (Friedel 2016): "I'm tired from these games, and if I was playing against
a human, he would be exhausted too. But I'm playing against something that knows
no such feelings and is always playing with the same strength."

The pressure was building for Kasparov. He was expected to win… and time was
running out. As game one showed, anything could happen.

Deep Blue – Kasparov, Garry (2795)

Four Knights Game C47
Philadelphia match (5), 16.02.1996

1.e4 e5 2.♘f3 ♘f6 3.♘c3 ♘c6 4.d4 e×d4 5.♘×d4 ♗b4 6.♘×c6 b×c6 7.♗d3 d5 8.e×d5 c×d5 9.0-0 0-0 10.♗g5 c6 11.♕f3 ♗e7 12.♖ae1 ♖e8 13.♘e2

13.h3 is the main line.

13...h6 14.♗f4 ♗d6 15.♘d4 ♗g4 16.♕g3

16.♘×c6?? runs into 16...♕b6.

16...♗×f4 17.♕×f4 ♕b6

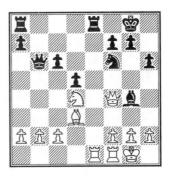

18.c4?!

Now Deep Blue opens the position for Black. Maybe the computer overestimates the weakness or importance of the resulting isolated pawn. After 18.b3, the position is completely equal.

18...♗d7 19.c×d5

19.b3 is met by 19...♕a5 and Black has no problems due to his activity.

19...c×d5 20.♖×e8+ ♖×e8 21.♕d2 ♘e4 22.♗×e4 d×e4 23.b3 ♖d8

"The position is slightly better for Black, but Kasparov offered a draw. Deep Blue also realized this and showed -0.10 to -0.15 for itself, but advisor Joel Benjamin decided to decline the offer. 'The draw offer came much too early,' said project manager C.J. Tan. 'We are scientists and wanted to continue the experiment.' But quite apart from that, with queens on the board and a bit of tactics left Benjamin wanted to see if Kasparov would go astray." (Friedel 2016) Hsu (2002a) adds: "Meanwhile DEEP BLUE had made up its mind on which move it wanted to play, unaware of the draw offer. Mike Valvo, the arbiter, made a snap ruling insisting that we either had to accept the draw offer immediately or make DEEP BLUE's intended move." The offer was declined.

24.♕c3 f5 25.♖d1?

White will run into a lot of trouble as a result of the upcoming pin on the d-file. After 25.g3 ♖c8 26.♕e3, "the game would end in four or five moves in a draw." (Kasparov quoted in Friedel 2016)

25...♗e6 26.♕e3? ♗f7

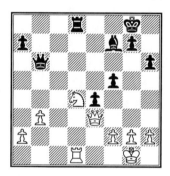

27.♕c3?

Allows the f-pawn to advance for free. But good advice is hard to give as White does not play 27.g3 lightly. But here it is probably necessary sooner or later.

27...f4 28.♖d2 ♕f6!

The direct 28...♖d5?? runs into the deadly double attack 29.♘f5 ♖xf5 30.♕c8+ and White wins.

29.g3?

29.♘e2 ♖xd2 30.♕xd2 ♕a1+ 31.♘c1 was forced, to reduce the pressure by exchanging rooks. But after 31...f3, Black should win in the long run because of White's passive, dominated knight. But to break down White's defenses would certainly not be easy.

29...♖d5!

Kasparov introduces the possibility that his rook might swing over to the kingside quickly.

30.a3 ♔h7 31.♔g2?! ♕e5

White is defenseless against Black's well-centralized forces.

32.f3

32.g×f4 ♕×f4 33.♕e3 is met by 33...♖g5+ 34.♔h1 ♕g4 35.♕g3 ♕c8 and Black wins.

32...e3

Kasparov wins a piece and converts easily.

33.♖d3 e2 34.g×f4 e1♕ 35.f×e5 ♕×c3 36.♖×c3 ♖×d4 37.b4 ♗c4 38.♔f2 g5 39.♖e3 ♖d2+ 40.♔e1 ♖d3 41.♔f2 ♔g6 42.♖×d3 ♗×d3 43.♔e3 ♗c2 44.♔d4 ♔f5 45.♔d5 h5 0-1

On Benjamin's recommendation to decline the draw offer after move 23 (Benjamin 2007), "Kasparov would later describe this as my main contribution to the first match. I didn't find it amusing."

Kasparov, Garry (2795) – DEEP BLUE
Slav Defense D30
Philadelphia match (6), 17.02.1996

1.♘f3 d5 2.d4 c6 3.c4 e6 4.♘bd2 ♘f6 5.e3 c5

This loss of a tempo is one of the main lines. DEEP BLUE wants to open up the game. But the price is quite high as Kasparov gets a comfortable position.

6.b3 ♘c6 7.♗b2 c×d4 8.e×d4 ♗e7 9.♖c1 0-0 10.♗d3

10...♗d7?

Hsu (2002a) explains this error as follows: "DEEP BLUE was supposed to develop its light-square bishop to b7, but after being taken out of the opening book by Garry's transposition, it moved the bishop to the d7-square instead. DEEP BLUE liked to put its bishops on open diagonals...and it did not understand that sometimes it is acceptable to put the bishop on a closed diagonal...The modifications, implemented as a result of this game...to improve the handling of the bishops and, similarly, the rooks turned out to be critical in the 1997 rematch." 10...dxc4 11.bxc4 b6, as in Shkliar-Beshukov, Krasnodar 2002, is called for.

11.0-0

11...♘h5?

An odd move. The knight will now be floating around aimlessly.

12.♖e1 ♘f4 13.♗b1 ♗d6 14.g3 ♘g6 15.♘e5 ♖c8 16.♘×d7 ♕×d7 17.♘f3 ♗b4 18.♖e3 ♖fd8 19.h4?!

19.c5 ♗a5 20.a3 ♗c7 21.b4 is a more precise.

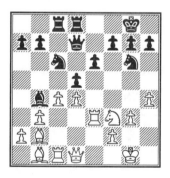

Kasparov playing Game 6, as seen from the television monitor.
(Monroe Newborn)

19...♘ge7?

Now Kasparov's pawns will roll all over Black. 19...d×c4 20.b×c4 ♗e7 is objectively also better for White because of his pair of bishops but much easier to play for the machine as the position is more open.

20.a3 ♗a5 21.b4

A good choice under the circumstances. Kasparov had considered the tempting piece sacrifice 21.♗×h7+! ♔×h7 22.♘g5+, but was not sure and wanted to take no risks. Kasparov (2017) took a pragmatic approach:

> …I considered a tempting piece sacrifice against its king that looked winning. But could I be sure? Ninety percent sure, yes. Ninety-five percent, maybe. But against DEEP BLUE, and needing only a draw to win the match, I would have to be 100 percent sure. Analysis later showed that it was indeed a winning blow, although there is no way to guarantee that I would have played it perfectly. And there was no reason for me to take any risks, since I was crushing it already.

21...♗c7 22.c5 ♖e8 23.♕d3 g6 24.♖e2 ♘f5 25.♗c3 h5 26.b5

"Keene calls this 'Kasparov's strategy of strangulation' and points out that 26.b5 doesn't just attack the knight but establishes 'a giant, crawling mass of white pawns, rather resembling a colossal army of soldier ants on the move.'" (Friedel 2016)

26...♘ce7 27.♗d2 ♔g7 28.a4

28...♖a8?

28...a6 is a better version of Deep Blue's concept as it is not good to grab the pawn with 29.b×a6? b×a6 30.♕×a6 ♖a8 31.♕b5 ♘c6 and Black has finally found good roles for all his pieces. A pawn is a very cheap price for this. But after 29.♕b3, White is clearly for choice.

29.a5 a6?

This amounts to strategic capitulation. But good advice is really hard to give.

30.b6 ♗b8?!

A really miserable retreat, which shuts the bishop and the a8-rook out of the game. From a practical point of view, 30...♗d8 was preferable as Kasparov's job is more difficult then. But White is winning here as well, e.g., 31.♘e5 ♕c8 32.c6! ♘×c6 (32...b×c6 33.♗f4 f6 34.♘×c6 ♘×c6 35.♖ec2 ♕b7 36.♖×c6) 33.♘×c6 b×c6 34.♕c3 ♘e7 35.♗f4 ♕b7 36.♗e5+ ♔g8 37.♗c2 ♖c8 38.♗a4 ♖f8 39.♖ec2 and wins in both cases.

31.♗c2 ♘c6 32.♗a4 ♖e7 33.♗c3

33...♘e5?

Black is lost in the long run in any case. But exchanging this way eases White's task as he gets the d4-square.

34.d×e5 ♕×a4 35.♘d4!

A typical technique: exchanging the opponent's active pieces underscores the importance of the bad – perhaps even incarcerated – pieces.

35...♘×d4 36.♕×d4 ♕d7 37.♗d2 ♖e8 38.♗g5 ♖c8 39.♗f6+ ♔h7

40.c6!

Kasparov opens the floodgates. In principle he can choose which wing to open, but here opening the queenside is clearly called for and much easier. 40.g4?! wins as well, but would be bad technique especially against a machine.

40...b×c6

40...♖×c6 41.♖ec2 ♖×c2 42.♖×c2 ♕e8 43.♕b4 ♔h6 44.♕f4+ ♔h7 45.♕c1, and White will invade with decisive effect.

41.♕c5 ♔h6 42.♖b2 ♕b7

43.♖b4! 1-0

Good prophylaxis, compelling the DEEP BLUE team to resign. After the direct 43.♕e7? ♕×e7 44.♗×e7 ♗×e5, the b2-rook is hanging. Now after 43...♔h7, 44.♕e7 wins simply. The programmer of the strong chess program RYBKA, Vasik Rajlich (2010), summed it up as follows: "Kasparov's wins in this match were convincing and prototypical. After the loss in Game 1, Kasparov avoided great complications and played more in the style of his former rival Anatoly Karpov, often making DEEP BLUE look foolish in the process."

Kasparov endured huge emotional swings during this match, but in the end persevered. That is the hallmark of a great champion!

With the advantage of hindsight six years later, Hsu (2002a) presents a nice summary of the match from the DEEP BLUE team's perspective:

Today, whenever I look at…game six, especially with the help of the newer version of DEEP BLUE, I cannot help but wonder, "How the hell did the old DEEP BLUE manage to tie the match after four games?" The old DEEP BLUE made many positional mistakes in the game, and Garry, sometimes cajoling, sometimes pressuring, had everything to do with causing the mistakes. …

In the first four games, DEEP BLUE was treading on familiar ground and was able to avoid making overt positional mistakes, most of the time. In the last two games, Garry forced DEEP BLUE into unknown territory, probed for its weaknesses, exploited them, and played DEEP BLUE as if he were a virtuoso conductor.

Reflecting back on the match many years later, Kasparov (2017) was quite critical of the quality of his play. He summarized his performance as follows: "I did not play very well In Philadelphia, even if I did play well enough."

Charles Krauthammer (1996)
Time Magazine **writer**

Now, [DEEP BLUE] cannot see everything forever – just everything within its horizon, which for DEEP BLUE means everything that can happen within the next 10 or 15 moves or so. The very best human player could still beat it…because he can intuit – God knows how – what the general shape of things will be 20 moves from now.

But it is only a matter of time before, having acquired yet more sheer computing power, BLUE will see farther than Garry can feel. And then it's curtains. Then he gets shut out, 6-0. Then we don't even bother to play the brutes again. The world championship will consist of one box playing another. Men stopped foot racing against automobiles long ago.

BLUE's omniscience will make it omnipotent. It can play – fight – with the abandon of an immortal. Wilhelm Steinitz, a world chess champion who was even more eccentric than most, once claimed to have played chess with God, given him an extra pawn and won. Fine. But how would he have done against BLUE?

7
2750 (1996-1997)

There was no doubt that IBM wanted to see a rematch. Internal IBM assessment indicated that the match generated enormous and favorable publicity for the company, especially for the company's stock price. With that much value at stake, the decision to invest in the DEEP BLUE team way back in 1989 was beginning to look like a bargain!

The DEEP BLUE team did a postmortem analysis of the match and came to several conclusions:

- Search: No major issues arose. The searching capabilities appeared sufficient. The program was tactically strong.

- Knowledge: Kasparov clearly had a greater positional understanding of the game, and that was where major improvements were possible for the program. This meant 1) identifying more chess knowledge that would add value to the program, 2) putting that knowledge on the chip, and, most importantly, 3) tuning the program so that the knowledge was applied in the right circumstances with the appropriate weighting.

- Openings: One can never do too much opening preparation! However, there were special cases that were not properly planned. For example, the team should have had their opening book prepared for a line to play as Black in their "must win" game 6.

- Match strategy. Consider possible match scenarios that might arise and decide in advance how they will be handled. For example, the team did not know how to respond to Kasparov's draw request in game 5.

The chess knowledge aspects were the most challenging. Sometimes DEEP BLUE would play a "bad" move and the team would dive into the program's innards trying to figure out what when wrong. But sometimes things were not as they seemed (Campbell 2005):

> There were examples of that in the games against Kasparov -- moves that seemed counterintuitive or just wrong, just plain wrong. But there was a logic to them, and you could reconstruct that logic. I saw plenty of examples of that as we were programming and preparing DEEP BLUE to play the match against Kasparov – the two matches. Many cases where we were very upset about a move that it played, and we would assume it was a bug and conduct a deep investigation and find out it had to play that move – there was no choice. Any other move would have lost, or significantly worsened its position. But intuition sometimes let us down into thinking we knew what was going on, when we didn't always.

Further, even identifying possible errors was hard. The very nature of how a chess program works had an insidious property of hiding all but the most flagrant of errors (Campbell 2005):

…these chess programs are surprisingly robust. You can discover the most horrendous errors you can imagine in the code, but because of this brute force capability and searching, it seems to always do something reasonable. It may not be ideal, it may not be what you intended, but it seems to always do something reasonable, because it's optimizing – choosing a continuation that optimizes the material balance and some of the factors you know about. There may be this one evaluation function term that's pulling you in the wrong direction but it still ends up playing reasonable chess.

Hsu (2002a) describes an "Aha!" moment that would have important implications for creating the next version of Deep Blue. A typical chess program would assign a fixed bonus, say 0.1 of a pawn, to having a rook on an open file. Since the search was always trying to maximize the score, positions with one or both rooks on open file(s) would be preferred (0.1 or 0.2 extra evaluation score) over those where the rooks were behind pawns (possibly no bonus). To tune the evaluation function, the team had a program that could identify when Deep Blue evaluations seemed to differ significantly from those of human grandmasters:

> These experiments on evaluation function tuning uncovered some unexpected results. In particular, the weights assigned to "rooks on open files" by human grandmasters, appeared to be much lower than the ones traditionally used by chess programs. I knew about this before the Philadelphia match, but I thought the result an artifact of some software bugs that I introduced somewhere. Closer examination after the match indicated that the result was real. It was not that human grandmasters attached lower weights to "rooks on open files," but that they were far more discriminating about when "rooks on open files" were important. In other words, there were far more contexts used by human grandmasters, either consciously or unconsciously, than by typical chess programs. After this discovery, I went through the entire set of hardware evaluation features, and located all the features that had low evaluation weights according to the tuning program. All these features might be in need of improvement.

Deep Blue was about to graduate from novice to more advanced in terms of its chess understanding. Rooks on open files are one of the rules used by novice players to help place pieces on good squares. Most chess programs do something similar. The important insight for the Deep Blue team was that this would not be good enough to beat Kasparov. Simplistic rules were insufficient to cover the depth and breath of knowledge that grandmasters used in their analysis. It would be critical to add greater sophistication to Deep Blue's "understanding" of chess. However, in no way would they be able to replicate the knowledge of a Kasparov. The question was whether better knowledge combined with incredible search depth would be sufficient to defeat the very best of the best chess grandmasters.

Evaluation Function Tuning

Evaluation functions consist of two parts. First, there are the features that get evaluated. They typically correspond to some recognizable chess property (doubled pawns, open file, king safety, etc.). Second, there is the importance, or *weight*, associated with each feature. The former is a matter of deciding on what chess knowledge is important for a program to recognize; the second is a mathematics optimization problem.

What weight should be associated with a feature? Are isolated doubled pawns more important than a rook on an open file? Is a safe king more important than a pawn? How do you decide? And, more importantly, can the computer make that decision automatically?

Many techniques to have the computer refine its evaluation function weights have been proposed in the literature. The DEEP BLUE team used an approach of tuning the weights to better predict the moves of strong grandmasters. Given a database of representative positions from grandmaster games, the goal was to have DEEP BLUE maximize the number of times that its search was able to select the same move as played by the grandmaster. Assume there are 1,000 positions in the database test set and that DEEP BLUE correctly predicts 600 of the grandmaster moves. The software can then analyze the 400 "errors" and make a small modification to one or more of the evaluation function weights to push the program into getting more correct matches. Then the test is run again, in the expectation of seeing improved performance. Unfortunately, it is not that simple. The evaluation function change may result in some of the 400 now being "correct," but it may also lead to having some of the 600 becoming incorrect.

Whereas in the past, such tuning would have been done by hand, the above process can be left to run for days, even weeks, on multiple computers. When the computations are completed, the set of weights achieving the highest score could be used as a new, "improved" evaluation function.

There are many problems with this approach, not the least of which is the blind nature of deciding which feature weights to change and by how much. More sophisticated techniques were soon to come.

If the DEEP BLUE team was going to make a major improvement in the quality of their evaluation function, then the program needed more chess features, and just as important, more context for those features. To Hsu, that meant building yet another version of the chess chip. The DEEP BLUE machine that would play Kasparov for the third time would have 8,000 features (or patterns) built into the silicon chip that was being designed.

Murray Campbell (2005) describes the hard work and frustration that he and Joel Benjamin experienced trying to get the evaluation function just right:

So given these 8,000 patterns that can be recognized, you have to decide first of all [in] what context are they [relevant], and in each of those contexts how important are they, what value they should be given. As an initial pass we just, off the top of our head, came up with some numbers based on our experience from DEEP THOUGHT and assign[ed] numbers. Some of the…patterns we weren't quite sure how to use initially and certainly in [1996] we didn't assign any values to them at all. Over time we started using them more and more. So we gave them initial values and tried to determine which contexts were appropriate and assign the values appropriate to the context, and let it play and observe its play and find out how it does against grandmasters, how it does against other programs, and find weaknesses, re-tune the values.

We also had a large test set of positions that we would rerun every so often to make sure that nothing was broken, that it was still solving the positions that it should solve and maybe it's got a few new ones that it hasn't been able to solve in the past; maybe not. These were a combination of tactical and positional types of issues because whether or not you find the right move is a complex combination of the search and the evaluation. So evolving those values and contexts we actually had a simpler problem in some sense than software programmers, who in principle can add new patterns any time they want. However, of course, each time you add a new pattern it slows down the system a little bit which tends to weaken its tactical ability and there's this delicate balance between evaluation and search that you're always playing. We don't have that problem. The evaluation is executed in the fixed amount of time and whatever patterns we have are evaluated in that amount of time or detected in that amount of time. If we needed to add more patterns, like we did between [1996] and [1997], we just put them in and it doesn't take any longer, because it's all executing in parallel on the chip.

So the big problem was, given some feedback from the grandmaster…Joel Benjamin, that [DEEP BLUE]'s playing a stupid move in this position, figuring out what's the cause of the stupid move. Sometimes it isn't a stupid move and it's his mistake. Sometimes it's the fault of the search, sometimes it's the fault of the evaluation, and we had to [diagnose the problem]. Literally everyday [Joel] would come in and start playing games, send us notes about moves that he thought were suspicious. And this wasn't [just] moves that [DEEP BLUE] played, but moves that it was considering. It's always printing out, as it's playing, what it expects to be the normal continuation. And if you see a weird move in that – it may just appear for an instant, for one iteration, and it's gone – it's off on another track. But it's a sign that there's something wrong and you have to zero in on those and track them down. A very slow, very painful process [that] took the vast majority of my time.

Murray and Joel had their work cut out for them.

DEEP BLUE doing some sightseeing on the way to the Kasparov match.
(IBM)

As the chess professional on the team, Benjamin (2007) was able to observe the computer scientists and provide a unique perspective on their abilities.

> Though modest about his abilities, Murray [Campbell] was an accomplished chessplayer, appearing in two Canadian Junior Championships and winning the Alberta Championship. He phased out tournament chess after high school but peaked at a level around USCF master.

> Murray quit playing largely because his nervous system couldn't take it. He would be somewhat less worried about his computer program crashing or spitting out bad moves. As far and away the best chessplayer on the team, Murray took charge of "hard" chess aspects of the program like the evaluation function and opening book. His chess knowledge made watching DEEP BLUE and its predecessors play all the more difficult, as he knew all the mistakes a chessplayer could make!

> Murray's anxiety starkly contrasted with the supreme confidence of Hsu, the father of DEEP BLUE. To Hsu, anything is possible. In [a] 1992 panel discussion, he boasted DEEP BLUE would be ready for Kasparov in a year or two. I thought he trivialized the process of playing chess at the grandmaster level. He had the kind of intellectual arrogance that chess players often find insulting in many programmers.

> After getting to know Hsu…I realized he means no disrespect towards chess players. He just has tremendous faith in his vision… When I asked him why he began the chess project, he said, "because I saw a way to do it."…

> [Hsu]'s confidence often produced a relaxed attitude that tried the patience of his colleagues. … But when crunch time approached, or an idea exploded in his brain, [Hsu] could produce a month's worth of work in a brief flurry. …

> … Joe Hoane joined the chess project at IBM in 1990. By then he had accumulated good experience in parallel processing, and Murray and [Hsu] liked his understanding of search, which became his main focus.

> If [Hsu] is guided by inspiration, Joe [Hoane] thrives on perspiration. He is a master of articulation, the process of taking a problem in the computer's behavior and formulating a solution. He might not solve the problem on the first try, but he would start the ball rolling. …

> The core of the team had clearly defined responsibilities…but they shared insights with one another. The ultimate success in the Kasparov war effort would hinge on how well they could work together, and how well they could incorporate the observations of a computer layman [Benjamin] in their midst. It took a while to get the process down pat.

The rematch with Kasparov took place in May 1997 in New York City. The prize fund was $1.1 million, with $700,000 going to the winner. The match format remained the same as the previous year – six games were to be played.

Kasparov seemed to be in fine form prior to the match. He had a superb result at the annual Linares tournament, where he scored 8.5/11 against the world's elite grandmasters, including wins against the number 2 through 6 finishers in the event. Since playing DEEP BLUE in 1996, Kasparov's results had been steadily improving.

And what of DEEP BLUE? One of this book's authors wrote that (Schaeffer 1997):

> While much is known about Kasparov's activities during the past year, the same
> cannot be said for DEEP BLUE. After the Philadelphia loss, the DEEP BLUE team
> retreated to their laboratory just north of New York City and did extensive secret
> preparations. (Although it must be said that DEEP BLUE JUNIOR, a small version of its
> big brother, toured the country and played many exhibition games.) ...
>
> Prior to the match, only two things were known about the new DEEP BLUE
> (affectionately called DEEPER BLUE): their chess-playing...chip had been re-fabricated,
> presumably to make it faster and add extra evaluation function capabilities, and
> Grandmaster Joel Benjamin was hired to work full-time...on testing and developing
> the chess knowledge. The new hardware consisted of...512 chess chips. IBM said that
> the new configuration was twice as fast as the previous year, evaluating roughly 200
> million positions per second.

1997 Kasparov – DEEP BLUE Match Predictions[8]

International Master David Levy: I predict [Kasparov] will win by at least 4.5-1.5.
Kasparov will find it easier to put into practice what he learned last time than the
DEEP BLUE team will.

Grandmaster Yasser Seirawan: I'd put my money on Kasparov. Kasparov will win,
and win quicker and easier than he did last time.

DEEP BLUE project manager C.J. Tan: I truly think we have a system which is far
superior to what we had last year. ... We will win this match overwhelmingly.

World Champion Garry Kasparov: I'm going to beat it absolutely. We will beat
machines for some time to come.

Shaking hands before game 1: Kasparov (left) and Hsu.
(Monroe Newborn)

In the following games, comments are used from Feng-hsiung Hsu (2002a), Grandmaster John Nunn (2017), and Joel Benjamin (2007). Benjamin (2014) describes the opening preparation for the match:

> We spent a lot of time preparing to play against the Najdorf, which of course was his signature opening (it was going to be 6.♗e2). We put time into the Dragon as well, because he had played it, though it didn't seem likely. Maybe we studied other openings but I don't remember. For most defenses to 1.e4 we just put in main lines, including, rather serendipitously, ♘×e6 in the Caro-Kann.

> With Black we had to put in a lot more work because he was quite capable of playing 1.e4 or 1.d4. We prepared to defend the Ruy Lopez, playing the variation with ♗c5 that Shirov was always playing back then. We were going for a Traxler (Wilkes-Barre) against the Giuoco Piano if we could get it. Against 1.d4 our main opening was the Grünfeld. I believe we were going to answer 1.c4 with 1...e5 and follow up with ♘f6 and d7-d5.

> I never dreamed in a million years that he would play none of these openings. His awesome opening knowledge was the biggest advantage he had. Against flank openings we had bare bones prep. We gave it the system it used in the match, d5, c6, ♘f6, ♗g4, etc. and left it as that since there weren't really any variations to work on.

Kasparov, Garry (2785) – Deep Blue
Reti Opening A07
New York match (1), 03.05.1997

1.♘f3 d5 2.g3 ♗g4 3.b3 ♘d7 4.♗b2 e6 5.♗g2 ♘gf6 6.0-0 c6 7.d3 ♗d6 8.♘bd2 0-0 9.h3 ♗h5

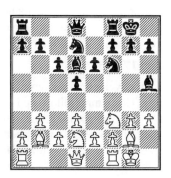

10.e3

"A very unusual move, indeed I can find no examples of it from practical play. The normal moves here are 10.e4 and 10.♕e1. Of the two, I would judge 10.e4 to be the more flexible. In this way White can reserve the option of either ♕e1 or ♕e2, depending on Black's reply. The merits of 10.e3 are rather hard to find; Kasparov soon adopts the ♕e1 and e4 plan, but having lost a tempo in the process. Perhaps his idea was simply to take DB out of its opening book." (Nunn)

10...h6?

Kasparov's trick directly pays dividends. This move not only does not help but it creates fresh problems for the light-square bishop.

11.♕e1 ♕a5?

This misplaces the queen. The plan to exchange the bishops with ♗a3 is easily stopped; the move not only has no point, but Black even has problems with the unprotected queen in several lines.

12.a3 ♗c7?!

Another odd move, but it is already not easy. One sample line in which Black has problems as a result of the unprotected queen is 12...♗g6 13.e4 e5 14.exd5 cxd5 15.♘e4 ♕xe1 16.♘xf6+ gxf6 17.♖xe1 ♘b6 18.f4 and White has a dangerous initiative.

13.♘h4!

This threat to hunt the bishop with g4 provokes a serious weakening.

13...g5 14.♘hf3 e5

"All this looks absolutely horrible to the human eye. Having pushed both e- and g-pawns, the f5-square has become a serious weakness. If White could plant a knight there, then the game would be decided. However, DB isn't as stupid as that; there is no straightforward route by which a knight can reach the key square. Nevertheless, this long-term weakness remains a lasting burden for Black." (Nunn)

15.e4

Fixing the weakness on Black's kingside.

15...♖fe8 16.♘h2

Kasparov follows a slow but clear plan to regroup a knight to f5 with ♕c1, ♖e1, and ♘h2-f1-e3-f5. This schematic thinking is typical for humans. Here it works very well as Black has no clear targets or aims. So it is difficult for DEEP BLUE to find a plan.

16...♕b6 17.♕c1 (17.♘g4!?) **17...a5**

"At last DB hits upon a plan for developing counterplay, although in this particular position it is not very effective. The natural follow-up is ...a4 to induce b4, and then ...c5. However, ...c5 is hard to arrange because of the pressure on d5, and if Black exchanges first on e4, then the route ♘c4-e3-f5 is opened up for the knight on d2. We can see how, time and time again, Black's natural plans are frustrated because they would seriously expose the weakness on f5." (Nunn)

18.♖e1 ♗d6 19.♘df1 dxe4 20.dxe4 ♗c5 21.♘e3 ♖ad8 22.♘hf1 g4?

The computer weakens its kingside unnecessarily. Hsu explains it as follows: "The move was the result of a bug we had introduced just before the rematch. An automatic tuning run for the evaluation function pointed out to us that the weighting for one class of king safety terms should be increased...What we did not realize was that, in extreme cases, the new weights reached the maximum allowed values and become saturated. In other words, DEEP BLUE no longer distinguished between a very bad and an even worse position. Tossing away the g-pawn therefore meant nothing to DEEP BLUE as long as it eliminated Garry's h-pawn."

After 22...♗g6, Black's activity compensates for the kingside weaknesses and the position is about equal.

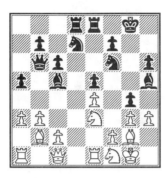

23.h×g4

The slightly surprising 23.♘d2!?, to protect e4 in case of 23...g×h3 24.♗×h3, was a very serious alternative, which also gives White an advantage and is probably even better than the game.

23...♘×g4 24.f3?!

This slight weakening of the kingside is not necessary. It will give DEEP BLUE counterplay, which seems to be sufficient. But it has to be admitted that the following bishop maneuver ♗c5-e7-g5 was difficult to foresee. 24.♘×g4 ♗×g4 25.♘e3 (Nunn) is slightly preferable to the game continuation as White has made no concession and has kept his kingside shield completely intact.

24...♘×e3 25.♘×e3

25...♗e7!

A strong regrouping of the bishop. From g5 it also shields the weaknesses on the kingside, while the pressure on the diagonal a7-g1 leads to nothing tangible.

26.♔h1 ♗g5 27.♖e2 a4 28.b4

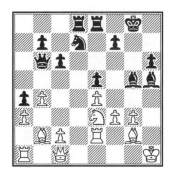

28...f5!!

"Correct. Black must make use of his temporary piece activity to make some inroads. Passive play would allow White to get back on track exploiting his strategic advantages." (Nunn)

29.e×f5!?

Kasparov chooses the principled approach, which involves an exchange sacrifice. The alternative 29.♕e1 is met by 29...f×e4 30.♘c4 ♕a6! (revealing one point of 27...a4) 31.♖×e4 ♘f6 32.♘×e5 ♖d2 33.f4 ♘e4 34.♕×e4 ♕e2 35.♕×e2 ♖×e2 36.f×g5 ♖×c2 37.♗d4 ♖d2 38.♗c3 ♖c2 with a draw by repetition.

29...e4 30.f4 ♗×e2

The greedy 30...♗×f4? is punished by 31.g×f4 ♗×e2 32.♕d2 (Nunn) and wins.

31.f×g5 ♘e5

31...h×g5?? runs into 32.♘c4.

32.g6!

Kasparov keeps his pawns united. 32.g×h6? is met by 32...♘f3 (Not 32...♖d6?? 33.♘c4! (Nunn)) 33.♗×f3 (33.♘g4 ♖d1+ 34.♕×d1 ♗×d1 35.♖×d1 ♖d8) 33...♗×f3+ 34.♔h2 ♖d6 35.♘g4 e3 and Black's counterattack prevails in both cases.

32...♗f3 33.♗c3!?

Kasparov protects d2, preparing to transfer the queen to the kingside. The direct 33.♕e1 is answered by 33...h5! (33...♕b5? 34.♗c3 transposes to 34.♕e1, which is better for White. After 33...♗×g2+? 34.♘×g2 ♘f3 35.♕c3 ♕d4 36.♘e3, Black cannot maintain the blockade.) 34.♗c3 ♕c7 with equality.

33...♕b5?

Hsu explains this mistake as follows: "Deep Blue was willing to trade the queens as its king was less safe. But Garry also had two connected passed pawns...that could become very valuable in the endgame phase...The ability to use this endgame feature existed in the chess hardware but was not in use...Afterwards Deep Blue played 33...h5 instead." 33...h5? is probably a misprint and Hsu means 34...h5! as 33...h5? runs into 34.f6 ♘×g6 35.♗×f3 e×f3 36.♘g4 h×g4 37.♕h6 ♔f7 38.♕h7+ ♔e6 39.f7 and White wins. 33...♖d7, to prepare the retreat ♕d8, equalizes, e.g., 34.♗×e5 (34.♕e1 ♕d8 35.♗×e5 ♖×e5 36.♕c3 ♖dd5) 34...♖×e5 35.♗×f3 e×f3

36.♘g4 ♕d4 37.♘f6+ ♔g7 38.♘h5+ ♔g8 39.♘f6+ with a draw by repetition.

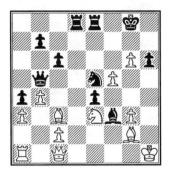

34.♕f1!?

Logical from a human point of view and in the game this move worked well. Maybe Kasparov has smelled that DEEP BLUE is going to exchange queens. Objectively a bit stronger was 34.♕e1! when White is for choice, but it is not clear, if he can win, e.g., 34...♘×g6 (34...♘g4? is refuted by an amazing queen sacrifice, 35.♗×f3 e×f3 36.♘×g4 ♖×e1+ 37.♖×e1.

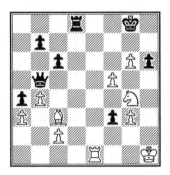

Now follows a line which is a trademark of the machines: 37...♔f8 38.♗g7+ ♔g8 39.♗f6 ♔f8 40.♗e7+ ♔g8 41.♔g1 f2+ 42.♘×f2 ♕×f5 43.♗×d8 and White has good winning chances.) 35.f×g6 ♕h5+ 36.♔g1 ♗×g2 37.♔×g2 (37.♘×g2?! is met by 37...e3 38.♕f1 ♕×g6 39.♕f3 e2 40.♔f2 e1♕+ 41.♖×e1 ♕×c2+ 42.♔g1 ♖×e1+ 43.♘×e1 ♕g6 when Black has good drawing chances.) 37...♕f3+ 38.♔h2 ♕h5+ 39.♔g1 ♕×g6 40.g4 ♖f8 41.♕h4 ♖d7 42.♖f1 ♖×f1+ 43.♔×f1 ♕g5 44.♕×g5+ h×g5 45.♔e2 and White is in control.

34...♕×f1+?

Bringing White's rook into play with gain of time. After the direct 34...h5, Black is not worse.

35.♖×f1 h5 36.♔g1!

A very strong move which shows that Kasparov's trumps are long term. 36.♗×c5? allows Black to blockade the pawns after 36...♖×e5 37.♗×f3 e×f3 38.♖×f3 ♔g7.

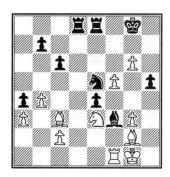

36...♔f8?

An odd move. Black must play 36...♘g4! which keeps the balance according to Keene (2002) and Hsu. This is a bit too optimistic as after 37.f6 ♖e6 38.♗h3 (38. ♘f5? is met by 38...♘xf6 39.♗h3 ♖de8 40.♗d4 ♗e2 with equality.) 38...♖xf6 39.♗xg4 ♖xg6 40.♗h3 ♖xg3+ 41.♔h2 ♖g5 42.♖f2

…as given by Keene, White is still for choice, as he is in full control and dominates the dark squares. But Black might be able to defend since White has only queenside pawns left. It is an open question and more analysis is needed.

37.♗h3! b5 38.♔f2 ♔g7?!

This makes White's job easier, but as g4 cannot be stopped in the long run, Kasparov is winning in any case. 38...♖d6 39.♖g1 ♔g8 (39...♘g4+ 40.♗xg4 hxg4 41.♖f1 ♖ed8 42.♔g1) 40.g4 hxg4 41.♗xg4 ♗xg4 42.♖xg4 and White wins in both instances because of the strength of his passed pawns as the blockade is broken.

39.g4! ♔h6 40.♖g1 hxg4

40...h4 41.g5+ ♔g7 42.♘g4 wins as well.

41.♗xg4 ♗xg4 42.♘xg4+ ♘xg4+ 43.♖xg4 ♖d5 44.f6

44...♖d1?

This random move was the result of a bug and loses easily. So Kasparov was wondering after the game why the machine had not played 44...♖f5+!. Together with Frederic Friedel, FRITZ, and his second, Grandmaster Yury Dokhoian, he found the line 45.♔e3! ♖f3+ 46.♔e2 ♖xc3 47.f7 ♖d8 48.g7 ♖xc2+ 49.♔e1 ♖c1+ 50.♔f2 ♖c2+ (50...e3+ 51.♔g2 e2 52.g8♕ ♖xg8 53.fxg8♕ ♖g1+ 54.♔f3 ♖xg4 55.♕h8+ ♔g6 56.♕e8+ ♔f5 57.♕f7+ ♔e5 58.♔xg4) 51.♔g3 ♖c3+ 52.♔h4 ♖c1 (52... ♖d1 53.g8♘+) 53.g8♕ ♖h1+ 54.♔g3 ♖g1+ 55.♔f4 ♖f1+ 56.♔e5 ♖d5+ 57.♔e6 ♖f6+ 58.♔xf6 and White wins in all cases. It is of course not that surprising that White's attack is quicker. But to work out the details is another matter. Naturally the Kasparov camp could not know that the computer's choice was the result of a bug and not of deep calculation.

45.g7 1-0

To many knowledgeable observers, this game went exactly as expected. Kasparov made strong moves and applied pressure, while the computer made numerous second-best moves and dug itself into a hole. That a computer bug reared itself in this game is unfortunate but it does not detract from Kasparov's strong performance.

This game must have increased Kasparov's confidence that he would live up to his pre-match prediction that he would "beat it absolutely."

DEEP BLUE – Kasparov, Garry (2785)
Ruy Lopez C93
New York match (2), 04.05.1997

1.e4 e5 2.♘f3 ♘c6 3.♗b5 a6 4.♗a4 ♘f6 5.0-0 ♗e7 6.♖e1 b5 7.♗b3 d6 8.c3 0-0 9.h3 h6

The Smyslov variation is slightly passive but solid and most often leads to closed positions. It is quite slow and allows White to reach the set-up with d4 followed by ♘b1-d2-f1-g3 without problems.

10.d4 ♖e8 11.♘bd2 ♗f8 12.♘f1 ♗d7

12...exd4?! 13.cxd4 ♘xe4? runs into the typical 14.♗d5.

13.♘g3 ♘a5 14.♗c2 c5 15.b3 ♘c6 16.d5 ♘e7 17.♗e3 ♘g6

17...♛c7 is the alternative.

18.♛d2

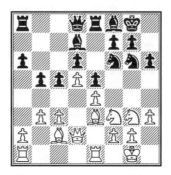

18...♘h7

Kasparov wants to exchange pieces to reduce the problem of White's space advantage. But the plan is quite slow and this gives White a pleasant initiative, which DEEP BLUE exploits strongly.

19.a4

DEEP BLUE thought for 10 minutes on this theoretical move. According to Grandmaster Miguel Illescas (2009), this was a trick so that Kasparov could never know if the machine was playing theory or on its own.

19...♘h4 20.♘×h4 ♛×h4 21.♛e2 ♛d8

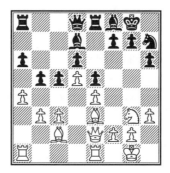

22.b4!

This move is natural from a human point of view – it is a well-known pattern for this kind of position. This is also the reason why the annotators did not highlight it when the game was played. But according to Joel Benjamin, for DEEP BLUE, this move was not clear at all. The computer played it as now the a1-rook is active on the a-file, which cannot be closed by Black anymore as a×b5 is always possible. DEEP BLUE had this information directly encoded in its hardware evaluation function as a result of the work on the activity of rooks done by Benjamin.

22...♛c7 23.♖ec1

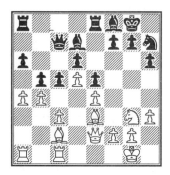

23...c4?

Kasparov closes the position, something that he certainly would not have done against a human. He hopes the DEEP BLUE will not know what to do in the resulting closed position. But this will prove to be a mistake as the DEEP BLUE team, and especially Joel Benjamin, has done a lot of work in this area. Also wrong is 23...♗e7? because of 24.c4 (Nunn) and the queenside opens up in White's favor. 23...cxb4?! also gives White the initiative after the typical 24.cxb4 ♕b7 25.axb5 axb5 26.♖a5; 23...♕b7 seems to be relatively best.

24.♖a3 ♖ec8 25.♖ca1 ♕d8

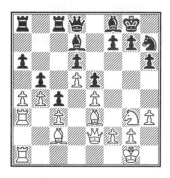

26.f4

"A stunning move played by a computer. Human beings know very well that opening a second front against a position under pressure can often cause it to collapse completely, but for a computer to find this idea is exceptional. None of the home computer programs I tested found this move at a tournament time-limit." (Nunn) With the advantage of 20 years of hindsight, Kasparov (2017) criticizes DEEP BLUE's move choice: "This move 26.f4 in game two is given a 'great move' exclamation point annotation in several books on the match, but analysis shows that it's far from the best move in the position. Instead, it could have retreated its bishop and tripled its pieces on the a-file, gaining a dominant position without giving me any counter-chances. Indeed, this superior plan is the first choice of any good engine today in just seconds." This echoes Anatoly Karpov's famous maneuver 26.axb5 axb5 27.♗a7 from his game against Grandmaster Wolfgang Unzicker, from the Nice Olympiad 1974. But Kasparov's 26.♗d1! is even better.

26...♘f6

Kasparov wants to keep the position as closed as possible. 26...exf4 27.♗xf4 is also very unpleasant for him, e.g., 27...g6 28.♕d2 ♘g5 29.♘e2 ♕e8 30.♘d4 with a strong initiative.

27.f×e5 d×e5

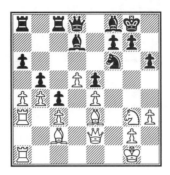

28.♕f1?!

DEEP BLUE wants to prevent the a5-lever. This is a very deep and difficult problem. From the human perspective, 28.♕f2! is more logical and would also have been a better choice from the psychological point of view, as this virtually forces Kasparov to play the lever ...a6-a5, opening the position, but the computer of course does not think this way. The following sample line shows that White is clearly for choice: 28...a5 29.a×b5 a×b4 30.c×b4 ♗×b4 31.♖a7 ♖×a7 32.♖×a7 ♗×b5 33.♘f5 ♗d7 34.♗b6 ♕×b6 35.♕×b6 ♗c5+ 36.♕×c5 ♖×c5 37.♖a8+ ♔h7 38.♘d6 ♔g6 39.♖a7 and Black will fall into zugzwang sooner or later. The preventive 28.♖3a2, to avoid the a5-lever, is also very strong.

28...♘e8

28...♗d6? sets a trap, if the machine is too materialistic and grabs the pawn with 29.a×b5? a×b5 30.♖×a8? (30.♗a7 *à la* Anatoly Karpov is better) 30...♖×a8 31.♖×a8 ♕×a8 32.♗×h6 ♕a2 33.♗b1 ♕b3 34.♗d2 ♗×b4 with counterplay. But White has 29.♘f5 ♗×f5 30.♕×f5 with a clear advantage (Nunn). The lever 28...a5!? on the other hand is much more interesting than it seems at first sight: 29.a×b5 a×b4 30.♖×a8 ♖×a8 31.♖×a8 ♕×a8 32.♕×c4 ♕a1+

33.♔f2 (after 33.♔h2, 33...♕e1 is more precise than 33...♕×c3 which is given by Keene) 33...♕b2 34.♕b3 b×c3 35.b6 ♗c8 36.♔f3

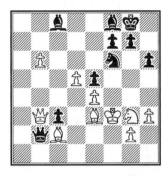

…and White is better, but Black still has drawing chances because of his activity, e.g., 36...♗a6 (36...♗b4?! allows dangerous options: 37.♕c4!? (37.♘f5 and 37.♘e2 are also interesting.) 37...♕×c2 38.♕×c8+ ♔h7 39.♕f5+ ♔g8 40.b7 ♗d6 41.♕c8+ ♔h7 42.b8♕ ♕d1+ 43.♔f2 ♗×b8 44.♕×b8 ♕c2+ 45.♔g1 ♘×e4 46.♕×e5 ♘×g3 47.♕×g3 ♕d1+ 48.♔f2 ♕×d5 49.♕f3 and only White can harbor hopes to win.) 37.♘e2 (37. ♘f5 ♕a1 38.♕b1 ♕b2 39.d6 ♘d7 40.♗c1) 37...♗b4 and Black is still alive.

29.♕f2 ♘d6

Now it is too late for 29...a5? in view of 30.♗b6 ♘c7 (The queen sacrifice 30... ♕×b6 31.♕×b6 a×b4 is interesting, but is simply insufficient.) 31.a×b5 a×b4 32.♖×a8 ♖×a8 33.♖×a8 ♕×a8 34.♗×c7 ♕a1+ 35.♔h2 b3 36.b6 ♕b2 37.b7 b×c2 38.b8♕ ♕×b8 39.♗×b8 c1♕ 40.♕a7 and White is clearly better.

30.♗b6 ♕e8 31.♖3a2 ♗e7 32.♗c5 ♗f8

Kasparov takes his last move back. This was criticized, but good advice is hard to give and, in fact, the move may not be that bad after all.

33.♘f5 ♗×f5 34.e×f5

34...f6?

This weakens the light squares in the long term, which is especially critical as Black has no light-square bishop. Another disadvantage of this move is more remote, but will be very relevant in the game. In many endings, White's king has a road on the light squares into Black's camp on the kingside. Black will almost always face a fight on two fronts that will overload the defense more often than not. 34...a5 35.f6 g6 was called for. White is also for choice of course, but as in the game Black is strategically lost as he has no counterplay, Kasparov should have opted for this line from an objective point of view. On the other hand it can be argued that he could hope that the machine might grab a queenside pawn. He could not expect that DEEP BLUE would apply a very effective "do not rush" concept.

35.♗×d6 ♗×d6

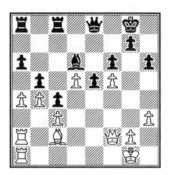

36.a×b5!

The greedy 36.♕b6?! ♕e7! 37.a×b5 ♖ab8 38.♕×a6? (38.♕e3 a×b5 39.♗e4 (King 2017) is necessary and clearly better for White) 38...e4 39.♕a7 ♕e5 40.♕e3 ♖e8 (DEEP BLUE) gives Black strong counterplay.

36...a×b5

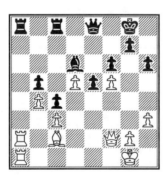

37.♗e4!!

A typical human preventive move, which must have been a big shock for Kasparov. There is no need to rush with 37.♕b6? ♖×a2 38.♖×a2 ♖a8.

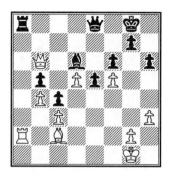

Matters are not as easy as Benjamin describes. White now has 39.♖a5! (Benjamin only mentions 39.♖×a8? ♕×a8 40.♕×d6 ♕a1+ 41.♔h2 ♕c1 with a draw, according to DEEP BLUE.) 39...♖×a5 40.b×a5.

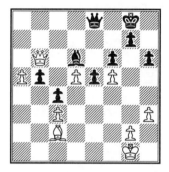

Now Black faces the difficult question whether or not to exchange queens. Pure opposite-color bishops have a large drawish tendency, but here it is not so easy as White has two passed pawns and the plan to invade with the king on the kingside. So 40...♕e7 might be better, but matters are not clear.

37...♖×a2?!

Kasparov is visibly shocked and concedes the a-file to White completely. The preventive 37...♕d8 was more tenacious.

38.♕×a2 ♕d7 39.♕a7 ♖c7

39...♕×a7+ does not help as Black is too passive, e.g., 40.♖×a7 ♖d8 41.♖a5 ♖b8 42.♖a6 ♖d8 43.♖b6 (Nunn).

40.♕b6 ♖b7 41.♖a8+ ♔f7 42.♕a6 ♕c7 43.♕c6 ♕b6+

44.♔f1?!

This is no mistake in itself, as White can trade queens the next move and then win the ending. But if White wants to realize the game plan, then 44.♔h1! is correct: 44...♖b8 45.♖a6 as now 45...♛e3?! is refuted by 46.♛×d6 ♖e8 47.♖a1 ♛×e4 48.♖a7+ ♔g8 49.♛d7 +− (Nunn).

44...♖b8

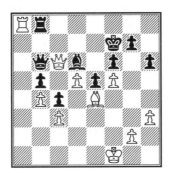

45.♖a6?

...and Kasparov believed that the machine had seen everything and resigned, just at the very moment when he had good chances to fight for a draw. **1-0**

DEEP BLUE should have killed all counterplay first with 45.♛×b6 ♖×b6 46.♔f2 when White's king will invade successfully, e.g., 46...♖b8 47.♖a7+ ♔g8 48.♖a6 ♗f8 49.♔g3 ♖d8 50.♔g4 ♖d6 51.♖a5 ♖b6 52.♔h5 ♔f7 53.♖a7+ ♗e7 54.♖c7 ♖d6 55.♖b7 and the b-pawn is lost. With additional rooks the drawish tendency of pure opposite-color bishop endings is much reduced and a slight initiative can even prove to be very unpleasant.

Surprisingly in this bleak position, Black has excellent chances to save the game! Instead of resigning, continue:

A triumphant DEEP BLUE team after game 2.
From left to right: Feng-hsiung Hsu, Murray Campbell, Joe Hoane, Jerry Brody, Chung-Jen Tan, Joel Benjamin.
(Monroe Newborn)

45...♕e3! 46.♕×d6 ♖e8

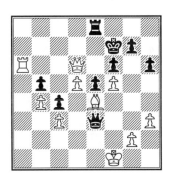

47.♕d7+!

47.h4? h5! closes the net, and White's king cannot escape from perpetual check (but not 47...♖e7? 48.♗f3 ♕c1+ 49.♔f2 ♕d2+ 50.♔g3 ♕e1+ 51.♔g4 h5+ 52.♔×h5 ♕g3 53.♕e6+ ♖×e6 54.d×e6+ ♔g8 55.♖a8+ ♔h7 56.♖h8+ ♔×h8 57.e7 ♔h7 58.e8♕+−). From a human point of view this pattern is relatively easy to see. But for a computer it is far from easy as it quite long before the draw is certain. According to Joel Benjamin, computer expert Ed Schroeder produces a variation in which is 35 ply deep before a repetition occurs: 48.♗f3 ♕c1+ 49.♔f2 ♕d2+ 50.♗e2 ♕f4+ 51.♔g1 ♕e3+ 52.♔h2 ♕f4+ 53.♔h3 ♕×f5+ 54.♔h2 ♕f4+ 55.♔g1 ♕e3+ 56.♔f1 ♕c1+ 57.♔f2 ♕f4+ 58.♔e1 ♕c1+ 59.♗d1 ♕×c3+ 60.♔f1 ♕c1 61.♔e2 ♕b2+ 62.♔f1 ♕c1 and finally the draw is absolutely clear.

47...罝e7 48.豐c6 豐×e4 49.d6

Black is at a major crossroads with two main alternatives.

49...豐×f5+

49...豐d3+ 50.曺g1 罝e8

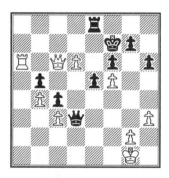

and now White's rook can stop the perpetual check with 51.罝a1!, making Black's life very difficult, e.g., 51...h5 (51...豐×c3? 52.罝d1 豐c2 53.罝f1 豐d2 54.罝f3 豐d4+ 55.曺h2 豐a7 56.罝g3 and wins; or 51...曺f8 52.豐c7 曺g8 53.曺h2 豐d2 54.d7 罝f8 55.罝f1 h5 56.豐c6 罝d8 57.豐b5 豐d3 58.罝f3 豐×d7 59.豐×c4+ with good winning chances.) 52.曺h2 (52.豐×b5?! 罝d8 53.豐b7+ 曺g8 54.豐e7 豐×d6 55.豐×d6 罝×d6 56.罝a8+ 曺f7 57.罝c8

and this rook ending should be drawn in view of Black's activity, despite the fact that he loses the c4-pawn) 52...h4 53.♕×b5 ♖d8 54.♕c6 ♔g8 55.b5 ♕g3+ 56.♔h1 ♕×c3 57.♖d1 ♕c2 58.♖e1 ♕d3 59.♖e4

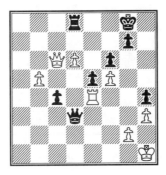

and White still has chances to win as his passed pawns are more dangerous.

50.♔g1 ♖d7 51.♕×b5 ♕e6 52.♕c5 ♔g6 53.♖c6 e4

54.♕×c4

The alternative 54.♕d4 leads, after 54...e3 55.♕×c4 ♕e5 56.♖c5 ♕×d6 57.♕e4+ ♔f7 58.♕×e3 ♖e7 59.♕f2 ♕d1+ 60.♔h2 ♖e1

to a major piece ending, where Black's counterplay promises him good drawing chances.

54...♛×c4 55.♖×c4 ♚f5 56.b5

Now Black has a choice between 56...♚e5 and 56...♖×d6. It is likely that Black can hold the rook ending but by no means obviously clear. In a practical game White still has chances to win. So there is no proof that White is winning – in fact the position is most likely a draw – but Black certainly also has no forced draw. A computer will assess all critical positions above to be in White's favor.

Joel Benjamin writes that "In this case the logs offer no illumination. DEEP BLUE never assessed 45...♛e3! as the best move, so it didn't appear in its output. We had to run DEEP BLUE from the diagram position (where Kasparov resigned) for ten minutes to get it to recognize the draw." As the above analysis proves that there is no forced draw, this seems to be another of the puzzling mysteries surrounding the rematch. Hsu states that "There was a way for White to avoid an outright repetition draw, but the resulting ending, even though better for White, might not be winning." Unfortunately Hsu does not give the concrete line of analysis, which he had discovered together with DEEP BLUE JUNIOR, a tuned-down version of the program.

For the DEEP BLUE team, it was no real problem that the machine had erred and given up a clearly winning position. But Kasparov's helpers had the problem of how to tell Garry that he may have resigned a drawn game. Benjamin (2007) relates the story:

> Kasparov's second Yuri Dokhoian did the deed as he and Kasparov walked to lunch to an Italian restaurant. "Garry stopped in his tracks and grabbed his head," [Frederic] Friedel told [*New York Times* writer] Bruce Weber. "There was no shouting, no obscenities. He eventually walked on, didn't say anything." At the restaurant I could see he was analyzing in his head – click-click, click-click-click – and after five minutes he glanced at me. And he said, "Rook e8, h4, h5. That was all? That simple? How could the computer not see that?"

This second game puzzled Kasparov and he used the press conference after the third game to voice his doubts. Benjamin relates that:

> [Grandmaster and match commentator] Maurice Ashley picked up on Kasparov's apparent insistence that DEEP BLUE's play in game two was unexplainable. He seemed to be insinuating something. Maurice followed his journalistic instincts and asked the most provocative possible question. "Do you think there may have been some kind of human intervention during this game?"

Kasparov replied: "It reminds me of the famous goal which Maradona scored against England in 1986. He said it was the hand of God."

He spoke a little further; I hardly heard the rest. The implication was very clear: he was accusing us of cheating!

Benjamin thinks this conspiracy theory is not even plausible and gives the following reasons:

1. The DEEP BLUE team and all their actions were observed by an impartial referee, Ken Thompson. How could cheating occur?

2. If the computer plays better than almost any human, why would you want to overrule it? Most likely you would just be making a mistake.

3. What would be IBM's motivation? The risk-reward analysis doesn't add up. ...

4. ... Why would IBM take the chance that anyone would confess?

After the third game, Garry demanded an answer to his question and wanted the logs of the computer to verify that no human intervention had occurred. The DEEP BLUE team refused this but after some negotiations agreed that the arbiter Ken Thompson could have the logs during the match, and Kasparov after the match. Here Benjamin again is convincing: "For ten years I've owned printouts from all six games...There is no smoking gun, just a lot of numbers most people would find incomprehensible." Then he goes on to explain DEEP BLUE's decisions in the second game and it seems that it just made the right moves for the right reasons.

Regarding the amazing 37.♗e4!!, it is interesting to note that DEEP BLUE found it in its normal allocation of time. According to Hsu it scored 37 points compared to 32 points for 37.♕b6?. This is a remarkable result for a computer program. For a human the score would be higher and the decision in favor of 37.♗e4 easier.

Sadly, Kasparov's accusations dominated the rest of the match. Yet they should not detract from a remarkable game – any grandmaster would be proud to have played this game. The DEEP BLUE team, especially with the chess input of Joel Benjamin, had produced a major improvement in the program's ability to play positional chess. The result was a stunning and historic accomplishment. Bravo!

The question on everyone's mind was how would Kasparov recover from the enormous blow to his ego and confidence? Here the computer has a big advantage. Not having an ego makes a difference!

Kasparov, Garry (2785) – DEEP BLUE
English Opening A29
New York match (3), 06.05.1997

1.d3!?

Kasparov wants to throw DEEP BLUE out of its opening book as soon as possible.

1...e5 2.♘f3 ♘c6 3.c4 ♘f6 4.a3 d6

After 4...d5? 5.cxd5 ♘xd5, Kasparov would get his Najdorf Sicilian with an extra tempo.

5.♘c3 ♗e7

5...♘d4 and 5...g6 are the alternatives. Hsu explains DEEP BLUE's choice: "In this position, British Grandmaster Michael Adams once played ♗e7 as Black. DEEP BLUE was given a hefty bias to play 5...♗e7 as a result of this one single game played by Michael."

6.g3 0-0 7.♗g2 ♗e6 8.0-0 ♕d7 9.♘g5

9.♗g5 ♘d4 10.♘d2 ♗h3 11.e3 ♗×g2 12.♔×g2 ♘e6 13.♗×f6 ♗×f6 14.♘de4 was Kortschnoi-Adams, Moscow 1994 that was later drawn.

9...♗f5 10.e4 ♗g4 11.f3 ♗h5 12.♘h3 ♘d4 13.♘f2 h6 14.♗e3 c5 15.b4 b6 16.♖b1

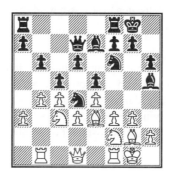

16...♔h8

A typical computer move. A human would try to prepare on the queenside for example with 16...a6.

17.♖b2 a6 18.b×c5

This opens roads for Black but it is difficult to make progress otherwise.

18...b×c5 19.♗h3!?

Kasparov plays for the full point. 19.g4 ♗g6 20.♕a4 ♖fb8 21.♕×d7 ♘×d7 22.♖fb1 ♖×b2 23.♖×b2 ♖b8 is completely equal.

19...♕c7!

DEEP BLUE reacts by preparing play on the queenside. 19...♘×f3+? 20.♔h1 ♕c7 21.g4 loses for Black and 19...♗×f3? 20.♗×d7 ♗×d1 21.♘f×d1 ♘×d7 22.♖b7 (Nunn) gives White more than enough compensation for the pawn.

20.♗g4 ♗g6!?

Taking on g4 would open the kingside for White.

21.f4 e×f4 22.g×f4 ♕a5

DEEP BLUE has managed to drum up counterplay in time.

23.♗d2 ♕×a3

24.♖a2

Kasparov (2017) is candid in his opinion of his play here: "Another moment that showed I was far from my best was when I forced the exchange of queens instead of playing my rook deep into black's position. It wasn't much of an improvement, analysis shows, but it would have been much more in keeping with my style. I was playing scared." 24.♖b7 ♘xg4 25.♕xg4 ♗f6 26.♘d5 ♕a2 27.♗e3 ♕e2 (Nunn) is also dynamically balanced.

24...♕b3 25.f5 ♕xd1 26.♗xd1 ♗h7

Kasparov has enough compensation for the pawn because of his space advantage and initiative, but Black's position is very solid.

27.♘h3 ♖fb8 28.♘f4 ♗d8 29.♘fd5 ♘c6 30.♗f4 ♘e5 31.♗a4 ♘xd5 32.♘xd5 a5 33.♗b5 ♖a7 34.♔g2

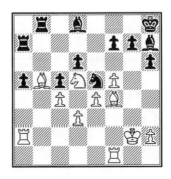

34...g5!

DEEP BLUE takes measures before Kasparov can build up an attack on the kingside. 34...♘xd3? runs into 35.♗xd6 ♖c8 36.♖d1 ♘b4 37.♗xc5 and wins.

35.♗xe5+ dxe5 36.f6 ♗g6

37.h4!?

Kasparov tries to open a second front but he cannot break through and the game peters out to a draw:

37...gxh4 38.♔h3 ♔g8 39.♔xh4 ♔h7 40.♔g4 ♗c7 41.♘xc7 ♖xc7 42.♖xa5 ♖d8 43.♖f3 ♔h8 44.♔h4 ♔g8 45.♖a3 ♔h8 46.♖a6 ♔h7 47.♖a3 ♔h8 48.♖a6 ½-½

A well-played game by both sides.

Deep Blue – Kasparov, Garry (2785)
Modern Defense B07
New York match (4), 07.05.1997

1.e4 c6 2.d4 d6

Kasparov again avoids his normal lines and plays anti computer chess.

3.♘f3 ♘f6 4.♘c3 ♗g4 5.h3 ♗h5 6.♗d3 e6 7.♕e2 d5 8.♗g5 ♗e7 9.e5

9.0-0? runs into 9...♘xe4 10.♗xe7 ♘xc3 11.♕e5 ♕xe7 (Nunn).

9...♘fd7 10.♗xe7 ♕xe7 11.g4 ♗g6

12.♗×g6?!

Bringing the h8-rook into the game. 12.0-0-0 is more logical.

12...h×g6 13.h4 ♘a6 14.0-0-0 0-0-0 15.♖dg1 ♘c7

The spectator's view of Game 4, with DEEP BLUE computing its 16th move.
(Monroe Newborn)

16.♔b1

DEEP BLUE seems to like prophylactic king moves. But it difficult to stop Black's kingside play in any case.

16...f6! 17.e×f6 ♕×f6!?

Now Black's position is easier to play than after 17...g×f6?!, as Kasparov will follow up with ♖de8, ♖hf8 and e5.

18.♖g3 ♖de8 19.♖e1 ♖hf8 20.♘d1

20...e5!!

A strong pawn sacrifice that activates Black's whole army with one strike.

21.d×e5

21.♘×e5? ♛×h4 plays into Black's hand.

21...♛f4 22.a3 ♘e6

22...♖e6!? is the alternative, which may even be better than the game continuation.

23.♘c3 ♘dc5

24.b4!

This move is probably strong as it takes away the c5-square from Black's knights.

24...♘d7 25.♛d3 ♛f7

26.b5?

A big positional mistake, which made the DEEP BLUE team hunt for the software bug causing it and the related mistakes in the first game. Joe Hoane finally found the problem and fixed it. Hsu relates the following story, which certainly pleased him: "At this juncture we had a surprise guest at the operations room. IBM chairman and CEO, Lou Gerstner, had decided to pay the team a visit and Gerstner commented, 'I think we should look at this as a chess match between the world's greatest chess player and...,' a short pause, 'Garry Kasparov.'" Gerstner certainly knows his business as *New York Times* writer Bruce Weber was present and the quote appeared in print the next day. After 26.♘a4, White is not worse.

26...♘dc5 27.♕e3 ♕f4!

Kasparov is willing to trade queens despite his pawn deficit, as White has so many weaknesses and Black can activate his whole army quickly and harmoniously while White has no real targets in an endgame.

28.b×c6 b×c6 29.♖d1 ♔c7 30.♔a1 ♕×e3?!

An understandable decision against the machine. But objectively 30...♖f7, as given by Kasparov later, was stronger as White now has problems finding a plan, while Black's position plays itself.

31.f×e3 ♖f7

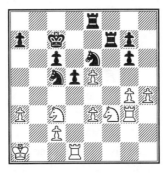

32.♖h3?

A very strange move, after which DEEP BLUE is in deep trouble. Probably it is planning to play h4-h5 to try to exchange all the kingside pawns. But this plan is too slow and allows a dangerous activation of Black's forces, as now the g-pawn is weak in many lines. After a normal move like 32.♔b2, the position is more or less equal.

32...♖ef8 33.♘d4 ♖f2 34.♖b1 ♖g2 35.♘ce2 ♖×g4

After 35...♖ff2?! 36.♘×e6+ ♘×e6 37.♘d4 ♘×d4 38.e×d4 ♖×c2 (Nunn), White defends with 39.♖e1.

36.♘×e6+ ♘×e6 37.♘d4!

DEEP BLUE tries to escape into a rook ending, where the drawish tendency will help it to survive.

37...♞×d4

The alternative 37...♖e8!? 38.♖f3 ♞d8 deserves serious attention as with knights the drawish tendency is much less and a slight initiative may prove to be extremely annoying.

38.e×d4 ♖×d4 39.♖g1 ♖c4 40.♖×g6 ♖×c2 41.♖×g7+ ♔b6 42.♖b3+ ♔c5 43.♖×a7

43...♖f1+?

This loses valuable time. 43...d4! gives better practical chances, e.g., 44.♔b1 (44. e6? ♖f1+ 45.♖b1 ♖ff2 is very dangerous in view of Black's activity.) 44...♖e2 45.♖a5+ ♔c4 46.♖b4+ ♔d3 47.♖b3+ ♔e4 48.♖c5 ♖e3 and Black can fight on, but it should most probably be a draw in the end. Deep Blue had self-terminated on Kasparov's move and had to be restarted (while its clock was running).

44.♖b1 ♖ff2

45.♖b4!

But this strong resource might have been overlooked by Garry. It threatens mate and destroys his concept. Now he must exchange one pair of rooks, which leads to a draw.

45...♖c1+ 46.♖b1 ♖cc2 47.♖b4 ♖c1+ 48.♖b1 ♖×b1+ 49.♔×b1 ♖e2 50.♖e7 ♖h2 51.♖h7

51...♔c4

51...d4 is also insufficient, e.g., 52.e6 ♖e2 53.♖e7!!. An amazing move! 53...d3 54.♖d7 ♔c4 55.e7 ♔c3 56.♖c7 ♖e1+ 57.♔a2 d2 58.♖×c6+ ♔d3 59.♖d6+ ♔c2 60.♖c6+ ♔d1 61.a4 ♖e3 62.♖d6 ♔e2 63.h5 d1♕ 64.♖×d1 ♔×d1 65.h6 ♖×e7 66.♔b3 with a draw.

52.♖c7! c5 53.e6 ♖×h4 54.e7 ♖e4 55.a4 ♔b3 56.♔c1 ½-½

Kasparov must have been disappointed in the result. His strong initiative petered out into a draw. He was in the same match position as in 1996 – all even with only two games to go. The pressure for him to win must have been growing in his mind. And DEEP BLUE? No pressure. Every game was played independent of the match circumstances. The DEEP BLUE team members were not as lucky. Surely they must have felt the pressure. Please, no more bugs!

Kasparov, Garry (2785) – DEEP BLUE

Reti Opening A07
New York match (5), 09.05.1997

1.♘f3 d5 2.g3 ♗g4 3.♗g2 ♘d7 4.h3 ♗×f3

Kasparov was surprised that DEEP BLUE gave up the bishop so easily. The main line is 4...♗h5.

Kasparov contemplating move 5 in Game 5.
(Monroe Newborn)

5.♗×f3 c6 6.d3 e6

Black has given up and light-square bishop and now puts its pawns on the light squares to compensate for it.

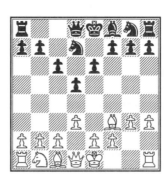

7.e4?!

"White's general strategy is to play e4, which serves two purposes. Firstly, it may help to break up Black's solid central pawn structure, and secondly a subsequent e4-e5 will gain space and may form the basis of a kingside attack, should Black castle on that side of the board. However, it is unusual for White to play e4 so quickly, the usual logic being that e4 cannot be prevented, so White may as well play 0-0 and bring his king into safety before taking action in the center." (Nunn) 7.♘d2, followed by e4 later gives White a slight advantage.

7...♘e5 8.♗g2 d×e4 9.♗×e4 ♘f6 10.♗g2 ♗b4+ 11.♘d2

11...h5!?

"A surprising move from a computer, but a good one. The computer puts its finger on the slight weakness created by the move h3. This means that after a later ...h4, White will be forced to either defend the g3-pawn or play g4, but then the f4-square is accessible to Black's pieces, especially the knight on g6. Some human players who like pushing their rook's pawns (Grandmaster John Speelman, for example) might also have played this move, but it is certainly interesting that DEEP BLUE finds this quite sophisticated positional idea." (Nunn)

Hsu explains that DEEP BLUE can safely play the move as Black can always castle queenside later; he had programmed the king safety evaluation of DEEP BLUE in such a way that the program recognized this. At the time several other programmers discouraged their brainchildren from playing such moves, which weaken the king's position in case of castling short.

Kasparov (2017) has a different opinion. "It turns out that ...h5 wasn't very good and that I could have gotten a large advantage by moving my knight to the e4 square, but I responded weakly." Kasparov probably refers to 16.♘e4! instead of 16.♘f3.

12.♕e2 ♕c7 13.c3 ♗e7 14.d4 ♘g6 15.h4

Kasparov must stop the h4 advance.

15...e5!

DEEP BLUE frees its position, exploiting its lead in development. The side combating the bishop pair, but having a lead in development, usually tries to open the position to find prospects for the knight before the bishops take control first and reign supreme later.

16.♘f3 e×d4 17.♘×d4 0-0-0 18.♗g5 ♘g4 19.0-0-0 ♖he8

19...♗×g5+ 20.h×g5 ♕a5?? runs into 21.♖×h5 (Nunn).

20.♕c2 ♔b8?!

20...♗×g5+ 21.h×g5 ♘6e5 is more precise.

21.♔b1?!

Kasparov copies the standard DEEP BLUE prophylactic king move. But 21.♗×e7 ♘×e7 22.♖he1 gives him a slight initiative, while after the text, the game is just dead equal.

21...♗×g5 22.h×g5 ♘6e5 23.♖he1

23.♖×h5? runs into 23...c5 24.♘b5 ♕b6 25.♖×d8+ ♖×d8 26.a4 a6 27.♘a3 ♘×f2 and Black is better.

23...c5 24.♘f3 ♖×d1+ 25.♖×d1 ♘c4 26.♕a4 ♖d8 27.♖e1

27.♖×d8+? ♕×d8 28.♕×c4?? runs into 28...♕d1#.

27...♘b6 28.♕c2 ♕d6 29.c4

29...♕g6?

An odd move which spoils the pawn structure and gives White some initiative. After 29...♕d3, the position is completely equal.

30.♕×g6 f×g6 31.b3 ♘×f2 32.♖e6 ♔c7?

Regrouping the knight with 32...♘c8 has a higher priority.

33.♖×g6?

Are we humans too materialistic and not the machines? But the decision was difficult of course, as Black's h-pawn becomes a force after 33.♘e5! ♖d1+ 34.♔c2 ♖g1 35.♗f3 ♖×g3 36.♖×g6 h4, but it seems that White is on top as a result of his strong bishop: 37.♖×g7+ ♔d6 38.♘f7+ ♔e6 39.♗×b7.

33...♖d7 34.♘h4 ♘c8 35.♗d5

If 35.♘f5?, then 35...♘e7.

35...♘d6 36.♖e6

36...♘b5!

DEEP BLUE correctly exchanges the knight for the powerful d5-bishop.

37.c×b5 ♖×d5 38.♖g6 ♖d7 39.♘f5 ♘e4 40.♘×g7 ♖d1+

"By move forty, DEEP BLUE assessed the position as being even." (Hsu) This seems to be correct. But unfortunately Hsu says nothing about the 43rd move.

41.♔c2 ♖d2+ 42.♔c1 ♖×a2 43.♘×h5

43...♘d2?

Does the computer have problems with perpetual check patterns here? 43...♖g2 draws, e.g., 44.♘f6 ♘c3 45.♖h6 ♖e2 and Black has installed the famous perpetual check mechanism ♘a2-c3.

44.♘f4?

This allows DEEP BLUE to escape with a very deep plan. 44.♖g7+ ♚d6 45.♖×b7 ♘×b3+ 46.♚b1 ♖h2 47.♘f6 is critical and White still has winning chances. Garry Kasparov (2017) claims it to be a win.

44...♘×b3+ 45.♚b1 ♖d2 46.♖e6 c4 47.♖e3

47.♖e4!? is another try, but Black can draw by 47...♚d6 48.♖×c4 ♖d3 49.♘×d3 ♘d2+ 50.♚a2 ♘×c4 51.♘c5 ♚e5.

47...♚b6!!

Black's king enters the attack just in time. An amazing concept!

48.g6 ♚×b5 49.g7 ♚b4 and a draw was agreed. ½-½

White can try to win but against best defense it does not work: 50.♖e2 ♖d1+ 51.♚b2 c3+ 52.♚c2 ♖c1+ 53.♚d3 ♖d1+ 54.♚c2 54.♘e4 ♘c5+ 55.♚f5 ♖d8 56.♚g6 ♚b3 57.♖h2 c2 58.♘e2 ♚b2 59.♖h8 ♖d6+ 60.♚f5 ♖d5+ 61.♚f4 ♖d4+ 62.♚e3 ♖d3+ 63.♚f4 ♘e6+ 64.♚e4 ♘c5+; or 54...♖c1+ 55.♚d3, with a draw by repetition in both cases.

Again, Kasparov must have been disappointed in the game result. He had initiative to play with and ended up with nothing to show for it. DEEP BLUE was proving to be a tenacious opponent.

Deep Blue – Kasparov, Garry (2785)

Caro-Kann B17

New York match (6), 11.05.1997

1.e4 c6 2.d4 d5

This time Kasparov goes for the real Caro-Kann, which he had played in his youth.

3.♘c3 dxe4 4.♘xe4 ♘d7

But previously he had only employed 4...♗f5.

5.♘g5 ♘gf6 6.♗d3 e6 7.♘1f3 h6?!

A provocative move, which was probably a gamble by Kasparov.

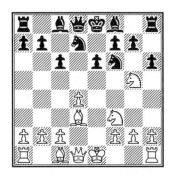

7...♗d6 is the main line, which was often employed by none other than Kasparov's arch rival Anatoly Karpov.

Two decades later, Kasparov (2017) revealed his thought process when considering 7...h6 and the danger posed by the possible sacrifice 8.♘xe6:

> While looking at the horrible positions for Black that resulted, I realized that only a computer would be able to defend them, and that was the point. Computers love material and are incredible defenders. I was sure that Deep Blue would apply its fantastic defensive prowess to my position, evaluate it as fine for Black, and therefore would decline to sacrifice the knight. I lost this bet, obviously, and spectacularly so, but the reason I lost it would not be clear for over a decade.

8.♘xe6!!

Played instantly from Deep Blue's opening book. The book had been set up to force the computer to play the sacrifice.

How did this sacrifice get into Deep Blue's opening book? This question remains unresolved to this day. Hsu's and Benjamin's accounts are similar but Miguel Illescas' (2009) version contradicts both completely.

Hsu states that: "Deep Blue was out of its opening book on move 11.♗f4...The position on the playing board had actually shown up in our lab a month earlier, when the other grandmasters (not Illescas) were working on Deep Blue's opening book." Benjamin says that "11.♗f4! This was the first decision for Deep Blue, and a good one" and "Our Caro-Kann preparation consisted of a few main lines entered by [Grandmaster] Nick De Firmian. While he was inputting I added a notation to answer 7...h6 with 8.♘×e6."

How long was Benjamin's preparation exactly? Did he only force the machine to take on e6 and looked at the evaluation, or did he check more lines as Hsu's account implies? Benjamin (2009) reacted to Illescas' version and elaborated: "But I think 8.♘×e6 had been prepared well before the match. Nick De Firmian was given the task of inputting lines in openings we weren't expecting, like the Caro-Kann. When we got to this position I stuck in 7...h6 8.♘×e6 ♕e7 9.0-0."

But what about the critical 8...f×e6? Benjamin does not mention it. He continues with "just to be thorough...I think Miguel was in the office at the time and that's how he remembers." This contradicts Hsu's version: "Miguel was not in the United States at the time of the discussion, so he had not yet seen DEEP BLUE's evaluation of the position after 11.♗f4." Benjamin continues: "After so many years I'm not 100% confident about my memories...Miguel's version is certainly a better story."

Illescas' version is: "On the morning of the last game, Joel and I were making a last effort, trying to improve the book...We were looking at all kinds of rubbish such as 1.e4 a6 and 1.e4 b6, giving as many forced moves to the computer as we could...That very morning we told DEEP BLUE, if Garry plays h6, take on e6 and don't check the database. Just play, don't think." The puzzling question is: Why did Illescas contradict Benjamin and Hsu, as he certainly was aware of the earlier accounts? Illescas' version gives Kasparov more options to voice his doubts. If Benjamin's and Hsu's versions are correct, then the matter could safely be closed.

Garry Kasparov's (2009) reaction to Illescas' claim that the book was altered "on the morning of the last game" was predictable:

> … is it really harder to believe that a giant corporation pulling out all the stops with many millions of dollars at stake stooped to dirty tricks...than to believe it's a coincidence the DEEP BLUE team was working on the 4...♘d7 Caro-Kann I'd never played before that morning...I feel he (Manuel Illescas) is asking for a much greater leap of faith than I am.

In preparing for their 2017 book *Deep Thinking*, Kasparov and co-author Mig Greengard contacted Joel Benjamin:

> GM Benjamin wrote to contradict his colleague Miguel Illescas's published recollections about game six, saying that it was he (Benjamin) who entered the fateful 8.♘×e6 move into DEEP BLUE's opening book, "a month or so before the match." That is, not "that very morning" of game six, as emphasized by Illescas with such vigor that his revelation was the headline of the interview. Benjamin said that he didn't dissent when the interview, and my incredulous response, were published in 2009 due to not wanting to publicly contradict his old teammate. This dispute between twelve-year-old and twenty-year-old human memories is another reason that all DEEP BLUE's files and logs should have been released by this time…

This issue could have been easily resolved twenty years ago by looking at the backup file of DEEP BLUE's opening book from before the match. Has anyone asked specifically for this file?

This riddle is still unsolved. Has Nick De Firmian given his account? Who is right, Illescas or Benjamin and Hsu? Are Kasparov's suspicions founded following Illescas version that ♘xe6 was entered on the very morning of the game because his preparations were somehow known to the DEEP BLUE side? But Kasparov has no hard evidence, no real proof of his theory, so until this is clarified, everyone has to come to their own conclusion. Be that as it may, the fact is that Kasparov gambled and it backfired.

8...♕e7?!

A shocked Kasparov answers quite quickly. So probably this was still prepared. But it seems that the queen is too badly placed here and creates a traffic jam on the kingside. 8...fxe6 9.♗g6+ ♔e7 10.0-0 ♕c7 11.♖e1 ♔d8 is the critical alternative. White's attack is very dangerous and over the board it is extremely difficult to defend but objectively matters are not totally clear.

9.0-0 fxe6 10.♗g6+ ♔d8 11.♗f4!

11.c4 and 11.♖e1 are the alternatives.

Now Kasparov is at a major crossroads. As he always prepares very thoroughly, it may be that he still had decided before the game to continue here with

11...b5?

Joel Benjamin has the following theory to explain Kasparov's decision: "...I tested the position against the contemporaneous version of FRITZ after the match...It actually played ♕d1-e2, ♖f1-e1, and ♕e2xe6, exchanging into a losing endgame." But the problems with 11...b5? are well described by John Nunn: "The idea of Kasparov's move is to secure the d5-square for his knight against the thrust c2-c4. However, it gives White the chance to open new lines on the queenside and bring his a1-rook into play without loss of time. Moreover, it fails to deal with the main problem of Black's position – his inability to move his queen. The only square available to her is b4, but this not only leaves the e6-pawn undefended, it also allows White to gain time by chasing the queen."

The line 11...♘d5 12.♗g3 ♕b4

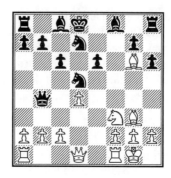

had been played in a match between a team of mathematics professor Ingo Althöfer and FRITZ against Grandmaster Gennadi Timoshchenko, Jena 1996, with the latter publishing extensive analysis in the *ICCA Journal* in March 1997. 13.♖e1 (13.♕e2 ♗e7 14.c4 ♘5b6 15.b3 ♗f6 16.♖ad1 ♕e7 17.♖fe1 as in Dvoirys-Zakharevich, Kursk 1987, with compensation according to Timoshchenko. But White appears better.) 13...♗e7 14.♕e2 ♗f6 15.c4 ♘e7 16.a3 ♕b3 17.♗d3 as in Chandler-Hübner, Biel 1987, and now 17...♘f8 18.♖ad1 ♗d7 19.♘e5 ♗e8 is playable according to Timoshchenko but 20.d5 wins for White.

However, matters are not so simple. Even today's engines have problems with the sacrifice as given by RYBKA author Rajlich (2010): "Black's position (after 11.♗f4!) is critical but playable – for example, Jeroen Noomen and Dagh Nielsen, RYBKA's opening book authors, aimed for exactly this position with Black in our 2007 match versus Zappa in Mexico City."

12.a4!

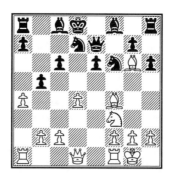

DEEP BLUE wants to bring its a1-rook in to play and open roads against Black's king. Now the game is effectively over; it is practically impossible to defend such an open position with an insecure king against a powerful calculating machine that acts like a shark that smells blood.

12...♗b7 13.♖e1 ♘d5

13...b4 loses to 14.c4 bxc3 15.bxc3 ♘d5 16.♗g3 ♘xc3 17.♕b3 (Nunn).

14.♗g3 ♔c8 15.axb5 cxb5 16.♕d3 ♗c6

17.♗f5!

"DEEP BLUE's evaluation went flying over +200 when it found this move." (Benjamin)

17...e×f5 18.♖×e7 ♗×e7?!

18...♘e7 is more tenacious but White's attack will still win after 19.♕c3.

19.c4!

...and after talking to his mother Clara for some time, Kasparov resigned as he will lose truckloads of material. **1–0** For example, 19...b×c4 (19...♘b4 20.♕×f5 b×c4 21.♘e5 [Nunn] and White simply has too many attackers) 20.♕×c4 ♘b4 (20...♔b7?? runs into 21.♕a6#) 21.♖e1 ♖e8 22.♗d6 ♗×d6 23.♖×e8+ ♔b7 24.♖×a8 ♔×a8 25.♕e6 ♗b8 26.d5 and it is all over.

Edward Fredkin (1997)
Computer scientist

Announcing that DEEP BLUE is to be awarded the $100,000 Fredkin Prize: "There has never been any doubt in my mind that a computer would ultimately beat a reigning world chess champion. The question has always been when."

A disconsolate Garry Kasparov (left) after resigning Game 6. Deep Blue's C.J. Tan on the right. (Monroe Newborn)

History was made! A "grand challenge" problem in artificial intelligence, indeed all of computing science, had finally been realized. It had been 50 years since Shannon first conceived of his ideas for a chess-playing program. Over that period of time, literally hundreds of researchers – academics, industry investigators, computer hobbyists, and chess players – had made contributions that slowly advanced our understanding of how to create a chess-playing machine. The Deep Blue team – principally Feng-hsiung Hsu, Murray Campbell, and Joe Hoane – made the last great leap forward in this remarkable quest. Campbell (2005) generously credits one person in particular who was not part of the team, yet whose influence had a profound effect:

> *Interviewer*: What is the debt of Deep Blue to Belle?
>
> *Campbell*: There's a large debt. The original design of the Deep Thought chip, which provided a good part of the Deep Blue chip, was based on the Belle design. A somewhat improved design of the Belle move generator was done for Deep Thought. And of course Ken Thompson was always there at these [computer chess] events. And if you asked Ken the right question, he'll tell you the answer – it's figuring out the right question to ask him and that was always the joke. Because Ken was very open, he didn't keep a lot of secrets, but he didn't volunteer a lot of information either. So if you could figure out the right question to ask Ken you could get a goldmine.

An analogy to summiting Mount Everest is appropriate. Numerous people enabled the success of Tenzing Norgay and Edmund Hillary. These people pioneered the route to the top, devised the equipment necessary, studied the food and water requirements, understood the ice and weather conditions, and so on. For over 50 years, many tried for the top, only to be defeated by exhaustion, equipment, and/or the elements. In 1953 the summit was conquered.

In chess, many people pioneered the steps needed for success, devised the algorithms required, studied the domain knowledge, understood the computational requirements, and so on. For over 50 years, many tried for the top, only to be defeated by lack of computing power, insufficient chess knowledge, and/or bugs. In 1997 the grand challenge of created a world-championship-caliber chess-playing computer was achieved.

Why did so many take up the computer chess challenge? As was true for Mount Everest, "because it's there" (George Mallory, mountaineer) applies in this case too. Circa 1950, the notion that it might be possible to create a non-human "intelligence" that could play chess was intriguing. Taking this to the logical conclusion of defeating the human World Chess Champion was the ultimate goal. Researchers and hobbyists became obsessed with this quest. Far be this a defeat for mankind, the DEEP BLUE victory is a testament to the ingenuity and tenacity of the human species. The work that culminated in DEEP BLUE represents a crowning achievement and a deeper understanding of what it means to be human.

Jack Peters (1997)
International Master and *Los Angeles Times* chess columnist

The exhibition match between Garry Kasparov and DEEP BLUE in Philadelphia has generated more publicity for chess than anything since Bobby Fischer's return in 1992. Unfortunately, our wonderful game has been reduced to serving as a benchmark for the progress of computers. Future generations may benefit from the new knowledge of computer design; at the moment, though, chess is suffering. Its artistic component no longer seems important, and the worth of our centuries of tradition decreases daily. Kasparov's 4-2 victory [in the 1996 match] seems beside the point, as DEEP BLUE has demonstrated that it can play at or beyond the level of Kasparov in fairly ordinary positions. How sad that chess can be conquered by mere calculation.

Kasparov was the unfortunate victim. There is no question that he is a brilliant chess player, quite likely the best human player yet seen. That he would agree to play computers is a testament to his character and confidence. He could easily have said "No" to playing computers. He bravely put his reputation on the line repeatedly. He must have known that one day his brilliant string of successes would come to an end. The computer chess community and, indeed, mankind owe him a debt of gratitude. *Salut!*

The DEEP BLUE team. From left to right: Gerry Brody, Murray Campbell, Feng-Hsiung Hsu, Joe Hoane (standing),
Joel Benjamin, Chung-Jen Tan (seated).
(IBM)

1997: Othello/Reversi

Michael Buro's (NEC) program LOGISTELLO defeats World Champion Takeshi Murakami 6-0 in an exhibition match. Computers are performing at a super-human level.

One of this book's authors (KM) provides his grandmaster opinion of the match:

DEEP BLUE was ahead of the programs of that era in several respects. It played closed positions better, it had several functions implemented in the hardware, and it was faster. It profited a lot from Joel Benjamin's work. Usually it is not so easy for grandmasters and programmers to find a common language, but the DEEP BLUE team managed to establish just that. Man as toolmaker had defeated man as player.

When the man versus machine matches commenced, there was a clear difference in playing strength – humans were stronger when it came to strategy, the endgame, and maintaining the balance tactically. But DEEP BLUE certainly was a large leap forward and so it makes sense to compare both sides and to see why DEEP BLUE was stronger than the software-based programs of the time.

Kasparov in general won the opening battles in both matches. Only his anti-computer strategy in the second game and his gamble in the sixth game of the rematch backfired. In the second game, he underestimated the ability of DEEP BLUE to play closed positions. This was easily understandable, as many commercial programs of that era could not handle closed positions well. He could not know how well the DEEP BLUE team had managed to include Joel Benjamin's suggestions on pawn levers, and rook and bishops on closed files and diagonals respectively.

The DEEP BLUE team used a more refined strategy regarding its opening book. The extended book was more human-like. Illescas (2009) writes that:

> For example, the treatment of the opening strategy which we used for the match was completely new. At that time all programs played the moves that were in the book. If the move was in the book, the program would play it immediately. If it was not in the book the program would think. There were only two possibilities. With DEEP BLUE, we decided...the approach should be much more human...We gave DEEP BLUE a lot of knowledge of chess openings but we also gave it a lot of freedom to choose from the database with statistics.

In short-term tactical calculations, the machine was stronger than Kasparov, as can be seen in the first game [of the 1996 match] in which it refuted Kasparov's mistake 27...d4? by precise calculation. But the horizon problem reared its head as well as in the famous second game of the rematch, where Kasparov resigned instead of trying to give perpetual check. A relative strength of Kasparov was also the feel for dynamic pawn sacrifices, e.g., 20...e5 in game four and 21.f4 in game five of the rematch.

While the machine would play some positions as if divinely inspired, Kasparov apparently had problems occasionally getting into the proper frame of mind. This was especially the case before the sixth game of the rematch. The pressure on him was enormous while the machine just does not have such a problem.

On the other hand, DEEP BLUE had problems with its king safety and the moves 22... g4? in the first game and 26.b5? in the fourth game of the rematch were due to a bug. It overestimated the value of an unchallengeable bishop outpost and its bias against the queen trade backfired in the second game of the first match. Using biases and contempt factors is always a risky business of course.

A few weeks after the match, Garry Kasparov (1997) presented a reasoned discussion of what happened:

> This was a very tough match, which demanded a lot of my energy. It was also a very interesting match that captured the imagination of millions of people all over the world. Unfortunately, they also got to see some errors on my part. ...

> I admit that I was probably too optimistic at the start of the match. I followed the conventional wisdom when playing computers of playing 'ugly' openings [non-theoretical] to avoid early confrontation, to accumulate positional advantages and then I was confident that my calculation would stay at a high level once the confrontation occurred.

My whole preparation was a failure because DEEP BLUE played very differently from what I expected. My preparation was based on some wrong assumptions about its strategy; and when after Game 2 it proved to be a disaster, I over-worked myself. I actually spent more energy on the games in this match than for any before in my life. Every game in this match took a lot out of me. There was enormous pressure because I had to keep my eye on every possibility, since I didn't want to miss any single shot.

This is also partly why I lost this match. When Game 6 finally came, I had lost my fighting spirit. I simply didn't have enough energy left to put up a fight. At the end of Game 5 I felt completely emptied, because I couldn't stand facing something I didn't understand. If I had been playing against a human whom I knew, then it would have been different. For example, I was one game down against Anand in the 1995 world championship, but I fought back. Here, I was fighting the unknown.

Despite the score of this match, I am firmly convinced that this thing is beatable. Having said that, I don't think there are that many players in the world who would be able to beat it. I think only four or five players in the world would stand a chance against DEEP BLUE. You need outstanding chess qualities to play it – you simply can't make comparisons with other chess computers. Take my case: I have an enormous score in training against the best PC programs, but it didn't help me to prepare for DEEP BLUE. As a matter of fact, I think I made a mistake in doing that. In the future I have to prepare specifically for DEEP BLUE, and play normal chess, as well as normal openings.

Is there a future? Yes, I think so! I just challenged IBM for a rematch, to take place later this year, under slightly different conditions, such as 10 games, with one rest day between each game. Further, I want to receive ten practice games played by DEEP BLUE against a grandmaster, as well as the nomination of an independent panel to supervise the match and DEEP BLUE, making sure there are no suspicions whatsoever. If this match takes place, and I hope it will, I am so confident I can win it, that I am even willing to play for a "winner takes all" prize. My score prediction? 6-4 in my favor!

With the passage of time, he has been able to reflect on the significance of the match, and his role in history (Kasparov 2010b):

The result was met with astonishment and grief by those who took it as a symbol of mankind's submission before the almighty computer. ("The Brain's Last Stand" read the *Newsweek* headline.) Others shrugged their shoulders, surprised that humans could still compete at all against the enormous calculating power that, by 1997, sat on just about every desk in the first world.

It was the specialists – the chess players and the programmers and the artificial intelligence [AI] enthusiasts – who had a more nuanced appreciation of the result. Grandmasters had already begun to see the implications of the existence of machines that could play—if only, at this point, in a select few types of board configurations— with godlike perfection. The computer chess people were delighted with the conquest of one of the earliest and holiest grails of computer science, in many cases matching the mainstream media's hyperbole. The 2003 book DEEP BLUE by Monty Newborn was blurbed as follows: "a rare, pivotal watershed beyond all other triumphs: Orville

Wright's first flight, NASA's landing on the moon…."

The AI crowd, too, was pleased with the result and the attention, but dismayed by the fact that DEEP BLUE was hardly what their predecessors had imagined decades earlier when they dreamed of creating a machine to defeat the world chess champion. Instead of a computer that thought and played chess like a human, with human creativity and intuition, they got one that played like a machine, systematically evaluating 200 million possible moves on the chess board per second and winning with brute number-crunching force. As Igor Aleksander, a British AI and neural networks pioneer, explained in his 2000 book, *How to Build a Mind:*

> By the mid-1990s the number of people with some experience of using computers was many orders of magnitude greater than in the 1960s. In the Kasparov defeat they recognized that here was a great triumph for programmers, but not one that may compete with the human intelligence that helps us to lead our lives.

It was an impressive achievement, of course, and a *human* achievement by the members of the IBM team, but DEEP BLUE was only intelligent the way your programmable alarm clock is intelligent. Not that losing to a $10 million alarm clock made me feel any better.

With the publication of Kasparov's and Greengard's 2017 book *Deep Thinking*, we see a side of Kasparov that the general public has not seen before – a man who has mellowed over time. When at the top of his game, he oozed confidence and was often viewed as being arrogant – he was the best and any loss was a minor bump in the road and an opportunity to improve. He was relentless in his drive for perfection, and unapologetic about his actions and public statements. But in writing *Deep Thinking* it is obvious that Kasparov has done a lot of deep thinking and reflection about the match. Accusations have been replaced by admissions. The big surprise is that in several places he apologizes for his actions. The following text undoes many of the claims made by Kasparov in the heat of the battle:

> I have been asked, "Did DEEP BLUE cheat?" more times than I could possibly count, and my honest answer has always been "I don't know." After twenty years of soul-searching, revelations, and analysis, my answer is now "no."

He still has the competitive fire in his belly, as evidenced by his anger with the aftermath of the match. He did not get the rematch that he expected and that the public wanted. Instead of belaboring on this point, he laments that "the real victim of this betrayal was science." There was a data point suggesting that machine was better than man at chess, but the scientific evidence was inconclusive. The DEEP BLUE team was soon to be disbanded and the hardware dismantled. Of what value was a scientific data point that cannot be reproduced?

One of this book's authors summed up the perspective from the artificial intelligence point of view (Schaeffer 1997):

> … Of course, a loss by Kasparov is not a defeat for mankind, but a triumph: man has found a way to master complex technology to create the illusion of intelligence. The press is the gullible audience that has been fooled by a sleight of hand; the DEEP BLUE team is Harry Houdini, and IBM, his agent.

True intelligence in silicon had not yet been achieved. Massive calculations and deep search triumphed over appropriate application of chess knowledge. The victory of machine over man in chess showed that mimicking the human approach was not necessarily best. After all, does it make sense to build airplanes that flap their wings?

Diego Rasskin-Gutman (2009)
Professor

DEEP BLUE's victory increases even more the stature of Kasparov and the rest of us mortals, who with our emotions, dreams, hungers, desires, hopes, and fears are able to face monsters of such mythological proportions.

Endgame

8
2850 (1998-2003)

Although machines challenging humankind at chess grabbed all the headlines, the growing strength of these programs was beginning to have a profound effect on human-versus-human competition. This showed up in several ways.

First, human players now had a sparring partner that they could play whenever they wanted. The ability to practice more often meant players could improve their rating more quickly than previously. As well, their "friendly" opponent had no qualms about endless postmortem analysis of a game, giving insights as to what went right, opportunities missed, alternatives not considered, and, well, entertainment. Often watching the computer play itself (self play) could be fun to watch and educational. The more time a human player spent engaged with their chess computer, the more likely it would translate into rating points.

Second, players of all strengths used computers to assist with their opening preparation. Databases of games allowed players to look for new or rarely played moves to surprise an opponent. Computer analysis was used to uncover errors in the openings, or to find strong moves that had been overlooked. The result was that the 1990s saw the computer's status change from being a novelty item to becoming an indispensible aid for assisting the preparation of top-flight players.

Third, computers could influence the outcome of adjourned games. The ability to stop a game, do some private analysis of the adjourned position with a computer, and then resume the game meant that technology was being unfairly used to possibly influence the game result.

Shirov, Alexei (2670) – Lautier, Joel (2635)
Munich, 1993

In days gone by, games would be adjourned, usually after the 40th or 60th move, and then analyzed at home before they were continued, typically the next day. For example, in 1993, Alexei Shirov's start at the Munich tournament did not go well. After two rounds he had scored only a half-point, and in the third round his position against Joel Lautier was very bad. When the second time control was reached, Lautier became greedy and had to seal a move in the following position:

Although Black is three pawns ahead, he is on the brink of disaster in view of White's strong attack. After analyzing this position for a long time, the co-author of this book (KM) shared his thoughts with the German chess trainer and journalist Claus Dieter Meyer. Meyer later wrote an article on this for the German *Schach Magazin 64* (12/1994), which Shirov included in his book *Fire on Board* (Everyman 1997):

61...♔g8?! Lautier had indeed sealed the move we expected. For about 15 years we thought that it lost, but computers, using the six-man tablebases, cannot be defeated.

62.♔g6 ♗c6 63.♗c5!?

Lautier had overlooked this tricky move in his adjournment analysis and did not find the necessary retort.

63...♖d3? FRITZ 3 running on Alexei's notebook had found the paradoxical "only" move 63...♔h8!!, probably by eliminating all alternatives. This is of course much more difficult for humans. 64.♗d4 (after 64.♖×g7?!, 64...♗e8+ is the point, which destroys the coordination of the attacker) 64...♔g8 65.♖×g7+ ♔f8 66.♖c7 ♗g2! (not 66...♗d5? 67.♖c5!+– Müller's improvement found later in 1993 (67.♔f6 ♔e8 68.♖c5 ♗b7! 69.♖e5+ ♔d7 70.♖e7+ ♔c6 71.♖e6+=, Shirov & Lautier in their post-mortem analysis)) 67.♔f6 ♔e8 68.♔e6 ♔d8 69.♖c5 ♗b7 70.♗f6+ ♔e8 71.♖c7 ♖e3+ 72.♗e5 ♖×e5+ 73.♔×e5 ♗e4 74.♔f4.

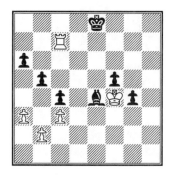

With the help of the six-man tablebases, C.D. Meyer revised the former analysis (see *The Magic of Chess Tactics* ChessBase DVD 2009, correcting the analysis in Mayer and Müller (2003)) and came to the conclusion that Black is probably able to survive, for example: 74...♔d8 75.♖a7 ♔c8 76.♖xa6 ♔b7 77.♖g6 ♗d3 78.♔e5 ♔c7 79.♔d4.

Here 79...♗c2!= is called for; it was found in 2015 in joint analysis with Vincent Keymer. Now it seems that White cannot win. The influence of the six-man tablebase is only indirect as it is used in the search (for leaf nodes that have six or fewer pieces). Meyer's original suggestion 79...♗e2? loses in view of 80.♖f6 ♗d3 81.b3 g3 82.bxc4 bxc4 (82...♗xc4 83.♖xf5 g2 84.♖g5 ♗f1 85.c4 bxc4 86.♖g6+−) 83.♔e3 ♗e4 84.♖g6 g2 85.♔f2+−.

64.♖xg7+ ♔h8 65.♗d4 ♖xd4 66.cxd4 f4 67.♖c7 ♗e4+ 68.♔h6 ♗d5 69.♖c5 ♗g8 70.d5 f3 71.d6 ♗e6 72.♖e5 ♗d7 73.♖e7 f2 74.♖xd7 ♔g8 75.♖g7+ ♔f8 76.d7 1-0

Needless to say, today adjourned games are effectively a thing of the past. This removes the *threesome* potential and ensures that the games are *mano a mano*.

Fourth, there is using computers to correct human analysis and increase our understanding of certain positions, endgames in particular. Consider the following example, an instance of an important and practical class of rook and pawn endgames.

Lautier, Joel (2645) – Salov, Valery (2660)
Madrid, 1993

Black to move. An easy win? Not so simple! In his classic book *Secrets of Rook Endings* (Gambit Publications, 1999), Grandmaster John Nunn used this position to glean insights from the KRPKP endgame. He teased his readers with a quiz: "In this position Salov found a sequence of 11 consecutive 'only' moves to win the game. Your challenge is to find the first two moves of the solution." Try it, and prepare to be surprised. There is a lot you can learn by studying the winning and drawing sequences from tablebases.

In the following position, tablebases help correct human analysis in this fight of rook versus bishop.

Tiviakov, Sergei (2480) – Korsunsky, Rostislav (2390)
Frunze, 1989

Human analysts thought that this position was a fortress, something that one of the authors (KM) also claimed many times (e.g., in *Endgame Corner 70*). However, White can win, as first pointed out by Jonathan Hawkins in his excellent book *Amateur to IM – Proven Ideas and Training Methods* (Mongoose Press, 2012). This is accomplished either by invading with his king to c6 (this winning method was known to human theory) or – and this is really surprising – by a properly timed exchange of pawns by a3-a4:

45.♔e4 ♗f2 46.♖f5 ♗g1 47.♖f1 ♗c5 48.♔d5 ♗e3 49.♖f7+ ♔b6

50.♖f3 ♗g1 51.♖f1

51.♖f6+ ♔b7 52.♖f4 ♔b6 is more direct.

Now White should amazingly exchange pawns with 53.a4!! b×a4 54.♖×a4 ♗e3.

White's rook now wins a very long domination duel (mate in 73 moves according to the tablebase), e.g., 55.♖a1 ♗f2 56.♖f1 ♗e3 57.♖f6+ ♔b7 58.♖f3 ♗g1 59.♔d6 ♗h2+ 60.♔e6 ♔c6 61.♖f1 ♗g3 62.♔f5.

This is really incredible! White's king moves to f5 to win the domination fight. Chess really is a rich game! 62...♗d6 63.♖c1+ ♔b6 64.♔e4 ♗c5 65.♔d3 ♔b5 66.♖a1 ♔b6 67.♔c4 ♗e3 68.♖a3 ♗g1 69.♖g3 ♗f2 70.♖f3 ♗g1 71.♔b4 ♗d4 72.♖b3 ♗e5 73.♖a4+ ♔a7 74.♔a5 ♗f6 75.♔b4 ♔b6 76.♔a4+ ♔a7 77.♖b4 ♗e5 78.♔b3 ♗d6 79.♖g4 ♗e5 80.♖e4 ♗g3 81.♔b4 ♔b6 82.♖g4 ♗d6+ 83.♔c4 ♗b8

84.♖g6+ ♔b7 85.♔d5 ♗f4 86.♖g4 ♗b8 87.♔c5 ♗a7+ 88.♔d6 ♗b8+ 89.♔d7 a5 90.♔e6 ♔c6 91.♖c4+ ♔b5 92.♔d5 a4 93.♖c5+ ♔b6 94.♔c4 ♗f4 95.♖b5+ ♔a6 96.♔c5 ♗e3+ 97.♔c6 ♗c1 98.♖b8 ♔a5 99.♔c5 ♗e3+ 100.♔c4 ♔a6 101.♖a8+ ♔b6 102.♖×a4 +−

51...♗e3 52.♔e4 ♗g5 53.♖f5 ♗c1 54.♖f2 ♗g5 55.♔d4 ♗c1 56.♖e2 ♔a5 56...♗g5 57.♖e6+ ♔b7 58.♔c5 ♗d8 59.b4 ♗h4 60.♖b6+ ♔a7 61.♔c6 +− **57.♔c3 ♔b6 58.♔d4 ♔a5 59.♖c2 ♗h6 60.♖g2 ♗c1 61.♖c2 ♗h6**

62.♖c7?!

Allowing Black to put up more resistance. 62.♖g2 wins quicker, e.g., 62...♗c1 (62...♗f8 63.♔c3 ♔b6 64.♖g6+ ♔b7 65.b4 +−; 62...♔a4 63.♖g6 ♗c1 64.♔c3 +−) 63.♖e2 ♔b6 (63...♗h6 64.♔c3 ♗g7+ 65.♔b3 ♗f6 66.♖e6 ♗d4 67.♔a2 b4 68.a×b4+ ♔b5 69.♔b3 +−) 64.♔d5 ♗g5 (64...a5 65.♔d4 a4 66.♔d5 b4 67.♖c2 ♗e3 68.a×b4 ♔b5 69.♖c8 +−) 65.♖e6+ ♔b7 66.♔c5

and White's king invades to c6. 66...♗d8 67.b3 ♗g5 68.♖b6+ ♔a7 69.♔c6 +−

62...♔b6 63.♖e7 ♗c1 63...♗g5 64.♖e6+ ♔b7 65.♔c5 ♗d8 66.b3 ♗h4 67.♖b6+ ♔a7 68.♔c6 +− **64.♖e6+ ♔b7 65.♖e2**

Even 65.♔c5 is playable: 65...♗×b2 66.♖e7+ ♚b8 67.♖e3 (67.♚b6? ♗d4+ 68.♚×a6 ♗c5=) 67...♚c7 68.♖f3 ♚b7 69.♖h3 ♚c7 70.♖h7+ ♚b8 71.♚b6+−

65...♚b6?!

Now the bishop is dominated. 65...♗g5!? 66.♚c5 ♗h4

was more tenacious, e.g., 67.a4 b×a4 68.♚b4 ♗g3 69.♚×a4 ♗c7 70.♚b4 ♗b6 71.♚c4 ♚c6 72.♖e6+ ♚b7 73.♚d5 ♗f2 74.♖f6 ♗g1 75.♖f1 ♗e3 76.♖f3 ♗g1 77.♚d6 ♗h2+ 78.♚e6 ♚c6 79.♖f1 ♗g3 80.♚f5

and White wins as shown above, 65...♗f4?! 66.♖e7+ ♔b6 67.♖e6+ ♔b7 68.♔c5 ♗g5 69.♖b6+ ♔a7 70.♔c6+−

66.♔d5 ♗g5 66...a5 67.♔d4 a4 68.♔d5 b4 69.♖c2 ♗e3 (69...b×a3 70.♖×c1 a×b2 71.♖b1 a3 72.♔c4+−) 70.a×b4 ♔b5 71.♖c8+− ; 66...♔a5 67.♖c2 ♗e3 (67...♗f4 68.♖c6+−) 68.♖c6 b4 69.a×b4+ ♔b5 70.♖c8 ♗f4 71.♖c5+ ♔b6 72.♔c4+− **67.♖e6+ ♔b7 68.♔c5 ♗d8** 68...♗h4 69.♖b6+ ♔a7 70.♔c6+− **69.b3 ♗h4 70.♖b6+ ♔a7 71.♔c6**

White's king has reached the key square c6 and it is over:

71...♗f2 72.♖b7+ ♔a8 73.♖f7 ♗g1 74.♖f4 ♔a7 75.a4 b×a4 76.♖×a4 ♗f2 77.b4 ♗e3 78.b5 ♔b8 79.♖×a6 1-0

This analysis was first published in the *ICGA Journal* (December 2013).

Then, of course, there are the bizarre positions found in tablebases – flights of fantasy; mere curiosity without any pedagogical value.

White to play and mate in 262 moves. We leave the solution as an exercise to the reader. Good luck!

Tim Krabbé (1991)
Chess writer

Regarding the sequences of perfect play in endgame tablebases:

The moves are beyond comprehension. A grandmaster wouldn't be better at these endgames than someone who had learned chess yesterday. It's a sort of chess that has nothing to do with chess, a chess that we could never have imagined without computers. The [winning] moves are awesome, almost scary, because you know they are the truth, God's Algorithm – it's like being revealed the Meaning of Life, but you don't understand a word.

Finally, there is cheating. If there is a way to use a computer during a game, someone will find a way to skirt the rules to their advantage. The first widely publicized case of using computers to cheat in a tournament occurred in 1993. Although never proven, it was quite likely that a player was communicating with a computer during his games (Friedel 2011a):

At the World Open 1993 in Philadelphia a completely unknown player appeared, unsubtly calling himself John von Neumann [the name of a famous mathematician]… He played excellently, drawing against GM Helgi Olafsson in the second round.

Von Neumann, J. – Olafsson, Helgi (2530)
Sicilian Defense B96
Philadelphia Open, 1993

1.e4 c5 2.♘f3 d6 3.d4 c×d4 4.♘×d4 ♘f6 5.♘c3 a6 6.♗g5 e6 7.f4 b5 8.e5 d×e5 9.f×e5 ♕c7 10.e×f6 ♕e5+ 11.♘de2?! 11.♗e2 is critical. **11...♕×g5 12.♘e4 ♕h4+?!** 12...♕e5 is the refutation of White's concept.

13.♘2g3 g×f6? 13...♕f4 limits the damage. **14.♕d4** Now White is winning, but von Neumann takes the repetition. Probably the winning lines are too deep.

14...♔e7 15.♕c5+?! 15.♕b4+ ♔d8 16.♕a5+ ♔e7 17.0-0-0 ♘d7 18.♗×b5 −+
15...♔d8 16.♕b6+ 16.0-0-0+ still wins. **16...♔e8 17.♕d4 ♔e7 18.♕c5+**

♔d8 19.♕b6+ ♔e8 20.♕d4 ♔e7 21.♕c5+? ½–½

But in round four he suddenly stopped at move nine and lost on time. Here's the game:

J. von Neumann – D. Shapiro [C44] Philadelphia Open, 1993: **1.e4 e5 2.♘f3 ♘c6 3.d4 e×d4 4.e5** A very strange move. Maybe von Neumann had the wrong position, with ♘f6 instead of ♘c6 on his computer. **4...♘ge7 5.♗e2 ♘f5 6.0-0 ♗e7 7.♘bd2 0-0 8.♘b3 d6 9.e×d6 ♕×d6** and now White stopped playing and lost on time. **0-1.**

This is how the game from round nine went:

J. von Neumann – NN [B40] Philadelphia Open, 1993: **1.e4 c5 2.♘f3 e6 3.d4 c×d4 4.♘×d4 ♘f6 5.♘c3 ♗b4 6.e5 ♘d5 7.♗d2 ♘×c3 8.♗×c3 ♗×c3+.** Here von Neumann thought for forty minutes, although there is only one reasonable move (pawn takes bishop). Then he disappeared for a while, came back, played **9.b×c3** and won the game. Obviously there was some communication problem that had to be solved.

Von Neumann won a prize in the category of players without an ELO rating. Naturally people had become suspicious of this unknown and highly unorthodox player. Before the organizers handed over the $800 check they asked him to solve a simple chess puzzle. He refused, turned and left, and has never been seen again at chess tournaments.

Perhaps the most visible case was that of Clemens Allwermann (Friedel 2011b):

At the Hoogovens super-tournament in Wijk aan Zee, in January 1999, there was one main topic of conversation. Every morning at breakfast Garry Kasparov would come over to Vishy Anand's table to discuss the matter with him. The object of their interest was the new German chess star, Clemens Allwermann. This hitherto unknown player had won the Böblinger Open, ahead of GMs and IMs. He had played wonderfully courageous attacking chess, scoring 7.5 points from nine games, without a single loss. His ELO performance was 2630. This sensational result made the headlines all over Germany…

So who is this Clemens Allwermann? If I said this was a 17-year-old super-sharp kid, rising meteorically, as they sometimes do, you might still find the sheer magnitude of his success difficult to believe. It turns out that Allwermann was 55 years old and had had a stable rating of around 1900 for the last twenty years. He ranked around number 10,000 in Germany, but his remarkable performance could theoretically elevate him to number two (behind [Grandmaster] Artur Jussupow) in this country.

News of Allwermann's achievement spread quickly – but perhaps not in the way the player himself may have anticipated. "Was a pocket DEEP BLUE used for brain doping" asked one newspaper, while *Der Spiegel* put it more sarcastically: "Move over Goethe, Beethoven and Einstein, here comes a new pinnacle of Teutonic genius."

Nobody was willing to believe that the amateur had done it all on his own. Especially not when other players discovered that you could reproduce virtually all of Allwermann's moves with the chess program FRITZ. Hartmut Metz revealed all of this in newspapers and *Schach-Magazin 64*. He gave many examples that show it was not just the tactically brilliant shots played by Allwermann but also bad, anti-positional moves that FRITZ will duplicate.

The game that caused the greatest suspicion was the one Allwermann played in the last round. It was an encounter that would decide the winner of the tournament, and the amateur player was facing the leading grandmaster. Completely undaunted Allwermann proceeded to outplay his opponent in fine attacking style, reaching an easily winning position.

Allwermann, Clemens – Kalinitschev, Sergey (2505)
Sicilian Defense B32
Boeblingen, 1999

1.e4 c5 2.♘f3 ♘c6 3.d4 c×d4 4.♘×d4 e5 5.♘b5 d6 6.c4 ♗e7 7.♗e2 a6 8.♘5c3 ♘f6 9.0-0 ♗e6 10.♗e3 0-0 11.♘a3 ♘d7 12.♕d2 ♘c5 13.♘c2 f5 14.e×f5 ♗×f5 15.♗f3 ♔h8 16.♗d5 ♕e8 17.♖ad1 ♕g6 18.♘a3 e4 19.f3 Modern engines prefer 19.♘e2. **19...e×f3 20.♗×f3 ♘e5** 20...♗f6!? **21.♘d5 ♗h4 22.♘f4 ♘×f3+ 23.♖×f3 ♕e8 24.♘d5 ♘e6 25.♖df1 ♕g6 26.b3 ♖f7?!** After 26...♗e4!?, Black is certainly not worse. **27.♘c2**

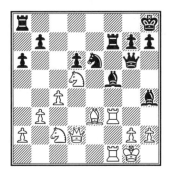

Modern engines prefer 27.c5!?. **27...♘g5?** A tactical oversight. After 27...♖af8, it is more or less equal. **28.♗×g5 ♗×g5 29.♕f2!** ♗×c2 29...♖af8 30.♘d4 ♗e6 31.♘×e6-+ **30.♖×f7 ♗f6**

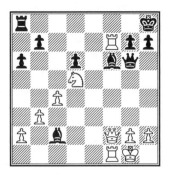

31.♕a7 A typical flashy computer move, which is totally unnecessary. The normal 31.♖×b7 wins as well. **31...♖g8 32.♕×b7 ♗e4 33.♘f4 ♕f5 34.♕d7 ♕e5**

35.♔h1 g5 36.♘h3 g4 37.♘f2 ♗f5 38.♘×g4 ♗e4 38...♗×d7 39.♘×e5 ♗×e5 40.♖×d7 –+ **39.♖7×f6 ♗×g2+ 40.♔×g2 ♕e4+ 41.♔h3 1–0** Allwermann announced mate in eight moves, which is correct but unbelievable to human eyes. From that moment on it was more or less clear that he had used a computer but it was not so clear, how it was done.

> Here Kalinitschev resigned. While they were shaking hands Allwermann couldn't resist mentioning that the final position was mate in eight. "I don't think so," said Kalinitschev. "Check it out, you'll find I'm right," replied Allwermann with a wry smile. …
>
> After the Böblinger Open a number of experts also got to work, analyzing Allwermann's games. They all discovered the same thing: on tournament time controls FRITZ plays most of the other moves Allwermann executed on the board. There was a lot of speculation on how he might have got the moves from the computer. The tournament director in Böblinger recalls that although the temperature in the playing hall was usually 32 degrees Centigrade Allwermann always appeared with a tie and a dark blazer. Some participants speculated that a miniature camera might have been hidden in his tie. The long hair and spectacles could easily have hidden a receiver. Hartmut Metz reports that Allwermann used to run a store for electronic equipment, so the expertise was probably available.

Once technology gets its tentacles enmeshed in something, the changes that occur are dramatic and irreversible. Witness what has happened to the music industry, book stores, newspapers, and the stock exchange, to name only a few. And so it is with chess. By the end of the twentieth century, it was obvious that computers were inexorably changing chess – mostly in good ways.

1998: Backgammon

Gerald Tesauro's program TDGAMMON narrowly loses a 100-game match against World Champion Malcolm Davis. However, a programming error caused a huge point swing in favor of the human. Post-mortem analysis of the match showed that the program made many fewer mistakes than the World Champion. Within a few years, computers were acknowledged to be stronger than humans.

1998: Scrabble

Brian Sheppard's program MAVEN defeats United States Champion Adam Logan by a score of nine wins to five in a match. The following year, MAVEN defeats World Champion Joel Sherman and World Championship Runner-up Matt Graham by a score of six wins to three in a match sponsored by the *New York Times*. MAVEN is considered to be a stronger Scrabble player than any human.

When the aftershocks of Kasparov's loss to DEEP BLUE had subsided, a new round of carbon-based versus silicon-based matches got underway. After all, the Kasparov match result had to be an anomaly. It was inconceivable that DEEP BLUE really was a better player than the man many considered to be the greatest (human) chess player of all time. Chess fans clamored for a rematch.

Alas, it was not to be. IBM concluded that it had "already reaped the equivalent of more than $100 million worth of favorable and free publicity." Playing another match had little media upside, but a huge potential downside if the computer lost. Further, IBM was not all that impressed with Kasparov, as Feng-hsiung Hsu (2005) later related:

> Well, we stop doing serious work on DEEP BLUE a few months after the 1997 match. We were preparing for a new match, as any good sportsman would do. But Kasparov was making all sorts of accusations, and IBM decided not to go on with it. When I left IBM, I got sufficiently mad at Kasparov's accusations and licensed the DEEP BLUE chip technology just in case. I actually tried to set up a match with him at one point but it didn't work. Kasparov wasn't really interested in playing. [He was right to decline. I was planning to create something a hundred to a thousand times faster and capable of beating him with a 100 to 1 time odds. Of course, without telling him first.]

Hence, the decision was made to end the project. The DEEP BLUE machine was dismantled with parts of it being sent to the Smithsonian Museum. A smaller, portable version of the machine with 1/16th of the horsepower, DEEP BLUE JUNIOR, stayed around for a few years to play exhibitions before it too was archived. The DEEP BLUE team was disbanded with most of the members choosing to eventually leave IBM. As Michael Corleone (*The Godfather*) would have said: "It's not personal, [Feng-hsiung, Murray, and Joe]. It's strictly business." It was an ignoble ending to a noble effort.

From the scientific point of view, IBM's decision to end the project was poorly received. There was one scientific data point – a short six-game match – suggesting that computers were better than humans at chess. One of the core tenets of research is to repeat experiments to validate the results for correctness. With the possibility of a rematch eliminated, the world was left to wonder whether the Kasparov result was indicative of the competitor's relative strength, or a mistake that would have been corrected in a rematch. To most scientists (and chess players), the matter of who was better – man or machine – was not yet settled.

With DEEP BLUE out of the way, numerous chess programs rose to the forefront, aided by faster computers, the use of multiple computers, extensive testing, and the careful refinement and addition of chess knowledge. Many of the top teams employed a grandmaster to help prepare the opening book, play test games against the program, and help identify areas for improvement.

Temporal Difference Learning

Consider a simple evaluation function with 100 features. Assume each feature can have an integer weight in the range of -100 (strongly avoid) to 100 (actively encourage). Thus there are 100 features each of which has to be assigned one of 201 values. You can try deciding on the "importance" of each feature by hand, but manually tuning an evaluation function is an incredibly time-consuming processes. Typically you would decide on values based on a chess-player's intuition. This may result in numbers that are close to where they need to be (bishop is worth 3 points), but not completely accurate (3.3 may be a better default). Further the numbers are complicated by interactions; many features interact with other features, resulting in a complexity that is hard for a human to understand, let alone assign definitive values (the real value of a bishop depends on the nature of the position). There had been attempts to automate the process, but none of them led to significant success.

Reinforcement learning is based on a simple idea: good behavior gets positive reinforcement (reward) and bad behavior gets negative reinforcement (penalty). Over time, the entity being trained learns to strive for positive rewards and avoid negative feedback. In the chess context, a feature that is somehow related to success (winning) gets a higher weight (reward) and if correlated with failure (losing) gets a lower weight (penalty). When combined with lots of data, a program "learns" which features are good and which are bad -- and weights them appropriately.

How do you get the data? Self play. Have a program play against itself millions of times. When a game is decisive, have the program analyze the games moves to identify the role that each feature played in the final result. Features which contributed significantly to the result can have their weight increased or decreased appropriately. If you play enough times, the value of a feature will converge to a final result.

Reinforcement learning had been an active subject of research since the 1950s (primarily in Arthur Samuel's checkers-playing program). But in the 1980s Richard Sutton made important improvements to the idea and turned it into a high performance learning algorithm. Gerald Tesauro used Sutton's ideas to build his super-human backgammon program TDGAMMON.

The version of reinforcement learning used in game-playing programs is called temporal difference learning. When the program is in a lost position, say at move 40, one can identify the feature(s) relevant to the position that are responsible for the loss and assign appropriate penalty(s). But the real culprit for the loss may have happened many moves beforehand. Hence, some of the blame has to be passed back to move 39, and then to move 38, and so on. But as you go back further in the game, the certainty about the result lessens. Whereas on move 40 you are 100% confident that you are lost, perhaps on move 39 you are less confident – 95% -- and on move 38 even less – 90%. Thus the credit/blame assigned to features is lessened the further back the analysis goes.

In 1998, Jonathan Baxter, Andrew Tridgell, and Lex Weaver published their results of using temporal difference learning to tune the evaluation function weights of their chess program KNIGHTCAP. Programmers immediately saw it as a way to eliminate the tedium of manual tuning of evaluation functions. Today's learning algorithms scale up to thousands of features: all one has to do is play enough games to allow the learning to converge to stable values for the feature weights.

The most time-consuming and tedious aspect of building a high-performance chess program had been solved.

Other chess knights stepped forward to do battle with the silicon monsters. In 1998, soon-to-be World Champion Viswanathan Anand played an 8-game exhibition match against Ed Schröder's multiple World Computer Chess Champion program,

REBEL. The match featured three time controls, with the computer defeating the human 4½ to 1½ at the fast pace, but losing ½ to 1½ under normal tournament conditions. Many regarded Anand as the best speed chess player in the world, so the computer's domination was disconcerting.

A year later, Anand faced off against FRITZ, drawing a game that gave an insight into a fundamental limitation of computer chess programs (circa 1999, but still true to this day).

Anand, Viswanathan (2781) – FRITZ 6
Frankfurt (2), 03.07.1999

Is it not easy to convert Black's extra bishop because of the reduced material, but no strong human would play the greedy **32...♖×a2?** as it is easy to see that the pin will be eternal after **33.♖dd2** and so a draw was agreed. ½-½

In 2000, for the annual Netherlands Chess Championship, the Dutch Chess Federation made the unprecedented decision to allow a computer into the event. The 12-player round robin featured eight grandmasters, three masters, and FRITZ SSS. The human side was divided over the decision (Ree 2000):

> [Grandmaster Paul] van der Sterren took the principled stand and refused to play FRITZ from the beginning. Known computer killer [Grandmaster John] van der Wiel sums up the reasons he decided to play: "...not only because of the considerably improved prize fund (which was a condition *sine qua non*, of course) but also because I was hoping for two side-effects: firstly this was an opportunity for us to demonstrate to non-experts that Kasparov-DEEP BLUE was a deplorable accident; secondly, if FRITZ did reasonably well in the championship, some computer firms might say: 'Why don't we organize an event with human players and computers?'"

Van Wely, Loek (2646) – FRITZ SSS
English Opening A25
Netherlands Championship (7), Rotterdam, 14.05.2000

1.c4 e5 2.g3 ♘f6 3.♗g2 ♘c6 4.♘c3 ♗b4 5.a3 ♗×c3 6.b×c3 0-0?!

Objectively the move is good and the main line. But under the circumstances FRITZ will not be able to handle the resulting closed position well.

7.e4!

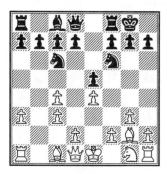

McShane (2000): "This slightly stodgy, positional set-up is ideal computer hunting territory."

7...a6 8.a4!

Prophylaxis is very important. Van Wely handles this aspect very well in the game and keeps matters as simple as possible. This will make FRITZ really look bad.

8...d6 9.d3 ♗g4 10.f3 ♗d7?!

10...♗e6 11.♘e2 ♘d7 with the idea f5 is much more natural. Van Wely was planning 12.g4 to keep the position blocked.

11.♘e2 ♕c8 12.h3!

Again strong prophylaxis.

12...b6?! 13.f4

13...♗e6??

McShane (2000): "It is moves like this that make me wonder if silicon will ever catch the carbon. Van Wely undoubtedly wanted to play [f5] anyway, and instead of seeking counterplay with something like ♕b7 and b5 FRITZ hands over more tempi."

14.f5 ♗d7 15.g4 ♘e8 16.♘g3 ♕d8 17.g5 ♗c8 18.h4 f6 19.♕h5 ♘a5 20.♖a3!

McShane (2000): "I really like this move – nothing spectacular but it sums up the whole strategy, which is ruling out counterplay. ♖b1 would undefend a4 and van Wely is in no hurry to deliver mate."

20...♕e7 21.♘f1

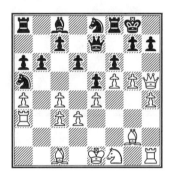

21...♘c6?!

21...g6! 22.f×g6 h×g6 23.♕×g6+ ♕g7 was the last chance to continue the fight. Otherwise White's attack will crash through, which is easy to see or feel for a human but not for a computer.

22.♘e3 ♕d7 23.g6 h6 24.♘g4 ♖a7 25.♖g1 1-0 A very well played anti-computer game.

Van Wely went on to win the Dutch championship and prevented FRITZ from earning the title of Dutch Champion (which would have happened had this game result gone the other way).

In 2000, Amir Ban's and Shay Bushinsky's many-time World Computer Chess Champion program JUNIOR (and its multi-processor variant DEEP JUNIOR) played in a category 19 chess tournament in Dortmund. Against the likes of World Champion Vladimir Kramnik (who defeated Kasparov for the title in 2000), former FIDE World Champion Alexander Khalifman, and challengers Michael Adams, Viswanathan Anand, and Peter Leko, the program scored an impressive 4½ out of 9 for a 2703 performance rating.

Bareev, Evgeny (2702) – DEEP JUNIOR
Queen's Gambit Declined D46
Dortmund SuperGM (1), 07.07.2000

The source for the game moves is ten Geuzendam (2000).

1.c4 e6 2.♘c3 d5 3.d4 c6 4.e3 ♘f6 5.b3 ♘bd7 6.♗b2 ♗d6 7.♘f3 0-0 8.♗d3 ♕e7 9.0-0?!

9.♕c2 scores better.

9...e5! 10.♗e2

Against a human, Bareev would certainly not have played the opening like this as 8.♗e2 would be more consistent. 10.d×e5?! ♘×e5 11.c×d5 ♘×f3+ 12.g×f3 is dangerous against a computer of course.

10...e4 11.♘d2 a6 12.c×d5 c×d5

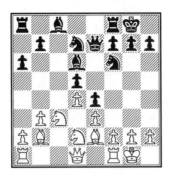

It is already not easy for White, so Bareev tries to get activity by sacrificing a pawn with...

13.b4!?

…which is not quite correct but works in the game.

13...♗×b4 14.♕b3 ♘b8 15.♘a4?!

15.a3 ♗a5 16.a4 gives White more compensation.

15...♕d6!

15...♗×d2? 16.♘b6 ♖a7 17.♗a3 ♕d8 18.♗×f8 ♔×f8 19.♕c2 ♗e6 20.♖ab1 ±

16.♖fd1 ♘c6 17.♗c3 ♗×c3 18.♕×c3 ♗g4 19.♗×g4 ♘×g4 20.♘f1 b5 21.♘c5 ♖fc8 22.♖dc1

22...h5?!

Junior just likes to move its rook's pawns. 22...♘f6 23.♖c2 ♘d7 gives more hope for a black advantage.

23.♖c2 ♘f6 24.♖ac1 ♘e8 25.a4 b4 26.♕e1 h4 27.h3 ♕h6 28.♘b3 ♖c7 29.♕e2 ♖aa7 30.♕g4 ♔f8 31.♘fd2 ♘e7 32.♖×c7 ♖×c7

33.♘c5!

Bareev correctly avoids the exchange of the second rook and has almost sufficient compensation for the pawn.

33...♖a7 34.♘db3

34.a5!?, to regroup with 34...♘d6 35.♕d1 ♘b5 36.♕b3 ♘×d4 37.♕×b4 ♘dc6 38.♕b6, is even more precise.

34...♔g8 35.♕e2 ♘c7 36.a5 ♘b5 37.♕d2 ♘c6 38.♘a4 ♕f6 39.♖c5 ♖c7 40.♕e2

40.♖×d5? is very messy and risky and so Bareev correctly avoids it, e.g., 40...♕e6 41.♘b6 ♘×a5 42.♖d8+ ♔h7 43.♘d5 ♘×b3 44.♕×b4 ♖c1+ 45.♔h2 ♘c5, with unclear consequences.

40...g6 41.♕c2?

41.♘b6 ♕e6 42.♘×d5 ♘c×d4 43.♕c4 ♘e2+ 44.♔f1 ♖d7 45.♘×b4 ♘ec3 46.♘d4=.

41...♔g7?

The preventive 41...♕d6 stops White's counterplay.

42.♕e2?

The more active 42.♘b6 leads, after some complications – 42...♘×a5 43.♘×d5 ♖×c5 44.♘×c5 b3 45.♘×b3 ♕d8 – to equality.

42...♔h8?

A very strange move from the human point of view

42...♕d6 is again called for.

43.♕c2?

Too slow. The more direct 43.♘b6 and 43.♖×d5 ♕e6 44.♕c4 both lead to complete equality.

43...♕d6 44.♕e2 f5 45.♕d1 ♔h7 46.♕e2 ♖f7 47.f4 e×f3 48.♕×f3

48...♘e7?!

The alternative 48...♖e7!? is preferable as the following more or less forced line is difficult to find for a human and the resulting endgame is very promising: 49.♘b6 ♘c×d4 50.♕f2 ♕g3 51.♘×d4 ♘×d4 52.♘×d5 ♖e6 53.♖c7+ ♔h6 54.♔f1 ♕×f2+ 55.♔×f2 ♘c6 56.♘f4 ♖d6 57.♖b7 ♖d2+ 58.♔e1 ♖a2.

49.♕f4 ♕×f4 50.e×f4 ♖f6 51.♘b6 ♖d6 52.♔f2

52...♔h6?!

Quite slow. The direct 52...g5 53.f×g5 ♔g6 54.♘c8 ♘×c8 55.♖×c8 ♔×g5 offers better winning chances as in endings with rooks and knights already a slight initiative is very unpleasant.

53.♘c8 ♘×c8 54.♖×c8 ♔g7 55.♔e3 ♖e6+ 56.♔d3 ♖e1

57.♖c1!

Very precise calculation or good intuition by Bareev. Not 57.♖a8? ♖g1 58.♘c5 b3 59.♘×b3 ♖×g2 60.♖×a6 ♖g3+ 61.♔c2 ♖×h3 62.♖b6 ♘a3+−+.

57...♖×c1 58.♘×c1 ♔f6

58...♘a3 59.♘b3 ♘c4 60.♘c5 ♘×a5 61.♘×a6 ♘c6 62.♘c7 ♔f7 63.♘×d5 b3 64.♔c3 ♔e6 65.♘c7+ ♔d6 66.♘b5+ ♔d5 67.♘c7+=.

59.♘a2 b3 60.♘b4 ♔e6 61.♘×a6 ♔d6 62.♘b4 ♘×d4 63.♔c3 ♘e2+ 64.♔×b3 ♘×f4 65.a6 ♔c7 66.♔c3 g5 67.♔d4 g4

68.♔c5!

His activity saves Bareev. 68.♘×d5+?? runs into the breakthrough 68...♘×d5 69.♔×d5 f4 70.♔e4 f3 71.g×f3 g×h3−+.

68...d4 69.♔×d4 ♘×g2 70.♘d3 g×h3

70...g3 71.♘e5 ♔b6 72.♘f3 ♔×a6 73.♔e5 f4 74.♔e4 ♔b5 75.♘g1 ♔c4 76.♘e2=.

71.♘f2 h2 72.♔e5 f4 73.♔e4 ♔b6 ½-½ A tough battle!

Kramnik, Vladimir (2770) – DEEP JUNIOR
Queen's Pawn Game D00
Dortmund SuperGM (5), 12.07.2000

1.d4 d5 2.e3!? ♘f6 3.♗d3 e6 4.f4 ♗e7 5.♘f3 c5 6.c3 0-0?! 7.♘bd2

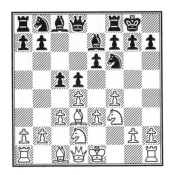

7...♞g4

"The following idea is typical 'computer chess.' I think that a player of master strength would never come up with such an anti-positional idea, but we are talking about the computer program whose playing strength is about 2700! Black closes the center giving White an opportunity to develop the attack without any effort or counterplay" (Finkel 2000). This is a bit harsh as objectively Black's play is not bad as Kramnik later points out. But JUNIOR does not play the resulting positions well, so it is likely that the programmers disallowed c5-c4 after this game.

8.♕e2 c4?! 9.♗c2 f5 10.♖g1

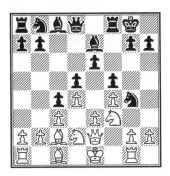

Kramnik (quoted in ten Geuzendam 2000): "A typical anti-computer move I enjoyed playing a lot. A human would immediately understand that my plan is to play h3 and g4 but the computer doesn't."

10...♞c6 11.h3 ♞f6 12.g4 ♞e4 13.♕g2 g6?!

13...♖f7 is preferable according to Kramnik, as in the game he can open lines by advancing his h-pawn.

14.♕h2 ♚h8?! 15.h4

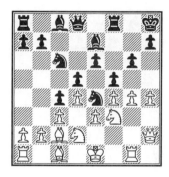

Kramnik (ten Geuzendam 2000): "Actually around this point I was talking to Jeroen Piket and I told him that sooner or later I expected the computer to take on d2, a decision which no human would ever make."

15...♘×d2??

15...f×g4 16.♘×e4 g×f3 17.♘f2 (Kongstad 2003) (17.♘g5 e5) 17...e5 is much stronger and also suits the computer's style better.

16.♗×d2 f×g4 17.♘g5

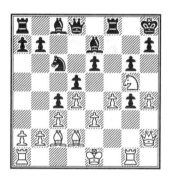

17...♕e8?

Junior played this move instantly. Kramnik (ten Geuzendam 2000): "After the game Amir Ban said that the computer had missed my reply." This is a small surprise, as usually Junior likes to move rook's pawns. In any case it should have taken more time. 17...h6? is also bad because of 18.h5±; So Black should choose between 17...♗×g5 18.h×g5 ♘e7 19.♖×g4 ♘f5 and 17...e5 18.f×e5 ♗f5 19.0-0-0, when White is for choice in both cases but Black can still fight.

18.h5! g×h5 19.♖×g4 ♖f6

19...e5 20.♖h4 e×f4 21.♖×h5 ♗×g5 22.♖×h7+ ♔g8 23.0-0-0+−.

20.♖h4 ♖h6 21.0-0-0 a5

The counterattack is far too slow but Black is lost in any case.

22.♖h1 b5

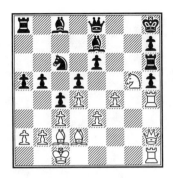

23.♗d1!

Kramnik (ten Geuzendam 2000): "The technical solution 23.♖×h5 ♖×h5 24.♕×h5 ♕×h5 25.♖×h5 ♖a7 26.♖×h7+ ♔g8 was also winning, but I was in a good mood and looking for a direct mate."

23...♖a7 24.♗×h5 ♕f8 25.e4!

Continuing the attack is much stronger than 25.♘f7+ ♕×f7 26.♗×f7 ♗×h4 27.♗e8.

25...♗d8 26.f5 b4

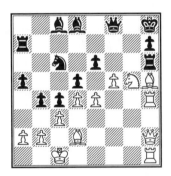

27.♗g6! ♖×h4 28.♕×h4 b×c3 29.b×c3 ♗f6 30.♕×h7+ ♖×h7 31.♖×h7+ ♔g8 32.♗f7+ ♕×f7 33.♖×f7 1-0

JUNIOR resigned in view of 33...♗×g5 34.♖c7 +−. The ease with which Kramnik won this game perhaps instilled a sense of overconfidence. He would soon find out that this game was not typical of what to expect from computers!

Grandmaster Robert Hübner had a spotty record against computers. But in 2001 he agreed to play a six-game match against DEEP FRITZ. He wanted to prove a point that the time had not yet come for a human grandmaster playing solidly to be overthrown by the likes of FRITZ. He played the match in his usual steadfast style.

DEEP FRITZ – Hübner, Robert (2612)
French Defense C01
Dortmund match (3), 18.07.2001

1.e4 e6 2.d4 d5 3.e×d5 e×d5 4.♘f3 ♘f6 5.c4 ♗b4+ 6.♘c3 0-0 7.♗e2 d×c4 8.♗×c4 ♗g4 9.0-0 ♘c6 10.♗e3 ♕d7 11.a3 ♗a5 12.♖c1 ♖ad8 13.♘a4 ♗b6 14.♘×b6 a×b6 15.b4 ♕d6

16.b5?

FRITZ overplays its hand. This just weakens the whole queenside while Black's a5-knight is not as bad as it looks. The game is equal after 16.h3 ♗h5 17.♖e1 ♖fe8 18.g4 ♗g6 19.♕b3.

16...♘a5 17.♗e2 ♘d5 18.♕d3 ♖fe8

19.♘g5!?

FRITZ plays a Tal-like speculative piece sacrifice, which is probably not correct! White's position is uncomfortable in any case.

19...♗×e2 20.♕×h7+ ♔f8 21.♖fe1 ♘×e3 22.♖×e2 ♕h6 23.f×e3 ♕×g5 24.♖×c7 ♕h6 25.♕×h6 g×h6 26.♔f2

26...♖c8?

26...♖d5 27.a4 ♖f5+ 28.♔g1 ♘b3 29.g4 ♖g5 30.h3 ♖e7 is a more precise realization of Hübner's plan, with some winning chances.

27.♖ec2 ♖×c7 28.♖×c7 ♖e7 29.♖c8+ ♖e8 30.♖c7 f5

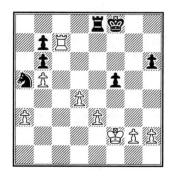

31.♔f3?

31.g3, with the idea 31...♖e7 32.♖c8+ ♔f7 33.♔e2 ♔f6 34.♔d3, offered much better drawing chances.

31...♖e7 32.♖c8+ ♔f7 33.♔f4 ♔e6 34.♖f8?! ♖f7 35.d5+?!

Weakening the d-pawn, but White's position is very difficult in any case.

35...♔e7

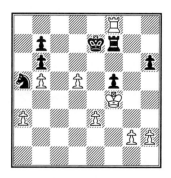

Now FRITZ exchanges into a technically lost endgame with...

36.♖×f7+?

The rook should be kept on the board with 36.♖h8 or 36.♖g8 with better practical chances.

36...♔×f7 37.♔×f5 ♘c4 38.e4 ♘×a3 39.g4 ♘×b5 40.e5

40.h4 ♘d4+ 41.♔f4 b5 42.♔e3 ♘c2+ 43.♔d2 ♘b4 44.h5 ♘a6 45.g5 h×g5 46.e5 ♘c7 47.e6+ ♘×e6−+ .

40...♘c7 41.d6

41.e6+ ♔e7 42.♔e5 ♘e8−+ (Hübner and Hecht 2001).

41...♘e6 42.h4 b5 43.g5 ♘g7+ 44.♔e4

And now Hübner misses his chance with...

44...h×g5?

He should keep as many pawns on the board as possible with 44...h5! 45.♔d5 b4 46.g6+ (46.♔c4 ♘e6 47.♔×b4 ♘f8 48.♔c5 ♔e6−+).

46...♔f8!! (Of course not 46...♔×g6?? 47.d7+−) 47.♔c4 ♘e6 48.♔×b4 ♔g7 49.♔b5 ♔×g6 50.♔b6 ♔f5 51.♔×b7 ♔×e5−+.

45.h×g5 b4 46.♔d3 ♔g6 47.♔c4 ♔×g5 48.♔×b4 ♔f5 49.♔c5 ♔×e5 50.♔b6 ♔×d6 ½-½ A far from perfect game, but entertaining nevertheless.

The final score was 3 to 3 – all games were drawn. Hübner was never in trouble in the match, thereby proving his point that solid play was a drawing (but not winning) recipe against computers.

David Bronstein (2002)
Grandmaster

In discussing whether humans should play computers at chess, Bronstein replied:

We must, because you'll never find a better teacher. In the first place, it brings humans down to earth: don't stick your nose in the air, don't think that you can see something. You're not a magician! Secondly, by its actions, which are absolutely free of prejudice, it can teach us not to be afraid of difficult positions... The computer suggests to humans new technical methods and helps teach us not to think like a stencil. For example, ever since the time of Capablanca it has been accepted that it is not good to move the same piece twice in the opening, or that you shouldn't bring your queen out early in the game. The computer is phenomenal at refuting these human misconceptions, which have become firmly embedded in our brains. It takes ideal advantage of the strength of the queen, making it do unbelievable pirouettes on the board. Humans cannot play that way. That means we have to learn. The computer teaches humans to sense the geometry of the chessboard better. It reminds us that it isn't necessary to play with plans and ideas, but it's possible to play one move at a time… Can humans learn? They can. There are many capable students. Yes, man has something to learn from the computer. He must always keep it available as a partner. Not making it into an enemy, not trying to slay the Dragon. I could end on this optimistic note if I didn't know for a certainty that they won't be satisfied with this. They are the people who have an insatiable desire to slay the Dragon, and the programmers who want to prove that their Dragon can subdue the imagination of Man.

Surely someone could restore the chess world order and put the upstart computers in their place. World Champion Vladimir Kramnik bravely took up the challenge. He agreed to play an 8-game match against DEEP FRITZ in Bahrain. FRITZ was given the right to play Kramnik by virtue of winning a match against its electronic rival JUNIOR in 2001.

Kramnik had an advantage that Kasparov did not. The DEEP FRITZ software was frozen several months before the start of the match, and Kramnik was given that version to practice against. He could learn its strengths, probe it for weaknesses, and test out how effective different strategies would fare against the program.

Would Kramnik be able to restore the honor of humanity? Chess fans had waited five long years since the stinging defeat of Kasparov for a chance to get revenge. The hope was that Kramnik would erase the stain on chess by beating DEEP FRITZ. Then the ball would be back in the computer's court.

Game one was a draw. And then the fireworks started.

2002: Awari

Henri Bal and John Romein create a program to solve the African pebble game of Awari. Perfect play by both sides leads to a draw.

Kramnik, Vladimir (2807) – DEEP FRITZ
Queen's Gambit Accepted D27
Bahrain match (2), 06.10.2002

Kramnik has crafted a good strategy with the white pieces against DEEP FRITZ. It is one he also has used in his regular games with good success. He exchanged queens quickly and set up a closed position with just two open files, both of which were easy to control. This minimized the danger of tactical surprises by the computer and retained the chance of winning the endgame with his fantastic technique.

1.d4 d5 2.c4 d×c4 3.♘f3 ♘f6 4.e3 e6 5.♗×c4 c5 6.0-0 a6 7.d×c5 ♕×d1 8.♖×d1

This does not look ambitious, but Kramnik knows how to keep increasing the slight advantage in such positions.

8...♗×c5

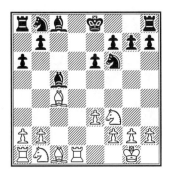

9.♔f1!?

Did Kramnik want to throw FRITZ out of its openings book? Here are some of the games Kramnik has played against his opponents after Black's 8th move: 9.♘bd2 b6 10.♗e2 ♘bd7 11.♘c4 (11.♘b3 ♗e7 12.♘fd4 ♗b7 13.f3 0-014.e4 ♖fc8 15.♗e3 ♔f8 16.♘d2 ♘e5 17.♘4b3 ♖c6 18.♖ac1 ♖ac8 19.♖×c6 ♖×c6 20.g4 h6 21.h4 ♗c8 22.g5 h×g5 23.h×g5 ♘fd7 24.f4 ♘g6 25.♘f3 ♖c2? 26.♗×a6 with a clear White advantage in Kramnik-Kasparov, Braingames World Championship London 2000, which was drawn later.) 11...♗b7 12.b3 ♔e7?! (12...0-0 13.♗b2 ♗d5 14.♖ac1 ♖fc8 15.♘fe5 b5 16.♘×d7 ♘×d7 17.♘d2 ♗b4 18.♘b1 ♘b6 19.f3 ♖×c1 20.♖×c1 ♖c8 21.♖×c8+ ♘×c8 22.♗a3 ♗×a3 23.♘×a3 b4 24.♘c2 a5 25.♗a6 ♘b6 26.e4 ♗c6 27.♔f2 ½-½ Kramnik-Lautier, Monte Carlo 1997) 13.♗b2 ♖hd8 14.♘e1 b5 15.♘a5 ♗e4 16.♗f3 ♗×f3 17.g×f3 ♖dc8 18.♘d3 ♖ab8 19.♘×c5 ♖×c5 20.♖ac1 ♔e8 21.♗d4 ♖×c1 22.♖×c1 ♖a8 23.♔f1 e5 24.♗b2 ♘d5 25.♖d1 ♘e7 26.♘b7 and White had a pleasant initiative in Kramnik-Karpov, Frankfurt 1999 and he went on to win.

9...b5?!

Giving White the a4-lever directly. 9...♘bd7 is more precise.

10.♗e2 ♗b7 11.♘bd2 ♘bd7 12.♘b3

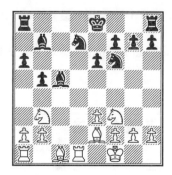

12...♗f8?!

This move is not entirely convincing. In any case, a human being would hardly have played this "undeveloping" retreat. They would choose between 12...♗b6 and 12...♗e7.

13.a4!

A typical strategy to fight for squares on the queenside and to create weaknesses in the opponent's position.

13...b4 14.♘fd2!

Kramnik mobilizes his knight to occupy the c4-square, which he has just secured. From here it can keep a dangerous watch on Black's position.

14...♗d5?!

This move is hard to like, as White wants to play f3 followed by e4 anyway. But good advice is already difficult to give as, e.g., after 14...♘c5 15.♘a5, White is also pressing.

15.f3 ♗d6 16.g3 e5 17.e4 ♗e6 18.♘c4 ♗c7 19.♗e3

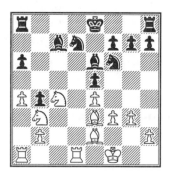

19...a5

This kind of move is never pleasant, because the b5-square and the a5-pawn become very weak. But there was no real alternative. White has achieved a nicely dominating position, the kind that is very comfortable against a computer because Black has hardly any counterplay. Black would like to complete his development by castling and then mobilize his king's rook. It is for this reason that Kramnik executes the following maneuver; he is determined to keep the initiative.

20.♘c5

20.♖ac1!?

20...♘×c5 21.♗×c5 ♘d7 22.♘d6+ ♔f8

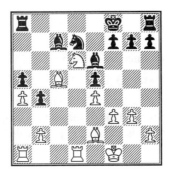

22...♔e7? 23.♘f5+ ♔f6 24.♗e7+ ♔g6 25.♖ac1±.

23.♗f2?

Kramnik misses the direct 23.♘b5+ ♘×c5 24.♘×c7 ♖c8 25.♖ac1 ♗h3+ 26.♔g1 ♘b3 27.♗a6 that gives him a strategically won position.

23...♗×d6

DEEP FRITZ gives up the pair of bishops in order to release some of the pressure. But Kramnik gets a permanent advantage. 23...♔e7 24.♘f5+ is also very pleasant for White.

24.♖×d6 ♔e7 25.♖ad1

25.♖c6 is the alternative.

25...♖hc8 26.♗b5 ♘c5!!

This looks like a tactical blunder. But we must remember that Black is a computer that will never overlook something as shallow as this.

27.♗c6 ♗c4+!

Kramnik confessed later that he had completely overlooked this move and was horrified because he thought he was lost. "But after a few seconds I saw a way to force the draw with perpetual check, and so I calmed down and started to look for a way to win." He found it in a very subtle rook endgame. 27...♖a6?? 28.♗×c5 ♖a×c6 29.♖×c6++– with check; 27...♖×c6? 28.♖×c6 ♘×a4 29.♖d2±.

28.♔e1 ♘d3+ 29.♖1×d3 ♗×d3 30.♗c5!

30.♖×d3?? ♖×c6–+.

30...♗c4

30...♗c2 31.♔d2 ♗×a4?? is refuted by 32.♖d5+ ♔f6 33.♗×a4+–.

31.♖d4+ ♔f6 32.♖×c4 ♖×c6 33.♗e7+ ♔×e7 34.♖×c6

The resulting rook endgame is better for White because the black rook is tied to the passive defense of the a-pawn. One of the main principles of rook endings is activity. The rook is useless if it is engaged in passive defensive tasks.

34...♔d7

34...♖d8 35.♔e2 doesn't help.

35.♖c5

35...f6?

After this Black is condemned to passivity. Maxim Notkin (2002) proved that 35...♖c8 is better because after 36.♖×a5 ♖c2 it is a draw. The point, however, is so deep that even DEEP FRITZ would have difficulty finding it. This is the main line continuation of Notkin's analysis: 36.♖×c8 ♔×c8 37.♔d2 ♔d7 38.♔d3 ♔d6 39.♔c4 ♔c6.

Black has the opposition and White cannot win the tempo battle: 40.h4 g6 41.g4 h5 42.g5 ♔d6 43.♔b5 f6 44.g×f6 g5 45.h×g5 ♔e6 46.♔×a5 h4= and the final queen endgame is drawn.

36.♔d2 ♔d6 37.♖d5+ ♔c6 38.♔d3 g6?!

In the next phase Deep Fritz only weakens its own position. 38...♖a7 seems to me to be tougher.

39.♔c4 g5 40.h3 h6 41.h4 g×h4 42.g×h4 ♖a7

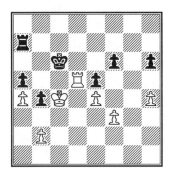

43.h5!

Do not rush! Kramnik has all the time in the world to improve his position before resorting to ♖d8. In such positions, it is wise to restrain oneself and first maximize the strength of one's position.

43...♖a8

Now Kramnik embarks on a maneuver in order to force Fritz to concede ground. He could achieve this with b3, but that gives up a possible waiting move later on. Kramnik really plays this endgame superbly. Rubinstein or Capablanca would have loved to watch it!

44.♖c5+

44.♔d3 with the plan ♔e3 and f4 was also a possibility.

44...♔b6 45.♖b5+

Naturally not 45.♔d5?? ♖d8+ 46.♔c4 ♖d4+ −+ .

45...♚c6 46.♖d5

Zugzwang.

46...♚c7?

46...♖a7 47.♖d8 ♖c7 48.♖f8 ♚b6+ should also be lost for Black, but it is more active and less pleasant for Kramnik.

47.♚b5 b3 48.♖d3 ♖a7 49.♖×b3 ♖b7+ 50.♚c4 ♖a7

The pawn ending after 50...♖×b3 51.♚×b3 ♚b6 52.♚c4 ♚c6 53.b4 +− is lost because of the outside white passed pawn.

51.♖b5 ♖a8 52.♚d5 ♖a6 53.♖c5+ ♚d7 54.b3 ♖d6+

54...♖a7 55.♖b5 ♚e7 56.♚c6 ♖a8 57.♚b7 ♖d8 58.♖×a5 +− .

55.♚c4 ♖d4+ 56.♚c3 ♖d1 57.♖d5+ and the FRITZ team resigned as the transition into the pawn ending is the simplest way to victory. **1-0** For example, 57...♖×d5 58.e×d5 ♚d6 59.b4 a×b4+ 60.♚×b4 ♚×d5 61.♚b5 ♚d6 (61...f5 62.a5 e4 63.f×e4+ f×e4 64.a6 e3 65.a7 e2 66.a8♕ +−) 62.a5 f5 63.a6 ♚c7 64.♚c5 e4 65.f×e4 f×e4 66.♚d4 ♚b6 67.♚×e4 ♚×a6 68.♚f5 ♚b6 69.♚g6 ♚c7 70.♚×h6 ♚d7 71.♚g7 +− .

Kramnik is now up by one game in the match.

Deep Fritz – Kramnik, Vladimir (2807)
Scotch Game C45
Bahrain match (3), 08.10.2002

DEEP FRITZ avoided the Berlin Wall (which Kramnik so successfully used to defeat Kasparov in their 2000 title match) by opting for the Scotch. But Kramnik has a good anti-computer strategy prepared for that as well. One must agree that his preparation for this encounter is excellent.

Vladimir Kramnik (left) versus Deep Fritz, operated by co-author Matthias Feist, in the "Brains in Bahrain" match.
(ChessBase)

1.e4 e5 2.♘f3 ♘c6 3.d4 e×d4 4.♘×d4 ♗c5 5.♘×c6

The main continuation. White hopes to thwart the black initiative with b×c6 and then to mobilize his kingside pawn majority.

5...♛f6 6.♛d2 d×c6 7.♘c3

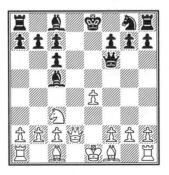

7...♘e7

Kramnik probably wants to throw Fritz out of its openings book. Did he know at this point that it would later play a2-a3? In the world championship match Kasparov-Short, the following line was "debated": 7...♗e6 8.♘a4 ♜d8 9.♗d3 ♗d4 10.0-0 ♘e7 (10...a6 11.♘c3 ♘e7 12.♘e2 ♗b6 13.♛f4 ♘g6 14.♛×f6 g×f6 15.♘g3 h5 16.♗e2 h4 17.♘f5 ♗×f5 18.e×f5 ♘e5 19.♖e1 ♔f8 20.♗f4 ♖d4 21.g3 ♔g7 22.♖ad1 ♖e4 23.♔g2 h×g3 24.h×g3 ♗×f2 25.♔×f2 ♖h2+ 26.♔f1 ♖e×e2 27.♖×e2 ♖h1+ 28.♔f2 ♖×d1 29.b3 ♖d7 30.♖d2 ♖×d2+ 31.♗×d2 c5 32.♔e3 c6 33.♔e4 c4 34.b4 b5 35.♗f4 ♘d7 36.♔d4 ♔f8 37.♗c7 ♔e7 38.g4 ♔f8 39.♗d6+ ♔g7 40.♗c7 ♔f8 41.a3 ½-½ Kasparov-Short, London 1993) 11.c3 b5 12.c×d4 ♕×d4 13.♕c2 ♕×a4 14.♕×a4 b×a4 15.♗c2 ♗c4 16.♖e1 ♗b5 17.♗e3 ♘c8 18.♗c5 ♘b6 19.♖ad1 ♖×d1 20.♖×d1 a6 21.f4 ♘d7 22.♗a3 h5 23.♔f2 ♖h6 24.e5 c5 25.♗f5 ♖b6 26.♖d2 g6 27.♗c2 ♖e6 28.♔g3 ♘b6 29.♗×c5 ♘c4 30.♖d5 ♘×b2 31.f5 ♗c6 32.♖d2 g×f5 33.♔f4 ♘c4 34.♖e2 f6 35.♗×f5 ♖×e5 36.♗d3 ♗d5 37.♗d4 ♖×e2 38.♗×e2 ♔e7 39.♗×h5 ♗×g2 40.♗d1 a3 41.h4 ♗d5 42.h5 ♘e5 43.h6 ♗×a2 44.♗c5+ ♔f7 45.♗c2 ♗c4 46.h7 ♔g7 47.♗f8+ ♔h8 48.♗e7 ♗d3 49.♗×f6+ ♔×h7 50.♗×e5 ♗×c2 ½-½ Kasparov-Short, London 1993.

8.♕f4 ♗e6 9.♕×f6

Naturally FRITZ does not fall for 9.♕×c7?? ♕×f2+ 10.♔d1 ♖d8+ −+ .

9...g×f6

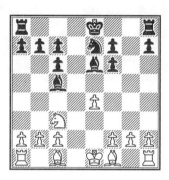

Once again Kramnik has succeeded in reaching a position without queens, one which he understands much better than FRITZ. Somehow it all looks so easy when he does it, but if I (KM) think of my blitz games against the program, things are very different there.

10.♘a4 ♗b4+

It is good to provoke ...c3 and weaken the d3-square for White. Apart from that, the knight on a4 now looks a little strange.

11.c3 ♗d6 12.♗e3 b6 13.f4 0-0-0 14.♔f2 c5 15.c4 ♘c6 16.♘c3 f5!

The position should remain closed.

17.e5 ♗f8

Introducing the idea of ♗g7 and f6.

18.b3?!

This weakens the position more than being useful. 18.♘d5 was also possible and may have been better suited to FRITZ's "natural" abilities.

18...♘b4!

This move came after a 30-minute think by Kramnik and was hailed in the pressroom as pure brilliancy. "It is as though Kramnik was the computer, finding a fantastic resource that no human would ever consider," said one leading grandmaster. Others speculated that Kramnik has learned a lot from his preparation with the computer. After 18...♗g7?!, the move 19.♘d5 would have been better, e.g., 19...♗xd5 20.cxd5 ♖xd5 21.♗c4 ♖d7 22.♖ad1 and Fritz would have had a better understanding than in the game.

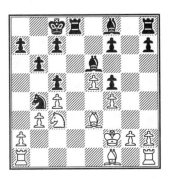

19.a3?

This move in not appealing. The pawns on a3 and b3 are weak, and Black can remove one of the two bishops. 19.♖c1 makes a better impression. White should first try to get the situation under control and then work Black's kingside weakness.

19...♘c2 20.♖c1 ♘xe3 21.♔xe3 ♗g7!

With the idea of playing f6, in order to open the position for the bishop.

22.♘d5?

Now it is too late and loses too much time. 22.♗d3 f6 23.exf6 ♗xf6 24.♖he1 is the lesser evil.

22...c6! 23.♘f6 ♗xf6 24.exf6 ♖he8

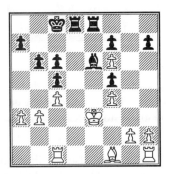

Black is much too active. Fritz has neglected its development and does not have the situation under control.

25.♔f3 ♖d2 26.h3

A human being would hardly have played this move. But there are not any reasonable alternatives. Now Kramnik's excellent technique comes into play.

26...♗d7 27.g3

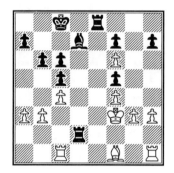

27...♖e6

Any potential counterplay with the pawn on f6 is eliminated – exactly what Capablanca would have done in this position.

28.♖b1 ♖xf6 29.♗e2

Now the bishop has moved, but it still makes a sad impression.

29...♖e6 30.♖he1

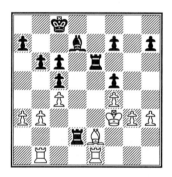

30...♔c7!

First bring all your pieces into play, remembering that the king is an important attacking entity in the endgame. Then advance on the queenside, or attack the enemy pawns. This plan cannot be stopped.

31.♗f1 b5!?

31...♖xe1 32.♖xe1 ♖b2 33.♖e3 b5 was also possible, but Kramnik does not want to allow White any counterplay at all. After all he does not need to!

32.♖ec1 ♔b6 33.b4?!

And this backfires. But White was lost in a higher sense anyway.

33...c×b4 34.a×b4 ♖e4! 35.♖d1 ♖×d1 36.♖×d1 ♗e6! 37.♗d3 ♖d4 38.♗e2?!

38.♔e3 c5 39.b×c5+ ♔×c5 40.c×b5 ♗c4 41.♗c2 ♖×d1 42.♗×d1 ♗×b5 should also be winning for Black.

38...♖×d1 39.c5+ ♔b7 40.♗×d1 a5!−+

…and it is all over…

41.b×a5 ♔a6 42.♔e3 ♔×a5 43.♔d4 b4 44.g4 f×g4 45.h×g4 b3 46.♔c3 ♔a4 47.♔b2 f6 48.♗f3 ♔b5 49.g5 f5 50.♔c3 ♔×c5 51.♗e2 0-1

The FRITZ team resigned in view of 51...♔b6 52.♗d1 ♔b5 53.♗e2+ ♔a4 54.♔b2 ♔b4 55.♗f3 c5−+. A wonderful performance!

The rout was on! These are the kind of results that chess players around the world had hungered for since 1997.

Game 4 was draw, and Kramnik led by a score of 3 to 1 at the halfway point in the match. Given Kramnik's reputation for solid play, the rest of the match was a mere formality.

DEEP FRITZ – Kramnik, Vladimir (2807)
Queen's Gambit Declined D57
Bahrain match (5), 13.10.2002

Is Kramnik again able to exchange queens early and keep everything under control? No. This time it is different…

1.d4

No more 1.e4 as FRITZ's experience with it in this match was not pleasant.

1...♘f6 2.c4 e6 3.♘f3 d5 4.♘c3 ♗e7 5.♗g5 h6 6.♗h4 0-0 7.e3 ♘e4

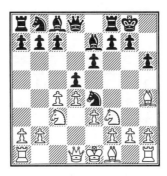

The Lasker Variation has a rock solid reputation. Another advantage is that some pieces are usually exchanged early.

8.♗×e7 ♕×e7 9.c×d5 ♘×c3 10.b×c3 e×d5 11.♕b3 ♖d8 12.c4 d×c4 13.♗×c4 ♘c6 14.♗e2

DEEP FRITZ does not want to exchange its bishop after ♘a5, of course.

14...b6!?

The following bishop fianchetto secures Black's queenside.

15.0-0 ♗b7

Curiously this position had already arisen in the game between Kramnik (White) and his second in Bahrain, Christopher Lutz, in 1994. Kramnik (2002a) evaluated it as completely equal.

16.♖fc1

16.♖ac1 ♘a5 17.♕b2 ♖ac8=, Kramnik-Lutz, Germany 1994.

16...♖ac8 17.♕a4 ♘a5

A typical maneuver to get rid of the backward pawn on c7 and to activate Black's rooks.

18.♖c3 c5 19.♖ac1 c×d4 20.♘×d4

In the game Kosyrev-Podgaets, Moscow 2002, a draw was agreed at this point.

20...♖×c3 21.♖×c3 ♖c8

Kramnik wants to exchange more pieces, underscoring his queenside majority.

22.♖×c8+ ♗×c8 23.h3

23...g6?!

There is not much to like about this move, as White gets pressure and the initiative. Worthy of consideration is 23...♕d7!?.

24.♗f3

"DEEP FRITZ has some pressure. The ♘a5 is badly placed." (Schulz 2002)

24...♗d7 25.♕c2 ♕c5

26.♕e4!

FRITZ does not want to exchange queens, of course. 26.♕×c5? b×c5 and Black has the clearly better endgame.

26...♕c1+ 27.♔h2 ♕c7+ 28.g3 ♘c4

The knight has to come back to help defend the dark squares around Black's king.

29.♗e2 ♘e5 30.♗b5

30.♗f1 is interesting as well, to keep more pieces on the board.

30...♗×b5 31.♘×b5 ♕c5 32.♘×a7

32...♕a5?!

The active 32...♕c3 33.♕a8+ ♔g7 34.♕d5 ♔g8 35.♘c8 ♕c2 36.♔g1 ♘d3 gives Black more counterplay.

33.♔g2 ♕×a2 34.♘c8

289

34...♛c4??

An unbelievable tactical blunder. One suspects that Kramnik would have seen this against a human. 34...♞c4?! 35.♞e7+ ♚g7 36.♛d4+ ♚h7 37.♞d5 looks dangerous.; 34...♛e6!? was called for as the endgame after 35.♞xb6 ♛xb6 36.♛xe5 gives Black's drawing chances. But DEEP FRITZ has access to the endgame database Q+P vs. Q so Kramnik would have to defend extremely long and tenaciously to escape, if this is possible at all.

Kramnik (2018) describes how hard it is to play against a computer, and the level of concentration required can lead to blunders:

> I can stress one thing which I understood playing with computers these kind of matches, that basically you spend much more energy. I mean, it's much more tiring than playing a human being, because you need to keep a very high level of concentration for the full game. Against a human player, you can miss something. First of all, he might also not see some hidden tactics. Secondly, even if he sees you're much worse, but you can maybe trick him in time trouble. There is always a chance. With a computer, if you miss something tactical, simply, you have no chance. I mean, you are much worse, and you will lose. So that's why it requires much higher level of concentration. You're sitting there, and you just check for any kind of possible small tactics, which you wouldn't do against a human being, because it obviously shouldn't work. But with computer, you check everything. And then, of course, I think that's why…I was making these bad blunders, which I usually was not making at this time at least against human players. So I think that this kind of high level of concentration, it leads to some blackout at some point.

35.♞e7+ and Kramnik resigned as after 35...♚f8 36.♛xe5 +−, the knight e7 is protected by White's queen. **1−0**

A stunning end to a hard fought game. Grandmasters aren't supposed to make trivial blunders. But Kramnik is human after all, and we can all be forgiven for the occasional *faux pas*. *Time Magazine* reported on the surprising result (Hoffman, 2002):

> Vladimir Kramnik made the worst blunder of his career and arguably the biggest error ever made by a world chess champion. He lost a knight in a one-move combination on the thirty-fourth move and resigned immediately. …

> After the game, a dejected Kramnik did his best to appear unfazed. "I do not

blunder often," he told the spectators. "It's not a big problem. I just need to be more concentrated. Such things can happen any time." He conceded that he was tired. "We will go back to the hotel," he said, "and reconsider our approach."

Although Kramnik hung himself in this game, the machine deserves credit for putting him under so much stress that he collapsed.

But… being human meant that Kramnik was vulnerable to the psychological impact of his blunder. Could he maintain his equanimity?

The grandmasters who were watching said that it may be psychologically difficult for him to recover from such a colossal mistake. In the next game, they said, he'll waste time and energy second-guessing even obvious moves.

Kramnik, Vladimir (2807) – Deep Fritz
Queen's Indian Defense E15
Bahrain match (6), 15.10.2002

1.d4 ♘f6

This time Fritz avoids d7-d5, which makes it easier for Kramnik to choose quiet systems.

2.c4 e6 3.♘f3 b6 4.g3 ♗a6 5.b3 ♗b4+ 6.♗d2 ♗e7

This looks like a loss of tempo, but White's bishop on d2 is badly placed.

7.♗g2 c6 8.♗c3 d5 9.♘e5 ♘fd7 10.♘×d7 ♘×d7 11.♘d2 0-0 12.0-0 ♖c8 13.a4

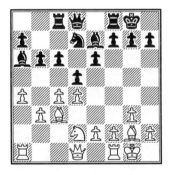

13...♗f6?!

This gives white a dangerous initiative. 13...c5 is better.

14.e4 c5 15.e×d5 c×d4 16.♗b4 ♖e8 17.♘e4!? e×d5

Deep Fritz is playing with fire. But it has managed to lead the play into tactical complications, an area where it feels like a fish in water.

18.♘d6 d×c4

19.♘×f7?!

A Tal-like sacrifice and an amazingly bold and courageous decision. But not a good one, as FRITZ is a very tenacious defender. 19.♗d5! was the right way, e.g., 19...♘c5 20.♗×f7+ ♚f8 21.♗×e8 ♛×d6 22.♗b5 and White is for choice.

19...♚×f7 20.♗d5+ ♚g6 21.♛g4+

21.b×c4? is answered by 21...♘e5 and Black defends.

21...♗g5 22.♗e4+

22.h4? ♘c5 23.b×c4 h5!−+ ; 22.f4? h5 23.♗f7+ ♚×f7 24.f×g5+ ♚g8 25.♛×h5 ♘e5 26.g6 ♘×g6 27.♛×g6 ♛d7 −+ (Schulz 2002).

22...♖×e4 23.♛×e4+ ♚h6!

FRITZ avoids the draw by 23...♚f7 24.♛d5+ as it has found amazing defensive resources in its calculations.

24.h4 ♗f6 25.♗d2+ g5

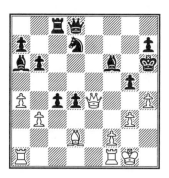

26.h×g5+?

After this mistake the game is lost in the long run, as White's attack will peter out. It is a pity that Kramnik's courage was not rewarded! The last real chance to fight for a draw was 26.b×c4 ♚g7 (26...d3 27.♛×d3 ♚g7 28.♗×g5 ♗×c4 29.♗×f6+ ♘×f6 30.♛×d8 ♖×d8 31.♖fc1) 27.h×g5 ♗×g5 28.♗×g5 ♛×g5 29.a5 and White still has drawing chances in both cases.

Kramnik (2018) reflects on the key decisions he made in this game:

FRITZ, at that time, like practically all chess programs, they were underestimating attack and piece sacrifice. So I started to calculate variations. I had a safe way to play probably a little better, equal, whatever. And then I saw that, it might simply win. And actually, it was not winning by one little move. There was some defense that I missed in the calculation. But then I thought it might be a way to trick the computer. It simply underestimated, and then it didn't look very deeply into this variation, into this sacrifice, and finally maybe after one, two moves, it will realize that it simply lost. Which was happening. I played quite a lot of training games, rapid training games before the match, and it was happening pretty often in fact with the computer. So I thought it might be a good chance for me to win a game, to get in plus two, and most probably to win a match, because then I needed only one draw out of two games. And, okay, I decided I was calculating. I spent a lot of time calculating. I thought everything works, and then I need some defense, and so on. So, I would say that it was not a kind of speculative thing or it was not a blunder. I mean, it was basically quite well thought and well measured decision, which didn't work. ... So I was trying not to sit in defense, but maybe to try to win another game.

26...♗×g5 27.♕h4+?!

Kramnik had planned 27.♕e6+ ♘f6 (27...♕f6? 28.♗×g5+ ♔×g5 29.♕×d7 +−) 28.f4.

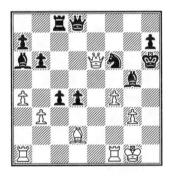

...but had missed the beautiful 28...♗h4!!, the point being 29.g×h4 ♕g8+. (Note that 28.♕h3+ is better than the game but Black is nevertheless clearly for choice after 28...♔g6! 29.f4 ♗h6 30.f5+ ♔f7 31.♕×h6 c×b3) A typical computer defense! In this respect humans do not stand a chance against the brute-force approach of the machines. You just cannot calculate every possible move in your head.

27...♔g6 28.♕e4+ ♔g7 29.♗×g5 ♕×g5 30.♖fe1 c×b3 31.♕×d4+ ♘f6 32.a5

32...♕d5?

The result of a misevaluation of the resulting endgames. This is one of the few areas where humans are still superior to the machines. But Kramnik has most probably lost hope and does not fight to the end. One of the many disadvantages of mortals. 32...♕c5 wins easily, as after 33.♕×c5, Black can take back with the pawn, 33...b×c5−+ .

33.♕×d5 ♘×d5 34.a×b6 a×b6

and Kramnik resigned. **0–1**

But the position is drawn!

The computer most probably evaluated the subsequent fortresses incorrectly because of its large material superiority: 35.♖×a6 b2 36.♖a7+ ♚g6 (36...♚f8 then 37.♖d7 ♘c3 38.♖d2 b1♕ 39.♖×b1 ♘×b1 40.♖b2 ♘c3 41.♖×b6

294

…and Black's winning potential has been reduced too much) 37.♖d7 ♖c1 38.♖d6+ ♘f6 39.♖dd1 b1♕ 40.♖xc1 ♕f5 41.♖c6! b5 42.♖ee6 b4 43.♖b6 h5 44.♖xf6+ ♕xf6 45.♖xb4=

and White's fortress is impregnable.

The British newspaper *The Independent* (2000) chimed in with a philosophical look at the result of game six:

> You thought it was all over. Man versus machine, that great theme of science fiction, played itself out when Garry Kasparov lost to DEEP BLUE in 1997. But just when computers thought they ruled the (chess) world, Man changed the rules. That is the thing about Men: they may not be able to calculate 3.5 billion moves per second, but they are clever. So when Vladimir Kramnik took on DEEP BLUE's successor, DEEP FRITZ, he was given two weeks to study his opponent's playing style. Mr. Kramnik started well, but lost yesterday, bringing the score to 3-3. His reaction was a substantial contribution to the archive of sport as philosophy. "I am not so depressed – the result is not positive, but the game was a pleasure," he said. "There were some beautiful moves. I did the right thing from a human point of view." When they invent a computer that can improvise that kind of solace in defeat, then and only then will machine's battle for supremacy have been won.

One line needs repetition: "the result is not positive, but the game was a pleasure." These are the words of a worthy champion and a great sport.

The last two match games were drawn, resulting in a final score of 4 points to 4. Once again, a World Champion failed to defeat a computer program in a match.

Kramnik (2002b) was interviewed soon after the match and had this to say about the play:

Are you happy with the quality of the games?

I showed a good level of chess, especially in the first half of the match. But even in the games I lost I cannot say that I played badly. I made one mistake in each of those games, but only one, and that was enough.

What did you think of FRITZ's play?

There were not so many games where it played strangely. In many games it was simply like playing a strong human grandmaster, it was absolutely normal, absolutely human play.

In game five FRITZ played very well, better than any human. It seemed almost equal, but it managed to keeping putting on this pressure all the time, it kept finding these very precise moves, not giving me a chance to get away. I played that game really well, and I shouldn't have blundered, but the position was not so pleasant anyway. I must admit it simply played very well.

…

Is playing against computers good for your regular chess? How is it different?

Playing computers can have a positive influence. My tactical feelings are very high after this match. You really see every little thing. I was managing a level of concentration that I could never manage before. Because you know that if you lose concentration for just one moment, it's over. One mistake and it's just over.

For instance in game six, after ♘xf7, I'm sure against most humans this would work very well. I couldn't say it was a mistake, but I realized afterwards that against a computer there is no way to save the game after that. You don't even realize it, but the game is already over! You are still playing, but the game is over!

…

Now that it's over how do you feel about the result?

I don't know how to assess the result. I cannot say I'm extremely happy with the result because I was leading 3-1. But I cannot say I am unhappy because after the match I know how difficult it was.

Now it was Gary Kasparov's chance to return to center stage and try to regain his honor. The period 1997-2002 had not been kind to him, with painful match losses to DEEP BLUE and Vladimir Kramnik. Beating a computer could restore his pride and help build momentum for recapturing the World Championship. In January 2003, he played a six-game match against Amir Ban's and Shay Buschinsky's DEEP JUNIOR in New York City. This was played under the banner of the first (and only) official FIDE/ICGA (International Computer Games Association) Man versus Machine World Championship.

There was enormous hype and considerable optimism surrounding Kasparov's return to the battle against the silicon monsters. The prestigious scientific journal *Nature* (2003) weighed in on the excitement:

New York City is gearing up for an unprecedented clash between intellectual heavyweights: Grandmaster Garry Kasparov will take on reigning World Computer Chess Champion DEEP JUNIOR, beginning on Sunday.

For chess and programming buffs, the $1-million, man-versus-machine match carries the glitz of a Las Vegas boxing bout. DEEP JUNIOR hasn't lost to a human in two years; Kasparov has been the world's top-rated human player for the past 18.

Kasparov is hoping to make up for his widely publicized 1997 defeat at the keyboard of IBM's chess supercomputer DEEP BLUE. This time he has been able to practice on a version of DEEP JUNIOR – which any buff can run on their laptop – for several months.

Unlike its silicon predecessors, DEEP JUNIOR has human qualities. "It plays more like Kasparov – doing daring, dangerous chess," says Frederic Friedel of Hamburg company ChessBase, which manufactures another chess program called DEEP FRITZ.

Analysis of the following games is largely taken from ChessBase (2003a) and Müller (2003).

Kasparov, Garry (2843) – DEEP JUNIOR

Slav Defense D45
New York match (1), 27.01.2003

1.d4 d5 2.c4 c6 3.♘c3 ♘f6 4.e3 e6 5.♘f3 ♘bd7 6.♕c2 ♗d6

7.g4!?

No anti-computer chess this time. Kasparov plays like Kasparov! A courageous but justifiable decision as he needs dynamic play to reach his best performance.

7...d×c4 8.♗×c4 b6 9.e4 e5

JUNIOR was surprisingly out of book and thought about 10 minutes now.

10.g5 ♘h5 11.♗e3 0-0 12.0-0-0 ♕c7

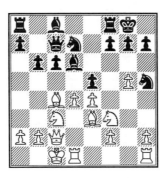

13.d5!

A strong novelty.

13...b5?

Too aggressive, as Black is not ready for a direct counterattack. 13...♗b7 was called for, e.g., 14.d×c6 ♗×c6 15.♘b5 ♗×b5 16.♗×b5 ♘c5 17.b4 ♘e6 18.♕×c7 ♗×c7 19.♔b2 and White's pair of bishop's gives him some advantage but much less than in the game.

14.d×c6 b×c4

15.♘b5!

Kasparov's knight will be a tower of power on d6. 15.c×d7? ♗×d7 16.♕d2 ♗g4 17.♕×d6 ♕×d6 18.♖×d6 ♗×f3 is not much for White.

15...♕×c6 16.♘×d6 ♗b7

Black hopes to get play against the e4-pawn.

17.♕c3!

17.♘f5? leads to nothing: 17...♕×e4 18.♘e7+ ♔h8 19.♕×e4 ♗×e4 20.♖×d7 ♗×f3=.

17...♖ae8?

Sacrificing the exchange to keep the e5-pawn. JUNIOR probably evaluates the d6-knight to be as strong as a rook. 17...♖ab8 18.♘×e5 ♘×e5 19.♕×e5 ♕a4 was better, at least creating some confusion.

18.♘×e8 ♖×e8 19.♖he1 ♕b5

19...♕×e4? 20.♖×d7 ♕×f3 21.♕×e5 +− .

20.♘d2 ♖c8 21.♔b1 ♘f8 22.♔a1

Kasparov brings his king in safety and plans to increase the pressure on the weak c4-pawn.

22...♘g6 23.♖c1 ♗a6

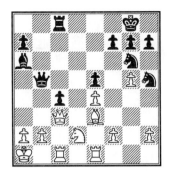

24.b3!

Liquidating into an endgame is good as the exchange is a powerful, long-term advantage. With Kasparov's technique the win is then only a matter of time.

24...c×b3 25.♕×b3 ♖a8?!

A strange move, but Black was lost in any case.

26.♕×b5 ♗×b5 27.♖c7 1-0

The resignation is a bit early, but there is no doubt about the final result anyway.

It had been a long six years since Kasparov last defeated a computer in a tournament game. The result must have been especially sweet for him!

Kasparov, Garry (2843) – DEEP JUNIOR
Slav Defense D45
New York match (3), 30.01.2003

Game 2 was a draw, giving Kasparov a one-point lead going into this game.

1.d4 d5 2.c4 c6 3.♘c3 ♘f6 4.e3 e6 5.♘f3 ♘bd7 6.♕c2 b6

The programmers of DEEP JUNIOR obviously hope to circumvent g2-g4 with this move. But Kasparov finds a way nevertheless. In the first game, 6...♗d6 was played.

7.c×d5 e×d5 8.♗d3 ♗e7 9.♗d2

Kasparov chooses to deviate from the well-trodden path to get g4 in.

9...0-0?!

9...♗b7 is more flexible.

10.g4!?

He plays courageously for an attack against the machine!

10...♘×g4 11.♖g1

This sharpens the play further. "The speculative 11...♘×f2 has been suggested as a possibility in reply to 11. h3, but it seems difficult to justify" (D. Levy). 11.♗×h7+ ♔h8 12.♗d3 came into consideration as well.

11...♘df6?

A very surprising move for the commentators. Junior makes the play even sharper. Why not? It is the computer! But objectively this goes too far. 11...♘gf6 is better, e.g., 12.e4 d×e4 13.♘×e4 ♘×e4 14.♗×e4 ♘f6 15.♗×c6 ♗e6 and Black has sufficient counterplay.

12.h3 ♘h6 13.e4! d×e4

14.♗×h6?

14.♗×e4! ♔h8 (14...♘×e4? 15.♗×h6 ♗f5 16.♖×g7+ [16.♗×g7!?] 16...♔h8 17.♘×e4 ♕d5 18.♖g4!? should be better for White) 15.♗×h6 g×h6 16.♗×c6 ♖b8 17.0-0-0 was more promising.

14...e×d3 15.♖×g7+

Obviously Kasparov did not like 15.♗×g7 ♘g4 (Of course, not 15...d×c2?, which allows a beautiful mate, 16.♗×f6+ ♗g4 17.♖×g4#) 16.♕×d3 ♔×g7 17.h×g4 because of 17...♗g5!.

15...♔h8 16.♕×d3 ♖g8!

16...♕e8? 17.♘g5 ♗a3+ 18.♔d2 ♗×b2 19.♖×h7+ ♔g8 20.♖g1 +– .

17.♖×g8+ ♘×g8

17...♕×g8? 18.0-0-0 ♕g6 19.♕e3 +– , with the idea of ♖g1.

18.♗f4 f6

Black has to control e5. Doing live commentary on schach.de, German Grandmaster Rainer Knaak was now sure that Kasparov would not win this game.

19.0-0-0 ♗d6

Black allows the halving of its bishop pair. The ♗c8 is the strong one anyway, as it has no counterpart and the light squares in White's camp are weak. 19...♗e6!? is worth consideration.

20.♕e3!?

Sacrificing the h3-pawn. 20.♗×d6 ♕×d6 21.h4 came into consideration as well.

20...♗×f4 21.♕×f4 ♗×h3 22.♖g1

22.♘d2!?.

22...♕b8 23.♕e3 ♕d6 24.♘h4

24.♘e4 is answered by 24...♕f8.

24...♗e6 25.♖h1 ♖d8 26.♘g6+

White's attack looks dangerous, but DEEP JUNIOR has everything under control.

26...♔g7 27.♘f4 ♗f5

28.♘ce2

Kasparov brings his queen's knight into the attack, but he just does not have enough firepower left to win.

28...♘e7 29.♘g3

This threatens ♕×e7+ (which will not work against a machine of course).

29...♚h8 30.♘×f5 ♘×f5 31.♕e4 ♕d7!

The game should now end in a draw, but in time trouble Kasparov blunders.

32.♖h5?

Kasparov overlooks the mating threat on the 35th move. 32.♘g6+ ♚g7 33.♘f4 ♚h8 (33...♖e8 34.♕g2+ ♚f8 35.♘g6+ h×g6 36.♕×g6 ♕d8 37.♖h7 ♖e1+ 38.♚d2 ♕×d4+ 39.♚×e1 ♕e4+=) 34.♘g6+ is equal.

32...♘×d4! 33.♘g6+?

Retreating with 33.♖h1 was best.

33...♚g8

33...♚g7?? 34.♖×h7+ ♚×h7 35.♘f8++−.

34.♘e7+ ♚f8 35.♘d5

Kasparov wanted to go in for 35.♖×h7, but he had overlooked 35...♘b3+ 36.♚c2 (36.a×b3 ♕d1#) 36...♘a1+ 37.♚c3 ♕d2+ 38.♚c4 b5+ 39.♚c5 ♕d6# when playing 32.♖h5?.

35...♕g7!

White was hoping for 35...cxd5? 36.♕xd4.

36.♕xd4 ♖xd5

and Kasparov resigned as it is over after 37.♖xd5 cxd5 38.♕xd5 ♕g5+ 39.♔d2 ♕xd2+ 40.♔xd2 h5 because of Black's outside passed h-pawn. **0-1**

New York Times reporter Grant McCord (2003) reported the end of the game as follows:

> Playing with the white pieces, the Azerbaijan-born Kasparov blundered with a rook move on his 32nd turn of the third game, allowing the machine to go two pawns up in material and establish a winning endgame.

> "This was a time pressure move that is ridiculous by his high standards," US Grandmaster Maurice Ashley said. "It makes the greatest player of all time look very human."

The same can be said about Kramnik and his mistakes against DEEP FRITZ two months earlier! The article continued:

> Kasparov's furious reaction at the board when he realized his mistake left no doubt he had betrayed himself after playing an enterprising game that appeared drawn even though the human player had less time on his clock.

> The former world champion who is still ranked number one, shook his head vigorously, stared up at the ceiling and covered his face with his hands as the computer crunched out the win.

And there was no time for sympathy from the DEEP JUNIOR team. This game was the realization of a dream for them.

> The human programmers of the Israeli-built software program that runs on a PC were excited by the victory.

> "Behind this is the accumulation of a lot of effort and this is the epitome of what we are doing," said programmer Shay Bushinsky, who along with fellow Israeli Amir Ban have worked on DEEP JUNIOR for 10 years. "Deep down in our hearts we are happy."

The match was now tied 1½-1½ and the next win would carry enormous weight. This is similar to the situation in the Kramnik-DEEP FRITZ match, which ended with two relatively uninteresting draws. Here it was a bit different. Game four was a draw and then…

Kasparov, Garry (2843) – DEEP JUNIOR
Nimzo-Indian Defense E48
New York match (5), 05.02.2003

1.d4 ♘f6

The DEEP JUNIOR team has changed its opening strategy. They obviously don't want to see g2-g4 against the Semi-Slav again.

2.c4 e6 3.♘c3 ♗b4 4.e3 0-0 5.♗d3 d5

From the Nimzo-Indian Defense, a structure from the Queen's Gambit has arisen.

6.c×d5

Freeing the ♗c8, but giving White the opportunity to launch a majority attack with f3 followed by e4 or a minority attack (e.g., with b4-b5, if Black plays ...c6).

6...e×d5 7.♘ge2 ♖e8 8.0-0 ♗d6 9.a3

Rather tame.

9...c6 10.♕c2

This makes the sacrifice on h2 more forceful as ♖h1 is no longer possible in many important lines. Did Kasparov want to provoke it?

After the game Kasparov suggested 10.f3 c5 11.♘b5.

10...♗×h2+!?

A very courageous sacrifice by DEEP JUNIOR! An audible gasp went up from the gallery when it was played.

Which other computer program would have played like this? By the way: "The Hungarian Grandmaster Joseph Horvath reached this position via a different move order already in 1989 and thought that Black can force a draw." (Kavalek 2003)

11.♔×h2

This is necessary as 11.♔h1? ♗c7 is just bad.

11...♘g4+ 12.♔g3

The only move. 12.♔g1? ♕h4 13.♖d1 ♕×f2+ 14.♔h1 ♖×e3−+ ; 12.♔h1?? ♕h4+ 13.♔g1 ♕h2#; 12.♔h3?? ♘×e3+ 13.♔h2 ♘×c2−+ .

12...♕g5 13.f4

13.♗×h7+?! ♔h8 14.f4 ♕h5 15.♗d3 ♕h2+ 16.♔f3 ♕h4 17.♘g3 ♘h2+ 18.♔f2 ♘g4+ 19.♔f3=.

13...♕h5

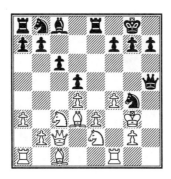

14.♗d2!?

"Suggested by Carsten Hansen in his 2002 Gambit Publications book *The Nimzo-Indian 4.e3* as an improvement on Horvath's 14.♘g1?! ♕h2+ 15.♔f3 ♕h5 18. ♔g3, repeating the moves." (Kavalek 2003)

14...♕h2+

14...♖xe3+? 15.♗xe3 ♘xe3 16.♕d2 ♘xf1+ 17.♖xf1 ±.

15.♔f3 ♕h4

16.♗xh7+

Kasparov contents himself with a draw and puts his hopes in the last game. The alternative, 16. g3!?, probably involved complications that were just too wild to try against a machine: 16.♘g3 ♘h2+ 17.♔f2 ♘g4+ 18.♔f3= (Gulko 2003); Is Black's compensation after 16.g3! really sufficient? This is certainly not easy to say and we have to wait for more detailed analysis. This doesn't prevent us from looking at some interesting lines: 16...♕h2 (Or 16...♘h2+ 17.♔f2 ♘g4+ 18.♔e1 – "I don't like this for Black at all" (Gulko 2003). One sample line runs: 18...♕h3 19.♘d1!? ♘d7 [19...♘h2 20.♗xh7+ ♔h8 21.♖f2±] 20.♘f2 ♘xf2 21.♔xf2 ♕h2+ 22.♔e1 ♘f6 23.f5 ♘g4 24.♕c5 ♘xe3 25.♗xe3 ♖xe3 26.♔d2 b6 27.♕c2 ♖xg3 28.♔c1 ±).

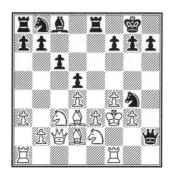

Now White is at a crossroads. It is certainly understandable why Kasparov did not want to try his luck against the machine. 17.♖ae1!?.

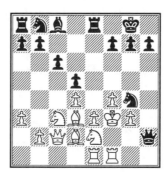

Also (a) 17.♖h1?? ♕f2#; (b) 17.f5!? ♘d7! (17...h5? is just too slow, e.g., 18.e4 ♘d7 19.♗g5 [19.♗f4!?] 19...c5 20.♘×d5 (suggested by Malcolm Pein in the *Daily Telegraph*) 20...c×d4 21.♘×d4 ♘de5+ 22.♔f4 f6 [22...♘f2 23.♖×f2 ♕×f2+ 24.♕×f2 ♘×d3+ 25.♔e3 ♘×f2 26.♔×f2 ♖×e4 27.♖d1 +−] 23.♗×f6 ♘×d3+ 24.♕×d3 ♘×f6 25.♘×f6+ g×f6 26.♕e2 +−).

18.♔×g4? This bold capture was the main focus of attention directly after the game. But now it seems that (b1) 18.e4! is called for, e.g., 18...♘de5+ (18...g6 19.♔×g4 d×e4 20.♘×e4 ♕h5+ 21.♔f4 g×f5 22.g4 ♕×g4+ 23.♔e3 +−; 18...c5 19.♔×g4 c×d4 20.♗f4 d×c3 21.e5±) 19.d×e5 ♘×e5+ 20.♔e3 b6 21.♖f4 g5 22.f×g6 h×g6 23.♘×d5 c×d5 24.♗c3 d×e4 25.♗b5 ♘g4+ 26.♖×g4 ♗×g4 27.♗×e8 ♖×e8 28.♖e1±; (b2)

18.♖h1? ♘de5+ 19.dxe5 ♘xe5+ 20.♔f4 ♕f2+ 21.♔g5 ♕f3 22.♕a4 f6+ 23.♔h4 b5−+; (b3) 18.♖ae1? ♘de5+ 19.dxe5 ♘xe5+ 20.♔f4 ♕h6#; 18...♕g2 19.e4 (One possible line after 19.♖h1? is 19...♘f6+ 20.♔h4 g5+ 21.♔xg5 ♕f3 22.♔xf6 ♕g4 23.♖xh7 ♔xh7 24.♖h1+ ♔g8 and Black mates.) 19...♘f6+ 20.♔f4 dxe4 21.♗xe4 ♖xe4+ 22.♘xe4 ♘d5+ 23.♔e5 (23.♔g4? ♕xe2+ 24.♔h3 ♘e3−+)

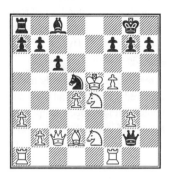

...and now Black does not play 23...♗xf5? but has 23...♕xe2 24.♖ae1 f6+ 25.♔d6 ♕a6 26.♘xf6+ ♘xf6 27.♕b3+ ♔h8 28.♔e5 c5 29.dxc5 ♗d7 with sufficient counterplay.

17...g6

(17...♘xe3? 18.♗xe3 ♕h5+ 19.♔g2 ♗h3+ 20.♔f2 ♗xf1 21.♖xf1 ♕h2+ 22.♔f3 ♕h5+ 23.g4 ♕h3+ 24.♘g3 ♖xe3+ 25.♔xe3 ♕xg3+ 26.♔d2+−; 17...♕h5? 18.♖h1+−; 17...f5? 18.♗xf5 ♕h5 19.♗xh7+ ♕xh7 20.♕xh7+ ♔xh7 21.♖h1+ ♔g8 22.e4 and White is better.)

Now 18.e4!? seems to be playable despite the problem with White's exposed king.

Alternatives:

(a) 18.♗c1?? ♘xe3 19.♗xe3 ♗g4+ 20.♔xg4 ♕h5#;

(b) 18.♘d1 plays it safe: 18...♕h5 19.♖h1 ♘xe3+ (19...♘e5+? 20.♔g2 ♕f3+ 21.♔g1 ♘xd3 22.♕xd3 ♗f5 23.♕b3 b6 24.♖h2 and Black's compensation is not sufficient.) 20.♖xh5 ♗g4+! a very important zwischenschach. 21.♔f2 ♘xc2 22.♗xc2 ♗xh5 and the position is more or less equal;

18...♘d7 (18...♕h5? 19.f5 g5 20.♗xg5 ♕xg5 [20...♘h2+? 21.♔g2 ♘xf1 22.♕c1 +−] 21.♘f4±) 19.e5 ♘df6 20.f5 ♖xe5 21.dxe5 ♘xe5+ 22.♔e3 c5 23.♗c1 ♕h6+ 24.♘f4 ♘xd3 25.♕xd3 ♗xf5 26.♕d1 d4+ 27.♔d2 ♖d8 28.♕f3 dxc3+ 29.♔xc3 ♕f8 30.♖e5±.

16...♔h8 17.♘g3 ♘h2+ 18.♔f2 ♘g4+ 19.♔f3 ♘h2+

Deep Junior has added a new, fascinating chapter to the ancient chapter of ♗xh2+/♗xh7+ Greek gift sacrifices! ½-½

ChessBase (2003b) nicely summarized the drama of game 5.

> When Deep Junior played 10... ♗xh2+ it smashed Garry Kasparov's kingside and many of our conceptions about computer chess with a single spectacular move.... From a quiet opening in a standard-looking position, the Israeli brainchild of Amir

Ban and Shay Bushinsky sacrificed a bishop out of a clear blue sky to drag Kasparov's king out into the open. Attacking with only a queen and knight, JUNIOR put the white king under heavy fire.

When a machine plays something like 10... ♗×h2+ against you, one thought goes through your mind. Unfortunately this is a family website and I can't print that thought here. Your second thought is, "So should I just resign?" You could tell from Kasparov's always-expressive face that he, like everyone in the room, was having painful flashbacks to game six against DEEP BLUE in 1997, when he was blown off the board after a piece sacrifice by the machine.

Kasparov collected himself, realized he wasn't being mated, and played the next few forced moves quickly. He captured the bishop and played his king from the frying pan into the fire on g3. JUNIOR feinted with its queen, keeping it close to Kasparov's king. The climax was reached on move 16, when it was becoming clear that Kasparov could allow a perpetual check draw or play a dangerous line and continue the game with his king in the center.

… Kasparov thought for over half an hour and allowed the perpetual check after 16.♗×h7+. The game was agreed drawn on move 19. A short draw with black against Kasparov cannot be called anything other than a tremendous success for JUNIOR, and the spectacular method in which it was achieved is an extra feather in JUNIOR's yarmulke.

Game six was an easy draw and, again, man had failed to defeat machine in a match. All was not right with the world!

Feng-hsiung Hsu (2002b) opined on the relative strengths of the opponents after the Kramnik and Kasparov matches:

Neither Vladimir Kramnik, the…World Champion, nor Garry Kasparov, the titleless number-one player, won their 2002 [and 2003] matches against the computers. Both matches followed the same pattern. The humans won games easily at first and led by more than one game. Then disaster struck. They both fell after uncharacteristic rudimentary blunders. After the computers levelled the matches, the humans offered early draws that were promptly accepted by the computer operators, and both matches ended up drawn.

Were the two computers really playing at Vladimir's or Garry's level? The match scores said so. Do I believe that? Yes and no. Vladimir and Garry were playing at the computers' level, but the computers were not playing at the level that Vladimir and Garry were capable of.

The repeated blunders certainly indicated that the humans were not playing at their peaks, and the quick draws suggested that both had lost their fighting spirit by the end of the 2002 [and 2003] matches. Nonetheless, the computers did play at a reasonably high level. The question is whether they played at the world championship level. This is harder to answer.

My intuition says no, but I am not 100 percent sure.

Not satisfied with the JUNIOR result, Kasparov again attempted to prove his superiority. In November he played a four-game match against the latest version of DEEP FRITZ. The games used the time control of 40 moves in two hours, followed by one hour for the next 20 moves and then 15 minutes for the rest of the game. A three-second increment was added after each move. The reason for the increment was that Kasparov was playing with a board that was "floating" in front of him – a form of virtual reality. The sponsor of the match, X3D Technologies Corp., had developed a three-dimensional technology, and, equipped with special glasses, Kasparov would see the board "floating" in space. There were no real pieces to touch and move – Kasparov's moves were made by his voice command.

This was a bizarre way to play a match. One has to wonder whether the novel interface affected Kasparov's play in the match.

In the first game, Kasparov won a pawn and had what many people thought was a winning advantage. Unfortunately for him, he let it slip and the game was drawn.

FRITZ X3D – Kasparov, Garry (2830)
Ruy Lopez C66
New York match (2), 13.11.2003

The game notes are based on Karsten Müller's posts on chessbase.de.

1.e4 e5 2.♘f3 ♘c6 3.♗b5 ♘f6

Kasparov follows Kramnik's footsteps to reach a Berlin Defense (also called the "Berlin Wall") to the Ruy Lopez.

4.d3

Surprise! 4.0-0 ♘×e4 5.d4 ♘d6 6.♗×c6 d×c6 7.d×e5 ♘f5 8.♕×d8+ ♔×d8 leads to the Berlin Defense.

4...d6 5.c3 g6 6.0-0 ♗g7 7.♘bd2 0-0 8.♖e1 ♖e8

Kasparov probably wants to throw FRITZ out of its book with this novelty. But in the ensuing positions, the rook would be better placed on f8, so I think that he would not play it against a human. 8...♗d7 9.a4 (9.♘c4 a6 10.♗×c6 ♗×c6 11.♘a5 ♕d7=) 9...a6 10.♗c4 ♗e6 11.a5 ♗×c4 12.d×c4 ♘h5 ½-½, Ponomariov-Grischuk, Panormo 2001.

9.d4 ♗d7

Kasparov wants to provoke the next move. In closed positions, the machine is not as strong as in open positions.

10.d5 ♘e7 11.♗×d7 ♘×d7

The structure is now similar to the King's Indian and many programs can't play that well. But Black's important light-square bishop is missing and White can expand quickly on the queenside. But FRITZ does not subsequently execute this plan. I am sure that Kasparov wouldn't play like this against Kramnik.

12.a4 h6

12...f5? is too early in view of 13.♘g5 ♘xd5 14.♘f1 ♘5f6 15.exf5 gxf5 16.♘e3.

13.a5

This advance is typical. The threat is a5-a6, to weaken the light squares on the queenside.

13...a6 14.b4 f5

The logical counterplay, which was prepared by h6.

15.c4 ♘f6 16.♗b2?!

Many commentators criticized this move, since the bishop does not yet know where it belongs. Flexibility is important! 16.♕b3!? is more logical. 16.c5? runs into 16...fxe4 17.♘xe4 ♘xe4 18.♖xe4 dxc5 19.bxc5 ♕xd5.

16...♕d7 17.♖b1

17.♖c1 followed by c5 was expected by the commentators.

17...g5!?

Very obliging. The main disadvantage is that FRITZ now knows what to do – a knight must head for e4 and its queenside pawns must advance. But the move is probably better than it looks at first sight and shows Kasparov's deep insight into the King's Indian structure. Khalifman preferred 17...f4, but after 18.c5, White's play is quite quick.

18.exf5

Necessary, otherwise Black's pawns will roll down the kingside.

18...♕xf5 19.♘f1! ♕h7

19...g4!? 20.♘g3 ♕g6 21.♘d2 h5 with counterplay according to IM Heiko Machelett.

20.♘3d2 ♘f5!?

20...♘g6?! 21.♘g3 ♘f4 22.♘de4 looks good for White. Schematic play with 20...♖f8?! 21.♘g3 ♖f7 22.♘de4 ♖af8 leads to trouble due to 23.c5! ♘fxd5 24.cxd6 cxd6 25.♘xd6 ♖xf2 26.♘ge4±.

21.♘e4 ♘xe4

The knight has to take immediately. Otherwise ♘g3 will follow and the knight will take on e4.

22.♖xe4 h5 23.♕d3 ♖f8 24.♖be1?!

FRITZ does not follow-up consistently now and in the following moves. The direct 24.c5 was called for.

24...♖f7 25.♖1e2 g4 26.♕b3 ♖af8 27.c5?!

27.b5 was better according to Khalifman.

27...♕g6 28.cxd6 cxd6

The alternative, 28...♘xd6 29.♖4e3 ♖f3!?, is also very interesting but, as in the game, Black has the initiative but White should be able to defend. As this is one of the strengths of the machines, FRITZ probably would have drawn here. The direct 29...h4 30.♗xe5 peters out to a draw: 30...♗xe5 31.♖xe5 ♖xf2 32.♖xf2 ♖xf2 33.♕e3 [33.♔xf2?! runs into 33...♕f6+] 33...♖f5=.

29.b5 axb5 30.♕xb5

30...♗h6?

Kasparov plans h5-h4-h3 (or g3) with an attack. But this move loses too much time. He had at least two other promising alternatives: The direct 30...h4, when one sample line runs 31.♕b4 (31.♘e3?? ♘d4–+) 31...g3 32.f3 gxh2+ 33.♔h1 ♘g3+ 34.♘xg3 hxg3 35.♖e1 ♖xf3 36.gxf3 ♖xf3 37.♖g4 ♕d3 with a draw. Or the enterprising 30...♖c7!?, when Black has some initiative after 31.♘g3 ♘d4 32.♗xd4 exd4 33.♖e6 ♖c1+ 34.♖e1 ♖xe1+ 35.♖xe1 ♕c2.

31.♕b6

Threatening to take on e5 as the queen on g6 is not protected and the d6-pawn d6 is pinned.

31...♔h7 32.♕b4

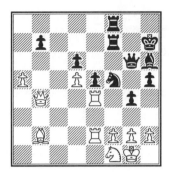

Preventing h5-h4. With his next move Kasparov renews the threat, but overlooks the importance of his unprotected f8-rook. He was in slight time trouble.

32...♖g7??

Shortly after playing this move, Kasparov stood up shaking his head. 32...♖g8 was necessary.

33.♖×e5!

FRITZ never misses such tactics! Anand opined on the ChessBase server: "Tricky beast."

33...d×e5 34.♕×f8

34...♘d4?!

Kasparov is still in shock and makes it easy for FRITZ. A typical human problem that the machines do not have of course. Tenacious defense is one of their big strengths compared to humans. But objectively Black is lost in any case, e.g., 34...♖d7 35.♕c8 ♕f7 36.♗×e5 ♖×d5 37.♕h8+ ♔g6 38.♖b2+–; or 34...♖e7 35.♕c8 ♗g7 36.♗a3 ♘d4 37.♖b2 ♖f7 38.d6+–.

35.♗×d4 e×d4 36.♖e8

Threatening mate on h8.

36...♖g8 37.♕e7+

FRITZ keep its attacking potential on the board of course. 37.♕×g8+? ♕×g8 38.♖×g8 ♔×g8 39.♘g3 is better for White but its largest advantage, the attack against Black's king, has vanished.

37...♖g7

The alternatives are no better: 37...♗g7 38.♖×g8 ♔×g8 39.♕×b7 +– ; 37...♔h8 38.♖×g8+ ♔×g8 39.♕×b7 +– ; 37...♕g7 38.♕e4+ ♕g6 39.♖e7+ ♖g7 40.♕e5 ♗g5 41.♖e6 ♕c2 42.♕×d4 +– .

38.♕d8

Again threatening mate.

38...♖g8 39.♕d7+ 1-0

Kasparov resigned in view of 39...♖g7 40.♕c8 ♖g8 41.♕×b7 ++– .

Another stunning defeat for Kasparov.

Kasparov, Garry (2830) – FRITZ X3D
Slav Defense D45
New York match (3), 16.11.2003

1.♘f3 ♘f6 2.c4 e6 3.♘c3 d5 4.d4 c6 5.e3 a6?!

This very principled (but highly dubious) move is the novelty compared to the second game.

6.c5!?

Kasparov closes the position immediately and emphasizes the weakness of b6 and the dark squares on the queenside.

6...♘bd7 7.b4

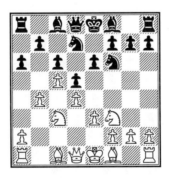

7...a5?

A strategic mistake. May be even the losing move in a higher sense as the position is now closed and FRITZ does not understand it at all.

8.b5!

Black's a5-pawn is now very weak.

8...e5 9.♕a4

9.d×e5? ♘c4 gets tactical and plays into FRITZ's hands (or should that be, into FRITZ's circuits?).

9...♛c7 10.♗a3!

This is aimed against sacrifices on c5 or b6. Furthermore, the bishop can go to b4 after ♘×a5 to free the queen.

10...e4?

FRITZ closes the center. Not a good idea for a computer.

11.♘d2 ♗e7 12.b6!

What a pawn chain! An ideal structure against FRITZ! 12.♗e2 h5 13.b6 ♛d8 14.h3 ♘f8 15.0-0-0 ♘e6 16.♘d×e4 ♘×e4 17.♘×e4 h4 18.♘d2 was also clearly better for White in Reshevsky-Keres, World Championship Den Haag/Moscow 1948.

12...♛d8 13.h3

A dream position! Completely closed and a waiting prey on a5.

13...0-0 14.♘b3 ♗d6?!

A little joke. The bishop can't be taken. But the trap is much too obvious for Kasparov and only valuable time is lost. 14...♘b8 with the idea ♘f6-d7 followed by f5 was better.

15.♖b1!?

Protecting b6. 15.c×d6?? ♘×b6 loses the queen, and 15.♘×a5? is too early: 15...♘×b6! 16.c×b6? ♗×a3 17.♛×a3 ♛×b6.

15...♗e7?!

15...♗b8 would be consistent. But a similar configuration was DEEP BLUE's undoing in its first match against Kasparov.

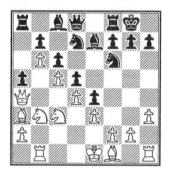

16.♘×a5!

Take courage! This pawn has to be taken at some moment. It is very surprising that FRITZ does not give a big disadvantage for itself. Any human playing Black would be shaking in his shoes.

16...♘b8

Probably to protect c6 and to blockade on a6.

17.♗b4

Kasparov frees his pieces on the queenside with the following maneuvers.

17...♛d7

After 17...♞e8?, FRITZ calculated 18.♞xc6 ♜xa4 19.♞xd8 ♜a8 20.c6 ♝xd8 21.c7 ♝xc7 22.bxc7 ♞xc7 23.♝xf8+−.

18.♜b2

Prophylaxis.

18...♛e6?!

FRITZ plays like a fish out of water. 18...♞e8 19.♛d1 f5 is the right plan, now or even later. But FRITZ does not move its f-pawn until the end of the game. Have the programmers prohibited it from "weakening" its king's position?; 18...♛f5? is refuted by 19.♞xc6!! (Reeh 2004).

19.♛d1 ♞fd7

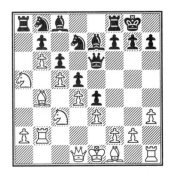

20.a3

Slowly, slowly! Secure everything! Allow no tactic! Very well done. FRITZ shall be adrift at sea.

20...♛h6 21.♞b3 ♝h4

21...f5 is better again.

22.♛d2

♛xe3+ was threatened.

22...♞f6 23.♚d1

This castling by hand is very fine and reminds me of the great Tigran Petrosian. Quite nice!

23...♝e6 24.♚c1 ♜d8

FRITZ has no plan and plays completely random moves. It is very hard to believe that such a powerful program does not know anything about this position.

25.♜c2 ♞bd7 26.♚b2

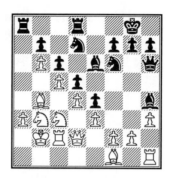

The king is very secure here. This is a well-known concept: the king is better placed behind its own advanced pawn wall than crushed by the enemy pawn front. FRITZ has not even begun advancing his kingside pawns.

26...♘f8 27.a4 ♘g6

Black's moves make no real sense.

28.a5 ♘e7 29.a6!

Very strong. Black will be completely dominated soon and its queenside is in ruins.

29...b×a6

29...♖d7 30.a×b7 ♖×b7 31.g3 ♗g5 32.♗g2 and White wins as the game.

30.♘a5

What a knight! A real monster!

30...♖db8 31.g3 ♗g5 32.♗g2

32.h4? ♘g4 gives Black counterplay, which it does not deserve.

32...♕g6 33.♔a1!?

Slowly, slowly! Do not allow any tactics.

33...♔h8

FRITZ is in free-fall. In the meantime, Kasparov prepares the decisive strike on the queenside, slowly and calmly but steadily.

34.♘a2

Heading for b4.

34...♗d7 35.♗c3 ♘e8 36.♘b4 ♔g8 37.♖b1 ♗c8 38.♖a2 ♗h6 39.♗f1 ♕e6

40.♕d1

The queen heads for a4 to increase the pressure on a6 and c6. The time trouble is over, and so is the game in a higher sense.

40...♘f6 41.♕a4 ♗b7 42.♘×b7 ♖×b7 43.♘×a6!?

An adventure like 43.♗×a6 ♖bb8 44.♘×c6 is of course not necessary.

43...♕d7 44.♕c2 ♔h8 45.♖b3 and the FRITZ team resigned for the machine. **1-0**

A possible finish would have been 45...♔g8 46.♖ba3 g6 47.♘b4 ♖×a3 48.♖×a3 ♔g7 49.♖a8 ♘c8 50.♕a2 ♘×b6 51.c×b6 ♖×b6 52.♕a7 ♖b7 53.♕c5+−. A superb performance by Kasparov. FRITZ had no chance.

With a draw in game four, yet another match between the *creme de la creme* of chess-playing humanity ended in a draw with the electronic creations of humanity. All these matches followed a similar pattern. Humans play well and win a game or two. Computers play well and cash in when the humans make a slip or two. Some might argue that the humans played, on average, better moves. However, in the end all that matters is the final result. Given the Kramnik and two Kasparov match results, there was now enough evidence to assert that computers were the equals of the best of humanity.

But… computer programs continued to improve. They get faster hardware or more processors. They get access to more memory. They play more games and learn from their mistakes. Their opening book continues to expand. The programmers continue to refine the chess knowledge. And all this is happening on a daily basis.

As evidence of the continued improvement, witness the following game. In computer science, there is the so-called Turing Test (Alan Turing's invention, of course). In the context of chess, it poses the question as to whether you can tell which player is the man and which is the machine. For much of the history of computer chess it has been easy – computers have telltale weaknesses and play "non-human" moves. Can you tell whether the computer played White or Black in the following game snippet? Black is to play.

21...♗×f2+!!

An intuitive Tal-like sacrifice.

22.♔×f2 ♘fg4+ 23.♔g1 ♕h6 24.♖c3 ♕×h2+ 25.♔f1

25...h5!?

Another surprise. the Black player neglects the forced draw to be had by 25...♕h5 26.♔g1 (26.♕d4 h6 27.♘d2 ♘h2+ 28.♔g1 ♕d1+ 29.♔×h2 ♘g4+ 30.♔h3 ♘f2+ 31.♔h2 ♘g4+=) 26...♕h2+ and goes for the kill, which is an excellent practical decision and makes White's task much more difficult.

26.♕d4?

A typical error when under pressure. 26.♕e2 h4 27.♗c1 h3 28.♗b7 ♕×e2+ 29.♔×e2 ♘c4+ 30.♔f3 ♘ce5+ 31.♔e2 leads to a draw by repetition.

26...h4 27.g×h4 ♕×h4 28.♖h3 ♘h2+ 29.♔g1?

29.♖×h2 is forced, but after 29...♕×h2 30.♘d2 ♕g3, it is next to impossible to hold such a position.

29...♘hf3+ 30.♗×f3 ♕×h3 31.♘d2 0-1

Only humans play Tal-like sacrifices, right? Wrong! The missing header for this game is:

Romanishin, Oleg (2561) — Brutus
Lippstadt (1), 07.08.2003

Computers had come a long way. And they were continuing to improve…

9
3000+ (2004-present)

It was just a matter of time. Since the DEEP BLUE victory, computers had repeatedly shown that this result was not a fluke and, indeed, was a portend of the future. Man versus machine games would only hold public interest as long as there was the unresolved question of superiority. The previous years had clearly shown that it was increasingly difficult for the human side to win an event, let along a single game. Arguments that computers were not as good as the human World Champion, while often heard for a few years after the DEEP BLUE result, quietly disappeared. It is almost with morbid fascination that man-machine events continued to happen, in part motivated by ego (humans are not good at admitting defeat) and in part for scientific curiosity (when does the line of superiority get crossed). Anyone with any knowledge of technology knew that it was just a matter of time before technology would overwhelm humanity. After all, with algorithms where the programs could learn from self-play it was clear that the software would incrementally improve literally every single day, whereas humans could not. The inherent advantages of computer technology were inexorably making the programs stronger – fast computing, large memories, endless computations, and continual learning. This was daunting, to say the least!

Nevertheless, strong grandmasters continued to bravely throw themselves into the fray against the computers. There was no shame in losing any more – that psychological barrier had long ago been broken. Rather one could achieve glory by defeating the electronic behemoths, and that was a mighty accomplishment in and of itself.

As if the humans already did not have enough to deal with, a new electronic "beast" emerged. Chrilly Donninger honed his chess programming skills by creating the NIMZO program. In the early 2000s, he became interested in computer hardware for chess. He believed that technology had advanced to the point whereby relatively inexpensive hardware could be used to build a machine that played chess at a level well beyond anything that had been seen before.

Field-programmable gate arrays (FPGAs) are computer chips that provide generic computer logic and wires that the user can customize. This allows you to create a computer chip that does what you want it to do (such as play chess). Because it has been tailored to do one task, it will be much faster at performing that task than a general-purpose computer. However, because it is customizable, it will not be as fast as a specially fabricated chip (such as was done for DEEP BLUE). The end result was that Donninger built an FPGA-based chess machine that offered a major performance boost over what conventional personal computers could achieve. The machine had enough FPGAs to achieve performance (positions per second) that was roughly comparable to DEEP BLUE's speed. When you combined that with the carefully honed chess software that Donninger been developing for over a decade and the latest advances in search algorithms, the end result was a chess "monster." Hence, Donninger called the machine HYDRA, the many-headed serpent of Greek mythology. The project started in 2002, but by late 2004 the machine had proven itself against other computer programs and was ready to challenge the best humans.

In October 2004, Bilbao hosted the First Man Versus Machine World Championship. The human side had former FIDE World Champion Ruslan Ponomariov, future FIDE World Champion Veselin Topalov, and a young (12 years old!) but future World Championship Challenger Sergey Karjakin. They were up against a strong computer lineup that featured enhanced commercial products FRITZ 8 and DEEP JUNIOR, and the special-purpose machine HYDRA.

The event had an odd schedule. Each human played four games against the computers: two against one program, and one against each of the other two programs. Thus a total of 12 man-machine games were played.

Ponomariov, Ruslan (2722) – HYDRA
Queen's Indian Defense E15
Bilbao (1), 06.10.2004

1.♘f3 ♘f6 2.c4 b6 3.d4 e6 4.g3 ♗a6 5.b3 ♗b4+ 6.♗d2 ♗e7 7.♗g2 c6 8.♗c3 d5 9.♘e5 ♘fd7 10.♘×d7 ♘×d7 11.♘d2 0-0 12.0-0 b5 13.c5 e5 14.b4

Ponomariov closes the position. The other main line, 14.d×e5, scores better for White in carbon-based games.

14...e4 15.e3 ♕c7 16.♖e1 ♗g5

17.a4?!

Ponomariov rushes things. The preparatory 17.♗f1 is preferable.

17...b×a4 18.♖×a4 ♗b5 19.♖a3 ♘f6 20.♗f1

20.f4? e×f3 21.♘×f3 ♘e4 plays into Black's hands.

20...a6 21.♕a1 ♖ab8 22.♗×b5 a×b5 23.♖a7 ♕c8 24.♕a6 ♕e6

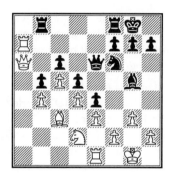

25.罝a1?!

White should take defensive measures, e.g., 25.堂g2 h5 26.h3 h4 27.包f1 包h7
28.豐a2 魚d8 29.豐e2 包g5 30.豐g4 and he is at least not brought down by a mating
attack.

25...h5!

The battering ram is coming.

26.罝c7

26.h4? can even be met by 26...魚×h4.

26...h4 27.罝×c6 豐f5

28.豐a2?

Now Black's attack crashes through. Ponomariov had to take the emergency exit
with 28.罝×f6 when he can continue to fight an uphill struggle.

28...包g4 29.包f1 豐f3 30.h3

30.g×h4 does not help because of 30...魚×h4 31.包g3 魚×g3 32.h×g3 g5 33.魚e1
堂g7 34.豐×d5 罝h8 35.豐×g5+ 堂f8–+ .

30...♘×e3! 31.f×e3 ♗×e3+ 32.♔h2 ♗f2!

The killer.

33.g×h4 e3

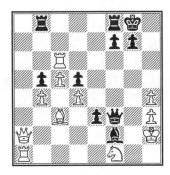

White is totally helpless despite his extra piece. **0–1**

A beautiful game by HYDRA; it is not often that you see a grandmaster being so easily "man"handled. With 3½ out of 4 games against these elite players, the machine was clearly ready for stronger opposition.

The following game shows that it is not easy to win a won game against a computer.

Topalov, Veselin (2737) – HYDRA
Queen's Pawn Game D00
Bilbao Human-Comp Bilbao (2), 07.10.2004

1.d4 d5 2.c3 ♘f6 3.♗f4 e6 4.e3 ♗d6 5.♗g3 0-0 6.♘d2 b6 7.♘gf3 c5 8.♘e5 a5 9.♗h4 ♗e7 10.♗d3 ♘fd7 11.♗g3 ♘×e5 12.d×e5 ♗a6 13.♗c2 ♖a7 14.♕g4 d4 15.h4

Very original. Topalov lures the d-pawn forward.

15...d3?!

15...♖d7 is more consequent and flexible.

Hydra author Chrilly Donninger
(ChessBase)

16.♗b3 ♛c7?! 17.a4 ♛c8 18.♗c4 ♖d8 19.♗×a6 ♛×a6 20.♛c4 ♛c8 21.0-0-0♛c6 22.f3 ♛a8 23.♘b1 ♖ad7 24.♖d2 ♘c6 25.♘a3 ♖d5 26.f4 ♖5d7 27.♔b1 ♘a7 28.e4 ♛c6 29.♖hd1 ♖b7 30.♘b5

30.♖×d3 ♖×d3 31.♖×d3 b5 32.a×b5 ♘×b5 33.♘×b5 ♖×b5 34.♖d2 was the alternative.

30...♘×b5 31.a×b5 ♛c8 32.♗f2

32.h5!?

32...h5

Topalov has outplayed the multi-headed monster. Chrilly Donninger recalls: "Facing Veselin Topalov the program got into difficulties against a human player for the first time...The position was objectively lost; a human opponent would probably have resigned on the spot. Thirty moves in the organizers pleaded with Topalov if he'd be so kind as to offer a draw, please. They made reservations in the best restaurant in town...Topalov refuses. He prefers to be the Hercules of chess and complete his tasks. The tournament train leaves for the restaurant... After 95 moves, HYDRA escapes with a perpetual. The substitute [restaurant] Bocuse[9] lets us in after all: he knows that 'chess players aren't quite right in the head.'" (Donninger 2009)

33.♖×d3 ♖bd7 34.♖×d7 ♖×d7 35.♖×d7 ♕×d7 36.♔c2 ♕f8 37.♕e2 g6 38.c4 ♕d8 39.g3 ♔e8 40.♕f3 ♗f8 41.♕e3 ♕c7 42.♗e1 ♕d7 43.♗d2 ♗h6 44.♔d1 ♔f8 45.♔e2 ♕d8 46.♗c3 ♕d7 47.♕f3 ♔e8 48.g4 h×g4 49.♕×g4 ♕e7

49...♕c7? 50.f5 g×f5 51.e×f5 e×f5 52.♕g8+ ♗f8 53.♕g2+−

50.♔f3 ♕d8 51.♔e3 ♕e7 52.h5 g×h5 53.♕×h5 ♕f8

54.♔f3?!

54.♗e1 ♕g7 55.♗f2 ♕h8 56.♔f3 was a more precise order of moves. It is not clear if White can break through, but he has better chances than in the game.

54...♕g7 55.♕g4 ♕h7 56.f5 ♔d7 57.♕h5 ♕g7 58.b3

58.f6 ♕g6 59.♕×g6 f×g6 60.♔e2 ♗f4=

58...♗c1 59.♗e1 ♗b2 60.♗g3 ♗c3 61.♗f4

61.f6 is met by 61...♕g6! 62.♕×g6 f×g6 63.f7, as otherwise Black constructs a fortress by transferring its king to c7: 63...♔e7 64.♗h4+ ♔×f7 65.♗d8 a4 66.b×a4 ♗a5=.

61...♗d4 62.♗h2 ♕g8 63.♕h6 ♗c3 64.♗g3 ♔c7 65.♕f6 ♔d7 66.♗f4 ♕h7 67.♔g4 ♕g8+ 68.♗g5 ♗d2 69.♕h6 ♗c3 70.♕f6 ♗d2 71.♔h5 ♗×g5 72.f×e6+ f×e6 73.♕×g5 ♕h8+! 74.♔g4 ♕h7

75.♕f4

75.♕f6!? was a better try, but 75...a4 76.b×a4 ♕×e4+ 77.♔g5 ♕×c4 also seems to be drawn.

75...♔e8 76.♔g5 ♕g7+ 77.♔h5 ♕h8+ 78.♔g4 ♕h7 79.♕f6 ♕×e4+ 80.♔g5 ♕g2+ 81.♔h6 ♕h1+ 82.♔g7 ♕b7+ 83.♔g8 ♕g2+ 84.♕g7 ♕f3 85.♕g6+ ♔e7 86.♕g7+ ♔e8 87.♕g6+ ♔e7 88.♕g7+ ♔e8 ½-½

Karjakin, Sergey (2591) – Deep Junior
Sicilian Defense B90
Bilbao (2), 07.10.2004

1.e4 c5 2.♘f3 d6 3.d4 c×d4 4.♘×d4 ♘f6 5.♘c3 a6 6.f3 e5 7.♘b3 ♗e6 8.♗e3 ♗e7 9.♕d2 h5

This is one of the main lines here.

10.♘d5 ♗×d5?!

Very risky. Now Black must be extremely careful that White's bishop will not dominate the board sooner or later. 10...♘×d5 11.e×d5 ♗f5 scores better.

11.e×d5 ♘bd7 12.♗e2 ♖c8 13.c4 h4 14.0-0 h3 15.g3

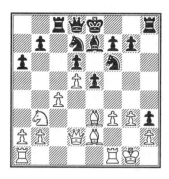

15...0-0?!

This is inconsistent with the previous play. 15...b6 16.a4 a5 is more logical.

16.♘a5 ♕c7 17.b4 ♖fe8 18.♖fd1 ♘b8 19.♖ac1 e4?! 20.f4 ♕d7 21.c5

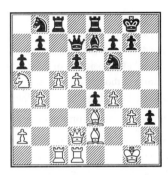

White has achieved a dream position and is strategically winning.

21...d×c5 22.b×c5 ♗f8 23.d6 ♘c6 24.♘c4 ♖b8 25.♖b1 ♕e6 26.♖b3 g6 27.♘b6 ♗g7

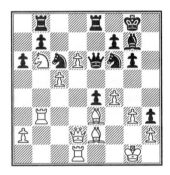

28.♘d5!?

Karjakin plays a safe and strong strategy. Next he will activate his light-square bishop and his d1-rook. The alternative 28.d7 ♖ed8 29.♕d6 is less clear from a human point of view, but better from a computer point of view.

28...♕d7 29.♘×f6+ ♗×f6 30.♗c4 a5?!

JUNIOR just likes to move its rook pawns.

31.a3 ♖a8 32.♖b5 a4 33.♕e2 ♗g7 34.♗d5 ♖a7 35.♔f2 ♗f6 36.♖b6 ♔f8?! 37.♖db1 ♗g7 38.g4 ♗h8 39.♔g3 f5 40.g5 ♕h7 41.♗×c6 b×c6 42.♖×c6 1-0

The final score: Man 3½, Machine 8½. Despite very strong opposition, the computers thoroughly dominated their human opponents. Only Karjakin was able to score a full point in a game.

And what did we learn from this event? Even as knowledgeable an expert as David Levy (2004) expressed doubts as to whether the humans did as well as they should have:

> What have we learned from this crushing defeat of the grandmaster team? I do not believe that the 8½-3½ total score is a true reflection of the relative strengths of the two teams. Instead I feel that some of this disparity is due to insufficient preparation

on the part of the grandmasters. Before the start of the event I had expected that all of the GMs would have analysed two of the programs in great depth (HYDRA is not available for purchase so no advance preparation was possible for Chrilly Donninger's monster). But whatever the level of preparation of team GM it did not show itself to good effect in most of the games, although Topalov appeared to have a much better understanding of how computers play chess than did either of his team-mates.

In the end, however, he reached the right conclusions:

Above all, we learned in Bilbao how difficult it is for a GM to play the best moves often enough to win against a top program. When two GMs play each other, each can expect his opponent to make some inaccuracies during a game, so that one mistake will often be balanced by a subsequent mistake from the opponent. Programs are not like that. The best programs play at a consistently high level, so much so that, after a program leaves its openings book, only very rarely will it make a move that gives much away. A human player, even though he might be able to play 2750 level chess for 95% of his moves, is somewhat more fragile, and for the remaining 5% of the time he will often play the second best or third best move when only the best will do. It is moments like that that frequently determine the outcome of a GM vs computer game – give a beast a single chance and it will pounce.

Even making allowances for inadequate preparation on the part of some of the human players, it is clear that the computer team was significantly stronger than the GMs. This first Man vs Machine Team Championship has indicated a level at which we can witness a highly dramatic contest, but with the average strength of the GMs at this level the contest will inevitably be one-sided. For the next event in this series, the average strength of the human team will need to be raised.

HYDRA's success meant that Donninger looked for a more challenging event to showcase his monster. He quickly found a willing opponent in Grandmaster Michael (Mickey) Adams, one of the best players in the world at the time. In June 2005, they played a six-game match in London.

Mig Greengard (2005)[10]
Chess writer

I remember seeing the impressive amount of preparation done by Kasparov and Kramnik for their matches against JUNIOR and FRITZ. A team of seconds helped analyze the programs' games, looking for weaknesses and tendencies. This went on for months in advance. Months! Adams has been playing a lot lately and of course he didn't have HYDRA or its previous incarnations available for training. With his full tournament schedule it's hard to imagine he did anything near the sort of preparation required to battle a machine this tough.

HYDRA – Adams, Michael (2737)

Petroff Defense C42
London m (1), 21.06.2005

In the following, material is used from Donninger (2009).

1.e4 e5 2.♘f3 ♘f6 3.♘×e5 d6 4.♘f3 ♘×e4 5.d4 d5 6.♗d3 ♘c6 7.0-0 ♗e7 8.♖e1 ♗g4 9.c3 f5 10.♕b3 0-0 11.♘bd2 ♘a5 12.♕c2 ♘c6 13.b4 a6

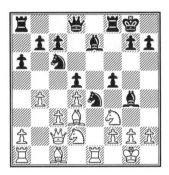

14.♖b1!?

The prepared novelty that HYDRA had already played in a training game against Christopher Lutz, who played it trying to simulate Adams' style as best he could. Previously Ponomariov and Leko had tried 14.a4 against Adams.

14...♗d6

14...♔h8 is an alternative.

15.h3 ♗h5 16.b5!

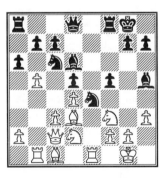

Now Adams thought for a very long time and came up with the strong...

16...♘a5!

In the training game, Lutz had taken with exchange with 16...a×b5?! 17.♖×b5 ♘a5?! 18.♖×d5 ♗×f3 19.♘×f3 ♗h2+ 20.♔×h2 ♕×d5 but went down later.

17.c4

Black also has counterplay after 17.b×a6 b×a6 18.c4 ♞c6 (Huzman 2005).

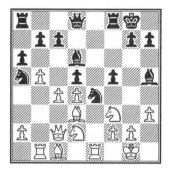

17...d×c4?!

This gives White a slight initiative, a dangerous situation against a computer. 17...a×b5!? 18.c×d5 ♞×d2 19.♞×d2 c6 is better than the game, as the harmony of White's army is slightly disrupted. The position seems to be dynamically balanced.

18.♞×c4 ♞×c4

Now 18...a×b5? 19.♖×b5 c6 runs into 20.♖×f5! ♖×f5 21.♗×e4±.

19.♗×c4+ ♚h8 20.b×a6 b×a6 21.♞e5 c5 22.♗d5 ♖c8 23.♗e6

23...♖c7?

Adams had to sacrifice an exchange with 23...c×d4! 24.♕×c8 ♕f6 when Black's compensation keeps him afloat, e.g., 25.♕c4 ♕×e5 26.g3 d3 27.♗d5 d2 28.♗×d2 ♞×d2 29.♖×e5 ♞×c4 30.♖e6 ♗f7 31.♗×c4 ♗×e6 32.♗×e6 ♗c5.

24.♗×f5

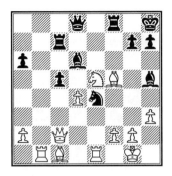

24...⌐×e5?

Adams probably hoped that the opposite-color bishops make it easier to play for him and would give him drawing chances. But this is deceptive and HYDRA presses its initiative very forcefully. 24...⌐×f5 25.♕×e4 ⌐f8 26.⌐d2 ♕f6 was the last real chance to fight for a draw.

25.d×e5 ⌐×f5 26.♕×e4 ⌐g6 27.⌐b6 ⌐f8 28.♕e3 ⌐cf7 29.⌐d6 ♕a5?! 30.e6 ⌐e7 31.⌐a3 ⌐fe8 32.⌐×c5 ♕×a2?!

32...⌐f5 33.⌐×a6 ♕×a6 34.⌐×e7 ♕a5 was more tenacious.

33.⌐d2 1-0 A surprise to Adams, but probably not to Donninger.

Adams, Michael (2737) – HYDRA
Sicilian Defense B80
London m (2), 22.06.2005

1.e4 c5 2.♘c3 e6 3.♘f3 ♘c6 4.d4 c×d4 5.♘×d4 ♕c7 6.g3 a6 7.♗g2 d6 8.♘×c6 b×c6 9.0-0 ♘f6 10.♘a4 e5 11.c4 ♗e7 12.♗e3 12.c5!? **12...♗e6 13.⌐c1 0-0 14.b3 ♕b7 15.♕e2 ⌐fe8 16.h3 ⌐ab8 17.⌐fd1 ♗f8**

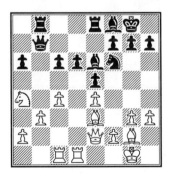

18.♔h2?!

Against a human Adams would probably have played 18.c5 d5 19.e×d5 ♘×d5 20.♘b6, which gives White a strong initiative.

18...h6 19.⌐c2 ♗e7 20.♗c1 ♕c7 21.♗b2 ♘d7 22.♗c3 ♘f8 23.♕e3 c5 24.♗b2 ♗d7 25.♘c3 ♘e6 26.♘d5 ♕d8 27.f4 ♘d4 28.⌐f2 ♗c6

29.f×e5?!

This gives up flexibility. 29.♖df1 is more logical.

29...d×e5

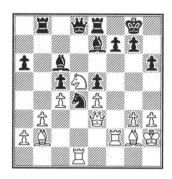

30.♗×d4

Adams plans to construct a fortress based on his control of the light squares, which works out. Objectively better is 30.♗f3!? a5 31.♗h5 ♖f8 32.♗c3 with complete equality. But from a practical point of view, Adams' choice is not bad against HYDRA.

30...c×d4 31.♕f3 ♖f8 32.♕h5 f6 33.h4 ♗e8 34.♕f3 ♗f7 35.♗h3 ♖b7 36.h5 a5 37.♔g2 ♕e8 38.♗g4 ♗c5 39.♖h1 ♕c6 40.♖b2 ♖fb8 41.♗f5 ♔h8 42.♖hb1 ♕e8 43.g4 ♕c6 44.♕d3 ♗g8 45.♕d1 ♕a6 46.♖d2 a4 47.♖db2 ♕a8 48.♔h2 ♗f7 49.♔g2 ♗f8 50.♔h2 ♗e8?!

50...♗a3 is a better practical choice.

51.b4!

Adams prepares to sacrifice an exchange to construct an impregnable fortress. Even if it could be taken, it was unlikely that the machine would storm it, as often material sacrifice and a certain way of thinking is necessary for this and the computer does not think in this manner..

51...a3 52.♖b3 ♗a4 53.b5 ♕a7 54.♔g2 ♕c5 55.♕d3 ♗×b3 56.♕×b3 ♖a8 57.♖d1 ♕d6 58.♖c1 ♕b8 59.♔f3 ♗d6 60.♔e2 ♗c5 61.♔d3 ♕a7 62.♖b1 ♕a5 63.♕c2 ♕d8 64.♖h1 ♕d6 65.♕b3 ♖e8 ½-½

HYDRA — Adams, Michael (2737)

Ruy Lopez C91
London m (3), 23.06.2005

1.e4 e5 2.♘f3 ♘c6 3.♗b5 a6 4.♗a4 ♘f6 5.0-0 ♗e7 6.♖e1 b5 7.♗b3 d6 8.c3 0-0 9.d4 ♗g4 10.d5 ♘a5 11.♗c2

HYDRA is out of its opening as the team had planned, as they assumed that the resulting positions would suit the program well.

11...c6 12.h3 ♗c8 13.d×c6 ♕c7 14.♘bd2 ♕×c6 15.♘f1 ♗e6 16.♘g5

16...♗d8?

A novelty but not a good one. 16...♗d7 is the main line.

17.♘e3 ♗d7 18.a4

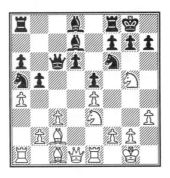

18...h6?

This weakens the kingside in the long term. White now has motifs like ♘f3-h4-f5 and ♗×h6. But Black's position is very precarious in any case. I suggest 18...♘e8, but I do not claim that it equalizes of course.

19.♘f3 ♖c8

19...♗b6 is answered by 20.♘h4 with strong pressure. One sample line runs 20...♗×e3 21.♖×e3 ♔h7 22.♖g3 ♗e6 23.♕f3 ♕c8? 24.♗×h6 and White's attack crashes through.

20.a×b5 a×b5 21.♘h4! ♘c4?!

Allowing the following invasion on the light squares. But good advice is already hard to give, as 21...g6 22.b4 ♘b7 23.♗b3 ♔h7 24.♘d5 is also clearly in White's favor.

22.♘×c4! b×c4

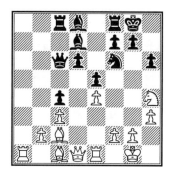

23.♗a4!

A very strong exchange as the d7-bishop is Black's main defender of the weak light squares.

23...♕c7 24.♗×d7 ♕×d7 25.♘f5 d5

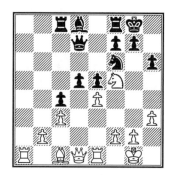

26.♖a6! ♕b7?

Adams had to play 26...d×e4 27.♕×d7 ♘×d7 28.♖×e4 ♗f6 to reduce HYDRA's attacking potential. But the endgame is clearly better for White.

27.♖d6 ♗e7?

27...g6 is relatively best, but against HYDRA, it cannot be defended in the long run of course. 27...♘×e4? runs into 28.♖×e4 d×e4 29.♗×h6+− .

28.♗×h6!!

What a hammer blow!

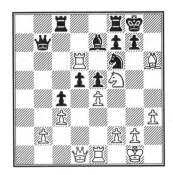

and Adams resigned in view of 28...g×h6 29.♕f3 ♔h7 30.♕e3+− . **1-0**

How can one possibly recover from such a humbling defeat?

Adams, Michael (2737) − Hydra
Sicilian Defense B70
London m (4), 25.06.2005

1.e4 c5 2.♘c3 d6 3.♘ge2 ♘f6 4.g3 g6 5.♗g2 ♘c6 6.d4 c×d4 7.♘×d4 ♘×d4 8.♕×d4 ♗g7 9.0-0 0-0 10.a4 ♕a5 11.♕d3 ♗d7 12.♘d5 ♘×d5 13.♕×d5 ♕×d5 14.e×d5 ♗f6 15.c3 a5!

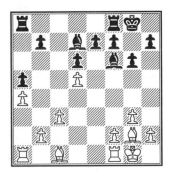

Black already has taken the initiative. But the ending will remain in the bounds of a draw for a long time until Adams cracks under the pressure.

16.♖e1 ♖fb8 17.♗f1 b5 18.a×b5 ♗×b5 19.♗×b5 ♖×b5 20.♖d1 ♖c8 21.♖a4 ♖cc5 22.c4 ♖b3 23.♗e3 ♖c8 24.♗d4 ♔g7 25.♔f1 ♗×d4 26.♖×d4 ♖×b2 27.♖×a5 f5 28.♖a7 ♔f6 29.g4 ♖b4 30.g5+ ♔×g5 31.♖×e7 ♖c×c4 32.♖×c4 ♖×c4 33.♖×h7 ♔f6 34.♖d7 ♔e5 35.♖g7 ♖g4 36.f3 ♖g5 37.♔f2 ♔×d5 38.h4 ♖h5 39.♔g3 ♖h6 40.♖e7

40.♔f4 ♖×h4+ 41.♔g5 ♖h3 42.♔f4= is also playable.

40...♔d4

41.♖e1?!

Adams makes it difficult for himself. 41.♖e6! d5 42.h5 ♖×h5 43.♖×g6 ♚e3 44.♖e6+ ♚d3 45.♚f4 d4 46.♖a6 draws more easily.

41...d5 42.♖d1+ ♚e5 43.♖e1+ ♚d6

44.♖d1?

Losing an important tempo that HYDRA exploits by protecting the d5-pawn indirectly. The straightforward 44.♖a1 draws: 44...d4 45.♖a5 ♚c6 (45...♖h8 46.♖a6+ ♚d5 47.♖×g6 d3 48.♚f4=) 46.♖e5 f4+ 47.♚f2 ♖×h4 48.♚e2 ♖h5 49.♖e4 ♚d5 50.♚d3 g5 51.♖×d4+ ♚e5 52.♖d8=.

44...♖h5! 45.♖a1 ♚c5 46.♖c1+ ♚b4 47.♖d1

47.♖c6 ♖h6 48.♚f2 f4 49.♚e2 ♚b5 50.♖f6 ♖×h4 51.♖×g6 ♚c4–+

47...♚c4 48.♖c1+ ♚d3 49.♖c6 ♖h6 50.h5 f4+ 0–1

HYDRA – Adams, Michael (2737)
Ruy Lopez C87
London m (5), 26.06.2005

1.e4 e5 2.♘f3 ♘c6 3.♗b5 a6 4.♗a4 ♘f6 5.0-0 ♗e7 6.♖e1 d6 7.c3 ♗g4 8.d3 ♘d7 9.♗e3 ♗×f3?!

A slight concession. 9...h6 is the main line.

10.♕×f3 ♗g5

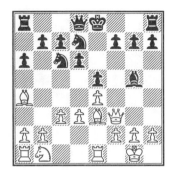

11.♗×c6!?

After this novelty HYDRA has a slight positional advantage and goes on to win a very instructive game by collecting small advantages. A real positional masterpiece! It is very difficult to highlight a single Black mistake from now on. It is just extremely difficult to escape from HYDRA's grip. 11.♘d2 was played, e.g., in Anand-Short, Dortmund 1997.

11...b×c6 12.♘d2 0-0 13.♕g4 ♗×e3 14.♖×e3 ♖b8 15.b3 ♘c5 16.f4 e×f4 17.♕×f4 ♘e6 18.♕f2 ♖b5 19.♖f1 ♖g5 20.d4 ♖g6 21.a4 ♖f6 22.♖f3 ♖×f3 23.♕×f3 ♕g5 24.♘c4 ♕g6

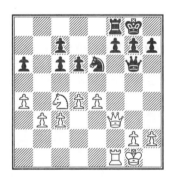

25.h4!!

HYDRA gains more space and increases the pressure. It does not care that its kingside is weakened, as this cannot be exploited by Black.

25...f6 26.♘e3 ♖e8 27.♘f5 h5 28.b4!

HYDRA seizes more space, makes c6-c5 more difficult and prepares to open a second front later.

28...♔h7 29.♘g3 c5

29...♕g4 30.♕f5+ ♔h6 31.♕×g4 h×g4 32.♖f5 is also clearly better for White.

30.d5 ♘d8

31.♖b1!

The right order of moves as 31.b×c5? can be met by 31...♘b7.

31...♘f7 32.b×c5 d×c5 33.♖b7 ♖c8

33...♖e7 34.♘f5 ♘e5 35.♕g3 +−

34.♖a7 ♘d6 35.♖×a6 ♖e8 36.♖c6 ♘×e4 37.♕×h5+ ♕×h5 38.♘×h5 ♔h6 39.♖e6! ♖d8 40.♖×e4 ♔×h5 41.a5 1-0

Adams, Michael (2737) − Hᴅᴅʀᴀ
Sicilian Defense B42
London m (6), 27.06.2005

1.e4 c5 2.♘f3 e6 3.d4 c×d4 4.♘×d4 a6 5.♗d3 ♗c5 6.♘b3 ♗a7 7.0-0 ♘e7 8.c4 d6 9.♘c3 ♘bc6 10.♕e2 0-0 11.♗e3 e5 12.♖ad1 ♘d4 13.♗×d4 e×d4 14.♘d5 ♘c6 15.f4 ♕h4 16.♘d2 ♗e6

17.♘c7?!

In principle, the opening has worked quite well for Adams. But this exchange takes the sting out of his initiative. 17.♘f3 ♕d8 18.♕d2 f6 19.b4 gives him a slight edge.

17...♖ac8 18.♘×e6 f×e6 19.g3 ♕e7 20.a3 e5 21.f5 ♘b8 22.♔g2 ♘d7 23.b4 ♔h8 24.♗c2 ♘f6 25.♖c1 ♖c7 26.♗b3 ♖fc8 27.♖c2 a5 28.♖fc1 ♕e8 29.h3 a4 30.♗a2 ♖e7

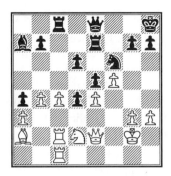

31.c5!?

Adams decides to open the queenside to activate his forces. If he just waits, then Black can eventually try to open the kingside.

31...d×c5 32.b×c5 ♖ec7 33.♗e6 ♖d8 34.♕d3 g6!?

Creating the option to open a second front on the kingside into play.

35.♔h2?!

35.♘f3 is more aggressive, e.g., 35...g×f5 36.♗×f5 ♘h5 37.h4 and White is not worse.

35...♕c6 36.♕f3?!

Adams starts to drift under the constant pressure. The direct 36.g4 is better when the position is more or less dynamically balanced.

36...♖f8 37.g4?!

This weakens many squares, but good advice is hard to give.

37...♕b5

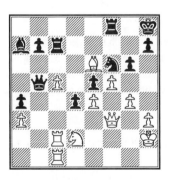

38.♕g3?

Allowing the decisive invasion of Black's queen. After 38.♖b1 ♕a5 39.♖bc1 ♖×c5 40.♕d3, it is not easy to break White's blockade.

38...♕e2+ 39.♕g2 ♕e3 40.♕g3

40.♖f1 d3 41.♖c3 ♗×c5 42.♔h1 g×f5 43.♖×f5 ♖c6–+

40...♖×c5 41.♕×e3 d×e3 42.♘f3 ♘×e4 43.♔g2 ♔g7 0-1

The match was thankfully over. The final score of 5½-½ in favor of the machine echoed the performance of Bobby Fischer. In his 1970-1972 world championship title quest, Fischer was often compared to a machine. Grandmaster Mark Taimanov, after losing 6-0 to Fischer, was quoted as saying, "The terrible feeling that I was playing against a machine which never made any mistake shattered my resistance." Michael Adams probably had a similar feeling. After all, his opponent had a performance rating of roughly 3000!

One has to empathize with Adams, who had to sit on a stage in front of the world media, play a largely unknown but exceptionally strong adversary, and endure the onslaught of technology. Much to his credit, he gave it his best shot and took defeat in stride.

Some commentators were of the opinion that Michael Adams' debacle was the result of insufficient preparation. In an interview given shortly after the match ended, Adams gave no excuses for the final result (ChessBase 2005a):

How extensive was your preparation for the match?

It was a question of time really. I worked about a week with [Grandmaster] Yasser [Seirawan], and that was quite intense. But by that time we were coming quite close to the match…

So you didn't really have much time to prepare for the match at all?

Well, we actually signed the contract one month before the match, which is not really enough for preparation. Maybe you could say I would've been better off with better preparation, but I don't think it would've made a great deal of difference. Perhaps I would've lost 1:5 instead of 0.5:5.5, but I doubt if it changed anything radically.

And the future of man versus machine competitions at chess?

Do you think Adams versus HYDRA 2005 is going to be remembered as THE turning point in the race against machines?

I think it proves that HYDRA is a much stronger 'player' than any other computer in the world. We may not be able to measure its strength in ELO, but it is huge. I also suspect HYDRA is stronger than any other human opponent. Okay, it has to be proved in the future, but this is my impression at the moment and I suspect it is accurate. I mean from my point of view I don't think I played terribly. I did my best and it just wasn't good enough.

Grandmaster David Norwood (2005) had a more "big picture" perspective on the match:

Last week saw the end of humanity. When DEEP BLUE beat Kasparov eight years ago, there was still a great deal of doubt. If top human grandmaster focused on the weaknesses of their artificial opponents, they could still win. The Wembley match between Britain's Michael Adams and HYDRA finally buried that notion. The Terminators have won.

Mickey is one of the best players in the world and HYDRA made him look like an amateur. If computers can totally dominate one of the world's oldest and most complex games, where is the limit for artificial intelligence? Hopefully, we will never have a real war against the machines.

Reaction to the 2005 Adams-HYDRA match[11]

Grandmaster John Nunn:

I really can't see much point in further man-machine contests under the present rules (in which the computer is allowed an unlimited opening book and access to endgame tablebases). However, even changing the rules would probably only delay the inevitable dominance of the machines. Let's get back to humans playing humans, which I for one find more interesting than man-machine contests.

International Master David Levy:

...We are clearly facing, very soon, a situation in which man vs machine Chess, as we currently know it, is no longer of any spectator interest, because soon the time will come, if it has not already arrived, when the gladiator will always be eaten by the lion. What then?

In my opinion the answer is simple – odds games. When the strongest human players have no chance at even games, let us give the human pawn odds.

Chess writer Mig Greengard:

One useful thing this match showed is that strong humans can lose to machines consistently without blundering. This is relatively new. Technical play and grinds with equal material of this sort were relatively rare in machine wins over grandmasters. Sure, they would grab a pawn and win all the time, but here HYDRA never really had a strategically inferior position. It made a few odd "computer" moves, but for the most part it held the balance positionally. When that happens, it's almost inevitable that the computer's error-free play will eventually triumph. To win, or even draw, a human needs a considerable head-start by reaching positions the computer doesn't understand.

A few months later, the Second Man versus Machine World Championship was held, again in Bilbao. This time the human side featured three former FIDE World Chess Champions: Rustam Kasimdzhanov, Alexander Khalifman, and Ruslan Ponomariov. The computer side remained the same (HYDRA, FRITZ and JUNIOR), albeit benefitting from an additional year of improvements. The final score was a decisive 8-4 in favor of the computers (five wins, one loss, six draws). Here is a sample of the high-quality play of HYDRA.

HYDRA – Ponomariov, Ruslan (2704)

French Defense C06
Bilbao (3), 22.11.2005

1.e4 e6 2.d4 d5 3.♘d2 ♘f6 4.e5 ♘fd7 5.♗d3 c5 6.c3 ♘c6 7.♘e2 a5 8.0-0

8...c4?

This concession is too large against HYDRA, as Black's play is too slow. 8...c×d4 and 8...a4 are the main lines. Postny (2006) assesses it as follows: "Ponomariov decided to close the center in order to reduce the number of concrete variations to a minimum. This kind of strategy was quite successful against computers some years ago, but in the last few years computer's ability to play well and consequently in closed positions has increased dramatically."

9.♗c2 b5

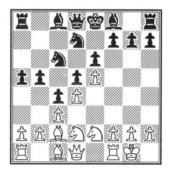

10.b3!

A very strong novelty. Now HYDRA can play on both wings.

10...♘b6 11.b×c4 b×c4 12.♖b1

12...♔d7!?

Ponomariov wants to hide on the queenside, which is not bad in itself. Black's situation is already quite difficult anyway.

13.♘f4 ♔c7 14.♕f3 ♖b8 15.♘h5 ♕e7 16.♖e1 ♗a6 17.♕g3 g6?

Ponomariov should have executed his plan to escape with the king now with 17...♔b7.

18.♘f6 ♔b7?

This allows a mighty strike. 18...h6 is called for.

19.♘de4!! and it is all over!

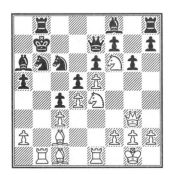

19...♔a7

19...d×e4 runs into a thunderstorm: 20.d5 ♘a7 21.♖×b6+ ♔×b6 22.♗e3+ ♔b7 23.d6 ♕d8 24.♗×e4+ ♔c8 25.♗×a7+− (Postny 2006).

20.♘d6

Hydra's knights rule.

20...♘c8 21.♗a3 ♖×b1 22.♖×b1 ♘×d6 23.♗c5+ ♔a8

24.♗a4

Hydra executes with utmost precision and plunges   with all its heads – into the attack.

24...♗b7 25.e×d6 ♕×f6 26.♗×c6 ♗×c6 27.d7! ♗×c5 28.♕c7 e5 29.d×c5

343

1-0

Postny (2006) provides a nice assessment of the play:

> A very brutal and impressive performance. I would say that White's level of play in this game was something unreachable. Therefore, one should not blame a human and particularly great player like Ruslan Ponomariov for his seemingly poor performance, but praise the chess engine for the great game. In my opinion, the question about the better player, human or computer is becoming rhetorical. Therefore, people should concentrate on competing between themselves.

Monte Carlo Tree Search

Adding knowledge to a game-playing program is challenging, unless you have an expert in that game who can help you. Even then, it can be difficult as the human expert typically talks one language (the game) and the computer scientist another (algorithms). Would it not be wonderful to eliminate the game knowledge from the program?

Wait! That is hearsay. How can you possibly write a program to play strong chess without using chess knowledge? Not possible. But it is! All you need to know is when a game is won, lost, or drawn.

Assume the computer is given a position and asked to assess how good it is. From this position, play a series of random moves all the way to the end of the game. In other words, play a random legal move for White, then a random move for Black, then a random move for White, and so on. When you get to the end of the game you know the final result. Now repeat the process with a new series of random moves and record the result. Pretend you do this 100 times. What can you conclude if these random move sequences lead to a win 76 times, a loss 18 times, and a draw 6 times?

The Monte Carlo Tree Search algorithm is based on the idea of using the power of statistics. If a position favors one side over the other, then this advantage will eventually show itself if you gather enough data. It is the same principle as seen with election polling. Polling companies sample the general population to decide who is ahead in an election. There may only be a few thousand people surveyed in a poll from a population of many million, but that may be enough to determine with high probability the result. So it is with game-tree search. If we do enough random move sequences, we may be able to determine with high probability the best move or the final result.

The computer is out of its opening book and now has to decide on its move. It has, say, 40 alternatives to choose from. Do 100 Monte Carlo move sequences on the first choice to find out its winning percentage. Repeat that process with the second choice, then the third, and so on. Finally, select the move to play with the highest winning chance. Simple! And it uses no knowledge.

Okay, so it is not quite as simple as described above. First, if you want a statistically significant result, you may need to obtain a lot of search results. Second, you cannot afford to consider all moves, so you might need some knowledge to be more selective. Third, using truly random move sequences may not be the most informative search method; using knowledge to eliminate obviously stupid moves will improve efficiency.

Bruce Abramson explored the idea of using Monte Carlo methods in games in 1987. In 2006, Levente Kocsis and Csaba Szepesvári presented their UCT (Upper

---

Confidence bounds applied to Trees) algorithm as a way to elegantly decide how to intelligently apply Monte Carlo search in a game-tree. Their algorithm balances exploration (new moves to consider) and exploitation (deciding when to concentrate on improving the statistics).

In principle, one can build a strong chess program using only Monte Carlo Tree Search – with no chess knowledge. This method uses lots of computing power to get meaningful move-sequence samples. In practice, chess knowledge is used to avoid wasting resources on hopeless lines and concentrating the search on portions of the tree that are more likely to be informative.

Beating "ordinary" grandmasters seemed to be routine. But two grandmasters held a special place in the public's eye: Kasparov and Kramnik. These two players were viewed as being in a league of their own. Surely machine supremacy could not be declared until these great players had been put in their place. In 2006, Vladimir Kramnik agreed to play a six-game match with DEEP FRITZ. If anyone could reassert human supremacy at chess, surely it was the reigning World Champion Vladimir Kramnik.

Vladimir Kramnik (right) vs DEEP FRITZ.
(ChessBase)

Kramnik, Vladimir (2750) – Deep Fritz 10
Catalan Opening E03
Bonn m (1), 25.11.2006

1.d4 ♘f6 2.c4 e6 3.g3

"In my opinion the Catalan Opening is a good choice against a computer. In the structures which generally arise from it, concrete calculation is not at such a premium; more important are strategic nuances." (Braun 2006)

3...d5 4.♗g2 d×c4

Fritz tries to open the position but the resulting structure is also easy to play for Kramnik.

5.♕a4+ ♘bd7 6.♕×c4 a6 7.♕d3 c5 8.d×c5 ♗×c5 9.♘f3 0-0 10.0-0 ♕e7 11.♘c3 b6 12.♘e4!

Kramnik simplifies further and probably already aims for the coming endgame.

12...♘×e4 13.♕×e4 ♘f6

14.♕h4!?

14.♕×a8 ♗b7 15.♕×f8+ ♔×f8 is too risky against a computer.

14...♗b7 15.♗g5 ♖fd8 16.♗×f6 ♕×f6 17.♕×f6 g×f6 18.♖fd1

18...♔f8?

The result of a misevaluation of the resulting endgame. In this respect strong humans are still superior to the machine. Kramnik just knows that his knight is better than the dark-square Black bishop. After 18...♗xf3 19.♗xf3 ♖ab8, the game would have ended in a draw soon.

19.♘e1!

A typical retreat also often employed by Grandmaster Ulf Andersson in similar positions. White has a sustainable strategic initiative.

19...♗xg2 20.♔xg2 f5 21.♖xd8+ ♖xd8 22.♘d3 ♗d4 23.♖c1 e5!?

This try to get counterplay is good. But FRITZ follows a misguided plan with it.

24.♖c2

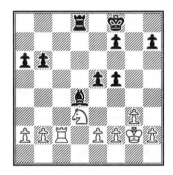

24...♖d5?

FRITZ 10 misevaluates the resulting bishop versus knight ending. Without the rooks, the knight reigns supreme. After 24...a5!, White has only a minimal advantage.

25.♘b4! ♖b5 26.♘xa6 ♖xb2

Black does not want to exchange the rooks of course, but it has no choice, as after 26...♗xb2!?, White can force the exchange with 27.♘c7 ♖c5 28.♖xc5 bxc5.

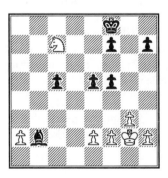

...and White should be winning, but matters are more difficult than they seem at first sight: 29.a4 (29.♘d5!?) 29...♗d4 (29...♔e7? 30.a5 ♔d6 31.♘b5+ ♔c6 32.a6 ♔b6 33.a7 ♔b7 34.♔f3 ≠) 30.c3 (30.a5?! c4 31.♘b5 c3 32.♘xd4 exd4 33.a6 c2 34.a7 c1♕ 35.a8♕+ ♔g7 36.♕d5 ♕b2 is most likely only drawn.) 30...c4 31.♔f3 ♗c5 32.♘a6 ♗d6 33.♔e2 ♔e7 34.♔d2 ♔e6 35.a5 ♔d5 36.♔c3 e4 37.♘b4+

♔c5 38.a6 ♗e5+ 39.♔d2 ♔b6 40.a7 ♔b7 41.♘c6 and White is better but it is not completely clear if he can win.

27.♖×b2 ♗×b2 28.♘b4 ♔g7

29.♘d5

29.♔f3 b5 30.♘d5 ♗d4 31.e3 ♗c5 32.♔e2 e4 33.♔d2 ♔g6

At first I (KM) thought that 34.♔c3? wins and in fact published it in *ChessBase Magazine*, but Kasparov proved me wrong. He gave a convincing line: 34.♘c7! b4 35.♘d5 ♔g5 36.h3 h6 37.♘f4 ♗d6 38.♔c2 h5 39.♘g2+− and White has complete control and will invade with his king (Kasparov 2007). Kasparov's idea is right, but his execution is wrong. 33.♔d2? is the real mistake of my line. In Kasparov's line (34.♘c7!) 36...h5! draws instead of 36....h6?. Kasparov's idea should be played in the form 33.♘c7! b4 34.♘d5 and White wins.

So, what is wrong with 34.♔c3? Continue 34...♔g5 35.♘c7 ♔g4 36.♘×b5 ♔f3 37.♔c4 ♗b6 38.♘d4+ ♔×f2 39.♘×f5 ♔f3 40.♔d5 ♗×e3 41.♘h4+ ♔g4 42.♔×e4 ♗b6 43.a4

348

This is surprisingly drawn because of the strength of the bishop in an open position: 43...h5! (Kasparov; but not 43...♗d8? 44.♞g2 ♚h3 45.♞f4+ ♚g4 46.♚e3 ♗b6+ [46...h5 47.♞g2 ♗b6+ 48.♚e2 ♗a5 49.♚f2 ♗d8 50.h3+ ♚xh3 51.♚f3+−] 47.♚e2 ♗d8 48.♚f2 ♚f5 49.♚f3+− [M.Feist]) 44.♞g2 f5+ 45.♚e5 ♗c7+ 46.♚e6 ♗b6 47.♚f6 ♗d8+ 48.♚g6 ♚f3 49.♞e1+ ♚g4 50.♞d3 ♗c7 51.♞f2+ ♚f3 52.♚xf5 ♚xf2 53.♚g5 ♚f3 54.♚xh5 ♚e4=.

29...♗d4 30.a4?

Pawn moves do not have priority here.

30...♗c5 31.h3?! f6 32.f3 ♚g6 33.e4 h5! 34.g4 h×g4 35.h×g4 f×e4 36.f×e4 ♚g5 37.♚f3 ♚g6 38.♚e2 ♚g5 39.♚d3 ♗g1 40.♚c4 ♗f2 41.♚b5 ♚×g4 42.♞×f6+

42.♞xb6 ♗xb6 43.♚xb6 f5=

42...♚f3 43.♚c6 ♗h4 44.♞d7 ♚×e4 45.♚×b6 ♗e1 46.♚c6 ♚f5 47.♞×e5 ♚×e5 ½-½

Deep Fritz 10 − Kramnik, Vladimir (2750)
Queen's Gambit Accepted D10
Bonn m (2), 27.11.2006

1.d4 d5 2.c4 d×c4 3.e4 b5 4.a4 c6 5.♞c3

5.a×b5 c×b5 6.♞c3 ♗d7 is the alternative.

5...b4 6.♞a2 ♞f6 7.e5 ♞d5 8.♗×c4 e6 9.♞f3

9...a5!?

Kramnik has managed to get a relatively closed position with a clear plan for Black: the lever c6-c5 can be prepared in the long-term. For White, it is much more difficult to use the advantage in development.

10.♗g5 ♛b6 11.♘c1 ♗a6 12.♕e2 h6 13.♗e3 ♗×c4 14.♕×c4 ♘d7 15.♘b3

15.♘d3 ♗e7 16.♖c1 ♖c8 17.♘d2 0-0 18.♘e4 ♛b8 is also okay for Black.

15...♗e7 16.♖c1

16...0-0!

As White cannot take on c6, Kramnik brings his king into safety and his king's rook into play.

17.0-0

17.♕×c6? runs into 17...♛×c6 18.♖×c6 ♘7b6 (Braun 2006).

17...♖fc8 18.♕e2 c5

Finally Kramnik has managed to execute this freeing advance. He is by no means worse and White has to act carefully. So Kramnik has won the opening battle again.

19.♘fd2?

The start of a misguided attack. 19.d×c5 ♗×c5 (19...♘×c5 20.♗d4 ♖c7 21.♘fd2

Ξac8 22.g3=) 20.♗d4 ♗xd4 21.♘fxd4 ♘c5 22.♘xc5 Ξxc5 23.♘b3 Ξxc1 24.Ξxc1 is almost equal.

19...♕c6 20.♕h5?!

Deep Fritz consistently follows its plan to attack. 20.Ξa1? runs into 20...c4–+; 20.♕g4?! ♘xe3 21.fxe3 ♕xa4 also favors Black: 22.♕f4 (22.Ξxf7? ♔xf7 23.Ξf1+ ♔g8 24.♕e6+ ♔h8 25.♕e7 c4 26.♘f7 Ξe8 27.♕xd7 ♕xd7 28.Ξxd7 cxb3 and Black is for choice according to (Braun 2006).) 22...♖f8 23.♘xc5 ♘xc5 24.dxc5 ♕a2 and Black's counterplay gives him the advantage. 20.♘xc5 ♘xc5 21.dxc5 ♘xe3 22.fxe3 ♗xc5 23.b3 Ξd8 24.♘c4 was probably the best way to limit the damage.

20...♕xa4 21.♘xc5 ♘xc5 22.dxc5

22...♘xe3!

Kramnik does not fear any ghosts.

23.fxe3 ♗xc5 24.♕xf7+ ♔h8 25.♕f3 Ξf8 26.♕e4 ♕d7!

The queen rejoins Black's forces. White will have to fight hard for the draw.

27.♘b3 ♗b6 28.Ξfd1 ♕f7 29.Ξf1

29...♕a7!?

29...♕e7 is the alternative.

30.Ξxf8+ Ξxf8 31.♘d4 a4 32.♘xe6 ♗xe3+ 33.♔h1

33...♗×c1?

Now it is a clear draw. After 33...♖e8!, amazing complications can arise: 34.♖d1 (34.♖f1 ♛a6 35.♖f3 ♛×e6 36.♖×e3 ♛a6) 34...a3 35.♘×g7 a2 36.♘×e8 a1♛ 37.♛f3 ♗f4.

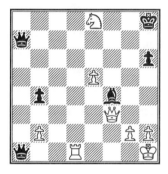

...and in both cases Black is clearly for choice but both may still be tenable for White with tenacious defense that can be expected from the machine.

34.♘×f8

34...♛e3??

An embarrassing oversight. Kramnik would never have allowed such a mate against a human. Only after 34...♚g8 35.♘g6 can Black play 35...♛e3 36.♛d5+ ♚h7 37.♘f8+ ♚h8 with equality. Frederic Friedel (2006) witnessed the dramatic turn of events and described it as such:

> Kramnik played the move 34...♕e3 calmly, stood up, picked up his cup and was
> about to leave the stage to go to his rest room. At least one audio commentator also
> noticed nothing, while FRITZ operator Mathias Feist kept glancing from the board to
> the screen and back, hardly able to believe that he had input the correct move. FRITZ
> was displaying mate in one, and when Mathias executed it on the board Kramnik
> briefly grasped his forehead, took a seat to sign the score sheet and left for the press
> conference, which he dutifully attended.

35.♕h7# 1-0

A dazed Kramnik describes what happened in the post-game press conference
(Friedel 2006):

> It was actually not only about the last move. I was calculating this line very long in
> advance, and then recalculating. It was very strange, some kind of blackout. I was
> feeling well, I was playing well, I think I was pretty much better. I calculated the line
> many, many times, rechecking myself. I already calculated this line when I played
> 29...♕a7, and after each move I was recalculating, again, and again, and finally I
> blundered mate in one. Actually it was the first time that it happened to me, and I
> cannot really find any explanation. I was not feeling tired, I think I was calculating
> well during the whole game... It's just very strange, I cannot explain it.

It takes a strong personality to recover from such a devastating blow!

Kramnik, Vladimir (2750) – DEEP FRITZ 10
Catalan Opening E03
Bonn m (3), 29.11.2006

**1.d4 ♘f6 2.c4 e6 3.g3 d5 4.♗g2 d×c4 5.♕a4+ ♘bd7 6.♕×c4 a6 7.♕c2
c5 8.♘f3 b6**

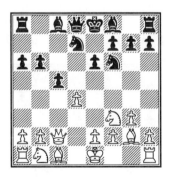

9.♘e5!

Kramnik starts his play immediately.

**9...♘d5 10.♘c3 ♗b7 11.♘×d5 ♗×d5 12.♗×d5 c×d5 13.0-0 ♘×e5
14.d×e5**

14...♕c8

A computer move, which is justified by FRITZ's excellent 16th move. 14...♗e7 would probably be the choice of most humans and is also playable.

15.♖d1 ♕e6 16.♕d3

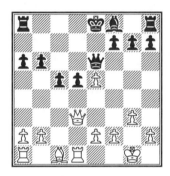

16...♗e7!

FRITZ finds the best way to complete its development. 16...d4?! 17.e3 d×e3 18.♗×e3; 16...♖d8?! 17.♕×a6; and 16...♕×e5?! 17.♗f4 all play into White's hand.

17.♕×d5 ♖d8 18.♕b3 ♖×d1+ 19.♕×d1 0-0 20.♕b3

20...c4!

FRITZ plays actively and energetically. 20...♕×e5?! 21.♕×b6 ♕×e2 22.♗e3 is easier to play for Kramnik.

21.♕c3 f6 22.b3 ♖c8 23.♗b2 b5 24.♕e3

24.e×f6? ♗×f6−+

24...f×e5 25.b×c4 ♖×c4 26.♗×e5 h6 27.♖d1 ♖c2

28.♕b3?!

The resulting endgame should be drawn of course but only Black can play for a win. Against a human, Kramnik would most probably have played something else here such as, e.g., 28.a3, when White is slightly better but all three results are still possible.

28...♕×b3 29.a×b3 ♖×e2 30.♗d6 ♗f6 31.♗c5 a5 32.♗d4 ♗e7 33.♗c3 a4 34.b×a4 b×a4 35.♖d7 ♗f8 36.♖d8 ♔f7 37.♖a8 a3?!

From a practical point of view 37...♖c2 was better.

38.♖×f8+! ♔×f8 39.♗b4+ ♔f7 40.♗×a3

White has constructed an impregnable fortress. The machine cannot understand the very nature of this concept, which is easy for Kramnik.

40...♖a2

40...g5 is more principled, marking the f- and h-pawns as weaknesses, but it does not change the result in this case.

41.♗c5 g6 42.h4 ♔f6 43.♗e3 h5 44.♔g2 ½-½

Deep Fritz 10 – Kramnik, Vladimir (2750)
Petroff Defense C43
Bonn m (4), 01.12.2006

**1.e4 e5 2.♘f3 ♘f6 3.d4 ♘×e4 4.♗d3 d5 5.♘×e5 ♘d7 6.♘×d7 ♗×d7
7.0-0 ♗d6 8.♕h5 ♕f6 9.♘c3 ♕×d4 10.♘×d5?!**

10.♗e3 is played more often but White's advantage is very small even in that case.

10...♗c6 11.♘e3 g6 12.♕h3

12...♘g5?!

12...0-0 is more precise as White cannot profit from the bishop pair after 13.♘c4 ♖fe8 14.♗e3 ♕f6 15.♘×d6 ♘×d6 because of Black's activity.

13.♕g4 ♕f4 14.♕×f4 ♗×f4 15.♘c4 ♘e6

15...♗×c1?! 16.♖e1+ ♘e6 17.♖a×c1 0-0 18.♘e5 (Braun) is easier to play for White who has a strategic initiative.

16.♗×f4 ♘×f4 17.♖fe1+ ♔f8 18.♗f1 ♗b5

19.a4

19.♘a5?! is neutralized by 19...♗×f1 20.♔×f1 ♔g7=, but 19.♖e5!? was a serious alternative.

19...♗a6 20.b4 ♗×c4 21.♗×c4 ♖d8 22.♖e4 ♘h5 23.♖ae1 ♖d7

24.h3?!

24.g3!? is a bit more precise: 24...♘g7 25.b5 h5 26.♔g2, and White's initiative is not so easy to neutralize.

24...♘g7 25.♖e5

After 25.g4, Black frees his knight by 25...h5 26.♔g2 h×g4 27.h×g4 f5 28.g×f5 ♘×f5.

25...♘f5 26.♗b5 c6 27.♗d3 ♘d6 28.g4 ♔g7 29.f4

29.♖e7?! is met by 29...♖×e7 30.♖×e7 ♔f6 31.♖c7 ♖c8=.

29...♖hd8 30.♔g2 ♘c8 31.a5 ♖d4 32.♖5e4 ♔f8 33.♔f3 h6 34.♖×d4 ♖×d4 35.♖e4 ♖d6 36.♔e3 g5

37.♖d4

Usually the side with rook and bishop does not want to exchange rooks, so 37.c4!? is a better practical choice. But objectively it should be tenable for Black as well.

37...♔e7 38.c4 ♖×d4 39.♔×d4 g×f4 40.♔e4 ♔f6 41.♔×f4 ♘e7 42.♗e4 b6 43.c5 b×c5 44.b×c5 ♘g6+ 45.♔e3 ♘e7 46.♔d4 ♔e6 47.♗f3

With his next moves, Kramnik builds an impregnable fortress

47...f5! 48.♗d1 ♔f6! 49.♗c2 f×g4 50.h×g4 ♔e6 51.♗b1 ♔f6 52.♗e4 ♔e6 53.♗h1 ♔f6 54.♗f3 ♔e6 ½-½

Kramnik, Vladimir (2750) – Deep Fritz 10
Nimzo-Indian Defense E51
Bonn m (5), 03.12.2006

1.d4 ♞f6 2.c4 e6 3.♞f3 d5 4.♞c3 ♝b4 5.e3 0-0 6.a3 ♝×c3+ 7.b×c3 c5 8.♝b2 ♞c6 9.♖c1 ♖e8 10.♝d3 d×c4 11.♝×c4 e5 12.d×e5 ♛×d1+ 13.♖×d1 ♞×e5 14.♞×e5 ♖×e5 15.♝e2 ♝d7 16.c4 ♖e7

17.h4?!

17.♝×f6 g×f6 18.♖d6 ♔g7 19.♔d2 ♝c6, Geller-Spassky, Riga 1965, was a better choice against Fritz. After 20.♝f3, White cannot lose and indeed presses for some time.

17...♞e4! 18.h5 ♝a4 19.♖d3

19...b5!

FRITZ activates play on the queenside before Kramnik can consolidate and bring the power of his bishop pair into full force.

20.c×b5 ♗×b5 21.♖d1 ♗×e2 22.♔×e2 ♖b8 23.♗a1 f5 24.♖d5 ♖b3 25.♖×f5 ♖×a3 26.♖b1 ♖e8

27.♖f4

27.♖e5 ♖a2+ 28.♖b2 ♘c3+ 29.♔d3 ♖×e5 30.♖×a2 ♖×e3+! 31.f×e3 ♘×a2 32.♔c4 "was evaluated by Kramnik as a draw" (Braun 2006).

27...♖a2+ 28.♔e1 h6 29.♖g4 g5! 30.h×g6 ♘×f2 31.♖h4 ♖f8

32.♔f1!!

The only defense as Black has no dangerous discovered check.

32...♘h3+ 33.♔e1 ♘f2 34.♔f1 ♘h3+ 35.♔e1 ½-½

Deep Fritz 10 – Kramnik, Vladimir (2750)
Sicilian Defense B86
Bonn m (6), 05.12.2006

1.e4 c5 2.♘f3 d6 3.d4 c×d4 4.♘×d4 ♘f6 5.♘c3 a6 6.♗c4 e6 7.0-0 ♗e7 8.♗b3 ♕c7 9.♖e1

9.f4 is the main line.

9...♘c6 10.♖e3!?

An original concept. Objectively, the rook lift should not be too dangerous for Black, but Kramnik cannot use most of his experience and pattern recognition for the Sicilian from this point forward.

10...0-0 11.♖g3 ♔h8 12.♘×c6 b×c6 13.♕e2

13...a5!?

Kramnik keeps his center flexible to be able to react there later and develops counterplay on the queenside.

14.♗g5 ♗a6 15.♕f3 ♖ab8 16.♖e1 c5 17.♗f4 ♕b7 18.♗c1 ♘g8

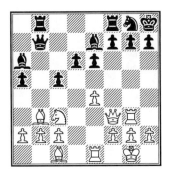

19.♘b1!?

A highly original preventive regrouping to deal with Black's play on the queenside.

19...♗f6 20.c3 g6

20...♗e5 21.♖h3 ♘f6? runs into 22.♕d1!!± (Ftacnik 2006).

21.♘a3 ♕c6 22.♖h3 ♗g7 23.♕g3 a4?!

This exposed the pawn. 23...c4 24.♗c2 e5 25.♕h4 h6 is more precise.

24.♗c2 ♖b6?

Kramnik probably missed the following shot. Otherwise he would have chosen 24...e5 25.♕h4 h6 with chances for both sides.

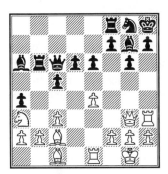

25.e5!!

FRITZ opens the way for his pieces and disrupts Black's pawn structure.

25...d×e5 26.♖×e5 ♘f6

Of course not 26...♗×e5? 27.♕×e5+ f6 28.♖×h7+ ♚×h7 29.♕h5+ ♚g7 30.♕×g6+ ♚h8 31.♕h7#.

27.♕h4 ♕b7 28.♖e1 h5 29.♖f3

A good practical decision, as Kramnik now faces a difficult choice. It is really remarkable that FRITZ did not take the pawn with 29.♕×a4 as objectively this may well be better than the text move, e.g., 29...♖a8 30.♕h4 ♖×b2 31.♖f3±.

29...♘h7?

Too passive. Kramnik had to try to get counterplay by 29...e5!!.

30.♕×a4 (30.♖×e5 ♘g4 31.♖e1 ♕b8) 30...e4 and White is better but Black has drawing chances in both cases because of his activity. But a move like 29...e5!! is of course difficult to play against a machine. This is one of the human disadvantages in these matches. FRITZ had it easier when it put the e-pawn on that very same square with 25.e5!!.

30.♕×a4 ♕c6 31.♕×c6 ♖×c6

32.♗a4!

"The program will now give an impressive lecture in chess technique; without precision the task could have been much more complicated." (Ftacnik 2006)

32...♖b6 33.b3 ♔g8 34.c4 ♖d8 35.♘b5 ♗b7 36.♖fe3

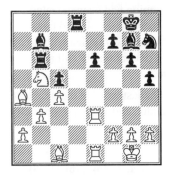

36...♗h6?!

The exchange of bishops helps White, but good advice is already hard to give.

37.♖e5 ♗×c1 38.♖×c1 ♖c6 39.♘c3 ♖c7

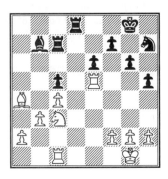

40.♗b5!

FRITZ starts the decisive regrouping. Its pressure against c5 will allow it to take over the d-file so that its rook can invade.

40...♘f8 41.♘a4 ♖dc8 42.♖d1 ♔g7 43.♖d6 f6 44.♖e2 e5 45.♖ed2 g5 46.♘b6 ♖b8 47.a4 1–0

Complete domination by White. A masterpiece of the machine. It takes a 3000 ELO performance rating to defeat a World Champion by a score of 4 to 2.

The human world chess champion had been defeated by a computer in 1997. Surely it was a fluke, or so many believed. And now, in 2006, it happened again. In that decade in between, man had struggled with no major successes and many embarrassing failures. Could one rationally still argue that humans were the better players? The data did not lie.

In many ways, this game is the last word in the titanic struggles of Man versus Machine at chess. Public, media, and – most importantly – sponsor interest in these battles was gone.

Garry Kasparov (2010)
Former World Chess Champion

It was my luck (perhaps my bad luck) to be the world chess champion during the critical years in which computers challenged, then surpassed, human chess players. Before 1994 and after 2004 these duels held little interest. The computers quickly went from too weak to too strong. But for a span of ten years these contests were fascinating clashes between the computational power of the machines (and, lest we forget, the human wisdom of their programmers) and the intuition and knowledge of the grandmaster.

Post-Game

The Kramnik – Fritz match effectively closed the book on serious man-machine chess contests. The state of the art was reflected in a series of 2007 and 2008 events where Rybka gave pawn-and-move odds to grandmaster opposition. It did quite well, despite the significant handicap. How insulting! Not only were the machines our masters at chess, these games served to show how wide the gap had grown.

Joel Benjamin (2014) played a match against Rybka giving draw odds. His conclusions are quite sobering.

> I lost one such match against Rybka, with White in all the games. Afterwards Larry Kaufman told me he didn't think anyone in the world could draw Rybka with Black. Quite a sobering thought. The bottom line is that handicap matches can be humiliating to grandmasters (oh what a beating I took for science and a little bit of money). Top players won't be too interested. I think that the ship has sailed on man vs machine. We know that our way of thinking is often superior in chess but over the course of a game the big advantages the computers have cannot be overcome. There is no new ground to cover.

Monty Newborn (2006), whose work in computer chess goes back to the late 1960s, was asked to comment on the Kramnik match result.

> Today's outcome may end the interest in future chess matches between human champions and computers, according to Monty Newborn, a professor of computer science at McGill University in Montreal. Professor Newborn, who helped organize the match between Mr. Kasparov and Deep Blue, said of future matches: "I don't know what one could get out of it at this point. The science is done."
>
> Mr. Newborn said that the development of chess computers had been useful.
>
> "If you look back 50 years, that was one thing we thought they couldn't do," he said. "It is one little step, that's all, in the most exciting problem of what can't computers do that we can do."
>
> Speculating about where research might go next, Mr. Newborn said, "If you are interested in programming computers so that they compete in games, the two interesting ones are poker and go. That is where the action is."

2007: Checkers

A team led by Jonathan Schaeffer (University of Alberta) announces that Checkers is solved: perfect play by both sides from the starting position leads to a draw.

Computers continue to this day to play against each other online. The result is that the top programs have gaudy ratings over 3300 ELO with no limit to how high they might climb within sight (circa 2018). Even as talented a player as World Champion Magnus Carlsen would be a massive underdog in a match against an electronic super-grandmaster. With a 500 rating point deficit, one would expect a lop-sided result. *C'est la vie.*

Many players attribute the outstanding success of computer chess programs to the hardware – faster computers and/or more computing resources translates into additional ELO points (as per Ken Thompson's result). There is no doubt that hardware performance dominated the outstanding success of computer players in the 1980s and 1990s. However, always behind the scenes were talented programmers and knowledgeable chess experts who were continually refining the software, adding chess knowledge where appropriate, or devising new algorithms to allow the program to overcome a weakness. Has the success been due to hardware speed (brute-force search) or software intelligence (knowledge and algorithms)? In car racing parlance, is winning a race the result of a faster car or a more skillful driver?

In 2014 an interesting experiment took place. Albert Silver ran a short match between KOMODO 8 and SHREDDER 10 to see if he could demonstrate the relative contributions of hardware and software in the program's performance. At the time of the experiment KOMODO 8 had a gaudy 3232 rating. SHREDDER 10 was a dominant program in 2006 (8 years previously), with a rating of 2855 (Carlsen strength). Was the rating difference of 375 points due to faster hardware, better software, or a combination of both. As Silver (2014) observes:

> Over the last 20 years, and even more so the last decade, we have seen technology advancing by leaps and bounds in ways that would shock someone from only 1990. Hardware has advanced so much that our smartphones of today (the first iPhone dates back only seven years) are far more computer than phone, but software has also advanced hand-in-hand with this process. The strength of chess engines has also taken off, but it is sometimes hard for the layman to differentiate how much of the progress is due to hardware and how much to software. The answer is both of course.

> Still, it was a bit of a shock to listen to a conversation between two strong players, one of whom is a grandmaster, claim that engines had really not progressed at all in the past ten years, and that the ELO leaps the programmers were taking credit for, were entirely due to the faster hardware. Needless to say, for someone who knows several of these programmers, and the enormous time and effort expended, to see them classified as con artists did not sit well with me.

> I realized the statements were not meant maliciously, and were sincere in their utter ignorance. After some thought I realized the vast majority of users are probably unclear on just how much progress has been made in pure programming terms.

Silver pitted KOMODO running on a smart phone versus SHREDDER using a state-of-the-art desktop machine. In terms of hardware, KOMODO was completely out-gunned, running at only 2% of the speed it could achieve on a desktop. Clearly SHREDDER had an enormous compute advantage that should have translated into an easy match win. The result? KOMODO scored four wins and two draws in six games: a decisive 5-1 victory. In other words, all the quiet, unassuming, and often incremental work being done behind the scenes to produce better search algorithms and incorporate more knowledgeable software had paid off. DEEP BLUE, even though its 1997 hardware is faster than a 2017 desktop computer, would lose to today's top chess programs.

Given that the machine is now superior to man at chess, some players, including Kasparov, advocated for a new style of chess that was a symbiotic relationship between the two. Under the moniker of "advanced chess" (and other similar names and variants), a few events were held where the human entrant was aided by a computer. While interesting, such events failed to capture the public's imagination. It seemed to be a forlorn attempt to return chess and computer chess to the media spotlight.

Bent Larsen (2010)
Grandmaster

…These Kasparov-computer matches exasperate me. And as for advanced chess, it's simply inadmissible! It's a road to nowhere. Chess loses its mysticism. Nobody will consider chess as an art. It's a pity that it's the very champion who destroys chess.

Grandmasters Anand and Shirov playing Advanced Chess
(ChessBase)

With computers having a 3000+ rating, the obvious question to ask is whether they will ever be "perfect." If chess is a draw, as most experts believe, then perfect play means that both sides never make a losing move.

How difficult is it to solve chess? Circa 2018, checkers is the largest game solved that is of interest to competitive humans. It has roughly 10^{21} possible positions:

$$1,000,000,000,000,000,000,000.$$

To make it more concrete, the number is more than one billion times larger than the size of Bill Gates' wealth.

Chess is a much harder game computationally: a larger board (64 playable squares versus 32), more piece types (six versus two), and additional special-case rules. No one knows how many possible legal chess positions there are, but the estimates all hover around 10^{45}, plus or minus a factor of one thousand:

$$1,000,000,000,000,000,000,000,000,000,000,000,000,000,000,000.$$

This is not quite the number of atoms in the universe, but not that far off (relatively speaking)!

The reality is that current technology cannot solve chess. Even with a computer one million times faster and with one million times more storage, the task is hopeless. A major technological breakthrough is needed before solving chess becomes a possibility. If it is one lesson the past century has taught mankind, never underestimate the advances in technology. A new computer paradigm, such as quantum computing, may hold the key.

So, for now and the foreseeable future, computers are not perfect and the elite programs may occasionally make a mistake and lose a game. It does not really matter; it is undisputable that computers are much stronger than humans and that gap will only grow over time.

2015: Poker

The University of Alberta's Computer Poker Research Group (CPRG), led by Michael Bowling, announces that they have solved two-player limit Texas Hold'em.

In October 2016, the CPRG demonstrates super-human play for two-player no-limit Texas Hold'em. In February 2017, a team from Carnegie-Mellon University also demonstrates super-human play.

Does it really matter that there are chess-playing machines that can beat the best of humanity? Not really. People play chess for many reasons: social, to be with friends; intellectual, to understand the mysteries of the game; pleasure, to enjoy competition; artistic, to create beauty over the board; and many other reasons. None of these is affected by having a super-GM electronic opponent. Indeed, the computer can be used to enhance our enjoyment. We can use it to accelerate our learning, uncover new knowledge about the game, have a tireless and adaptable sparring partner, and so on.

But chess aficionados lament that some aspects of the game may have been diminished as a result of the advent of computers. For example, consider psychology. Could Mikhail Tal have dominated the world with his risky, complex tactical play? The computer would have ruthlessly and unemotionally laid bare all the holes in his analysis. Yet Tal's games, even the ones that are flawed, have enormous entertainment value. Psychology is still a relevant factor in human play, but its importance is limited by the impervious board assessments of the machine.

Then there are the beautiful gems of the past. Deep search would have deprived us of being witness to the elegant dance of the Black pieces in Reti versus Alekhine from Baden-Baden, 1925. Cold objective analysis would have led White to play differently in Larsen's first game against Petrosian at the Second Piatigorsky Cup, 1966. How much poorer would the chess literature be?

Garry Kasparov (2017)
Former World Chess Champion

Chess computers don't have psychological faults, but they do have very distinct

---

strengths and weaknesses, far more distinct that any equivalently strong human player would have. Today, they are so strong that most of their vulnerabilities have been steamrolled into irrelevancy by the sheer speed and depth of brute-force search. They cannot play strategically, but they are too accurate tactically for a human to exploit those subtle weaknesses decisively. A tennis player with a 250-m.p.h. serve doesn't have to worry very much about having a weak backhand.

Finally, here is one last game in the battle for chess supremacy between man and machine. For this encounter go back to 2005 and the Second Man versus Machine World Championship in Bilbao.

Ponomariov, Ruslan (2704) – Fʀɪᴛᴢ
Queen's Pawn Game D00
Bilbao (2), 21.11.2005

1.d4 ♘f6 2.c3 d5 3.♗f4 ♗f5 4.e3 e6 5.♕b3 ♘bd7?!

This should not be correct but the computer can try it against a human as it gets activity as compensation. 5...♕c8 is the main line.

6.♕×b7 ♗d6 7.♗×d6 c×d6 8.♕a6 ♖b8 9.♕a3 ♕b6 10.b4 0-0 11.♘d2 e5 12.♘gf3 ♕c7 13.♗a6 e4 14.♘g1 ♖b6 15.♖c1 ♘b8 16.♗e2 ♖c8

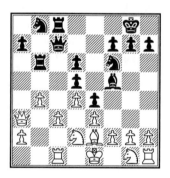

17.♗d1!

Ponomariov's point. He manages to consolidate and his extra pawn gives a slight advantage but it is difficult to make that count.

17...♗d7 18.♘e2 ♗b5 19.0-0 ♘bd7 20.♘b3 h5 21.♖e1 h4 22.h3 ♖b7 23.♘a5 ♖bb8 24.♗a4 a6 25.♗b3 ♘b6 26.♕b2 ♕d7 27.a3 ♖c7 28.♕a2 ♖bc8 29.♘f4 ♕f5

The alternative 29...♖×c3 30.♖×c3 ♖×c3 31.♘×d5 ♘b×d5 32.♗×d5 ♗a4 also gives Black some compensation for the pawn.

30.a4 ♗d3

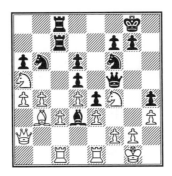

31.g4?

Ponomariov overreaches and runs into a powerful counterblow. After 31.♕d2 ♘c4 32.♘×c4 d×c4 33.♗d1, White is certainly not worse.

31...h×g3 32.f×g3 g5! 33.g4 ♕h7 34.♘h5 ♘×h5 35.g×h5 ♕×h5 36.♔h2 ♕h4 37.♔g2 ♖×c3 38.♖×c3 ♖×c3 39.♔g3

39...♗c2??

FRITZ was running on a relatively slow machine and might have been in time trouble. 39...♘c4 is simply winning.

40.♕×h4 g×h4 41.♖c1

41...♖×b3?

This move loses, as White's queenside pawns will queen. The choice between 41...
♗×b3, 41...♖×e3 and 41...♘c4 is very difficult. Black retains practical drawing
chances in all cases.

42.♘×b3 ♗×b3 43.a5 ♘c4 44.b5 ♗a4

44...a×b5 45.a6 ♘b6 46.♖c6 ♘a8 47.♖c8+ +−

45.b×a6 ♗c6 46.a7 ♔g7 47.a6 ♗a8 48.♖b1 1−0 Bravo Ruslan!

Why is this game so important? The computer played well until blundering and
losing a won position. Not the best-played game by either side.

At the time of this writing (2018), this game represents the last victory by a human
against an elite chess program when played under tournament conditions.

Garry Kasparov (2017b)
Former World Chess Champion

Winning against a computer today is virtually impossible. The level of precision that
is required, the level of vigilance... it's impossible.

Technology does not stand still. Every day there are new advances reported in the
literature. The field of artificial intelligence is one of the most exciting areas for
innovation these days. In particular, the past decade has seen the emergence of so-
called "deep learning" and reinforcement learning as powerful AI tools. This was
amply demonstrated in 2016 and 2017 when DeepMind's program ALPHAGO came
out of nowhere and crushed all human opposition at the difficult game of Go.

In 2017 the DeepMind team generalized their program to play chess and shogi
(Japanese chess). The result was staggering. With four hours of computing (albeit
using a massive amount of computing power), the new program, ALPHAZERO,
was able to master chess – with no human input other than the rules of the game.
ALPHAZERO then played a 100-game match against STOCKFISH, one of the strongest
programs in the world at that time with its 3200+ ELO rating. The result was
stunning: the learning program won by the mind-boggling score of 24 win to 0 with
76 draws. Analysis of the games show that ALPHAZERO has an internal model for
evaluating positions that is unlike anything ever seen in human play. The games
are deep, mysterious, and, well, amazing! At the time of this writing there are no
published games between ALPHAZERO and humans, but surely the result of any such
contest is a foregone conclusion.

2017: Go

The program ALPHAGO, the product of Google's DeepMind and led by David Silver,
defeated 18 time World Go Champion Lee Sedol by a score of 4 wins to 1 in a 2016
exhibition match. In 2017, the program defeated the current World Champion Ka Jie
by a score of 3-0.

Go has been considered the "Holy Grail" of board games for artificial intelligence
research. Success could not be achieved by deep alpha-beta search (19×19 board

meant 361 possible moves at the start of the game) or by extensive knowledge (humans argue that strong play requires numerous pieces of refined knowledge). In the end, the winning recipe was Monte Carlo tree search combined with machine learning (deep learning and reinforcement learning). By playing millions of games, the program was able to refine its evaluation function to the point where it has achieved super-human abilities. The result is a *tour de force* for artificial intelligence research.

Computer domination at chess is complete. It has been a 60 year journey, starting with the germination by Claude Shannon, and breaking the novice barrier by MacHack, the club player of Chess X.Y, the mastery of Belle, the leap forward of Deep Blue, to, finally, the elite and super-elite grandmaster programs of today. It is a testament to mankind's quest for scientific knowledge and determined pursuit of a grand challenge. But it is also a tribute to the human grandmasters, and their ability to navigate through the complexities of chess and hold at bay for so many years the massive computational power of technology.

But it really has been a contest between man and man. On the one hand we have the extraordinary abilities of human players such as Garry Kasparov and Vladimir Kramnik who set the standard for human excellence at a challenging domain. Given the slow computing power at their disposal (the brain) and the limited data storage ability (memory), what they achieved at chess is remarkable.

On the other hand, we have a generation of scientists whose intellectual curiosity and competitive spirit allowed them to create ideas and invent new technology. The game of chess has played a pivotal role in the advances of artificial intelligence, many of which are now part of our daily lives. For many involved in creating strong chess-playing machines, the goal was to conduct leading-edge research; chess was the application domain used to demonstrate the research. Some of the ideas pioneered by computer-chess researchers or by using chess as an experimental test bed include transposition tables, alpha-beta search enhancements, "brute-force" search, Monte Carlo tree search, parallel search, search-knowledge trade-offs, constructing large databases, reinforcement learning, annual competitions, etc. This work has found applications in deciphering the human genome, health-related applications, global positioning satellite (GPS) systems, robot navigation, optimization algorithms, and electronic entertainment ("video" games). And, of course, the grand result – super-human chess-playing computers – represents the realization of a 60+ year quest to achieve a goal once thought unattainable. It is not too grandiose to claim that this is a milestone in the history of mankind.

Garry Kasparov (2017a)
Former World Chess Champion

If we feel like we are being surpassed by our own technology it's because we aren't pushing ourselves hard enough, aren't being ambitious enough in our goals and dreams. Instead of worrying about what machines can do, we should worry more about what they still cannot do.

A
References

Several references have been invaluable to this work:

- David Levy (1976). *Chess and Computers*, Computer Science Press.
- David Levy (1988). *Computer Chess Compendium*, Springer-Verlag. This book collects all the key historical papers on computer chess into one reference book.
- Computer History Museum (ComputerHistory.org). A repository of historical photographs, important documents, and oral histories of the computer chess pioneers.
- Chess Programming Wiki (chessprogramming.wikispaces.com). A vast amount of well-organized information.
- Bill Wall's Chess Page (billwall.phpwebhosting.com). An eclectic collection of everything to do with chess, with lots of valuable computer chess resources.

Georgy Adelson-Velsky, Vladimir Arlazarov, and Mikhail Donskoy (1975). "Some Methods of Controlling the Tree Search in Chess Programs," *Artificial Intelligence*, vol. 6, no. 4, pp. 361-371.

Viswanathan Anand (2003). In *ChessBase Magazine*, no. 94.

Thomas Anantharaman, Murray Campbell, and Feng-hsiung Hsu (1990). "Singular Extensions: Adding Selectivity to Brute-Force Searching," *Artificial Intelligence*, vol. 43, no. 1, pp. 99-109.

Lawrence Aung (2010). "DEEP BLUE: The History and Engineering behind Computer Chess," illumin.usc.edu/188/deep-blue-the-history-and-engineering-behind-computer-chess.

Charles Babbage (1864). *Passages from the Life of a Philosopher*, Longman, Green, Longman, Roberts, & Green.

Alexander Baburin (2000). "Putting on the Blitz in Frankfurt," *New in Chess Magazine*, no. 5, pp. 32-45.

Alex Bell (1978). *The Machine Plays Chess?*, Pergamon Press.

Joel Benjamin (2007). *American Grandmaster*, Everyman Chess.

Joel Benjamin (2009). Letter published in *New in Chess Magazine*, no. 6.

Joel Benjamin (2014). Email exchange with Karsten Müller.

Hans Berliner (1988). Quoted at www.chessclub.com/user/help/Quiz18.

Hans Berliner (2005). "Oral History of Hans Berliner," Computer History Museum.

Alex Bernstein and Michael de Van Roberts (1958). "Computer v. Chess-player," *Scientific American*, June, pp. 96-105.

Mikhail Botvinnik (1968). Edward Winter (2014) reports Mikhail Botvinnik's remarks from *Chess*, October issue.

Mikhail Botvinnik (1994). Quoted in Dirk Jan ten Geuzendam's *Finding Bobby Fischer*, New In Chess.

Arik Braun (2006). In *ChessBase Magazine*, no. 116.

David Bronstein (1973). *200 Open Games*, Batsford.

David Bronstein (1996). Quoted by Grandmaster Larry Evans in his syndicated column "Larry Evans on Chess," November.

David Bronstein (2002). A 2002-03 interview with Bronstein by Yuri Vasiliev given at chesspro.ru with a translation at www.danamackenzie.com/blog.

Robert Byrne (1993). "Chess," *New York Times*, March 9.

Mackenzie Carpenter (1990). "Computer Chalks Up Its Greatest Win," *Pittsburgh Post-Gazette*, June 5.

ChessBase (2003a). "Kasparov-DEEP JUNIOR Draw After Stunning Sacrifice," *ChessBase*, online at en.chessbase.com/post/kasparov-deep-junior-draw-after-stunning-sacrifice.

ChessBase (2003b). Various material contributed by Karsten Müller, *ChessBase*, online at chessbase.de.

ChessBase (2005a). "An Exclusive Interview with Michael Adams by Aryan Arghandewal," *ChessBase*, online at en.chessbase.com/post/-hydra-is-the-kasparov-of-computers-.

ChessBase (2005b). "Adams vs HYDRA: Man 0.5 – Machine 5.5," *ChessBase*, online at en.chessbase.com/post/adams-vs-hydra-man-0-5-machine-5-5.

Peter Hugh Clarke (1963). Edward Winter (2014) reports the following quote from Clarke's article "From the USSR," *British Chess Monthly*, April, pp. 117-118.

Chrilly Donninger (2009). "Flying Hours with Ken Thompson," *New in Chess Magazine*, no. 1, pp. 46-57.

Mikhail Donskoy (undated). *A History of Kaissa*, www.computer-museum.ru/games/kaissa1.htm. Translation using Google.

Hubert Dreyfus (1965). "Alchemy and Artificial Intelligence," available at www.rand.org/content/dam/rand/pubs/papers/2006/P3244.pdf.

Education Testing Service (1959). "Horizons of Science: Thinking Machines," vol. 1, no. 4. Available as "Alex Bernstein at the IBM 704" at YouTube.com.

Max Euwe (1970). www.chessclub.com/user/help/Quiz18.

Alexander Finkel (2000). In *ChessBase Magazine*, no. 78.

Edward Fredkin (1997). Carnegie Mellon University press release, July 25.

Peter Frey (1978). "Appendix CHESS 4.5: Competition in 1976," in *Chess Skill in Man and Machine*, Peter Frey (editor), Springer-Verlag.

Frederic Friedel (2006). "How Could Kramnik Overlook the Mate?," *ChessBase*, online at en.chessbase.com/post/how-could-kramnik-overlook-the-mate-.

Frederic Friedel (2011a). "A History of Cheating in Chess (2)," *ChessBase*, online at en.chessbase.com/post/a-history-of-cheating-in-che-2-.

Frederic Friedel (2011b). "A History of Cheating in Chess (3)," *ChessBase*, online at en.chessbase.com/post/a-history-of-cheating-in-che-3-.

Frederic Friedel (2016). In *ChessBase MEGABASE*.

Lubomir Ftacnik (2006). In *ChessBase Magazine*, no. 116.

Richard Greenblatt, Donald Eastlake III, and Stephen Crocker (1967). "The Greenblatt Chess Program," AFIPS Fall Joint Computer Conference, pp. 801-810.

Richard Greenblatt (1992). "Wedgitude," *International Computer Chess Association Journal*, vol. 15, no. 4, pp. 192-198.

Richard Greenblatt (2005). "Oral History of Richard Greenblatt," Computer History Museum.

Boris Gulko (2003). In *ChessBase Magazine*, no. 94.

Hal (1968). Taken from the movie *2001: A Space Odyssey.*

Jeremy Hanken (1989). "DEEP THOUGHT has Miles to Go Before It Sleeps," *Chess Life*, March, pp. 22-28.

Paul Hoffman (2002). "Brains in Bahrain Report: Kramnik Is All Too Human," *Time Magazine*, October 12.

Israel A. Horowitz and Philip L. Rothenberg (1963). Edward Winter (2014) reports the quote from Horowitz's and Rothenberg's *The Personality of Chess*, MacMillan Company.

Feng-hsiung Hsu (1990). rec.games.chess posting, March 2.

Feng-hsiung Hsu (2002a). *Behind DEEP BLUE*, Princeton University Press.

Feng-hsiung Hsu (2002b). *Behind DEEP BLUE*, afterword in the paperback edition, Princeton University Press.

Feng-hsiung Hsu (2005). "An Interview with Feng-hsiung Hsu," *Ubiquity*, July issue. ubiquity.acm.org/article.cfm?id=1086452.

Feng-hsiung Hsu, Thomas Anantharaman, Murray Campbell, and Andreas Nowatzyk (1990). "A Grandmaster Chess Machine," *Scientific American*, October, pp. 44-50.

Robert Hübner and Hans-Joachim Hecht (2001). "Robert Hübner Neutralisert 'FRITZ'," *Schach*, no. 9.

Alexander Huzman (2005). In *ChessBase Magazine*, no. 108.

Robert Hyatt (1984). "Cray Blitz Versus David Levy," *International Computer Chess Association Journal*, vol. 7, no. 2, pp. 102-105.

Miguel Illescas (2009). Interview by Dirk Jan ten Geuzendam, *New in Chess Magazine*, no. 5.

The Independent (2002). "Artificial Intelligence," editorial, October 17.

Peter Jansen (1989). "Levy - DT Match (1)," rec.games.chess postings, December 12 and 13, 1989.

Garry Kasparov (1988). Paris press conference, as quoted in Hsu (1990).

Garry Kasparov (1989). Quoted from Edward Winter (2014).

Garry Kasparov (1997). Email posted in rec.games.computer.chess, May 27.

Garry Kasparov (2007). "Human Malfunction," *New in Chess Magazine*, no.1, pp. 95.

Garry Kasparov (2009). Letter published in *New in Chess Magazine*, no. 7.

Garry Kasparov (2010). "The Chess Master and the Computer," *New York Times*, February 11.

Garry Kasparov and Mig Greengard (2017a). *Deep Thinking*, PublicAffairs.

Garry Kasparov (2017b). "Deep Thinking," talk at Google, available on YouTube.

Lubomir Kavalek (2003). "Chess," *Washington Post*, February 10.

Raymond Keene (2002). *Brains in Bahrain*, Hardinge Simpole Publishing.

Daniel King (2007). As quoted in Benjamin (2007).

James Kister, Paul Stein, Stanislaw Ulam, William Walden, and Mark Wells (1957). "Experiments in Chess," *Journal of the ACM*, vol. 4, no. 2, pp. 174-177.

Christian Kongsted (2003). *How to Use Computers to Improve Your Chess*, Gambit Publications.

Danny Kopec (1990). "Advances in Man-Machine Play," *Computers, Chess, and Cognition*, Tony Marsland and Jonathan Schaeffer (editors), Springer-Verlag, 1990.

Alan Kotok (1962). "A Chess Playing Program for the IBM 7090 Computer," B.Sc. thesis, Massachusetts Institute of Technology, Department of Electrical Engineering.

Tim Krabbé (1991). "Stiller's Monsters," online at timkr.home.xs4all.nl/chess/perfecttxt.htm.

Lawrence J. Krakauer (2010). "MacHack VI Competes," blog posting at ljkrakauer.com/LJK/60s/machack.htm.

Vladimir Kramnik (2002a). In *ChessBase Magazine*, no. 43.

Vladimir Kramnik (2002b). "Mig Talks to Kramnik," *ChessBase*, online at en.chessbase.com/post/mig-talks-to-kramnik.

Vladimir Kramnik (2018). Conversation with Karsten Müller, Hanon Russell, and Jonathan Schaeffer. April 25.

Charles Krauthammer (1996), "Kasparov: DEEP BLUE Funk," *Time Magazine*, February 26.

Richard Lang (1987). Quoted in Kaare Danielsen, "The 7th World Microcomputer Chess Championship," *International Computer Chess Association Journal*, vol. 10, no. 3.

Bent Larsen (1988). Quoted in David Levy, "Computer Beats Grandmaster," *International Computer Chess Association Journal,* vol. 11, no. 3, pp. 168-170.

Bent Larsen (1993). Quoted at www.chessclub.com/user/help/Quiz18.

Bent Larsen (2010). "Chess Legend Bent Larsen Turns 75," *ChessBase*, online at en.chessbase.com/post/che-legend-bent-larsen-turns-75/4.

Bent Larsen (2014). *Bent Larsen's Best Games*, New In Chess.

David Levy and Monroe Newborn (1980). *More Chess and Computers*, Computer Science Press.

David Levy (1988). "Computer Beats Grandmaster," *International Computer Chess Association Journal*, vol. 11, no. 3, pp. 168-170.

David Levy and Monroe Newborn (1991). *How Computers Play Chess*, W.H. Freeman.

David Levy (2004). "Bilbao Man vs Machine – A Resume," *ChessBase*, online at en.chessbase.com/post/bilbao-man-vs-machine-a-resume.

David Levy (2005). "Oral History of David Levy," Computer History Museum.

David Levy (2016). Email sent to Jonathan Schaeffer.

Thomas Luther (2000). In *ChessBase Magazine*, no. 77.

T. Anthony Marsland (2007). webdocs.cs.ualberta.ca/~tony/ICCA/wita-history-readme.txt.

Claus Dieter Mayer and Karsten Müller (2003). *The Magic of Chess Tactics*, Russell Enterprises.

Grant McCord (2003). "Kasparov Blunders as DEEP JUNIOR Draws Level," *New York Times*, January 31.

Luke McShane (2000). In *ChessBase Magazine*, no. 77.

Karsten Müller (2003). "Man Equals Machine," *International Computer Games Association Journal*, vol. 26, no. 1, pp. 9-13.

Harry Nelson (2005). "Oral History of Harry Nelson," Computer History Museum.

Monroe Newborn (2003). *DEEP BLUE. An Artificial Intelligence Milestone*, Springer.

Monroe Newborn (2006). Quoted in "Once Again, Machine Beast Human Champion at Chess," by Dylan Loeb McClain, *New York Times*, December 5.

Allen Newell, John Shaw, and Herbert Simon (1958). "Chess-Playing Programs and the Problem of Complexity," *IBM Journal of Research and Development*, vol. 2, pp. 320-335.

David Norwood (2005). "Adams Was No Hercules Against HYDRA," *The Telegraph*, July 2. Online at www.telegraph.co.uk/culture/chess/3644589/David-Norwood-records-that-Adams-was-no-Hercules-against-Hydra.html.

Maxim Notkin (2002). In *Chess Today,* no. 699.

John Nunn (2017). In *ChessBase MEGABASE*.

Jack Peters (1997). Original quote appeared in a 1997 *Los Angeles Times* article, quoted in Jack Peters (2011), "Involuntary Retirement," *Chess Life*, February 18.

Lev Polugaevsky (1968). "Poebinok c Uralskim Robotom," *Chess in the USSR* (*Shakhmaty v SSSR*), no. 8, pp. 18-19. The translation is taken from David Levy (1976).

Evgeny Postny (2006). In *ChessBase Magazine*, no. 111.

Vasik Rajlich (2010). "Man vs. Machine," *New in Chess Magazine*, no. 2.

Diego Rasskin-Gutman (2009). *Chess Metaphors*, MIT Press.

Hans Ree (2000). "Dutch Bargain," *New In Chess Magazine*, no. 4, pp. 36-53.

Oliver Reeh (2004). In *ChessBase Magazine*, no. 98.

Fred Reinefeld (1948). *Relax with Chess*, Pitman, New York, 1948, page 116. Quoted at Edward Winter (2014).

Jonathan Schaeffer and Aske Plaat (1997). "Kasparov Versus DEEP BLUE: The Rematch," *International Computer Chess Association Journal*, vol. 20, no. 2, pp. 95-101.

André Schulz (2002). *ChessBase* web site.

Harry Schüssler (1989). In *ChessBase Magazine*, no. 16.

Claude Shannon (1950). "Programming a Computer for Playing Chess," *Philosophical Magazine*, vol. 41, no. 314, pp. 256-275.

Albert Silver (2104). "KOMODO 8: The Smartphone Versus Desktop Challenge," *ChessBase*, online at en.chessbase.com/post/komodo-8-the-smartphone-vs-desktop-challenge.

Herbert Simon and Allen Newell (1958). "Heuristic Problem Solving: The Next Advance in Operations Research," *Operations Research*, January, page 10.

Herbert Simon (1967). "Cool It, Friend! (An Open Letter to Herbert Dreyfus)," available at digitalcollections.library.cmu.edu/awweb/awarchive?type=file&item=33715. Undated, but unquestionably composed in 1967.

Herbert Simon (1978). "Rational Decision-Making in Business Organizations," *Nobel Memorial Lecture*, December 8. Available at: www.nobelprize.org/nobel_prizes/economic-sciences/laureates/1978/simon-lecture.pdf.

David Slate and Lawrence Atkin (1977). "CHESS 4.5 – The Northwestern University Chess Program," in *Chess Skill in Man and Machine*, Peter Frey (editor), Springer-Verlag.

Kathleen and Dan Spracklen (2005). "Oral History of Kathleen and Dan Spracklen," Computer History Museum.

Günter Stertenbrink (2002). In *ChessBase Magazine*, no. 91.

Dirk Jan ten Geuzendam (2000). "The Growing Pains of JUNIOR," *New in Chess Magazine*, no. 5, pp. 27-31.

Ken Thompson (2005). "Oral History of Ken Thompson," Computer History Museum.

Sergei Tiviakov (2000). In *ChessBase Magazine*, no. 77.

Jaap van den Herik and Richard Greenblatt (1992). "An Interview With Richard D. Greenblatt," *International Computer Chess Association Journal*, vol. 15, no. 4, pp. 200-207.

John van der Wiel (2000). *New in Chess Magazine*, no. 4.

Karl Gottlieb von Windisch (1783). *Briefe über den Schachspieler des Hrn. von Kempelen, nebst drei Kupferstichen die diese berühmte Maschine vorstellen* (Inanimate Reason; Or Circumstantial Account of that Astonishing Piece of Work, M. de Kempelen's Chess-Player). The image is public domain and came from commons.wikimedia.org/wiki/File:Tuerkischer_schachspieler_windisch4.jpg.

Louis Constant Wairy (1895). *Memoirs of Constant – First Valet de Chambre to the Emperor on the Private Life of Napoleon*, Charles Scribner's Sons, New York.

Bill Wall (2014). "IBM and Chess," available at www.chessmaniac.com/ibm-and-chess.

Norbert Weiner (1948). Quoted from an article by William Lawrence, *New York Times*, December 19.

Edward Winter (2014). "Chess and Computers," chesshistory.com/winter/extra/computers.html.

B
Games

1
Robert J. Fischer – MacHack
exhibition match (1977)

The first game is in Chapter 3. Here are the remaining two games.

Fischer, Robert – MacHack
King's Gambit Accepted C33
Exhibition match (2), 1977

1.e4 e5 2.f4 e×f4 3.♗c4 d5 4.♗×d5 ♘f6 5.♘c3 ♗b4 6.♘f3 0-0 7.0-0 ♘×d5?!

Again the computer overestimates the value of the pair of bishops. In human games this move has not been repeated. 7...♗×c3?! 8.d×c3 c6?! 9.♗c4 ♕b6+ 10.♔h1 ♘e4 11.♕e1 ♖e8? 12.♗×f4! (12.♘g5 +−) 12...♘d6? (12...♘f6 13.♕g3 +−) 13.♗×d6 ♖×e1 14.♖a×e1 ♗d7 15.♘g5 ♘a6 16.♖×f7 1-0 Fischer-Nyman, Cicero simultaneous exhibition 1964; 7...c6 is the main line.

8.♘×d5 ♗d6? The dynamic 8...f5! 9.♘×b4 f×e4 10.c3 e×f3 11.♕×f3 a5 12.♘d3 g5 13.b3 is only slightly worse.

9.d4 g5? This runs into an amazing refutation. But Black has big problems in any case due to White's strong center.

10.♘×g5!! ♕×g5 11.e5 ♗h3 12.♖f2 ♗×e5 12...♗e7 13.♗×f4 ♕h4 14.g3 +−.

13.d×e5 c6?! 14.♗×f4 ♕g7 15.♘f6+ ♔h8 16.♕h5 ♖d8 16...♗e6 17.♗h6 +−.

17.♕×h3 ♘a6 18.♖f3 ♕g6 19.♖c1 ♔g7 20.♖g3 ♖h8?! 21.♕h6# 1-0

MacHack – Fischer, Robert
Sicilian Defense B34
Exhibition match (3), 1977

1.e4 c5 2.♘f3 g6 3.d4 ♗g7 4.♘c3 c×d4 5.♘×d4 ♘c6 6.♗e3 ♘f6 7.♘×c6 b×c6 8.e5 ♘g8 9.f4 f6 10.e×f6 ♘×f6 11.♗c4?

This just wastes valuable time as the resulting black backward e-pawn is not as important as the dynamics. 11.♗e2 is the main move.

11...d5 12.♗e2 ♖b8 13.b3? White does not have time for this.

13.♗d4 is called for as 13...♖×b2?! can then be met by 14.♘×d5=.

13...♘g4 14.♗d4 e5 14...♘e3!?

might be even better, but is much more complicated.

15.f×e5 0-0?! 15...♕h4+ 16.g3 ♕h3 17.♗f1 ♕h5 applies more pressure.

16.♗×g4 ♕h4+ 17.g3 ♕×g4 18.♕×g4 ♗×g4

19.♖f1?

The computer, ahead in material, wants to exchange pieces and most likely misses the strong dynamic blow 20...c5!!. 19.h3 ♗d7 20.0-0-0 ♖be8 21.♘a4 ♗×e5 22.g4 is more or less equal.

19...♖×f1+ 20.♔×f1 c5!! 21.♗f2 21.♗×c5 ♗×e5 22.♖d1 ♗×c3 23.♖×d5 ♖e8 24.♗×a7 ♖e1+ 25.♔g2 ♖e2+ 26.♔g1 ♗h3–+ **21...♗×e5 22.♗e1 ♖f8+ 23.♔g2 ♖f3 24.h3 ♖×c3 25.♗×c3 ♗×c3 26.♖f1 ♗f5 27.♖f2 h5 28.♖e2 ♔f7 29.♖e3 ♗d4 30.♖f3 ♔e6 31.c3 ♗e5 32.♖e3 d4 33.c×d4 c×d4 34.♖e1 d3 35.h4 d2 36.♖d1 ♗c3 37.♔f2 ♗g4 38.♖h1 ♗d4+ 39.♔g2 ♔d5 40.a3 ♔e4 41.♖f1 ♔d3 42.♔h2 ♔e2 43.♔g2 ♗h3+ 44.♔×h3 ♔×f1 45.g4 d1♕ 46.♔h2 ♕e2+ 47.♔h3 ♕g2# 0-1**

2
David Levy – Cʜᴇss 4.5 exhibition game (1977)

Cʜᴇss 4.5 – Levy, David (2320)
Sicilian Defense B77
Levy challenge game, 01.04.1977

Played at Carnegie Mellon University in Pittsburgh. David Levy manages to expose the program's weakness in a strategic endgame.

1.e4 c5 2.♘f3 d6 3.d4 c×d4 4.♘×d4 ♘f6 5.♘c3 g6 6.f3 ♗g7 7.♗e3 0-0 8.♕d2 ♘c6 9.♗c4 a6 10.♘×c6 b×c6 11.0-0 ♘d7 12.f4 ♘b6 12...♖b8!?.

13.♗e2 ♗e6 14.b3 ♘c8 15.a3 15.♖ad1!?.

15...♕a5 16.b4 ♕c7 17.f5 ♗d7 18.♗h6?

Exchanging attacking potential is wrong. After 18.♖ad1 a5 19.b5 ♖b8 20.♖f3, White is certainly not worse.

18...♕b6+ 19.♔h1?! Allowing a queen exchange. Under the circumstances, 19.♗e3 was more circumspect.

19...♕d4 20.♕×d4 ♗×d4 21.♖f3 ♗g7 22.♗×g7 ♔×g7 23.♖b1 ♘b6

A good move against the machine. Objectively 23...a5 is probably more precise.

24.♖ff1?!

The computer has no idea what to do. It has no long-term strategic plan. 24.a4 is more or less equal, e.g., 24...♗e8 25.a5 ♘d7 26.♘a4=.

24...♖fb8 25.♖bd1?! f6 26.a4?

The beginning of the end as now Black can open the queenside on his terms.

The prophylactic 26.罩b1 limits the damage.

26...a5! 27.b5?! 27.b×a5 offers better practical chances, e.g., 27...罩×a5 28.f×g6 罩c5 29.e5 but objectively it should lose as well.

27...c×b5 28.a×b5?

White should try to exchange the bad bishop with 28.盫×b5 but after 28...罩c8 his weak queenside should be the downfall anyway.

28...罩c8 29.罩d3 罩c5 30.罩g3? This misplaces the rook as White's attack on the king is an illusion, but White is already lost in any case.

30...罩ac8 31.罩ff3 a4 32.h4 a3 33.f×g6 h×g6 34.罩e3 盫e6 35.h5 g5 36.公d5 a2 37.罩a3 盫×d5 38.e×d5 罩×c2 39.盫d1 罩d2 40.堂h2 罩c1 41.盫b3 a1營 42.罩×a1 罩×a1 43.罩e3 0-1

3
David Levy – CHESS 4.7 match (1978)

Games 1, 3 and 4 are in Chapter 3.

CHESS 4.7 – Levy, David (2320)
Sicilian Defense B23
Toronto match (2), 27.08.1978

1.公c3 c5 2.e4 公c6 3.f4 a6 4.公f3 g6 5.d4 c×d4 6.公×d4 盫g7 7.盫e3 d6 8.公×c6?!

8.盫e2 is the main line.

8...b×c6 9.盫e2 罩b8 10.營c1 營a5

11.盫d2?!

Very tame. The dynamic 11.0-0 盫×c3 12.b×c3 營×c3 13.罩d1 is more in the spirit of the position.

11...營b6 12.公a4 營a7

13.公c3?

This regrouping of the knight is too slow. 13.盫f3 盫d4 14.c3 盫f2+ 15.堂e2 followed by 盫e3 is better.

13...盫d4 14.公d1 公f6 15.c3 盫b6 16.營c2 公g4?!

16...0-0 is more flexible.

17.♕a4?

Pawn hunting is not good here. White should address the problem of its unsecure king with 17.♗×g4 ♗×g4 18.♕d3 a5 19.♘e3 ♗c8 20.b3 0-0 21.f5 a4 22.0-0.

17...0-0 18.♗×g4 ♗×g4 19.♕×c6?

This greedy capture opens roads for Black's attack. 19.h3 is better but Black is for choice after 19...♗d7.

19...♗×d1 20.♔×d1 ♗e3 21.b3 ♗×d2 22.♔×d2 ♖bc8

22...♖fc8 is slightly stronger.

23.♕a4?

23.♕d5 ♕f2+ 24.♔d3 ♕×g2 25.c4 was the lesser evil.

23...♕f2+ 24.♔d3 ♕×g2 25.♕d4?!

25...♕f3+?

25...e5 26.♕e3 d5 27.e×d5 ♕×d5+ 28.♔c2 ♕g2+ 29.♕d2 ♖×c3+ wins on the spot.

26.♔c2 ♕e2+?!

The direct 26...e5!? 27.♕d2 ♕×e4+ 28.♔b2 ♕×f4 was still better.

27.♔c1 e5

Finally Levy delivers this blow.

28.f×e5?

This opens roads for Black's attack. 28.♕d2 ♕×e4 29.♖f1 e×f4 30.♔b2 was the last real chance to fight.

28...d×e5 29.♕×e5?

This greedy capture loses directly. 29.♕d2 is the only move to continue the fight but for a lost cause of course.

29...♖fe8 30.♕g3 ♖×e4 31.♕h3 ♖d8 32.♕f1 ♕d2+ 33.♔b1 ♖e2 34.♕×e2

34.♕c1 ♕d3+ 35.♔c2 ♕×c2#.

34...♕×e2 35.♖e1 ♕×e1+ 36.♔b2 ♖d2+ 37.♔a3 ♕×a1 0-1

Levy, David (2320) – Chess 4.7
English Opening A00
Toronto match (5), 30.08.1978

1.c4 ♘f6 2.a3 c6 3.d3 d5 4.♕c2 d×c4 5.♕×c4 e5 6.♘f3 ♗d6 7.g3 ♗e6 8.♕c2 ♘bd7 9.♗g2 0-0 10.0-0 ♕b6?!

10...h6 is more natural.

11.♘bd2 ♕c5 12.♕b1 h6?! 13.b4 ♕b5 14.♕c2 ♘b6 15.♗b2 a5

16.a4 ♛a6

16...♛×b4? runs into 17.♗a3 ♛×a3 18.♖×a3 ♗×a3 19.♘×e5±.

17.b×a5 ♛×a5 18.♗c3 ♛c5 19.♖fc1 ♘bd7 20.a5 ♛a7

21.♛b2

Against a human, Levy most probably would have opened the position with 21.d4!?, which is objectively stronger.

21...♘g4?

This premature attack is easily repelled. Black should just maintain the position with, e.g., 21...♖fe8.

22.♘e4 ♗c7 23.h3?!

23.♗b4! ♖fe8 24.h3, to meet 24...f5 with 25.♘c5, is even better.

23...f5 24.h×g4 f×e4 25.d×e4 ♗×g4 26.♗e1 ♘c5?! 27.♖cb1

27...♖ae8?

The wrong rook. Black should either play

27...♖fe8 or 27...♘×e4. In both cases, White advantage is kept within bounds.

28.♗d2 ♖f7?

Allowing a deadly pin on the e3-a7 diagonal. But good advice is already hard to give.

29.♗e3 ♗d6 30.♛c2 ♗×f3?! 31.♗×f3 ♖a8 32.♖c1 b6 33.♔g2

A cold-blooded move. Levy can afford this prophylaxis as he wins in any case.

33...♛b7 34.a×b6 ♖×a1 35.♖×a1 ♘e6 36.♖a7 ♛c8 37.♛a2 ♖f6 38.♖a8 ♗b8 39.♗g4 ♔f7 40.♛a7+ ♗×a7 41.♖×c8 ♗×b6 42.♗×e6+ ♖×e6 43.♗×b6 1-0

4
Additional Man-Machine Games (1970s)

Levy, David (2320) – Chess 4.8
King's Gambit Rosentreter Gambit C37
Hamburg, 02.1979

The following exhibition game pitted man against machine – brains and brawn. Not only did the computer have to decide on its moves, it also had to play them. David Levy (2016) gives some insights on this publicity stunt.

> The TV station wanted an exciting game and asked me how we could achieve that. I suggested that I pick an opening variation in which one side makes a sacrifice, and that [Slate and Atkin] could then choose which colour they wanted to play. That's what we did. I looked through my old King's Gambit book [by Keres] and picked the line we played, which I felt offered roughly equal chances.

The recording session lasted about 10 hours. If you look at my chin at the start and the end of the game you might see that a bit of stubble grew in the interim.

The robot came from a car factory in Sweden. The TV station was worried about it accidentally hitting me, so a micro-switch was added so that the arm would stop moving if the pincers got to near me.

1.e4 e5 2.f4 e×f4 3.♘f3 g5 4.d4 g4 5.♗×f4 g×f3 6.♕×f3 Levy was asked to play enterprising chess and so he chooses the Rosentreter Gambit, which is most likely not correct but dangerous over the board.

6...♘c6! 7.d5 ♕f6! The computer does indeed play the refutation.

8.d×c6 ♕×b2 9.♗c4 9.♕b3 is answered by 9...♗g7 10.c×b7 ♗×b7 11.c3 ♕×a1 12.♕×b7 ♗×c3+ 13.♔d1 ♖d8 14.♗×c7 ♘f6 15.♗×d8 ♔×d8 and Black is better.

9...♕×a1 10.♗×f7+ 10.♗e5? ♕×b1+ 11.♔d2 ♕b4+ 12.♔d3 f6−+ **10... ♔d8** 10...♔×f7?? 11.♗e5++− **11.0-0 ♕g7 12.♗d5** 12.♕h5 ♗d6−+ **12... ♗c5+ 13.♗e3 ♗×e3+ 14.♕×e3 d×c6 15.♖f7 ♕h6 16.♕d4 c×d5 17.♕×h8 ♕b6+ 18.♔f1** 18.♖f2 is met by 18...♕×b1+ 19.♖f1 ♕b6+ 20.♔h1 ♗e6−+ .

18...♕b1+ 19.♔f2 ♕×c2+ 20.♔g3 ♕d3+ 21.♖f3 ♕×e4 22.♕×g8+ ♔d7 23.♕g7+ ♔c6 24.♖c3+

24...♔b5?! The first step in the wrong direction. 24...♔d6 25.♕×c7+ ♔e6 wins.

25.♖b3+ ♔a4? Now White's attack wins the queen and this should lead to a draw. 25...♔c6 26.♖c3+ ♔d6 transposes and wins.

26.♕c3 ♕g4+ 27.♔f2 ♕c4 28.♖a3+ ♔b5 29.♕a5+ ♔c6 30.♖c3 ♗e6 31.♕a4+ ♔d6 32.♖×c4 d×c4 33.♕b4+ ♔c6 34.♕a4+

34...b5? It seems as if the computer is playing for a win and overestimates the passed c-pawn. After 34...♔d6, White has a draw, but not more.

35.♕a6+ ♔d7 36.♕×b5+ ♔d6 37.♕b4+ c5 38.♕d2+ ♔c7 39.♕h6 ♗g8 40.♕g7+ ♔c6 41.g4 a6 42.♕f6+ ♔b5 43.♕d6 ♔b4?! **44.♕b6+?** Both sides underestimate the importance of king activity. 44.♔e2 was called for.

44...♔a3? 44...♔c3 45.♕×c5 ♔c2 should defend.

45.♕c6? 45.♔e2 ♔×a2 46.♔d2 ♖f8 47.♕×a6+ ♔b3 48.♕b7+ ♔a4 49.♔c3 +− **45...♖f8+ 46.♔e3 ♖b8?** 46...♔b2 47.♕×c5 ♖e8+ 48.♔f3 ♔c2 is the way to go.

47.♕×a6+? Too greedy. 47.♕d6 ♖e8+ 48.♔d2 is necessary to control Black's counterplay.

47...♔b2 48.♕d6

48...♖a8? Now Black is stuck and White can just advance the kingside pawns. The active 48...♖e8+ 49.♔f4 c3 50.♕b6+ ♔c1 51.♕×c5 c2 draws.

49.♕d2+ ♔a3 50.h4 ♖a6 51.g5 ♖a8 52.h5 ♖e8+ 53.♔f4 ♖a8 54.♔e5 ♖a6 55.g6 h×g6 56.h×g6 ♖a8 56...♖×g6 57.♕c1+ ♔×a2 58.♕c2+ +− . **57.♔f6 ♖a4 58.♔g7 ♖a8** 58...♗e6 59.♕e3+ c3 60.♕×e6 c4 61.♕e2+ +− . **59.♕g2 ♖d8 60.♕c6 ♖d3 61.♕a6+ ♔b4 62.♔×g8 ♖a3 63.♕b6+ ♔c3 64.g7 ♖×a2 65.♔f7 ♖f2+ 66.♔e7 ♖g2 67.♕f6+ ♔c2 68.♕f5+ ♔b2 69.♔f7 c3 70.♕e5 c4**

71.♕b5+? This careless check gives the win away. After 71.g8♕ ♖×g8 72.♔×g8, Black's c-pawns are not dangerous, e.g., 72...♔c2 73.♔f7 ♔d2 74.♕d4+ ♔c2 75.♔e6 ♔b3 76.♔d5 c2 77.♕a1 +− .

71...♔c1 72.♕×c4 ♖×g7+ 73.♔×g7 c2 74.♔f6 ♔d2 An odd move, but it does draw as White's king is just outside of the winning zone g1-g4-d4-d5-a5. Going to the safe short side with 74...♔b2 is the human approach.

75.♕d4+ ♔c1 76.♔e5 ♔b1 77.♕b4+ ♔a2 78.♕c3 ♔b1 79.♕b3+ ♔a1 80.♕a4+ ♔b2 81.♕d4+ ♔b1 82.♕d3 ♔b2 83.♕b5+ ♔c3 Another odd move, but it also draws.

84.♕c5+ ♔b2 85.♕b6+ ♔a1 86.♕g1+ ♔b2 87.♕b6+ ♔a1 88.♕a7+ ♔b1 89.♕b7+ ♔a1

What a fight, which lasted about 10 hours! ½-½

Levy (2016) provides a postscript to the game:

> After the game was over I was presented with a chessboard motif baby costume because [my wife and I] were expecting a baby a couple of months later.
>
> The TV station announced at the end that anyone who wanted the moves of the game with notes by both

players should write in to them. They received 70,000 requests.

Several years later I was on the autobahn somewhere in the southwest of Germany and stopped at a cafe. The person who served us recognized me from the TV programme.

5
David Levy – Cʀᴀʏ Bʟɪᴛᴢ match (1984)

Cʀᴀʏ Bʟɪᴛᴢ – Levy, David (2320)
Modern Defense Irregular Variation B00
London match (1), 1984

1.e4 a6 2.d4 g6 3.♘f3 ♗g7 4.♘c3 b5 5.♗d3 ♗b7 6.0-0 d6 7.♗f4 e6 8.e5 d5 9.b4 ♘d7 10.♕d2 ♘e7 11.a4 c6 12.a×b5 c×b5 13.♗h6 0-0 14.♗g5 ♖e8 15.♖a3 ♘b6 16.♘d1 ♘c4 17.♗×c4 d×c4 18.♘b2 ♕c7 19.♖fa1 ♖ec8 20.c3 ♗×f3 21.g×f3 ♘f5 22.♖×a6 ♖×a6 23.♖×a6 ♕b7 24.♖a5 ♕×f3 25 ♖×b5 h6 26.♗f4 ♕h3 27. ♗g3 h5 28.♖c5 ♖a8 29.♕c1 h4 30.♗f4 ♕f3 31.h3 ♕×h3 32.♖×c4 ♕f3 33.♗h2 h3 34.♕f1 ♖a1 35.♘d1 ♖×d1 0-1

Levy, David (2320) – Cʀᴀʏ Bʟɪᴛᴢ
London match (2), 1984

1-0 (forfeit). A fast game was played later that day, won by Levy.

Cʀᴀʏ Bʟɪᴛᴢ – Levy, David (2320)
Hippopotamus Variation B07
London match (3), 1984

1.e4 d6 2.d4 ♘d7 3.♘f3 g6 4.♗c4 e5 5.♘c3 ♗g7 6.♗f4 ♘e7 7.0-0 h6 8.h3 a6 9.♕d2 b6 10.♖fd1 ♗b7 11.♗b3 g5 12.♘×g5 h×g5 13.♗×g5 ♘f6 14.♕f4 ♘h7

15.♗h4 ♕d7 16.♖d3 ♘g6 17.♕g3 ♘f6 18.♗×f6 ♗×f6 19.♕f3 ♕e7 20.♕e3 ♗g5 0-1 Computer crashed.

Levy, David (2320) – Cʀᴀʏ Bʟɪᴛᴢ
Hippopotamus with White A00
London match (4), 1984

1.d3 e5 2.♘d2 ♘c6 3.g3 ♘f6 4.♗g2 ♗c5 5.e3 d5 6.♘e2 0-0 7.a3 ♗f5 8.b3 ♘g4 9.h3 ♘f6 10.♗b2 ♕d6 11.g4 ♗e6 12.♘g3 a5 13.♕e2 ♘d7 14.♘f5 ♗×f5 15.g×f5 ♘f6 16.h4 ♖fe8 17.♗h3 a4 18.b4 ♗×b4 19.a×b4 ♕×b4 20.♗a3 ♕×h4 21.♘f3 ♕h5 22.♘d2 ♕×e2+ 23.♔×e2 b5 24.c3 h6 25.♗g2 ♖a5 26.♖ab1 ♖b8 27.♖b2 ♖b6 28.♖hb1 ♕h7 29.♗c5 ♖b8 30.♗a3 ♘a7 31.♘f3 ♘d7 32.♘e1 c6 33.♘c2 ♖a8 34.♘b4 ♖d8 35.♘a2 ♘c8 36.c4 d×c4 37.d×c4 b×c4 38.♗×c6 ♘a7 39.♗e4 ♘f6 40.♗e7 ♖c8 41.♗×f6 g×f6 42.♖b6 c3 43.♖×f6 ♔g7 44.♖fb6 a3 45. ♖g1+ 1-0

6
David Levy – Dᴇᴇᴘ Tʜᴏᴜɢʜᴛ match (1989)

The first game is in Chapter 5. Here are the remaining three games.

Dᴇᴇᴘ Tʜᴏᴜɢʜᴛ – Levy, David (2320)
Modern Defense A42
London match (2), 12.12.1989

1.c4 d6 2.♘c3 g6 3.d4 ♗g7 4.e4 a6?! 5.♗e3 ♘f6 6.♗e2 0-0 7.f4 c6?! 8.e5 ♘e8 9.♘f3

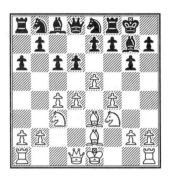

9...d5?

It is not enough to get a closed position against a computer. It should not be completely passive and the machine should have no dangerous short-term plans to improve. So 9...b5 was more in the spirit of the previous play.

10.0-0 ♘c7 11.♖c1 e6?! 12.♕e1 b5?

12...d×c4 13.♗×c4 ♘d7 14.♗f2 f5 15.e×f6 ♘×f6 is probably the lesser evil.

13.c×d5 c×d5 14.♘d1!

A strong regrouping.

14...♖a7 15.♘f2 ♘d7 16.♕a5 ♘a8

17.♕a3?!

This concedes space. The bind should be maintained by 17.♗d2 ♕×a5 18.♗×a5 ♘ab6 19.b3± (Schüssler 1989).

17...♕b6 18.♗d2

18.♘d3!?.

18...a5 19.♕d6 b4 20.♖c6 ♕d8 21.♖fc1 ♗b7 22.♖6c2 ♘db6 23.♕×d8 ♖×d8 24.♗e3 ♖c8 25.♖c5 ♗f8 26.♗d3?!

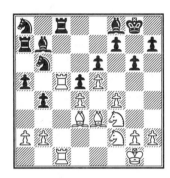

A surprisingly bold exchange sacrifice. But the risk is not necessary as 26.♖×c8 ♗×c8 27.♘g4 gives White a solid advantage.

26...♖d8?

As Black's position is very passive, Levy should have tried 26...♗×c5 27.d×c5 ♘a4 28.c6 ♘8b6 29.♗b5 ♗c6 30.♗×b6 ♘×b6 31.♖c6 ♖×c6 32.♗×c6 ♖c7 33.♘d4 ♘c4 34.♘d3 ♘e3 with practical drawing chances.

27.♖5c2 ♖c8 28.♖×c8?!

The direct 28.♘g4 is more precise.

28...♗×c8 29.♘g4 ♗e7 30.♘f6+

30...♗×f6?

Now the dark squares are fatally weak. 30...♔g7, to answer 31.♘e8+ ♔f8

389

32.♘d6 ♗xd6 33.exd6 with 33...f6, was the last chance to fight.

31.exf6 ♖c7 32.♘e5 ♖xc1+ 33.♗xc1 ♗b7 34.a3!

DEEP THOUGHT opens a second front.

34...♘c7?

34...bxa3 35.bxa3 Nc7 36.Bd2 Nc4 was more tenacious.

35.axb4 axb4 36.♗d2

36...♘a4?

Losing quickly. Levy had to try 36...♗a6 or 36...♘a6. But both should lose in the long run as well, as Black has too many problems, not the least of which is his king, which is difficult to activate and may even be attacked later.

37.♗xb4 ♘xb2 38.♘g4

Peter Jansen (1989), the operator of DEEP THOUGHT during the match, comments on this position.

> I was told that [Grandmaster] Jonathan Speelman saw 38. ♘g4!! even before [DEEP THOUGHT (DT)] played it, causing quite some commotion in the analysis room. After that, people were speculating why DT took so long to make its moves. What happened was that, although DT did see a mate in 12 at move 38, I did not announce this to Levy, because I expected DT to come

up with a shorter mate soon. And so it merrily went on looking for one at the rate of 3 minutes per move, until Levy resigned...

After the game Speelman declared himself quite depressed that something as beautiful as 38. ♘g4 turned out to be reducible to mere stupid calculations....

38...e5 39.♘h6+ ♚h8 40.♘xf7+ ♚g8 41.♘h6+ ♚h8 42.f5 and Levy resigned as 42...♘xd3 is met by 43.f7 +− . **1-0**

Levy, David (2320) – DEEP THOUGHT
Dutch Defense A80
London match (3), 13.12.1989

Peter Jansen (1989):

> During the game, Levy seemed clearly more nervous than the two previous days, and also showed signs of a bad cold (not too surprising given the magnitude of the flu epidemic London was going through). He may also have been disturbed by the TV people, who were packing their equipment (fairly noisily) just when Levy was considering his 6th move. In any case, Levy did not look for excuses: he called [DEEP THOUGHT] "a very strong opponent" and said he had fully expected to lose against it.

1.d4 f5 2.♗g5 c6 3.c3 h6 4.♗f4 ♘f6 5.♘d2 d6 6.e4?

Too optimistic as the machine is a very strong defender. 6.e3 is normal.

6...g5 7.e5 ♘h7!

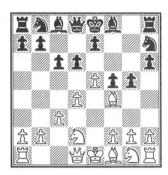

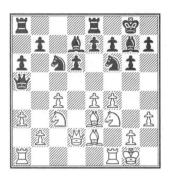

8.♘c4?

Levy will not get enough compensation for the piece as Black's king will escape to the queenside. 8.♗g3 f4 9.♕c2 fxg3 10.♗d3 gxf2+ 11.♔xf2 ♘d7 12.♗xh7 ♕c7 13.♘e2 is only slightly worse.

8...gxf4 9.♕h5+ ♔d7 10.♕xf5+ ♔c7 11.♕xf4 ♗e6 12.♘f3 ♖g8 13.♘e3?! ♘g5 14.exd6+ exd6 15.d5 ♗xd5 16.♘xd5+ cxd5 17.♘d4?!

17.0-0-0 is preferable but White does not have enough compensation even in this case of course.

17...♕e7+ 18.♗e2 ♘c6 19.♘b5+ ♔b8 20.h4 ♘e6 21.♕f3 ♘e5 22.♕xd5?! ♘f4 0-1

Levy resigned because of 23.♕xg8 ♘f3+ 24.♔d1 ♕xe2+ 25.♔c1 ♘d3+ 26.♔b1 ♕xb2#.

Deep Thought – Levy, David (2320)
Modern Defense A31
London match (4), 13.12.1989

1.c4 d6 2.♘c3 ♘d7 3.d4 g6 4.♘f3 ♗g7 5.e4 c5 6.♗e2 cxd4 7.♘xd4 ♘gf6 8.♗e3 0-0 9.0-0 a6 10.f3 ♖e8 11.♕d2 ♘e5 12.h3 ♗d7 13.f4 ♘c6 14.♘f3 ♕a5 15.a3

15...♖ad8?

This just wastes time and takes away the d8-square from the queen. 15...♘h5 is much more in the spirit of the Hedgehog, e.g., 16.♗f2 ♗h6 (16...♗xc3!?) 17.b4 ♕d8 18.♘g5 ♘xf4 19.♕xf4 f6 20.h4 fxg5 21.♕d2 ♗e6 22.hxg5 ♗g7.

16.b4 ♕c7 17.♖ac1 b6?! 18.♗d3 ♕b7 19.♕f2

19...♖b8?!

Levy loses a piece but good advice is already hard to give.

20.e5 ♘h5 21.b5

21.g4+− is also playable immediately.

21...axb5?! 22.cxb5 ♘d8 23.g4 ♗h8 24.gxh5 ♗xh3 25.hxg6 hxg6 26.♖fd1 ♕d7 27.♘g5 ♗g4 28.♕h4 ♗g7 29.♖d2 ♗h5 30.♘d5 ♕a7 31.♖c7 ♖h7 32.exd6 exd6 33.♖c8 ♕xa3 34.♘e4 1-0

7
Additional Man-Machine Games (1980s)

In 1985 Garry Kasparov played a simultaneous exhibition against 32 computer programs. Kasparov (2010) recalls that experience:

> The four leading chess computer manufacturers had sent their top models, including eight named after me from the electronics firm Saitek.
>
> It illustrates the state of computer chess at the time that it didn't come as much of a surprise when I achieved a perfect 32–0 score, winning every game, although there was an uncomfortable moment. At one point I realized that I was drifting into trouble in a game against one of the "KASPAROV" brand models. If this machine scored a win or even a draw, people would be quick to say that I had thrown the game to get PR for the company, so I had to intensify my efforts. Eventually I found a way to trick the machine with a sacrifice it should have refused. From the human perspective, or at least from my perspective, those were the good old days of man vs. machine chess.

Three games from the exhibition follow.

Kasparov, Garry (2715) – Superstar 36K
Benko Gambit A57
Hamburg Spiegel simultaneous exhibition (32 opponents), Hamburg, 1985

One of the authors (KM) made the moves for the machine and already had the impression in 1985 that the computer was much better after 17... ♘c6, which is confirmed by modern engines.

1.d4 ♘f6 2.c4 c5 3.d5 b5 4.c×b5 a6 5.b6 ♗b7 6.♘c3 ♛×b6 7.e4 g6?

This is too provocative. 7...d6 is the main move.

8.e5 ♘g8 9.♘f3 ♗g7 10.♗c4 ♘h6 11.0–0 0–0 12.♖e1 12.♗g5!?.

12...♘f5 13.♛d3 f6

14.d6+?

The time has not come yet to decide how to use White's mighty center. After 14.♘a4 ♛a5 15.b3, White is winning.

14...e6 15.♘e4?! 15.e×f6 ♖×f6 (15... ♗×f6 16.♗g5) 16.♗g5 ♖f7 17.♖×e6 d×e6 18.♗×e6 limits the damage.

15...f×e5 16.♘fg5 h6 17.♘f3 ♘c6 18.♗e3 ♘b4 19.♛b1 ♗×e4 20.♛×e4 ♘×d6 21.♛×g6

21...♘f5?

A tactical error. After 21...♖f6! 22.♛g4 ♘×c4 23.♛×c4 ♛b5, Black is much better. Of course, not 21...♘×c4?? 22.♗×h6 ♖f7 23.♘g5 +– .

22.♘×e5 ♖f6?!

The computer misjudges the resulting endgame and underestimates the strength of White's bishops. 22...d5 23.♗b3 ♖f6 24.♕h5 ♘e3 25.♘d7 ♕d8 26.♘×f6+ ♕×f6 27.♖×e3 c4 28.♗a4 ♘d3 gives better practical chances.

23.♘×d7 ♖×g6 24.♘×b6 ♖e8 25.♖ad1?! 25.♖e2 +– is more precise.

25...♘h4 26.♗×c5 ♘f3+

The computer is materialistic, which was the rule in those days, and takes the exchange. 26...♘×g2 27.♖×e6 ♖e×e6 28.♗×e6+ ♖×e6 29.♖d8+ ♔f7 30.♔×g2 ♘×a2 31.♖d7+ should also be lost in the long run.

27.♔f1 ♘×e1 28.♖×e1 a5 29.a3 ♘c2 30.♖e2 ♘d4 31.♖e4 ♘c6?

This voluntary retreat is odd. 31...♖d8 is called for.

32.b4?! Kasparov misses the more precise 32.♗b5 e5 33.♗c4+ ♔h7 34.♗f7 +– .

32...a×b4 33.a×b4 ♘e5?! 33...♗f8 to reduce the pressure by exchanges is necessary.

34.♗e2 ♘f7?!

Again this voluntary retreat is odd. 34...♖d8 offers more resistance, e.g., 35.f4 ♘c6 36.b5 ♘a5 37.♗h5 ♘b3 38.♗×g6 ♘×c5 39.♖c4 ♗f8 and White should be winning, but it is not easy.

35.f4 35.♘d5!? +– was even better.

35...e5

This opening of the a2-g8 diagonal looks too dangerous to human eyes. 35...h5 36.♗×h5 ♖h6 37.g4 ♖d8 was probably a better practical chance.

36.♗c4 ♖g4 This rook is misplaced,

but 36...♗f8 37.♘d7 ♗×c5 38.b×c5 ♔g7 39.f5 +– does not help either.

37.g3 ♖d8 38.♗e6 ♖g6 39.f5 ♖g5 40.♗e7 ♖d1+ 41.♔e2 ♖h1 42.♗×g5 ♖×h2+ 43.♔f3 h×g5 44.♘d7 ♖b2 45.♖c4 e4+ 46.♔×e4 ♖d2 47.♖c8+ ♔h7 48.♘f8+ ♗×f8 49.♖×f8 ♘h6 50.b5 ♔g7 51.♖c8 ♖e2+ 52.♔d5 ♖b2 53.♔c6 1-0

Kasparov, Garry (2715) – Mephisto Exclusive S
King's Indian Attack A08
Hamburg Spiegel simultaneous exhibition (32 opponents), Hamburg, 1985

1.e4 c5 2.♘f3 e6 3.d3 d5 4.♘bd2 ♘c6 5.g3 ♘f6 6.♗g2 ♗d6 7.0-0 0-0 8.♖e1 ♘g4?! 8...♕c7 is the main line.

9.h3 ♘ge5 10.♘×e5 ♗×e5 11.c3 11.♘b3!?.

11...d4 12.c4 b6?! 13.f4 ♗b8 14.e5 ♗b7 15.♘e4 a5 16.♕h5

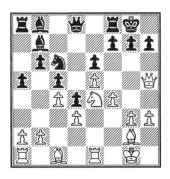

16...♕d7??

This allows a forced mate. Probably the computer did not really look at the coming knight sacrifice, which is very easy for Kasparov of course. After 16...♖a7, White still has good long-term attacking chances, but matters are not completely clear.

17.♘f6+ g×f6 18.e×f6 ♔h8 18...♘e7 19.♕g5+ ♘g6 20.♕h6 ♗×g2 21.♕g7#. **19.♗e4 h6 20.♕×h6+**

♔g8 21.♕g7# 1–0

Kasparov, Garry (2715) – Turbostar 432
Hamburg Spiegel simultaneous exhibition (32 opponents), Hamburg, 1985

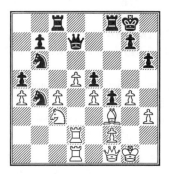

White is not better and Kasparov now starts to muddy the waters to try and win this game. He wanted to win the exhibition by a score of 32-0.

31.g5?!

Highly risky. Better is 31.♖c1 ♘xc4 32.♖dd1 ♘b2 33.♖d2 ♘c4=.

31...♘×c4 32.♖a2?

Objectively this move is bad and Kasparov would never have played it against a human, but against a computer of those times it was a good try as the machines tended to take too much material and neglect king safety. 32.♖e2 limits the damage but is of course not the point of Kasparov's previous move.

32...♘×a2 33.♘×a2 ♕×a4 34.g×h6 ♕×a2?! This greedy capture does win, but 34...g×h6–+ is much easier as now Black's king is safe.

35.♕g2 ♖c7 36.d6 ♖d7 37.♗g4

37...♕b3??

The blunder Kasparov wanted to provoke, probably caused by the horizon effect. 37...♘e3! leads to a technical win after 38.f×e3 ♕×g2+ 39.♔×g2 f3+ 40.♔f2 ♖dd8–+.

38.♗×d7 ♕×d1+ 39.♔h2 ♖f7 40.♗e6 ♔f8 41.h7 ♘×d6 42.h8♕+ ♔e7 43.♗×f7 ♘×f7 44.♕h×g7 1–0

Novag Monster Y – King, Daniel (2425)
Sicilian Defense B92
Commonwealth Championship (2), London, 17.02.1985

1.e4 c5 2.♘f3 d6 3.d4 c×d4 4.♘×d4 ♘f6 5.♘c3 a6 6.♗e2 e5 7.♘b3 ♗e7 8.0-0 0-0 9.a4 ♘c6 10.f4 ♘b4 11.♔h1 ♗d7 12.♗e3 ♗c6 13.♗f3 b5 14.a×b5 a×b5 15.♕e2 ♕c7 16.♖×a8

A new move. 16.♖fc1 d5= was known from Mestel-Tarjan, Buenos Aires 1978.

16...♖×a8 17.♕d2 ♕b7 18.♗g1 ♗f8 19.f×e5 d×e5 20.♘c5 ♕c7 21.♖d1 ♘a6?! 22.♘×a6?!

Exchanging the active knight like this is a mistake. 22.♘d5 ♗×d5 23.e×d5 ♗d6 24.b4 is slightly better for White.

22...♖×a6 23.g3?! The prophylactic 23.♕d3 ♕b7 24.h3 is more circumspect.

23...b4! 24.♘d5 ♗×d5 24...♘×d5!?

25.e×d5 ♗b5 is the alternative.

25.e×d5 e4?!

Opening the position plays into White's hand. 25...♗d6!? was called for, when Black is slightly more comfortable.

26.♗g2 ♖d6 27.♕e2 ♘×d5 28.♗×e4 ♘f6 29.♗f3 ♖e6 30.♕d3 h5 31.♖a1 ♘g4 32.♖a7 ♕b8 33.♕f5 33.♖a8 ♕e5 34.♕d2 applies more pressure, but White's advantage is not very large.

33...♖f6?!

33...♘h6 34.♕×h5 ♖e1 is more or less equal. Now a typical computer error follows.

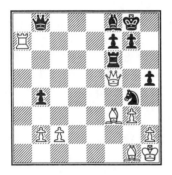

34.♕×h5?

This wins a pawn, but Black's initiative on the light squares wins the game. After 34.♕d5, White is better because of the powerful bishops, especially the play on the light squares.

34...♖×f3 35.♕×g4 ♖f1 36.♕d4 ♕b5 37.♖c7 37.♔g2 ♕e2+ 38.♗f2 ♖×f2+ 39.♕×f2 ♕×f2+ 40.♔×f2 ♗c5+ -+.

37...♕f5 38.♕d2 ♗c5 39.♖×c5 39.♕d8+?! is refuted by 39...♔h7 40.♕h4+ ♔g6 41.♖c6+ f6-+.

39...♕×c5 40.♕d8+ ♔f8 41.♕d5 41.♕×f8+ ♔×f8 42.♔g2 ♖c1 43.♗c5+ ♔g8 44.♗×b4 ♖×c2+ 45.♔g1 ♖×b2-+

41...♖d1!? A nice "joke."

42.♕c6 42.♕×d1? ♕a8+ 43.♕f3 ♕×f3#.

42...♕d8 43.h4 ♕d5+ 44.♕×d5 ♖×d5 45.♗e3 ♖d1+ 46.♔g2 ♖b1 47.♗d4 ♖c1 48.c3 b3 49.♔f3 ♖c2 50.c4 0-1

Yanofsky, Daniel – Phoenix
French Defense C10
Canada Open, Edmonton, 1985

1.e4 e6 2.d4 d5 3.♘c3 ♘c6 4.♘f3 ♘f6 5.e5 ♘e4 6.♗b5 ♗b4 6...♗d7 is the alternative.

7.♗d2 ♗×c3

This has not been played, but it might not be that bad. 7...♘×d2 is chosen by the humans exclusively.

8.b×c3 0-0 9.0-0 f6 10.e×f6 ♕×f6 11.♕e2

11...♘×d2?

The direct capture plays into White's hand, who gets full control and a dark-square bind. Only after 11...♗d7 12.♗d3 is the capture good: 12...♘×d2 13.♕×d2 e5 which is almost equal.

12.♕×d2 ♗d7 13.♖fe1 a6 14.♗×c6 ♗×c6 15.♖ab1 ♗b5 16.♘e5 ♖a7? A very odd move.

17.♖e3 ♕e7 18.♖be1 c5?

The beginning of a misguided concept, which in the end plays into White's

hands. 18...♖f6 19.♖h3 ♖a8 20.♕g5
♖e8 brings more defenders to the
kingside.

19.♘f3 ♖f6 20.♖e5

20.♘g5!? ♗d7 21.c4 applies even more
pressure.

20...♗c4?

The wrong direction as the a2-pawn
does not matter. Black must bring back
all men to the defense with 20...♖a8
21.♘g5 ♗d7. Then White is still much
better, but it is not so easy to breach the
walls of Black's house.

21.♘g5 ♗×a2?

This greedy capture loses by force,
but White's attack should also crash
through after 21...c×d4 22.c×d4 h6
23.♘×e6 as Black's bishop cannot join
the defense in time.

22.♘×e6 c×d4 23.♘×d4 ♕d7 24.♖e7 ♕d6 25.♕g5 g6 26.♕h6 1-0

Mephisto – Spraggett, Kevin (2525)
Sicilian Defense, French Variation B40
Wenen Open, 1986

1.e4 c5 2.♘f3 e6 3.♗e2 ♘c6 4.0-0
♘f6 5.♘c3 d6 6.d4 c×d4 7.♘×d4
♗e7 8.♗e3 a6 9.♘×c6 b×c6
10.♕d2 ♕c7 11.♗f4 0-0 12.♖ad1
♖d8 13.♗c4 ♗b7 14.♖fe1 c5
15.♕d3 ♘h5 16.♗c1 g6 17.♗h6

♗f6 18.♕d2 ♗e5 19.♗g5 ♖d7
20.h3 ♗c6 21.f3 ♕b7 22.♖b1
♗d4+ 23.♔h1 d5 24.e×d5
e×d5 25.♗d3 ♗g7 26.♗h6
c4 27.♗×g7 ♔×g7 28.♗e2 d4
29.♘d1 c3 30.♕g5 ♖e8 31.♕h4
♖de7 32.♕×d4+ f6 33.♘×c3
♘g3+ 34.♔g1 ♘×e2+ 35.♖×e2
♖×e2 36.♘×e2 ♖×e2 37.c4 ♗×f3
38.♔f1 0-1

Mephisto – Ivanov, Igor (2515)
Modern Defense: Queen Pawn Fianchetto A40
U.S. Open, Long Beach, 1989

Ivanov was a very strong player, but he
seemed to be regular fodder for strong
computer opponents.

1.d4 g6 2.c4 ♗g7 3.♘c3 c5 4.♘f3
c×d4 5.♘×d4 ♘c6 6.e3 ♘f6
7.♘c2 b6 8.♗e2 ♗b7 9.0-0 ♖c8
10.♗f3 ♗a6 11.b3 ♘e5 12.♗b2
♘×f3+ 13.♕×f3 ♖c5 14.♘d5 ♖×d5
15.c×d5 ♗×f1 16.♖×f1 0-0 17.d6
e6 18.e4 ♘e8 19.♗×g7 ♔×g7
20.♕c3+ ♕f6 21.e5 ♕f4 22.g3
♕e4 23.♘e3 f6 24.♕c8 ♘×d6
25.e×f6+ ♖×f6 26.♕×d7+ ♘f7
27.♕×a7 h5 28.♖d1 h4 29.♕×b6
♘g5 30.♔f1 h×g3 31.h×g3 ♕f3
32.♖d7+ ♔h6 33.♘d1 ♘e4
34.♔g1 ♘g5 35.♕d4 ♘h3+
36.♔f1 g5 37.♕d3 ♕h1+ 38.♔e2
♖f5 39.♕c3 ♘g1+ 40.♔d2 ♖e5
41.♘e3 ♕e4 42.♕c8 1-0

8
Bent Larsen – DEEP BLUE Match (1993)

Game 1 is in Chapter 6.

DEEP BLUE NORDIC – Larsen, Bent (2540)
Sicilian Defense: Accelerated Dragon B38
Exhibition match (2), Copenhagen, 26.02.1993

Hsu (1993):

> The machine had good chances to
> win the second Larsen match game,
> but could not pull it off. This game,
> together with the first game, made us
> realize that the machine needed to be
> told to open up the position when it
> had the bishop pair. Something also
> needs to be done about unlike bishops
> endings. The machine knows that one
> pawn up in bishops of opposite color
> ending is drawish. Unfortunately,
> some time one extra rook each does
> not change the result either.

**1.e4 c5 2.♘f3 g6 3.c4 ♗g7 4.d4
c×d4 5.♘×d4 ♘c6 6.♗e3 ♘f6
7.♘c3 0-0 8.♗e2 d6 9.0-0 ♗d7
10.♕d2 ♘×d4 11.♗×d4 ♗c6
12.f3 a5 13.b3 ♘d7 14.♗e3 ♘c5
15.♖ab1 ♕b6 16.♖fc1 ♖fc8
17.♖c2 h5 18.♘d5 ♗×d5 19.c×d5
♕b4 20.♕×b4 a×b4 21.♗d2 ♘a6
22.♖bc1 ♗d4+ 23.♔f1 ♖×c2
24.♖×c2 ♗c5 25.♗d3 ♔f8 26.♗b5
♘c7 27.♗h6+ ♔g8 28.♗d3 ♘e8
29.♗d2 ♘f6 30.♔e2 ♔g7 31.♗b5
h4 32.h3 ♖d8 33.♗g5 ♖h8
34.♔d3 ♖h5 35.♗f4 e5 36.d×e6
f×e6 37.♗a4 b6 38.♗c6 ♔f7
39.♗d2 d5 40.e×d5 e×d5 41.♗f4
♖f5 42.♗c7 ♘h5 43.♖e2 ♘f4+
44.♗×f4 ♖×f4 45.♗×d5+ ♔g7
46.♗e4 ♖f7 47.♔c4 ♖d7 48.♗d5
♖e7 49.♖c2 ♖c1 50.♗b7 ♔f6
51.♗e4 ♖d1 52.♔b5 g5 53.♖e2
♖a1 54.♗d3 ♖g1 55.♗h7 ♖a1**

**56.♔c4 ♖g1 57.♔d5 ♖d1+ 58.♔c6
♖f1 59.♗d3 ♖f2 ½-½**

Larsen, Bent (2540) – DEEP BLUE NORDIC
Scandinavian Defense B01
Exhibition match (3), Copenhagen, 27.02.1993

Hsu (1993):

> We did not choose the Scandinavian
> Defense, Danish variation to honor
> our host. The 1.e4 e5 defense was
> busted (well, sort of), and nothing
> else was ready. 8...0-0-0?? is a horrible
> mistake by the machine. Probably
> the only chess player at the match
> site that did not think that Larsen was
> winning was the machine. 13...♗d6!
> is critical. If 13...e×d5, then ♗c7! is
> annihilating. Larsen could have won
> a pawn by 14.♗d6, but might have to
> give up the attack. The attack petered
> out into a better ending for Black,
> but the ♕♘ vs ♕♗ ending would
> probably require the likes of Karpov
> to win it.

**1.e4 d5 2.e×d5 ♕×d5 3.♘c3 ♕a5
4.♘f3 ♘f6 5.d4 ♗f5 6.♗e2 e6
7.0-0 ♘bd7 8.a3 0-0-0 9.♗f4
♕b6 10.♘b5 ♘d5 11.♗g3 a6
12.c4 a×b5 13.c×d5 ♗d6 14.♕b3
♗×g3 15.h×g3 ♘f8 16.a4 ♖×d5
17.a×b5 ♔d7 18.♗c4 ♖d6 19.d5
♔e7 20.♖fe1 ♘d7 21.♕c3 ♘f6
22.♘h4 ♗g4 23.♖e3 ♖hd8
24.d×e6 f×e6 25.♖ae1 ♖d1 26.♕e5
♖×e1+ 27.♖×e1 ♖d2 28.♘f5+
♗×f5 29.♕×f5 ♖d1 30.♕e5 ♖×e1+
31.♕×e1 ♕d6 32.♕e2 h6 33.b3
♕d7 34.♕f3 b6 35.♕e2 ♔f7 36.g4
♕d6 37.g3 ♘d5 38.♔g2 ♔f6
39.♕f3+ ♔e7 40.♕e4 ♘f6 41.♕g6
♔f8 42.g5 h×g5 43.♕×g5 ♕d4
44.♕c1 ♔c7 45.♕g5 ♔f7 46.♕c1
♕e5 47.♕d2 ♔e7 48.♕b4+ ♔d7
49.♕d2+ ♘d5 50.♕d3 g5 51.♕f3**

♔e7 52.♔g1 ♕d4 53.♕h5 ♕g7
54.♕g4 ♔d6 55.♕e4 ♕a1+
56.♔g2 ♕f6 57.♕c2 ♕e5 58.♕c1
♔d7 59.♔g1 ♔e7 60.♔f1 ♔f6
61.♕a3 ♔f7 62.♕c1 ♔e7 ½-½

Deep Blue Nordic – Larsen, Bent (2540)
Sicilian Defense Najdorf Variation B74
Exhibition match (4), Copenhagen, 28.02.1993

Hsu (1993):

> Larsen got into early trouble
> underestimating 14.f5. Machine
> probably had a winning edge at move
> 25. But it willingly went into another
> unlike bishops ending without proper
> assessment. The resultant queen and
> bishop ending might be winnable had
> the queen been traded and the [king's
> knight] pawn (but not the [king's
> rook] pawn) become passed. The
> machine, however, was trying hard
> to avoid trading the queen. This time,
> it did not know that certain unlike-
> bishops endings are winnable.

1.e4 c5 2.♘f3 d6 3.d4 c×d4 4.♘×d4
♘f6 5.♘c3 a6 6.a4 g6 7.♗e2
♗g7 8.0-0 0-0 9.f4 ♘c6 10.♗e3
♗d7 11.♘b3 ♗e6 12.♖a3 ♖c8
13.♔h1 ♖e8 14.f5 ♗×b3 15.♖×b3
♕d7 16.f×g6 h×g6 17.♘d5 ♘×d5
18.e×d5 ♘e5 19.a5 ♗f6 20.c3 ♔g7
21.♖b4 ♖h8 22.♕b3 ♖c7 23.♗b6
♖cc8 24.♔g1 ♖h4 25.♗d4 ♖c7
26.♗×e5 d×e5 27.♖×h4 ♗×h4
28.♖×f7+ ♔×f7 29.d6+ ♔g7
30.d×c7 ♕×c7 31.♕b4 ♗g5 32.♗f3
b5 33.a×b6 ♗e3+ 34.♔h1 ♗×b6
35.♕e4 ♕c5 36.♕b1 a5 37.♗e4 g5
38.♗h7 ♔h8 39.♗f5 ♕f2 40.♗g6
♔g7 41.♗h7 ♔h8 42.♗f5 ♔g7
43.♗d3 ♗e3 44.♗h7 ♔h8 45.b3
♗d2 46.c4 ♗e3 47.♗g6 ♗d4
48.♗f5 ♗c5 49.♗e4 ♗e3 50.♕d1
♔g7 51.♕a1 ♗d4 52.♕c1 ½-½

9
Additional Man-Machine Games
(1990s)

Novag – Bronstein, David
King's Indian Defense, Exchange Variation E92
Aegon, 1992

A beautiful example of a grandmaster
doing nothing, waiting for the program
to make enough small positional
mistakes, and turning it into a decisive
advantage.

1.c4 g6 2.♘f3 ♗g7 3.d4 d6 4.e4
♘f6 5.♘c3 0-0 6.♗e2 e5 7.d×e5
d×e5 8.♕×d8 ♖×d8 9.♗g5 ♖e8
10.♗×f6 ♗×f6 11.♘d5 ♗d8
12.0-0-0 c6 13.♘e3 ♘d7 14.a3
♘c5 15.♘d2 ♘e6 16.♗g4 h5
17.♗×e6 ♗×e6 18.♘f3 ♗c7
19.♘g5 ♗c8 20.♘f3 a5 21.♖d2
♗b6 22.♖hd1 a4 23.♔c2 ♔g7
24.♔b1 ♔f6 25.♖c2 ♗c5 26.h3
♗e6 27.♘d5 c×d5 28.c×d5 ♗×h3
29.g×h3 b6 30.♖d3 ♖a5 31.♘d2
♖a7 32.♘c4 ♔g5 33.♖g3+ ♔h6
34.♔c1 ♖c7 35.♖d3 f6 36.d6
♖d7 37.♔d1 ♔g7 38.♔e2 ♔f7
39.♖d1 ♔e6 40.h4 ♖g8 41.♖f1
♗d4 42.♖g1 g5 43.h×g5 ♖×g5
44.♖gc1 ♖g4 45.♖h1 ♖×e4+
46.♔d3 ♖f4 47.♖×h5 ♗×f2
48.♖h2 ♗c5 49.♖c3 ♗d4 50.♖cc2
b5 51.♘d2 ♗×d6 52.♖g2 ♔d5
53.♔e2 e4 54.b4 ♖h7 55.♖c8 ♗b6
56.♖b8 ♔c6 57.♖e8 e3 58.♖e6+
♔b7 59.♘f1 ♖f2+ 60.♖×f2
e×f2 61.♖×f6 ♖e7+ 62.♔f3 ♖e1
63.♖f7+ ♔c8 64.♔g2 ♖a1 65.♖f5
♖×a3 66.♖×b5 ♔c7 0-1

Seirawan, Yasser (2600) – Rebel
Slave Defense D45
The Hague, 1995

**1.d4 d5 2.c4 c6 3.e3 ♘f6 4.♘c3 e6
5.♘f3 ♘bd7 6.b3 ♗b4 7.♗d2 0-0
8.♗e2 b6 9.0-0 c5?** Black exchanges
the bishop for the knight, which is very
problematic as the bishops have strong
long term potential. 9...♕e7 is the main
move.

**10.c×d5 e×d5 11.a3 ♗×c3 12.♗×c3
♘e4 13.♗b2 ♗b7 14.♘d2 f5?**
This weakens the dark squares on the
kingside too much. 14...♘d6 is the
lesser evil.

**15.♖c1 ♕e7 16.♘×e4 f×e4 17.d×c5
b×c5**

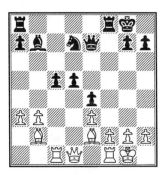

18.b4!? A nice strategic point, which
is tactically justified, typical for strong
human grandmasters. **18...c4** 18...cxb4?
runs into 19.Rc7 bxa3 20.Ba1 Rab8
21.Rxb7 Rxb7 22.Qxd5+i.

**19.♕d4 ♘b6 20.f4 e×f3 21.♖×f3
♖×f3 22.g×f3**

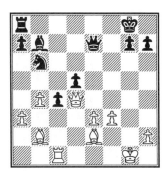

22...♖c8? Black should bring the
knight to the kingside with 22...♘d7
23.♔f2 ♘f6 24.♖g1 ♖f8 to limit the
damage.

**23.♔f2 ♖c6 24.♖g1 ♖c7 25.♗d1
♘c8 26.♗c2 ♘d6 27.a4 a6 28.♖g4**
28.♗c3!? ♘e4+ 29.♗×e4 d×e4 30.f4 +−

**28...♕f8 29.♖f4 ♕e7 30.♗c3 ♕e6
31.♖g4 ♘e8 32.♖g5 ♖f7 33.♖e5
♕d7 34.♗f5** Seirawan clarifies
matters. The alternative 34.♕g4 ♘d6
35.♕×d7 ♖×d7 36.h4 is also very
strong.

**34...♖×f5 35.♖×e8+ ♖f8 36.♖×f8+
♔×f8 37.b5 a×b5 38.a×b5 ♕c7
39.f4 ♕e7 40.♔e2 ♕d7 41.♔d2
♔g8 42.♕e5 ♗c8 43.b6 h6
44.♗d4 ♔h7 45.♔c3 ♗b7 46.f5
♕f7 47.♕e6 ♔g8 48.♗c5 h5?!**
Black is lost in any case, but this is not
so easy to calculate even for modern
engines, e.g., 48...g6 49.♗d4 ♕×e6
50.f×e6 g5 51.♗c5 ♔g7 52.♗e7 ♔g6
53.♔d4 ♔f5 54.♗×g5 ♔×e6 55.♗×h6
♔d6 56.h4 ♔c6 57.h5 ♗c8 58.♗f8 ♗f5
59.♗b4 +− .

49.h4 g6 50.♗d4

50...♕×e6? The resulting pure opposite-color bishop ending is just lost. 50...gxf5 was the last chance to fight, albeit for a lost cause, e.g., 51.♔h6 ♕e7 52.♕×h5 ♕a3+ 53.♔c2 ♕d3+ 54.♔c1 ♕a3+ 55.♔d1 ♕a4+ 56.♔e2 ♕c2+ 57.♔e1 ♕c1+ 58.♔f2 ♕c2+ 59.♔g1 ♕c1+ 60.♔g2 ♕d2+ 61.♔h3 +−.

51.f×e6 ♔f8 52.♗f6 ♗a8 53.♔d4 ♔e8 54.e4 d×e4 55.♔×c4 ♗b7 56.♔d4 ♔f8 57.♗g5 ♔e8 58.♔e5 ♗c6 59.♔d6 ♗a8 60.♔c7 e3 61.♗×e3 1-0

Stangl, Markus (2560) − Zugzwang
Slav Defense, Czech Variation D19
Lippstadt (11), 1995

In the 1990s it was still possible to win with a long-term king attack.

1.♘f3 d5 2.d4 ♘f6 3.c4 c6 4.♘c3 d×c4 5.a4 ♗f5 6.e3 e6 7.♗×c4 ♗b4 8.0-0 0-0 9.♕e2 ♘bd7 10.e4 ♗g6 11.♗d3 ♗h5 12.♗f4 ♖e8 13.e5 ♘d5 14.♘×d5 c×d5 15.h3 a6 16.g4 ♗g6 17.♗×g6 f×g6 18.♔g2 ♕b6 19.h4 ♖f8 20.♗e3 ♖ac8 21.♖h1 ♗e7 22.♕d3 ♕b4 ♖he g±eed± 22...♕×b2? +−∞ ⇄ e∓ b± 23.♖hb1 ♕c2 24.♕×c2 ♖×c2 25.♖×b7 ♖d8 26.♘g5 ♖c6 27. ♖c1 +− (Stangl), which is no problem to find out for the machine of course.

23.h5 g×h5? The machine

underestimates the coming storm. 23...♘c5! 24.♕a3 ♘b3 is almost equal.

24. ♖×h5 g6

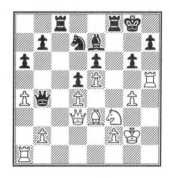

25.♖×h7!! A surprise for the machine, which had expected 25.♖hh1?=.

25...♔×h7 26.♖h1+ ♔g7 27.♗h6+!? After a long think Stangl finds a winning continuation. The machine had planned to meet its main expectation 27.♖h6 with 27...♖f5 but White also wins after 28.g×f5 e×f5 29.♕f1 ♘f8 30.♕h1 +−.

27...♔f7

28.♗d2! This double threat is Stangl's point.

28...♕×b2 29.♖h7+ ♔e8 30.♕×g6+ ♔d8 31.♖×e7 ♕a3! 31... ♖×f3 32.♕e8+ ♔c7 33.♗a5+ ♔b8 34.♕c8+ ♔×c8 35.♖e8# (Stangl); 31...♔×e7 32.♗g5+ +−.

32.♗e3 ♔×e7 33.♗g5+ ♘f6

**34.exf6+ ♔d8 35.f7+ ♔d7
36.♘e5+ ♔c7 37.♕xe6 ♖h8
38.♘f3 ♕d6 39.♕f5 ♔b6 40.♗f4
♕c6 41.g5 ♕c2 42.♕xc2 1–0**

Van der Wiel, John (2535) – PANDIX
English Opening A13
The Hague, 1996

The computer is guilty of two typical mistakes: having no plan, and underestimating attack potential. An even game quickly turns ugly.

**1.c4 e6 2.♘f3 ♘f6 3.b3 d5 4.♗b2
♗e7 5.e3 0-0 6.♗e2 b6 7.cxd5
exd5 8.0-0 ♗g4 9.d3 c5 10.h3
♗h5 11.♘e5 ♗xe2 12.♕xe2
♘bd7 13.♘c6 ♕e8 14.♘xe7+
♕xe7 15.♘d2 d4 16.e4 ♖ac8
17.♖ae1 ♖fe8 18.♕d1 ♘e5
19.♘c4 b5 20.♘xe5 ♕xe5 21.f4
♕e6 22.♕f3 h6 23.e5 ♘d5 24.f5
♕c6 25.♗c1 ♘b4 26.♕g3 ♘xa2
27.f6 g6 28.♗xh6 ♕e6 29.♗g7
1–0**

DRAGON – Seirawan, Yasser (2630)
French Defense C05
The Hague, 1997

**1.e4 e6 2.d4 d5 3.♘d2 ♘f6 4.e5
♘fd7 5.f4 c5 6.c3 ♘c6 7.♘df3 c4
8.♘e2 b5 9.g4 ♘b6 10.♘g3 h6
11.♗e2**

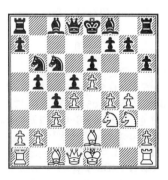

11...♕d7! A strong move against the computer. The program is "happy" as Black can no longer castle. However, this is irrelevant because the position is closed position. When using chess knowledge in a program, the context is important!

**12.♗e3 a5 13.♕c2 ♔c7 14.f5
b4 15.♖g1?** 15.0-0 is much more natural as the king is very safe here.
15...♕e8 16.♖g2? 16.b3 (Kongstad 2003) is called for to avoid the coming queenside bind. **16...a4 17.♗f1
b3 18.♕b1 bxa2 19.♖xa2 ♘a5
20.♘h5 ♔b8**

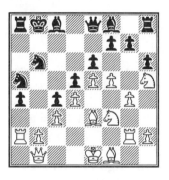

21.f6? Closing the kingside is a big mistake, as Black then plays on the queenside for free. "When playing against a computer, what you want are messy strategic conditions," Seirawan was once quoted as saying (Kongstad 2003). **21...g6 22.♘g7?** This exchange plays into Black's hands.

**22...♗xg7 23.fxg7 ♖h7 24.♖a3
♕g8 25.g5 h5 26.♔f2 ♕xg7
27.♔g1 ♖h8 28.♖f2 ♖e8 29.♘d2
♖e7 30.♗e2 ♕g8 31.♖f3 ♗d7
32.♗f2 ♕c8 33.♕c1 ♗e8 34.♕d1
♖b7 35.♗f1 ♕c6 36.♗g2 ♘c8
37.♕a1 ♖aa7 38.♖f4 ♕b6 39.♖a2
♘b3 40.♘xb3 axb3 41.♖xa7 ♖xa7
42.♕c1 ♖a2 43.♗f1 ♕a5 44.♗e1
♖a1 45.♕d2 ♖b1 46.♗g3 ♕a1**

47.♖f2 ♘b6 48.♕e2 ♔c8 49.♕d2
♘a4 50.♕e3 ♘×b2 51.♖f3 ♘a4
52.♕f4 b2 0-1 A fine anti-computer
game!

McShane, Luke (2467) – ConNers
King's Indian Attack B10
Lippstadt, 1999

An example of underestimating an
attack on the king.

**1.e4 c6 2.d3 d5 3.♘d2 e5 4.♘gf3
♗d6 5.g3 ♘f6 6.♗g2 0-0 7.0-
0 ♖e8 8.h3 ♘bd7 9.♘h4 ♘c5
10.♖e1 ♗e6 11.a3 a5 12.♘f1
♕d7?!** Already wrong, as 13 ♗g5
is difficult to deal with, regardless of
whether the pawn is captured on h3.
12...h6.

13.♗g5! ♗×h3?? 13...♗e7! was
possible: 14.e×d5 ♘×d5 15.♗×e7
♖×e7 16.♖×e5 ♗×h3 17.♖×e7 ♘×e7.
**14.♗×h3 ♕×h3 15.♗×f6 g×f6
16.♘e3 ♕e6 17.♘hf5 ♔h8
18.♔g2** White has a winning kingside
attack. **18...♖g8 19.♖h1 ♖g5
20.♖h4 ♘d7 21.♕h1 ♘f8 22.♕h2
d×e4 23.♖h1 ♔g8 24.d×e4 ♖a7
25.♘g4 ♖a8 26.♘gh6+ ♔h8
27.♘×d6 1-0**

10
Dortmund (2002)

Rounds 1 and 5 can be found in Chapter 8.

Deep Junior – Hübner, Robert (2615)
French Defense C04
Dortmund SuperGM (2), 08.07.2000

**1.e4 e6 2.d4 d5 3.♘d2 ♘c6
4.♘gf3 ♘f6 5.e5 ♘d7 6.♘b3 ♗e7
7.♗b5 0-0 8.0-0 ♘cb8 9.c3 b6
10.♘bd2 ♗a6 11.a4 c6 12.♗×a6**
♘×a6 13.♕e2 ♘c7 14.b3 c5
15.♖e1 ♘b8 16.♗a3 ♘c6 17.♕d3
♖c8 18.a5 ♖a8

19.♔h1

A strange move from the human point
of view.

19...♕d7?

19...♕c8 is called for, when Black is
not worse and has a good anti-computer
position. One possible option for the
point of view of the machines now is
20.♔g1.

20.d×c5 1-0

Dr. Hübner was shocked by missing
the coming ♘e4 and resigned. But he
should have played on as White has the
initiative but matters are not clear after
20...b×c5 21.♘e4 c4 22.b×c4 ♗×a3
23.♖×a3 ♕e7, when White can choose
between 24.c×d5 and 24.♘eg5.

Adams, Michael (2755) – Deep Junior
Ruy Lopez C68
Dortmund SuperGM (3), 09.07.2000

**1.e4 e5 2.♘f3 ♘c6 3.♗b5 a6
4.♗×c6 d×c6 5.d4 e×d4 6.♕×d4
♕×d4 7.♘×d4 c5 8.♘e2 ♗d7
9.♗e3 ♘f6 10.f3 0-0-0 11.♘d2
h6 12.0-0-0 g6 13.h4 b6 14.♘f4
♗g7 15.♘f1 ♖he8 16.♘g3 a5
17.♗d2 h5 18.c4 ♗a4 19.b3 ♗c6
20.♔c2 ♘d7 21.♗c3 ♗h6 22.♘h3**

a4 23.♖he1 ♘e5 24.♖×d8+ ♔×d8
25.♘e2 ♔c8 26.♘ef4 ♗d7 27.♖d1
♘c6 28.♘g5

28...f5!?

JUNIOR activates his bishops and
calculates that its counterplay
compensates the resulting weaknesses
on the kingside.

**29.e5 ♘×e5 30.♗×e5 ♖×e5
31.♘×g6 ♖e2+ 32.♖d2 ♖e8
33.♘f4 ♗g7 34.♖e2**

34.♘×h5 ♗d4 35.g3 ♖e3 36.♖d3 ♖e2+
37.♖d2 ♖e3 also leads to a more or less
forced draw.

**34...♖×e2+ 35.♘×e2 a×b3+
36.a×b3 ♗e8 37.♔d3 ♔d7
38.♘h3 ♗f6 39.g3 ♗e5 40.♘hf4
♗f7 41.♔e3 ♔d6 42.♘d3 ♗f6
½-½**

DEEP JUNIOR – Khalifman, Alexander (2667)
Modern Defense B08
Dortmund SuperGM (4), 10.07.2000

**1.e4 g6 2.d4 ♗g7 3.♘c3 c6 4.♘f3
d6 5.♗e3 ♘f6 6.♕d2 b5 7.♗d3
♗g4?!**

Very risky. 7...♘bd7 is the main line.

**8.e5! b4 9.♘e4 ♘×e4 10.♗×e4 d5
11.♗d3 ♗×f3 12.g×f3 ♕b6 13.h4!**

White has a strong initiative.

13...♘d7

If 13...h5?, then 14.e6±.

**14.h5 c5 15.d×c5 ♘×c5 16.♗e2
0-0 17.♕×d5 ♖ac8 18.h×g6 h×g6
19.♕d4**

19...g5?!

Objectively this move is a mistake but
in the game it works well as the queens
are exchanged. 19...♖fd8 20.♕h4 ♗e5
21.♕h7+ ♔f8 22.♗h6+ ♔e8 23.♕g8+
♔d7 24.0-0-0+ ♔c7 25.♕×f7 ♕f6±.

20.♗×g5?!

20.♕g4 is much stronger: 20...♕g6
21.♖h5 ♖fd8 22.♖×g5 ♕h6 23.♗c4+−.

20...♘e6 21.♕×b6 a×b6

22.♗×e7?

Too greedy 22.♗e3 ♗×e5 23.0-0-0
gives White a winning attack.

22...♖fe8 23.♗d6 ♘d4

403

24.♗d3

JUNIOR decides to attack with opposite-color bishops. A very difficult decision. With hindsight, it would have been better for JUNIOR to go for the endgame arising after 24.♖d1!?, as in the game fortresses may arise on the dark squares, while after 24...♘xe2 25.♔xe2 ♖xc2+ (25...♗xe5 26.♖hg1+ ♗g7+ 27.♔d2) 26.♖d2 ♖xd2+ 27.♔xd2 ♗xe5 28.♗xe5 (28.♖e1?? runs into the shot 28...♗c3+) 28...♖xe5 29.♖h6, JUNIOR will have practical winning chances.

24...♗xe5 25.0-0-0 ♗xd6 26.♗h7+ ♔f8 27.♖xd4 ♗c5 28.♖g4 ♔e7 29.♖e1+

29.♖e4+ is answered by 29...♔f6 30.♖f4+ ♔e7 31.♖e1+ ♔f8 and Black's walls are by no means easy to breach.

29...♔d6 30.♖d1+ ♔c7 31.♗d3 ♖cd8 32.♖f1

32.♖f4!?.

32...♖d4 33.♗e4 ♖e5 34.♖h1 ♖e7 35.♖g5 ♖d6 36.♖g2 ♖ed7 37.♗f5 ♖e7 38.♖f1 ♖e5 39.♗e4 ♖e7 40.♖h2 ♖ed7 41.f4 ♖d4 42.f3 ♗d6 43.♖h4 ♗c5 44.♖hh1 ♖d2 45.♔b1 ♖g2 46.f5 ♗d4 47.♖d1 ♗c5 48.♗d3 ♖g3 49.♖df1 ♖e7 50.♗e4 ♖d7 51.♔a1

A strange move.

51...♗d4 52.♗d3 ♖e7 53.♗c4 f6 54.♔b1 ♖eg7 55.♖h4 ♗c5

56.♖e4?

After this move it is next to impossible to break Black's solid set up. 56.c3 gives much better practical chances.

56...♖g1! 57.♖c1 ♖7g5 58.♗e2 ♖xc1+ 59.♔xc1 ♖xf5 60.♔d2 ♖d5+ 61.♗d3 ♗d4 62.♔c1 ♗c5 63.♖e6 ♖d6 64.♖e2 ♖d7 65.♖g2 ½-½

Deep Junior – Akopian, Vladimir (2660)
Owen's Defense B00
Dortmund SuperGM (6), 13.07.2000

1.e4 b6 2.d4 ♗b7 3.♗d3 ♘f6 4.♕e2 e6 5.♘f3 d5 6.e5 ♘fd7 7.♘g5 ♗e7 8.♕g4 h5 9.♕g3 ♘f8 10.0-0 ♗a6 11.♗xa6 ♘xa6 12.c3 c5 13.♖d1

At first sight slightly strange, but JUNIOR plans to open the d-file in some lines.

13...c4 14.♖e1 ♖c8 15.h4 ♘h7 16.♘f3 ♖g8

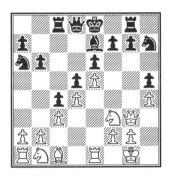

17.♗g5?

Allowing Black to exchange his problem knight h7. It is better to open a second front immediately with 17.b3 b5 18.b4 ♘c7 19.a4.

17...♘×g5 18.♘×g5 ♘b8 19.♘d2 ♘c6 20.b3 ♘a5 21.♖e3 ♗×g5 22.h×g5 g6 23.♖f3 ♖c7 24.♖f6 ♕c8 25.♕f4 ♖f8 26.b4 ♘c6 27.♘f3 ♖e7 28.♘h4

28.g4!? h×g4 29.♘h2 is more open.

28...♖g8 29.a4 ♖g7 30.♕c1 ♖c7 31.a5?! b5 32.♕e3 ♔d7

Now that the queenside is closed, Akopian heads for it.

33.♔h1 a6 34.♖d1 ♕e8 35.♔h2 ♘e7 36.♖h1 ♘g8 37.♖f3 37.♘f3!? **37...♘e7 38.♖h3 ♘f5 39.♘×f5 e×f5 40.♖e1 ♖c6 41.♕f3 ♕e6 42.♖h1 ♖c8 43.♕e3 ♕e7 44.♕f4 ♕e6 45.♖e1 ½-½**

Anand, Viswanathan (2762) – Deep Junior
Colle System D05
Dortmund SuperGM (7), 14.07.2000

1.d4 d5 2.♘f3 ♘f6 3.e3 e6 4.♗d3 c5 5.c3 ♘c6 6.♘bd2 ♗e7 7.a3

Anand tries everything to provoke c5-c4 by weakening the b3-square, but it seems that the programmers have explicitly forbidden this advance after the game against Kramnik.

7...♕c7 8.♕e2 0-0 9.0-0 ♖d8 10.♖e1 a6 11.h3 b5 12.d×c5

Now Anand cannot wait any longer for c5-c4.

12...♗×c5 13.e4 ♘h5 14.♘b3 ♘g3 15.♕c2 d×e4 16.♘×c5 e×d3 17.♘×d3 ♘f5 18.♗f4

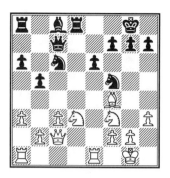

White is slightly better, but as computers are difficult to beat, Anand decided to call it a day: "You're not going to outplay a computer in this position. It is just too open." ½-½

Deep Junior – Piket, Jeroen (2649)
Modern Defense B15
Dortmund SuperGM (8), 15.07.2000

All quotes are Jeroen Piket's taken from ten Geuzendam (2000).

1.e4 g6 2.d4 ♗g7 3.♘c3 c6 4.♘f3 d5 5.h3 a6

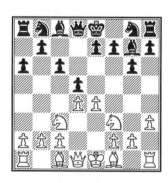

"A move that I would not allow myself to play against any of the other participants in the tournament. Against a computer such a waiting move is not such a bad idea. Of course a certain risk is involved and the effect may be both positive and negative."

6.♗f4 ♘f6 7.e5 ♘fd7 8.♕d2 e6 9.♗g5?! ♕b6 10.0-0-0 h6 11.♗e3

♕c7

"At this point I was most satisfied. My plan has worked. Gradually I can built up an attack with b5...The only counter-plan it has is a sacrificial attack on the kingside, but I knew that this goes against its nature."

12.h4 b5 13.♗f4?!

"When you see such purposeless moves you know that you are doing fine."

13...♘b6 14.a3?! ♘8d7 15.♔b1 a5 16.♘a2

16.♗xb5 is objectively not completely correct, but would have been a much better choice, e.g., 16...cxb5 17.♘xb5 ♕c6 18.♘d6+ ♔f8 19.h5 g5 (19...♘c4 20.♘xc4 dxc4 21.hxg6 c3 22.♕e3) 20.♗xg5 and at least chaos rules.

16...♕a7 17.g4?! ♗f8 18.c3 ♗a6 19.♕e1 ♘c4

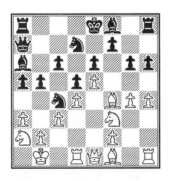

20.♗d2

"Another defensive move that a human would not easily come up with." But matters are very unpleasant in any case.

20...♗e7 21.♘c1 ♘db6 22.h5 g5! 23.♘a2 ♔d7 24.♗c1 ♖hb8

Piket invites everyone to the party. A very good strategy against a computer.

25.♔a1?!

The king is of course not really safe here. But good advice is hard to give anyway.

25...b4! 26.♘d2

26.cxb4 axb4 27.♘xb4 ♘a4-+.

26...♘xd2 27.♗xd2 ♗xf1 28.♖xf1 ♘c4 29.♖b1 b3 30.♘c1

30...♗xa3!

"Time to haul in the point."

31.♕d1

31.bxa3 b2+ 32.♔a2 bxc1♘+ 33.♕xc1 ♖xb1 34.♔xb1 ♖b8+ 35.♔c2 ♕a6-+.

31...♕b6 32.bxa3 b2+ 33.♔a2 bxc1♕ 34.♕xc1 ♕xb1+

Dirk ten Geuzendam (2000) comments that, "Again it was a heavy case of anti-computer chess which made Shay Buschinsky remark, 'We are seeing a new kind of chess. Eight pawn chess.'"
0-1

Leko, Peter (2740) – Deep Junior
Four Knights Game C48
Dortmund SuperGM (9), 16.07.2000

1.e4 e5 2.♘f3 ♘c6 3.♘c3 ♘f6 4.♗b5 ♘d4 5.♗c4 ♗c5 6.d3 c6 7.♘×d4 ♗×d4 8.♕f3 h5?!

JUNIOR likes to move its rook's pawns. Here it seems premature and does not fit well with 0-0 which will follow later.

9.h3 d5 10.e×d5 ♗×c3+ 11.b×c3 c×d5 12.♗b3 ♕c7 13.0-0 0-0

13...♗e6 14.♕g3 0-0-0 fits better with ...h5.

14.♕g3 a5!?

14...♕×c3? 15.♖b1 gives White a strong initiative.

15.a4 ♗e6 16.♗h6

16.♖e1!? ♕×c3 17.♕×e5 is a very interesting alternative.

16...♘e8 17.♗d2 f6 18.f4! e×f4 19.♕×f4 ♘d6 20.♖ae1 ♗f7 21.♕d4 ♕c6

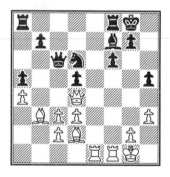

22.♖e7

White should be better, but it is by no means easy to make real progress. Other candidate moves here are 22.♗h6 and 22.g4, but to defeat a machine in this kind of position is not easy of course.

22...♖fe8?

This provokes the following strong

exchange sacrifice. 22...♖ad8 prevents the sacrifice.

23.♖×f7! ♘×f7 24.♗×d5 ♕d7 25.♖b1 ♖ad8 26.c4

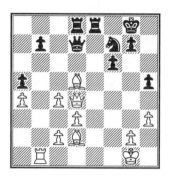

26...♕×a4?

Decentralizing the queen. The direct counterattack 26...♖e2? runs into 27.♗×a5+–. So the preparatory 26...♕c8 should be played.

27.♖×b7 ♖d7

28.♖×d7?

Leko fails to seize the moment: 28.♗×f7+ ♖×f7 29.♕d5 ♖ef8 (29...♕a1+ 30.♔f2 ♖ef8 31.♗f4 ♕c3 32.♗d6 ♕d2+ 33.♔g1 h4 34.♔h2 ♕e3 35.c5+–) 30.♗f4 and his active army gives him a winning advantage, e.g., 30...♕e8 31.c5 a4 32.♗d6 a3 33.♔f2+–.

28...♕×d7 29.♗×a5 ♖e2 30.♗b6 ♕e8 31.♗c7 ♖×c2 32.c5

32...♚h8!?

JUNIOR plays for a win by unpinning its knight. 32...♛e1+ 33.♚h2 ♜c1 34.♗f4 ♛h1+ 35.♚g3 ♛e1+ 36.♚h2 draws immediately.

33.♗g3 ♛d8 34.♗f2 ♜c1+ 35.♚h2 ♛b8+ 36.g3 ♘h6 37.♚g2 ♜c2 38.♗e4 h4 39.♛e3

39.g×h4? ♛f4 plays into Black's hands.

39...f5 40.♗d5 h×g3 41.♛×g3 ♛b5!

JUNIOR correctly avoids the exchange of queens.

42.♛e3 ♛b4 43.d4 ♛b2 44.c6 ♚h7 45.♛f4 ♛a3

46.♗e4!?

Very risky – courageous – against a computer. Leko is still trying to win at any price. 46.♗f3 ♛b2 47.♛e3 ♜c3 48.♛f4 draws easier.

46...♜×f2+!? 47.♚×f2 f×e4 48.c7

♛a8 49.d5 ♛a7+ 50.♚g2 ♛a2+ 51.♚f2 ♛c4 52.d6 ♛c6 53.♚f8 e3+ 54.♚f3 ♛c2+ 55.♚f1 ♛c4+ 56.♚g2?

56.♚e2 ♛c1+ 57.♚e1 ♛c5 58.♛b1+ g6 59.♛b7=.

56...♛e6

57.♛c6?

Mistakes always seem to come in pairs. The preventive 57.♚f1! was called for to deal with the e-pawn. But it seems that Black can win nevertheless, e.g., 57...♘f5 58.♚h5+ ♚g8 59.♛g4 ♛f7 60.d7 ♛×d7 61.♛c4+ ♚g6 62.♛c2 ♛c8.

57...♛a2+ 58.♚h1 ♘f5 59.♛e4

59.c8♛ runs up against 59...♘g3+ 60.♚g1 ♛f2#.

59...♛a1+ 60.♚h2 ♛b2+ 0-1

Leko resigned because of 61.♚h1 g6−+. After the game Leko was very impressed (ten Geuzendam 2000): "I outplayed the machine in the opening, but already when I made the exchange sacrifice I was not too happy with the position. I was better, but this is the kind of position that is very difficult to win against a computer. I believe that I would win this position against Garry but a computer just holds on." This position is not good from a psychological point of view. If you assume that your opponent is superior to you then it will become a self-fulfilling prophecy.

11
Hübner versus Deep Fritz (2002)

Game three of the match is given in Chapter 8.

Deep Fritz – Hübner, Robert (2612)
English Opening A18
Dortmund match (1), 15.07.2001

1.e4 e6 2.c4 e5 3.♘f3 ♘c6 4.♘c3 ♘f6 5.d4 ♗b4 6.d5 ♘e7

7.♘×e5?!

Making it relatively easy to equalize. 7.♕c2 is more dangerous for Black.

7...♗×c3+ 8.b×c3 d6 9.♘f3 ♘×e4 10.♗d3 ♘c5 11.♗b1 ♗f5 12.0-0 0-0 13.♖e1 ♗×b1 14.♖×b1 ♖e8 15.♗a3 b6 16.♗×c5 d×c5 17.♖b2 ♘g6 18.♖×e8+ ♕×e8 19.♖e2 ♕d7 20.♘e5 ♘×e5 21.♖×e5 ♖e8 22.f4 f6 23.♖e2 ♔f8 24.g3 ½-½

Hübner, Robert (2612) – Deep Fritz
Ruy Lopez C96
Dortmund match (2), 16.07.2001

1.e4 e5 2.♘f3 ♘c6 3.♗b5 a6

4.♗a4 ♘f6 5.0-0 ♗e7 6.♖e1 b5 7.♗b3 d6 8.c3 0-0 9.h3 ♘a5 10.♗c2 c5 11.d4 c×d4 12.c×d4 e×d4 13.♘×d4 ♗b7 14.♘f5 ♖c8 15.♗f4 ♘c4 16.b3 ♘e5 17.♘d2 ♖e8 18.♖c1 ♗f8 19.♗b1 ♖×c1 20.♕×c1 b4

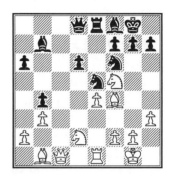

21.♕d1?!

21.♖d1 is more precise.

21...d5!

The typical freeing advance.

22.♘f1 ♘g6 23.♗g5 h6 24.♗×f6 ♕×f6 25.e×d5 ♖×e1 26.♕×e1 ♗×d5 27.♕d2 ♗e6 28.♘d4 ♗d7 29.♗e4 ♘f4 30.♘e2 ♘×e2+ 31.♕×e2 ♗c5 32.♘e3

32...♕a1+?!

From a practical point of view, it was better to keep the queens on the board to make it more difficult for Hübner by playing a move like 32...g6.

33.♕d1 ♛×d1+ 34.♘×d1 f5 35.♗d3
♗c8 36.♘b2 ♔f7 37.♗c4+ ♔f6
38.♘d3 ♗d6 39.f4 ♗b7 40.g3 a5
41.♔f2 g5 42.h4 ♗e4 43.h×g5+ h×g5
44.♗b5 g×f4 45.g×f4 ♗×d3?! ½-½

Of course not a very good try to for a
win, but White's fortress should hold in
any case.

Hübner, Robert (2612) – Deep Fritz
Ruy Lopez C96
Dortmund match (4), 19.07.2001

1.e4 e5 2.♘f3 ♘c6 3.♗b5 a6
4.♗a4 ♘f6 5.0-0 ♗e7 6.♖e1
b5 7.♗b3 d6 8.c3 0-0 9.h3 ♘a5
10.♗c2 c5 11.d4 c×d4 12.c×d4
♗b7 13.d5 ♘c4 14.b3 ♘b6 15.a4
b×a4 16.b×a4 ♕c7 17.♘a3 ♘bd7
18.♘d2 ♖ab8 19.♘dc4 ♘c5

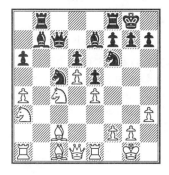

20.♖b1

Hübner is probably satisfied with a
draw. With 20.♕f3!?, he could play a
slightly favorable more complex game.

20...♗a8 21.♖×b8 ½-½

Deep Fritz – Hübner, Robert (2612)
Slav Defense D17
Dortmund match (5), 20.07.2001

1.d4 d5 2.c4 c6 3.♘f3 ♘f6 4.♘c3
d×c4 5.a4 ♗f5 6.♘e5 ♘bd7
7.♘×c4 ♘b6 8.♘e5 e6

Quite risky. 8...a5 is the main line.

9.f3 ♘fd7 10.a5 ♘×e5 11.a×b6
♘d7 12.e4 ♗g6 13.b×a7?!

13.♖×a7 is critical, e.g., 13...♘b6
14.♖×b7 ♖a1 15.♗e2 ♗d6 16.0-0
and it is not clear if Black has enough
compensation.

13...♕b6

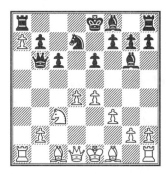

14.f4?!

This move is hard to explain. I strongly
doubt that a human would play it, as
it is not consistent with the strategy of
playing against the ♗g6 with the granite
wall f3-e4. But Fritz does not think in
this way of course.

14...♗b4 15.♕d3 0-0 16.♗e2 ♘f6
17.f5 e×f5 18.e×f5 ♗h5 19.♗×h5
♘×h5 20.0-0 ♖×a7 21.♖×a7 ♕×a7
22.♗g5 ♖e8 23.g4 ♗×c3 24.b×c3
♘f6 25.♗×f6 g×f6 26.♕g3 h6
27.♖e1 ♖×e1+ 28.♕×e1 ♕a2 29.h3
½-½

Hübner, Robert (2612) – Deep Fritz
Caro-Kann Defense B17
Dortmund match (6), 21.07.2001

In the last game Hübner uses a bug in
the opening book to draw quickly:

1.e4 c6 2.d4 d5 3.♘d2 d×e4
4.♘×e4 ♘d7 5.♘f3 ♘gf6 6.♘×f6+
♘×f6 7.♘e5 ♘d7 8.♘f3 ♘f6
9.♘e5 ♘d7 ½-½

12
Kramnik versus Deep Fritz (2002)

Rounds 2, 3, 5, and 6 are in Chapter 8.

Deep Fritz – Kramnik, Vladimir (2807)
Ruy Lopez C67
Bahrain match (1), 04.10.2002

1.e4 e5 2.♘f3 ♘c6 3.♗b5 ♘f6

The Berlin Defense. 3...a6 is the main line.

4.0-0 ♘×e4 5.d4 ♘d6 6.♗×c6 d×c6 7.d×e5 ♘f5 8.♕×d8+ ♔×d8

The bishop pair gives Black compensation for the pawn structure weakened by the doubled c-pawns (normally the pawn ending would be lost) and for White's advantage in development. Whether this is enough is currently being vigorously debated in the chess world. Here the main question is how Deep Fritz will be able to handle the position. The opening choice was excellent. It is reasonable to assume that Kramnik will be satisfied to draw with the Black pieces and to attack as White.

9.♘c3 h6 10.b3

Grandmaster Ronen Har Zvi also played the Berlin in a Man-versus-Machine event at KasparovChess.com. He did quite well with it, and I'm sure that Kramnik has studied this game carefully. 10.♗d2 ♔e8 11.♖ad1 ♗e6 12.♖fe1 ♖d8 13.a4 ♗b4 14.♘e4 ♗×d2 15.♖×d2 ♖×d2 16.♘f×d2 ♔e7 17.f3 ♖d8 18.♔f2 b6 19.b4 g5 20.g3 ♖d5 21.c4 ♖d3 22.♖b1 ♖a3 23.a5 ♖a2 24.g4 ♘h4 25.♔e3 ♖a3+ 26.♖b3 ♖×b3+ 27.♘×b3 ♗×c4 28.♘d4 ♗d5 29.a6 ♘g6 30.♘f5+ ♔e6 31.♘×h6 ♗×e4 32.♔×e4 ♘×e5 33.♘f5 f6 34.♘d4+ ♔d7 35.h3 c5 36.b×c5 b×c5 37.♘e2 c4 38.f4 ♘d3 39.f×g5 f×g5 40.♔f5 ♘f2 41.♔×g5 ♘×h3+ 42.♔h5 ♔d6 43.g5 ♘×g5 44.♔×g5 ♔c5 45.♔f4 ♔b6 46.♔e5 ♔×a6 ½-½ Deep Junior-Har Zvi, KasparovChess Internet 2000. Kasparov was apparently so impressed with Kramnik's treatment of the Berlin Defense that he has surprisingly introduced it into his own repertoire.

Kramnik has done well against 10.h3: 10...♗d7 (10...♔e8 11.♘e4 c5 12.c3 b6 13.♖e1 ♗e6 14.g4 ½-½ Kasparov-Kramnik, Braingames World Championship, London 2000) 11.b3 ♔c8 12.♗b2 b6 13.♖ad1 ♘e7 14.♖d2 c5 15.♖fd1 ♗e6 16.♘e2 g5 17.h4 g4 18.♘h2 h5 19.♖d8+ ♔b7 20.♖×a8 ♔×a8 21.♖d8+ ♔b7 22.♘f4 ♘g6 23.g3 c4 24.b×c4?? An incredible blunder. 24...♘×f4 25.g×f4 g3!! 26.♘f1 (26.f×g3 ♗c5+ 27.♔g2 ♖×d8-+) 26...g×f2+ 27.♔h2 ♗×c4 0-1 Anand-Kramnik, Mainz 2001.

Judit Polgar was able to defeat Garry Kasparov with 10.♖d1+!? in a rapid chess event. 10...♔e8 11.h3 ♗e7 (11...a5 12.♗f4 ♗e6 13.g4 ♘e7 14.♘d4 ♘d5 15.♘ce2 ♗c5 16.♘×e6 f×e6 17.c4 ♘b6 18.b3 a4 19.♗d2 ♔f7 20.♗c3 ♖hd8 21.♖×d8 ♖×d8 22.♔g2 ♖d3 23.♖c1 g5 24.♖c2 a×b3 25.a×b3 ♘d7 26.♖a2 ♗e7 27.♖a7 ♘c5 28.f3 ♘×b3 29.♖×b7 ♘c1 30.♘×c1 ♖×c3 ½-½ Kasparov-Kramnik, Braingames World Championship, London 2000) 12.♘e2

♘h4 13.♘×h4 ♗×h4 14.♗e3 ♗f5
15.♘d4 ♗h7 16.g4 ♗e7 17.♔g2 h5
18.♘f5 ♗f8 19.♔f3 ♗g6 20.♖d2 h×g4+
21.h×g4 ♖h3+ 22.♔g2 ♖h7 23.♔g3 f6
24.♗f4 ♗×f5 25.g×f5 f×e5 26.♖e1 ♗d6
27.♗×e5 ♔d7 28.c4 c5 29.♗×d6 c×d6
30.♖e6 ♖ah8 31.♖e×d6+ ♔c8 32.♖2d5
♖h3+ 33.♔g2 ♖h2+ 34.♔f3 ♖2h3+
35.♔e4 b6 36.♖c6+ ♔b8 37.♖d7 ♖h2
38.♔e3 ♖f8 39.♖cc7 ♖×f5 40.♖b7+
♔c8 41.♖dc7+ ♔d8 42.♖×g7 ♔c8 1-0
J.Polgar-Kasparov, Moscow 2002.

10...♔e8

Kramnik voluntarily leaves the d-file
and goes for a very solid setup with his
bishops on e7, e6 and rook's pawns on
h5 and a5. This position can only be
stormed with long-term plans that are
difficult for the computer to find. So it
is an ideal position against DEEP FRITZ,
but a disappointment for chess fans that
wanted to see fiery combinations.

11.♗b2 ♗e7

Kramnik had certainly studied the game
Klovans-Dautov, Minsk 1986 which
continued 11...a5 12.♘e2 a4 13.♘f4
♗e6 14.g4 ♘e7 15.♘×e6 f×e6 16.♘d4
(16.♔g2!?) 16...♔f7 17.c4 (17.f4 ♘d5
with counterplay.) 17...h5!= .

12.♖ad1

12...a5

Kramnik cleverly holds back with his
Bishop on c8, so that his bishop pair

may not be prematurely cut in half.
The following game is an example,
how Black can go down, if he allows
to many exchanges and is not placed
actively enough: 12...♗e6 13.♘e2 ♖d8
14.♖×d8+ ♗×d8 15.♖d1 ♖g8 16.♘f4
g5 17.♘×e6 f×e6 18.g4 ♘e7 19.♘d4
♖g6 20.c4 c5 21.♘e2 ♖g8 22.♘g3
♘g6 23.♘h5 ♗e7 24.♔g2 ♗f8 25.♔g3
♖f7 26.♖d3 ♗d8 27.f3 b6 28.♔f2 ♖d7
29.♖×d7 ♔×d7 30.♔e3 ♔e8 31.♔e4
♔f7 32.♗c1 c6 33.♗e3 ♘f8 and now
the white pawn majority is a clear
danger. 34.f4 g×f4 35.♗×f4 ♔g6 36.♘f6
♗×f6 37.e×f6 ♘d7 38.h3 b5 39.f7 h5
40.g×h5+ ♔×f7 41.♗d3 ♘f6 42.a4 a6
43.a5 ♔f5 44.♔e3 ♘f6 45.h6 b×c4
46.b×c4 ♔g6 47.♗e5 ♘h7 48.♗f4 ♘f6
49.♔f3 ♔f5 50.h4 ♔g6 51.♗e5 ♘g8
52.♗g7 ♘e7 53.♔e4 ♘f5 54.h5+ ♔f7
55.♗e5 ♘×h6 56.♔f4 ♘f5 57.♔g5 ♔g8
58.♔g6 ♘h4+ 59.♔f6 1-0 Klovans-
Reichenbach, Berlin 1998.

13.a4

13.g4?! does not achieve anything: 13...
♘h4 14.♘×h4 ♗×h4 15.h3 h5 and
Black has no problems.

13...h5

Securing the knight on f5 and allowing
a possible ♖h6.

14.♘e2 ♗e6 15.c4

15.♘f4!? g5 16.♘×e6 f×e6 17.♘d2 (or
17.♖d3) was also possible.

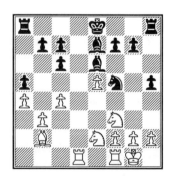

15...♖d8!

This is a good strategy since Black's rooks are not coordinated and White has control of the d-file.

16.h3 b6 17.♘fd4 ♘×d4 18.♘×d4 c5 19.♘×e6 f×e6

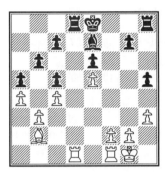

The bishop pair has been decimated, but the Black position is very solid. An important detail is that the pawn on e5 is on the same color square as the bishop on b2. This makes the bishop a weak piece with no prospects on either wing. Does FRITZ understand this?

20.♖×d8+ ♔×d8 21.♗c1 ♔c8

Kramnik is planning to exchange the other rook as well, so that FRITZ will be left with just the bishop.

22.♖d1 ♖d8 23.♖×d8+ ♔×d8 24.g4 g6

After 24...h×g4?! 25.h×g4, White has the plan f4, ♔g1-g2-h3 and ♗c1-d2-e1-h4 etc. For this reason Kramnik leaves the white pawn on h3.

25.h4?

A human being would have hardly played this move, since it makes the draw quite evident. An alternative strategy would have been 25.♔g2 ♔e8 26.♔f3 ♔f7 27.♔e4 with the idea of f2-f4-f5. Kramnik will certainly have checked such endgames, but the correct defense is not obvious.

Here are some of the ideas and the dangers that lurk in the following lines:

(a) 27...h×g4! (27...♗d8 28.f4 ♗e7 29.f5 h×g4 30.h×g4 c6 31.f6 ♗d8 and the black position should be quite impenetrable, since the following plan does not succeed: 32.♗e3 ♗c7 33.b4? a×b4 34.a5? b3−+.

(b) 27...h×g4?! (28.h×g4 g5 29.f4 g×f4 30.♗×f4 ♔g6 31.♔f3 c6 32.♔g3 ♗d8 33.♔h3 with the idea ♗f4-g3-h4) 28.h×g4 White plans ♔f3-g3-h3 followed by ♗g3-h4, so 28...♗h4 has to be played (28...g5 29.f4 g×f4 30.♗×f4 ♔g6 31.♔f3 c6 32.♔g3 ♗d8 33.♔h3 with the idea ♗f4-g3-h4) 29.♗e3 (29.f4 ♗e1 30.f5 g×f5+ 31.g×f5 ♔e7 32.♗g5+ ♔d7 (Notkin 2002) 33.f6 [33.♗f6 ♗c3 34.♔f4 ♗d2+ 35.♔g4 ♗e3=] 33...♔e8 34.f7+ ♔×f7 35.♗d8 c6 36.♗×b6 ♗b4 37.♔f4 ♔g6 38.♔g4 ♔h6=) 29...♔e8 (29...g5? is wrong, e.g., 30.♔d3 ♔g6 31.♔e2 ♔h6 32.♗d2 ♔g6 33.♗e1 ♔h6 34.f3 ♗×e1 35.♔×e1 ♔g6 36.♔f2 ♔h6 37.♔g3 ♔g7 38.f4 g×f4+ 39.♔×f4

413

♔g6 40.♔g3 ♔g5 41.♔h3 ♔f4 42.♔h4 ♔xe5 43.g5 ♔f5 44.♔h5 +–) 30.♔f3 (30.g5 ♗xf2 31.♗xf2

...is drawn (Stertenbrink 2002): 31... ♔d7 32.♔d3 ♔c6 33.♔c2 ♔b7 34.b4 axb4 35.a5 ♔a6 36.axb6 cxb6 37.♔b3 ♔b7 38.♔a4 ♔c6 39.♗e1 ♔c7 40.♔b5 ♔b7 41.♗d2 ♔c7 42.♔a6 ♔c6 and White can make no progress as 43.♔a7?? runs into 43...b5 –+) 30... ♔f7 31.♔g2 ♗e7 32.f4 ♗d8 33.♔h3 ♗e7 34.♗f2 ♔g7 35.♗h4 (35.♔g2 ♔f7 36.♔f3 ♗d8 37.♔e4 ♗e7 38.f5 gxf5+ 39.gxf5 ♗g5=) 35...♗xh4 36.♔xh4 ♔h6 37.♔g3 ♔g7 38.♔f3 ♔f7 39.♔e4 ♔e7 40.f5 g5= and Black's fortress cannot be taken because of the reserve tempo c7-c6.

Finally, 25.gxh5?! gxh5 26.♔g2 ♔e8 27.♔f3 ♔f7 28.♔e4 ♔g6 29.f4 c6 is of course totally drawn.

25...hxg4!

If DEEP FRITZ were human, one would think that it was hoping for 25...♗xh4. But this blunder was too obvious for Kramnik. The danger is 26.g5 and the bishop will never see the light of day. However Kramnik later said that he actually considered this, because, although White can capture the bishop with ♔g1-g2-h3, this does not give him an inroad. In fact an immediate 26...♗xf2+ 27.♔xf2 makes the draw

obvious.

26.♗g5 ♗xg5 27.hxg5

The pawn ending is completely drawn since both kings cannot move into the enemy space.

27...♔e8 28.♔g2 and the draw was agreed. ½-½

Kramnik, Vladimir (2807) – DEEP FRITZ
Queen's Gambit Declined D34
Bahrain match (4), 10.10.2002

Somehow Kramnik once again succeeds in getting the queens off the board, and to create a clear-cut position. He really seems to have prepared extremely well for this game.

1.d4 d5 2.c4 e6 3.♘f3 c5

It is understandable that FRITZ will not go into a Queen's Gambit Accepted once again. So we cannot assume that the Tarrasch Defense would come as a complete surprise to Kramnik.

4.cxd5 exd5 5.g3

This is considered the most effective, since the white bishop can apply optimum pressure from g2.

5...♘c6 6.♗g2 ♘f6 7.0-0 ♗e7 8.♘c3 0-0 9.♗g5 cxd4 10.♘xd4 h6 11.♗f4

Kramnik keeps the pair of bishops, which can become very dangerous for FRITZ.

11...♗g4 12.h3 ♗e6 13.♖c1 ♖e8

14.♘×e6!? f×e6 15.e4

A typical transformation that is quite advantageous against a computer, because once again a queen exchange is looming.

15...d4 16.e5 d×c3 17.e×f6 ♗×f6 18.b×c3 ♕×d1 19.♖f×d1

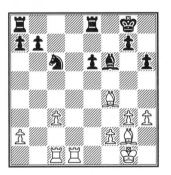

The pair of bishops and the more active pieces give White a pleasant position. FRITZ will find it very difficult to find tactical shots.

19...♖ad8 20.♗e3 ♖×d1+ 21.♖×d1 ♗×c3 22.♖d7 ♖b8

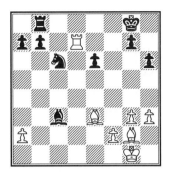

Kramnik now decides to cash in and win the pawn back, which is easily understandable from a human point of view. But according to Keene (2002) FRITZ was "anticipating the curious advance 23.f4, when it assessed the subsequent positions as being highly favorable for White. However no human grandmaster could make any sense of this pawn move, which seems to have little to do with the current situation." A very interesting remark! Are we humans more materialistic than the machines?

23.♗×c6

23.f4!? may give better practical chances as it is more difficult to play now for Black (but also for White of course) and the bishop pair is a dangerous weapon. Another interesting option is 23.♗e4!?.

23...b×c6 24.♖×a7 ♖b2 25.♖a6

25...♗d2!

FRITZ understands this endgame perfectly. Because of the open position and its active pieces it can hold easily.

26.♖×c6

Kramnik is putting safety first, which is hardly surprising in view of the match score. 26.♗d4 ♖c2 27.♖a7 g5 is equal.

26...♗×e3 27.f×e3 ♔f7

27...♖×a2 28.♖×e6 ♔f7 is also a draw.

28.a4 ♖a2 29.♖c4 ♔f6 30.♔f1

30...g5

FRITZ correctly initiates counterplay on the kingside, to have options if things become dangerous. It is important to know this technique, even if the position is a draw and even if the program doesn't use it.

31.h4 h5 32.h×g5+

32.♖c5 g×h4 33.g×h4 ♖×a4 34.♖×h5 ♔g6 35.♖h8 ♔g7 36.♖h5 ♔g6=.

32...♔×g5 33.♔e1 e5 34.♔f1 ♔f5 35.♖h4 ♔g6 36.♖e4 ♔f5 37.♖h4 ♔g5 38.♔g1 ♔g6 39.g4

Kramnik trades down to a dead draw, which is clear because with his king completely cut off on the back rank, he cannot make any progress.

39...h×g4

39...♔g5 40.♖×h5+ ♔×g4 41.♖e5 ♖×a4=.

40.♖×g4+ ♔f5 41.♖c4

Here Kramnik offered a draw, which was immediately accepted by the operator. ½-½

DEEP FRITZ – Kramnik, Vladimir (2807)
Queen's Indian Defense E19
Bahrain match (7), 17.10.2002

FRITZ again chooses 1.d4 to avoid the Berlin Wall. But Kramnik's variation of the Queen's Indian is very solid.

1.d4 ♘f6 2.c4 e6 3.♘f3 b6 4.g3 ♗b7 5.♗g2 ♗e7 6.0-0 0-0 7.♘c3 ♘e4

Black occupies the center and plans to reduce the pressure by exchanging knights.

8.♕c2 ♘×c3 9.♕×c3 c5 10.♖d1 d6 11.b3 ♗f6 12.♗b2 ♕e7 13.♕c2 ♘c6 14.e4 e5 15.d5

Good news for Kramnik: the position is closed.

15...♘d4 16.♗×d4 c×d4 17.♗h3

17.a4 a5 18.♘e1 ½-½, Vaganian-Petrosian, Tallinn (Keres Memorial) 1983.

17...g6 18.a4

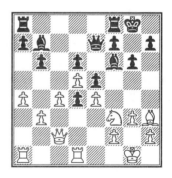

18...a5!?

Stops a5 and makes it much more difficult for White to open the queenside. It seems that Kramnik doesn't want to go into an firefight again. 18...♗g7?! 19.a5!? b×a5 20.♖×a5 f5 21.♘d2 ♗c8 22.c5 with a white initiative in Polugaevsky-Gulko, USSR Championship Moscow 1976.

19.♖ab1

Planning b3-b4…

19...♗a6!

…against which Kramnik takes measures.

20.♖e1

FRITZ did not like 20.b4?! ♕c7, as it is very difficult to make further progress on the queenside then.

20...♔h8 21.♔g2 ♗g7 22.♕d3 ♖ae8 23.♘d2 ♗h6

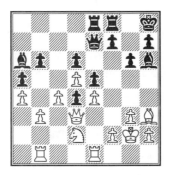

24.f4!?

FRITZ does not just want to wait. But he can't simply proceed and open the position as this might as well favor Black's bishops.

24...♕c7

Kramnik just waits with good prophylactic moves.

25.♖f1 ♔g8 26.♖be1 ♕d8 27.♔g1

FRITZ does not see a way to make progress. Its pieces are on good squares but it is not easy to realize pawn breaks.

27...♗b7 28.♖e2 ½-½

Kramnik, Vladimir (2807) – DEEP FRITZ
Queen's Gambit Declined D68
Bahrain match (8), 19.10.2002

Kramnik allows simplifications right from the opening, avoiding risks (you certainly should remember Kasparov's disastrous last game against DEEP Blue).

1.d4 ♘f6 2.c4 e6 3.♘f3 d5 4.♘c3 c6 5.♗g5 ♗e7 6.e3 0-0 7.♗d3 ♘bd7 8.0-0 d×c4 9.♗×c4 ♘d5

An old maneuver to reduce the pressure.

10.♗×e7 ♕×e7 11.♖c1 ♘×c3 12.♖×c3 e5

This solves the problem of Black's c8-bishop.

13.♗b3 e×d4 14.e×d4 ♘f6 15.♖e1 ♕d6

16.h3

Not very aggressive. 16.♘e5 ♘d5 17.♖g3 is played more often, but it seems that Black can defend by 17...♗e6 18.♕h5 ♕b4 19.♖e4 ♕d2 20.♘f3 ♕c1+ 21.♖e1 ♕f4=, McPhillips-Kobayashi, Gaziantep 2008.

16...♗f5 17.♖ce3 ♖ae8 18.♖e5 ♗g6 19.a3

White has an isolated d-pawn, but as all his pieces are active, this weakness does not make itself felt at the moment.

19...♕d8 20.♖×e8 ♘×e8 21.♕d2

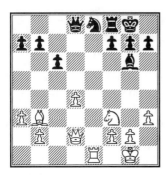

...and Kramnik's draw offer was accepted. ½-½

13
Kasparov versus Deep Junior (2003)

Games 1, 3 and 5 of the match are in Chapter 8. The following games analysis is largely taken from ChessBase (2003) and Müller (2003).

Deep Junior – Kasparov, Garry (2847)
Sicilian Defense B42
New York match (2), 28.01.2003

1.e4 c5 2.♘f3 e6

Normally Kasparov prefers the Najdorf variation, 2...d6 3.d4 c×d4 4.♘×d4 ♘f6 5.♘c3 a6.

3.d4 c×d4 4.♘×d4 a6 5.♗d3 ♗c5

Another set up is 5...♘f6 6.0-0 d6 7.c4 ♗e7 8.♘c3.

6.♘b3 ♗a7 7.c4 ♘c6 8.♘c3 d6 9.0-0 ♘ge7 10.♖e1 0-0 11.♗e3 e5 12.♘d5

White's play in the following game is more convincing: 12.♗×a7 ♖×a7 13.♕d2 ♗e6 14.♗f1 b6 15.♖ed1 ♖d7 16.♖ac1 f5 17.f3 f4 18.♘d5 g5 19.♕f2 ♘c8 20.c5 b×c5 21.♗×a6 ♗×d5 22.e×d5 ♘6e7 23.♗d3 ♖a7 24.♕c2 ♔g7 25.♗×h7 c4 26.♘d2 and White

won later in Kogan-Bezold, Würzburg 1996.

12...a5!?

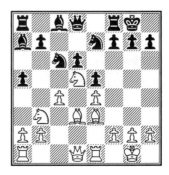

Kasparov has managed again to reach a position, which is not easy to play for the computer. He plans a4 to fight for the d4-square.

13.♖c1 a4 14.♗×a7 ♖×a7 15.♘d2

15.♘a1!? ♘×d5 16.c×d5 ♘b4 17.♘c2 was the alternative and is also more or less equal.

15...♘d4 16.♕h5?!

More a gesture than a threat.

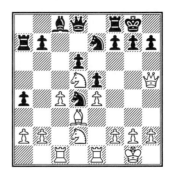

16...♘e6!?

Aiming for the very strong c5-square. 16...♘×d5 was the alternative.

17.♖c3

17.b4?! a×b3 18.a×b3 ♘d4 19.♖a1 ♖×a1 20.♖×a1 ♘×d5 21.e×d5 (21.c×d5 ♕b6) 21...f5 and Black is slightly better.

17...♞c5 18.♗c2 ♞×d5

This is easier than trying to ignore and play around the ♞d5 with 18...♞c6.

19.e×d5 g6?!

This weakens the kingside, something that will be felt later. After the direct 19...f5, Black's central pawn mass is very impressive.

20.♕h6 f5 21.♖a3 ♕f6!?

A devilish trap into which Deep Junior falls. It just likes the material too much. Kasparov gives 21...e4 22.h4 ♕f6 23.h5 b6 in *Informant 87* without evaluation. After 24.b4, it is not so easy to equalize.

22.b4?

Consequent – and wrong. Post-game analysis by Deep Junior revealed that 22.♞f3! was called for and gives White a good game: 22...e4 23.♞g5 ♕g7 (23...b6? 24.b4 ♕b2 25.♖h3 ♕×b4 26.♖d1 +– ; 23...♕h8 is answered by 24.♖b1, and White is for choice.) 24.♕×g7+ ♚×g7 25.b4 a×b3 26.♖×a7 b×c2 27.♖c1 h6 28.♞e6+ ♗×e6 29.d×e6 ♚f6 30.♖×c2 ♚×e6 with compensation according to Kasparov. Black should be able to hold but he would still have had some work to do. "At the end of the match, the programmers said that during the match they made some changes to Deep Junior

as a result of which it would now play ♞f3 in game 2." (D. Levy from Müller (2003))

22...a×b3 23.♖×a7 b×c2

The c2-pawn is very strong and White's back rank is weak. In addition, the h6-queen and the a7-rook are very far away. This spells disaster.

24.♖c1 e4 25.♖×c2

25.♕e3? f4 26.♕a3? ♕d4 –+ .

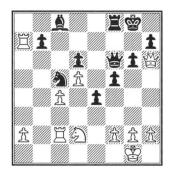

25...♕a1+?

Kasparov played this move too fast. 25...f4! threatens e3 and cuts the queen off from the defense of White's first rank: 26.♞f1 (or (a) 26.h4? ♕a1+ 27.♞f1 e3 28.h5 ♗f5 –+ ; (b) 26.h3? ♕a1+ 27.♚h2 [27.♞f1 ♕d1 28.♖d2 ♕e1 29.♖a3 e3 30.f×e3 ♞e4 –+] 27...♕d1 28.♖b2 ♕e1 29.♖b6 ♕×d2 30.♖×d6 ♕b2 31.♕g5 ♞d7 32.♖a8 ♕e5 33.♕×e5 ♞×e5 34.♖b6 ♞d3 –+ ; (c) 26.♖a8? e3 27.♞f1 ♞d3 28.f×e3 f×e3 29.♕×f8+ ♕×f8 30.♖e2 ♚g7 31.♞×e3 ♕d8 32.h3 ♕c7 –+) 26...e3 27.♞×e3 (27.f×e3? f×e3 28.♕×f8+ ♚×f8 29.♖a8 ♚e7 30.♖×c8 ♕f5 –+) 27...♗f5 28.♖c1 ♕b2 29.♖d1 f×e3 30.♕×e3 ♗c2 and Black's minor pieces dominate the board.

26.♞f1 f4

27.♖a8!

The only defense, with the idea of ♕×f8+ followed by ♖×c8+. Kasparov had probably missed this resource.

27...e3

27...♘d3 also leads to a draw by perpetual check: 28.h4 e3 29.h5 e×f2+ 30.♖×f2 ♕d4 31.h×g6 ♕×f2+ 32.♔h2 h×g6 33.♕×g6+.

28.f×e3 f×e3

After 28...♘e4, White defends with 29.♖e2 ♕d1 30.♖b2 f×e3 31.♕×f8+ ♔×f8 32.♖×b7 ♘f6 33.♖×c8+ ♘e8 34.♖bb8 e2 35.♖×e8+ ♔g7 36.♖b7+ ♔h6 37.♖f7= (Kasparov).

29.♕×f8+! ♔×f8 30.♖×c8+ ♔f7
½-½

A draw was agreed in view of 31.♖c7+ ♔f8 (31...♔e8? 32.♖e2 ♔d8 33.♖f7 is dangerous for Black) 32.♖c8+ ♔f7 with perpetual check.

Deep Junior – Kasparov, Garry (2847)
Sicilian Defense B44
New York match (4), 02.02.2003

1.e4 c5 2.♘f3 ♘c6 3.d4 c×d4 4.♘×d4 e6 5.♘b5 d6 6.c4

White has installed the Maroczy Bind. It has more space, but Kasparov just sets up a hedgehog.

6...♘f6 7.♘1c3 a6 8.♘a3

This knight is not well placed here and has already moved three times. Black should have equality.

8...♘d7

A novelty to throw Deep Junior out of its opening book. 8...Be7 is usual.

9.♘c2 ♗e7 10.♗e2 b6 11.0-0 ♗b7

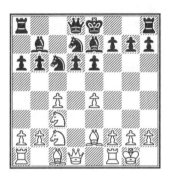

12.h3?!

One of those weakening pawn moves first players make so easily in the hedgehog. It does not fit into the subsequent white play.

12...0-0 13.♗e3 ♖c8 14.♕d2 ♘ce5

The ♘c6 was a small problem in Black's position. Normally it is redeployed to d7 via e5 but thanks to h3, Kasparov does just this now.

15.b3 Nf6 16.f3

The does not fit in with h3 (the dark squares on the kingside are now weak), but signals that Junior wants to play on the queenside, which is correct here, in my opinion.

16...♕c7 17.♖ac1 ♖fe8

17...b5?! plays with the fire in view of 18.c×b5 ♕×c3 19.♕×c3 ♖×c3 20.♗d4 ♖c7 21.b×a6.

18.a3 ♘ed7

Black has reached a typical hedgehog position.

19.♖fd1 ♛b8

Vacating the *vis-à-vis* of the ♖c1 and increases the harmony in Black's camp. 19...♘c5!? 20.♖b1 d5 came strongly into consideration.

20.♗f2

20.♘d4?! allows 20...d5.

20...♖cd8?!

Inviting JUNIOR to play on the queenside, which is not good as the computer then follows a strong plan. 20...♗a8 is preferred.

21.b4

21.♗g3 is easily fended off with 21...♘e5.

21...♗a8 22.a4

White takes the initiative on the queenside.

22...♖c8 23.♖b1 ♛c7

24.a5!?

According to Anand (2003), a correct and strong maneuver by the machine.

24...b×a5 25.b5! ♗b7

25...a×b5? 26.♘×b5 ♛d8 27.♘×d6±

26.b6

26.♘d4 came strongly into consideration as well.

26...♛b8 27.♘e3 ♘c5 28.♛a2 ♘fd7 29.♘a4 ♘e5

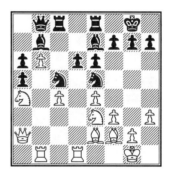

30.♘c2

Good prophylaxis. 30.♘×c5?! d×c5 31.♛×a5 ♘c6 is not what White wants.

30...♘cd7 31.♘d4 ♖ed8

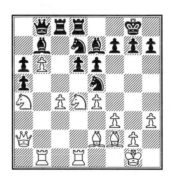

32.♔h1

Such a computer move always shows that the machine does not see a way to improve its position.

32...♘c6 33.♘×c6 ♖×c6 34.♔g1 h6 35.♛a3!?

Junior fights again!

35...♖dc8

Kasparov did not have much time left and had to play quickly.

36.♗g3 ♗f8?!

Now ♗d8 is no longer an option. 36...♘e5?? 37.♗xe5 dxe5 38.♕xe7+−; 36...♔f8!? (Anand 2003).

37.♕c3 ♘e5

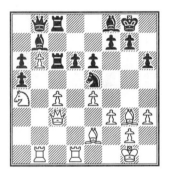

38.c5!

Opening the floodgates.

38...♘d7 39.♕xa5 ♘xc5 40.♘xc5 ♖xc5 41.♕a4 ♖5c6

41...a5 42.♗b5 is very good for White as well.

42.♗f2

42.♗xa6? is met by 42...♕a8 43.♗b5 ♖xb6.

42...d5 43.♗xa6 ♗c5 44.♗xc5 ♖xc5

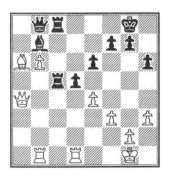

45.♗xb7?

45.exd5 exd5 (45...♗xa6 46.♕xa6 exd5 47.b7 and the b-pawn is a powerful force.) 46.♗d3 (Knaak) was much better. Now it is rather questionable if Black can survive.

45...♕xb7 46.exd5 exd5 47.♕a7 ♖5c7

Kasparov sets a very deep trap. 47...♖b8 48.♖e1 ♖c7 came into consideration as well.

48.♕xb7?!

48.♕a5!?.

48...♖xb7 49.♖xd5

Now this double rook ending is completely drawn.

49...♖c6! 50.♖db5 h5

Black has an impregnable fortress as White's rooks are tied to the defense of the b-pawn. Deep Junior does not understand the very nature of this conception and plays on.

51.♔f2

51...♖e6!

This assures that White's king remains out of play.

52.f4 g6 53.♔g3 ♔g7 54.♔h4 ♔h6 55.♖1b4 ♖d6 56.g3 f6

Threatening 57...♖bxb6 58.♖xb6?? g5 followed by mate.

57.g4 h×g4 58.h×g4 ♔g7 59.♖b3

59.f5 g5+ leads to nothing as 60.♔h5?? is refuted by 60...♖b8 61.b7 ♖h8#.

59...♖c6 60.g5 f5 61.♖b1 ½-½

A narrow escape by Kasparov. Playing against the hedgehog used to be very difficult for computer programs, but DEEP JUNIOR played it quite well. Its attack on the queenside was forceful and Kasparov could only survive by an ingenious defense.

The last game was not boring, but its peaceful end was quite early as both sides decided not to fight it out to the bitter end.

DEEP JUNIOR – Kasparov, Garry (2847)
Sicilian Defense B92
New York match (6), 07.02.2003

1.e4 c5 2.♘f3 d6 3.d4 c×d4 4.♘×d4 ♘f6 5.♘c3 a6 6.♗e2 e5

One of the main lines. 5...a6 was played to deny White's pieces the important b5-square.

7.♘b3 ♗e7 8.0-0 0-0 9.♔h1 ♗d7 10.♗e3 ♗c6 11.♗f3

In my opinion, this does not fit well with ♔h1.

11...♘bd7 12.a4

12.♘d5 can be answered with 12...♘×d5 13.e×d5 ♗b5.

12...b6

12...♘c5!?.

13.♕d3 ♗b7 14.h3

Not the strongest move, but JUNIOR likes moving its rook's pawn.

14...♖c8

14...♘c5!? came into consideration again.

15.♖ad1 h6 16.♖fe1 ♕c7 17.g3

♖fd8 18.♔h2 ♖e8

Both sides have reached their ideal set ups and it is not easy for either to make further progress.

19.♖e2 ♕c4 20.♕×c4 ♖×c4 21.♘d2 ♖c7 22.♗g2 ♖ec8 23.♘b3

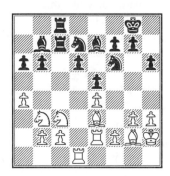

23...♖×c3!?

Kasparov combined this typical Sicilian exchange sacrifice with a draw offer.

24.b×c3 ♗×e4!

24...♘×e4?! was too risky because of 25.♗×b6 ♘×g3 26.♗×b7 ♘×e2 27.♗a5 ♖f8 28.♗×a6 ♘f4 29.♗b4.

25.♗c1 ♗×g2 26.♔×g2 ♖×c3 27.♗a3 ♘e8

27...♘c5?! is answered by 28.a5.

28.f4 ½-½

The draw offer from the DEEP JUNIOR team, which was accepted by Kasparov to avoid further risk. One sample line

runs 28...f6 29.a5 b5 30.♗b4 ♖c8
31.♘d4 g6 32.c3 ♔f7 33.♘c2 ♘b8
34.♘e3 ♘c6 35.♘d5 ♗d8 with equality.

14
Kasparov versus Deep Fritz (2003)

Games 2 and 3 are in Chapter 8. Notes
are based on Karsten Müller's posts on
chessbase.de.

Kasparov, Garry (2830) – Fritz X3D
Slav Defense D45
New York match (1), 11.11.2003

1.♘f3

Does Kasparov play like this to avoid
the Tarrasch Variation of the Queen's
Gambit or is this the best move order in
his opinion to reach the Meran?

**1...d5 2.c4 c6 3.d4 ♘f6 4.♘c3 e6
5.e3 ♘bd7 6.♕c2 ♗d6 7.g4 ♗b4
8.♗d2 ♕e7 9.♖g1**

9.a3 leads to the famous game Gelfand-
Kramnik Berlin 1996: 9...♗xc3
10.♗xc3 b6 11.♗d3 ♗a6 12.♕a4 dxc4
13.♕xa6 cxd3 14.♕xd3 0-0 15.g5 ♘d5
16.♗d2 f5 17.0-0-0 c5 18.♔b1 b5
19.♕xb5 ♖ab8 20.♕a5 ♖b3 21.♔a2
♖fb8 22.♖b1 e5 23.♖hc1 ♕e6 24.♔a1
exd4 25.♖xc5 ♘xc5 26.♕xc5 ♘c3
27.♘xd4 ♖xb2 28.♖xb2 ♕a2+ 0-1
Gelfand-Kramnik.

9...♗xc3

9...b6 is played more often.

10.♗xc3 ♘e4

10...b6 was again an alternative, e.g.,
11.♗d3 dxc4 12.♗xc4 ♗b7 13.g5 ♘d5,
Szeberenyi-Izsak, Budapest 1997.

11.0-0-0!? ♕f6?! 12.♗e2

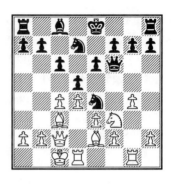

12...♘xf2?

Did Kasparov hope for this greedy
pawn grab to happen? He gets now
a murderous initiative based on his
advantage in development, his mighty
pair of bishops and the unsafe black
king. A human would be shaking in his
boots with Black here. 12...♘b6!? was
the alternative.

13.♖df1 ♘e4 14.♗b4!

This prevents Black from castling short
Black's weak dark squares.

14...c5

Or 14...♘g5 15.cxd5 cxd5 16.♔b1 with
powerful compensation. Throwing in
14...a5?! 15.♗a3 helps only White, e.g.,
15...c5 16.cxd5 exd5 17.dxc5 ♕e7
18.c6 ♘dc5 19.cxb7 ♗xb7 20.♗b5+
♔d8 21.♘d4±.

15.cxd5

Why did Kasparov think so long here?
The alternative, 15.dxc5, leads, after
15...♕e7 16.cxd5 exd5 17.♘d4, to a
transposition to the game.

15...exd5

15...cxb4? 16.♕xe4±.

16.dxc5 ♕e7

Oliver Reeh in his live comments on the
match suggested solving the problems
of Black's king radically with 16...0-
0?!, but after 17.c6 bxc6 18.♗xf8 ♘xf8,

White has 19.♗d3 with nice prospects.

17.♘d4!

A mighty square for White's knight, which is liked an octopus here. It can for instance jump to f5 to increase the pressure on the dark squares.

17...0-0!

This human-looking move, which was again suggested by Oliver Reeh, was a surprise. FRITZ evacuates his king at the cost of an exchange Not 17...b6? 18.♘f5+− . IM Heiko Machelett, Prof. Dr. Althöfer, and Karsten Müller, commenting live from Friedrich Schiller University Jena, thought the more "FRITZ-like" 17...♘d×c5? 18.♗b5+ ♔f8 19.♖f4 b6 would follow. Black keeps its pawn and cements its knights. But the h8-rook is out of game at the moment.

This is a typical shuffle chess problem by the way. So Heiko suggested options like h7-h6 followed by ♔f8-g8-h7 or g7-g6 and ♔g7. But the whole line has a hole, which was seen by FRITZ in time: 20.♗c6! ♗b7? (20...♘d6! 21.♔b1 ±) 21.♘f5+− ♕c7 22.♗×b7 ♕×b7 23.♖×e4 d×e4 24.♕×c5+ b×c5 25.♕×c5+ ♔g8 (25...♘e8 26.♖d1 ♖c8?! 27.♘×g7#) 26.g5 h6 (26...♖c8? 27.♘h6+ g×h6 28.g×h6#) 27.♘e7+ ♔f8 28.♘d5+ ♔e8 29.♘c7+−; 17...♘e×c5? 18.♘f5 ♕f8 19.♖d1 g6 20.♖×d5 g×f5 21.♗b5 ♘d3+ 22.♕×d3 ♕×b4 23.♕×f5+− .

18.♘f5 ♕e5 19.c6 b×c6 20.♗×f8

Kasparov invests again a lot of time. Later he will be a bit short of time. 20.♘e7+? ♔h8 21.♘×c6 is strongly met by 21...♕g5! , e.g., 22.♗×f8 ♕e3+ 23.♔b1 ♘d2+ 24.♔a1 ♘×f1 25.♗×g7+ ♔×g7 26.♖×f1 ♗h7.

20...♔×f8

Played quickly by FRITZ. It must have

had enough time to calculate it in advance, on Kasparov's time. 20...♘×f8 21.♗d3 is very pleasant for White(21. ♕×c6? ♖b8 gives Black strong attack).

21.♘g3!

Not 21.♗d3? ♘dc5 and Black has good counterplay, or 21.♕×c6? ♘b6 22.♕c2 ♗d7 and Black can fish in muddy waters.

21...♘dc5 22.♘×e4 ♘×e4 23.♗d3 ♗e6

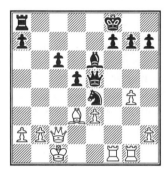

24.♗×e4

Kasparov clarifies the situation by exchanging. But objectively it was better to deal this directly and play 24.♔b1 ♖b8 25.♖g2 first. White is clearly better because of the long-term strength of his rooks.

24...d×e4 25.♖f4

The preventive 25.♔b1!? is a bit more precise as Black will most probably play ♗d5 in any case while it is not clear if White's rook is well placed on f4.

25...♗d5

After 25...♗×a2?! 26.♕×c6, White profits more from the opening of the queenside as his rooks can operate quickly on the files.

26.♕c5+ ♔g8

The key of White's strategy in this

position is the prevention of any counterplay by slow, restrictive improvement of his pieces based upon dominance on the dark squares. This is very strong especially against FRITZ, which needs activity like a fish needs water.

27.♖gf1

Threatening ♖xf7, which FRITZ of course would never overlook. 27.g5?! ♕e6 28.a3 ♕h3 a ↕d 27.♖g2?! ♕g5 gives Black counterplay.; The preventive 27.h4!? ♖b8 28.♖g2 also came strongly into consideration. If g4-g5 is played later, then the three white pawns make it very difficult to mobilize Black's kingside majority and may even be used to launch an assault on the dark squares by h4-h5-h6 (White's queen threatens to land on g7 and back rank mates loom large).

27...♖b8

27...a5?? 28.♖xf7 ♗xf7? (28...a4?? 29.♖f8+ ♖xf8 30.♕xf8#) 29.♕xe5+−.

28.♖1f2

28.♖xf7?? ♕xb2+ 29.♔d1 ♗xf7−+.

28...♕c7 29.♖c2 ♕d7

29...h6!? is tactically playable as 30.♕xd5? can be met by 30...♕xf4.

30.h4

30.b3!? is aimed against the ♗d5, but can be answered by 30...♖b5 31.♕d4 ♕e7, when the lever a7-a5-a4 is in the air. Nevertheless, White is for choice after 32.♖f5.

30...♕d8

Threatening to take on h4 and on a2.

31.g5 ♗xa2 32.♖xe4

Played after 15 minutes of thought. It seems that Kasparov is now satisfied with a draw. Here or on the next move

he could still play for the full point. 32.♖d2!? would have probed Black's wound again – the weak dark squares, e.g., 32...♕e8 (32...♗d5? 33.♖xe4 a5 [33...♖b5? 34.♕xc6+−] 34.♖ed4 f5 [34...♕e8? 35.e4+−] 35.e4±) 33.h5 a6 (33...♗d5 34.h6) 34.♖d6 ♗d5 35.♕a7 ♕f8 36.♕c7 ♖c8 37.♕d7 and White is clearly for choice in both cases.

32...♕d3!

Pressing the attack.

33.♖d4?

Not 33.♕xc6? ♕f1+ 34.♔d2 ♖d8+ 35.♖d4 ♕f2+ 36.♔d3 ♕f1+=. However, with 33.♕f5! ♖f8 34.♖e5 ♕d6 35.♕e4. Kasparov could have avoid the perpetual check and continued the game with winning chances as his extra exchange is a solid long-term advantage.

33...♕xe3+ 34.♖cd2 ♕e1+

34...♖f8?! is answered by 35.♕c3.

35.♖d1 ♕e3+

35...♕e8?! helps only White, e.g., 36.♖b4 ♖a8 37.♖b7.

36.♖1d2 ♕g1+ 37.♖d1 ½-½

FRITZ X3D – Kasparov, Garry (2830)
Queen's Gambit Accepted D27
New York match (4), 18.11.2003

1.d4 d5!?

No King's Indian? A surprise!

2.c4 d×c4 3.♘f3 e6 4.e3 a6 5.♗×c4 c5 6.0-0 ♘f6 7.♗b3 c×d4 8.e×d4 ♘c6 9.♘c3 ♗e7 10.♖e1 0-0 11.♗f4 ♘a5 12.d5 ♘×b3 13.♕×b3 e×d5

13...♘×d5 14.♖ad1 ♘×f4 was too risky against a machine.

14.♖ad1 ♗e6 15.♕×b7

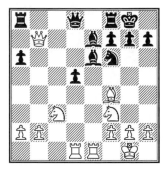

15...♗d6!

This is a strong novelty compared to 15...♗c5 16.♗e5 ♕a5 17.♘d4, when White was slightly better in Kramnik-Anand, Monte Carlo 2001.

16.♗g5 ♖b8 17.♕×a6 ♖×b2 18.♗×f6

The winning potential diminishes more and more. The draw is now clear.

18...♕×f6 19.♕×d6

19.♘×d5?? ♗×d5 20.♖×d5? ♗×h2+ 21.♔×h2 ♕×a6−+.

19...♕×c3 20.♘d4

20.a4 ♖a2=.

20...♖×a2 21.♘×e6 f×e6 22.♕×e6+ ♔h8 23.♖f1

The usual trick 23.♕f7 is parried by 23...♕c8 (23...♖×f7?? 24.♖e8+ ♖f8 25.♖×f8#) 24.♕×d5 ♖a×f2−.

23...♕c5!

24.♕×d5

24.♖×d5?? is nicely refuted by 24...♕×f2+ 25.♖×f2 ♖a1+ 26.♖d1 ♖×d1+ 27.♔e1 ♖×e1+ 28.♖f1 ♖e×f1#.

24...♖f×f2! 25.♖×f2

25.♕×c5?? ♖×g2+ 26.♔h1 ♖×h2+ 27.♔g1 ♖ag2#; 25.♕d8+ ♖f8+ 26.♕d4=; 25.♕×a2?? ♖×a2+ 26.♔h1 h6−+.

25...♕×f2+ 26.♔h1 h6! ½-½

15
Bilbao (2004)

Additional games can be found in Chapter 9.

Junior – Topalov, Veselin (2737)
Ruy Lopez C65
Bilbao (1), 06.10.2004

1.e4 e5 2.♘f3 ♘c6 3.♗b5 ♘f6 4.d3 ♗c5 5.c3 d6 6.d4 e×d4 7.c×d4 ♗b4+ 8.♔f1 d5 9.e5 ♘e4 10.a3?!

Junior likes to move its rook's pawns. But here it has no real point and gives Topalov a comfortable game. 10.♕a4 is the main line.

10...♗e7 11.♕c2 0-0 12.♗e3 f5 13.♘c3 ♔h8 14.♘e2 g5 15.h3 f4 16.♗d2 ♗f5 17.♕d1 a6 18.♗a4 ♕d7 19.♖c1 ♔g7 20.♗e1 h5

21.♘h2 h4

21...♗×h3?! is met by 22.f3 ♗e6 23.♖×c6 b×c6 24.♕c1 ♘g3+ 25.♘×g3 f×g3 26.♗×c6.

22.♔g1

22...b5

Black has no problems but it is also not easy to break White's solid set-up, as the sacrifice 22...♗×h3?! is again not a good choice against a machine because of 23.♗×c6 b×c6 24.g×h3 f3 25.♘g4 f×e2 26.♕×e2 ♖f4 27.f3 ♘g3 28.♗×g3 h×g3 29.♔g2 ♖×d4 30.b4 and White's strategic initiative is dangerous.

23.♗c2 ♘d8 24.♗b4 ♗×b4 25.a×b4 c6 26.♘f3 ♕e7 27.♕e1 ♘e6 28.♗d1 ♖ac8 29.♖a1 ♕a7 30.♗c2 ♖f7 31.♖a3 ♖g8 32.♕a1 ♖a8 33.♗d3 ♔g8 34.♕b1 ♖af8 35.♕c2 ♕b6 36.♖a1 ♖g7 37.♖c1 ♖c8 38.♖d1 ♖f8 39.♔f1 ♖gf7 40.♖c1 ½-½

Fritz – Karjakin, Sergey (2591)
Scotch Game C45
Bilbao (1), 06.10.2004

1.e4 e5 2.♘f3 ♘c6 3.d4 e×d4 4.♘×d4 ♘f6 5.♘×c6 b×c6 6.e5 ♕e7 7.♕e2 ♘d5 8.c4 ♘b6 9.♘d2 d6 10.e×d6 c×d6 11.b3 ♗g4 12.f3 ♗e6 13.♗b2 d5 14.c×d5 ♘×d5 15.0-0-0 ♕g5 16.h4 ♕e3 17.h5 h6

18.♖e1 ♕×e2 19.♗×e2 f6 20.♖h4 ♔d7 21.♗c4 ♗d6?!

21...a5 22.♘e4 ♗b4 23.♘c3 ♖he8 is preferable.

22.♘e4

22...♖he8?!

The bishop pair should be preserved with 22...♗e7. But this kind of open position should be avoided against a computer altogether, as the machine is like a shark in the water.

23.♘×d6 ♔×d6 24.♖he4 ♗d7 25.♗d4 a5 26.a3 ♗e6 27.g4 ♗f7 28.♗f2 ♖e6 29.♔d2 ♖ae8 30.b4 a×b4 31.a×b4

31...g6?

loses by force. 31...Kc7 was the only move to continue the fight but it will be an uphill struggle of course.

32.♖×e6+ ♖×e6 33.♗c5+ ♔d7 34.♖a1 g×h5 35.♖a7+ ♔e8 36.b5

h×g4 37.b×c6 and Karjakin resigned in view of 37...♖×c6 38.♗b5 +– . **1-0**

Ponomariov, Ruslan (2722) – Fritz
King's Indian Defense E97
Bilbao (2), 07.10.2004

1.♘f3 ♘f6 2.c4 g6 3.♘c3 ♗g7 4.e4 d6 5.d4 0-0 6.♗e2 e5 7.0-0 ♘c6 8.d×e5 d×e5 9.♗g5 ♕×d1 10.♖f×d1 ♗g4 11.h3 ♗×f3 12.♗×f3 ♘d4 13.♘d5 ♘×d5 14.c×d5 f5 15.♖d2 ♖f7 16.♗e3 ♘×f3+ 17.g×f3 ♗f8 18.♖c1 a5 19.♔f1 ♗d6 20.♔e2 ♔f8 21.♖dc2 a4 22.♖c4 ♔e7 23.h4 ♔d7

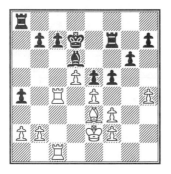

24.h5!?

Ponomariov opens a second front in typical fashion. Altogether he plays a good game, but as the machine does not crack under his pressure, in the end he only reaches a draw.

24...g×h5 25.♖h1 f4 26.♗d2 a3 27.b3 h4 28.♖×h4 ♖c8 29.♔d3 ♖g8 30.♖c1 ♖g2 31.♔e2 ♖gg7 32.♗c3 ♖e7 33.♖h5 ♖g6 34.♖ch1 ♖gg7 35.♖f5 ♖g2 36.♔f1 ♖g8 37.♖hh5 ♖ge8 38.♔e2 ♖g8

39.♔f1

39.♗×e5?! would not be a good choice of course as 39...♗×e5 40.♖×e5 ♖×e5 41.♖×e5 ♖g1 42.♖h5 ♖a1 43.e5 ♖×a2+ 44.♔d3 is drawn. With 39.♖f6, White can play for more than a draw, but in the end it is most probably also insufficient to win. Ponomariov stops all counterplay but, without taking some risks, Black's castle certainly cannot be stormed.

39...♖ge8 40.♖fg5 c6 41.d×c6+ ♔×c6 42.♖h6 b5 43.♔e2 ♔d7 44.♖gh5 b4!

This imprisons White's bishop and closes the gates of the fortress.

45.♗d2

45.♖×d6+ ♔×d6 46.♗×b4+ ♔c6 47.♗×e7 ♖×e7 48.♔d3 ♔b5 is also drawn.

45...♖f7 46.♖×h7 ♖×h7 47.♖×h7+ ♔c6 48.♖h6 ♔c7 49.♖h7+ ♔c6

50.♖h6 ♔c7 51.♖h7+ ½-½

Junior — Ponomariov, Ruslan (2722)
Sicilian Defense B90
Bilbao (3), 08.10.2004

**1.e4 c5 2.♘f3 d6 3.d4 c×d4
4.♘×d4 ♘f6 5.♘c3 a6 6.♗e3 e5
7.♘b3 ♗e6 8.f3 ♘bd7 9.♕d2 b5
10.0-0-0 ♗e7 11.g4 ♘b6 12.g5
♘h5 13.♘d5 ♘×d5 14.e×d5 ♗d7
15.♘a5 0-0 16.♔b1 f5**

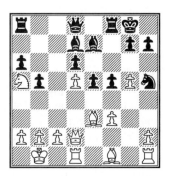

17.♘c6

Probably 17.g×f6 ♘×f6 18.♖g1, as in Motylev-Zulfugarli, Swidnica 1999, was a better choice against a human, as in the game Junior does not manage to pose Ponomariov any real problems.

**17...♕e8 18.♘×e7+ ♕×e7
19.♖g1 f4 20.♗b6 g6 21.♗d3
♗f5 22.♗×f5 ♖×f5 23.♕b4 ♖f7
24.♖d3 ♘g7 25.♖c3 ♘f5 26.♖c6
♖e8 27.♕e4 ♕d7 28.♗f2 ♖a8
29.♖b6 ♘e7 30.h4 ♘c8 31.♖c6
♘e7 32.♖b6 ♘c8 33.♖c6 ♘e7 ½-½**

Hydra — Karjakin, Sergey (2591)
Ruy Lopez C65
Bilbao (3), 08.10.2004

**1.e4 e5 2.♘f3 ♘c6 3.♗b5 ♘f6
4.d3 ♗c5 5.0-0 d6 6.c3 0-0
7.♘bd2 a6 8.♗a4 ♗a7 9.h3 ♘e7
10.♖e1 ♘g6 11.♘f1 ♗d7 12.♗×d7**

♕×d7 13.♗g5 ♕d8

13...♘h5!?.

**14.♘h4 ♖e8 15.♘×g6 h×g6
16.♘h2 ♕d7 17.♕b3**

17.♗×f6 g×f6 18.♘g4 is parried by 18...♔g7 19.♕d2 ♖h8.

**17...♕b5 18.♕c2 ♘h7 19.♘f3
♘×g5 20.♘×g5 ♖ad8 21.♖ad1 d5
22.♘f3**

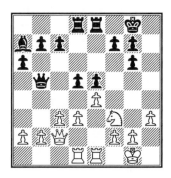

22...♖e6?

This runs into a powerful opening of the position. After a normal move like 22...f6, it is more or less equal.

**23.c4! d×c4 24.d×c4 ♕e8 25.c5
♖e7**

25...♖×d1 26.♖×d1 f6 27.♖d5 c6 28.♖d3±.

26.♖×d8 ♕×d8 27.♖d1 ♕e8?!

27...♖d7, to exchange attacking potential, is preferable but White remains clearly on top after 28.♖×d7 ♕×d7 29.♕c4.

28.♖d3 c6 29.♕d1!

Hydra begins to prepare the coming invasion on the kingside.

**29...♕f8 30.b4 ♗b8 31.♖d8 ♖e8
32.♖d7 ♖e7**

33.♘g5!

HYDRA starts the attack for real.

33...♗c7 34.♕g4 ♕e8

34...♖xd7 35.♕xd7 ♗d8 36.♘f3 ♕e7 37.♕xe7 ♗xe7 38.♘xe5±.

35.♖xe7 ♕xe7 36.♕h4 ♕d8 37.♕h7+ ♔f8 38.♕h8+ ♔e7 39.♕xg7 ♕f8 40.♕h7 a5 41.a3 axb4 42.axb4

42...♔e8?

42...b6 and 42...♔f6 were more tenacious. But to defend such a position against this very strong computer seems to be too much for a human.

43.♘e6! fxe6 44.♕xc7 ♕f4 45.♕c8+ ♔e7 46.♕xb7+ ♔f6 47.g3 ♕xe4 48.♕c8 ♔f7 49.♕d7+ ♔f6 50.♕e8 g5

Black has no perpetual because of 50... ♕e1+ 51.♔g2 ♕e4+ 52.♔h2+−.

51.♕h5 ♕xb4 52.♕f3+ ♔e7

53.♕xc6 e4 54.♕d6+ ♔f6 55.♕d8+ ♔g6 56.♕g8+ ♔f6 57.♕f8+ ♔g6 58.♕e7 ♕c4 59.h4
1-0 and Karjakin resigned as White will make progress, e.g., 59...gxh4 60.gxh4 e3 61.♕g5+ ♔f7 62.fxe3 ♕c1+ 63.♔g2 ♕c2+ 64.♔g3 ♕c1 65.h5 ♕g1+ 66.♔f4 ♕h2+ 67.♔f3 ♕h1+ 68.♔f2 ♕h2+ 69.♔g2+−.

FRITZ – Topalov, Veselin (2737)
French Defense C06
Bilbao (3), 08.10.2004

1.e4 e6 2.d4 d5 3.♘d2 a6 4.♘gf3 ♘f6 5.e5 ♘fd7 6.♗d3 c5 7.c3 ♘c6 8.0-0 g5 9.♗b1 g4 10.♘e1 h5 11.♘b3

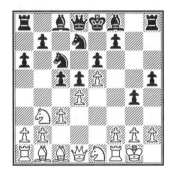

11...a5?!

11...c4 12.♘d2 b5 was preferable, keeping the position more closed.

12.♘xc5 ♘xc5 13.dxc5 ♗xc5 14.♘d3 ♗a7 15.♕a4 ♗d7 16.♕f4 ♗b8

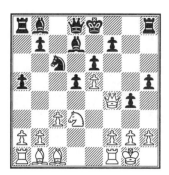

17.♖d1

This is slightly strange from a human point of view, as the rook seems to belong on e1, and for reasons of flexibility, may not move now at all.

17...f5 18.c4 d4 19.♖e1 ♕e7 20.♗c2 h4 21.♗d2 ♗c7 22.♗d1 ♖g8 23.a3 a4 24.f3 g×f3 25.♗×f3 ♗a5 26.♗×a5

26...♖×a5?

From now on it will be an uphill struggle. 26...♘×a5 was called for.

27.♕d2 ♕g5 28.♕f2 ♖g7 29.c5 ♔f8 30.♖ac1 ♔g8 31.♔h1! ♖a8 32.♖c4 ♗e8 33.♗d1 ♕h6 34.♘f4 ♖d8 35.♖×a4 d3

35...h3!? 36.♘×h3 ♘e7 was an alternative.

36.♗b3 ♗f7 37.♕e3

37...♕g5?

Just loses time and Topalov soon has to retreat. 37...d2 38.♖d1 ♔h7 was the last chance to fight.

38.♖d1 ♔h7 39.♖d2 ♔h6

40.♔g1

Slightly strange from a human point of view, but it wins.

40...♕g5 41.♗c4 ♗e8

41...♖d4 42.♗b5 +− .

42.♗×e6 ♖e7 43.♖×d3 ♖×d3 44.♕×d3 ♘×e5 45.♕×f5+ ♕×f5 46.♗×f5+ ♔h6 47.♘d5 1-0

Topalov, Veselin (2737) – Junior
Sicilian Defense B56
Bilbao (4), 09.10.2004

1.e4 c5 2.♘f3 d6 3.♘c3 ♘c6 4.d4 c×d4 5.♘×d4 ♗d7 6.♗e3 ♘f6 7.f3 e6 8.g4 h6 9.♕d2 a6 10.0-0-0 b5 11.h4 b4 12.♘ce2

12...♕a5?

This may already be the source of the forthcoming problems. The queen is not doing much on a5 but the pin of the b4-pawn is very problematic. 12...♘e5 is the main line.

13.♔b1 ♖c8 14.♖g1 ♘e5 15.♘c1 g6 16.g5 h×g5 17.h×g5 ♘h5 18.a3

Topalov just wins a pawn and JUNIOR does not get enough compensation.

18...♘c4 19.♗×c4 ♖×c4 20.♘a2 ♖c8 21.♘×b4 ♕a4 22.♔a2 ♕a5 23.♕d3 ♘g7 24.c3

24.♖h1!?.

24...e5 25.♘b3 ♕b5 26.♘d5 ♕×d3 27.♖×d3 ♗b5 28.♖d2 ♖h3 29.♖f2 ♗d7 30.♘a5 ♗e6 31.c4 ♘h5 32.b3

32.♖d1!?, to take back on d5 with the rook, was also strong.

32...♗×d5 33.e×d5 ♘g3 34.♘c6 ♔d7 35.b4 ♘f5 36.♗d2 ♘e7

37.♘a5

Topalov decides to keep his knight. Probably a good decision as in the game he can exchange it under more favorable circumstances.

37...♘f5 38.♖e1 ♗g7 39.♘c6 ♘d4 40.♘×d4 e×d4 41.♔b3 d3 42.♖e4

42.f4+− is even better.

42...♖h1

43.♖f4?

Topalov rushes. After the prophylactic 43.♗e1 White is strategically winning.

43...♗e5!!

Such options are never missed by a computer. JUNIOR forces a draw with its active play.

44.♖×f7+ ♔e8 45.♖b7 ♖b1+ 46.♔a4 ♖b2 47.♖h7

47.c5 d×c5 48.f4 ♗d4 49.♖h2 c4 50.d6 ♖d8 51.f5 ♖d7 52.♖b8+ ♖d8 53.♖×d8+ ♔×d8 54.f6 ♗e5 55.f7 ♗×d6 56.♖h8+ ♔d7 57.♗c3=.

47...♗f4 48.♗×f4 ♖×f2 49.♖h8+ ♔d7 50.♖h7+ ♔e8 ½-½

Karjakin, Sergey (2591) − FRITZ
Sicilian Defense B80
Bilbao (4), 09.10.2004

1.e4 c5 2.♘f3 d6 3.d4 c×d4 4.♘×d4 ♘f6 5.♘c3 a6 6.f3 e6

**7.&e3 b5 8.g4 h6 9.&d2 &bd7
10.0-0-0 &b7 11.h4 b4 12.&a4
&a5 13.b3 &c5 14.a3 &c8 15.a×b4**

15.&×b4 is the main line.

**15...&×b3+ 16.&×b3 &×a4
17.&b2 d5 18.c3 d×e4 19.&a5
&d5 20.&a1 &d7 21.&×a6 e×f3
22.&×c8 &×c8 23.g5 &e4 24.&d3**

24.&c2, as in Acs-van Wely, Hoogeveen
2002, is the alternative.

**24...&b8 25.&f4 &d6 26.&×d6
&×d6 27.&×f3**

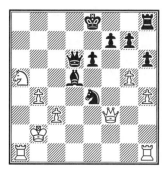

27...&×g5?

Is FRITZ programmed to stir up
complications and avoid a draw? 27...
h×g5 leads to a repetition after 28.h×g5
&h2+ 29.&×h2 &×h2+ 30.&a3 &c2
31.c4 &d6 32.&b3 &b5+ 33.&a4
&c3+.

**28.&d3 &e4 29.&he1 &h2+
30.&e2 &×h4 31.&b5+ &e7
32.&c6+ &f6**

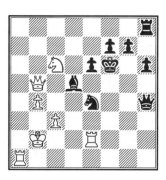

33.&g2?

Karjakin wants to cut off the king's
escape route but FRITZ just opens a new
one. After 33.&d3 &g6 (33...&×c6?
34.&d4+ &e7 35.&a7+ &f8 36.b5 &d5
37.c4 &g4 38.&c2 &g8 39.c×d5 &h7
40.&×f7 +–) 34.&e5+ &h7 35.&×f7
&c8 36.&a3 White is clearly better.

33...g5!

FRITZ sets its majority in motion and
prepares a retreat for its king.

**34.&f1+ &g7 35.&e5 &f6 36.&c5
&e4 37.&×f6**

37...&a8!

A deadly counterattack. 37...&×g2+? is
met by 38.&f2 &c8 39.&c6 and matters
are unclear, but White is not worse.

38.&g6+

38.&×f7+ is parried by 38...&g8
39.&g7+ &h8 40.&h7+ &×h7 41.&f2
&g7 42.&g4 &a7–+ .

**38...&h7 39.&×h6+ &×h6
40.&×f7+ &g6 41.&×g5+ &×f7
42.&f2+**

42.&c7+ &f8 43.&d6+ &e8 44.&g8+
&f7 45.&×a8 &×a8 46.c4 should lose
in the long run as well but was more
tenacious.

**42...&f3 43.&×f3+ &×f3 44.c4
&c8 45.&c3 &e2 46.c5 &b5
47.&g1 e5 48.&d1 &e8 49.&e1**

♔f6 50.♕d2 ♖d8+ 0-1

HYDRA – Ponomariov, Ruslan (2722)
Sicilian Defense B85
Bilbao (4), 09.10.2004

1.e4 c5 2.♘f3 d6 3.d4 c×d4
4.♘×d4 ♘f6 5.♘c3 a6 6.♗e2
e6 7.0-0 ♗e7 8.f4 0-0 9.a4 ♘c6
10.♗e3 ♗d7 11.♘b3 b6 12.♕d2
♕c7

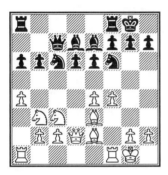

13.♖f3

Slightly strange from the human point
of view, but far be it for me to argue
with the mighty HYDRA.

13...♘g4 14.♖d1 ♘×e3 15.♖×e3
♖fd8 16.♖g3 ♗e8 17.f5 ♗f6
18.♖f1 ♕e7 19.♗d3 ♘e5 20.♔h1
♖dc8

20...b5!?, to get counterplay quicker,
was probably stronger.

21.♘d4

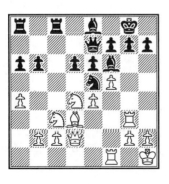

35...b×c4?

Running into a powerful attack.

21...♔h8

It was risky to enter the complications
after 21...♘c4 22.♕e2 ♘×b2 23.e5
d×e5 24.f×e6 against such a calculating
machine as HYDRA.

22.♖h3 ♘c4 23.♕e2 ♗×d4
24.♗×c4 ♗×c3 25.b×c3 e×f5
26.♖×f5 g6 27.♖f4 ♖c5 28.♕f1
♖a7 29.♗d5 ♔g7 30.c4 b5 31.♕c1

31...h5?.

Now Black has to follow a very narrow
path to stay afloat. After 31...♕g5, to try
to disrupt the harmony of the attacking
army, the game is more or less equal.

32.g4! f6!

Ponomariov keeps a clear head and
finds the best defense.

33.g×h5 g5 34.♖g3 ♔h7 35.♖f2

Attacking potential had to be exchanged with 35...♗f7.

36.♕f1! ♗f7 37.♖×f6 ♗×d5?

Walking into a forced mate. But 37...♖×d5 38.e×d5 ♗×d5+ 39.♔g1 ♕e4 40.♕f5+ ♕×f5 41.♖×f5 ♗e4 should lose in the long run as well, but some technical problems may arise and fortresses lurk here and there, so Ponomariov should have tried it.

38.♕f5+ 1-0

16
Bilbao (2005)

The Ponomariov – FRITZ game from round 2 is in Chapter 9 and the HYDRA – Ponomariov game from round 3 is given in Chapter 10.

Ponomariov, Ruslan (2704) – JUNIOR
King's Indian Attack B10
Bilbao (1), 20.11.2005

1.♘f3 d5 2.d3 ♘f6 3.g3 c6 4.♘bd2 ♘bd7 5.♗g2 e5 6.0-0 ♗d6 7.e4 0-0

8.♔h1?!

Ponomariov wants to throw JUNIOR out of its book but in a way this backfires. 8.♖e1 is the main line.

8...♖e8 9.♕e1 a5 10.a4 b6 11.♘h4 ♘c5 12.f3?!

12.b3 is more natural.

12...g6 13.♖f2 ♖a7 14.♖e2 ♖ae7 15.♕f1 ♘h5 16.♗h3 ♘e6 17.♘b3 ♖a7 18.♘g2 ♖c7 19.♗e3?!

Allowing the following opening shot, after which it is easier for JUNIOR to play, but it is quite difficult to defend White's position in any case.

19...♘ef4!?

A typical move for JUNIOR's aggressive style.

20.♗×f4?

20.g×f4 ♗×h3 21.♗×b6 ♘×f4 22.♗×a5 ♕g5 gives Black dangerous compensation but just had to be played.

20...♗×h3 21.♗d2 f5

22.♕g1?

22.e×f5 g×f5 23.♕e1, to use the pin in the e-file, was the last chance but Black remains for choice of course.

22...f×e4 23.f×e4 ♖f7 24.♖f1 ♖×f1 25.♕×f1 ♗e7 26.e×d5 ♕×d5

Black's active army rules the board. It is almost impossible to defend such a position against a machine.

27.♔g1 ♘f6 28.♕e1 ♘g4 29.♘e3 ♘×e3 30.♗×e3 ♖f8 31.♖f2 ♖×f2 32.♕×f2 e4 33.♘c1 c5 34.b3 g5

436

**35.c4 ♕c6 36.♘e2 e×d3 37.♘c3
♗d8 38.♘d5 ♕e6 39.♗d2 ♕e4
40.♘c3 ♕g4 41.♘d5**

41.♕e3 ♗f6 42.♕×d3 ♗d4+ 43.♔h1
♕e6–+ .

**41...h5 42.♕e3 ♕d1+ 43.♗e1?!
♔g7 44.♔f2 ♗g4 45.♗c3+?!
♔f7 46.♕d2 ♕×d2+ 47.♗×d2
♗d1 48.♔e3 ♗×b3 49.♔×d3
♗×a4 50.h4 g×h4 51.g×h4 ♗b3
52.♔c3 a4 53.♗g5 ♗×g5 54.h×g5
b5 55.♘f4 b4+ 56.♔b2 ♗×c4
57.♘×h5 a3+ 0–1**

Hydra – Kasimdzhanov, Rustam (2670)
King's Indian Defense E94
Bilbao (1), 20.11.2005

**1.d4 ♘f6 2.c4 g6 3.♘c3 ♗g7 4.e4
d6 5.♘f3 0-0 6.♗e2 e5 7.♗e3
♘a6 8.0-0 c6 9.d5 ♘g4 10.♗g5
f6 11.♗h4 c5 12.♘e1 ♘h6 13.a3
♗d7 14.♘d3 g5 15.♗g3 ♕e7 16.f3
f5 17.♗f2 f4 18.b4 b6 19.h3 ♘f7
20.♖b1 h5 21.♖b2 ♘h6 22.♗e1
♗f6 23.♘f2 ♔h8 24.♕d3 ♖g8
25.♘b5 ♖g6 26.♗d1**

Kasimdzhanov has finished the
mobilization of his forces on the
kingside. He has two options now. He
can at least for the moment just wait and
see what Hydra will do, or he can start
the typical attack. He boldly attacks,
which should be correct and logical.

**26...♖ag8 27.♘×a7 g4 28.f×g4
♗h4 29.♘c6 ♕g7 30.♗c3 h×g4
31.♘×g4 ♘×g4 32.♗×g4 ♗×g4**

32...♖×g4? 33.h×g4 ♗g3 is parried by
34.♗e1+– .

33.♖×f4!?

Hydra decides to sacrifice a piece
to open roads for its counterattack.
33.h×g4 ♖×g4 34.♕h3 ♕g5 also gives
Black good compensation.

33...♗h5 34.♕f1

34...♗g3?

Kasimdzhanov miscalculates. After
34...♗f6, the position seems to be
dynamically balanced.

**35.♖f7 ♕h6 36.♗d2 ♗f4 37.♗×f4
e×f4**

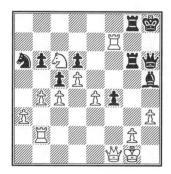
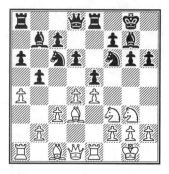

38.罩×f4

It is interesting that HYDRA prefers this over 38.豐×f4. Does HYDRA have prejudiced against the exchange of queens? But not 38.②e7? because of 38...罩×g2+.

38...罩g3?

Losing directly. 38...豐g7 offers more resistance, but HYDRA would have won later anyway.

39.②e7

and Black resigned in view of 39...豐g7 40.②×g8 豐×b2 41.②e7 豐e5 42.罩g4 豐×e7 43.罩×g3+−. **1-0**

Fritz – Khalifman, Alexander (2653)
Ruy Lopez C77
Bilbao (1), 20.11.2005

1.e4 e5 2.②f3 ②c6 3.奧b5 ②f6 4.d3 d6 5.c3 奧e7 6.0-0 0-0 7.②bd2 a6 8.奧a4 b5 9.奧c2 罩e8 10.罩e1 奧f8 11.d4 h6?!

This slow move allows FRITZ to regroup without problems. 11...e×d4 12.c×d4 奧g4 creates more pressure.

12.②f1 奧b7 13.②g3 g6 14.a4 奧g7 15.奧d3!

FRITZ asks an unpleasant question.

15...b×a4?

Now Black's structure is in ruins. 15...e×d4 16.a×b5 a×b5 17.罩×a8 豐×a8 18.c×d4 豐a4 was preferable.

16.豐×a4 e×d4 17.c×d4 ②d7 18.奧e3 ②b6 19.豐b3 a5 20.奧b5 罩f8 21.d5! ②b4 22.奧d4 奧×d4 23.②×d4 奧c8 24.②c6 ②×c6 25.奧×c6 罩a7 26.②e2 奧d7 27.②d4 a4 28.豐d3 奧c8 29.豐e3 ⚔h7 30.f4 豐e7 31.豐c3 豐f6?!

This move runs into the following powerful central advance. But good advice is hard to give.

32.e5 d×e5

32...豐×f4? 33.②b5 罩a6 34.e6+−.

33.f×e5 豐e7 34.②b5 罩a6 35.罩ad1 a3

Desperation.

36.b×a3 罩a4 37.d6 c×d6

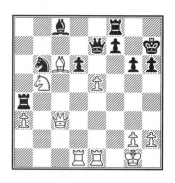

38.♘×d6

This wins, but from a human point of view 38.e×d6+− is just much more natural.

38...♖a6 39.♗b5 ♖a8 40.♕d4 ♕a7 41.♗c6 ♖b8 42.♖b1 ♗e6 43.♗b7

43.Rec1 is even stronger.

43...♖×b7 44.♘×b7 ♕×b7 45.♖×b6 ♕a7 46.a4 ♖c8 47.♖b4 ♕a8 48.♕f2 ♖c3 49.♖f4 ♕b7 50.♖f1 ♔g7 51.a5 ♕c7 52.♕d4 ♔g8 53.a6 1-0

Khalifman resigned because of 53...♖c4 54.♕d6. But not 54.a7? in view of 54... ♖×d4 55.a8♕+ ♖d8; but not 54...♕a7+ 55.♔h1 ♖c8 56.♖b4 ♖a8 57.♖b6+−.

Khalifman, Alexander (2653) – HYDRA
Queen's Pawn Game D11
Bilbao (2), 21.11.2005

1.d4 d5 2.♘f3 c6 3.e3 ♘f6 4.♗d3 ♗g4 5.♘bd2 e6 6.c4 ♗d6 7.♕b3 b6 8.♕c2 ♘bd7 9.h3

Posing an unpleasant question to the monster.

9...♗×f3

The machine has probably calculated than it gets the initiative. As the bishop pair is a long-term advantage, 9... ♗h5 might be preferable. It is hard to criticize the program so "?!" could be

appended to the game continuation.

10.♘×f3 0-0 11.0-0 ♖c8 12.b3 c5 13.♗b2

13...b5!

HYDRA opens the queenside to get squares for its dark knights before White's bishop pair takes complete control. A typical technique.

14.♕e2 b×c4 15.b×c4 c×d4 16.c×d5 ♘×d5 17.♘×d4 ♘c5 18.♗c4 ♗b8 19.♘f3 ♘e4

20.♕d3

Khalifman heads for an endgame, a good choice against the monster. 20.♖ac1 is the alternative approach.

20...♘dc3 21.♖fc1 ♕×d3 22.♗×d3 ♖fd8 23.♗f1 f6 24.♖c2 ♘a4 25.♖×c8 ♖×c8 26.♖c1 ♖×c1 27.♗×c1 ♔f7 28.♗c4 ♗c7 29.♘d4 ♘ac5 30.♔f1 ♗b6 31.g4 ♔e7 32.♔g2 ♘d6 33.♗f1 e5 34.♘b5

♘×b5 35.♗×b5 ♗a5

So far Khalifman had played very strongly, but instead of...

36.♗b2?!

...he should have now played 36.♗a3 to apply more pressure. Objectively it might still be drawn, but White can play on for a very long time with his bishops.

36...♔d6 37.♗c4 ♗b4 38.f4 ♘a4 39.♗c1 e4 40.♔f1 a5 41.h4 ½-½

Kasimdzhanov, Rustam (2670) – JUNIOR
Sicilian Defense B31
Bilbao (2), 21.11.2005

1.e4 c5 2.♘f3 ♘c6 3.♗b5 g6 4.0-0 ♗g7 5.♖e1 e5 6.♗×c6 d×c6 7.d3 ♗g4 8.♘bd2 ♘f6 9.♘c4 ♗×f3 10.♕×f3 ♕e7 11.a4 ♘h5 12.♗d2 0-0 13.♖ab1 b6 14.b4!

The typical plan to play on the queenside. Kasimdzhanov has reached a good anti-computer position.

14...c×b4 15.♗×b4 c5 16.♗c3 ♖ab8

17.♕g4

17.g3!? ♕c7 18.♖b3 ♖fe8 19.♖eb1, to follow up with a5, creates more pressure.

17...♘f4 18.♗d2 ♘e6 19.♘e3 ♕d7 20.a5 b×a5?!

A structural concession. 20...b5 is more natural.

21.♗×a5 h5

JUNIOR just likes to push its rook's pawns. But here it is not bad, as Black may attack on the kingside later.

22.♕d1 ♘f4 23.♖a1 ♖b7 24.♗c3 ♖fb8 25.♘c4 ♕e7?

Was this really played or was 25...♕c7 the game continuation? *ChessBase MEGABASE* 2017 gives ♕e7 but ♕c7 is more likely.

26.♗d2?

This allows the regrouping of the knight to d4, after which Black's position is difficult to storm. 26.g3! ♞h3+ 27.♔g2 ♛e6 28.♗d2 gives White a solid advantage.

26...♞e6 27.h3 ♞d4 28.♗e3 ♔h7 29.♔h2 ♖d8

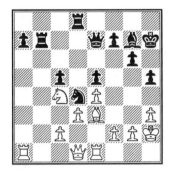

30.♔g1

Kasimdzhanov is satisfied with a draw. He is slightly better and could play on with 30.♛d2 ♖dd7 31.♖a6 ♗f6 32.♖ea1 but it is of course not easy to defeat the machine.

30...♖db8 31.♔h2 ½-½

Junior – Khalifman, Alexander (2653)
Ruy Lopez C90
Bilbao (3), 22.11.2005

1.e4 e5 2.♞f3 ♞c6 3.♗b5 ♞f6 4.d3 d6 5.c3 ♗e7 6.0-0 0-0 7.♖e1 a6 8.♗a4 b5 9.♗b3 ♞a5 10.♗c2 c5 11.♞bd2 ♞c6 12.♞f1 ♖e8 13.♞g3 ♗f8 14.h3 g6 15.a3 ♗g7 16.♗e3 ♛e7 17.b4 ♗b7 18.♗b3 h6 18...a5!? **19.♛d2 ♔h7 20.♖eb1**

20...♞b8?!

This regrouping is quite slow. 20...♖ed8 21.a4 (21.♛a2 ♖d7) 21...c×b4 22.c×b4 ♛e8 is almost equal.

21.♛a2!

Hitting Black's Achilles' Heel.

21...♖f8 22.b×c5 d×c5 23.a4 ♞bd7 24.♛b2

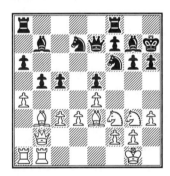

24...♗c6?!

Now White's pressure is mounting. 24...♖fc8 is more precise, to answer 25.a×b5 a×b5 26.♖×a8 ♗×a8 27.♖a1 with 27...c4.

25.a×b5 a×b5 26.♖×a8 ♖×a8 27.♖a1 ♖×a1+ 28.♛×a1 c4

28...♞b6 29.♛a6 ♞fd7 30.h4 gives White a strong initiative.

29.d×c4 b×c4 30.♗c2!

The c4-pawn remains weak, so JUNIOR keeps his valuable e-pawn.

30...♗f8

30...♘c5 31.♕a3 ♘fd7 32.♕b4 is also very unpleasant.

31.♕a6! ♕e6 32.♘d2 ♘c5 33.♕×c4 ♕×c4 34.♘×c4

34...♘c×e4?

After 34...♘fd7 35.f3 ♗b5 36.♘b2 ♔g7, it is much more difficult to make progress against Black's blockade.

35.♘×e5 ♘×g3 36.f×g3 ♗e4 37.♗×e4 ♘×e4 38.c4 ♘×g3

38...f5 39.♘d7 ♗d6 40.g4±.

39.♘d7 ♔g8?!

39...♔g7 is more tenacious but should lose as well after 40.♗d4+ f6 41.♗×f6+ ♔f7 42.♗e5.

40.♘f6+ ♔g7 41.♘e8+ ♔g8 42.c5 ♘f5 43.c6 ♘e7 44.c7 f5 45.♘d6 ♗g7 46.♔f2 ♗e5 47.c8♕+ ♘×c8 48.♘×c8 ♔g7 49.♔e2 g5 50.♘e7 ♔f6 51.♘c6 ♗d6 52.♗d4+ ♔e6 53.♗g7 ♔f7 54.♗c3

Of course, not 54.♗×h6? because of 54...♔g6.

54...h5 55.♗b4 ♗c7 56.♘d4 ♔f6 57.♔d3 ♔e5 58.♗c3 ♔f6 59.♗d2 ♗b6 60.♔c4 f4 61.♔d5 ♗×d4 62.♔×d4 ♔f5 63.♗e1 g4 64.h×g4+ h×g4 65.♔d3 1-0

FRITZ – Kasimdzhanov, Rustam (2670)
Caro-Kann Defense B12
Bilbao (3), 22.11.2005

1.e4 c6 2.d4 d5 3.e5 ♗f5 4.♘c3 h5 5.♗d3 ♗×d3 6.♕×d3 e6 7.♘f3 ♘h6 8.a4?!

Slightly strange. 8.♗g5 is more natural.

8...♗e7 9.0-0 ♘f5 10.♘d1 ♘d7?!

The knight will be in the way later. 10...c5 is necessary to develop the knight on c6.

11.♘e3 g6 12.a5 a6 13.c4 ♘h4?!

13...d×c4 14.♕×c4 ♘×e3 15.♗×e3 0-0 was a better choice as it is easier to play.

14.♘×h4 ♗×h4 15.b3 ♗e7 16.f4 ♖g8!?

Not best, but Black's position is very difficult and in the game the move works quite well.

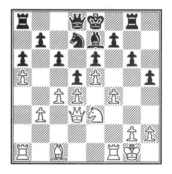

17.♕e2?

Very slow. The direct 17.c×d5 c×d5 18.f5!!, to meet 18...g×f5? with 19.♘×f5, makes much direct more pressure.

17...f5 18.♗a3 ♗×a3 19.♖×a3 ♕e7

442

20.♖aa1

The direct 20.b4!?, with the idea of meeting 20...♕×b4?! with 21.♕a2, contains more poison.

20...0-0-0 21.b4 d×c4

21...♕×b4? 22.♖fc1 is of course out of the question.

22.♘×c4 ♚b8 23.♖ac1

23.♘d6?! allows 23...♘f6.

23...g5!

Black needs counterplay.

24.♘d6 g×f4 25.♖c2

25.♘×b7? ♚×b7 26.♖×c6 is refuted by the coldblooded 26...♘b8!.

25...♘f8 26.♕×h5 ♘g6 27.♕f3

27...♘h4?!

Treading on very dangerous tactical territory. 27...♖h8 was needed: 28.b5 a×b5 29.a6 ♖×d6 30.e×d6 ♕×d6 31.♕c3 b×a6 32.♕×c6 ♕×d4+ 33.♔h1 ♘e5=.

28.♕×f4 ♖g4 29.♕h6 ♖dg8 30.g3 ♖×d4 31.♕e3

31...♖×b4

31...♖d5 is probably objectively better, but a human can hardly play it against a machine, e.g., 32.b5 a×b5 33.a6 f4 34.♕×f4 ♘f5 35.a×b7 ♘×d6 36.e×d6 ♕×b7 37.d7+ e5 38.♕f6 ♕b6+ 39.♔g2 ♔b7 40.♖fc1 ♖×d7 41.♖×c6 ♕d8.

32.♔h1 ♘g6

33.♕a3?

The wrong way to trap the rook. Better is 33.♕c3 ♖b5 34.♘×b5 c×b5 (34... a×b5 35.a6±) 35.♖fc1±.

33...♖b5! 34.♘×b5 a×b5

35.♕d6+?!

The endgame is most probably drawn in view of Black's dangerous counterplay with his passed pawns. FRITZ probably overestimates the value of its resulting passed a-pawn on a7 (see move 38). The alternative 35.♕e3 is probably better from a practical point of view, at least against a human, e.g., 35...♕c7 36.a6 b×a6 37.♖d1 ♘e5 38.♖e2 ♘c4 39.♕×e6 ♖g7 40.♕×f5 ♔b7 and White is better, but matters are not totally clear.

35...♕×d6 36.e×d6 ♔c8! 37.a6 ♔d7 38.a7 ♖a8 39.♖a1 ♔×d6 40.♖d2+ ♔e7 41.♖e2 ♔d6 42.h4 b4 43.h5

43...♘f8!

The knight halts White's progress while the advance of both sides' pawns will neutralize each other, leading to a draw.

44.♔g2 c5 45.♖b2 ♔c6 46.h6

♔b5 47.g4 c4 48.g×f5 b3 49.f×e6 ♘×e6 50.h7 ♘g5 51.h8♕ ♖×h8 52.a8♕ ♖×a8 53.♖×a8 ♘e6 54.♖h8 ½-½

Khalifman, Alexander (2653) – FRITZ
Queen's Indian Defense E12
Bilbao (4), 23.11.2005

1.d4 ♘f6 2.♘f3 e6 3.c4 b6 4.♘c3 ♗b7 5.♗g5 h6 6.♗h4 ♗e7 7.e3 ♘e4 8.♘×e4 ♗×e4 9.♗×e7 ♕×e7 10.♗e2 0-0 11.0-0 d6 12.♘d2 ♗b7 13.♗f3 c5 14.♗×b7 ♕×b7 15.♘f3 ♘d7 16.d×c5 d×c5 17.♕c2 ♖ad8 18.♖fd1 ♖fe8 19.h3 ♕c7 20.b3 ♘f6 21.♖ac1 e5

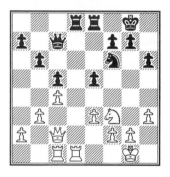

22.♖×d8?!

This exchange gives Black a long lasting initiative, which is always dangerous against a machine. 22.♘d2 e4 23.♘b1 is more or less completely equal and much easier to play than the game.

22...♖×d8 23.e4 ♕d6 24.♖e1 ♘h7 25.♘h2 f6 26.♘f1 ♕d3 27.♕×d3 ♖×d3 28.h4 ♘f8 29.♖e2 ♘e6

29...♖d1 30.♖d2 ♖a1 31.f3 ♘e6 32.♔f2 ♘d4 was the alternative, keeping more winning potential on the board.

30.♖d2 ♖d4 31.♖×d4 c×d4 32.♘d2 ♔f7 33.g3 g6 34.♔f1 f5

35.♔e2 ♘c5 36.f3?!

36...h5

36...a5!? was probably a better practical choice, as now it is more difficult for White to find a plan.

37.b4 ♘e6 38.e×f5 g×f5 39.♔d3 ♔e7 40.a3 a6 41.♘b3 ♔d6 42.♘d2 b5 43.♘b3! f4 44.g4 h×g4 45.f×g4 b×c4+

45...e4+ 46.♔×e4 b×c4 47.♘d2 c3 48.♘b3 f3 49.♔×f3 ♔d5 50.♘c1 ♔c4 51.♔e4=.

46.♔×c4 e4 47.♘×d4 f3

48.♘×f3!

The saving resource.

48...e×f3 49.♔d3 ♔e5 50.♔e3 ♘d4 51.h5 ♔e6 52.h6 ♔f7 53.g5 ♔g6 ½-½

Kasimdzhanov, Rustam (2670) – HYDRA
English Opening A30
Bilbao (4), 23.11.2005

1.♘f3 ♘f6 2.c4 b6 3.g3 c5 4.♗g2 ♗b7 5.0-0 e6 6.♘c3 ♗e7 7.d4 c×d4 8.♕×d4 d6 9.♖d1 a6 10.b3 ♘bd7 11.e4 ♕c8 12.♕e3 ♕c7 13.♗b2 0-0 14.♘d4 ♖ac8 15.h3 ♖fe8 16.♖e1 ♗f8 17.♖ad1 ♕b8 18.♖e2 h6 19.♕d2 ♘c5 20.♖de1 ♕a8 21.♔h2 ♖ed8 22.♕e3

22...d5

One of the typical freeing advances in the Hedgehog. But here White manages to keep control and a slight advantage. But to defeat the mighty H**YDRA** is another matter.

23.c×d5 e×d5 24.e5! ♘fe4 25.♖d1 b5 26.♖c2 ♕b8 27.♘ce2 ♖e8 28.f3 ♘f6 29.♘f5 ♘fd7 30.f4 g6 31.♘h4 ♘f6 32.♘d4 ♘fe4 33.♖dc1 ♕a7 34.♘e2 ♕b8 35.♘d4 ♕a7 36.♘e2 ♕b8 ½-½

Junior – Ponomariov, Ruslan (2704)
French Defense C18
Bilbao (4), 23.11.2005

1.e4 e6 2.d4 d5 3.♘c3 ♗b4 4.e5 c5 5.a3 ♗×c3+ 6.b×c3 ♕a5 7.♗d2 ♕a4 8.♕b1 c4

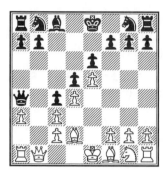

9.♘h3

9.h4 is played most often; usually JUNIOR likes to advance its rook's pawns. But White scores better with the game continuation which may be the reason for the choice.

9...f5!?

This takes JUNIOR out of its opening book. A clever choice!

10.♗e2 ♘c6 11.0-0?!

Quite tame. Now a very long maneuvering phase follows, until Ponomariov finds a good moment to open roads. 11.♘f4!? b6 12.h4 ♗d7 13.♗h5+ g6 14.♗f3 creates more pressure.

11...b6 12.♗h5+ g6 13.♗f3 ♗d7 14.♕c1 0-0-0 15.♘g5 ♖f8 16.h4 h6 17.♘h3 ♖f7 18.g3 ♖fh7 19.♗g2 ♘ge7 20.♖b1 ♔c7 21.♖e1 ♗c8 22.♗f3 ♗d7 23.♗e3 ♗c8 24.♕b2 ♗d7 25.♗c1 ♗e8 26.♗d2 ♗d7 27.♖ec1 ♗e8 28.♖a1 ♗d7 29.♖e1 ♗e8 30.♗g2 ♗d7 31.♗c1 ♗e8 32.♗e3 ♗d7 33.♗d2 ♗e8 34.♕b1 ♗d7 35.♕c1 ♗e8 36.♗f4 ♔c8 37.♖b1 ♗d7 38.♗d2 ♔c7 39.♗e3 ♗e8 40.♗f3 ♗d7 41.♗d2 ♗e8 42.♗f4 ♗d7 43.♖a1 ♗e8 44.♗d2 ♗d7 45.♖e3 ♗e8 46.♖b1 ♗f7 47.♖e2 ♗e8 48.♗g2 ♗d7 49.♕b2 ♖g8 50.♗h1 ♖gh8 51.♗f3 ♗e8 52.♗g2 ♗d7 53.♕c1 ♗e8 54.♗e3 ♗d7 55.♖a1

♗e8 56.♗f3 ♔d7 57.♖e1 ♔c7 58.♗f4 ♗d7 59.♕b2 ♖g8 60.♗d2 ♗e8 61.♕c1 ♖gh8 62.♕d1 ♖g8 63.♗e3 ♗d7 64.♕c1 ♖gh8 65.♗g2 ♔c8 66.♕d2 ♔c7 67.f3 ♗c8 68.♖e2 ♗d7 69.f4 ♖b8 70.♘f2 b5 71.♘d1 ♘c8 72.♖e1 ♘b6 73.♗f3 ♕a5 74.♕f2 ♘a4 75.♖b1 ♕a6 76.♗d2 ♕c8 77.♘e3 ♘e7 78.♔g2 ♗c6 79.♘d1 ♕f8 80.♘b2 ♘xb2 81.♖xb2 ♖b6 82.♔g1 ♗e8 83.♖bb1 ♘c6 84.♗c1 ♘d8

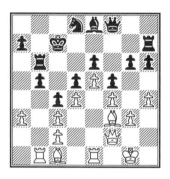

85.♔f1

The following transfer of the king to e3 is a bit strange for human eyes. Be that as it may, this position is not easy to play for White. Ponomariov's strategy has been a success. But to defeat the machine is another very difficult matter.

85...♘f7 86.♔e2 ♖g7 87.♕h2 ♕e7 88.♔e3 ♗c6 89.♖g1

89...g5!

Finally the time has come to open roads against White's king.

90.h×g5 h×g5 91.罝h1 罝b8 92.豐f2 罝h8 93.罝×h8 ②×h8 94.象b2 ②g6 95.罝g1 象e8 96.象c1 罝h7 97.f×g5 豐×g5+ 98.會e2 豐e7 99.會d1 ②f8 100.g4 f×g4 101.象×g4 ②d7 102. 豐g3

102...象h5?!

After this exchange it seems to be completely drawn. With 102...②b6 103.象h3 ②a4, Ponomariov could have pressed for a win.

103.象×h5 罝×h5 104.豐g6 罝f5 105.象e3 豐f7 106.豐×f7 罝×f7 107. 罝g6 ②f8 108.罝g8 會d7 109.會d2 會e8 110.象h6 罝f1 111.象g7 a6 112.會e2 罝f7 113.會e1 罝f3 114. 會d1 罝f1+ 115.會d2 a5 116.會e2 罝f7 117.象h6 a4 118.象g7 罝f5 119.罝h8 罝f7 120.象h6 罝f5 121. 象d2 罝f7 122.象e1?!

After the following exchange of rooks, only Black can play for a win, so it was better to play 122.象h6 and make a draw soon.

122...罝h7!? 123.罝×h7 ②×h7 124. 象h4 ②f8 125.會f3 ②d7 126.象g5 ②b8 127.會e2 會f7 128.象d8 ②c6 129.象b6 會g6 130.象c5 會f5 131. 會f3 ②d8 132.象d6 ②f7 133.象e7

會g6 134.會g4 ②h6+ 135.會f4 ②f5 136.象b4 會h5 137.象f8 會h4 138. 象d6 會h5 139.象f8 ②h4 140.會g3 ②g6 141.象d6 會g5 142.象c7 會f5 143.會f3 ②h8 144.象d8 ②f7 145. 象e7 會g6 146.會g4 ②h6+ 147.會f4 會h5 148.象d6 ②g4 149.會f3 會h4 150.象e7+ 會h5 151.象d6 ②h6 152.會f4 ②f5 153.象f8 ½-½

17
Additional Man-Machine Games (2000s)

Piket, Jeroen (2633) – FRITZ SSS
Reti Opening A07
Netherlands Championship (1), Rotterdam, 07.05.2000

1.g3 e5 2.象g2 d5 3.d3 ②f6 4.②f3 ②c6 5.0-0 象e7 6.c3 a5 7.豐c2 0-0 8.e4 d×e4 9.d×e4 象e6 10.罝d1 豐e8 11.象g5 罝d8 12.②bd2 ②d7 13.象f1 象×g5 14.②×g5 象g4 15.②gf3 豐e7 16.h3 象e6 17.②c4 豐f6 18.②fd2 豐h6 19.h4

19...f5!?

FRITZ opens roads. The dynamic advantage should compensate the resulting static weakness of the e-pawn.

20.e×f5 象×f5 21.象d3 象×d3

22.♕×d3 ♕h5?!

22...♘c5 23.♕e2 ♕g6 24.♘e3 b6 is more harmonious.

23.♘e3 ♔h8 24.♕c2 ♘c5 25.♘b3 ♖×d1+ 26.♖×d1 ♘e6

27.♖d5?!

The centralizing 27.♕e4 creates much more pressure, e.g., 27...♕e8 (27...♕e2 can be met by 28.♖d2 ♕e1+ 29.♔g2 ♘ed4 30.♕d3 e4 31.♕f1) 28.a4 with initiative in both cases.

27...♕f7 28.♕e2 b6 29.♖d1 a4 30.♘d2 ♘c5 31.♘dc4 e4 32.♖d5 ♘e7 33.♖d4 ♔g8

This is a sign that the computer sees no way to make progress.

34.a3 ♕e8 35.♘e5 ♘c8 36.♘5c4 b5 37.♘d2?!

Giving Black's knights the option to create some confusion by hopping around. 37.♘g2 is completely equal.

37...♘d6 38.♖d5 ♘d3 39.♘×e4 ♘c1 40.♕c2 ♘×e4 41.♕×c1 ♘×f2

41...♕e6!? was probably a better choice from the practical point of view, e.g., 42.♖×b5 ♘×f2 43.♕d2 ♘h3+ 44.♔g2 ♖f2+ 45.♕×f2 ♘×f2 46.♔×f2, and the position should be drawn; however defending against a queen is always difficult for a human.

42.♖f5!

Piket consistently exchanges attacking potential.

42...♖×f5 43.♘×f5 ♘g4 44.♕d2 h5 45.♘d4 c5 46.♘f3 ♕e3+ 47.♔g2 ♕e4 48.♕e1! ♕×e1 49.♘×e1 ♘e5 ½-½

Van den Doel, Erik (2522) – Fritz SSS

English Opening A22
Netherlands Championship (3), Rotterdam, 09.05.2000

1.c4 ♘f6 2.♘c3 e5 3.e4?! ♗c5 4.g3 0-0 5.♗g2 ♘c6 6.♘ge2 d6

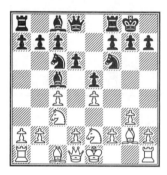

7.d3??

7.0-0 was obligatory when White can hope to realize his anti-computer strategy in the long run.

7...♘g4 8.0-0 f5 9.♘a4?!

Allows a mighty blow but it is too late anyway as 9.h3 is met by 9...f4! 10.h×g4 ♗×g4 with a winning attack. In such positions computers are like a shark or bloodhound that has caught the scent.

9...♘×f2!!

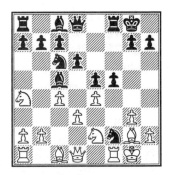

Thomas Luther (2000): "As soon as things are getting tactical, Fritz's strength shoots up from ELO 1000 to 3000. White is already lost."

10.♖×f2 ♗×f2+ 11.♔×f2 f4!

John van der Wiel (in Ree (2000)): "This is what separates today's Fritz from the ancient programs, which would doubtlessly have played 11...f×e4 seeing another pawn."

12.g×f4

12.♘g1!? f×g3+ 13.♔×g3 ♕e8 14.h4 ♕g6+ 15.♔h2 ♖f2 16.♗g5 ♗d7 17.♔g3 ♖af8–+ ; 12.♗f3? f×g3+ 13.♔×g3 ♕f6 14.♘g1 ♕g6+ 15.♔f2 ♘d4 16.♗e3 ♘×f3 17.♘×f3 ♗g4–+ .

12...e×f4 13.♘g1?

13.♘×f4 g5 14.♕h5 g×f4 15.♗f3 offers more resistance but White is already defending a lost cause.

13...♕h4+ 14.♔f1 f3!

The final blow. van der Wiel writes (Ree 2000), "After this Fritz suffered a brief system breakdown ('Just in time,' commented van den Doel)."

15.♘×f3

15.♗e3 ♗g4–+ .

15...♕×h2 0–1

Fritz SSS – Reinderman, Dimitri (2561)
King's Indian Defense E82
Netherlands Championship (4), Rotterdam 10.05.2000

1.d4 ♘f6 2.c4 g6 3.♘c3 ♗g7 4.e4 d6 5.f3 0-0 6.♗e3 b6

To throw Fritz out of its opening book.

7.♗d3 e5 8.d×e5?!

This opens the position somewhat but looks can be deceiving as the d-file with be closed by the knights soon. 8.d5 is of course called for if White were a human player.

8...d×e5 9.♘ge2 c5 10.♕d2 ♘c6 11.♖d1 ♘d4 12.♗g5 ♗b7 13.♘d5 ♕d6 14.♘×d4 c×d4 15.♘×f6+?!

15.0-0 is more natural.

15...♗×f6 16.0-0 ♗×g5 17.♕×g5 ♔g7 18.f4 f6 19.♕h4 ♖ae8 20.f5 ♕e7 21.♕g3 g5 22.a3 h5 23.♕f3 ♔h6 24.♗e2 g4 25.♕d3 ♕g7 26.♖de1 ♕g5

Black is slightly better but probably did not have much time left and decided to draw in view of his slightly exposed king. ½-½

Nijboer, Friso (2540) – Fritz SSS
Scandinavian Defense B01
Netherlands Championship (5), Rotterdam, 12.05.2000

1.e4 d5 2.e×d5 ♘f6 3.♘f3 ♘×d5

4.d4 ♗f5 5.♗e2 e6 6.0-0 ♗e7 7.c4 ♘b6 8.♘c3 0-0 9.♗e3 ♘c6 10.h3 ♗f6 11.♕d2 ♗g6 12.♖fd1 ♖e8 13.♖ac1 ♕e7 14.c5!

Leading to a closed position in which White has full control and Black no easy short term plans.

14...♘d5 15.♘×d5 e×d5 16.b4 a6 17.a3 ♕d7 18.♖e1 ♖e7 19.a4 ♘a7

19...a5 can be met by 20.b5 ♘b4 21.c6.

20.♖a1 ♖ae8 21.♖a3 ♖e4

FRITZ does not know what to do.

22.♗d3 ♖4e6 23.♗f1 ♘c6 24.♖ea1

Against a human, Nijboer would have played the direct 24.b5 of course.

24...♗e4 25.♘h2

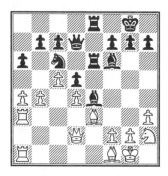

25...♗e7?

This move is hard to understand from the human point of view and the source of the coming problems where Nijboer can press almost for free. One alternative is 25...h5, to play against the h2-knight, e.g., 26.b5 ♘e7 27.♗g5 ♗×g5 28.♕×g5 ♘f5 29.f3 ♘×d4 30.f×e4 ♖e5 31.♕c1 d×e4 32.b×a6 b×a6 33.♗×a6 ♕e7 and Black has much better practical chances than in the game where chaos rules.

26.b5 ♘a7 27.♖b3 ♗h4 28.♘g4 ♕d8 29.♖a2 b6 30.c×b6 ♖×b6

31.♘e5 ♗e7?! 32.♖ab2 a×b5 33.♕a5 ♕a8 34.a×b5 ♕b7 35.♖a2 ♘c8 36.♘d7 ♖e6?! 37.♕a8

37.♗f4! is objectively stronger, but it is hard to criticize Nijboer as his choice is simpler and safer.

37...♕×a8 38.♖×a8 ♗d6

39.♘c5?

A tactical error. After the preparatory 39.♖c3, White is clearly better.

39...♗×c5 40.d×c5 d4! 41.♖×c8 ♖×c8 42.♗×d4 ♖d8 ½-½

Even if White might be slightly better after 43.♖b4, under the circumstances, it is almost impossible to beat the machine from this position and so a draw was agreed.

FRITZ SSS – Grooten, Herman (2393)
Czech Benoni A44
Netherlands Championship (6), Rotterdam, 13.05.2000

1.d4 c5! 2.d5?! e5

A very good choice against FRITZ.

3.e4 d6 4.♘c3 ♗e7 5.♘f3 a6 6.a4 ♗g4 7.♗e2 b6 8.♘d2! ♗c8 9.♘c4 ♘f6

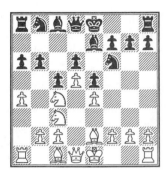

10.a5?

"Overcompensating for its 8th move, which appeared to show deep understanding. First White avoided ♗g4×f3, now he goes for the bishop after all, helping Black on the queenside in the process" (Van der Wiel in Ree (2000)). 10.f4! (Luther 2000) is much stronger and gives Black headaches.

10...b5 11.♘b6 ♖a7 12.♘×c8 ♕×c8 13.♕d3 0-0 14.♘f3 ♘e8 15.0-0 ♕d8 16.♕h5

Luther (2000): "The queen moves are typical for chess programs. FRITZ doesn't know what to do."

16...h6 17.♘d1 ♗g5 18.♘e3 g6 19.♕h3 ♘f6 20.♕f3?

20.g3! ♘e4 21.f3 ♗×e3+ 22.♗×e3 ♘f6 23.♗×h6 ♖e8 24.c4 gives White's bishops much better prospects.

20...♘h7 21.c4 ♕d7 22.♗d3 b4 23.♗c2 h5 24.♕d1 h4 25.h3?

Taking away many options. 25.g3 is a much better choice.

25...♕d8 26.b3 ♘d7 27.♖e1?!

FRITZ has absolutely no clue what to do in the long-term and just moves around aimlessly.

27...♘df6 28.♗b1 ♗f4 29.♗b2 ♕e7 30.♗c2

30...♔h8?!

Luther (2000): "Black has achieved a lot. But in order to win this position, he has to open up the kingside. To this purpose I find the king to be badly placed on h8. My suggestion would be a king's march to the queenside, followed by realizing f7-f5. FRITZ would continue playing passively."

31.♘g4 ♘g8 32.♕e2 ♕g5 33.♘h2 ♕h6 34.♖ad1

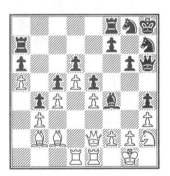

34...f5!?

Luther (2000): "Brave! Opening the position is playing into FRITZ's chips."

35.♔h1 ♖af7 36.e×f5 g×f5 37.♖g1 ♖g7 38.♘f3

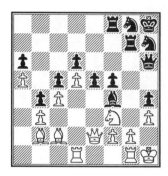

38...♕f6?

This destroys the harmony of Black's army. 38...♘e7 39.♘e1 ♘f6 40.♘d3 ♘g6 is better and more or less equal.

39.♘e1!

Now the computer has found a clear, short-term way to open the game.

39...♘e7 40.♘d3 ♘g6 41.g3 ♗h6 42.f4!

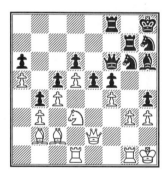

Opens the floodgates. To defend such a position under time pressure is almost impossible against a machine.

42...h×g3 43.f×e5 ♕h4! 44.♕g2 f4?!

44...♘xe5 45.♘xe5 dxe5 46.♗xe5 f4 47.♖df1 ♕h5 48.♗xg7+ ♗xg7 49.♗xh7 ♕xh7 50.♖f3 ♗e5 is probably better as Black can keep his powerful pawn duo.

45.e6?

FRITZ overestimates the value of the protected passed e-pawn. It should

simply grab the d-pawn with 45.exd6 ♘g5 46.♘xf4 ♖xf4 47.♗xg7+ ♗xg7 48.♕xg3 ♘xh3 49.♕xh4+ ♖xh4 50.♖ge1 ±.

45...♘f6

45...♘g5 was the alternative: 46.♘xf4 ♘xf4 (46...♖xf4? 47.♗xg7+ ♗xg7 48.♕xg3 ♖f3 49.♕xh4 ♘xh4 50.♖d3 ±) 47.♕xg3 ♕xh3+ 48.♕xh3 ♘gxh3= (Luther 2000).

46.♖df1

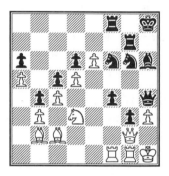

46...♕g5?!

Thomas Luther's 46...♕h5 and John van der Wiel's 46...♘g4 were both better practical choices and should lead to dynamic equality.

47.♘e1 ♘h4?

47...♕h4 48.♘f3 ♕h5 was the last chance to fight. Then it is not easy for White to break through. But given the circumstances it was almost impossible for Gooten to defend now.

48.♕e2 ♖e7

48...f3? 49.♖xf3 ♘xf3 50.♘xf3 +−.

49.♘g2 f3?

This allows the direct elimination of both kingside pawns for which the exchange is a cheap price to pay. But 49...♘xg2 50.♗xg2 ♗g8 51.♕f3 is also lost in the long run.

50.♖×f3! ♘×f3 51.♕×f3 ♗g7

51...♔g8 52.♗c1 ♕g7 53.♘e3 ♗xe3 54.♗xe3 ♘e8 55.♕h5+– .

52.♗c1 ♕h5 53.♕xg3 ♖g8 54.♘f4 ♗h6 55.♕xg8+ ♘xg8 56.♘xh5 ♗xc1 57.♖xc1 1-0

Kongstad (2003) sums this game up in the spirit of 2003: "A very typical man vs. machine game. At first the human outplays the computer positionally, and then outplays himself tactically... The computer plays the first part of the game like a total amateur, but wakes up to execute an elegant finish with very precise calculations."

Fʀɪᴛᴢ SSS – Tiviakov, Sergei (2567)
Sicilian Defense B51
Netherlands Championship (8), Rotterdam,
15.05.2000

All quotes are from Tiviakov (2000).

1.e4 c5 2.♘f3 ♘c6 3.♗b5 d6 4.0-0 ♗d7 5.c3 ♘f6 6.♖e1 a6 7.♗f1 ♗g4 8.h3 ♗h5 9.d3 e6 10.♘bd2 ♗e7 11.g4 ♗g6 12.♘h4 ♘d7 13.♘g2 h6 14.♘f4 ♗h7 15.♗g2 0-0

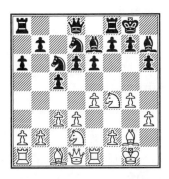

"Black has reached an optimal setup. According to David Bronstein, Black in the game against a computer must keep his pieces on the last 3 ranks, avoiding direct contact with the silicon opponent, waiting for him in the point of the eventual breakthrough. I've been trying

to follow the advice of D. Bronstein here."

16.♘f3 ♘de5 17.♗e3 ♘xf3+ 18.♕xf3 ♗g5 19.♖ed1 ♖c8 20.♕g3 ♘e5 21.b3 ♖e8 22.♘e2 ♗h4!? 23.♕h2 b5 24.d4 cxd4 25.♖xd4 ♕c7 26.♖ad1 ♗e7?! 27.♕g3 ♘d7

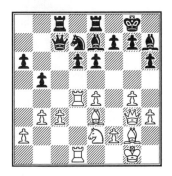

28.g5?!

"Positionally Fʀɪᴛᴢ is very weak, when he sees the opportunity to open the line, he does it." 28.h4 is called for.

28...hxg5 29.♗xg5 ♗f8 30.♖4d3 ♘c5 31.♖e3 ♔h8! 32.♗h4 e5 33.♕g4 ♕d7!?

A good anti-computer move. Against a human Tiviakov would probably have played 33...♘e6, which is also good for Black.

34.♕xd7 ♘xd7 35.♔f1?!

A very strange typical computer move for the time. But Black's position is easier to play in any case as he has a clear plan.

35...f6 36.♗g3 ♘c5?!

The direct 36...♗g8 followed by advancing the a-pawn is more precise.

37.h4 ♖c6 38.♗h2?! ♗g8 39.h5 a5 40.♗h3 ♖c7!

Good prophylaxis before continuing the play on the queenside.

453

41.♔e1

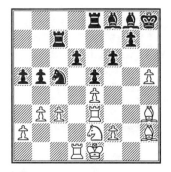

"Until this very moment the computer was still evaluating the position as at least not worse for him, completely not understanding what Black was aiming for."

41...a4

"And only after this move FRITZ suddenly understood it had the much worse position with the evaluation dropping from around 0.00 to something around –1.00."

42.b4 ♘d7 43.♘c1 ♘b6 44.♗f1 ♘c4 45.♖g3

45...♗e6?

Unnecessary prophylaxis. The immediate 45...♖ec8 was called for as 46.♗h3 can be met by 46...♘b2 (Tiviakov 2000).

46.♗h3 ♗f7

A difficult decision, as the alternative

46...♗xh3 47.♖xh3 ♘b6 is also better for Black and less complex.

47.♗f5 ♖b8!? 48.♖h3 ♖b6 49.f4 ♖bc6 50.♘e2 ♔g8?! 51.♗g6 ♗e6 52.f5?!

52.♗f5 is easier to play for FRITZ.

52...♗d7 53.♔f2

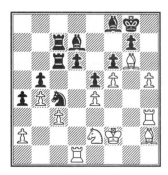

53...♔h8?!

In the game this works well but objectively it is not good as the king is not safe here. From the modern computer point of view, 53...♘b2 54.♖g1 ♖c4 55.h6 gxh6 56.♖hg3 ♗c8 is called for and Black is clearly better. But it is understandable that Tiviakov did not play this.

54.♖g3?

54.♗g3! ♘b2 55.♖g1, to attack with h6, is much more dynamic.

54...♘b2 55.♖d2 a3

56.♔g2?

After this slow move Black is strategically winning as White will be completely passive so that the position is relatively easy to play for a human. Fritz should try 56.h6! g×h6 57.♗f7 to confuse matters. Black is still better, but White has tactical counterplay.

56...♖c4 57.♖e3 ♗c6 58.♔f3 ♘a4 59.♗g1 ♘b6 60.♔g3 ♖b7 61.♔f3 ♔g8!

Such slow moves are good against a program when it has no clear short-term concept.

62.♔f2?!

"This is the last move one would expect to see from the computer. Fritz voluntarily, but not immediately necessarily, gives up a central pawn for nothing!!! Any human player, any other computer program would keep trying to defend it." And indeed it is very seldom that a machine violates the principles "do not rush and do not give up material unnecessarily." After 62.♖d1 d5 (62... ♖c7!?) 63.♔f2 d×e4 64.♔e1, for example, Black's job is much harder.

62...♖×e4

62...♗×e4 wins quicker but is also more tactical, e.g., 63.♗e8 ♘a4 64.♖×e4 ♖×e4 65.♗c6 ♖×e2+ 66.♔×e2 ♘c3+ 67.♔d3 ♖c7 68.♔×c3 ♖×c6+ 69.♔b3

♖c1 70.♗a7 ♖b1+ 71.♔×a3 g6 72.f×g6 ♗h6−+ .

63.♗e8 ♖c4 64.♗×c6 ♖×c6 65.♖g3 ♔f7

65...d5?! 66.♔f1 makes it easier for the computer.

66.♔e1 ♘a4 67.♖d5 ♖c4 68.♗f2 ♔e8 69.♖dd3 ♘b2 70.♖d2 ♖e4 71.♔f1 ♔d7 72.♖g6

72...♔e7!?

Tiviakov wants to stop any counterplay and retreats. 72...♔c6 73.h6 g×h6 74.♖×f6 ♘c4 should win as well but the tactical complications should be avoided if possible.

73.♖d5 ♔f7 74.♖g3 ♗e7 75.♖g6 ♗f8 76.♖g3 ♖c4 77.♖d2 ♖c8 78.♔g2 ♗e7 79.♖d5 ♖h8 80.♖h3 ♔e8 81.♖h4 ♔d7 82.♔f3!

"It is incredible how good computer defends his position. All his pieces are

455

being constantly reorganized, achieving full harmony. If FRITZ could have played so in other stages of the game!"

82...♔c6 83.♔e4 ♖bb8

83...♗d8!?.

84.♗a7 ♖a8 85.♗f2 ♖h7 86.♖h1 ♘c4 87.♘g3 ♗d8 88.♖hd1 ♗c7 89.♔f3 ♖d8 90.♔g4 ♗b6 91.♗×b6 ♔×b6!

91...♘×b6? is bad technique because of 92.♖c5+ d×c5 93.♖×d8 ♔c7 94.♖d1. In the game Black has the clear plan to achieve the advance d5, which cannot be stopped in the long run.

92.♖1d3 ♖hh8 93.♔f3 ♔c6 94.♖d1 ♘b6 95.♖5d3 d5

Tiviakov has managed to realize his main objective. Now it is clear that he is winning. But to defeat a computer is by no means easy.

96.♔e2 ♖c8 97.♔e1 ♔b7 98.♔f2 ♖c4 99.♔g2 ♖f4 100.♖f1 ♖×f1

It is easier to keep the active rook with 100...♖g4. But Black is winning both ways.

101.♔×f1 ♔c6 102.♔e2 ♘a4 103. ♔d2 e4 104.♖d4 ♘b2 105.♔e3 ♖e8 106.♔f4 ♔d6 107.♖d2 ♘d3+ 108.♔g4?! ♔e5?!

108...♖c8 109.♘e2 ♔e5–+ with a deadly zugzwang is easier.

109.♖g2 ♘b2 110.♘e2 ♘d1 111. ♖g3 ♖c8 112.♔h3 ♖c7

112...♔×f5 113.♖×g7 ♘×c3 wins as well but gives White counterplay.

113.♔g2

Tiviakov (2000) describes a common problem that happens when the computer is dependent on a third party to play its moves:

> Somewhere around here (I don't remember when exactly) the draw had been offered by the FRITZ SSS* operator Frans Morsch. I have had only a little bit more than 2 minutes on my clock and the draw offer completely ruined my concentration, making me to commit a blunder on the 115th move. I find the draw offer insulting because of the following points: (1) Under no circumstances should a player offer a draw in a lost position. It is considered unethical. (2) Under no circumstances should a player offer a draw at the moment when the opponent is in time-trouble. The draw offer destroys the concentration of a player and takes away a lot of valuable time necessary to make the decision. The draw offer is considered unethical. (3) According to the Quick Play Finish Rules the player who has the advantage has the right to claim the draw when he has less than 2 minutes on his clock. I could have always claimed the draw at any moment after if I wished to do so. (4) Frans Morsch is an operator, not a player. His task is only to input and make the moves on the board. Under no circumstances should he try to disturb a player, trying to influence the outcome of the game. I was shocked, my concentration was gone, but still I continued playing.

113...♖b7 114.♘d4 e3

Of course a computer would not allow 114...♘xc3?? if it worked, so 115.♘c6+ ♚d6? 116.♖xc3 ♖c7? 117.♘d4+−.

115.♘e2

115...♚xf5?

Too greedy. Black should put everything on his strongest trump the passed e-pawn with 115...♚e4! which wins comfortably.

116.♚f3! ♚e5 117.♖g1 ♘b2? ½-½

117...♘f2 118.♚xe3 ♘e4 still gives Black good winning chances but not under the circumstances because of Tiviakov's lack of time. He protested and claimed the full point due to Morsch's draw offer that had disturbed him. But the appeals committee turned it down and the draw stood as result.

De Vreugt, Dennis (2498) – Fritz SSS
Caro-Kann Defense, Advance B12
Netherlands Championship (9), Rotterdam,
17.05.2000

1.e4 c6 2.d4 d5 3.e5 ♗f5 4.♘f3 e6 5.♗e2 c5 6.♗e3 cxd4 7.♘xd4 ♘e7 8.c4 ♘bc6 9.♘c3?

9.♕a4 is the main line.

9...♘xd4 10.♗xd4 dxc4 11.♕a4+ ♘c6 12.♖d1 ♗d3 13.♗xd3 cxd3 14.♖xd3

14.♗e3 ♗b4 15.♕b5 0-0 16.f4 ♕a5 17.♕xa5 ♗xa5 18.♖xd3 ♘b4 is also unpleasant.

14...♗c5 15.♘e4 ♗xd4 16.♘d6+ ♚f8 17.♖xd4 ♘xd4 18.♕xd4 ♕a5+ 19.♚e2 ♚g8

20.h4?

Inserting the moves with the h-pawns helps Black a lot as the h8-rook can be activated via h6. 20.♖c1 was the last chance to fight.

20...h5 21.♖h3 ♕xa2 22.♖f3 ♕a6+ 23.♚e1 ♖d8 24.♖a3

24.♖xf7 ♖h6−+.

24...♕c6 25.♕f4 f6 26.♖xa7 ♖h6 27.♖xb7 ♖g6 28.♕e4 ♖xd6 29.♕xg6 ♕c1+ 30.♚e2 ♕d2+ 31.♚f3 ♖d3+ 0-1

Van der Wiel, John (2558) – Fritz SSS
Queen's Pawn Game D00
Netherlands Championship (11), Rotterdam,
19.05.2000

John van der Wiel had never lost to a computer program before using normal time controls. He had extensive experience playing computers as a result of playing in numerous AEGON events. He comments on what it is like to play the computer (Van der Wiel 2000): "Obviously, if you meet the computer in an open battle, with many tactical ideas and concrete calculations, you try to fight it with its strongest weapons and you might well have an opponent who plays the game at 2700 strength or better. However in certain other types of positions the quality of the computer's moves doesn't rise above, say, 1800!"

1.d4 d5 2.c3 ♘f6 3.♗g5 ♘e4 4.♗f4 g5 5.♗c1 h6 6.e3 ♗g7 7.♗d3 ♘d7?! 8.c4! ♘df6 9.f3 ♘d6 10.c5 ♘f5 11.♘e2 g4?!

It was better to aim for e5 in the long run.

12.f4 ♕d7 13.♘bc3 ♕e6 14.♕d2 ♗d7 15.b4 h5 16.a4

16...0-0-0??

Luther (2000): "Fritz castles into disaster. I guess every human would very much respect White's deployment on the queenside. Such emotions are unknown to Fritz. In this respect we humans will always be superior to computers. It's interesting that castling long features in nearly all variations calculated by Fritz."

Van der Wiel (2000): "This didn't surprise me that much (from a human opponent it would have)."

17.♔d1 h4 18.b5 ♔b8 19.♖b1

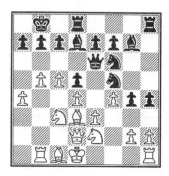

19...h3?!

Van der Wiel (2000): "This is the bonus for playing 'slow' moves against a computer, when it doesn't really have a plan. It selects a move which wins after all replies but one and fails to see the long-term choices that it loses."

20.g3 ♗e8 21.a5 ♔a8?

The king is not really safe here. Black should try to use his advantage in development by 21...♘e4 22.♘xe4 dxe4 23.♗c2 c6, to create more direct play before White can consolidate completely.

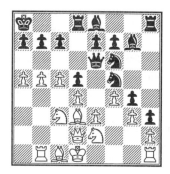

22.♔e1!

Luther (2000): "There is no need for White to rush things up. After even the kingside has been closed, [Van der Wiel] takes his time to move his king to f2 and then gets queen and bishop c1 into play. In due course White's attack on the queenside will be decisive.

Computer programs are very vulnerable to such attacks on the king which can be planned long in advance."

22...♗d7 23.♔f2 a6

This gives White many additional options to open the queenside, but just waiting by 23...♗c8 24.♕c2 ♔b8 25.♗d2 is also insufficient.

24.♕c2 ♖b8 25.♗d2!

Van der Wiel plays strong and simple chess.

25...a×b5 26.♘×b5 ♗×b5 27.♖×b5 ♘e4+ 28.♗×e4 ♕×e4

28...d×e4 29.♖hb1 ♖hd8 30.♖b6!+− (Luther 2000).

29.♕×e4 d×e4 30.♘c3 e6 31.♘×e4 ♘e7 32.♘g5 ♖hf8

32...♗f6!?, to exchange the bishop for the knight, was a better practical chance but loses as well in the long run of course.

33.♖hb1 ♔a7 34.a6!

A strong liquidation into an easily won endgame.

34...b×a6

34...b6 35.♗b4+− .

35.♖×b8 ♖×b8 36.♖×b8 ♔×b8 37.♘×f7 ♔c8 38.♘g5 ♔d7 39.♔e2 ♘f5 40.♘e4 ♔c6 41.♘f2 ♘h6 42.♗a5 ♗f6 43.♔d3 ♔d7 44.e4 ♗g7 45.♔c4 ♔c6 46.♗d2 1-0

A very well played anti-computer game. Nowadays this is much more difficult as the programs evaluate levers in closed positions better.

Fritz/Primergy K800 – Kramnik, Vladimir (2758)

English Opening A27
Frankfurt match (5), 18.06.2000

A rapid chess contest that brings out the best in humankind. Some of the comments are based on Baburin (2000).

1.c4 e5 2.♘c3 ♘c6 3.♘f3 f5 4.d4 e4 5.♘g5 ♗b4 6.♘h3 ♘f6 7.e3 ♗×c3+ 8.b×c3 d6 9.♘f4 0-0 10.h4 ♕e7?!

This gives Fritz the opportunity to open the position.

11.c5! ♘d8

11...d×c5? runs into 12.♗c4+ ♔h8 13.h5 ♘g8 14.♗a3 b6 15.♗×g8 ♔×g8 16.♘g6±.

12.♕b3+ ♘e6 13.♗c4 ♖e8 14.♗a3

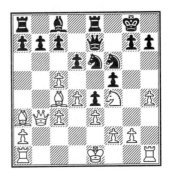

14...♔h8!?

In the game, this works out very good as Fritz gets too greedy. 14...♖b8 is objectively preferable but White still has a strong initiative.

15.♗×e6 ♗×e6 16.♕×b7 d5 17.♖b1 ♗f7 18.♖b3?!

After 18.h5, White is clearly better.

18...♖ec8 19.c6?! ♕d8 20.♕a6

20.♕h4 ♘h5 21.♕e7 is much safer of course.

20...♘h5 21.♘×h5 ♗×h5 22.♖b7 ♕f6

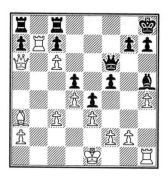

23.0-0?!

From a human point of view, this move is strange as White's king will always be in danger on the kingside. Objectively it is probably still playable.

23...h6!?

23...♕×h4? simply does not work against a machine and indeed it runs into 24.♗d6 c×d6 25.♖×a7 ♖ab8 26.c7+− .

24.♗c5?!

Hunting queenside pawns is not the order of the day. 24.♖fb1 is more natural.

24...♔h7!?

A typical human prophylactic move to try to preserve one rook.

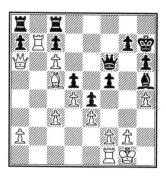

25.♗×a7?

As White must try to exchange attacking potential, this is the wrong way around. 25.♖×a7 seems to lead to a

draw more or less by force: 25...♕×h4 26.♖×a8 ♖×a8 27.♕b7 (27.♗e7!?) 27... ♕d8 28.♗e7 ♕×e7 29.♕×a8 ♗f3 30.g3 f4 31.♕c8 ♕g5 32.♔h2=.

25...♕×h4 26.♖fb1

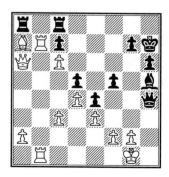

26...♗f3!!

A thunderous blow – relatively easy for a human but not so for a computer, especially from a distance when its searchlight does not shine so brightly.

27.♕f1

27.g×f3? e×f3 28.♕d3 (28.♕f1 ♖e8−+) 28...♖f8−+ .

27...♖e8

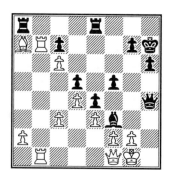

28.♗b8?

Running into a strong exchange sacrifice, something that computer programs of the time had difficulty in properly assessing. Nowadays they handle it better, but it is still one of its Achilles' Heels. Not 28.♖b8? ♖e6 29.♖×a8 ♖g6 30.♖bb8

Ξg5–+. The last chance was 28.Ξ×c7! but it is unlikely that White can survive after 28...Ξe6 29.$\triangle$b8 (29.Ξ×g7+? $\triangleq$×g7 30.$\triangle$b8 $\triangledown$g4 31.$\triangle$e5+ Ξ×e5 32.d×e5 $\triangle$e2–+) 29...Ξg6 30.Ξ×g7+ Ξ×g7 31.$\triangle$g3 $\triangledown$h5 as its pawns are not strong enough.

28...Ξa×b8! 29.Ξ×b8 Ξe6!

Finally all of Kramnik's long-term preparations pay off and his rook joins the party with decisive effect.

30.Ξf8 Ξg6 31.Ξ×f5

31.Ξbb8 Ξg5–+.

31...Ξ×g2+ 32.$\triangledown$×g2 $\triangle$×g2 0–1

Kongsted (2003): "After the game one of the ChessBase programmers was quoted as saying that the FRITZ king-safety evaluation was not optimized for rapid games as the program is usually tuned to compete with other programs about being number one on the computer rating list (apparently he considered king safety to be less important in computer versus computer games)."

In 2002, Dutch Grandmaster Loek van Wely played a four-game match against Ed Schröder's program, REBEL, a former World Computer Chess Champion.

REBEL CENTURY – Van Wely, Loek (2697)
French Defense C10
Maastricht match (1), 19.02.2002

This match was not that typical of carbon versus silicon battles. It was more typical of van Wely's aggressive approach. He was well prepared with White and managed to win both games. REBEL also showed a few typical computer weaknesses from the early computer-chess days.

1.e4 e6 2.d4 d5 3.$\triangle$c3 a6 4.$\triangle$d3

$\triangle$f6 5.$\triangle$f3 $\triangle$e7 6.0-0 c6 7.Ξe1 b5 8.$\triangle$e5 $\triangle$b7 9.$\triangledown$f3 0-0

10.e×d5?!

The direct 10.$\triangledown$h3 is better, e.g., 10...d×e4 11.$\triangle$×e4 $\triangle$×e4 12.$\triangle$×e4 f5 13.c3 f×e4 14.$\triangledown$×e6+ $\triangleq$h8 15.$\triangle$f7+ Ξ×f7 (15...$\triangleq$g8?? runs up against the famous 16.$\triangle$h6+ $\triangleq$h8 17.$\triangledown$g8+ Ξ×g8 18.$\triangle$f7#) 16.$\triangledown$×f7 $\triangledown$f8 17.$\triangledown$e6 c5 18.d5 and White is for choice. But evaluating such imbalances as rook, pawn and initiative against bishop and knight is not so easy of course.

10...c×d5 11.$\triangledown$h3 $\triangle$c6 12.$\triangle$g5 g6

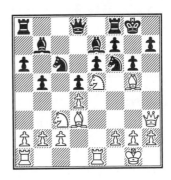

13.$\triangle$h6?

REBEL overrates winning the exchange. 13.$\triangledown$h4 gives it the initiative.

13...$\triangle$×d4 14.$\triangle$×f8 $\triangle$×f8 15.a4 b4 16.$\triangle$e2 $\triangle$×e2+

16...$\triangle$c6 17.$\triangle$×c6 $\triangle$×c6 18.$\triangle$d4 $\triangle$b7 is a bit more precise and Black is slightly better.

**17.♖×e2 ♘e4 18.♖d1 ♛c7
19.♗×e4 d×e4 20.♘g4**

20...♗g7?

Too optimistic. 20...♗e7 21.♛g3 ♖c8 is more or less equal.

**21.♖ed2 ♗d5 22.♘e3 ♗c6
23.♛h4 ♗×b2 24.♖d8+ ♖×d8**

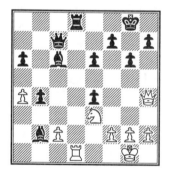

25.♖×d8+?!

This leads by force to a drawn endgame. 25.♛×d8+!? ♛×d8 26.♖×d8+ ♚g7 27.♖d6 ♗×a4 28.♖×a6 ♗e8 29.♘c4 ♗d4 30.♘d6 offers better winning chances.

25...♚g7 26.♘g4 ♛f4!

The only defense.

**27.♖g8+ ♚×g8 28.♘h6+ ♛×h6
29.♛×h6 ♗×a4 30.♛f4 ♗×c2
31.♛b8+ ♚g7 32.♛×b4 ♗f6
33.♛d6 ♗d3 34.f3 h5 35.♚f2 a5**

**36.♛d7 a4 37.♛×a4 e×f3 38.g×f3
g5 39.♛b4 ♗f5 40.♚g2 g4 41.f4
h4 42.♚f2 h3 43.♛e2 ♚g6**

43...g3 44.h×g3 h2 45.♛b7 ♗d4=.

**44.♛f8 ♗g7 45.♛d8 ♗f6 46.♛g8+
♗g7 47.♚e3 ♚f6 48.♛d8+ ♚g6
49.♚f2 ♗f6 50.♛g8+ ♗g7 51.♚g3
♚f6 52.♚h4 ♚g6 53.♛c8 e5**

53...♗f6+ 54.♚g3 ♚h5 55.♚f2=.

**54.♛c6+ ♗f6+ 55.♚g3 e×f4+
56.♚×f4 ♗e6 57.♛e4+ ♚h6
58.♛d3 ♗g5+ 59.♚e5 ♚g7
60.♛e4 ♗d8 61.♚d6 ♗f6 62.♚c7
♚h6 63.♚c6 ♚g5 64.♚d6 ♗f5
65.♛c6 ♗e6 66.♛c2 ♗f5 67.♛e2
♚g6 68.♚c5 ♗g7 69.♛a6+ ♗e6
70.♛d6 ♗b2 71.♚c6 ♗g7 72.♚c7
♚f5 73.♛d3+ ♚f4 74.♛d2+
♚f3 75.♚d6 ♗f8+ 76.♚c6
♗e7 77.♛d3+ ♚g2 78.♛g3+
♚f1 79.♚b6 ♗f8 80.♛c3 ♚g2
81.♛d2+ ♚g1 82.♛f4 ♗e7
83.♛g3+ ♚f1 84.♚c6 ♗f8
85.♛f4+ ♚g2 86.♚b5 ♚g1
87.♛e5 ♚g2 88.♛g3+ ♚f1 89.♚c7
♗h6 90.♛c3 ♚e2 91.♛c2+ ♗d2
92.♚c6 ♚e1 93.♛d3 ♗h6 94.♚c5
♚f2 95.♛g3+ ♚e2 96.♚d4 ♗g7+
97.♚e4 ♗h6 98.♛e5**

98...♗d2?

Probably fatigued, van Wely blunders. 98...♗f8 draws.

99.♔d4+ ♔f1 100.♔d3 ♗h6

100...♗e1 101.♕e2++−.

101.♕f6+ ♔g2 102.♕×h6 ♔×h2 103.♕d2+ ♔g1 104.♔e3 g3 105. ♔f3 1-0

Van Wely, Loek (2697) – REBEL CENTURY
Queen's Pawn Game A46
Maastricht match (2), 20.02.2002

1.d4 ♘f6 2.c3 e6 3.♗g5 h6 4.♗h4 b6 5.♘d2 ♗b7 6.e3 ♗e7 7.♘gf3 c5 8.♗d3 0-0?! 9.♕e2 d5 10.♘e5 ♘c6 11.f4 ♘e4 12.♗g3!?

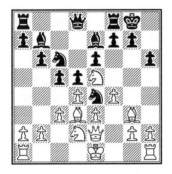

Against a human, this would probably not be a good move. But here it works as REBEL exchanges on g3 to get the bishop pair and to weaken White's pawns. But these factors are not relevant as White will just attack on the kingside. Van Wely had prepared this novelty, deviating from 12.♗×e7 ♘×e7 13.0-0 f6 14.♘g4 ♘×d2 15.♕×d2 ♘f5 16.♖f3 ♖c8 17.♖af1 van der Wiel-REBEL CENTURY 3.0, Match Maastricht 2001, when White was slightly better but the game was later drawn.

12...♘×g3?

12...f5 or 12...♘×e5 should be played.

13.h×g3 ♖c8?! 14.♘df3 ♗d6?!

Now White's attack plays itself; from a human point of view 14...♘×e5 was necessary.

15.g4 f6 16.♘g6 ♖f7 17.g5 ♖cc7 18.g×h6 g×h6 19.♖×h6 ♖h7 20.♖×h7 ♖×h7 21.0-0-0 c4 22.♗c2 ♕e8 23.g4 ♖h6 24.♘fh4 ♖h7 25.♔g2 ♘d8 26.♖h1 b5 27.♘f3 ♖×h1+ 28.♕×h1 ♘f7 29.♕h5 ♕d7 30.♘gh4 ♘h8 31.g5 f5 32.♘e5 ♗×e5 33.d×e5

33.f×e5 ♗c8 34.g6 ♕e7 35.♘g2+− is easier but van Wely continues to play simple chess and avoids complications.

33...♗c8 34.♘f3 ♕f7 35.♕h6 ♕g6 36.♕×g6+ ♘×g6 37.♘d4 ♗d7 38.b3 ♔g7 39.♗d1 ♘e7 40.♔b2 ♔g6 41.♗e2 ♘c8 42.a4! a6 43.a×b5 a×b5 44.♔a3 ♘e7 45.♔b4 ♘c6+ 46.♘×c6 ♗×c6 47.♔c5 ♗e8 48.b4 1-0

REBEL CENTURY – Van Wely, Loek (2697)
French Defense C04
Maastricht match (3), 21.02.2002

1.e4 e6 2.d4 d5 3.♘d2 ♘c6 4.♘gf3 ♘f6 5.e5 ♘d7 6.♘b3 ♗e7 7.♗b5 ♘cb8 8.0-0 b6 9.♕e2 a5 10.♗e3 ♗a6 11.a4 c6 12.♗×a6 ♘×a6 13.♖fc1 0-0

14.c4!

To make use of his advantage in development, White opens the position. This is more important than the weakening of the b4-square.

14...d×c4 15.♖×c4 ♘db8 16.♘bd2
♘b4 17.♘e4 ♘8a6

18.♘fd2!

Opening the roads to the kingside.

18...♘c7 19.♕g4 ♔h8 20.♖a3!

REBEL prepares to swing this rook into
the attack.. It plays the "build" phase
well and human-like.

**20...♘bd5 21.♗g5 f6 22.e×f6 g×f6
23.♖h3! ♕e8**

Of course the computer would never
allow 23...f×g5?? if it had no refutation
at hand 24.♕h5 +−.

**24.♕h4 ♖f7 25.♗h6 b5 26.a×b5
c×b5 27.♖c1 a4 28.♖g3 a3**

28...b4? runs into 29.♘c4 ♘b5 30.♘e5
f×e5 31.♕g4 ♘f4 32.♗g7+ ♔g8
33.♗×e5+ ♘g6 34.h4 +−.

29.b×a3 ♖×a3 30.♘f3 b4?

Black does not have time for this and
must take preventive measures on the
kingside with 30...♗f8, when Black can
hope to survive the attack.

31.♕h5 ♖×f3?

Mistakes always seem to come in pairs,
but 31...♗f8 is also insufficient in view
of 32.♘e5 ♖e7 33.♘×f6 ♘×f6 34.♕×e8
♘c×e8 35.♗×f8 ♖c7 36.♗c5, winning
in the long run.

32.g×f3 ♗f8

33.♔h1!

…and Black's days are numbered.

33...♖e7 34.♖cg1 1–0

Van Wely, Loek (2697) – REBEL CENTURY
English Opening C36
Maastricht match (4), 22.02.2002

**1.c4 c5 2.♘c3 ♘c6 3.g3 g6 4.♗g2
♗g7 5.a3 ♘f6 6.♖b1 a5 7.e3 d6
8.♘ge2 ♗f5 9.d3 ♘e5 10.e4 ♗g4
11.h3 ♗f3 12.0-0 ♗×g2 13.♔×g2
0-0 14.g4 e6 15.♘g3**

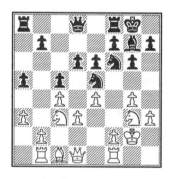

15...♘e8?!

Usually Black should try to open the
center to counter White's play on the
kingside, but here 15...d5? is met by
16.f4 ♘c6 17.g5 ♘d7 18.c×d5 e×d5
19.♘×d5. So the prophylactic 15...♘c6
was required.

16.f4 ♘c6 17.f5 ♕h4?!

As the queen will have to retreat soon,

this is just a waste of time.

18.♗e3 ♗e5 19.♘ce2 e×f5 20.e×f5 ♘g7 21.♘e4 ♕d8 22.f6 ♘e6 23.♘2c3 ♖e8 24.♕d2 ♔h8 25.b3 ♖b8 26.♗g1 ♖g8 27.a4 g5 28.♗e3 ♘b4 29.♘d5?!

Van Wely plays simple chess, which is not bad against a machine of course. Maybe he has already seen the coming exchange sacrifice. Objectively, 29.♖f5± is stronger.

29...♘×d5 30.c×d5 ♘f4+ 31.♗×f4

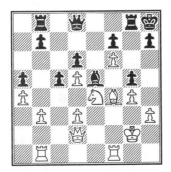

31...♗×f4?

REBEL underestimates the coming strong exchange sacrifice. It had to start counterplay with 31...g×f4 32.♖×f4 b5 with unclear consequences.

32.♖×f4! g×f4 33.♕×f4 b6

34.♕×d6

As the pawn cannot run away, it was more flexible to play 34.♖e1!±, which

also keeps the option open to leave the queen on the board.

34...♕×d6 35.♘×d6 ♖gf8 36.♘e4 ♖be8 37.♔f3 ♖e5 38.♘c3!

A strong retreat; 38.d6? ♖d5 plays into Black's hands.

38...♖fe8

38...♖d8 39.♔f4 ♖e×d5 40.♘×d5 ♖×d5 does not help because of 41.♖e1±.

39.♔f4 ♖e3 40.♖d1 ♖×h3 41.♘e4 ♖h2

41...h6 42.d6 ♖h2 43.♖e1±.

42.d4 c×d4?!

42...♖e2 43.♘d6 ♖f8 44.♘b7 ♖b8 45.d×c5 b×c5 46.d6 ♖×b7 47.d7 ♖f2+ 48.♔e5 ♖e2+ 49.♔d6 ♖×d7+ 50.♔×d7 loses as well, but at least Black reaches a technical rook ending.

43.d6 ♖d8 44.♖×d4

44...♖c2?!

This loses more or less by force. REBEL probably misevaluates the upcoming rook exchange as a result of an horizon effect. 44...♔g8?! is also weak because of 45.♔e5 h5 46.d7 h4 47.♔d6 ♖e2 48.♔c7+−; 44...h5 45.d7 ♖h4 46.♔e5 h×g4 47.♖c4 ♔h7 48.♔d6 ♔g6 49.♔e7 ♖×d7+ 50.♔×d7 ♖h3 gives better practical chances.

45.♖c4! ♖×c4 46.b×c4 ♔g8 47.♔e5 ♔f8 48.c5 b×c5 49.♘×c5

♔e8 50.♔d5 ♖b8 51.d7+ ♔d8
52.♔c6 ♖b2

52...h5!? is met by 53.g5+– (of
course not 53.g×h5?? ♖b6+ 54.♔×b6
stalemate).

**53.♘b7+ ♖×b7 54.♔×b7 ♔×d7
55.♔b6 1-0**

In 2003, Russian Grandmaster Evgeny
Bareev (now a resident of Canada)
played a four-game match with Mark
Uniacke's HIARCS program.

HIARCS X – Bareev, Evgeny (2729)
French Defense C01
Maastricht match (1), 28.01.2003

Not a lot went on in this match. Neither
side was able to create enough pressure
to overpower the other side.

**1.e4 e6 2.d4 d5 3.e×d5 e×d5 4.♘f3
♘f6 5.c4**

HIARCS opens the position. But Bareev
easily manages to deal with it.

**5...♗b4+ 6.♘c3 0-0 7.♗e2 d×c4
8.♗×c4 ♖e8+ 9.♗e3 ♗e6 10.♕b3
♗×c4**

The untested 10...♘d5 might be an idea
here.

**11.♕×c4 ♘c6 12.0-0 ♗×c3
13.b×c3 ♕d5 14.♕d3 ♘a5 15.♘d2
b5 16.a4 a6 17.a×b5 a×b5 18.♖fb1
c6 19.f3 h5 20.♖e1 ♘c4 21.♘×c4**

21...b×c4?!

21...♖×a1 22.♖×a1 b×c4 23.♕d2 ♕f5
creates slightly more pressure, but the
result would still most probably have
been a draw as computers are strong
defenders.

**22.♕d1 ♕f5 23.♗d2 ♖×e1+
24.♗×e1 ♖×a1 25.♕×a1 ♔h7
26.♕a2 ♕d3 27.♔f2 ♘d5 28.♕d2
♕×d2+ 29.♗×d2 ♔g6 30.g4!? f5
31.♔g3 ♘f6 32.g×h5+ ♘×h5+
33.♔f2 ♔f6 34.♔f1 ♔e6 35.♔g2
♘f6 36.♔g3 ♘d5 37.h4 g6 38.h5
f4+ 39.♔g4 g×h5+ 40.♔×h5 ♔f5
41.♔h4 ♘c7 42.♔h3 ♘e6 ½-½**

Bareev, Evgeny (2729) – HIARCS X
English Opening A25
Maastricht match (2), 29.01.2003

**1.c4 e5 2.g3 ♘c6 3.♘c3 g6 4.♗g2
♗g7 5.♖b1 a5 6.a3 d6 7.b4 a×b4
8.a×b4 f5 9.b5 ♘ce7 10.e3 ♘f6
11.♘ge2 ♗e6 12.♗×b7 ♖a7
13.♗g2 ♗×c4 14.d3 ♗e6 15.♗d2
h5?!**

Slightly strange. 15...0-0 is normal.

**16.h4 ♕d7 17.♕c2 0-0 18.0-0 ♖b8
19.♖fc1 ♗f7 20.♖b4 d5 21.d4 e4?!**

21...♘e4 is more active.

22.♘f4 ♘g4?!

The position of the other knight should
be improved first by 22...♘c8 as it is
more misplaced.

23.♗f1 ♖ba8 24.♖a4 ♗h6

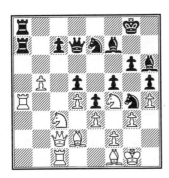

25.♖ca1?

This inaccurate move allows Black to exchange one pair of rooks easily. 25.♖a6 makes this much more difficult, e.g., 25...♗×f4 (25...g5 26.h×g5 ♗×g5 27.♘d1 ±) 26.e×f4 c6 27.♕b2 c×b5 28.♖×a7 ♖×a7 29.♘×b5 ♗b7 30.♕a3±.

25...♖×a4 26.♖×a4 ♖b8 27.♖a6 ♗×f4 28.e×f4 ♘c8 29.♗c1 ♘b6 30.♗e2 ♔g7 31.♕a2 ♘f6 32.♗a3 ♘e8 33.♗c5 ♘d6 34.♕a1 ♕d8 35.♕a3 ♘bc4 36.♕b4 e3

37.f3

At first sight it seems that White must have an advantage here, but that is by no means easy to prove as the following sample lines illustrate: 37.♗×c4 e×f2+ 38.♔×f2 ♘×c4 39.♗e7 ♕d7 40.♗f6+ ♔g8 41.♕g2 (41.♖a7 ♘d6 42.♗e5 ♘e4+) 41...♘e3+ 42.♔g1 ♘g4; or 37.♗×d6 e×f2+ 38.♔×f2 ♘×d6 39.♕c5 ♕e7 and Black has some counterplay in both cases. It is not easy at all to

defeat a machine, while Bareev proves that the time had not come yet when the machines were clearly stronger.

37...♘×b5 38.♘×b5 ♕d7 39.♖a5 ♗e8 40.♗×c4 d×c4 41.♕c3 ♖×b5 42.♖×b5 ♕×b5 43.d5+ ♔g8 44.♕×e3 ♗f7 45.♕e7 ♕b8 46.♗d4 ♕e8! 47.♕f6 ♕e1+ 48.♔g2 ♕e2+ 49.♗f2 ♗e8 50.♕e5 ♕×e5 ½-½

Hiarcs X – Bareev, Evgeny (2729)
French Defense C13
Maastricht match (3), 30.01.2003

1.e4 e6 2.d4 d5 3.♘c3 ♘f6 4.♗g5 d×e4 5.♘×e4 ♗e7 6.♗×f6 ♗×f6 7.♘f3 0-0 8.♗c4 ♘d7 9.♕e2 a6

10.0-0

Not very ambitious; 10.0-0-0 is the main line.

10...b5 11.♗d3 ♗b7 12.c3 ♗e7 13.b4 ♗d5 14.a4 c6 15.♖a3

15.Nc5!? was probably a better try.

15...a5!

Well calculated by Bareev. Black equalizes completely.

16.a×b5 c×b5 17.♖×a5 ♖×a5 18.b×a5 ♕×a5 19.♗×b5 ♘f6

19...♗×e4 20.♗×d7 ♕d5 (20...♗a8 21.♘e5=) 21.♘e5 ♗×g2 22.♖a1 ♗h3 23.♗c6 ♕b3=.

20.♘×f6+ ♗×f6 21.♕d3 ♗×f3 22.g×f3 ♖c8

and White's extra pawn cannot be converted because of Black's initiative.

23.c4 ♖d8 24.d5 e×d5 25.c×d5 ♕b4 26.♗c4 ♗e5 27.♕e4 ♕d6 28.h3 ♕f6 29.♖b1 h5 30.♔g2 ♗d6 31.♗d3 g6 32.h4 ♔f8 33.♖e1 ♖b8 34.♗c2 ♔g7 35.♖b1 ♖c8 36.♖b7 ♖c7 ½-½

Bareev, Evgeny (2729) – Hiarcs X
English Opening A20
Maastricht match (4), 31.01.2003

1.c4 e5 2.g3 ♘f6 3.♗g2 c6 4.d4 e×d4 5.♕×d4 d5 6.♘f3 ♗e7 7.c×d5 c×d5 8.0-0 ♘c6 9.♕a4 0-0 10.♗e3 ♗e6 11.♘c3 ♕d7 12.♖fd1 h6 13.♖ac1 ♖fd8 14.♘d4 ♗h3 15.♗h1 a6 16.♘×c6 b×c6

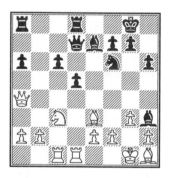

17.♘b1?!

Very slow and a bit too sophisticated; 17.♗d4 is more natural and applies more pressure.

17...♖dc8 18.♘d2 ♕b7 19.♘b3 ♕b5 20.♕×b5 a×b5 21.a3 b4 22.a×b4 ♗×b4 23.♘c5 ♗f5 24.♗g2 ♖a2 25.♘d3 ♗d6 26.♗d4 ♘e4 27.g4 ♗d7 28.f3?!

28.h3 ♖e8 29.♖a1 is more natural.

28...♘g5 29.f4 ♘e6 30.♗e3 ♖e8 31.♗f3 ♘g5 32.f×g5 ♖×e3 33.g×h6 g5?!

A bit strange, but the endgame is probably drawn in any case.

34.♖a1 ♖×a1 35.♖×a1 ♖e6 36.♖a8+ ♔h7 37.b4 ♔×h6 38.b5 c×b5 39.♗×d5 ♖f6 40.e4 ♗e6 41.♔g2 ♔g7 42.h3 ♗f8 43.♖b8 ♗×d5 44.e×d5 b4 45.♖b7 ♗d6 and a draw was agreed in view of **46.♘×b4 ♗×b4 47.♖×b4 ♖d6 48.♖d4 ♔f6 49.♔f3 ♔e5 = ½-½**

C

Games Index

D
End Notes

[1] For those with a computing interest, Cliff Shaw is credited with inventing the linked list, one of the most ubiquitous programming data structures.

[2] Jim Gillogly tried this idea earlier in his TECH program.

[3] One of the authors (JS) was in the audience for this game, attending his first computer chess event. He too had a good laugh at the expense of the KAISSA team. Three years later he was a participant in computer chess tournaments.

[4] In Levy and Newborn (1980).

[5] An interesting trivia item is that in the 1890s Emile Berliner, the brother of Hans Berliner's grandfather, invented the record (a music storage device) and the gramophone machine to play records.

[6] One millionth of a second.

[7] Quoted in Winter (2014).

[8] Quoted in Newborn (2003).

[9] Paul Bocuse, a famous chef and his self-named restaurant.

[10] From ChessBase (2005b).

[11] Quoted in ChessBase (2005b).

Signs & Symbols

1-0   White won

0-1   Black won

½-½   draw

!   strong move

!!   excellent move

?   poor move

??   blunder

!?   interesting move

?!   dubious move

=   equal game

±   White is slightly better

∓   Black is slightly better

±   White is clearly better

∓   Black is clearly better

+–   White is winning

–+   Black is winning

+   check

Learn Chess the Right Way: Book 3 – Mastering Defensive Technique by Susan Polgar

Learn Chess the Right Way: Book 4 – Sacrifice to Win! by Susan Polgar

Learn Chess the Right Way: Book 5 – Finding Winning Moves! by Susan Polgar

Legend on the Road by John Donaldson

Let's Play Chess by Bruce Pandolfini

The Life & Games of Carlos Torre by Gabriel Velasco

London 1922 by Geza Maróczy

Looking for Trouble (2nd ed.) by Dan Heisman

The Magic of Chess Tactics by Karsten Müller & Claus Dieter Meyer

The Magic of Chess Tactics 2 Karsten Müller & Claus Dieter Meyer

Man Versus Machine: Challenging Human Supremacy at Chess by Karsten Müller and Jonathan Schaeffer

Maneuvering: The Art of Piece Play by Mark Dvoretsky

Mastering Mates: Book 1 – One-move Mates by Jon Edwards

Mastering Mates: Book 2 – Two-move, Three-move and Four-move Mates by Jon Edwards

Masters of the Chessboard by Richard Réti

Max Euwe: Fifth World Chess Champion by Isaak & Vladimir Linder

Miniatures in the Sicilian Najdorf by Carsten Hansen*

Miniatures in the Queen's Indian by Carsten Hansen*

Miniatures in the Ruy Lopez – Main Lines by Carsten Hansen*

The Modern Chess Instructor by Wilhelm Steinitz

Modern Ideas in Chess by Richard Réti

Modern Morra Gambit (2nd. ed.) by Hannes Langrock

Music and Chess: Apollo Meets Caissa by Achilleas Zographos

My Best Games of Chess, 1908-1937 by Alexander Alekhine

My Best Games of Chess,1905-1954 by Savielly Tartakower

My Chess by Hans Ree

My First Book of Checkmate by David MacEnulty

My First Book of Checkmate Workbook by David MacEnulty

My First Book of Chess Tactics by David MacEnulty

Najdorf x Najdorf by Liliana Najdorf

New York 1924 by Alexander Alekhine

New York 1927 by Alexander Alekhine

Nottingham 1936 by Alexander Alekhine

Opening Originals: Strong Sidelines for Club Cats by Daniel Lowinger

Paul Morphy: A Modern Perspective by Valeri Beim

A Practical Guide to Rook Endgames by Nikolay Minev

Profession: Chessplayer – Grandmaster at Work by Vladimir Tukmakov

Reaching the Top?!: A Practical Guide to Playing Master-Level Chess by Peter Kurzdorfer

Reinfeld on the Endgame by Fred Reinfeld

The Rules of Chess by Bruce Pandolfini (free!)*

St. Petersburg 1909 by Emanuel Lasker

Sabotaging the Sicilian, French & Caro-Kann with 2.b3 by Konikowski & Soszynski

The Scotch Gambit by Alex Fishbein

Sicilian Defense: The Chelyabinsk Variation by Gennadi Timoshchenko

Strategic Opening Repertoire by John Donaldson & Carsten Hansen

Studies for Practical Players by Mark Dvoretsky & Oleg Pervakov

Tal-Botvinnik 1960 by Mikhail Tal

The Scotch Gambit: An Energetic and Aggressive System for White by Alex Fishbein

The Tactician's Handbook by Victor Charushin, Revised & Expanded by Karsten Müller

Topalov-Kramnik 2006 by Veselin Topalov with Zhivko Ginchev

Tragicomedy in the Endgame by Mark Dvoretsky

Vienna 1922 by Larry Evans

A World Champion's Guide to Chess: Step-by-Step Instructions for Winning Chess the Polgar Way by Susan Polgar and Paul Truong

Why You Lose at Chess by Fred Reinfeld

Wilhelm Steinitz: First World Chess Champion by Isaak and Vladimir Linder

Zürich 1953 by Miguel Najdorf

*Available only as an eBook